AF692809

Legal Interpretation of Tax Law

Series on International Taxation

VOLUME 46

Series Editors

Prof. Ruth Mason, University of Virginia School of Law
Prof. Dr Ekkehart Reimer, University of Heidelberg

Introduction & Contents

The Series on International Taxation deals with a wide variety of topics in the global tax arena. The authors include many of the field's leading experts as well as talented newcomers. Their expert views and incisive commentary has proven highly useful to practitioners and academics alike.

Objective

The volumes published in this series are aimed at offering high-quality analytical information and practical solutions for international tax practitioners.

Readership

Practitioners, academics and policy makers in international tax law.

Frequency of Publication

2-3 new volumes published each year.

The titles published in this series are listed at the end of this volume.

Legal Interpretation of Tax Law

Second Edition

Edited by

Robert F. van Brederode
Richard Krever

Wolters Kluwer

Published by:
Kluwer Law International B.V.
PO Box 316
2400 AH Alphen aan den Rijn
The Netherlands
Website: www.wolterskluwerlr.com

Sold and distributed in North, Central and South America by:
Wolters Kluwer Legal & Regulatory U.S.
7201 McKinney Circle
Frederick, MD 21704
United States of America
Email: customer.service@wolterskluwer.com

Sold and distributed in all other countries by:
Quadrant
Rockwood House
Haywards Heath
West Sussex
RH16 3DH
United Kingdom
Email: international-customerservice@wolterskluwer.com

ISBN 978-90-411-8473-3

e-Book: ISBN 978-90-411-8474-0
web-PDF: ISBN 978-90-411-8475-7

© 2017 Kluwer Law International BV, The Netherlands

All rights reserved. No part of this publication may be reproduced, stored in a retrieval system, or transmitted in any form or by any means, electronic, mechanical, photocopying, recording, or otherwise, without written permission from the publisher.

Permission to use this content must be obtained from the copyright owner. Please apply to: Permissions Department, Wolters Kluwer Legal & Regulatory U.S., 76 Ninth Avenue, 7th Floor, New York, NY 10011-5201, USA. Website: www.wolterskluwerlr.com

Editors

Dr Robert F. van Brederode (LLB, Utrecht University, 1982; LLM, Utrecht University, 1985; Ph.D., Amsterdam University, 1993) is a tax lawyer, scholar, and practitioner concentrating in the area of global indirect tax. He held senior positions in tax with several of the Big 4 firms. In addition, he served as Assistant Professor at Maastricht University, School of Law; Professor of tax law at the Erasmus University, School of Economics; and Adjunct Professor at New York University, School of Law, Graduate Tax Program. He is the author of *Systems of General Sales Taxation: Theory, Policy and Practice* (Kluwer Law International, 2009), editor of *Immovable Property Under VAT: A Comparative Global Analysis* (Kluwer Law International, 2011) and *Science, Technology and Taxation* (Kluwer Law International, 2012) and co-editor of *VAT and Financial Services: Comparative Law and Economic Perspectives* (Springer, 2017).

Richard Krever is a professor at the University of Western Australia Law School. He has previously held tax law drafting, design, and interpretation roles with the IMF, World Bank, Australian Treasury, and Australian Taxation Office, and provided tax law design and drafting assistance on behalf of international organizations in many Asian, African, Caribbean, South American, Pacific, and eastern European nations.

Contributors

Kim Brooks is a professor at the Schulich School of Law at Dalhousie University, where she served as Dean from 2010 to 2015, and a technical tax law expert with the IMF. Prior to her arrival at Dalhousie, she served as an associate professor and the H. Heward Stikeman Chair in the Law of Taxation at McGill University. She has also taught at the University of British Columbia's Faculty of Law and at Queen's University.

Wilson Chow is an associate professor at the HKU Faculty of Law since 1995 and is the first full-time local teacher of Hong Kong Taxation Law. His teaching now covers taxation systems in Hong Kong and Mainland China, as well as international taxation. He is the author of a range of publications, including a major *Halsbury's Laws of Hong Kong* volume on *Taxation and Revenue* and *Willoughby and Halkyard's Encyclopaedia of Hong Kong Taxation*. Mr Chow joined the Board of Review (Inland Revenue Ordinance) in 2003 and has been a Deputy Chairman of the Board since 2007.

Dr Thomas Dubut holds a Post-Graduate Master's degree (DEA) in Public Finances and a Ph.D. in International Tax Law from the University of Paris I Panthéon-Sorbonne. He has been teaching tax law at several French Universities for almost fifteen years (currently at the Sorbonne Law School and at Paris Dauphine University) and has been visiting Research Fellow at the Vienna University of Economics and Business (WU) and at the National University of Athens (Greece). He has been involved in tax reforms or tax modernization efforts in several developing countries (Burundi, Haiti, Mali, Mauritania, Rwanda, Senegal, Somaliland, Madagascar, China and Burkina-Faso) as an external expert/consultant for the International Monetary Fund (LEG, FAD), the World Bank (IFC, IDA), Trademark East Africa, the German Development Agency (GiZ), Adam Smith International, BDO East Africa and the French law firm Droit-Afrique. He has published around thirty articles in academic journals and books in French and English.

Dr Carlo Garbarino is Professor of Taxation at Bocconi University Milan and SDA Professor at the Bocconi Business School; Senior Emily Noel Fellow, NYU Law School, 2016–2017; Grotius Research Scholar, University of Michigan, 2014–2015; Hauser

Global Visiting Faculty, NYU Law School, 2013–2014. He is a member of Dipartimento di Studio Giuridici and of Steering Committee of the Ph.D., Program in International Economic Law of Bocconi University, and is an affiliated member of the Department of Accounting, Bocconi. He holds a Ph.D. in Comparative and International Taxation, and a Master of Laws from the University of Michigan. He served as visiting scholar at Yale University Law School and as visiting professor at the Université Sorbonne-Paris, University of Michigan Law School, New York University, University of San Paulo, and the University of Florida. Professor Garbarino also serves as a faculty member of Scuola Direzione Aziendale (SDA) – Bocconi, and on the Editorial Board of Alta Scuola Formazione ODC, Milan, and as Director of Osservatorio Fiscale e Contabile – SDA Bocconi. He did Internships at Caplin & Drysdale, Washington, DC (1986); and Roberts & Holland, New York (1987). Formerly he served as an associate with Studio Legale Bisconti, Milan (1989–2000), and as Of-counsel, Head of tax department, Allen & Overy, Milan (2001–2005). He is the editor of *EC Tax Review*, *Economia & Management* – SDA (2008–2010); *Diritto tributario internazionale*; *Editor-in-chief* of *Fiscalità e Commercio Internazionale*; and Director of the Series '*Comparative and International Taxation*', Bocconi University Press – Egea, Milan. Carlo is the editor of four volumes: *Aspetti fiscali delle operazioni internazionali* (1995); *Convenzione Italia-USA contro le doppie imposizioni, Commentario* (2001); *Le Convenzioni dell'Italia in materia di imposte su reddito e patrimonio, Commentario* (2002); *Aspetti internazionali della riforma fiscale* (Milano, 2004). He is the author of *Manuale di tassazione Internazionale* (2008) and of *Judicial Interpretation of Tax Treaties* (Elgar 2016), and of three monographs, as well as of more than hundred publications on comparative and international taxation.

Dr Caroline Heber is a senior research fellow at the Max Planck Institute for Tax Law and Public Finance, Department of Business and Tax Law, Munich as well as a Post-Doctoral Research Associate at the Institute for Austrian and International Tax Law, WU, Vienna. Prior, she was a Research Fellow of the Ross Parsons Centre, University of Sydney and of the Department of Fiscal Law, University of Graz. Caroline is specialized in the field of VAT Law, European and International Tax Law, and European Union Law. Currently, she lectures Austrian, German, and European Tax Law both at the University of Munich and WU Vienna.

Steve R. Johnson (B.A., St. Francis College (New York), 1976; J.D., New York University, 1981) is a university professor, Florida State University College of Law. He practised tax law from 1981 to 1986 in the New York City office of the Willkie Farr & Gallagher law firm, where his work included federal taxation as to corporations, partnerships, and international transactions as well as state and local sales and income taxation. From 1986 to 1994, Steve served in the Internal Revenue Service Chief Counsel's Office, litigating numerous cases on a wide range of substantive and procedural tax issues. He served as a Senior Attorney with that office as well as a Special Assistant United States Attorney for the Department of Justice. Before joining the Florida State faculty, Steve was a Professor at the Indiana University-Bloomington School of Law from 1994 to 2001 and was the E.L. Wiegand Professor at the

William S. Boyd School of Law at the University of Nevada from 2001 to 2011. He also has visited at the Illinois Institute of Technology, Chicago-Kent College of Law and the University of California, Hastings College of the Law. Since 2010, Steve also has been a member of the faculty of the Masters in Tax Law program at the University of Alabama School of Law. Steve has authored scores of tax and statutory interpretation articles and book chapters, has co-authored two books on tax law, and has been a featured speaker at numerous tax conferences throughout the United States. His published work has been cited by the United States Supreme Court, several federal circuit and district courts, the Court of Federal Claims, and the United States Tax Court.

Yoshihiro Masui is Professor of Law at the University of Tokyo. He served as an Expert Member for the Tax Commission of the Japanese government (2003–2006) and was a member of the Permanent Scientific Committee of the IFA (1999–2009). His monograph Taxation of Corporate Groups (University of Tokyo Press, 2002; in Japanese) won the Institute of Tax Research and Literature Award. He received an LL.B. in 1987 from the University of Tokyo and an ITP/LLM in 1992 from Harvard University.

Peter Mellor is a research fellow in the Taxation Law and Policy Research Institute and the Department of Business Law and Taxation at Monash University, Melbourne. Peter has previously worked as a solicitor in indirect taxation in the lead-up to the introduction of GST in Australia.

Gerard Meussen is Professor of Tax Law at the Radboud University Nijmegen, the Netherlands. He was a member and principal author of an EU Tax Expert Group advising the European Commission on lifting remaining tax obstacles for private individuals in the EU. He studied Law at the University of Nijmegen (present name Radboud University Nijmegen) in Nijmegen (The Netherlands) where he graduated in 1987. He specialized in tax law (Post Graduate LLM) at Tilburg University (The Netherlands) where he graduated in 1990.
He received his Ph.D. in 1997 in taxation at the Radboud University Nijmegen defending a thesis on Comparative Aspects of Valuation of Assets for Profit Taxation. He regularly gives lectures on topics covering different aspects of Dutch and European Tax Law and is a permanent contributor to European Taxation (correspondent European Union) and a number of Dutch scholarly tax journals including BNB, Weekblad voor fiscaal recht and Fiscaal weekblad FED. He was the final editor of *The Principle of Equality in European Taxation* (1999, Kluwer Law International) and *The Burden of Proof in Tax Law* (2013 IBFD).

Dr Dongmei Qiu (Ph.D., Xiamen University, China, 2009; LLM, Leiden University, the Netherlands 2010) is an associate professor at Xiamen University. She acquired her LLB, LLM, and Ph.D. at Xiamen University. During 2007–2008 and 2009–2010, she was based at the International Tax Center of Leiden University to pursue study on international taxation and she acquired her second LLM degree while at Leiden. During her stay in the Netherlands, she worked as an intern at Ernst & Young engaging in the Chinese business tax service. Since 2011, she serves at the Law School of Xiamen

University, first as assistant professor and now as associate professor, where she teaches courses including International Tax Law and Chinese Property Law. During July 2013 and again in July 2015 she worked as a post doctoral fellow at the Faculty of Law, Hong Kong University. Professor Qiu's main research interests are PRC taxation and international tax law. She is the author of a book on thin capitalization rules and has published dozens of articles in both English and Chinese in tax journals and periodicals.

Dr Luís Eduardo Schoueri holds the chair of tax law at University of São Paulo Law School, and, for 2017, he is Professor in Residence at the IBFD. After defending his thesis in the field of international tax law, he obtained his Master's degree at the University of Munich under the guidance of Professor Klaus Vogel. He achieved the Doctor's and Free Professor's degrees at the Law School of the University de São Paulo. He is partner of the law firm Lacaz Martins, Pereira Neto, Gurevich & Schoueri, vice president of the Brazilian Tax Law Institute, vice president of São Paulo's Commercial Association and author of several studies published in Brazil and abroad, including the books *Direito Tributário, Normas Tributárias Indutoras e Intervenção Econômica, Preços de Transferência no Direito Tributário Brasileiro, Distribuição Disfarçada de Lucros, Planejamento Fiscal através de Acordos de Bitributação: Treaty Shopping*, and *Ágio em Reorganizações Societárias (Aspectos Tributários)*.

Dr John Snape is an associate professor of Law at Warwick Law School, the University of Warwick. He was educated at St Mary's College, Blackburn, St Edmund Hall, Oxford (where he read Jurisprudence) and the University of Birmingham, from where he gained his doctorate on corporation tax. Though not practising, he is a qualified solicitor, with experience of corporate and commercial legal practice. He has also taught at Nottingham Trent, Leeds and City Universities. He has published widely on taxation matters, and especially on corporation tax and environmental taxes. He was the co-author, with the late Jeremy de Souza, of *Environmental Taxation Law: Policy, Contexts and Practice*, published by Ashgate, in 2006. His book, *The Political Economy of Corporation Tax: Theory, Values and Law Reform*, was published by Hart in 2011. His research interests encompass both the technical and policy aspects of tax law and its intellectual and historical roots in Early Modern and Enlightenment philosophy.

Christian Sternberg is a Research Fellow at the Max Planck Institute for Tax Law and Public Finance, Department of Business and Tax Law, Munich. Previously, he was a Research Fellow at the German-Dutch Research Centre for Taxation of Cross Border Business of the Universities of Münster, Osnabrück and Tilburg. Christian is a Ph.D. candidate in Law at the Institute for Tax Law, University of Münster; his research interests include European and International Tax Law, German and European Constitutional Law and Public International Law.

Dr Danil V. Vinnitskiy (LLM, USAL 1996; Ph.D., USAL 1999; habilitation, USAL 2003) is a Professor and Head of the Department of Tax and Financial Law at the Ural State Law University (USLU) and Head of the Research Centre for Comparative and

International Tax Law (Ekaterinburg, Russia). He is a member of the European Association of Tax Law Professors (EATLP) and of the Presidium of the International Association of Financial Law (which unites scholars from CIS countries). Danil Vinnitskiy is the author of more than 200 publications, including eleven monographs and seven textbooks on tax and financial law (including those prepared with co-authors). He is the general editor of the Russian Yearbook of International Tax Law, Member of the scientific councils of a number of the Russian Federation state bodies and has acted as an expert for the RF Constitutional Court. In 2015 he was elected Director of the BRICS Law Institute (Ekaterinburg, Russia).

Dr Robert C. (Bob) Williams holds the degrees BA, LLB (Cape), LLM (London), H Dip Tax (Witw), and Ph.D. (Macquarie). He is currently a professor in the School of Law, University of KwaZulu-Natal, Pietermaritzburg, South Africa. His areas of specialization are tax, trusts and corporate law, and he has published widely in each of these disciplines.

Summary of Contents

Table of Contents

Preface to the First Edition

As a direct result of the globalization of trade and business, tax departments and their external advisors are increasingly required to deal with the tax law of foreign jurisdictions. Effective consulting, regardless of whether internal or external, requires not only knowledge of the tax law per se, but also of how tax law is explained and interpreted in the courts of foreign jurisdictions. Legal interpretation has been a general subject of theoretical study for quite some time and is part of the curriculum of all or most law schools. Systematic study of the interpretation of tax law is not a separate 'discipline' within tax LLM programs, although the subject will be touched, implicitly or explicitly, when discussing specific court cases. Journal articles are, generally, focused on a single jurisdiction and/or a specific type of tax. This book tries to fill the void in tax literature by offering a comparative study into eleven jurisdictions as to the interpretation of law in the areas of VAT/GST or other general sales tax and of corporate income taxes.

Clearly, it is not practically feasible to cover each and every country in the world, nor would that be necessary. Essential is to offer a regional spread of jurisdictions and a balance between established and emerging economies, based on the relevance to the global cross-border investment world and their advisors.

The following jurisdictions were selected: Australia, Brazil, People's Republic of China, the European Union, Germany, Italy, Japan, Hong Kong, the Russian Federation, South Africa, and the United States of America. They are representative of six continents and cover a full spectrum of interpretation approaches and interpretation backgrounds that range from longstanding, but very different, common law systems (the USA and Australia), to very different civil law systems (Brazil, Germany and Japan) and two transitional economies shifting from socialist to market systems (China and Russia). Hong Kong, the gateway for investments into and out of China, stands on the doorway between old UK concepts inherited from its colonial past and very different Chinese concepts in the country of which it is now a special administrative region. South Africa is the leading economy of the African continent and has merged Roman-Dutch law with English common law. The EU is taken as a single jurisdiction because it operates as a single economic market and because of the realization of a fair degree of tax harmonization, especially in the area of indirect tax. However, harmonization of corporate income tax and personal income tax are both still in their infancy and for that reason we have decided to include as separate jurisdictions Germany and Italy, two founding Member States with the largest and fourth largest economy in the EU respectively.

An introductory chapter outlines theoretical approaches to legal interpretation in general and gives an overview of issues and topics specific for the area of taxation. As such, it provides contextual background and some guidance when reading the jurisdictional chapters. It also compares, to some extent, the variety of interpretative approaches applied in the eleven jurisdictions covered in this book.

The differences in legal systems and traditions did not allow us to design a common structure for all chapters. However, to facilitate comparisons between the interpretative approaches of the eleven jurisdictions, all authors followed guidelines as to the topics to be covered in each chapter.

We trust that this book will be a helpful reference for academics and practitioners when providing insight and counsel on how tax law generally and particular tax provisions specifically are likely to be applied to different types of cross-border transactions and investment.

The bibliography and register of case law are found in the back of the book, organized per chapter. This book is current with literature and case law through December 2013.

Robert F. van Brederode
Danbury, CT, USA

Richard Krever
Melbourne, VIC, Australia

Preface to the Second Edition

We are grateful for the opportunity to prepare a second edition of this book. The second edition includes updated materials from both original authors and, in two cases, new authors. We were fortunate to have the opportunity to extend the jurisdictional scope of the book by adding chapters on legal interpretation in Canada, France, and the United Kingdom. We trust this will increase the value of this book for the professional and academic readers. The second edition is current with literature and case law through November 2016.

Robert F. van Brederode
Atlanta, GA, USA

Richard Krever
Melbourne, VIC, Australia

List of Abbreviations

AC	Appellate Court (UK)
AC	*Appeal Cases* (UK)
ACT	advance corporation tax (superseded) (UK)
ACWS	All-Canada Weekly Summaries
AD or (A)	Appellate Division (SA)
ADI	Direct Action of Unconstitutionality (Ação Direta de Inconstitucionalidade)
AG	Attorney General (Canada)
AJ	Acting Justice
AJA	Acting Justice of Appeal
All ER Rep	All England Law Reports Reprint
Am. J. Comp. Law	American Journal of Comparative Law
AOA	Authorized OECD Approach
App Cas	Appeal Cases (superseded series) (England and Wales)
Ariz. St.	Arizona State
Art.	Article
ATO	Australian Taxation Office
ATO ID	Australian Taxation Office Interpretative Decision
ATR	Australian Tax Reports
B	Baron of the Exchequer (England and Wales)
Basic Law	Basic Law of the Hong Kong Special Administrative Region
BCLR	Butterworths Constitutional Law Reports
BFH	Bundesfinanzhof (Federal Fiscal Court)
BFHE	Entscheidungen des Bundesfinanzhofs (Decisions of the Federal Fiscal Court)

BGBl	Bundesgesetzblatt (Federal Law Gazette)
BGH	Bundesgerichtshof (Federal Court of Justice)
BGHZ	Entscheidungen des Bundesgerichtshofs in Zivilsachen (Decisions of the Federal Court of Justice in civil matters)
BLLR	Butterworths Labour Law Reports
BNB	Beslissingen in Belastingzaken
Boll. trib	Bollettino Tributario
BORO	Hong Kong Bill of Rights Ordinance
BTR	British Tax Review
BStBl	Bundessteuerblatt (Federal Tax Gazette)
BVerfG	Bundesverfassungsgericht (Federal Constitutional Court)
BVerfGE	Entscheidungen des Bundesverfassungsgerichts (decisions of Federal Constitutional Court)
BVerfGG	Bundesverfassungsgerichtgesetz (Federal Constitutional Court Act)
CA	Court of Appeal of England and Wales
CA 2006	Companies Act 2006 (UK)
CAA 2001	Capital Allowance Act 2001 (UK)
CACV	Court of Appeal Civil Appeal (Hong Kong)
Cap.	Chapter (Laws of Hong Kong)
CARF	Administrative Council of Administrative Appeals (Conselho Administrativo de Recursos Fiscais)
Cass.	Cassazione
C.B.	Cumulative Bulletin
CC	Constitutional Court (SA)
CC	Court Constitutionnel (France)
CE	Conseil d'Etat (France)
CEC	Customs and Excise Commissioners (UK)
cf	confer (see, compare)
CFA	Court of Final Appeal (Hong Kong)
CFC	Controlled Foreign Corporation
CGI	Code Général des Impôts (France)
CGT	Capital gains tax (UK)
ch.	Chapter
CIR	Commissioner of Inland Revenue (Hong Kong)
CJ	Chief Justice
CJEU	Court of Justice of the European Union (see also ECJ)
CLJ	Cambridge Law Journal

CJQ	Civil Justice Quarterly
CLR	Commonwealth Law Reports
CMLR	Common Market Law Review
C.L.B.	Commonwealth Law Bulletin
COFINS	Contribution to the Financing of Social Security (Contribuição para o Financiamento da Seguridade Social)
Colum.	Columbia
Conn.	Connecticut
Corr. trib	Corriere Tributario
Corte cost	Corte costituzionale
CPD	Cape Provincial Division
CR	Computer und Recht
CRA	Canada Revenue Agency
CRC	Revenue and Customs Commissioners (UK)
CTA 2009	Corporate Tax Act 2009 (UK)
CTA(s)	Corporate Tax Act(s) (UK)
CTC	Canada Tax Cases
CTPC	Customs Tariff Policy Commission (China)
d. lgs	decreto legislativo
DAU	Direct Action of Unconstitutionality (Brazil)
DB	Der Betrieb
DGFIP	Direction Générale des Finances Publiques (France)
DIPN	Departmental Interpretation & Practice Notes (Hong Kong)
Dir. comm. internaz	Diritto del commercio internazionale
Dir. prat. trib	Diritto e pratica tributaria
DLR	Dominion Law Reports (Canada)
DOTAS	Disclosure of Tax Avoidance Schemes (UK)
D.P.R.	decreto presidente della Repubblica
DStJG	Deutsche Steuerjuristische Gesellschaft (German Fiscal Association)
DStR	Deutsches Steuerrecht
DTA	Double Taxation Agreement
DTC	Dominion Tax Cases (Canada)
EA	Extraordinary Appeal (Brazil)
EC	European Community/Communities
ECHR	European Convention on Human Rights

ECJ	Court of Justice of the European Union (European Court of Justice)
ECR	European Court Reports
ECSC	European Coal and Steel Community
ECtHR	European Court of Human Rights
ECTJ	EC Tax Journal
ed.	Editor
eds	Editors
edn.	Edition
EDB 'KP'	Electronic Database 'Consultant-Plus'
EEA	European Economic Area
EEC	European Economic Community
e.g.	Exempli gratia (for example)
EITL	Enterprise Income tax Law (China)
EL Rev.	European Law Review
Enc. Giur. Treccani	Enciclopedia Giuridica Treccani
ER	English Report (England and Wales_
EStG	Einkommensteuergesetz (German Income Tax Act)
ETS	European Treaty Series
et seq.	et sequential (and the following)
EU	European Union
EWCA	England and Wales Court of Appeal
EWCA Civ	England and Wales Court of Appeal (Civil Division)
FA	Finance Act (UK)
FC	Federal Court
FCA	Federal Court of Australia decisions
FCA	Federal Court of Appeal (Canada)
FCAFC	Federal Court of Australia – Full Court decisions
FCJ	Federal Court Judgments (LexisNexis Quicklaw) (Canada)
FCT	Federal Commissioner of Taxation (Australia)
Finsocial	Social Investment Fund (Fundo de Investimento Social)
FKZ	Federalnyi Konstitutsionnyi Zakon (Federal Constitutional Law; Russia)
Fla. St. U.	Florida State University
Foro. it	Foro italiano
FTS	Federal Tax Service (Russia)

FZ	Federalnyi Zakon (Federal Law; Russia)
GAAR	General Anti-avoidance Rule
GAAR	General Anti Abuse rule (England and Wales)
GAC	General Administration of Customs (China)
Geo. Wash.	George Washington
GG	Grundgesetz (German Constitution)
Giur. cost.	Giurisprudenza costituzionale
Giur. It	Giurisprudenza Italiana
GmbH	Gesellschaft mit beschränkter Haftung
GST	Goods and Services Tax
Harv.	Harvard
Hastings Con. L.Q.	Hastings Constitutional Law Quarterly
HCA	High Court of Australia decisions
HCIA	High Court Inland Revenue Appeal (Hong Kong)
HK	Hong Kong
HKCFA	Hong Kong Court of Final Appeal
HKCFAR	Hong Kong Court of Final Appeal Reports
HKLJ	Hong Kong Law Journal
HKLR	Hong Kong Law Reports
HKLRD	Hong Kong Law Reports and Digest
HKPLR	Hong Kong Public Law Reports
HKSAR	Hong Kong Special Administrative Region
HKTC	Hong Kong Tax Cases
HL	Judicial committee of the House of Lords (superseded)
HM	Her Majesty's (UK)
HMRC	Her Majesty's Revenue and Customs (UK)
HMSO	Her Majesty's Stationery Office (UK)
How.	Howard
HR	Hoge Raad (Netherlands)
HRA 1998	Human Rights Act 1998 (UK)
IBFD	International Bureau of Fiscal Documentation
Ibid	Ibidem
I.C.L.Q.	International and Comparative Law Quarterly
ICMS	Sales Tax (Imposto sobre Operações _elatives à Circulação de Mercadorias e Prestação de Serviços de Transporte Interestadual e Intermunicipal e de Comunicação)

ICTA 1988	Income and Corporation Taxes Act 1988 (UK)
Id.	Idem
i.e.	id est (that is)
IHT	Inheritance tax (UK)
Ill. LR	Illinois Law Review
I.L.T.	Irish Law Times
IOF	Tax on Financial Operations (Imposto sobre Operações Financeiras)
IRC	Inland Revenue Commissioners (superseded) (UK)
I.R.C.	Internal Revenue Code (US)
IRD	Inland Revenue Department (Hong Kong and China)
IRO	Inland Revenue Ordinance (Hong Kong)
ISS	Tax on Services (Imposto sobre Serviços de Qualquer Natureza)
IStR	Internationales Steuerrecht
ITA 2007	Income Tax Act 2007 (UK)
ITEPA 2003	Income Tax (Earnings and Pensions) Act 2003 (UK)
ITLR	International Tax Law Reports
J	Justice
JA	Justice of Appeal
J. Emp. Legal Stud.	Journal of Empirical Legal Studies
JPY	Japanese Yen
jo	Juncto
JZ	Juristen Zeitung
KB	Kings Bench Division
KG	Kommanditgesellschaft
L. Rev.	Law Review
LC	Lord Chancellor (UK)
Legal I.E.I	Legal Issues of Economic Integration
Leg.	Legisprudence
LfT	Landfill tax
LGDJ	Librairie générale de droit et de jurisprudence (France)
LJ	Lord Justice of Appeal (England and Wales)
L.J.	Law Journal
LHK	Laws of Hong Kong
LPF	Livre des procédures fiscals (France)
LQR	Law Quarterly Review

LPBR	Law and Politics Book Review
LR Ex	Law Reports: Exchequer (superseded series) (England and Wales)
LR HL	Law Reports: House of Lords (superseded series) (UK)
MAP	Mutual Agreement Procedure (article 25 of the OECD Model Convention)
MC	Model Code
Mich. Comp. Laws Ann.	Michigan Compiled Laws Annotated
MLR	Modern Law Review
MNR	Minister of National Revenue (Canada)
MoF	Ministry of Finance
MTC	Model Tax Convention
Nat'l Tax J.	National Tax Journal
Nev. Law.	Nevada Lawyer
Nev. rev. Stat.	Nevada Revised Statutes
N.H. Bar J.	New Hampshire Bar Journal
N.H. Const.	New Hampshire Constitution
N.H. Rev. Stat. Ann.	New Hampshire Revised Statutes Annotated
NICs	National insurance contributions (UK)
NJW	Neue Juristische Wochenschrift
No.	Number
Nos.	Numbers
Nov.mo dig. it	Novissimo digesto italiano
NPC	National People's Congress (China)
NPJ	Non-Permanent Judge (Court of Final Appeal, Hong Kong)
NSWSC	Supreme Court of New South Wales decisions
NTA	National Tax Administration (Japan)
NV	Naamloze Vennootschap
Nw. U.	Northwestern University
N.Y.U.	New York University
OECD	Organisation of Economic Co-operation and Development
OG	Official Gazette (Brazil)
OJ	Official Journal of the European Union

Or.	Oregon
OUP	Oxford University Press
p	page
para	Paragraph
PCTA 1968	Provisional Collection of Taxes Act 1968 (UK)
PE	Permanent Establishment
pen	penale
PIS	Social Integration Program (Programa de Integração Social)
Pitt.	Pittsburgh
PJ	Permanent Judge (Court of Final Appeal, Hong Kong)
Plc	Public limited company (UK)
POTAS	Promoters of Tax Avoidance Schemes (UK)
pp	pages
PRC	People's Republic of China
Pt	Part (of a schedule) (UK)
PUF	Presses Universitaires de France
QB or QBD	Queens Bench Division (England and Wales)
QPC	Question prioritaire de constitutionnalité (France)
QSC	Supreme Court of Queensland decisions
R	Regina or Rex
R	Rhodesia
RA	Rhodesia Appeal Court
Rass. Trib.	Rassegna tributaria
R&D	Research and development
RE	Extraordinary Appeal (Recurso Extraordinário)
Rec.	Recueil
RF	Russian Federation
RF MTC	Russian Federation Ministry of Tax and Charges
RF SCC	Russian Federation Supreme Commercial Court
RF CPC	Russian Federation Commercial Procedure Code
Riv. Dir. Fin.	Rivista Diritto Finanziario
Riv. dir.trib	Rivista Diritto Tributarii
RJF	Revue de Jurisprudence Fiscale
RSC	Revised Statutes of Canada
s	Section
SA	South African Law Reports

SAAR	Specific Anti-avoidance Rules
SARS	South African Revenue Service
SAT	State Administration of Taxation (China)
SATC	South African Tax Cases
SCA	Supreme Court of Appeal
S. Cal.	Southern California
SCC	Supreme Court of Canada
Sch	Schedule (to a statute)
SCJ	Supreme Court Judgments (LexisNexis Quicklaw) (Canada)
SCNPC	Standing Committee of the National People's Congress (China)
SCR	Supreme Court Reports (Canada)
SCZ	Supreme Court of Zimbabwe
Sect.	Section
sez. Un	sezioni unite
Sing. J.L.S.	Singapore Journal of Legal Studies
S.L.G.	Scottish Law Gazette
SLS	Social and Legal Studies
SR	Southern Rhodesia
SR (NSW)	State Reports (New South Wales)
St.	Saint
Stat LR	Statute Law Review
Stat Realm	Statutes of the Realm (UK)
STC	Simon's Tax Cases (UK)
STC (STD)	Simon's Tax Cases (Special Commissioners' Decisions)
Sup. Ct. Econ. Rev	Supreme Court Economic Review
sv	Sub verbo (under the word)
(T)	Transvaal Provincial Division
TAAR	Targeted anti-avoidance rule (UK)
TASSC	Supreme Court of Tasmania decisions (media neutral citation)
Tax Law.	Tax Lawyer
TC	Tax Cases
TCC	Tax and Chancery Chamber (UK)
TCGA 1992	Taxation of Chargeable Gains Act 1992 (UK)
TEU	Treaty on the European Union
Tex	Texas

Tex. Tax Code	Texas Tax Code
TFEU	Treaty on the Functioning of the European Union
Thin Cap	Thin Capitalization
TNI	Tax Notes International
TPD	Transvaal Provincial Division
Treas. Reg.	Treasury Regulation
TS	Transvaal Supreme Court
U. Ill.	University of Illinois
UK	United Kingdom
UKFIT	UK First-tier Tribunal (UK)
UKHL	United Kingdom House of Lords (Judicial Committee) (superseded)
UKSC	United Kingdom Supreme Court
UKUT	United Kingdom Upper Tribunal
UN	United Nations
UNTS	United Nations Treaty Series
U. Ill. L. Rev	University of Illinois Law Review
U. Pa.	University of Pennsylvania
USA	United States of America
U.S.C.	United States Code
UTLJ	University of Toronto Law Journal
v.	Versus (against)
VADR	VAT Avoidance Disclosure Regime (UK)
VAT	Value Added Tax
VATA 1994	Value Added Tax Act 1994 (UK)
Va. Tax Rev.	Virginia Tax Review
VCLT	Vienna Convention on the Law of Treaties
VLR	Victorian Law Reports
Vol.	Volume
VCC	Vestnik of the Constitutional Court/
VSCC	Vestnik of the RF Supreme Commercial Court.
WASCA	Supreme Court of Western Australia - Court of Appeal decisions
WLD	Witwatersrand Local Division
WLR	Weekly Law Reports

World J. VAT/GST L.	World Journal of VAT/GST Law
WTD	Worldwide Tax Daily
WTJ	World Tax Journal
ZACC	Constitutional Court of the Republic of South Africa
ZLR	Zimbabwe Law Reports

CHAPTER 1

Legal Interpretation of Tax Law: A Reflection on Methods and Issues

Richard Krever & Robert F. van Brederode

§1.01 WHAT IS INTERPRETATION OF LAW?

This is not a book on legal philosophy, asking what law is or searching for its origins. It is, rather, a book on the most crucial step in the application of law, interpreting the meaning of the words that communicate law to the persons governed by law as well as those who administer and enforce the laws. There is, to be sure, a never-to-be-resolved debate on the source of law with those supporting positivist legal philosophy attributing the origin of law to collective action by the people to which the law applies and those adopting natural law philosophy claiming that law – at least underlying fundamental principles – derives from a higher authority be it a God or the social consciousness of a highly evolved humanity. All concede, however, that the art of interpreting law is clearly a matter of human action.

Interpretation of tax law is a subset of legal interpretation, a concept that has two aspects: it is *interpretation* – giving meaning to an object, sign, or, for our subject, the words used in a statute to communicate ideas – but done so in a way that is distinctly *legal* in nature. Interpretation is *legal* when it not only provides a shared understanding of the ideas intended by text, but also in the process of delivering that explanation actually establishes valid law, creating the rules that govern individual behaviour. Legal interpretation is thus dialectic in nature, both serving a communication role (the meaning of law) and a constructive purposive function, transmitting rules of behaviour and as a consequence influencing or regulating the social reality. The reality of that function cannot be ignored; the exercise is not simply one of choosing between semantically possible interpretations, but rather, within a procedural framework and interpretational tradition governed by legal definitions, norms, presumptions and legal precedent, establishing the operative consequences of words, raising the question of whether legal interpretation is actually a process of law-making. It is an exercise that must be pursued until a final result is achieved; the interpreter whether the person subject to a law, administering the law, or adjudicating the law has a legal obligation to reach a decision within an identified time frame.

It is difficult to provide a precise definition of legal interpretation, because the answer would depend on some basic ontological choices. Most scholars, therefore, prefer to distinguish between different philosophical theories of legal interpretation, and we will present some of those here in as far as we believe they are relevant for our discussion on tax law interpretation.

Analytic philosophy is not a single theory but comprises a variety of methods and conceptions. Traditionally, two branches of analytic philosophy are distinguished, namely formal and informal analytic philosophy,[1] which developed into the ordinary language philosophy. The formal approach to legal matters was introduced in the 1950s with the development of deontic logics, attempting to develop formal systems capturing the notions of, e.g., obligation, prohibition and permission.[2] Beyond the search for the logic of normative sentences, formal analytic legal philosophy also explored issues as the problem of normative systems, ontology of norms. Informal analysis is represented by Wittgenstein and the Oxford School of Ordinary Language Philosophy, in particular H.L.A. Hart.[3] The most important assumption of the analytic philosophy is that language is the key to any serious philosophising because language constitutes a medium between thinking and the world that seems to be objective in nature,[4] contrary to our thoughts that are throughout subjective. Where language is objective, the process of interpretation cannot be purely subjective. Analytic philosophers oppose any relativist views concerning the meaning of the words; in their view any given text has a set of determinable, possible interpretations.

Justification of an interpretational decision is also a crucial element of formal analytic philosophy. A distinction is made between internal and external justification. An argument is said to be justified internally if its conclusion follows logically from its premises. On the other hand, an argument is called externally justified, if it is internally justified and its premises are true. The problem with normative reasoning is that norms and other directive expressions are used as premises, which cannot be called false or true. If it is correct that norms are neither true nor false, then norms are outside the scope of logic, which has immense consequences for legal interpretation, as the

1. Generally, the linguistic turn in philosophy occurred at the beginning of the twentieth century with the publication of Bertrand Russell, *Principles of Mathematics* (Cambridge: Cambridge University Press, 1903); and George E. Moore, *Principia Ethica* (Cambridge: Cambridge University Press, 1903). Russell advocates formal analysis, while Moore represents common sense analysis that could be regarded as a predecessor of the ordinary language philosophy.
2. Jerzy Kalinowski, *La Logique des normes* (Paris: Presses Universitaires de France, 1972).
3. Herbert L.A. Hart, *The Concept of Law* (Oxford: Oxford University Press, 1961).
4. Ian Hacking, *Why Does Language Matter to Philosophy?* (Cambridge: Cambridge University Press, 1975).

conclusion of an interpretational argument is always a legal norm.[5] The purposefulness of legal interpretation poses some challenges for the logically oriented legal philosophy. The notion of a purpose is intimately linked with the pragmatic dimension of language. The pragmatic aspect of language has been given due attention in the informal analytic philosophy.

The contemporary theories of argumentation developed as an alternative to the logic-oriented account that tried to subject legal or normative thinking to the same rules that constitute the methods of natural sciences. Theories of argumentation are usually designed to give an account of the practical discourse, while the theoretical is left for logic and empirical epistemology. The most important theories in this category during the last century have been developed by Chaïm Perelman, Theodor Viehweg and Robert Alexy, which we will discuss briefly below.

The core of Perelman's approach is the concept of an audience.[6] In his view, the audience sets the criteria of the acceptance of an argument. This concept of audience is demonstrated (*see* Chapter 6) in the European Union where the European Court of Justice had to develop a 'European legal tradition' acceptable to all Member States (i.e., its audience); and where the national courts, acting within their own legal tradition, make legal rulings, that must adhere to the norms introduced at the European level and must be acceptable from the perspective of all other Member States (audience). Also, in China (*see* Chapter 5), the Ministry of Finance and the tax administration are the gravitational centres of legal interpretation and not the courts. However, in circumstances of cross-border trade and investments there is friction between this Chinese tradition and the perception of its international audience (foreign investors and businesses) expecting an independent judiciary to be charged with tax law interpretation and not what they may perceive as the opposing party of the tax conflict.

Viehweg perceives the process of legal interpretation as problem oriented, and, as a consequence, it cannot be a fully determined procedure to be applied in solving a legal issue; the judge is tasked with arguing for a particular solution.[7]

The main objective of Alexy's theory is to demonstrate that one can argue rationally being involved in a practical discussion provided a set of criteria is followed. Any discourse meeting the criteria can be called rational, and any decision made within such a discourse can also be called rational.[8]

The argumentation theories pay much attention to the problem of justifying the interpretational decision. For Alexy, an interpretational decision is justified if the

---

5. Legal procedure may also shift the burden of proof, which is difficult to incorporate in a logical model of legal reasoning that uses classical logic. To deal with this problem, such formal systems as defeasible logics were developed, *see* Bartosz Broz ek, *Defeasibility of Legal Reasoning* (Kraków: Zakamycze, 2004).
6. Chaïm Perelman and Lucie Olbrechts-Tyteca, *Traité de l'argumentation: La nouvelle rhétorique* (Paris: Presses Universitaires de France, 1958); *The New Rhetoric: A Treatise on Argumentation*, transl. by John Wilkinson and Purcell Weaver (Notre Dame: University of Notre Dame Press, 1969).
7. Theodor Viehweg, *Topik und Jurisprudenz* (5th edn, München: C.H. Beck, 1974).
8. Robert Alexy, *A Theory of Legal Argumentation*, transl. by Ruth Adler & Neil MacCormick (Oxford: Clarendon Press, 1989).

underlying argumentation process meets the criteria of practical discourse. For Perelman, an interpretational decision is justified if it is acceptable to its audience.

In practice, judges combine some or all of these approaches, depending on the particulars of each case. Generally, they will motivate their decision and demonstrate their line of reasoning while applying legal principles, doctrine, etc., in an effort to justify their decision in the eye of the audience (however defined) and satisfy at least the principle of the Alexy theory. The former may not always be possible, especially in highly charged cases such as those involving abortion, gay marriage or euthanasia, as the general audience may be divided in opposing factions, but then the decision may still be acceptable to the dissenting faction on the basis of solid argumentation. Moreover, apart from its universal audience, a court and justices will always seek to satisfy the legal community as its specific audience.

A useful demonstration of legal interpretation in action can be found in a probate case with which every US law student will be familiar, *Riggs v. Palmer*.[9] Francis Palmer executes a valid will, leaving most of his estate to his grandson, Elmer. Upon the remarriage of his widower grandfather, Elmer feared he would lose his inheritance, and murders his grandfather through poisoning. On the basis of the language of the New York Statute of Wills Elmer should, indeed, receive his grandfather's property as he is the named beneficiary in a valid will and the testator is dead. This was, unsurprisingly, Elmer's position, but also the reasoning of the dissent. However, what sets this case apart from normal probate cases is that the beneficiary killed the testator. Almost everyone, lawyer and non-lawyer, would agree that under such circumstances it would be 'unjust' for Elmer to receive his grandfather's inheritance. This injustice has found expression in the common law maxim 'No man shall profit from his own wrong'.[10] The fact of the murder is significant because it prevents the straightforward application of the wording of the statute of wills (i.e., an allocation of the testator's property to the testamentary beneficiary) and triggered a need for interpretation.

How did the majority opinion reason to justify its conclusion that Elmer should be denied his inheritance? On the basis of existing case law, it demonstrated that the above maxim is a constitutive general principle of law applied in the law of wills and in related departments of law, thus building a case for the legal proposition that precedents support an exception to the ordinary meaning of the words of the statute. The majority opinion makes a doctrinal argument that the words of a valid legislative enactment, *in casu* the New York Statute of Wills, should be allotted their normal force and effect unless the facts demonstrate a need for an exception. The law does not change, but is different in its application due to the circumstances.

Law is essentially an interpretive enterprise. To understand a corpus of law requires always an interpretation of the texts which comprise the law in question. Interpretivism is the view that a proposition of law is true in virtue of an interpretive fact, i.e., in virtue of the fact that the proposition follows from the best justification of a community's political practice. This view of law as integrity has been developed by

9. 115 N.Y. 506; 22 N.E. 188 (1889).
10. *See* Ronald Dworkin, *Taking Rights Seriously* (Cambridge: Harvard University Press, 1978): 14–45, containing an analysis of the legal reasoning followed in this case.

Ronald Dworkin.[11] Interpretivism says that it is not just political practice, such as a parliamentary majority vote for a statute that holds a certain legal proposition, or that such proposition is accepted by settled court practice, nor its moral appeal, that makes legal propositions true. Rather, legal propositions are made true by the best justification of political practice. Interpretivism therefore claims that legal requirements are sensitive to both the facts of the practice and the values served by it, but not fully determined by either.

Some interpretivists have developed the theory that through the act of reading, the reader creates the meaning of the text. Human understanding (whether it is a poem, symbol or a legal text) is not possible without interpretation.[12] If we need to visit a public lavatory, the respective signs on the doors, one depicting a human figure in a skirt and the other a human figure dressed in trousers, indicate to us as meaning that one group of lavatories is to be used by persons of the female gender and the other by persons of the male gender. Of course, understanding requires interpretation, but it seems that interpretivists posit that all understanding is interpretation. If that were the case, applying the same logic, interpretation itself would require an act of interpretation. Therefore, interpretation cannot explicate the very idea of understanding because it gives rise to an infinite regress of interpretations.[13] Moreover, the assumption that all understanding is interpretation makes it impossible to properly explain the existence of dissenting opinions. If a Scotsman in traditional dress enters the lavatory behind the door with the human figure in a skirt, his interpretation of the sign is not the correct understanding of the sign. The interpretation of, for example a legal text, and the understanding or meaning of it cannot be equivalent per definition. As Galileo posited, 'If Scripture cannot err, certain of its interpreters and commentators can and do in many ways',[14] echoing Saint Augustine who wrote:

> If it happens that the authority of Sacred Scripture is set in opposition to clear and certain reasoning, this must mean that the person who interprets Scripture does not understand it correctly. It is not the meaning of Scripture which is opposed to the truth but the meaning which he [the interpreter] has wanted to give to it. That which is opposed to Scripture is not what is in Scripture but what he has placed there himself, believing that this is what Scripture meant.[15]

---

11. Ronald Dworkin, 'Law as Interpretation', (1982) 60 *Texas Law Review* 527; Ronald Dworkin, *Law's Empire* (Cambridge: Harvard University Press, 1986).
12. *See*, Stanley E. Fish, *Is There a Text in This Class?: The Authority of Interpretive Communities* (Cambridge: Harvard University Press, 1980); and Stanley E. Fish, *Doing What Comes Naturally: Change, Rhetoric, and the Practice of Theory in Literature and Legal Studies* (Durham, NC: Duke University Press, 1989). For a critical evaluation of interpretivism, including the theories of Dworkin and Fish, *see*, e.g., Michael S. Moore, 'The Interpretive Turn in Modern Theory: A Turn for The Worse?', (1989) 41(4) *Stanford Law Review* 871–957.
13. Ludwig Wittgenstein, *Philosophical Investigations*, transl. G.E.M. Anscombe (3rd edn, New York: MacMillan Publishing Co., 1958), ss 141 and 198.
14. Letter of 21 November 1613 to Benedetto Castelli, in *Edizione nazionale delle Opere di Galileo Galilei*, edited by A. Favaro, edition of 1968, vol. V, p. 282.
15. Saint Augustine, *Epistula* (Letter) 143, Augustinus to Marcellinus. *The Work of Saint Augustine: A Translation for the 21st Century*, Part II/2, Letters (Epistulae) 100–155, transl. by Ronald Teske (Hyde Park, NY: New City Press, 2003).

In the case of legal interpretation, we are not searching for truth in any absolute sense, but we try to establish what is true as a matter of law, and this can vary with circumstances and in time. Law is in essence the reflection of a society's moral values and the vehicle by which its economic, political and social objectives are to be delivered. Given the crucial role of judges in the political, economic and social lives in a country, it comes as no surprise that a considerable percentage of contemporary empirical legal research is focused on the judicial decision-making process, i.e., what facts determine or explain judges' decisions. Over the last three decades studies use predominantly two research models, namely behaviouralism and attitudinalism.[16] Behaviouralism presumes a direct influence on judicial decisions by a judge's social-economic background, where attitudinalism ascribes an indirect influence, i.e., someone's background is formative on his or her ideology which, in turn, would influence a judge's decision. Indeed, studies in the US have frequently identified political affiliation as a determining factor – and thus a predictor – of judicial voting in ideologically divisive cases, but the difference overall between judges affiliated with the Democratic party and the Republican party respectively was relatively small.[17]

The limitations of both models have led to the development of more comprehensive models to explain and predict legal decision-making. The legal model points to the moderating influence of legal doctrine and precedence as well as a judge's role orientation as judicial officer, which would lead to increased impartiality and objectivity among judges. The public choice theory suggests that in addition to the socio-economic background of judges, the legal context of the case and their actual reasoning should be taken into account, because judges as rational persons pursue instrumental and consumptive goals like everyone else.[18] Institutionalism focuses on how judges are influenced by the institutional characteristics within which they operate. Instead of assuming that and studying how judges influence the institutions in which they work, this approach takes the opposite angle and studies the 'cultural' impact of the institution on the judge. Judges do not operate in isolation but function in intersecting relationships with other judges, and therefore they exercise strategic behaviour.[19] In Perelman's terms, a judge deals with a variety of audiences. First, a judge must convince at least a majority of the other judges of the court that his or her reading of the law is the correct one. Then his or her reasoning must be upheld by appeal courts; this is quite relevant as judges are protective of their reputation and do not like to be overruled. Subsequently, a judge faces the broader legal community of practitioners and academic commentators. Finally, the public at large, or society, forms the ultimate audience for any judge.

16. Michael Heise, 'The Past, Present, and Future of Empirical Legal Scholarship: Judicial Decision Making and the New Empiricism', (2002) 4 *University of Illinois Law Review* 819, 833.
17. *See*, for example, C.K. Rowland & Robert A. Carp, *Politics and Judgment in Federal District Courts* (Lawrence: University Press of Kansas, 1996), 24–57.
18. Richard A. Posner, 'What Do Judges Maximize? (The Same Thing Everybody Else Does)', (1993) 3(1) *Supreme Court Economic Review* 1.
19. *See*, for example, Howard Gilman, 'The New Institutionalism, Part I: More and Less Than Strategy: Some Advantages to Interpretative Institutionalism in the Analysis of Judicial Politics', (1997) 7(1) *Law & Cts.* 6; and Lee Epstein & Jack Knight, 'The New Institutionalism, Part II', (1997) 7(2) *Law & Courts* 4.

Because legal interpretation is the work of an individual, it would seem that interpretation never can be truly objective. The subjectivity of interpretation is advocated by many twentieth century philosophies of interpretation, like hermeneutics or postmodern movements. Those philosophies were developed in opposition to the idea of the objective interpreter as developed by the positivistic movement. Some conclude that interpretation is unavoidably subjective, and that the methodological elements used in the process such as 'plain meaning', 'purpose', 'intent', 'structure', 'strict construction', 'precedent' and other legal mysticisms are merely pieces manipulated in a game.[20] In our opinion, legal interpretation comprises both objective and subjective elements. The latter are found in the personal values, moral views, political philosophy, social-economic background and life experience of a judge. The former derive from the procedural framework in which legal interpretation takes place, the methodological approach, interpretational tradition and the parameters set by legal definitions, norms, presumptions and legal precedent. As such, interpretation can most accurately be characterised as being intersubjective. Interpretation is the subjective understanding of the interpreter of the law, which in itself is objective in nature (notwithstanding that its meaning may vary in time and factual context). The purpose of legal interpretation is to arrive at a legal decision on the basis of a coherent argumentation using generally accepted normative premises. Interpretation is constitutive as it determines what valid law is.

§1.02 SOME CONSIDERATIONS ON THE INTERPRETATION OF TAX LAW

Words are the building blocks for all human development, vehicles used to convey ideas, enabling two persons – the speaker and the listener – to share understandings. Tax law, like all law, is expressed in words. The meanings of words derive from the context in which they are used. Considered alone, they fail to communicate ideas. An assertion that someone is 'right' could mean they are physically located to the right side of the speaker. It could mean the person is politically conservative. It could mean the person is correct. In isolation, the word has no shared meaning. But in communication both the speaker and hearer share a common understanding because of the context in which the words are used. The words derive their meaning from the context.

A layperson unexposed to the remarkable world of tax law might be forgiven for starting with an assumption that tax law might resemble all other collections of words and interpreters of the law would look to the context to find the meaning of particular words. This would prove to be a naïve assumption. The world of tax law interpretation is in many ways one far removed from worlds of interpretation applied to other communications and even, in many cases, other laws. In all jurisdictions, the interpreters of tax law cite a wide range of interpretation doctrines, rules, or principles to explain decisions interpreting tax law. In the broadest terms, tax scholars speak of

20. Robert Benson, *The Interpretation Game: How Judges and Lawyers Make the Law* (Durham, NC: Carolina Academic Press, 2008).

literal interpretations versus purposive interpretations, decisions that respect legal form versus those looking to economic substance, interpretations based on civil law concepts versus those reflecting common law concepts, and interpretations ascribing unique tax law meanings to words versus those adopting meanings transplanted from other spheres of law.

Remarkably, apparently competing doctrines often coexist in the same jurisdiction at the same time and not surprisingly, in virtually all jurisdictions it is possible to find tax law interpretations along the entire spectrum of competing doctrines, whichever set of doctrines is used. Scholars seeking to better reconcile the resulting array of approaches may dig below the conventional distinctions such as literal versus purposive or form versus substance to cite a wide range of subordinate doctrines. In this volume (*see* Chapter15), for example, US cases are classified by reference to interpretation principles known as literalism, textualism, intentionalism, purposivism, dynamism and pragmatism. Further complicating attempts to characterise interpretation doctrines is the fact that different approaches may be used for different parts of the same law - in the income tax, income inclusion terms may be read broadly and deduction terms narrowly, or vice versa.

While they may lead to widely divergent outcomes, all the interpretation doctrines share a common aim - to give the meaning to the tax law that was intended by the legislature that enacted the law and thus communicated the ideas. Proponents of transplanted meanings argue the legislators intended the words used in tax laws to have the same meaning ascribed to the terms in others laws. Proponents of literalism assert the meaning must be found in the words themselves as set out in the articles in which they are found. Proponents of purposive interpretation argue the meaning must be the one that gives effect to the purpose of the provision. Whatever interpretation path is followed, the rationale remains the same - the goal is to give effect to the meaning intended by the legislators.

The premise on which the alternative interpretations rest is, of course, entirely a myth. The legislators intended no particular meanings for specific words in provisions passed into law. Almost certainly, the vast majority of the legislators had not read the exact words of the laws they passed. Their intention was to pass a law to give effect to policy, and the words chosen by the ministerial advisors and legislative drafters were intended to work together to telegraph that policy, not to be dissected and interpreted out of that broader context.

From a communication of policy perspective, it seems blindingly obvious that the words in tax law should be given meanings that protect the integrity of the policy they were intended to convey. As often as not, however, the interpreters of tax law look everywhere but at the underlying tax policy when interpreting the words of the law. Consider, for example, the income tax law distinction between employees and self-employed persons. Income tax laws impose withholding tax on the gross salary of the employees and allow the self-employed to determine net gains before remitting tax. The law assumes employees operate in an environment in which the costs of deriving gross income will be assumed by the employer while the self-employed will bear those costs directly, with the result that taxable income may be a small portion of gross receipts for the latter group. Imposing withholding tax on the self-employed might be grossly unfair, not to mention almost impossible to administer. Read in this context, the term employee would be understood to mean a person in a work environment in which remuneration comes from one source (making administration of a withholding tax feasible) and in which gross salary is quite likely to equal net gains from the provision of labour services. It would be illogical to ascribe to the term employee the meaning used in, say, a labour law code concerned with the relative rights of workers and the owners of capital or in vicarious liability tort law concerned with the extent to which a tortfeasor is acting independently of or in the service of another person.

And yet, as this volume shows, judges are as likely as not to read a term such as employee out of the context of the income tax law in which it is used and ascribe to the word a meaning from tort law or a labour law code. The process may not be as perverse as it appears painted in this way, however. Tax law is not drafted in a vacuum. The drafters know how administrators and courts interpret tax law and nevertheless used terms that they knew might be read out of the context of tax policy and ascribed meanings best suited to other policy objectives. In an idealised world, perhaps, judges would interpret words in tax laws in the context of tax policy. But in a world where judges have historically drawn upon a range of external sources for the meaning of words, it might only be logical to assume this is what the legislative drafters intended when they used terms with meanings in other areas of law and provided no separate tax law definitions for the terms.

§1.03 THE ADDITIONAL CHALLENGES OF TAX LAW INTERPRETATION

The interpreters of tax law face two significant challenges that are likely to arise more often in tax law than in other fields of law. The first is a combination of the inherent complexity of and easy substitutability of transactions subject to taxation. The second challenge is the phenomenon of legislative abdication or, to phrase it more delicately, legislative delegation, where the legislature knowingly walks away from difficult issues, leaving it to the administrators and then judiciary to give shape to the law.

The first challenge, that of complexity and substitutability, is not unique to tax law but undoubtedly may be observed more often in tax law than in other areas of commercial law. The infinite flexibility of modern commercial law allows for the replication of any particular economic transaction in an infinite number of legal forms. A simple secured debt, for example, can easily be structured as a finance lease or a repo transaction (a sale combined with a put option for the resale of the security asset to the borrower/seller). Whether the transaction is characterised as a loan, on the one hand, or a sale/repurchase or lease, on the other, has significant consequences for both tax law and company and securities law. The latter relies on accounting standards, so the finance lease or repo transaction will be treated as a loan for company and securities law purposes. Whether it will be treated this way for tax purposes depends first on whether the tax law measures profits using accounting standards and, if not, how the court characterises the multi-element transaction. A court looking at the substance of the transaction would recognise the fact that the parties intended the effect of all elements of the transaction taken and treat the arrangement as a loan. A court inclined to accept the paper form of the transaction will allow the parties to dissect the multistep arrangement into separate parts for tax purposes.

The example is merely the tip of a very large iceberg. Applications drawn from an array of modern financial tools such as derivatives, convertible notes, and put and call options can turn any contractual obligation into synthetic substitutes that replicate completely the effect of debt or equity. It is beyond the capacity of any legislature or legislation to anticipate every possibility and enact measures addressing the infinite legal possibilities. The best the legislature can hope for is that courts will understand the goals of the tax law and the reason it draws lines such as debt versus equity and apply the law to transactions in a way that protects the operation of the tax. If they do not, the challenge facing the legislature is even greater than that facing the court – drafting law so clearly that even recalcitrant judges can understand it.

The second challenge facing interpreters of tax law is the habitual abdication of law-making by the legislature in respect of areas of tax law most in need of legislature guidance. The ultimate example of legislative abdication is found in China (*see* further Chapter 5) where the legislature has delegated to the executive the power to enact tax laws and to provide all the substantive meat to skeletal legislation in the few cases where the legislature had passed tax legislation. The passivity of the judiciary in China effectively largely leaves the administration to create and interpret the tax law as it applies it.

In mature market economies, legislative abdication arises in two instances. One is where definitions and consequent line drawing create political hazards. The substantial legislative concessions for capital gains in some Anglo jurisdictions while the concept that enjoys the concessions remains undefined is a leading example.[21] Defining the gains eligible for concessional treatment would also entail offering plausible and persuasive explanation for the borderlines inherent in a definition. Seeking to avoid this step, the legislature leaves the term undefined, delegating the task of line drawing to the courts. The concept of capital gains is wholly a judicial concept in these jurisdictions.

Legislative delegation also arises in cases where the structure of the legislation creates the need for many borderlines and legislators with limited resources and time shy away from line drawing to concentrate on other priorities. An example is the need to distinguish hobbies from businesses in jurisdictions that have global income and deduction regimes. The issue rarely arises in jurisdictions in which the income tax is based on a schedular structure that makes no provision for the offset of excess expenses from business against employment income.[22] It is problematic in a global

21. For example, Australia and Canada provide an exemption for half of realised capital gains without providing any definition of the term, implicitly adopting the meaning of gains outside the juridical concept of ordinary income. New Zealand, Hong Kong and Singapore all exempt capital gains entirely from tax, again without any definition of the term, simply recognising as exempt amounts that are not ordinary income, a concept also not defined in the laws.
22. The global system is particularly common in English-speaking jurisdictions. Ironically, while the income tax of the United Kingdom started with and after more than two centuries retains a schedular system, virtually all other English-speaking jurisdictions have global tax systems. Continental tax systems most often are based on schedular tax structures. The boundaries between the systems have blurred in recent decades with the adoption of the dual income tax in

system, however, if expenses incurred to derive one type of income can be deducted from general taxable income comprising other types of income. In this case, a definition of business that excludes hobby-like activities is necessary to prevent taxpayers from deducting personal expenses from taxable income. In reality, there is no sharp line on the continuum with pure hobby activities at one end and profitable businesses at the other. Along the continuum are genuine businesses that lose money during start up phases or in economic downturns. Recognising the difficulty of characterising activities on a case-by-case basis, some jurisdictions resort to bright line statutory formulae – expenses from a business are deductible from other income only if the business realises a profit in a defined number of years within a wider number of years. Other jurisdictions leave the interpretation of business activities to the courts which devise judicial tests such as the 'reasonable expectation of profit' test that can be applied on a facts and circumstances basis to the facts of each case in which the tax administration challenges deductions from a money-losing operation.

The most significant instance of legislative delegation is the adoption of a general anti-avoidance rule (GAAR), a legislative measure that has spread widely in recent years. Most commonly, a GAAR provides authority for the characterisation of a transaction in a way that nullifies a tax benefit if two conditions are met. The first is a conclusion that access to the benefit for the particular transaction was not an intended outcome from the law. The second is that the taxpayer's dominant motive for structuring the transaction in the form taken was to obtain the tax benefit. In other words, the GAAR allows for an interpretation of tax law based on a taxpayer's subjective intent.

Both proponents and critics of GAARs agree the provisions authorise law-making by way of interpretation. Proponents of the measures argue the interpretative function of the courts is an appropriate extension of the courts' role in protecting the integrity of legislation. As independent arbiters, courts have responsibility to protect the legitimate rights and expectations of taxpayers and hold the state to account if laws purport to give the state powers beyond those granted in the constitution or administrators seek to impose obligations on taxpayers beyond those clearly set out in the law. At the same time, those courts are responsible for protecting the integrity of the law if taxpayers seek constructions or interpretations that clearly threaten the objectives of the law. The simplest resolution of this balancing act is to read the law so it yields the most appropriate outcome for the substance of a transaction – the courts calling a spade a spade, whether it is presented as a spade or as a series of independent steps intended to work together to create an instrument that serves the function of a spade. But if the law is not sufficiently robust to achieve this outcome, a GAAR provides a tool for the legislature to prevent manipulation by looking beyond the substantive rules to the subjective intent of taxpayers.

Critics of the GAAR argue creative law-making on the basis of taxpayer intention, as opposed to responsible interpretation of substantive provisions to reinforce the

---

Nordic countries (separating property income and business or labour income) and quarantining rules in global tax systems that create de facto schedular rules for particular types of income such as capital gains or passive losses.

integrity of a tax, is a step too far. The step from objective evaluation of the totality of facts of a transaction to deeming transactions that took place not to have occurred or vice versa on the basis of supposed taxpayer intent shifts the court's function from interpretation to legislator, the critics say. In almost every case the GAAR is invoked, an alternative solution would have been a legislative restructure to avoid the need for the rules that have been abused by the taxpayer. Under this viewpoint, the artificial process would be unnecessary if the law had been better drafted in the first place.

§1.04 COMPARATIVE STUDY OF TAX INTERPRETATION

This book does not deal with the line of argument used by courts to justify their rulings in individual tax cases. Rather, we are more generally interested in comparing the interpretative methodology applied in tax law. For example, our inquiry is into the external sources considered by courts when interpreting tax law, such as explanatory memoranda, administrative rulings, judicial precedents, judgments of foreign courts, legislative debates, OECD guidelines and commentary. We seek to establish whether courts prefer grammatical (literal) interpretation over teleological or purposive interpretation. The latter is generally assigned to interpretations that read provisions in a holistic fashion to achieve outcomes intended by sections as read in a wider context, looking at how the possible outcomes would fit into the wider aims of part of an Act or the entire Act. The former is used to describe the technique of reading the words in the section as they could conceivably literally apply, without considering whether that interpretation was consistent with the likely objective of the measure. There is unlikely to be a single approach adopted by all courts over all time – the pendulum often swings between the two approaches, and at any given time there are likely to be examples of both; and it is important to learn in what factual and/or statutory circumstances the one method is preferred over the other. A last example is the use of so-called transplanted categories, i.e., the situation where an undefined term in the tax law is clarified through the meaning of that same term in another law.

The approaches taken to interpretation of tax law vary greatly from nation to nation with a complex web of factors affecting the interpretation process. Cultural, constitutional, economic and historical influences unique to each country or region mould the process, often taking interpreters looking at similar issues in dramatically different directions. Is there any value to be gained by looking at the interpretation of tax law in other countries where the law and interpretation processes are built upon such dramatically different foundations and the outcomes may be on opposite sides of an interpretation spectrum? Are there any lessons to be learned, for example, from contrasting the interpretation in China of tax law built on tax administrative Circulars read by courts overseen in a one-party state by the Communist Party and the interpretation in the EU of tax law that derives from a multination treaty and is read by judges from a mix of civil law and common law jurisdictions?

The answer is an unambiguous yes. And the reason is not because of what we can learn of tax law in other countries – by itself a worthy outcome in the age of globalisation with cross-border investment flows and business activities – but rather what we learn about our own tax systems through comparative studies. As in all spheres of life, those who work most intensely in an area often fail to see the forest for the trees or, in the case of tax law, the underlying influences that have driven tax law interpretation from the time the taxes were adopted and that point the way to how it will be interpreted in the future.

The phenomenon is best illustrated with an example. Faced with the same question – what does income mean? – the judges in the highest courts in Australia and the US came to very different conclusions. The US Supreme Court interpreted the term to mean gross realised (and since expanded to some unrealised) gains from any source of any character. Truly windfall amounts are income for tax purposes in the US. The High Court of Australia interpreted the word to mean a particular class of gains that pretty much aligns with the type of gains to which a life beneficiary of a trust is entitled. The income concept is restricted to those gains clearly identified as returns from an investment, the product of personal services or business, or arriving as periodic payments expected by the recipient. It is not possible to imagine two more diametrically opposed views. But both Australian and US tax experts will assert with confidence that the judicial definitions of income in their respective jurisdictions reflect the 'ordinary' meaning of the term. Immersed in the subject on a daily basis to the extent that legal maxims and tax law interpretation principles become reflexive, tax experts often accept the peculiarities of their respective systems as the norm.

It is easy to overlook the factors that have guided tax interpretation in our home jurisdictions until we reflect upon the development of our tax systems from the perspective of experiences in other jurisdictions. Only then can we look beyond the cases and rulings to understand the logic behind the concepts. To the current scholar or practitioner, the income concept in the US or Australia is a tax law concept. But in neither country does the judicial definition or interpretation of the term come from tax law. The first cases on the meaning of 'income' in the US were constitutional law cases – the 16th amendment to the US Constitution was enacted with the specific objective of allowing the federal government to impose a progressive income tax on individuals. Early cases on the meaning of income in the income tax law were based entirely on constitutional grounds – what types of gains did the US Constitution envisage being taxed? The constitutional amendment had been passed to enable the government to appropriate on a progressive basis increments in economic power and in this context, the broad definition of income that lies at the heart of income tax jurisprudence in the US was the only logical one available to the court hearing constitutional law cases.

The Australian High Court, in contrast, considered the meaning of income in the context of a non-exclusive definition that set out eight types of receipts, including income derived under a trust. It was not an illogical leap for the Court to assume the word being defined had the same meaning as the familiar word used in the definition itself.

This, then, is the benefit of comparative studies – we need to look at the experience of other jurisdictions to open the door to a reconsideration of our own. The broader perspective can help us understand the forces that have driven interpretation of tax law in the past and that will continue to shape our understandings in the future.

The jurisdictions presented in this volume were chosen with this goal in mind. They comprise a full cross-section of interpretation backgrounds and outcomes, covering fourteen jurisdictions across six continents. The examples review tax law interpretation in civil law, common law and socialist legal systems. They include a jurisdiction where interpretation draws upon civil law and common law traditions within the same jurisdiction (the EU) and one in which history has left two parts of the same country with radically different interpretation approaches (China and Hong Kong). They include countries with long stable constitutional frameworks (the UK, US, Canada and Australia) and nations with significant constitutional and tax overhauls in medium (Germany and Japan) and shorter timeframes (Brazil and Russia). The story of tax interpretation in all these jurisdictions provides a rich tapestry of insights and perspectives that can help us to understand the development of tax interpretation in our own countries and the directions it may take going forward.

CHAPTER 2

Legal Interpretation of Tax Law: Australia

Richard Krever & Peter Mellor

§2.01 AUSTRALIA'S TAX SYSTEM: CONSTITUTIONAL BACKGROUND

[A] Introduction

Under Australia's federal system of government, taxes are imposed at the national (Commonwealth), subnational (State and Territory) and municipal levels. The Australian Constitution, which gave effect to Federation in Australia on 1 January 1901, provides for the taxation power of the Commonwealth government established at that time.[1] The Constitution also imposes a number of important restrictions on the tax powers of the State governments which, prior to Federation, were British colonies with parliamentary self-government and which continue to operate and impose taxes under their own Constitutions.[2] The mainland territory subnational governments of the Northern Territory and Australian Capital Territory impose taxes which are comparable to those of the States,[3] while local municipal governments in Australia operate pursuant to State and Territory legislation.

Court systems operate at both Commonwealth and State levels in Australia, the ultimate appeal court in all matters being the High Court of Australia.[4] Appeals on State taxes are considered by State administrative bodies and State courts, with an appeal

1. Constitution, s. 51(ii), which provides for power to make laws with respect to 'taxation; but so as not to discriminate between States or parts of States'.
2. *See* Peter Hanks, 'Constitutional Issues of Australian Taxation', in Richard Krever (ed.), *Australian Taxation: Principles and Practice* (Melbourne: Longman, 1987), pp. 37, 50-51.
3. These two territory governments are also parties to the Intergovernmental Agreement on Federal Financial Relations which provides for the distribution of GST revenue collected by the Commonwealth to the States, Northern Territory and Australian Capital Territory.
4. Prior to 1968, federal tax cases could be appealed (with leave) to the Privy Council sitting in the UK. Appeals from State Supreme Courts direct to the Privy Council in State tax matters also were no longer possible after 1986.

available to the High Court of Australia in some cases. Commonwealth legislation was once interpreted by a specialist tax administrative body known as the Board of Review and State courts or a single judge of the High Court. In 1986, the specialist Board of Review was folded into an Administrative Appeals Tribunal responsible for initial appeals of a broad range of Commonwealth administrative matters and since 1987, jurisdiction for appeals to a court has been shifted from the State Courts to a Federal Court. Appeal from the Federal Court is to the Full Court of the Federal Court and then, subject to a grant of special leave, to the High Court.

As Commonwealth statutes, interpretation of income tax and goods and services tax (GST) laws will be subject to the *Acts Interpretation Act 1901* (Cth.), which provides that an interpretation is to be preferred which 'would best achieve the purpose or object of the Act (whether or not that purpose or object is expressly stated in the Act)',[5] and that reference may be made to a variety of extrinsic materials in various circumstances.[6] Tax administrative legislation places the burden of proof on the taxpayer in tax disputes.[7]

One of the main features of Australia's taxation system is the substantial 'vertical fiscal imbalance' in the revenue raising by the Commonwealth and State levels of government, which sees the two most important taxes, income tax (personal and corporate) and GST, collected solely by the Commonwealth government and the States reliant upon substantial grants from the Commonwealth government (comprising all GST revenue collected and a portion of other Commonwealth revenue), in addition to the revenue collected under their taxes (payroll tax, land tax and various stamp duties). This imbalance, which existed in part from the outset at Federation and had led to the inclusion of constitutional provisions for revenue transfer to the States, has been greatly exacerbated by the course of interpretation of the broad financial provisions of the Constitution and the one-off event in 1942 when the Commonwealth, exercising wartime powers, effectively appropriated State income tax powers.

[B] Constitutional Restrictions on State Taxation

[1] Indirect Tax

At Federation, customs duties were one of the main sources of revenue to the States, and State income taxation was still in its infancy. To ensure there would be a single national customs law, the Constitution allocated to the Commonwealth the exclusive right to impose 'duties of customs and of excise'.[8] While the focus at the time was on the central government's assumption of all power to levy a customs tariff, the significant long-term impact came from the assignment to the central government of sole rights to impose excise duties. Subsequent interpretation of this measure that had the effect of denying States the power to levy most types of indirect taxes, along with

5. *Acts Interpretation Act 1901* (Cth.), s. 15AA.
6. *Acts Interpretation Act 1901*, s. 15AB.
7. *Taxation Administration Act 1953* (Cth.), ss 14ZZK and 14ZZO.
8. Constitution, s. 90.

the Commonwealth's de facto wartime appropriation of income tax rights, created the fiscal imbalance and need for extensive transfers from the central government.[9]

Over the course of nine decades, the Australian High Court interpreted the term 'duty of excise' widely to include any taxes imposed on goods at any stage in the process of production or distribution.[10] The interpretation imposed the condition that there be a direct relationship between the tax and a transaction involving the goods. State governments attempted to bypass the constitutional prohibition on excises by imposing 'franchise fees' on the sale of products normally subject to excise taxes. These fees were presented as licence fees, with the fee charged based on the volume of sales in the previous assessment period. The legality of these fees was finally settled in a 1990s decision that found them unconstitutional.[11] That decision necessitated a financial rescue package for the States from the Commonwealth government with the imposition of corresponding increases in federal commodity taxes and a windfall profits tax equal to the tax that would be refunded if any taxpayers sought refunds of what had turned out to be unconstitutional taxes, together with a complementary increase in central government financial support for the States.[12]

Following a consideration of Australian[13] and United States (US) precedents,[14] as well as interpretations of the US Constitution[15] and historic English commentaries on law,[16] the court in the franchise fees case settled on a definition of excise tax as an

9. *See* Cheryl Saunders, 'Vertical Fiscal Imbalance: Constitutional Origins', in David Collins (ed.), *Vertical Fiscal Imbalance and the Allocation of Taxing Powers* (Sydney: Australian Tax Research Foundation, 1993), pp. 55, 59–61; Cheryl Saunders, 'The High Court, Section 90 and the Australian Federation', in Neil Warren (ed.), *Reshaping Fiscal Federalism in Australia* (Sydney: Australian Tax Research Foundation, 1997), pp. 21, 22–27.

10. Saunders, 'The High Court, Section 90 and the Australian Federation', *supra* note 9, p. 28, citing *Parton v. Milk Board (Vic.)* (1949) 80 CLR 229 and the earlier judgment of Dixon J. in *Matthews v. Chicory Marketing Board (Vic.)* (1938) 60 CLR 263; Hanks, *supra* note 2, pp. 53–56. The *Matthews* and *Parton* cases included references to Privy Council decisions on the distinction between direct and indirect taxation under the Canadian Constitution.

11. *Ha v. New South Wales* [1997] HCA 34; 189 CLR 465; 36 ATR 319. In *Eclipse Resources Pty. Ltd. v. WA (No. 4)* [2016] WASC 62, paras [770]–[777] (upheld on appeal by the Western Australian Court of Appeal, [2017] WASCA 90, 12 May 2017), the Supreme Court of Western Australia concluded a levy imposed on waste disposed of to landfill was not an excise duty as there was no close connection between the levy and the waste including in circumstances where the recipient of the waste may later have used it after disposal to landfill in the production of valuable soil and structural fill products.

12. *See* Robert A. Dick, *A Loss of State Autonomy: Implications of the Ha and Hammond Decisions*, 27(1) Austl. Tax Rev. 30, 34 (1998), citing estimates that the revenue loss to the States for the 1997–1998 year would be greater than $5 billion; Michael Walpole, 'Sharing the "Magic Pudding" – An Australian Approach to Allocation of Taxing Rights', in Michael Lang & Peter Melz (eds), *Value Added Tax and Direct Taxation: Similarities and Differences* (Amsterdam: IBFD, 2009), pp. 1171, 1179–1180.

13. In particular, *Matthews v. Chicory Marketing Board (Vic.)* (1938) 60 CLR 263, per Dixon J. and *Parton v. Milk Board (Vic.)* (1949) 80 CLR 229 at 260, per Dixon J., referred to in *Ha v. New South Wales* [1997] HCA 34; 189 CLR 465; 36 ATR 319 at 326–328.

14. *Patton v. Brady, Executrix* 184 US 608, 617 (1902), cited in *Ha v. New South Wales* [1997] HCA 34; 189 CLR 465; 36 ATR 319 at 327, n. 37.

15. Joseph Story, *Commentaries on the Constitution of the United States* (1833), vol. 2, s. 940, cited in *Ha v. New South Wales* [1997] HCA 34; 189 CLR 465; 36 ATR 319 at 327, n. 37.

16. William Blackstone, *Commentaries on the Laws of England*, Bk. 1, Ch. 8, at 318, cited in *Ha v. New South Wales* [1997] HCA 34; 189 CLR 465; 36 ATR 319 at 327, n. 36.

inland tax on 'production, manufacture, sale or distribution of goods, whether of foreign or domestic origin'. The broad definition eliminated lingering uncertainty[17] about the possible constitutional validity of a State-based retail sales tax or value added tax (VAT) on the sale of new goods. A retail sales tax or VAT on used goods[18] or on supplies of services remains possible in theory but for practical reasons is unlikely to ever see the light of day.

[2] Income Tax

The vertical fiscal imbalance has been exacerbated by the fact that the Australian States also have not levied income taxes since the imposition of uniform income taxation by the Commonwealth in 1942. Income taxes had been imposed on a source basis from the late nineteenth century by the Australian colonies (all of which had income taxes in some form in place by 1901 when they became States in the newly created Commonwealth of Australia).

The Commonwealth also entered the income tax field in 1915, however, and the administrative complexities of this system for taxpayers, and significant differences in the income tax rules in each jurisdiction, led to efforts to bring about greater harmonisation over a long period.[19] One significant area of disagreement, for example, involved the allocation of income of multi-State businesses, which saw a variety of approaches taken by the States. Attempts were made to achieve a common basis for taxation in 1929 and again in 1936 when legislation was largely harmonised,[20] but differences had arisen again by 1942 when the Commonwealth government moved to monopolise the income tax field.

17. The uncertainty arose in part as a consequence of minority judgments such as that of Murphy J. of the High Court in *Hematite Petroleum Pty. Ltd. v. Victoria* (1983) 151 CLR 599 which led to the minority view that an excise duty was 'a selective tax on goods produced or manufactured locally': Saunders, 'The High Court, Section 90 and the Australian Federation', *supra* note 9, p. 30. A State retail *sales* tax would have been possible under this view.
18. In *Commissioner for Australian Capital Territory Revenue v. Kithock Pty. Ltd.* (2000) FCA 1098, the court concluded that a tax imposed on the sale of used motor vehicles was not an excise tax because the items sold had ceased to be part of the commercial production, distribution and sales chain once they were in the hands of final consumers.
19. *See* Cheryl Saunders, 'The Uniform Income Tax Cases', in H.P. Lee & George Winterton (eds), *Australian Constitutional Landmarks* (Cambridge: Cambridge University Press, 2003), pp. 62, 64–65; Rodney Maddock, *Unification of Income Taxes in Australia*, 28(3) Austl. J. Pol. & Hist. 354, 354–357 (1982).
20. New South Wales at this point accepted the harmonised scheme proposed in 1929 in relation to inter-State sales of goods by a manufacturer (two-thirds of profit to State of manufacture and one-third to State of sale); Queensland, however, legislated to tax 50% of the profit on sales of goods manufactured in another State and sold in Queensland: *Income Tax (Management) Act 1936* (N.S.W.), ss 37–38 and *Income Tax Assessment Act 1936* (Qld.), s. 28(7) and (8). New South Wales and the Commonwealth also could not reach agreement in 1936 on the method to be used to calculate tax on sales of goods by overseas manufacturers. *See* Richard Krever & Peter Mellor, 'The Development of Centralised Income Taxation in Australia, 1901-1942', in Peter Harris & Dominic de Cogan (eds), *Studies in the History of Tax Law, Vol. 7* (Oxford: Hart Publishing, 2015), pp. 363, 381–383.

The Commonwealth's initiative, the 'uniform tax scheme', which was originally expressed to apply for the period of the war and a year thereafter,[21] had two elements: increasing national rates to the point where additional State tax could not be sustained; and the payment of a fixed amount of financial assistance to the States based on the average of their income tax collections in the two previous financial years, less certain cost savings and other deductions.[22] The scheme was challenged by four of the States and upheld by the High Court in the year that the legislation was enacted.[23]

Significantly, the key features of the uniform tax scheme, including the payment of grants of financial assistance to each State on the condition that the State had not imposed income tax in the prior year, were found to be valid by the High Court on grounds other than the wartime defence power of the Commonwealth.[24] This outcome opened the door to continuation of the Commonwealth's exclusive role in income taxation after the war.[25] (By contrast, the extensive national price and wage controls imposed during the war were wound down in the post-war period.[26])

In January 1946, the Commonwealth announced its intention to continue to monopolise the income tax field. The central government was successful in a subsequent attempt by States to challenge the constitutionality of its move,[27] leaving the States with the constitutional power to impose income tax but no practical way of doing so while the Commonwealth retained its combined tax and grant scheme.[28]

21. *See*, for example, *States Grants (Income Tax Reimbursement) Act 1942* (Cth.), s. 8. *See also* the recommendation to this effect in Committee on Uniform Taxation, *Report* (28 March 1942), para. 1.
22. Saunders, 'The Uniform Income Tax Cases', *supra* note 19, p. 66, citing Treasurer Chifley, Debates, House of Representatives, vol. 170, p. 1290 (15 May 1942).
23. *South Australia v. Commonwealth* (1942) 65 CLR 373 (*First Uniform Tax Case*).
24. The Act providing for payment of grants to the States was upheld under s. 96, which relevantly provides that 'the Parliament may grant financial assistance to any State on such terms and conditions as the Parliament thinks fit'. However, the one-off transfer of State taxation office staff and equipment was upheld only under the wartime defence power of the Commonwealth. One judge would only have upheld the provision for priority in payment of Commonwealth income tax over State income tax under the defence power.
25. Saunders, 'The Uniform Income Tax Cases', *supra* note 19, p. 69, citing Kenneth H. Bailey, 'The Uniform Income Tax Plan (1942)', in Wilfred Prest & Russell L. Mathews (eds), *The Development of Australian Fiscal Federalism: Selected Readings* (Canberra: Australian National University Press, 1980), pp. 309, 323.
26. *See* Sydney J. Butlin & C. Boris Schedvin, *War Economy, 1942–1945* (Canberra: Australian War Memorial, 1977), Ch. 25. Efforts had been made by the Commonwealth on several occasions to secure constitutional power for such controls through referenda. More generally, in 1940 (prior to taking office) Australia's wartime Prime Minister John Curtin had set out a policy approach envisaging 'a greatly enlarged role for the Commonwealth in the management of the nation's affairs' both during and after the war: Chief Justice Robert French, 'If they could see us now – what would the founders say?', John Curtin Prime Ministerial Library Anniversary Lecture (18 July 2013), p. 4, available at: http://www.hcourt.gov.au/publications/speeches/current/speeches-by-chief-justice-french-ac (accessed on 6 September 2013).
27. *Victoria v. Commonwealth* (1957) 99 CLR 575 (*Second Uniform Tax Case*).
28. *First Uniform Tax Case* (1942) 65 CLR 373 at 416. Significantly, the Commonwealth had no power to outlaw State taxes where the revenue was to be used for State purposes but it could preclude the income tax at least through its own tax and grant powers. In this context, the 'New Federalism' policy of a conservative government in the late 1970s included legislation (since repealed) for the resumption of State income taxation, but for political reasons the option was not taken up by any of the States as the Commonwealth had not lowered its own rates to make

[C] Limitations on Commonwealth Taxation Powers

Unlike the case with the States, which are specifically excluded from some taxing fields by the Constitution, the Commonwealth suffers no constitutional restrictions on the nature of taxes it can impose under its taxing power.[29]

The apparently 'plenary and absolute' power of the Commonwealth government to impose taxation[30] does not provide constitutional immunity for all supposed Commonwealth tax laws, however. The validity of tax legislation has been attacked on the basis of the interpretation of 'tax', with taxpayers arguing so-called tax laws are in fact disguised regulatory rules designed to enforce Commonwealth incursions into subject areas that constitutionally belong to the States. Tax laws have also been attacked on the basis of two constitutional limitations on the Commonwealth's tax powers, namely a prohibition against discrimination and preference by the Commonwealth as between the States,[31] and another preventing taxation of property of any kind belonging to the States.[32]

The courts have interpreted the word 'tax' generously in respect of the Commonwealth's attempts to use 'taxing' measures as a means of enforcing intervention in areas of State competence.[33] For example, it may be that the Commonwealth government has no power to mandate all employers to provide superannuation (retirement pension) contributions for employees. It does so however by levying a tax, labelled the

room: Saunders, *supra* note 19, p. 77; Hanks, *supra* note 2, p. 53. Suggestions which have been made for limitation of the interpretation of the section 96 conditional grants power are also discussed in Peter Gerangelos, 'Tax Coordination Between Regions in Australia - Role of the Courts', in Michael Lang, Pasquale Pistone, Josef Schuch & Claus Staringer (eds), *Horizontal Tax Coordination* (Amsterdam: IBFD, 2012), pp. 53, 68–71.

29. *Roy Morgan Research Pty. Ltd. v. Federal Commissioner of Taxation* [2011] HCA 35; 244 CLR 97; 80 ATR 1 at 7, in which the High Court confirmed that a tax may be valid for constitutional purposes even though revenue raising is not the primary purpose of the impost. It had also been observed prior to this decision that the taxation power is '"plenary and absolute; unlimited as to amount, as to subjects, as to objects, as to conditions, as to machinery" so that "the Parliament has, prima facie, power to tax whom it chooses, power to impose such conditions as to liability or as to exemption as it chooses"': *Fairfax v. Federal Commissioner of Taxation* (1965) 114 CLR 1 at 12–13, approving the comments of Isaacs and Higgins JJ. in dissent in *R. v. Barger* (1908) 6 CLR 41. *See* Hanks, *supra* note 2, pp. 38–39.
30. *Fairfax v. Federal Commissioner of Taxation* (1965) 114 CLR 1 at 12–13.
31. Constitution, ss 51(ii) and 99 respectively; *see* Hanks, *supra* note 2, pp. 40–44.
32. Constitution, s. 114. A reciprocal prohibition applies against State taxation of property belonging to the Commonwealth.
33. A leading precedent defines tax as 'a compulsory exaction of money by a public authority for public purposes, enforceable by law, and ... not a payment for services rendered': *see Matthews v. Chicory Marketing Board (Vic.)* (1938) 60 CLR 263 at 276.

'superannuation guarantee charge' on employers who fail to do so,[34] an approach that has been upheld as a legitimate exercise of its taxing powers.[35]

The courts have in many cases taken a stricter view on whether various fees' imposed by the government or public authorities can be characterised as taxes for constitutional law purposes.[36] While a 'fee for immigration clearance' payable by airline operators in respect of arriving passengers has (at least where passengers are Australian citizens) been found to be a tax[37] as was a 'wool charge' imposed on farmers in respect of the sale of wool,[38] charges by a public authority to airlines for air services and facilities were considered outside the ambit of a tax,[39] as was a (State) commercial licence fee calculated by quantity for exploitation of natural resources.[40]

Courts have also been less sympathetic (to the Commonwealth) when interpreting the constitutional prohibition on the Commonwealth imposing tax on property of any kind belonging to a State.[41] They have, for example, invalidated a sales tax on

34. *Roy Morgan Research Pty. Ltd. v. Federal Commissioner of Taxation* [2011] HCA 35; 244 CLR 97; 80 ATR 1 at 13–14, in which the Full High Court unanimously upheld the validity of the superannuation guarantee charge in respect of shortfalls in employer superannuation contributions as a tax for constitutional purposes. *See also* the discussion of this case and of earlier comments on the scope of the taxation power by members of the High Court in Justice Michelle Gordon, *The Commonwealth's Taxing Power and Its Limits – Are We There Yet?*, 36(3) Melb. U. L. Rev. 1037, 1040–1044 (2013).
35. The High Court has indicated that for a levy to be treated as a tax it cannot be a penalty, or be arbitrary, and an impost which is enacted in a way that makes it incontestable will also be invalid: *see MacCormick v. Federal Commissioner of Taxation* (1984) 158 CLR 622 at 639–643. An impost payable if a particular behaviour is not carried out such as making superannuation contributions for employees appears to be neither a penalty nor arbitrary. A tax law applying retrospectively to facts which would not have been known to give rise to a tax liability at the time also will not generally be considered arbitrary or incontestable so as to be unconstitutional: see, most recently, *Chevron Australia Holdings Pty. Ltd. v. Federal Commissioner of Taxation* [2017] FCAFC 62 at [144] (Pagone J.).
36. In recent times, government imposts have also increasingly been described as 'levies', such as the Medicare levy, a state fuel levy in 1990 (to fund a partial bailout of depositors in a failed non-bank financial institution), a temporary increase in the Medicare levy in 1996–1997 to fund the 'Gun Buy-Back Scheme', the Air Passenger Ticket Levy of 2001 (known as the 'Ansett levy', to fund staff entitlements on that airline's insolvency), the Temporary Flood and Cyclone Reconstruction Levy of 2011 (Queensland flood levy), and many others. That these are, however, regarded as taxes by the government is shown by the fact that the levies are generally imposed under separate assessment and imposition Acts so as to comply with s. 55 of the Constitution (*see* further below in this section).
37. *Air Caledonie International v. Commonwealth* (1988) 165 CLR 462 at 467.
38. *Moore v. Commonwealth* [1951] HCA 10; 82 CLR 547. The charge was fully creditable against the farmer's income tax liability for the year and refundable if it exceeded the income tax liability.
39. *Airservices Australia v. Canadian Airlines International Ltd.* [1999] HCA 62; 202 CLR 133; 43 ATR 246.
40. *Harper v. Minister for Sea Fisheries* [1989] HCA 47; 168 CLR 314 (provided that there is a relevant relationship between the amount of the impost and the value of the privilege conferred). As the licence fee was found not to be a tax, it could not be an excise duty prohibited to the State under s. 90 of the Constitution.
41. One leading scholar nevertheless has argued that this restriction is generally applied under a 'fairly narrow definition' of the terms, 'focusing on the legal operation' of any legislation in question; *see* Vince Morabito, *The Constitutional Restriction on Taxes Imposed on Crown Property*, 1(1) J. Austl. Tax'n 41, 56 (1998).

goods created by a State instrumentality and then applied to own use[42] and income tax on gains realised on the sale of State assets, viewing the capital gain as an element of the underlying property which would make tax on the gain akin to tax on the underlying property.[43] By way of contrast, the Commonwealth has been allowed to impose income tax on interest payable to a State,[44] and States are liable to pay a fringe benefits tax on non-cash benefits provided to State employees as remuneration in lieu of cash salaries.[45] The other limitation on the Commonwealth's taxing power, the prohibition on discrimination between States, featured prominently in unsuccessful challenges to a clean energy excise tax imposed by the Commonwealth in 2011[46] and a minerals resource rent tax imposed by the Commonwealth in 2012.[47]

Important procedural requirements are also laid down in relation to Commonwealth taxation. In particular, it is provided that '[l]aws imposing taxation shall deal only with the imposition of taxation, and any provision therein dealing with any other matter shall be of no effect'.[48] This has been interpreted as requiring the Commonwealth to set out all taxes in two distinct Acts, an 'assessment' Act that sets out all the rules for calculating the base (e.g., taxable income for the income tax, taxable fringe benefits for the fringe benefits tax, and so on) and a separate 'imposition' Act that actually imposes a tax liability in respect of the base set out in the assessment Act.[49]

Another requirement is also imposed that Commonwealth taxation laws (other than duties of customs and of excise) 'shall deal with one subject of taxation only', and that 'laws imposing duties of customs shall deal with duties of customs only, and laws imposing duties of excise shall deal with duties of excise only'.[50] This measure has been interpreted in a restrictive fashion to limit the means by which the Commonwealth can levy indirect tax. For example, a provision imposing sales tax in respect of swimming pools constructed *in situ* was invalidated on the basis that the provision imposed a tax on land (as a subject distinct from the other provisions of the relevant law imposing a duty of excise).[51] However, the measure has been read generously in the case of

42. *Deputy Commissioner of Taxation v. State Bank of New South Wales* [1992] HCA 6; 174 CLR 219; 23 ATR 1.
43. *South Australia v. Commonwealth* [1992] HCA 7; 174 CLR 235; 23 ATR 10.
44. *South Australia v. Commonwealth* [1992] HCA 7; 174 CLR 235; 23 ATR 10.
45. *Queensland v. Commonwealth* [1987] HCA 2; 162 CLR 74; 18 ATR 158.
46. *Queensland Nickel Pty. Ltd. v. Commonwealth* [2015] HCA 12; 255 CLR 252. (By the time of the judgment, the relevant tax had been repealed with effect from 1 July 2014).
47. *Fortescue Metals Group Ltd. v. Commonwealth* [2013] HCA 34; 250 CLR 548. The alleged discrimination was said to arise in respect of credits provided under the tax for the various mineral royalties paid by taxpayers to the States. (The minerals resource rent tax was also repealed in 2014).
48. Constitution, s. 55.
49. *See* Hanks, *supra* note 2, pp. 46–49.
50. Constitution, s. 55.
51. *Mutual Pools & Staff Pty. Ltd. v. Federal Commissioner of Taxation* [1992] HCA 4; 173 CLR 450; 22 ATR 856. The statutory provision which added this tax in 1986 to the existing sales tax law was rendered void from the time of its introduction. The government implemented a scheme to refund an amount to the pool builder limited to the amount of the tax which had not been passed on or had been refunded to customers; the tax refund was otherwise payable to the customer directly. This scheme was upheld by the High Court in *Mutual Pools & Staff Pty. Ltd. v. Commonwealth* [1994] HCA 9; 179 CLR 155; 27 ATR 357.

income tax, with the High Court interpreting the subject of that tax broadly to include statutory assessments of gains that the Court had concluded fall outside the judicial concept of income in Australia (this interpretation is discussed further in §2.02[A] below),[52] an undistributed profits tax imposed on retained earnings of private companies to prevent shareholders from deferring indefinitely their income tax liability on dividends,[53] and imputed benefits enjoyed by taxpayers who owned their principal residences.[54]

§2.02 INCOME TAX INTERPRETATION

Australia has a common law system and many fundamental elements of the legal system such as contract law and tort law are based on principles developed by the courts through application of the doctrine of precedent. The tax law, in contrast, derives entirely from statute. The application of that statute, however, is guided to a significant extent by judicial interpretation of the words in the law and judicial characterisation of transactions in light of the interpretation of the terms of tax provisions.

Three aspects of interpretation by the courts of the income tax law have proved central to its application and development. The first two are the judicial interpretation of the fundamental building blocks of income and allowable deductions. The most basic terms in the law are undefined, leaving enormous scope for the courts to sculpt the shape of the Australian income tax system. On the receipt side, it was the courts interpreting the word 'income' that established the boundaries for the original income tax law and set the stage for all subsequent amendments to alter the base. On the outgoing side, the courts decided what types of expenses were 'capital' in nature and in consequence created both a boundary to the tax base and a guidepost to the later statutory rules to recognise expenses incurred to derive gross income.

The third aspect of interpretation of income tax law by the courts that has played a major role in the application of the law and, importantly, in the design of the income tax system as the legislature endorsed or reacted against court decisions, derives from the courts' alternating preference for a narrow or expansive interpretation of tax measures, sometimes described as 'literal' or 'purposive' interpretations.

52. *Resch v. Federal Commissioner of Taxation* (1942) 66 CLR 198, which included reference to US authorities on the meaning of income for tax purposes. *See also* Geoffrey Lehmann and Cynthia Coleman, *Taxation Law in Australia* (5th edn, Sydney: Australian Tax Practice, 1998), pp. 17–18, discussing the *Resch* case and arguments concerning the validity of the capital gains tax provisions in the context of the High Court decisions in *Mutual Pools & Staff Pty. Ltd. v. Federal Commissioner of Taxation* [1992] HCA 4; 173 CLR 450; 22 ATR 856 and *South Australia v. Commonwealth* [1992] HCA 7; 174 CLR 235; 23 ATR 10.

53. *Cornell v. Deputy Federal Commissioner of Taxation (South Australia)* (1920) 29 CLR 39.

54. *Harding v. Federal Commissioner of Taxation* (1917) 23 CLR 119.

[A] The Key Concept of 'Ordinary Income'

Australia's income tax legislation imposes tax on 'taxable income', which is calculated as gross income minus deductions.[55] From the introduction of income tax legislation in the late nineteenth century in Australia,[56] the term income was not defined in the law, and it was left to the courts to interpret the word and, in the course of doing so, decide what receipts should be included in gross income.[57] Not surprisingly given the use of precedent in Australian law and the influence of United Kingdom (UK) precedents in particular through much of Australia's legal history, the Australian judicial interpretation of the term was based on UK concepts.

The UK income tax at that time was a schedular tax applicable to 'profits' and 'gains' of various kinds, and the interpretation of the legislation in this form came to be based on a limited concept of income imported from the meaning of income for trust law purposes.[58] Importantly, the transplanted judicial meaning of income excluded amounts that would be considered 'capital' receipts or gains for trust law purposes. Capital gains, in this context, encompassed not only gains realised in respect of the sale of property other than inventory, but also capitalised receipts such as payments for the sale of investment income or employment income streams.

In contrast to the UK tax law, the early Australian income tax statutes taxed 'income' under a global statutory structure, on a model very similar to the US federal income taxes to that time.[59] In this context, some early Australian judicial decisions

55. The earliest income tax laws tended to speak directly of gross income – *see*, for example, *Taxation Act 1884* (South Australia), s. 12(V); *Income Tax Act 1895* (Victoria), s. 9(1), and *Income Tax Assessment Act 1915* (Commonwealth), s. 18(a) ('the gross income'). The Commonwealth legislation subsequently defined taxable income as assessable income less allowable deductions, with 'assessable income' in turn defined as meaning 'gross income' – *see*, for example, *Income Tax Assessment Act 1922* (Cth.), s. 4; *Income Tax Assessment Act 1936* (Cth.), s. 25(1).
56. *See* Peter Harris, *Metamorphosis of the Australasian Income Tax, 1866–1922* (Sydney: Australian Tax Research Foundation, 2002); Julie Smith, *Taxing Popularity* (Sydney: Australian Tax Research Foundation, rev. ed., 2004), pp. 36–44.
57. *See* Peter Mellor, *Origins of the Judicial Concept of Income in Australia*, 25(3) Austl. Tax F. 339 (2010).
58. Ross Parsons, *Income Taxation: An Institution in Decay*, 13(3) Sydney L. Rev. 435, 436–443 (1991); John Avery Jones, Luc De Broe, Maarten Ellis, Kees van Raad, Jean-Pierre Le Gall, Henri Torrione, Toshio Miyatake, Sidney Roberts, Sanford Goldberg, Jürgen Killius, Guglielmo Maisto, Federico Giuliani, Richard Vann, David Ward and Bertil Wiman, *Treaty Conflicts in Categorizing Income as Business Profits Caused by Differences in Approach between Common Law and Civil Law*, 57(6) Bull. Int'l Tax'n 237, n. 3 (2003); Richard Vann, 'Income as a Tax Base', in Richard Krever (ed.), *supra* note 2, p. 62; Richard Krever, 'Interpreting Income Tax Laws in the Common Law World', in Markus Achatz, Tina Ehrke-Rabel, Johannes Heinrich, Roman Leitner and Otto Taucher (eds), *Steuerrecht Verfassungsrecht Europarecht: Festschrift für Hans Georg Ruppe* (Vienna: Facultas Verlags- und Buchhandels AG, 2007), pp. 354, 357 (as noted in that chapter, the process of interpreting tax law provisions by reference to transplanted categories has been described as logically fallacious in Neil Brooks, 'The Responsibility of Judges in Interpreting Tax Legislation', in Graeme Cooper (ed.), *Tax Avoidance and the Rule of Law* (1997), pp. 93, 122–123); but *see also* John Prebble, *Income Taxation: A Structure Built on Sand*, 24(3) Sydney L. Rev. 301 (2002), contesting the view that the UK concept of income was drawn from limited trust concepts as opposed to the ordinary meaning of the term.
59. Mellor, *supra* note 57, 341.

interpreted the terms of income tax law differently from their meaning in trust law, adopting a broad view of assessable amounts, in one case even including accruing gains in the concept of income. The separate interpretation track for income in tax law lasted only briefly, however, and by the opening years of the twentieth century Australian courts had largely settled on an interpretation that for the most part aligned the meaning of income for tax and trust law purposes, excluding the range of gains and receipts that would be considered capital gains for trust law purposes.[60] An early decision by the High Court[61] that appeared to distinguish a key UK authority aligning income for tax and trust law purposes[62] was subsequently interpreted as an opinion based on the narrow facts of the case and ultimately had no impact on the judicial concept.[63] As noted in §2.01[C] above, the narrow judicial concept of income for tax purposes in Australia is in contrast to the broader view of the 'subject' of income taken by the High Court for the purposes of the constitutional requirement that laws imposing taxation must deal only with the one subject of taxation.[64]

The judicial concept of income that had been applied for tax law purposes clearly differed from the economic concept and the accounting concept of income. Following a 1935 decision that described the judicial concept of income for tax purposes as amounts 'determined in accordance with the ordinary concepts and usages of mankind', a new term came into use by the courts and from that time courts and commentators commonly described amounts that would be characterised by a court as income for tax purposes as 'ordinary income'.[65]

The relatively narrow judicial concept of income excluded from the tax base a wide range of receipts – gains on the sale of most assets other than inventory or assets actively traded in a business, employment income paid by way of non-convertible in kind benefits, capitalised employment benefits paid on termination of employment or as lump sum benefits from pension (superannuation, in Australian terminology) plans, compensation for the loss of income-generating property, discounts or premiums in lieu of interest or rent, and other 'capital' amounts.[66] There was little evidence to support the assertion made by some[67] that courts considered both legal and economic concepts in their decision making, at least in terms of the meaning of income.

The equity implications of and opportunities for avoidance from the narrow judicial concept of income were obvious and soon after the enactment of the first Commonwealth income tax Act the legislature embarked on a programme of base

60. *In re the Income Tax Acts (No 2)* (1901) 27 VLR 39 at 41–42.
61. *Commissioner of Income Tax (Queensland) v. The Brisbane Gas Company* (1907) 5 CLR 96. The case involved a provision of the *Income Tax Act 1902* (Qld.) for taxation of dividend payments relating to undistributed profits not previously taxed under the *Dividend Duty Act 1890*.
62. *Bouch v. Sproule* (1887) 12 App. Cas. 385 (H.L.).
63. The High Court applied the income tax provision of the 1902 Queensland Act to payments described by the company as dividends, and an analysis of the nature of those payments was unnecessary. In *Orr v. Wendt* [2005] WASCA 199, the *Brisbane Gas* case was put forward (unsuccessfully) to support the converse argument that the trust law meaning of income is always narrower than its tax law meaning in Australia.
64. *Resch v. Federal Commissioner of Taxation* (1942) 66 CLR 198.
65. *Scott v. Commissioner of Taxation* (1935) 35 SR (NSW) 215 at 219.
66. *See* Julie Cassidy, *Concise Income Tax* (5th ed., Sydney: Federation Press, 2010), pp. 174–175.
67. Lehmann and Coleman, *supra* note 52, pp. 79 and 82.

broadening by including specific types of gain into the calculation of income for tax purposes. Following 70 years of piecemeal inclusion measures, the legislature finally inserted into the income tax law a comprehensive inclusion regime subsequently renamed as the 'capital gains tax' rules that swept in many gains that had escaped the specific gain inclusion measures.

In 1997, the income tax legislation was largely replaced with a 'plain English' version of the tax law. In the new law the legislature formally recognised the judicial concept of income by setting out a new definition of taxable income with two elements to the inclusion side: 'ordinary income' and 'statutory income'. The former was not defined but was understood to mean income according to judicial concepts and the latter as all amounts included in the income tax base as a result of a specific inclusion provision in the income tax law. To avoid any overlap, when the inclusion measures were redrafted in plain English, a proviso was generally added stating that the provisions applied to amounts described in the sections to the extent they would not already be included in the tax base as ordinary income.

[B] The Concept of 'Capital' Expenses

From its inception, Australian income tax law established timing rules for the deduction of expenses by placing a restriction in the general deduction provision that allowed a deduction for expenses incurred in the derivation of gross income apart from 'capital' expenses. Separate depreciation rules then provided for the depreciation of capital expenses. There was no definition in the law of a capital expense, and once again the courts settled on a definition by importing tests from trust law, in this case the tests used to identify expenses of a trust that were charged against the interest of remainder or capital beneficiaries.

For accounting purposes or the measurement of economic income, a capital expense is one with a life longer than the current accounting year. These expenses are recognised over their effective lives through a depreciation or amortisation process. For tax law purposes, applying trust law tests the courts looked at a range of factors, including the longevity of any benefit acquired as a consequence of an expenditure. The life of the benefit is not determinative, however. More important is the form of the expense - one-off expenditures are likely to be considered capital outgoings while repetitive ones are most often treated as 'revenue' expenses, the judicial term for expenditures not characterised as capital in nature and thus deductible under the general deduction provision.

The frequency of payment test was supplemented in the 1940s by what remains the most important test, a distinction between expenses incurred in respect of an income-earning structure (treated as capital expenses) and those incurred in respect of an income-earning process (treated as revenue expenses). Ironically, when the test was first proposed by a single judge of the High Court, it was dismissed by the remainder of the bench,[68] but it was adopted as the predominant test following that judge's elevation to the position of Chief Justice.[69] Not surprisingly, the question of when an expense relates to a 'structure' or 'process' is at best problematic, and it is not uncommon for commentators describing outcomes to cite the often quoted observation from a UK decision that 'in many cases it is almost true to say that the spin of a coin would decide the matter almost as satisfactorily as would an attempt to find reasons'.[70]

The income-earning structure/process test did achieve appropriate results (from a tax policy perspective) in most cases where an expenditure resulted in the taxpayer acquiring tangible or legally recognised intangible property. Depreciation rules were then needed for the recognition of wasting assets with a limited life but the legislature moved slowly and in a very piecemeal fashion to address this issue. The original depreciation section only covered what was termed 'plant and equipment', meaning machinery or equipment other than buildings. Depreciation rules for buildings were added in several tranches over seven decades with separate depreciation regimes for mining buildings, forestry buildings, hotels and motels and finally other buildings used in the generation of income. Separate depreciation regimes applied to various types of intellectual property and further discrete rules applied to a range of services such as the cost for rural property owners of paying for connection to telephone or electricity lines. The legislature finally consolidated the depreciation and amortisation rules into a simplified set of capital allowances in 2001.

The interaction of the judicial tests and the limited range of depreciation or capital allowance measures meant many expenses commonly incurred in the course of a business could never be recognised for tax purposes. Some relief was provided in the course of tax reforms in 1985. For example, taxpayers were allowed to add the expense of defending title to property to the cost of the property, thus recognising the outgoing on the eventual disposal of the property. Indirect recognition of expenses incurred to acquire wasting intangible property such as contract rights not covered by the capital allowance rules was provided at the same time by allowing the taxpayers to recognise the expense as a capital loss (quarantined so it could only be deducted from a capital gain) when the rights expired. There remained a large number of expenses that could not be recognised, including outgoings that were characterised as capital because they were associated with an income-producing structure but generated no ongoing benefit or asset recognised in law. These were known colloquially as 'black hole' expenses, that is, expenses incurred for commercial purposes which disappeared into a black hole for tax purposes.

68. Dixon, J. in *Sun Newspapers Ltd. and Associated Newspapers Ltd. v. Federal Commissioner of Taxation* (1938) 61 CLR 337.
69. *Broken Hill Theatres Pty. Ltd. v. Federal Commissioner of Taxation* (1952) 85 CLR 423.
70. *Inland Revenue Commissioners v. British Salmson Aero Engines, Ltd.* [1938] 3 All ER 283. The case concerned a UK company that made payments to use a patent. The question to be determined was whether the taxpayer was required to withhold tax on the payments and the answer turned on the character of the royalty-like payments once received by the patent holder. It appears to have been assumed, however, that the character of the payments would be similar in respect of the payer and recipient if they were found to be capital amounts.

Decades of pressure from tax advisors and business taxpayers finally led in 2001 to the adoption of a residual expense capital allowance measure that permitted taxpayers to depreciate on a straight-line basis over five years the cost of capital expenses not recognised elsewhere as part of the cost base of an asset or depreciated under another specific capital allowance provision. The original version failed to catch a number of black hole expenses but since its amendment in 2005, the provision appears to achieve its goal.

While the multi-element system now in place for recognising expenses characterised as capital outlays under the judicial tests is an improvement over the original situation where none were recognised for tax purposes, none of the recognition rules are as generous as the immediate deduction allowed if the taxpayer can arrange a transaction in a way that presents the outgoing as a revenue expense. For example, expenses to secure multi-year contracts would be recognised only on the expiry of the contracts and then as capital losses only deductible against capital gains under the statutory recognition provisions. If the expenses are characterised as revenue outgoings regularly incurred in the ordinary course of business, they are immediately deductible.[71] Similarly, as noted, expenses incurred to protect title to an asset must be capitalised into the price of the asset if treated as capital in nature. If this happens, they will be recognised only when there is a disposal of the asset. If the expense is incurred to protect rights that are regarded as separate assets, the expense can only be recognised over five years through the residual capital allowance rule. But if the taxpayer can show defence of title expenses are regularly incurred as an incident of the income-earning process in the taxpayer's business, it will be characterised as an immediately deductible revenue outgoing.[72]

Most commonly, businesses incur expenses in response to commercial needs and only after the fact seek to attribute a particular character to the outlay. Well-advised enterprises able to plan before expenses can establish an evidentiary trail or pattern of behaviour that may assist in reinforcing a tax advantageous revenue characterisation of expenses.

---

71. An example of a taxpayer achieving this characterisation is found in *BP Australia Ltd. v. Federal Commissioner of Taxation* (1965) 112 CLR 386 where the taxpayer regularly paid gas station owners consideration to enter into multi-year 'tied house' agreements under which the operators agreed to sell the taxpayer's product exclusively for the life of the agreements.
72. A taxpayer who was able to do this is found in *Federal Commissioner of Taxation v. Consolidated Fertilizers Ltd.* (1991) 22 ATR 281. The taxpayer's right to use a technology under licence was challenged and the taxpayer incurred legal expenses to defend its right. It argued, successfully, that there was a continual risk of attack of this sort in its line of business and the expense was consequently a revenue outgoing.

[C] Literal and Purposive Interpretation of Substantive Provisions and the General Anti-avoidance Provision

In principle, the interpretation of a tax law should follow the same processes and doctrines as that of any other statute.[73] It is clear, however, that in practice interpretation of tax statutes may be subject to ideological and social perspectives that are unlikely to arise in other contexts.

Analysis of interpretation of tax law in Australia often seeks to place case law along a spectrum that has at one end a 'literal' interpretation approach and at the other a 'purposive' interpretation approach. Both approaches purport to give effect to the intent of the legislature in enacting a measure subject to interpretation and both rely on the meaning of the words used in the law. As the meanings of words are based primarily on the context in which they are used, the difference between the two approaches is fundamentally one of the extent to which judges look at words in isolation to attribute meaning to them or look at them in broader contexts and adopt the meaning most suitable for that broader context. Most often, the literal approach is argued by taxpayers seeking to avoid a liability on the basis that the words in the statute do not apply to their situation. Literal interpretation is thus often associated with successful tax avoidance arrangements.

For the first six decades of the twentieth century, Australian tax jurisprudence followed a middle path between extremes of so-called strict literalism or limited context interpretation and purposive interpretation looking at terms in the broader context of the legislation and the aim behind the provisions in which words were placed. A shift in the 1970s to the literalism extreme of the spectrum and a debate within the High Court over the relationship between statutory interpretation techniques and the role of a responsible judiciary led to a radical overhaul of the entire Australian income tax system and a significant shift in interpretation approaches back towards the central position taken by courts prior to the extreme literalism period.

The apex of strict literalism in Australia came in the late 1970s and early 1980s following the approach of the then Chief Justice of the High Court, Sir Garfield Barwick, who aligned a strict interpretation of tax law that considered the meaning of words in the law only in terms of the sentences in which they were found, without regard to the broader object of the sentences, with the maintenance of a free society.[74] This literal

73. '[The fact that an Act] is a taxing statute does not make it immune to the general principles governing the interpretation of statutes': *Cooper Brookes (Wollongong) Pty. Ltd. v. Federal Commissioner of Taxation* (1981) 147 CLR 297 at 323 (per Mason and Wilson JJ.).
74. 'It is for the Parliament to specify, and to do so, in my opinion, as far as language will permit, with unambiguous clarity, the circumstances which will attract an obligation on the part of the citizen to pay tax. The function of the court is to interpret and apply the language in which the Parliament has specified those circumstances. The court is to do so by determining the meaning of the words employed by the Parliament according to the intention of the Parliament which is discoverable from the language used by the Parliament. It is not for the court to mould or to attempt to mould the language of the statute so as to produce some result which it might be thought the Parliament may have intended to achieve, though not expressed in the actual language employed': *Federal Commissioner of Taxation v. Westraders Pty. Ltd.* (1980) 144 CLR 55; 11 ATR 24 at 26 (per Barwick C.J.).

approach led to a string of judgments in favour of taxpayers who had engaged in clearly artificial schemes entered into for the purpose of tax avoidance, prompting some commentators to conclude that the High Court under Sir Garfield was encouraging tax avoidance.[75]

The approach taken by the Chief Justice was strongly criticized in the dissenting High Court judgments of Lionel Murphy, who described the Court's 'absolutely literalistic' approach as an 'open invitation to artificial and contrived tax avoidance' that, rather than protecting the legal rights of citizens as asserted by the Chief Justice, could lead to great oppression as the Parliament responded by vesting tax officials with more and more discretion.[76] Justice Murphy's warning that the legislature would intervene if the literalist approach were to continue proved to be correct, though it did so not strictly in the manner he predicted.

The tax avoidance era of the late 1970s and early 1980s[77] and the vigorous debate over the relative merits of literalism and purposive interpretation that accompanied it led directly to three legislative developments.

The first was the amendment of the *Acts Interpretation Act*, the law setting out rules for the interpretation of Commonwealth statutes generally, so that it explicitly required courts to adopt a purposive interpretation when reading statutes.[78]

The second was the replacement of the previous anti-avoidance measure that had proved wholly ineffective in the face of complex and, in the words of the Chief Justice,

75. *See*, for example, Geoffrey Lehmann, *The Income Tax Judgments of Sir Garfield Barwick: A Study in the Failure of the New Legalism*, 9(3) Monash U. L. Rev. 115 (1983).
76. 'It has been suggested, in the present case, that insistence on a strictly literal interpretation is basic to the maintenance of a free society. In tax cases, the prevailing trend in Australia is now so absolutely literalistic that it has become a disquieting phenomenon. Because of it, scorn for tax decisions is being expressed constantly, not only by legislators who consider that their Acts are being mocked, but even by those who benefit. In my opinion, strictly literal interpretation of a tax Act is an open invitation to artificial and contrived tax avoidance. Progress towards a free society will not be advanced by attributing to Parliament meanings which no one believes it intended so that income tax becomes optional for the rich while remaining compulsory for most income earners. If strict literalism continues to prevail, the legislature may have no practical alternative but to vest tax officials with more and more discretion. This may well lead to tax laws capable, if unchecked, of great oppression': *Federal Commissioner of Taxation v. Westraders Pty. Ltd.* (1980) 11 ATR 24 at 40 (per Murphy J.).
77. Detailed in the comprehensive account of the era produced by a former Commissioner of Taxation, Trevor Boucher: *Blatant, Artificial and Contrived: Tax Schemes of the 70s and 80s* (Canberra: Australian Taxation Office, 2010), available at: http://www.ato.gov.au/super/content.aspx?menuid=39504&doc=/content/00244226.htm&page=3#P63_15145 (accessed on 8 March 2013). The second half of the 1970s saw a proliferation of evasion building upon successful avoidance schemes, the most famous of which were the 'bottom of the harbour' schemes that built upon dividend stripping schemes to avoid both primary company tax and tax on shareholder's gains; *see* further Richard Krever, *Tax Reform in Australia: Base-Broadening Down Under*, 34(2) Can. Tax J. 346, 369–375 (1986); *see also* Arie Freiberg, *Enforcement Discretion and Taxation Offences*, 3(1) Austl. Tax F. 55, 89 (1986), suggesting that the Australian Taxation Office to that time had 'sought the speedy and cost-effective resolution of problems at the cost of legitimating tax deviance'.
78. Section 15AA of that Act now says: 'In interpreting a provision of an Act, the interpretation that would best achieve the purpose or object of the Act (whether or not that purpose or object is expressly stated in the Act) is to be preferred to each other interpretation.'

'ingenious' tax avoidance schemes.[79] A new and sweeping general anti-avoidance rule[80] was adopted. It can be invoked by the tax authority whenever a taxpayer's predominant reason for any arrangement affecting tax is the reduction of a tax liability.

The third, and most important legislative response, was a sweeping overhaul of the Australian income tax system. A common feature of the tax avoidance cases at the heyday of the so-called strict literalism era was the structuring or restructuring of transactions with the aim of achieving a reduced tax burden. This was possible only because the tax law provided dramatically different outcomes for economically similar but legally different forms of transactions. For example, a gain on the sale of an asset was tax-free if characterised as a capital gain and fully taxed at marginal rates if characterised as business profits from a one-off business-like transaction. Arrangements could be made to achieve either characterisation and taxpayers found judges sympathetic to their de facto elections. The same was true of taxpayers extracting company profits by way of dividend stripping schemes that recharacterised fully taxable dividends as tax-free capital gains and taxpayers entering into a host of other arrangements designed to move arrangements across undefined borders or sharp divides with no economic substance.

Reforms adopted in the 1980s including adoption of a full company and shareholder imputation system that removed the double taxation of company profits distributed as dividends, inclusion of capital gains in the income tax base (albeit on an indexed cost base until 1999 and then on a half-inclusion basis), adoption of a comprehensive fringe benefits tax regime, replacement of the exemption for most foreign-source income with a comprehensive foreign tax credit system, the later adoption of attribution rules for income from investments in controlled foreign companies, trusts and investment funds in low tax jurisdictions, and implementation of a partial accruals regime for interest and interest substitutes, have greatly reduced the opportunities for game-playing by rearranging the legal form or character of a transaction to attract lower or nil tax rates. Some of the reform measures are remarkably complex, however, and the complexity has opened new avoidance opportunities that taxpayers, particularly large corporate taxpayers, have been able to exploit with some success.

The amendment of the *Acts Interpretation Act* to mandate 'purposive' interpretation of legislation and adoption of the replacement general anti-avoidance provision in 1981 helped shift the pendulum from the zenith of strict literalism it had reached, prompting the courts to read legislation generously where the purpose was clear, even if the language of the law was not.[81] It remained the case, however, that where the

79. *See Federal Commissioner of Taxation v. Westraders Pty. Ltd.* (1980) 11 ATR 24 at 25 (per Barwick C.J.).

80. Commonly called Part IVA (four A), based on its location in the *Income Tax Assessment Act 1936*. *See* discussion of Australia's general anti-avoidance rule (GAAR) in Richard Krever & Peter Mellor, 'Australia', in Michael Lang, Jeffrey Owens, Pasquale Pistone, Alexander Rust, Josef Schuch & Claus Staringer (eds), *GAARs: A Key Element of Tax Systems in the Post-BEPS World* (Amsterdam: IBFD Publications, 2016), p. 45.

81. For example, in *Cooper Brookes (Wollongong) Pty. Ltd. v. Federal Commissioner of Taxation* (1981) 147 CLR 297 the High Court departed from apparently defective wording in a statute to

legislature knowingly left gaps in the tax law and declined to delineate the borders of those gaps, the judges very often adopted interpretation techniques endorsing taxpayers' choices, throwing responsibility back to the legislature to tackle the politically sensitive issues it had sought to avoid.[82]

In recent years, as a general rule, where a transaction has no economic basis other than to generate tax benefits that will yield an after-tax profit from a pre-tax loss, courts recognise an abuse of the law and interpret substantive provisions or the general anti-avoidance sections to deny the tax benefits (deductions, exemptions, rollovers, deferrals, etc.) sought. At the same time, the courts have continued to respect the legitimacy of taxpayer choice where the law provides alternative tax treatments for legally different and economically similar transactions. Accordingly, the courts tend to deny the tax authority the ability to argue either substantive grounds or to invoke the general anti-avoidance measure if a taxpayer can show that valid economic objectives lay behind an impugned transaction that was carried out in a manner that sought to achieve the most favourable tax outcome.[83] Amending legislation adopted in June 2013 was intended to extend the reach of the general anti-avoidance provisions to any transactions implemented in a particular way with the aim of avoiding tax even if there is a sound commercial goal to the transaction. It remains to be seen, however, whether the amending legislation will achieve its intended goal if the taxpayer can show that the primary purpose of the transaction was to achieve a legitimate commercial outcome, with the tax benefits from a particular form of the arrangement arising only because the tax law provides alternative rules for legally different but economically similar undertakings.

[D] 'Plain English' and Principle-Based Drafting of the Income Tax Legislation

While technical changes to the tax law in the 1980s largely stemmed the extremes of tax avoidance Australia had experienced in the second half of the 1970s and changing judicial approaches in the 1980s showed a clear retreat from excessive literalism, concern remained over the difficulties judges faced in finding the 'purpose' of sections from the words in the provisions. At the same time, the many changes to the law in the

achieve a legislative intent and policy otherwise clear from the law. The case was decided when the 'purposive interpretation' amendments to the *Acts Interpretation Act* were before the Parliament.

82. For example, in *ANZ Savings Bank Ltd. v. Federal Commissioner of Taxation* (1993) 25 ATR 369, the taxpayer bank redrafted a standard blended loan agreement (a loan with equal payments comprising a diminishing interest component and increasing principal repayment component over the life of the loan) as a fixed term 'annuity' to take advantage of a rule that allowed banks to defer recognition of interest if the loan took the form of an annuity. The Full Federal Court allowed the taxpayer to structure the loan as an annuity and take advantage of the generous recognition rules for annuities. The decision forced the legislature to withdraw the concessional treatment of fixed term annuities.
83. *See*, for example, *Mills v. Federal Commissioner of Taxation* [2012] HCA 51; 250 CLR 171; 83 ATR 514. *See also* Anthony H. Slater, *Part IVA: An International Perspective*, 42(3) Austl. Tax Rev. 149 (2013).

1980s had expanded the legislation to several volumes of printed text and both taxpayers and tax administrators found the growing complexity daunting. The government, through the Australian Taxation Office (ATO), initially resisted the notion of simplified drafting, claiming plain English lacked the precision needed for the technicality of the tax law. Outside the Taxation Office, support for simplified language grew and a project undertaken by the Law Reform Commission in the State of Victoria to redraft a division of the income tax law in 'plain English' showed how much simpler the law could be while retaining technical accuracy.[84]

Finally, in late 1993, the government announced a project to 'simplify' the tax legislation by re-drafting the principal law in plain English. The project was funded to last three years from 1994 but the first tranche of redrafted law did not appear until 1997, when the project was originally scheduled to wind up. The tax and drafting experts seconded to the Taxation Law Improvement Project, as it became known, spent more than a year researching best drafting practice before sitting down to prepare the initial drafts using plain English and 'principle-based drafting' techniques. The process was a long one and sixteen years and many tranches later, there remain parts of the old law yet to be redrafted into the 1997 version.

While the structure of the 1997 law was very different from that of the predecessor legislation, most of the key terms in the earlier law with meanings based on judicial interpretations were used again in the new law to ensure continuity of the meaning given by the courts. To reinforce this intended outcome, a general statutory interpretation rule was also introduced in 1987 to provide that an idea expressed in an Act shall not be taken to have been changed as a result of the use of a 'different form of words for the purpose of using a clearer style' in a later Act.[85]

The new law, in the initial tranches at least, but no longer, used simpler construction and ordinary words and was generally accessible to non-tax experts, a group that would include the vast majority of judges sitting on the benches deciding tax cases. Some confusion, enduring to the present, resulted from the assertion by proponents of the new law that it was an example of what was labelled 'principle-based drafting',[86] a claim that obscured the extent to which the new law was in fact the antithesis of actual principle-based law. Each part of the law was prefaced with a 'purpose' section that apparently explained the objective of the part but in practice these sections did nothing more than explain briefly the operation of technical rules set out in more detail in following provisions. The provisions themselves set out technical rules but rigorously avoided explaining any principles underlying the rules and the

84. The Division redrafted in plain English by the Law Reform Commission Victoria in 1992 provided accruals recognition of deep discounts and the imputed interest component on zero coupon debt: *see* Law Reform Commission of Victoria, *Redraft of Division 16E of Part III of the Income Tax Assessment Act 1936* (Melbourne, 1992).

85. *Acts Interpretation Act 1901*, s. 15AC and, similarly, *Income Tax Assessment Act 1997*, s. 1-3; *see also* Ian M.L. Turnbull QC, *Clear Legislative Drafting: New Approaches in Australia*, 11(3) Statute L. Rev. 161, 165-166 (1990).

86. Greg Pinder, *The Coherent Principles Approach to Tax Law Design*, Econ. Roundup 75 (Autumn, 2005).

structure derailed any attempt a reader might have made to ascertain a purpose to the organisation.

The problem was best illustrated with the 'capital gains' provisions in the new law. As discussed in §2.02[A] above, the Australian courts had interpreted the term 'income', the foundation concept in the main charging provision, narrowly, excluding from the judicial definition of income a wide range of gains. The original capital gains measures included in the old legislation sought to overcome this with a single charging rule that, along with a small handful of deeming measures, effectively captured all the gains that had been excluded from the judicial concept of income. The replacement 'plain English' version reverted to the drafting style that had been used (and failed) for seven decades prior to the adoption of a capital gains regime, namely piecemeal identification of transactions intended to be covered by the capital gains inclusion rules, albeit this time in plain English. Gains to be brought into the tax base were identified as capital gains tax 'events' and new ones added every time a transaction revealed a type of gain that had been missed in the previous events. The 36 recognition events included in the capital gains measures inserted in the new law in 1998 had been expanded to 53 recognition events by 2013.

Ironically, in 1986 Australia had adopted a tax law that could have served as a model for principle-based tax law design. In the course of the mid-1980s tax reform, the decision was made to tax employee benefits by way of a separate excise tax imposed on employers rather than include the value of the benefits in the employees' assessable employment income. The 'fringe benefits tax' law, as it was known, was drafted in plain English and while the structure was awkward (the charging provision was inserted at section 66 of the *Fringe Benefits Tax Assessment Act 1986*, rather than up front!), the law was a model for principle-based drafting. The charging provision and associated definitions set out a clear default position imposing tax on all benefits of every kind other than salary that were received directly or indirectly by a past, present or future employee. The onus was thus on the taxpayer to show amounts fell into one of the explicit exemptions which were drafted to clearly delineate the limits for each concession. In contrast to the income tax law and the later GST law, the fringe benefits tax generated almost no requests for rulings or litigation, suggesting the principle-based drafting greatly simplified the task of interpreting the tax law. The income tax experience showed that the traditional Australian approach to defining a tax base using multiple separate narrow and specific rules for different transactions and different versions of transactions inevitably led to difficult to interpret borders that resulted in overlaps or lacunae in the law.

§2.03 INTERPRETATION OF GST/VAT

[A] Introduction

The GST in Australia is imposed on taxable supplies and taxable importations of goods and services[87] at the rate of 10%.[88] The GST was introduced with effect from 1 July 2000 and falls into the group of 'modern' VAT laws influenced by the example of the landmark New Zealand tax which was characterised by a single lower standard rate and limited exemptions, in contrast to the earlier traditional VAT laws imposed in European countries.[89]

While the Australian GST is considered to fall into the 'modern' VAT/GST camp because of its single rate and limited list of exempt supplies (called 'input taxed supplies' in the Australian legislation), in many respects it is more concessional than the dual-rate, multiple exemption European VAT laws. The Australian legislation contains a wide range of zero-rated supplies (known as 'GST-free supplies' in the Australian law) that includes food, health and education.[90] However, in line with the New Zealand precedent, it is comprehensive in its reach to all commercial and public entities so that government departments, charities and other bodies can register and claim potentially refundable input tax credits in the same manner as commercial enterprises.

87. *A New Tax System (Goods and Services Tax) Act 1999* (Cth.) (GST Act), ss. 9-5 and 13-5.
88. The GST is imposed under six separate imposition Acts so as to meet the constitutional requirements relating to imposition of different subject matters of taxation discussed in §2.01[C] above: *see A New Tax System (Goods and Services Tax Imposition – Customs) Act 1999* (Cth.), s. 4; *A New Tax System (Goods and Services Tax Imposition – Excise) Act 1999* (Cth.), s. 4; *A New Tax System (Goods and Services Tax Imposition – General) Act 1999* (Cth.), s. 4; *A New Tax System (Goods and Services Tax Imposition (Recipients) – Customs) Act 2005* (Cth.), s. 4; *A New Tax System (Goods and Services Tax Imposition (Recipients) – Excise) Act 2005* (Cth.), s. 4; *A New Tax System (Goods and Services Tax Imposition (Recipients) – General) Act 2005* (Cth.), s. 4. For further discussion of the introduction of GST in Australia, *see* Kathryn James, *The Rise of the Value-Added Tax* (New York: Cambridge University Press, 2015), ch. 6.
89. *See* Rita de la Feria & Richard Krever, 'Ending VAT Exemptions: Towards a *Post*-Modern VAT', in Rita de la Feria (ed.), *VAT Exemptions: Consequences and Design Alternatives* (Alphen aan den Rijn: Kluwer Law International, 2013), pp. 3, 4, citing Liam Ebrill, Michael Keen, Jean-Paul Bodin & Victoria Summers, *The Modern VAT* (Washington, DC: International Monetary Fund, 2001).
90. Of the taxes in the modern group, 'few have adhered as closely as New Zealand' to the principle of allowing no concessional exemptions from the tax base; in Australia's case in particular, there are 'many important gaps in the base as a result of what is quite probably the widest scope of GST-free (zero-rated) supplies of any VAT/GST system': Richard Krever, Book Review: *The Future of Indirect Taxation: Recent Trends in VAT and GST Systems Around the World* (Thomas Ecker, Michael Lang & Ine Lejeune, eds, Wolters Kluwer, 2012), 12(4) Austl. GST J. 186 (2012). As a result of '[c]onsumer caution and changes in spending patterns', the GST revenue pool has declined to the extent it has been described by the New South Wales government as a 'structural and significant collapse': New South Wales Treasury, *Budget Paper No. 2, Budget Statement 2012-13* (2012), p. 1-1.

[B] Approaches to Interpretation

A key issue which arose at an early stage in the application of the GST legislation[91] was the extent to which the legislation should be interpreted according to the broad economic principles of a VAT, to ensure that the GST is viewed as a tax on consumption and, as a corollary, that the tax is borne by consumers rather than the businesses involved in the supply chain under a principle of 'fiscal neutrality'.[92]

An important consideration in this regard was that the government's Explanatory Memorandum which accompanied the original Bill for the GST prefaced its discussion of the tax with the broad statements that GST 'is effectively a tax on final private consumption in Australia' and is 'effectively borne by consumers when they acquire anything to consume'.[93] The GST legislation itself, by contrast, did not contain an express statement of purpose to this effect along the lines of the introductory provision of the European Union's Directive governing the VAT system in its Member States, which (although not restricted to 'final' consumption) states that VAT is 'a general tax on consumption'.[94]

Before the courts had an opportunity to hear any appeals of GST assessments, a large number of cases concerning the application of the law were decided in the civil courts in the context of tort and contract cases – litigants arguing over whether GST was payable on supplies and should be or should not be included in amounts due under contracts or damages for tortious wrongs or breaches of contracts, and so forth. As these disputes did not involve assessments of tax liability, the Commissioner of Taxation was not party to the litigation and as a result, the initial interpretation of the GST legislation by the civil courts took place with no input from tax authorities.

The early cases had the effect of seriously narrowing the GST base by reading into the legislation a requirement that the supplier must take an active role in making the supply for it to satisfy the definition of a taxable supply.[95] Thus, if the supply were the consequence of an expropriation by a government authority (when the supplier was a passive supplier)[96] or a consequence of a court order,[97] the supply would not be viewed

91. *See* in particular the discussion by Justice Graham Hill in *Some Thoughts on the Principles Applicable to the Interpretation of the GST*, 6(1) J. Austl. Tax'n 1, 25–31 (2003).
92. Peter Hill, 'Taxation of Goods and Services in Australia: Past, Present, and Future', in Chris Evans & Richard Krever (eds), *Australian Business Tax Reform in Retrospect and Prospect* (Sydney: Thomson, 2009), pp. 547, 557–561; Michael Evans, 'Commentary: Taxation of Goods and Services in Australia', in Chris Evans & Richard Krever (eds), *ibid.*, pp. 563, 568–571, referring for example to the comments of the European Court of Justice in *Abbey National plc v. Customs and Excise Commissioners* (Case C-408/98) [2001] ECR I-1361. *See also* Rebecca Millar, *What's VAT Got to Do With It?*, 12(3) Austl. GST J. 99, 104–106 (2012), discussing the observations of Justice Hill in *HP Mercantile Pty. Ltd. v. Federal Commissioner of Taxation* [2005] FCAFC 126; 60 ATR 106.
93. Explanatory Memorandum to the A New Tax System (Goods and Services Tax) Bill 1998, p. 6.
94. Currently Council Directive 2006/112/EC of 28 November 2006 on the common system of value added tax, Article 1(2). *See* discussion in Chapter 5 of this volume.
95. *See* further Peter Edmundson, *GST and Involuntary Supplies*, 6(2) J. Austl. Tax'n 224 (2003); Christopher Sievers, *GST and Compulsory Acquisitions of Land: Can You Have an 'Involuntary Supply'?*, 12(4) Austl. GST J. 165 (2012); Richard Krever, *Involuntary and Statutory Supplies – The Australian GST Base Narrows*, 16(1) Int'l VAT Monitor 19 (2005).
96. *CSR Ltd. v. Hornsby Shire Council* [2004] NSWSC 946; 57 ATR 201.

as a taxable supply by the court. Among other things, this meant the supplier, even if it was registered and had been paid a tax-inclusive value for the supply, would not have to remit any GST, yielding a windfall for the supplier and a detriment to the buyer who would not be able to claim input tax credits despite having paid the tax-inclusive value for the supply.

These non-tax cases interpreting GST law had a dramatic effect on the interpretation of the GST when the reasoning set out in the cases was accepted by the ATO and incorporated into its private rulings for taxpayers.[98] The ATO subsequently decided, for example, that there would be no taxable supply if a former employer made a payment to a new employer to cover the costs that the new employer would automatically (and involuntarily) incur as a result of state employment law.[99] The tax authority became so enamoured with the logic of these 'no active supply' decisions that it even extended the reasoning to cases where taxpayers deliberately put themselves into a position that would require them to make a 'passive' supply. The ATO ruled, for example, that there was no taxable supply in the case of a supply that followed automatically in respect of an expired commodities future contact even though the arrangement followed an agreement by the supplier and was not a consequence of government or court compulsion.[100]

Two appeal decisions from mid-2005 were to prove of significant importance in guiding subsequent approaches to judicial reasoning in GST cases. The lead judgment by Hill J. in the first of these, the *HP Mercantile* case,[101] explained in detail the theory behind the GST – a multi-stage tax that was ultimately borne by final consumers only as a result of input tax credits that ensured there would be no cascading of tax prior to the supply to a final consumer. The approach reflected the principles set out in the Explanatory Memorandum prepared by the government to explain the purpose of the GST law when it was first submitted to Parliament. The Explanatory Memorandum introduced the GST as a tax on final consumption, collected via business. The second decision, the *Sterling Guardian* case, took a different approach. At first instance, the single judge hearing the case described the GST as a 'practical business tax', imposed on commercial transactions,[102] a conclusion endorsed by a higher court on appeal from the decision of the single judge,[103] with the appeal judgment explicitly rejecting the notion of the GST being a tax on consumption, ironically citing the *HP Mercantile* decision as authority for that conclusion.

97. *See*, for example, *Shaw v. Director of Housing and State of Tasmania (No. 2)* [2001] TASSC 2; 46 ATR 242; *Walter Construction Group Ltd. v. Walker Corporation Ltd. & Ors.* [2001] NSWSC 283; 47 ATR 48; and *Interchase Corporation Limited v. ACN 010 087 573 Pty. Ltd. & Ors.* [2000] QSC 13; 45 ATR 445.
98. ATO ID 2003/1172, ATO ID 2003/1173.
99. ATO ID 2002/1078.
100. ATO ID 2004/359.
101. *HP Mercantile Pty. Ltd. v. Federal Commissioner of Taxation* [2005] FCAFC 126; 60 ATR 106.
102. *Sterling Guardian Pty. Ltd. v. Federal Commissioner of Taxation* [2005] FCA 1166; 60 ATR 502.
103. [2006] FCAFC 12; 60 ATR 119.

Ultimately, with only a few exceptions, the second view prevailed in first instance and lower level appeal courts (but not in the High Court, as detailed further below),[104] with a narrow interpretation that read the GST legislation as a tax on business rather than consumption.[105] A court concluded, for example, that a supply of foreign currency to a customer exiting the country was a taxable supply while the policy intent of the GST law was arguably to treat the transaction as a GST-free (zero-rated) export.[106] In another case, the court found the tax office had no authority to delay a refund of GST where input tax credits exceeded output tax even when the tax authority was investigating the legitimacy of the transactions.[107] In a third case, the court allowed the full recovery of input tax by an agency paying part of the cost of taxi fares for a group of subsidised consumers, effectively eliminating the GST on the final consumption acquired with the payments.[108] In another case, the court found a business made no taxable supply when it provided a contract for sale of property and retained the deposit when the buyer failed to proceed with the transaction,[109] and in a further and not dissimilar case an appeal court found an airline had made no taxable supply when it retained payments for non-refundable discount airfares if the customer failed to board the flight even though the customers clearly acquired the rights they had sought with the discount fares.[110] In a case concerning a series of rebates provided by a manufacturer to an unrelated retailer based on sales of the manufacturers' products, the court concluded the payments were gifts and not consideration for supplies where the rebates were not expressly included in the dealership agreement.[111]

The narrow approach adopted by first instance and lower appeal courts has not been endorsed by the High Court, Australia's final court of appeal. The High Court has accepted the *Sterling Guardian* view that the GST may be a consumption tax in an economic sense but falls on supplies, not consumption in a legal sense, but nevertheless has interpreted the law in a manner consistent with the broader policy goal of the

104. One exception was *Saga Holidays Ltd. v. Federal Commissioner of Taxation* [2006] FCAFC 191; 64 ATR 602 (Federal Court of Appeal). The appeal court in that case rejected the taxpayer's argument that the supply of hotel accommodation in Australia was a tax-free export if sold through foreign travel agency packages when it was clear the consumption of the hotel services takes place in Australia.
105. In *Sterling Guardian Pty. Ltd. v. Federal Commissioner of Taxation* [2006] FCAFC 12; 62 ATR 119 (Federal Court of Appeal) at [10]–[15], the Court said, 'In economic terms it may be correct to call the GST a consumption tax, because the effective burden falls on the ultimate consumer. But as a matter of legal analysis what is taxed, that is to say what generates the tax liability (and the obligations of recording and reporting), is not consumption but a particular form of transaction, namely supply; *see* generally *HP Mercantile Pty. Ltd. v. Commissioner of Taxation*.'
106. *Travelex Ltd. v. Federal Commissioner of Taxation* [2009] FCAFC 133; 73 ATR 463 (Federal Court of Appeal).
107. *Federal Commissioner of Taxation v. Multiflex Pty. Ltd.* [2011] FCAFC 142; 82 ATR 153 (Federal Court of Appeal).
108. *Federal Commissioner of Taxation v. Secretary to the Department of Transport (Victoria)* [2010] FCAFC 84; 76 ATR 306 (Federal Court of Appeal).
109. *Reliance Carpet Co. Pty. Ltd. v. Federal Commissioner of Taxation* [2007] FCAFC 99; 66 ATR 117 (Federal Court of Appeal).
110. *Qantas Airways Limited v. Federal Commissioner of Taxation* [2011] FCAFC 113; 81 ATR 816 (Federal Court of Appeal).
111. *KAP Motors Pty. Ltd. v. Federal Commissioner of Taxation* [2008] FCA 159; 68 ATR 927 (Federal Court).

GST as a consumption tax. For example, the Court reversed the lower decision on currency conversion services to find no GST was payable on currency conversion services where the benefit of the service was enjoyed outside Australia.[112] Similarly, it reversed lower appeal court decisions on non-refundable deposits, concluding GST was payable where suppliers had received and kept deposits for the cancelled purchase of land and airline flights.[113]

It remains to be seen whether the broader purposive path apparently taken by High Court will permeate through to the lower level appeal and first instance tribunals. The assertion that the GST is a 'practical business tax' has been repeated time and again in GST cases but the impact of the business tax analogy on judicial analysis may yet prove to be limited. The outcomes in High Court decisions suggest there is room for interpretation that yields outcomes consistent with the GST being a tax on consumption despite the language suggesting it is a tax on business.[114]

[C] Interpretation: Some Specific Instances

[1] The Transitional Provisions and Long-Term Contracts

The application of the GST law to long-term contracts that had commenced prior to the introduction of the tax was controlled by a separate transitional law which deemed supplies made under pre-GST contracts to be zero-rated (GST-free in Australian terminology) until the earlier of five years after the introduction of the GST and the first review opportunity allowed under the contract.[115] The legislation did not define what

---

112. *Travelex Ltd. v. Commissioner of Taxation* was reversed by the High Court at [2010] HCA 33; 241 CLR 510; 76 ATR 329.
113. *Reliance Carpet Co. Pty. Ltd. v. Commissioner of Taxation* was reversed by the High Court at [2008] HCA 22; 236 CLR 342; 68 ATR 158; *Commissioner of Taxation v. Qantas Airways Ltd.* was reversed at [2012] HCA 41; 247 CLR 286; 83 ATR 1. The logic of the decision in *Reliance Carpet* was explored further by the High Court in *Commissioner of Taxation v. MBI Properties Pty. Ltd.* [2014] HCA 49, 254 CLR 376. For further discussion of the *Reliance Carpet, Travelex* and *Qantas Airways* cases, *see* Richard Krever & Jonathan Teoh, *Justice Edmonds and Interpretation of Australia's GST Legislation*, 45(2) Austl. Tax Rev. 121 (2016).
114. On the discussion of the 'practical business tax' arguments by the High Court in reaching its decision in *Travelex, see also* Michael Wigney SC, *Text, Context and the Interpretation of a 'Practical Business Tax'*, 40(2) Austl. Tax Rev. 94, 102–105 (2011) and Justice Richard Edmonds, *Interpretation of s 11-15: Significance of the Text, Context and History*, 12(3) Austl. GST J. 79, 81–83 (2012). A senior tax official, perhaps hopeful that the High Court unwinding the narrow 'practical business tax' outcomes of lower courts will become the norm, has described the approach as one that is consistent with general principles of statutory interpretation. *See* Robert Olding, 'Interpretation of the GST Act – Towards a Principled Basis?', in Christine Peacock (ed.), *GST in Australia: Looking Forward from the First Decade* (Sydney: Thomson, 2011), pp. 77, 88–91. The Explanatory Memorandum prepared by the government to accompany a recent amendment Act, the *Tax and Superannuation Laws Amendment (2016 Measures No. 1) Act 2016*, stated: 'The GST is a multistage tax with input tax credits (ITCs) generally available to businesses to prevent cascading of GST through each stage of production and to ensure that the incidence of the GST falls upon private consumption ...' (p. 67).
115. *A New Tax System (Goods and Services Tax Transition) Act 1999* (Cth.), s. 13. The rule was based on the earlier New Zealand transition rule: *Goods and Services Tax Act 1985* (N.Z.), s. 85. In contrast to the New Zealand legislation, however, a provision for recovery of GST after the

constituted a review opportunity and the issue generated litigation between taxpayers and the tax office and between suppliers and customers when suppliers interpreted contracts as allowing price adjustments to include the new tax.[116]

Ultimately, the results in the cases turned on the specific language in each contract, making it difficult to apply decided cases as precedents. While the confusing case law had been described as 'a minefield' for practitioners in this area[117] and the analysis often appears to be based on legalistic interpretation of private law features in contracts,[118] as well as precise quantification of the various components of consideration payable under the contracts,[119] there is considerable evidence that behind the legalism courts are very much aware of a guiding principle, namely the 'fundamental premise of the GST Act that a supplier is entitled, and indeed expected, to pass on to the recipient of the supply the burden of the GST'.[120] As a general rule, where the contract provides leeway for an alteration of consideration payable at a particular time or upon a particular event, the occasion will not be treated as a review opportunity if the terms of the contract would prevent the supplier from adding the full value of GST to the consideration otherwise payable at that time. It seems contractual terms are being interpreted to achieve outcomes consistent with the policy objectives of the GST law.

[2] Exemptions and Classifications

In the GST, as in all tax laws, many disputes arise in respect of transactions that fall near the statutory borderlines describing taxable and non-taxable events. For example, the GST law generally imposes a 10% rate of tax but food is zero-rated. A number of cases consider whether particular supplies do or do not constitute food. Similarly, the ordinary rate applies to most supplies of immovable property but supplies of some types of residential premises are specified as exempt (input taxed) supplies, and there are many cases on the character of premises.

While it may be possible to speculate on the broad objectives underlying concessional treatment of particular types of supplies, arguments about the merits of

---

five year period under long-term contracts was not included in the original legislation, and a rule for payment of GST by recipients under such contracts was only added after commencement of the tax, under amendments made shortly before the end of the period of transitional relief in 2005.

116. A case typical of long lease disputes between private parties is *Westley Nominees Pty. Ltd. v. Coles Supermarkets Australia Pty. Ltd.* [2006] FCAFC 115; 62 ATR 682.

117. Chris Bevan, *GST on Long-Term Non-reviewable Contracts: Unresolved Transitional Problems*, 9(1) The Tax Specialist 28, 30 (2005).

118. An example is *Federal Commissioner of Taxation v. DB Rreef Funds Management Ltd.* [2006] FCAFC 89; 62 ATR 699, which characterises supplies and payments under a lease.

119. A payment which could not be reviewed amounting to 17% of the total consideration prevented a finding that there had been an opportunity for a general review, but a payment amounting to 3% of the total did not: *Federal Commissioner of Taxation v. DB Rreef Funds Management Ltd.* [2006] FCAFC 89; 62 ATR 699 at 715 and *MTAA Superannuation Fund (R. G. Casey Building) Property Pty. Ltd. v. Federal Commissioner of Taxation* [2012] FCAFC 89.

120. *Federal Commissioner of Taxation v. DB Rreef Funds Management Ltd.* [2006] FCAFC 89; 62 ATR 699, referring also to *ACP Publishing Ltd. v. Federal Commissioner of Taxation* [2005] FCAFC 57; 59 ATR 98; *see also Westley Nominees Pty. Ltd. v. Coles Supermarkets Australia Pty. Ltd.* [2006] FCAFC 115; 62 ATR 682.

legalistic or literal interpretation, on one hand, and purposive interpretation, on the other, have no meaning where there are no signposts as to where particular supplies might fit within the general policy goals. Faced with borderlines that have not been clearly delineated by the legislature, courts must turn to other doctrines to classify transactions or supplies.

One approach is to adopt classifications or interpretation doctrines used in older laws on the assumption that by repeating distinctions used in past laws, the legislature was implicitly accepting the borders that had been drawn by courts when those predecessor laws had been applied. Reliance on this approach has been particularly noticeable in cases involving the definition of zero-rated (GST-free) food. For example, courts have referred to sales tax case law in the course of reaching decisions under the GST that a blackcurrant syrup product was not a beverage or ingredient 'of a kind marketed principally as food for infants',[121] that carbonated fruit juice drinks with 1% to 2% additives were not GST-free as 'non-alcoholic carbonated beverages [consisting] wholly of juices of fruits',[122] and that a product labelled by the manufacturer as Italian 'Mini Ciabatte' product was to be classified as a cracker, one of a list of items carved out of the general concession for food for human consumption.[123]

Another approach is for courts to recognise explicitly the political motivation for concessions and interpret cases on the basis of the political aims behind the law. For example, acknowledgement that the GST concession for food was the result of a 'political deal that gave partial exemption to food' paved the way for courts to interpret terms in the law using 'ordinary' or lay usage rather than consider the technical or industry meaning of terms.[124] In Australian law, an individual less than 18 is an 'infant' in terms of legal capacity for many purposes but clearly the layperson considering whether drinks are marketed principally as food for infants would have a very different view of an infant and on this basis would no doubt have reached the same conclusion as the court that blackcurrant syrup product that might be popular with younger persons was not a beverage or ingredient of a kind marketed principally as food for infants, or similarly that de-alcoholised wine is not fruit juice.[125] And while the manufacturer of Mini Ciabatte may label the product 'Italian flat bread', the fact that supermarkets stock the product on the shelves with crackers can be a more powerful and independent indicator of whether the consumers regard the product as being of the same kind as taxable crackers rather than non-taxable bread.[126] Put simply, the

---

121. *Cascade Brewery Company Pty. Ltd. v. Federal Commissioner of Taxation* [2006] FCA 821; 64 ATR 28.
122. *P. & N. Beverages Australia Pty. Ltd. v. Federal Commissioner of Taxation* [2007] NSWSC 338; 65 ATR 391.
123. *Lansell House Pty. Ltd. v. Federal Commissioner of Taxation* [2011] FCAFC 6; 79 ATR 22.
124. *Cascade Brewery Company Pty. Ltd. v. Federal Commissioner of Taxation* (2006) 64 ATR 28. *See also* the finding of a policy that 'basic fare should be GST-free', in *JMB Beverages Pty. Ltd. v. Federal Commissioner of Taxation* [2009] FCA 668; 73 ATR 191.
125. *JMB Beverages Pty. Ltd. v. Federal Commissioner of Taxation* [2010] FCAFC 68; 76 ATR 76.
126. *Lansell House Pty. Ltd. v. Federal Commissioner of Taxation* [2011] FCAFC 6; 79 ATR 22.

interpretation of items in terms of tax classifications adopted with lay usage in mind should not involve 'over-elaborate, almost mind-numbing, legal analysis'.[127]

A third approach adopted by courts when interpreting terms denoting a taxable or exempt borderline is to consider the practical administrative impact of the alternatives rather than focus on the effect of characterisation on the final price of supplies. This approach is evidenced in cases requiring the interpretation of the provision that treats the supply of residential premises that are 'to be used predominantly for residential accommodation ...' as exempt (input taxed) supplies.[128] Read literally, the reference to the use to which property is to be put implies a responsibility for the supplier to know the intention of the customer to determine whether GST is payable on the supply and in an early case involving a residential house and land marketed as a development site, a State court hearing a civil dispute relating to the sale of the property concluded that 'it does not accord with the natural meaning' of the provisions to determine the issue solely by reference to the physical characteristics of the property without also taking the purchaser's intention into account.[129] From an administrative perspective, however, this approach would have been unworkable in most cases. One of the principal advantages of the GST is the simplicity for the supplier who can calculate the tax liability by looking at the supply, without the need to know anything about the customer's status as a registered or not registered person or whether the supply will be used for taxable or private purposes. No doubt cognizant of these considerations, courts considering the question in the context of tax appeals have adopted a more pragmatic approach, interpreting the provision so the supplier can determine whether property is to be used for residential accommodation from its physical characteristics.[130]

§2.04 TREATIES

[A] Background

Australia maintains an extensive network of taxation treaties,[131] developed since the conclusion of its first such agreement with the UK, in 1946. The executive government of the Commonwealth has power to enter into treaties, and an approach of 'strict dualism' generally requires a legislative enactment by the Parliament for treaties to take effect in domestic law.[132] Proposed treaty actions are subject to review by the Joint

127. *Lansell House Pty. Ltd. v. Federal Commissioner of Taxation* [2011] FCAFC 6; 79 ATR 22 at 28–29, citing *Procter & Gamble U.K. v. Revenue and Customs Commissioners* [2009] STC 1990 at [14].
128. GST Act, s 40–65.
129. *Toyama Pty. Ltd. v. Landmark Building Developments Pty. Ltd.* (2006) 62 ATR 73 at 90–91.
130. *See*, for example, *Sunchen Pty. Ltd. v. Federal Commissioner of Taxation* [2010] FCAFC 138; 78 ATR 197.
131. For an analysis of the provisions of Australia's treaties, *see* Kathrin Bain, Richard Krever & Anthony van der Westhuysen, *The Influence of Alternative Model Tax Treaties on Australian Treaties*, 26(1) Austl. Tax F. 31 (2011).
132. *See* Alice de Jonge, 'Australia', in Dinah Shelton (ed.), *International Law and Domestic Legal Systems: Incorporation, Transformation, and Persuasion* (Oxford: Oxford University Press,

Standing Committee on Treaties of the Parliament before action is taken to bind Australia to the treaty at international law, and consultation in relation to treaty matters also takes place through a further standing committee comprising Commonwealth and State officials.[133]

[B] Interpretation of Australia's Taxation Treaties

Australia's income tax law and tax treaties are reconciled by the incorporation of the income tax law[134] and all tax treaties into a single International Tax Agreements Act[135] that provides in the event of inconsistency between the tax law and the treaties, apart from the application of the general anti-avoidance rule in the income tax law, the terms of the treaties prevail.[136]

Australia is a signatory to the Vienna Convention on the Law of Treaties, and the Convention governs the interpretation of tax treaties in the same manner as all other international agreements. Australian courts regard the Vienna Convention as reflecting customary interpretation rules and therefore the interpretation rules in the Convention also apply to the interpretation in Australia of a taxation treaty with a country that is not party to that Convention.[137] Reference can be made to the OECD Commentaries as 'supplementary means of interpretation' for the purposes of Article 32 of the Vienna Convention.[138] Significantly, Australian courts have explicitly endorsed a 'purposive' approach to the interpretation of treaties, looking beyond the words (which of course remain the primary consideration) to the broader object and purpose of the treaties.[139] They recognise this may mean that questions of interpretation arising under tax treaties may follow a more liberal approach to interpretation than would be adopted where all that was involved was a question of construction of domestic law.[140] A court will not, however, read a treaty in a manner that is wider than the clear words in the treaty. For example, a definition of real property that includes shares in a company with assets that consist wholly or principally of direct interests in land would not be read as

2011), pp. 23, 26–28, discussing also (pp. 42–50) the role of customary rules and principles of international law in relation to Australian law.

133. De Jonge, *supra* note 132, pp. 29–31.

134. *Income Tax Assessment Act 1936* and Income *Tax Assessment Act 1997.*

135. *International Tax Agreements Act 1953* (Cth.), s. 4(1).

136. *International Tax Agreements Act 1953*, s. 4(2).

137. *Thiel v. Federal Commissioner of Taxation* [1990] HCA 37; 171 CLR 338. This approach was applied recently by the Federal Court, for example, in a case involving the taxation treaty of 1991 between Australia and India (the latter country not a party to the Vienna Convention): *see Tech Mahindra Ltd. v. Federal Commissioner of Taxation* [2016] FCAFC 130 at [22].

138. *Thiel v. Federal Commissioner of Taxation* [1990] HCA 37; 171 CLR 338.

139. *Applicant A v. Minister for Immigration & Ethnic Affairs* [1997] HCA 4; 190 CLR 225, endorsed in *Federal Commissioner of Taxation v. Lamesa Holdings B.V.* [1997] FCA 785; 36 ATR 589 at 595–596 and *McDermott Industries (Aust.) Pty. Ltd. v. Federal Commissioner of Taxation* [2005] FCAFC 67; 59 ATR 358.

140. Justice Graham Hill, *The Interpretation of Double Taxation Agreements – The Australian Experience*, 57(8) Bull. Int'l Tax'n 320, 323 (2003).

catching interests in a company with indirect interests in land by virtue of ownership of another land-rich company.[141]

A primary purpose of tax treaties is to eliminate double taxation by requiring residence countries to provide credits for any tax levied on the income by the source country or to exempt the income from residence country taxation where it has first been taxed in the source jurisdiction. The relief only applies to prevent double 'juridical taxation', where both jurisdictions seek to tax the same person on the same income, one on the basis of the person's residence in the jurisdiction and the other because it claims the income had a source in the jurisdiction. Australian judicial interpretation follows the commonly accepted view that the treaties do not require residence countries to provide relief for double 'economic taxation' where each jurisdiction taxes a different entity on the same income. For example, if a foreign jurisdiction taxes a company resident in that jurisdiction on Australian source income while Australian law treats the individual resident in Australia who provided the actual services to the customer as the person deriving the income, an Australian court will not support the individual's bid to use a tax treaty to prevent the double taxation.[142]

The judicial process of interpreting treaties is similar to that employed when considering domestic legislation, starting with the words in the treaty and considering precedents and judicial authority for the meaning of terms used. While authority is drawn primarily from precedents considering treaties, there may also be regard to cases interpreting similar concepts in domestic law and authorities may be used in the same creative way, including drawing upon *obiter* in a precedent (conclusions or assumptions by the court not central to the decision) as authority for a proposition that is at the core of a later decision.[143]

Interestingly, a different approach has been taken to interpreting domestic law where interpretations of the treaty counterparts are available. For example, interpretation of transfer pricing adjustments allowed under tax treaties may take into account the transfer pricing guidelines prepared by the OECD to explain the operation of the adjustment rule in the model treaty.[144] In a recent case involving the application of the

141. *See*, for example, *Federal Commissioner of Taxation v. Lamesa Holdings B.V.* (1997) 36 ATR 589. Some Australian treaties provided explicitly for direct and indirect ownership of land through interposed entities. The legislature's response to the *Lamesa* decision was a treaty override measure that deemed all references in Australia's treaties to interests in companies with direct interests in land to mean interests in companies with direct and indirect interests in land! *See International Tax Agreements Act 1953*, s. 3A.

142. *Russell v. Federal Commissioner of Taxation* [2011] FCAFC 10; 79 ATR 31.

143. An example is the decision in *McDermott Industries (Aust.) Pty. Ltd. v. Federal Commissioner of Taxation* (2005) 59 ATR 358 considering the meaning of permanent establishment under the Australia–Singapore tax treaty, where the court looked at a precedent that considered the meaning of permanent establishment under domestic law (the starting point for the definition of permanent establishment in both the domestic law and treaties is the definition in the OECD model). The precedent relied upon, *Unisys Corporation Inc. v. Federal Commissioner of Taxation* [2002] NSWSC 1115; 51 ATR 386, concerned the question whether the storage of records in a location amounted to carrying on a business at the place. In the course of this judgment it was noted that the premises were rented on a temporary basis and the latter case drew upon this *obiter* when considering the question of what constituted ongoing presence in the jurisdiction.

144. OECD, Transfer Pricing Guidelines for Multinational Enterprises and Tax Administrations.

domestic transfer pricing rule, the court ruled that no regard could be had to the guidelines manual when interpreting the domestic law,[145] prompting a legislative amendment to specify that the guidelines are to be consulted when applying domestic law.[146]

The ongoing international law debate over 'ambulatory' or 'static' interpretations of treaties has not been decided definitively in respect of Australian tax treaties, though the courts appear to take a broadly 'ambulatory' approach to interpreting fundamental provisions in treaties. This is illustrated in the key decision on the tax authority's assertion that income tax treaties enacted prior to the inclusion of capital gains in the tax base have no application to later assessments of capital gains by non-residents. The assertion rests on an argument that the capital gains measures in the income tax law amount to a completely different tax from the income tax, and treaties that applied to income tax law therefore did not cover future capital gains tax measures. The foundation of the argument is the exclusion of all capital gains from the judicial concept of income for tax purposes. The penultimate court of appeal has rejected this argument, concluding that, for treaty purposes, the income tax extended to amounts that were outside the strict meaning of the term 'income' for tax law purposes.[147] The decision parallels the approach taken by the court for constitutional law purposes where courts have decided that income for constitutional law purposes will include capital gains outside the judicial concept of income as the term in the income tax law is interpreted.[148]

This is likely to be one of many treaty interpretation issues that will be developed further by the courts in the future. However, the ongoing commentary on this issue[149] remains cautious about any greater reliance on an ambulatory approach to extend the existing avenues of treaty interpretation.

145. *Federal Commissioner of Taxation v. SNF (Australia) Pty. Ltd.* [2011] FCAFC 74; 82 ATR 680 at 715.

146. *Income Tax Assessment Act 1997*, ss. 815-20, 815-135 and 815-235. The amended law at present allows reference to the guidelines as last amended on 22 July 2010; further legislation is proposed which would also allow reference to the OECD's recommended revisions to the guidelines set out in OECD, *Aligning Transfer Pricing Outcomes with Value Creation, Actions 8-10: Final Reports*, OECD/G20 Base Erosion and Profit Shifting Project (Paris: OECD Publishing, October 2015).

147. *Virgin Holdings S.A. v. Federal Commissioner of Taxation* [2008] FCA 1503; 70 ATR 478. An 'ambulatory' approach to interpretation of a tax treaty provision was also recently endorsed by the Federal Court in *Federal Commissioner of Taxation v. Seven Network Ltd.* [2016] FCAFC 70 at [83]; 103 ATR 253, a case involving the scope of the term 'other like property or right' for the purposes of the royalties withholding tax article of the treaty between Australia and Switzerland of 1981.

148. *See*, for example, *Resch v. Federal Commissioner of Taxation* (1942) 66 CLR 198; *see* text at *supra* notes 52 and 64.

149. *See*, for example, Peter Wattel & Otto Marres, *The Legal Status of the OECD Commentary and Static or Ambulatory Interpretation of Tax Treaties*, 43(7/8) Eur. Tax'n 222 (2003); Michael Lang & Florian Brugger, *The Role of the OECD Commentary in Tax Treaty Interpretation*, 23(2) Austl. Tax F. 95 (2008); Michael Kobetsky, *International Taxation of Permanent Establishments: Principles and Policy* (Cambridge: Cambridge University Press, 2011), pp. 167–178.

§2.05 SUMMARY

Judicial interpretation of tax legislation has had a profound effect on the development of tax law in Australia. The income tax base was determined originally by the transplanted judicial concept of 'income' on the revenue side (euphemistically called 'income according to ordinary concepts') and 'capital' on the expense side, with subsequent legislative changes respecting and building on the judicial concepts.

The many borderlines in the income tax law created opportunities for taxpayers to minimise tax by rearranging transactions and a period of narrow literal interpretation of provisions encouraged the growth of a tax avoidance industry. The resulting revenue losses and public disapproval led to dramatic legislative changes to the income tax system and the law governing statutory interpretation. The pendulum of interpretation subsequently swung back to a more moderate approach in which taxpayers' choices are respected where the law provides alternative treatments for economically similar and legally different versions of transactions, but courts invoke interpretations or allow the Commissioner to apply a general anti-avoidance provision where transactions would not be economically viable but for the tax benefits generated by the steps pursued.

The GST base was narrowed significantly by early judicial decisions interpreting key concepts in the context of civil cases at which tax authorities were not represented. Lower courts have continued to apply legalistic interpretations while ignoring the objective of taxing final consumption. The final court of appeal, the High Court, however has adopted an interpretative approach much more in alignment with the characterisation of the GST as a consumption tax, and this approach may gradually shift the approach of lower courts.

The judicial approach to the interpretation of treaties has been generous, looking at the underlying objectives of the law, similar to the approach adopted for the interpretation of income tax for constitutional purposes.

CHAPTER 3

Legal Interpretation of Tax Law: Brazil

Luís Eduardo Schoueri

§3.01 TAX JURISDICTION ALLOCATION WITHIN BRAZILIAN FEDERALISM

From the time of its first republican Constitution, Brazil has had a federal structure comprising three subdivisions (Union, States, and Municipalities), each with its own attributes and powers granted by the Constitution itself. Unlike the case with many other federal states such as Germany,[1] Brazil does not apply a primacy principle that would allow Federal law to prevail over State Law in case of conflict. This peculiarity of the Brazilian constitutional structure is also reflected in tax law.

As a consequence of the federal structure, a main characteristic of the Brazilian tax system is an exclusive allocation of tax jurisdiction among the federal subdivisions. The allocation of a tax base is accompanied by an allocation of exclusive rights to legislate in relation to that base. Thus, for example, the allocation of a tax base to a Municipality ensures there will be no interference by State or Federal Governments. Exclusivity means that only one federal Subdivision (Union, one of the 27 States or one of the more than 5,600 Municipalities) will be entitled to enact a tax on a specific source or transaction. The Constitution provides for a list of taxes allocated to the respective levels of government, i.e., the Union (Article 153), States (Article 155) and Municipalities (Article 156). Taxes are merely listed and identified by their names (e.g., import tax, inheritance tax, etc.). In some cases, the mere name of a tax may be enough to understand its subject area as it relates to concepts used in other areas of law (e.g., the inheritance tax); but that is not always the case.

The exclusive allocation of the tax legislating power has become a source of conflicts, usually because a federal subdivision exceeds its constitutional jurisdiction

1. As found in Art. 31 of the German Constitution (Grundgesetz); generally referred to as the principle of "*Bundesrecht bricht Landesrecht.*"

when it decides to enact a tax, thus encroaching upon the jurisdiction attributed by the Constitution to another subdivision.

This subject is called a "conflict of jurisdiction," and when it occurs between federal subdivisions of different levels (Union and State, or Union and Municipality, or State and Municipality), it is called a "vertical conflict." However, conflicts may occur, as well, between two States or two Municipalities, especially when it is not clear to which territory a taxable event is connected (the so-called "horizontal conflicts").

Since jurisdiction is distributed among federal subdivisions by the Constitution itself, one can immediately understand the importance of the interpretation in this subject. Constitutional issues may be examined in Brazil by any court, but lower courts' decisions are always subject to review by higher instances. For constitutional matters, the last instance is the Federal Supreme Court (Supremo Tribunal Federal (STF)) which therefore will finally decide who will be allowed to legislate (and collect) any tax.

The mere fact that jurisdiction is allocated by the Constitution does not mean that courts are allowed to interpret its terms freely. The Brazilian legal system has adopted a special category of statute, so-called "complementary law" ("lei complementar") which, although it does not constitute amendments to the Constitution, is a relevant instrument for the interpretation of the latter. Complementary law is enacted by the Federal Congress, but under a qualified quorum, and sets parameters within which all taxing entities (Union, States and Municipalities) are expected to act. Section §3.02 of this chapter provides an analysis of the complementary law.

The Brazilian tax system should be understood as a two-level structure. A higher level, comprising the Constitution and the complementary law, provides for a framework for the legislative actions in the area of taxation of the federal, subnational, and local governments. In essence, at the upper level, only taxing rights are allocated and taxpayers' rights are ensured. The lower level of legislation comprised the actual tax laws and rules enacted by the Union, States, and Municipalities. Additional rules have been implemented to ensure vertical redistribution of tax revenue from the federal level to the States, and from the latter to the Municipalities.

While the Federal Supreme Court is the court of last instance for the interpretation of the Constitution, the court of last instance for nonconstitutional issues is the Superior Court of Justice. Decisions of the latter may only be appealed to the Federal Supreme Court if a constitutional issue is raised. While one could expect, therefore, that several issues concerning the interpretation of tax law would be decided by the Superior Court of Justice, this does not occur as often as one might anticipate.

A good explanation for this phenomenon is the fact that upon any assessment, taxpayers are allowed to appeal before the Administration (Executive Branch) before going to courts. As will be explained in §3.04[A], this is very interesting, since, the tax is not subject to collection while the case is under review in Administration. In case taxpayers succeed, the Administration cannot bring the case to the Judiciary, since the principle "*nemo potest venire contra facto suum*" applies, thus not allowing the Administration to appeal against a decision of one of its organs. Within the Federal Administration, final decisions are found in the Administrative Council for Tax Appeals (Conselho Administrativo de Recursos Fiscais (CARF)), which replaced the so-called

"Taxpayers' Council." CARF, like its predecessor, is an organ within the Federal Administration, composed by an equal number of representatives of the Tax Administration and of taxpayers.[2] Its members are usually experienced tax professionals and therefore it is not surprising that most of its decisions are very well reasoned. In case a decision is made against taxpayers, the latter may bring the case to courts. However, the Judiciary is generally not as well read in tax law as CARF members and, therefore, the decisions of the latter tend to be confirmed. Similar structures to CARF exist in all States and in several Municipalities.

An important limitation to CARF, however, is that since it is an administrative organ, it is not allowed to declare the unconstitutionality of a statute. As a practical result, constitutional matters (like jurisdiction, for instance) are dealt with by the Federal Supreme Court and nonconstitutional matters are generally decided by CARF, although some important matters have occasionally been submitted to the Judiciary and finally decided by the Superior Court of Justice.

§3.02 THE COMPLEMENTARY LAW IN TAX MATTERS

The Constitution of 1988 provides in Article 59 for complementary law concerning the legislative process. Article 146 of the Brazilian Constitution assigns three fundamental tasks to a complementary law which deals with tax: (i) regulation of the limitations to taxing powers provided for in the Constitution; (ii) establishment of general tax rules; and (iii) arbitration of tax jurisdiction conflicts.

Article 69 requires complementary laws to be passed by an absolute majority for the Congress. Thus, while ordinary federal statutes are approved by simple majority of those present in the session at the time they are submitted, complementary law requires approval of more than 50% of all deputies and senators.

Complementary law is not exclusively applied to tax matters. However, it has a relevant role in the area of tax law. Not only the special quorum is required for the Union to create some taxes allocated to it by the Constitution but, more important, complementary law forms, as already explained, together with the Constitution itself, the upper level of the Brazilian tax system and, therefore, its rules must be observed by the Union itself, when it enacts statues to create federal taxes, as well as by the States and the Municipalities.

The regulation of taxing power limitations becomes particularly important in Brazil because the Constitution provides for explicit provisions intended to protect taxpayers' rights (e.g., legality, non retroactivity, etc.), which require some degree of clarification or complementation in order to be effective. A good example can be found in the tax immunities granted by the Constitution. The Union, States, and Municipalities must exclude persons or objects protected by immunity from their taxes. One of the immunities covers nonprofit educational entities. In this case, it is the role of the complementary law to "regulate" this limitation, determining the requirements that must be fulfilled by the entity for the immunity to be granted. Article 14 of the National

2. In the event of a tie, the view of the tax administration tends to prevail.

Tax Code (which is a complementary law) provides for three requirements: a qualifying entity: (i) must not distribute its profits; (ii) must apply its resources in the Country; and (iii) must maintain its books in regular order. If an educational entity fulfills these requirements, immunity is granted. The Federal Supreme Court has struck down a further federal statute that sought to establish additional requirements for the granting of immunity, on the basis that immunity cannot be qualified by an ordinary statute.[3]

The complementary law shall also establish general tax rules, which are binding to all federal subdivisions, to ensure national uniformity, notwithstanding the operative legislation enacted by different federal subdivisions. For instance, the National Tax Code (complementary law) establishes a five-year statute of limitation for tax matters. Since this matter is regulated on the upper level by a complementary law, Union, States, and Municipalities must observe this same period when regulating their own taxes.

The same idea of bringing some uniformity in spite of the constitutional decision to split jurisdictions may be found upon the constitutional regulation of some taxes. Emblematic is the Article 155, paragraph 2, of the Constitution. Although States have the jurisdiction to enact the most relevant Brazilian tax on consumption, the ICMS, a noncumulative tax on sales of goods and some services (energy, transport, and communication), the Constitution provides the general framework for this tax in order to provide a sufficient level of harmonization and conformity. The relevant constitutional provision is one of the longest in the Brazilian constitution, which already indicates that many questions concerning to ICMS tend to be constitutional in nature and must, therefore, be decided by the Federal Supreme Court. Notwithstanding its remarkable length, the provision does not by itself provide a complete framework for ICMS, ensuring uniformity and, therefore, the Constitution requires the enactment of a complementary law to further define crucial aspects of ICMS. Presently, Complementary Law No. 87 fulfills this constitutional task.

Finally, the complementary law plays an important role in tax coordination by providing arbitration rules in case of horizontal or vertical jurisdictional conflicts between the federal subdivisions.

The Constitution not only attributes tax jurisdiction to all of the federal subdivisions, but also distributes the taxing power between them. Such tax jurisdiction is nondelegable: even if the jurisdiction is not exercised (i.e., a federal subdivision did not impose a tax which is assigned to it under the Constitution), another subdivision is not entitled to take advantage of the vacuum and impose a tax that is outside its jurisdiction.

Despite the fact that the Constitution attributes tax jurisdiction to all the federal subdivisions and distributes the taxes between them, it does not establish rigid limits

3. The first decision of the Supreme Court on this matter was the Direct Action of Unconstitutionality No. 2028-5 (11 November 1999). The case had application only to the entity bringing the appeal and had no general application. More recently (19 October 2016), the majority of the Federal Supreme Court Justices held more generally that federal statutes establishing additional requirements for the granting of immunity would be unconstitutional. However, the decision has been suspended following a request for an adjournment by one of the judges and a final decision on the issue is still pending. *See* Supreme Court, Informative 844, 28 October 2016.

for the jurisdictions. Therefore, the complementary law has a fundamental role in drawing the definitive shape of each of the subdivision's jurisdiction.

A good example may be found in Complementary Law No. 116 dealing with composite supplies. The constitutional allocation of taxing rights provides Municipalities with the power to levy tax on the supply of services generally and States with the power to levy tax on the sales of goods as well as some specific services such as communications, transportation, and energy. Application the constitutional allocation of taxing rights is problematic in case of mixed transactions such as a bed and breakfast hotel which supplies both services and goods. Complementary Law No. 116 resolves the dilemma by deeming a breakfast that is included in hotel lodging fees as part of the lodging services and taxed accordingly.

An important issue when one considers interpretation of tax law is whether legal wording and terminology should be assigned their meaning under private law meaning, or whether they may have a specific meaning defined by tax law. This issue is specifically relevant in the area of tax jurisdiction, when the correct interpretation of Constitutional wording will be decisive. This explains the importance in Brazil of the conflict between Private Law and Tax Law, which was partially solved through complementary law, but in several cases has been resolved by the courts.

§3.03 CONCEPTS OF PRIVATE LAW AND INTERPRETATION OF THE CONSTITUTION

[A] The Role of Article 110 of the National Tax Code

Articles 153, 155, and 156 of the Constitution contain lists of taxes allocated to the Union, the States, and the Municipalities, respectively. Interpreting the content of these lists is crucial in order to establish tax jurisdiction.

As already mentioned above, the lists are not sufficient to determine the jurisdiction, since in several cases conflicts may arise. Therefore, a complementary law is needed to further define each jurisdiction. As complementary law is not the Constitution itself, it cannot exceed the jurisdictional scope or concept provided for in the Constitution. For instance, the ownership or real estate in urban areas is subject to Municipal taxes, while rural real estate is under Union's jurisdiction. The complementary law may well define what is urban, or rural real estate, but may not further define the concept of real estate.

When one comes to the National Tax Code, a golden rule appears in Article 110:

> Art. 110. The tax law cannot change the definition, the content and the range of the institutes, concepts and forms of private law used, expressly or implicitly, by the Federal Constitution, the Constitutions of the States, or by the Constitutions of the Municipalities, to change or bind the tax jurisdictions.

This article aims at protecting the distribution of tax jurisdiction by the Constitution. Clearly, if a sub-national legislator could define its own jurisdiction, through autonomous interpretation of concepts of private law chosen by the Constitution, the tax jurisdiction, as allocated by the latter, would become irrelevant.

As will be seen below, Article 110 is often quoted by the Federal Supreme Court to limit the application of tax laws. Interestingly, Article 110 is not only applied in cases where the Constitution clearly adopted a concept of Private Law, but Article 110 is also applied more generally in order to bind the interpretation of Constitutional terminology to ordinary statutes.

Article 110 does not provide a solution for all cases of conflict. Where it states that private law concepts employed by the Constitution may not be changed, a preliminary question arises: how to determine that the Constitution has employed a private law concept? There is no automatic presumption that similar or identical terminology has the same meaning when used in more than one set of laws. Each term needs to be understood within its specific context and in relation to other provisions of that particular law. It is not always the case that when a Constitutional term has already a predefined meaning for private law purposes, the term will also have that same meaning, including for tax law authorized under the Constitution.

For instance, the term "*propriedade urbana*" is found in the Constitution in relation to the allocation of tax jurisdiction to Municipalities. In Portuguese, ownership may be translated to "*propriedade*" and, therefore, if the Constitution allows Municipalities to tax urban "*propriedade,*" one may initially conclude that this expression refers to the right of ownership, what would imply that only the legal owner of an urban real estate is subject to this tax. In other words, the tax event would be the ownership of a real estate. However, the same expression "*propriedade*" may be translated into real estate. In this case, the term "*propriedade*" would not be a concept of private law (ownership), but rather refer to an object (real estate). Consequently, a tax on urban "*propriedade*" would not only comprise a tax on the ownership of a real estate, but on any other right to a real estate, like possession. Indeed, according to Article 32 of the National Tax Code not only the ownership of a real estate, but also the right of possession is taxable, and both fall within Municipal jurisdiction. Thus, the expression "*propriedade*" is understood not to refer to a concept of private law, but rather aimed at identifying several rights to real estate. The legislator focused not on the legal definition (right of ownership) but on the immovable good (real estate) itself.

This example demonstrates clearly how the distribution of tax jurisdiction in Brazilian federalism demands an adequate comprehension of the role of the complementary law, with specific reference to its relation with the Constitution. The interpretation of the Constitution and complementary law together establishes the scope of different tax bases.

Regarding the scope of Article 110 of the National Tax Code, some important former court decisions should be considered. The analysis of Supreme Court's precedents exemplifies the relation between the Constitution and the complementary law with respect to the concepts of private law.

[B] The Expression "Payroll"

The Brazilian Federal Government provides for healthcare and social assistance, granted as social rights under the Constitution. These are funded, amongst others, by the social contributions, i.e., federal taxes the revenue from which is exclusively assigned to such purpose.

The 1988 Constitution, in its original wording, provided for a social contribution levied on the "payroll" of "employers." The question arose in the context of payments made to company directors and self-employed professionals whether the terms "payroll" and "employers," as employed by the Constitution, refer to an employment relationship per se or whether a more general meaning should be given to these terms, allowing for broader taxation. The Federal Supreme Court adopted a very narrow interpretation of the terms, extending the labor law meaning of "employer" and "payroll" to tax law. The mandate in Article 110 to apply to terms used in the Constitution the meaning they enjoy in private law was extended to terms that have no specific definitions in private law but which are defined in labor law.[4] Relying on labor legislation, the court concluded that self-employed professionals and company directors would not be subject to the social contribution. The decision stated that the 1988 Constitution recognized as constitutionally valid concepts from the interpretation of earlier nonconstitutional legislation (in this case, from labor law, not private law), which could not be found to be unconstitutional. While the decision was based exclusively on the coincidence of the expression "payroll," it could draw on additional support from the constitutional reference to a payment made by "employers."

Accordingly, the reporting judge declared that "the expression 'employers' refers to those who keep a legal relation with service providers ruled by the Labour Laws Consolidation," stating, based on the labor law, that "company directors and self-employed professionals are not within the definition of employee, where, according to Article 3 of the Labour Laws Consolidation, employee is every individual that renders services on a non-eventual basis to an employer, under dependence of the latter, for remuneration."[5] One of the concurring opinions stated "the constitutional expression 'payroll' has a technical meaning and its conceptual signification does not allow its use in disagreement with the definition, content and scope adopted by the Labour Law."[6]

Interestingly, a dissenting opinion in this case was also based on the terms used in the Constitution. It stated that although there is a reference to "payroll" and "employer," there is also the term "workers," which has a broader meaning than the term "employees." Article 195, II refers, indeed, to workers' contributions, which is sufficient, according to this dissenting opinion, to conclude that when a self-employed person who is deemed to be a "worker" under the labor law personally pays a social services contribution, no additional liability should fall on the company that pays for the person's services.[7]

Another dissenting opinion is worth mentioning, since it assumed, contrary to the majority opinion, that the mere use in the constitution of the terms "employer" and "payroll" would not be enough to bind other legislation to the meaning of these terms in labor law. To support this reasoning, it was noted that within the legal system at

4. Supreme Court, Extraordinary Appeal No. 166.772-9-RS, decided on 5 December 1994.
5. *Supra*, Justice Marco Aurélio, concurring.
6. *Supra* note 4, Justice Celso de Mello, concurring.
7. *Supra* note 4, Justice Rezek, dissenting.

large a broader meaning had already been applied to these same terms. Hence, it was suggested that the constitutional language does not have necessarily a technical meaning where "'salary' in Social Security Law has the meaning of remuneration, the amount the insured person receives."[8] This argument is not very different from the previous ones, since the effort still was to examine the terms "payroll" and "employers" and to ascertain their meaning in ordinary statutes. While the majority opinion attested that the labor law meaning should be applied, the minority looked for other meanings, but also within the legal system. The hypothesis that the terms might be freely interpreted, i.e., without any reference to their meanings in ordinary statutes, was not taken into consideration.

From this decision, it is clear that by that time, the Federal Supreme Court was still very bound to Article 110 of the National Tax Code, confirming it as a general rule whereby, in synthesis, if an expression used by the Constitution would have a meaning in nonconstitutional law (generally meaning private law), this meaning should also prevail for the purpose of defining tax jurisdiction.

[C] The Leasing of Movable Goods and the Rendering of Services

Another instance where the Supreme Court had to investigate the content of a term used by the Constitution was when it had to decide whether the leasing (renting) of movable goods would be subject to the Municipal tax on services (ISS).

Traditionally, ISS has a very broad scope, under the generally accepted understanding that "services" would include all kinds of intangible supplies (utilities). This interpretation was challenged, however, by a taxpayer who argued that the expression "services" was employed in the Civil Code to refer to a narrow category of supply, the obligations of "doing."

As a legacy from Roman law, Brazilian private law distinguishes between two kinds of obligations: "giving" and "doing."[9] "Doing" obligations would demand an activity of the debtor, which may be a physical activity (e.g., painting a wall, repairing a machine), or an intellectual activity (e.g., writing a legal opinion, giving medical assistance). "Giving" obligations, on the other hand, imply the obligation of transferring the property of something to someone (e.g., selling a book).[10]

Since services were deemed to be "doing" obligations in private law, it was argued that this private law concept should prevail also in tax matters (as per the abovementioned Article 110 of National Tax Code) and therefore a tax on services would only be possible if the taxable event would comprise some "doing." In the case of leasing (renting) of movable goods, there was no "doing," but rather a "giving" and thus, no tax should be paid. The judges did not accept the argument that the

8. *Supra* note 4, Justice Carlos Velloso, dissenting.
9. *See* the Roman law concepts of *locatio-conductio operarum* and *locatio-conductio rerum*.
10. On the distinction, *see* Sílvio de Salvo Venosa, *Direito Civil* (*Civil Law*), vol. II (São Paulo: Atlas, 2001): 87–91; Silvio Rodrigues, *Direito Civil* (*Civil Law*), vol. II (São Paulo: Saraiva, 2002): 19–44; Caio Mário da Silva Pereira, *Instituições de Direito Civil* (*Civil Law Institutions*), vol. II (19th edn, Rio de Janeiro: Forense, 2000): 31–44.

Constitution did not necessarily refer to a private law institute to set the Municipalities' jurisdiction, in spite of the fact that a tax on services already existed when the 1988 Constitution was enacted and by that time there was no discussion as to its extension to all intangible supplies.[11]

There was a dissenting opinion pertaining that the ISS would cover the leasing of movable goods. Although not actually convinced that the expression "services" would include leasing, this opinion accepted the historical argument according to which in the original wording of the Article 71, paragraph 1, of the National Tax Code, the leasing of goods was referred to as a service. Also, it was mentioned that the ISS was the successor of the former "Tax on Industry and Professions," which also covered leasing. A final argument in the dissenting opinion was that the Constitution did not mention "tax on services," but rather "tax on services of any nature." The latter would imply a broader sense. According to this opinion, "one should extract a useful meaning from the expression 'of any nature' used in the Constitution."[12]

The majority opinion, however, was that Article 110 of the National Tax Code should "only be taken as pedagogical" and should be perceived as an "actual alert to the ordinary legislator, when facing the State's search for additional revenue." According to this opinion, the private law concept (rendering of services) should be seen as a limit to the tax legislator.[13]

The fact that the Constitution does not use the same terminology as used in private law, mentioning only "services," instead of "rendering of services," was not enough to convince the majority that the expression could have a broader meaning for municipal tax law purposes. Nor did the judges consider whether the concept of "services" was used consistently in all private law. The Consumer Defense Code (Law No. 8.072, of 11 September 1990), for instance, in Article 3, paragraph 2, defines service as "any activity provided in the consumer market, for remuneration, including those of banking, financial, credit and insurance, except for those resulting from labour relations."

[D] Revenues from Billings

In another decision regarding Article 110 of the National Tax Code the Supreme Court had to interpret the expression "revenues from billings" (*faturamento*) with respect to the COFINS, a social contribution.

At issue was the meaning of the term "revenues from billings" as used in Article 195, I, of the Constitution. This term, according to the taxpayers, should be given the same meaning as under private law, in accordance with Article 110 of the National Tax Code. Considering that a bill is an instrument typically used by traders in installment sales, it was argued, to this effect, that the Finsocial – predecessor of COFINS – could not be levied if the operation did not involve the issuing of a bill. The taxpayers argued that the Supreme Court in a previous case, examining Finsocial under the 1988

11. Supreme Court, Extraordinary Appeal No. 116.121/SP, decided on 11 October 2000.
12. *Supra*, Justice Octávio Gallotti, dissenting.
13. *Supra* note 11, Justice Marco Aurélio, concurring.

Constitution, concluded that the expression could not address financial revenues, as intended by the rule under analysis.[14]

A brief overview of the former legislation shows that the expression "faturamento" was even older. It had already been employed as early as 1970, when the contribution for the Social Integration Program (PIS)[15] was enacted. The PIS defined the tax base as "revenues from billings" of the sixth month before the occurrence of the taxable event. Prior to the enactment of the 1988 Constitution, Decree-laws No. 2.445 and 2.449 intended to modify this tax base, replacing it by the gross operational revenues of the month (including all revenues, even the financial). However, the Supreme Court deemed such Decree-laws unconstitutional.[16] Later, Provisional Measure No. 1212/95 provided for the social contribution to be levied on the revenues from billing of the month.

The expression was also used in Decree-law No. 1.940, of 25 May 1982, which instituted a tax, named Finsocial, for the purpose of financing federal government investments in the social area. Under the previous constitutional regime, the Finsocial, which was termed a contribution, was qualified as an unnamed tax, whose jurisdiction was allocated to the Union as far as it related to gross revenues of a company.[17]

After the 1988 Constitution, Law No. 7.690/88 referred to the Finsocial, "levied on companies' revenues from billings, based on Article 195, I, of the Constitution." Previously, Decree-law No. 2.397/87 had already set the gross revenues as the tax base of the Finsocial, which was also applied for service providers.

The Finsocial was succeeded by the COFINS, through Complementary Law No. 70, of 30 December 1991. Because its calculation basis (gross revenues) coincided with the calculation basis of the PIS, its constitutionality was challenged, arguing that the expression "revenues from billings," provided by the Constitution, would not allow the taxation of revenues not related to bills. This time, the Federal Supreme Court went a step further, not requiring the issuance of a bill for the tax to be valid. It was agreed that the taxable event, gross revenues of the sales of merchandise and of merchandise and services, "coincides with the concept of revenues from billings, which, for tax purposes, has always been understood as the product of all sales, not only of sales involving a bill, formality required only on installment sales (Art. 1 of Law 187/36)."[18]

It appears that the Federal Supreme Court rejects the idea that "revenues from billings" would require the issuance of a "bill" (as understood in Private Law), and adheres more relevance to the transactions (sales of merchandise and services).

It was in this context that, in 1998, Law No. 9.718 was enacted, unifying the calculation basis of the PIS and COFINS contributions in Article 2, to the revenues from billings. However, Article 3 clarified that revenues from billings would be equivalent to

14. *See* Supreme Court, Extraordinary Appeal No. 150.755, decided on 18 November 1992.
15. (*Programa de Integração Social* – "PIS"). Complementary Law No. 7, of 7 September 1970.
16. Supreme Court, Extraordinary Appeal No. 148.754-2/RJ, decided on 24 June 1993.
17. The Finsocial was levied according to the business activity carried out by the taxpayer; it was levied on the revenue of the sales of goods in case of commercial and industrial companies. *See* Supreme Court, Extraordinary Appeal No. 103.778, decided on 18 September 1985.
18. *See* Supreme Court, Direct Action of Unconstitutionality No. 1, decided on 1 December 1993, Justice Moreira Alves, concurring.

gross revenues, defined as (§ 1): "the totality of revenues derived by a legal person, being irrelevant the type of activity developed by it and the accounting classification adopted for such revenues."

This definition of a taxable event is much broader than the previous ones, since gross revenues would include any revenue of a company, even those not related to sales. The question was whether "billing" would include any such revenue (e.g., interest received on a loan). This raised the question whether the ordinary legislator has the discretion to include revenues that are not arising from sales of merchandise or the rendering of services in its redefinition of "gross revenues."

A complicating factor was that a few days after the enactment of Law No. 9.718/98, Constitutional Amendment No. 20/1998 was enacted, which modified Article 195, I, of the Constitution, by providing that the social contributions could be levied on "revenues or revenues from billings," in essence broadening the tax base. Put differently, if Law No. 9.718/98 had been enacted after the Constitutional Amendment, the ordinary legislator would not be tied to the expression "revenues from billings," and any revenue (including financial ones) would be taxable.

The Supreme Court found the enlargement of the tax basis by Law No. 9.718/98 to be unconstitutional.[19] This decision is an important source for the understanding of constitutional interpretation in Brazil as it relates to tax matters.

The reporter of the case based his opinion on the argument that Article 3, § 1, of Law No. 9.718/98 contains a legal fiction with a given meaning that was "discrepant from the one established by doctrine and jurisprudence,"[20] and his opinion was followed by those who argued that if a term is not defined in the Constitution, but is defined in another law, it should be assumed that the constitutional legislator is adhering the same meaning to the term as it is given in the other law.

This argument was not based on a concept existing in private law ("billing"), as one would expect from the wording of Article 110 of the National Tax Code, but rather on the fact that the term "revenues from billings" already existed in previous tax law itself. It was argued that "one shall [not] take the referential words used by the Constitution in a permanent, invariable, perpetual sense," but rather that since the concept of "revenues from billings" had already been defined by the Supreme Court in earlier decisions, an attempt by the tax legislator to impute a different meaning to the term would be incompatible with Article 110 of the National Tax Code.[21]

Article 110, in this case, seems to have been evoked not with the intent of "constitutionalizing" concepts of private law, but rather in the sense that tax legislators may not change meanings already accepted by the Federal Supreme Court. In other words, once said Court would accept a meaning for a word, this would be deemed as a constitutional concept, and could not be overruled by the tax legislation.

The dissenting opinions sustained that the Constitution does not define "revenues from billings." Therefore, the idea that the constitutional wording would provide

19. *See* Extraordinary Appeals No. 357.950, 390.840, 358.273 and 346.084, all decided on 9 November 2005.
20. *Supra*, Justice Marco Aurelio, reporting.
21. *Supra* note 19, Justice Cezar Peluso, concurring.

for a definite concept for the term should be rejected. The reference to revenues from billings, in this view, would be an open constitutional norm that would allow for meanings different from the one adopted under commercial law. It would not be acceptable to say that the 1991 legislator would have "the power to interpret the Constitution in a better or more appropriate sense" and the extent of the authentic interpreter's freedom, would only be limited by the "essential core." In this sense, it would not be acceptable that the mere use of a term provided by private law would imply that this institute of private law had been incorporated in the constitutional wording.[22]

Another line of reasoning could be found in the same case, which in spite of different arguments, finished by concluding for the constitutionality of the contributions. The reasoning was based on the argument that by introducing the expression "revenues or revenues from billings" in the Constitution, Amendment No. 20/98 had broadened the previous constitutional permissive. In this view, the Constitutional Amendment would have repaired any issue of unconstitutionality existing prior to the enactment of the Amendment.[23]

The judges in this case were primarily concerned with investigating the content of the term "revenues from billings," provided by the Constitution, without addressing the typological nature of the constitutional categories concerning tax jurisdiction, or the fact that it was a complementary law (Complementary Law 70/1991) which had defined the expression "revenues from billing." This argument could be important to conclude for the impossibility of ordinary federal law to broaden such concept, in order to include revenues beyond sales of merchandise and services.

[E] Financial Leasing and Rendering of Services[24]

When one takes into consideration the final position of the Federal Supreme Court on leasing (renting) of movable goods (*see* §3.03[C] above), one would believe that the Court would have definitively rejected the historic argument according to which ISS would tax any intangible supply, and that an obligation of "doing" was the core of the tax, thus not allowing ISS to be levied on renting.

Surprisingly, a different understanding was found some years later, when the Court examined financial leasing.[25] The question was raised whether financial leasing

22. This dissenting opinion, issued by Justice Gilmar Mendes, was diametrically opposed by Justice Celso de Mello's reasoning, despite reaching the same conclusion. He recurred to Art. 110 of the National Tax Code to argue for the primacy of concepts of private law used by the Constitution, "otherwise privileging, in the matter, the economic interpretation of tax law to the detriment of the postulate of typicality, which represents, in our normative system, a necessary and natural projection of the constitutional principle of the absolute reservation of the law in its material sense (...)." Despite his reference to the types in tax matters, for Justice Celso de Mello, Art. 110 constitutes a corollary of the primacy of private law over tax law.
23. *Supra* note 19, Justices Joaquim Barbosa and Eros Grau, dissenting.
24. For a critical review of the decision, *see* Hugo de Brito Machado, "ISS e o arrendamento mercantil (ISS and the leasing)", (in *Revista Dialética de Direito Tributário*, No. 185, 2011): 63–76.
25. Supreme Court, Extraordinary Appeal No. 547.245-SC, decided on 2 December 2009.

constituted the rendering of services. According to the taxpayers, a financial leasing contract comprises a lease and an option. Since there was no "doing" obligation, the precedent concerning rendering of movable goods was evoked. The taxpayers alleged that both cases were similar.

The prevailing opinion did not recognize that Court would change its opinion. The reporting judge preferred to declare that the ISS should be levied exclusively on "doing" obligations. However, in the case of financial leasing, it found that the underlying purpose[26] of a financial leasing contract is not the leasing of a good, but the provision of debt finance with the lessor acting as an intermediary between the supplier and the lessee. Thus, it was concluded, "financing is a service, on which the ISS may be levied," deeming as irrelevant the fact that the lessee could purchase the good in the end, since "any rendering of service involves, in distinct intensities, the utilization of a good." A further argument in this opinion was based on the expression "of any nature," which would allow one to get rid of the shackles of the concept of private law. The same argument had already been offered in a case concerning the leasing of movable goods, but was not accepted by the Court in that case.[27]

Another line of arguments also concluded for the possibility of ISS to be due on financial leasing, but this time clearly rejecting the equivalence of the expression "services of any nature" and the private concept of service. In other words, such statement simply disregarded the previous decision, which had been based on the identity of both expressions. According to this understanding, the term "services" would not constitute a concept insusceptible to change, but rather was subject to evolution. It was argued that "the rapid social evolution has lead to the obsolescence of certain established legal concepts, which may not remain immune to new valuations." Unlike the reporting Justice, this line of argument did not qualify the transaction as financing, but noticed that "in financial leasing, there is, for instance, the rendering of intermediary services between parties that have resources and those who need them, not in a general form as in a loan, but with the specific objective of granting the possibility of using a good." The characterization as a service of any nature would lie on the "characteristic note of approaching convergent interests (acquisition of the right to use a good, according to contractual dispositions and a specific tax regime)."[28]

[F] Software and the Concept of Merchandise

Another instance where the Supreme Court had to investigate the meaning of a Constitutional term regarded the concept of "merchandise" with respect to the tax on

26. Here understood as the economic and social function of the legal transaction. On the cause of legal transactions, *see* Caio Mário da Silva Pereira, *Instituições de Direito Civil* (*Institutions of Private Law*), vol. I (23rd edn, Rio de Janeiro: Forense, 2009): 431–436. The author addresses the problem as follows: "Every human action is attached to a reason. Every act is preceded by a more or less complex motivation. Every statement of intent has a reason, which may be purely inner and psychical, or outer and objective. In the search for the motivation of the act lays the problem concerning the *cause of legal transactions*."
27. *Supra* note 25, Justice Eros Grau, concurring.
28. *Supra* note 25, Justice Joaquim Barbosa, concurring.

sales, the ICMS.[29] The ICMS is a type of value-added tax levied on transactions involving the distribution of goods and the rendering of any type of intrastate or interstate transport services, as well as communication services. ICMS legislation is enacted by each State, within the limits set forth in the Constitution.

A State's jurisdiction to institute and charge the tax on sales (ICMS) derives from Article 155, II of the Constitution. The authorization allows for the imposition of ICMS on "operations related to the circulation of merchandise" as well as "interstate and inter-municipal rendering of transport and communication services."

In order to comprehend the scope of the tax jurisdiction set forth by the Constitution for the States on the institution of the ICMS, Brazilian doctrine analyzed the meaning of the expression "operations related to the circulation of merchandise." From the joint interpretation of the words "operations" and "circulation," it has been understood that the correct meaning of the expression would imply an "act of transmission," instead of a legal transaction. Thus, the word "operations" would be provided in the sense of an act of impulse, of transmission.[30]

However, according to the same doctrine not every "circulation operation" would give raise to the ICMS. The word "merchandise" would denote that the ICMS is not levied on the transmission of any and all goods; on the contrary, the tax incidence would be limited to operations related to merchandise.

The concept of "merchandise" with respect to ICMS-taxation has traditionally been tied to the private law, particularly commercial law, according to which merchandise should be corporeal, i.e., a physical good.[31] Alcides Jorge Costa, analyzing the previous Constitution, noted that, "to the effect of ICM,[32] merchandise is every corporeal movable good to be circulated or received to go on into the circulation process."[33]

The influence of the commercial law on the construction of the concept of merchandise remains strong. Roque Antonio Carrazza, for instance, notes, "merchandise, for the purpose of taxation under the ICMS, is what the commercial law considers as merchandise."[34] Similarly, José Eduardo Soares de Melo defines merchandise as the "corporeal good of the business activity."[35]

29. *Imposto sobre Operações relativas à Circulação de Mercadorias e sobre Prestações de Serviços de Transporte Interestadual e Intermunicipal e de Comunicação* – "ICMS."
30. "'Operations' configure the real sense of the juridicized fact, the exercise of a legal act as a transmission of a right (possession or propriety). (...) The concepts of 'circulation', 'operation' and goods' remain umbilical connected, and the interpreters and addressees of the ICMS shall consider them in their legal conception, to the effect of characterization of its incidence." *See*, José Eduardo Soares de Mello, *ICMS: teoria e prática* (*ICMS: theory and practice*) (São Paulo, Dialética, 2008): 11–19.
31. *See*, José Gomes Jardim Neto, 'Os produtos digitais vendidos na Internet e o ICMS' (The Digital Goods Sold via Internet and the ICMS), in Luís Eduardo Schoueri, *Internet: o direito na era virtual* (Rio de Janeiro: Forense, 2001): 279.
32. Former denomination of the ICMS.
33. Alcides Jorge Costa, *ICM na Constituição e na Lei Complementar* (*ICM in Constitution and in Complementary Law*) (São Paulo: Resenha Tributária, 1978): 99.
34. Roque Antonio Carrazza, *ICMS* (São Paulo: Malheiros, 2004): 42.
35. José Eduardo Soares de Melo, *supra* note 30, at 18.

Such understanding has influenced important decisions of the Supreme Court. When analyzing the taxation of software, the Supreme Court required as an imperative for taxation under ICMS of merchandise that it would have a physical form (*corpus mechanicum*). In the first decision of the Court on the matter,[36] the prevailing opinion was that "the concept of merchandise, actually, does not include the incorporeal goods, such as rights in general: merchandise is a corporeal good, an object of acts of commerce or intended to be so."[37]

From such assumption, the Court made a distinction between "customized software," which is adapted to each client's needs, and "standard software," produced massively and sold at retail. According to the Court's understanding, only the latter should be taxed under the ICMS, because they may be deemed as merchandise directed to the market, "materializing the *corpus mechanicum* of the intellectual creation of the program." This understanding of the Supreme Court was confirmed in later decisions.[38]

In summary, the jurisprudence followed its expected course. After defining the concept of merchandise as a movable good, it was understood that standard software operations should be taxed, since they would occur physically, i.e., there would be a *corpus mechanicum*, an object of the transaction. The consumer would acquire the *software*, as any other merchandise would be acquired, and the existence of intangible rights was deemed irrelevant.

Due to this understanding, it was expected that, absent a *corpus mechanicum*, ICMS could not be levied. For example, if software is acquired through an Internet download, the *corpus mechanicum* requirement would shield the transaction from the ICMS. However, in this regard it is important to consider the interlocutory injunction granted in a Direct Action of Unconstitutionality against a State law, in which the levy of the ICMS was allowed "on operations with software, even if made via download," i.e., without any physical support.[39]

In this case, the Court deemed it possible for the ICMS to be levied on software purchased via download, as it was necessary, in its view, to modify the Court's earlier position on the requisite of a *corpus mechanicum* to define "merchandise."

This was a very relevant step because, once more, the Court dismissed the necessary connection to private law: although the latter defines "merchandise" as a corporal good, it would make no sense to treat differently the sale of software via Internet, as opposed to physical sales. Equality seems to have forced the Court to once more leave aside the rigid terms of Article 110 of the National Tax Code.

36. Supreme Court, Extraordinary Appeal No. 176.626-3/SP, decided on 10 November 1998.
37. *Supra*, Justice Sepúlveda Pertence, concurring.
38. Supreme Court, Extraordinary Appeal No. 199.464-9/SP, decided on 2 March 1999; Supreme Court, Regimental Appeal in the Extraordinary Appeal No. 285.870-6/SP, decided on 17 June 2008.
39. *See* Supreme Court, Interlocutory Injunction in the Direct Action of Unconstitutionality No. 1.945/MT, decided on 26 May 2010.

§3.04 INTERPRETATION OF TAX PLANNING

[A] Administrative Procedures in Brazil

As already mentioned in §3.01, while constitutional tax matters are usually decided by the Supreme Federal Court, interpretation of tax legislation is usually decided at first instance at the administrative level of government itself. This section shall examine cases involving the Union, where Federal administrative procedure is applicable; all States and several Municipalities have similar rules and therefore main aspects of the former are also applicable to the latter.

Once a tax assessment is issued by the tax authorities, a taxpayer may appeal directly to judicial courts irrespective to any previous requirement or questioning before the tax administration, since section XXV of Article 5 of the Constitution ensures that any infringement of or threat to a right is subject to judicial overview.[40] In such a case, the lawsuit filed by the taxpayers against the Revenue Service is heard by general courts, which have no specialization in tax matters.

In addition to appealing directly to the Judiciary, a taxpayer may seek a review by the tax administration itself free from any costs.[41] Effectively, as from Decree No. 70,235 of 1972, Brazilian law provides for a comprehensive federal administrative review procedure. The internal review procedure has grown in relevance because of its quality due to the specialized knowledge of the agents involved in the area of taxation, exceeding the level of expertise commonly available with the judiciary.[42]

Accordingly, once the Revenue Service issues a tax assessment, the taxpayer may bring its claim to a body of trial within the local Revenue Service office composed of five tax agents. In case its request is not granted, the taxpayer is allowed to appeal to the so-called Administrative Council of Tax Appeals (*Conselho Administrativo de Recursos Fiscais* (CARF)), a body within the Ministry of Finance comprising a specialized group of experts chosen both among tax authorities and taxpayers[43] which is supposed to review the decision of the local body of trial.[44]

40. *See* Cleide Previtalli Cais, *O processo tributário* (*Tax Procedures*) (São Paulo: Revista dos Tribunais, 2004): 94.
41. In this respect, the Supreme Court has already deemed as unconstitutional the requirement, until then very common, for taxpayers to deposit the amount of tax charged as a condition for appealing to administrative bodies. The Court's binding ruling No. 21 states that "it is unconstitutional the requirement of previous deposit of money or goods for the admissibility of the administrative appeal."
42. One may thus say that the administrative review acts as a "filter" intended to decrease the number of suits against the Revenue Service brought to the Judiciary. *See*, Hugo de Brito Machado, *Mandado de segurança em matéria tributária* (*Writ of Mandamus in Tax Matters*) (São Paulo: Revista dos Tribunais): 303.
43. The bodies of trial within CARF are composed equally by tax agents and taxpayers, all appointed by the Minister of Finance.
44. The present CARF is the successor of the so-called "Taxpayers' Council." For the purpose of this chapter, references to the Taxpayers' Council shall be omitted as such, and generally referred to as CARF's decisions, irrespective of whether at the time of the decision, the body was still called Taxpayers' Council or already CARF.

Despite its specialization and celerity, caution is required when analyzing the merits of the administrative procedure. Although section LV of the Constitution, as is characteristic to the due process of law, grants a broad right of defense to litigators within the administrative review, one should say that this system is not adversarial. Indeed, and different from the judicial review under which the claims of both taxpayers and authorities are brought before a neutral judge, in its administrative counterpart the claim is brought to the tax administration itself. Since the chair of each body – to whom the casting vote is granted – is always an agent of the tax authority, it is not surprising that in several cases, where there is no consensus as to whether or not to uphold the assessment, the final decision will be against the taxpayer.

On the other hand, if the taxpayer's appeal is not granted by the CARF, the former may always resort to the Judiciary, where the debates will restart regardless of any opinions rendered during the administrative review. Of course the Judiciary will be aware of CARF's decision and, in case the decision is well argued, it is very unlikely that a regular (nonspecialized) judge will find a better reasoning that CARF itself. But one should insist on the fact that the regular judge is not bound by CARF's decision. If, however, CARF grants the taxpayer's request, the Revenue Service is not allowed to resort to the Judiciary, since by means of CARF's decision the tax administration would have extinguished the tax assessment it had issued itself. Also, it is worth mentioning that Brazilian law does not authorize tax transactions between the taxpayer and the fiscal authorities in order to reduce the amount of tax debt for a specific company or individual, other than that previously foreseen by law.

Previously, it was very common for Brazilian companies to appeal to the Judicial Branch to resolve tax assessments imposed by fiscal authorities, especially in order to avoid restrictions due to the nonpayment of the taxes discussed.

However, at present, we can observe that more and more companies are opting, when possible, for an administrative hearing. That is in part due to the fact that, since 2007, is not necessary anymore to deposit part of the amount of taxes under controversy.

[B] Tax Planning in CARF Case Law

For a long time, tax planning in Brazil benefited from an extremely formal approach, based on the notion of a taxpayer's freedom to arrange affairs as the taxpayer saw fit, which led to increasingly aggressive structures. Accordingly, until the mid-2000s, the administrative court jurisprudence largely respected the legal form of transactions, facilitating tax planning. Tax planning schemes were defended solely on the basis that, if no specific legal concept or tax event were applicable to the case, the structure would be legitimate. Brazilian scholars have rejected the application of an "economic interpretation," as it would "destroy what is legal in tax law."[45]

45. Alfredo Augusto Becker, *Teoria Geral do Direito Tributário* (*General Theory of Tax Law*) (2nd edn, São Paulo: Saraiva, 1972): 118. In the same sense, *see* Johnson Barbosa Nogueira, *A Interpretação Econômica no Direito Tributário* (*Economic Interpretation in Tax Law*) (São Paulo: Resenha Tributária, 1982): 44; Gilberto de Ulhôa Canto, *Elisão e Evasão* (*Avoidance and*

Recently, however, the CARF has substantially changed its position regarding tax planning. Few subjects have attracted such strong views among scholars and practitioners as the conditions under which a tax planning structure should be considered legitimate under Brazilian tax law.

Whenever challenging the transaction undertaken by the taxpayer, the members of CARF would likely base their position on the private law institute of "sham" as outlined by Article 167 of the Civil Code, i.e., the transaction would be disregarded on the basis of the malicious inveracities surrounding it and not due to its purpose, duration, or tax outcomes.

A good example is the so-called "reverse merger," i.e., a take-over of a profitable company by its loss-making counterpart as to allow the latter to carry forward its own tax losses (which would no longer be of any use if the loss-making company were absorbed by the profitable company, since under Article 514 of the Income Tax Ruling the successor is not able to offset tax losses from the merged company).

Under the formal approach, the CARF delivered several decisions validating the transaction and understood that tax losses could be carried forward as long as the formal conditions set by the Income Tax Ruling were met.[46] Paraphrasing the Superior Chamber of the court in a leading case regarding the matter:

> If the merger is not prohibited and the form in which it is executed constitutes, indeed, factually and legally a merger, there is no way to qualify the transaction as a sham.[47]

In "reverse merger" cases, it became common practice that the acquiring company (i.e., the successor) ended up resembling the merged company, as by assuming its activities, address, or even its name. It is interesting to see that, even when said circumstances led the judges to conclude for a sham transaction, the CARF, influenced by the legality argument, would deny the penalties applicable to fraud,

---

Evasion), in Ives Gandra da Silva Martins (ed.), Elisão e Evasão Fiscal (São Paulo: Resenha Tributária, 1988): 16; Antonio Roberto Sampaio Doria, *Elisão e Evasão Fiscal* (*Fiscal Avoidance and Evasion*) (2nd edn, São Paulo: José Bushatsky, 1977): 96; Paulo de Barros Carvalho, *O absurdo da interpretação econômica do "fato gerador" – direito e sua autonomia – o paradoxo da interdisciplinariedade* (*The Absurd Economic Interpretation of "Tax Events" – Law and Its Autonomy – The Interdisciplinarity Paradox*) (In Revista de Direito Tributário, No. 97, 2007): 16; Hugo de Brito Machado, *Curso de Direito Tributário* (*Tax Law Course*), (5th edn, Rio de Janeiro: Forense, 1992): 68; and Luciano Amaro, *Direito Tributário Brasileiro* (*Brazilian Tax Law*) (17th edn, São Paulo: Saraiva, 2011): 252–253. For a contrary position, admitting the economic interpretation in certain situations, *see* Rubens Gomes de Souza, *Interpretação no Direito tributário* (*Interpretation in Tax Law*) (São Paulo: Saraiva, 1975): 373; and Amílcar de Araújo Falcão, *Introdução ao Direito Tributário* (*An Introduction to Tax Law*) (Rio de Janeiro: Forense, 1959): 99.

46. The following judgments may be pointed in this respect: Administrative Council of Administrative Appeals, Judgments No. 101–94.127, decided on 28 February 2003; No. 105-15.822, decided on 22 June 2006; and 105-16.677, decided on 16 October 2007.
47. Administrative Council of Administrative Appeals, Judgment No. 01-01.874, decided on 15 May 1995.

reasoning that although there may have been intent to obtain tax advantages through elusive means, no bad faith is apparent inherent to the practice of fraud.[48]

Nevertheless, the Tax Code was amended in 2001, when a paragraph added to Article 116 that, in the eyes of some commentators,[49] incorporated a general anti-avoidance rule (GAAR).[50] One could easily claim this is not an anti-avoidance rule, but merely an anti-evasion rule, since it refers to cases involving dissimulation, while tax avoidance is usually referred to when it comes to real transactions, not simulated ones. However, even if this were a GAAR, one should note that this provision depends on a regulation to be issued by the Congress. In this sense, the government enacted, in August 2002, the Provisional Measure No. 66 (MP No. 66/2002), attempting to give the disregard procedure broad standards.

Effectively, the MP No. 66/2002 not only provided for a special procedure to disregard transactions for tax purposes, but also tried to introduce in the Brazilian legal system institutes and doctrines already adopted in other jurisdictions. In this sense, the MP No. 66/2002 included expressions such as "lack of business purpose" (defined as "the option for a more complex or more expensive form, between two or more forms available for the taxpayer") and "abuse of forms" (described by the statute as "the indirect act which produces the same economic result as the dissimulated act or legal transaction.")

This proposal from the Government, however, was rejected by the Congress and the regulation of the GAAR is still pending.[51] One reasonably expected that the rejection of the above doctrines by the Congress would be a benchmark for the definition of the current legal status of tax planning in the sense of enforcing the legality argument adopted by CARF.

Nevertheless, a movement of CARF towards a "substance versus form" approach emerged, using doctrines such as "business purpose" and "abuse of law" to disregard transactions undertaken by the taxpayer for no other purpose than tax reduction.

48. Administrative Council of Administrative Appeals, Judgment No. 103-21.046, decided on 16 October 2002.
49. Some scholars, as well as the Government, would argue that such provision should be understood as a GAAR, despite its clear provision demanding further regulation. *See* Ives Gandra da Silva Martins, "Norma Antielisão é incompatível com o sistema constitucional brasileiro" ("The Anti-abuse Rule Is Incompatible with Brazilian Constitutional System"), in Valdir Rocha Oliveira (ed.), *O planejamento tributário e a Lei Complementar 104* (São Paulo: Dialética, 2001): 125; and Marco Aurélio Greco, "Constitucionalidade do parágrafo único do artigo 116 do CTN" ("Constitutionality of the Sole Paragraph of Article 116 of the National Tax Code"), in Valdir Rocha Oliveira (ed.), *O planejamento tributário e a Lei Complementar 104* (São Paulo: Dialética, 2001); 194.
50. The mentioned paragraph reads as follows: "the Administrative Authority may disregard acts or legal transactions entered into with the aim of dissimulating the occurrence of a tax event or the nature of elements which constitute a tax obligation, *as per a procedure to be established by law*."
51. According to Art. 62 of the Federal Constitution, Provisional Measures are enacted by the Executive and are subject to a posterior approval of the Congress, which may reject or accept the Measure. Only in the latter case, it is converted into law.

Inspired by the common law experience, the business purpose doctrine has been extensively applied by the CARF and discussed by Brazilian authors.[52] In its contemporary meaning it may be defined as a judicial doctrine applied by tax authorities to recharacterize transactions that appear to fit within the literal words of a provision and thus achieve a tax outcome not different from the one intended by the legislature for transactions with a similar business outcome.[53] Notwithstanding the clear rejection of MP No. 66/2002 by the Congress, the CARF insisted on applying its doctrines as if they were part of the Brazilian legal system - which, of course, they are not. This led to great uncertainty for both taxpayers and tax authorities as to the borderline between valid tax planning and illegitimate tax evasion.

A comprehensive survey[54] of every decision handed down by the CARF on the matter from 2002 to 2008 revealed that, in light of tax planning charges, the judges not only asked (i) if the facts were deemed existent just as described by the taxpayer or (ii) if the applicable law was duly observed - two criteria usually linked to the legality argument - but also (iii) whether the transaction had nontax related purposes, in an evident departure from the previously prevailing understanding.

Moreover, the survey concluded that, while assessing the existence of a business purpose in the transaction, the CARF paid attention to (i) the independence of the parties involved, (ii) the time gap between the transactions and (iii) the coherence between the transaction and the business activity involved.

Returning to the "reverse merger" example, it will come as no surprise, in this context, that the CARF started to question what would be the business purpose justifying the merger of a profitable company into a loss-making one. This was the case, for instance, in Judgment No. 107-07.596, in which a transaction was held to be valid, *inter alia*, because of the nontax related purposes of the transaction as presented by the taxpayer:

> (...) no major effort is necessary to conclude that the company resulting from the transaction, in business terms, has gained efficiency and has reduced costs, namely those costs which are inherent to the mere fact of the existence of the company.[55]

---

52. *See* Hermes Marcelo Huck, *Evasão e Elisão: rotas internacionais* (*Tax Evasion and Tax Avoidance: International routes*) (São Paulo: Saraiva, 1997); Marco Aurélio Greco, *Planejamento Tributário* (*Tax Planning*) (São Paulo: Dialética, 2004); João Dácio Rolim, *Normas antielisivas tributárias* (*Anti-avoidance Tax Rules*) (São Paulo: Dialética, 2001); Miguel Delgado Gutierrez, "O Planejamento Tributário e o Business Purpose" ("Tax Planning and Business Purpose"), *Revista Dialética de Direito Tributário*, (São Paulo, n. 231, 2014): 75; Miquerlam Chaves Cavalcante, "O propósito negocial e o planejamento tributário no ordenamento jurídico brasileiro" ("Business Purpose and the Tax Planning in the Brazilian Law"), *Revista da PGFN*, (Brasília, n. 1, 2011): 139–162.
53. *See* Christopher M. Pietruszkiewicz, *Economic Substance and the Standard of Review*, Alabama Law Review, (vol. 60, (2009): 346–347. For a case law analysis, *see* Joshua Blank & Nancy Staudt, *Corporate Shams*, 87(6) *New York University Law Review* 1641 (2012).
54. *See* Luís Eduardo Schoueri, "O desafio do planejamento tributário" ("The Tax Planning Challenge"), in Luís Eduardo Schoueri (ed.), *Planejamento tributário e o "propósito negocial"* (São Paulo: Quartier Latin, 2010).
55. Administrative Council of Administrative Appeals, Judgment No. 107-07.596, decided on 14 April 2004.

The business purpose argument also became common in cases involving transactions carried out for the amortization for tax purposes of the goodwill accounted on the acquisition of investments. In this respect, the so-called "Carrefour case" is a good example, in which it was observed (summarizing):

> The facts accepted in this trial as proof demonstrate the absence of any business or corporate purpose of the merger other than for the transfer of goodwill to the merging company, thus reducing the taxable gain from the sale of the premises to Carrefour. (...) [T]he case should be qualified as sham and, therefore, a penalty should be applied.[56]

The above reasoning is symptomatic for the Court's approach. Although the main reason for the rejection of the tax planning is the lack of business purpose, which by itself has no legal bearing in the Brazilian legal system, the decision was ultimately based on the private law concept of sham. In other words, the passage indicates the will to hide behind concepts provided by law, the application of doctrines which currently do not have a legal basis in Brazilian law.

The analysis of other decisions involving similar transactions[57] shows that the CARF has been developing a concept of a "conduit company" – usually taken by the CARF's members as evidence of illegitimate tax planning. A "conduit company" is usually ephemeral and transitory, and does not have a purpose other than realizing a tax reduction.

To this effect, see what was observed in the judgment of the so-called "Santander case":

> The expression "conduit company" is used by tax authorities and scholars to define the legal entity, without business purpose, whose ultimate goal is not to produce goods and services, but serve as means to give an appearance of regularity to a situation which is not.[58]

Afterwards, however, the court decided in favor of the taxpayer although a conduit company (Gerdau Participações S.A.) was interpositioned solely to enable a tax reduction, arguing that the "artificial" behavior itself is not illegal insofar as the company acts by legal means. In this sense, the court stated:

> Within the tax law, there is no problem if a person acts to reduce his tax burden, provided that he acts by licit means. Indeed, one should expect persons to do so, being reprehensible the opposite behavior. (...) Provided that the taxpayer acts under the law, he may undertake his tax planning in order to reduce his tax burden.[59]

56. Administrative Council of Administrative Appeals, Judgment No. 103-23.290, decided on 12 May 2007.
57. In this sense, Administrative Council of Administrative Appeals, Judgments No. 101-96.724, decided on 28 May 2008 and No. 105-17.219, decided on 18 September 2008.
58. Administrative Council of Administrative Appeals, Judgment No. 1402-00.802, decided on 21 October 2011.
59. Administrative Council of Administrative Appeals, Judgment No. 1101-00.708, decided on 11 April 2012.

With its judgment in the "Gerdau case," the CARF seemed to have abandoned the trend towards the adoption of the "business purpose" and "substance versus form" doctrines and resorted to its previous position towards legality. However, in more recent decisions, the CARF has understood that the use of a conduit company is only justified in cases with where the interposition serves useful nontax purposes, such as business[60] and/or regulatory objectives.[61]

The CARF has accepted, for example, that there is a valid business reason to insert a conduit company into a business group of operational entities where the owners controlling the group wished to separate themselves from any direct ownership of one of the companies.[62] The CARF has also accepted regulatory considerations such as restrictions on obtaining governmental approvals or the need to comply with constraints established by regulatory entities as legitimate reasons for the use of conduit companies.[63]

Another aspect of an arrangement that has been used by the CARF as a relevant fact when considering the legitimacy of a conduit company arrangement is the timing of the arrangement. The CARF has decided, for example, that successive transactions, "especially when elapsed in only two days," imply an artificiality of a conduit company creation,[64] although it could be argued, that this aspect simply constitutes an indication of the lack of business purpose behind the arrangement.[65] A further consideration used by the CARF when deciding whether a conduit company arrangement had been adopted for business or tax minimization reasons is the "existence of alternative structures or ways available to the taxpayer that would lead to the same result".[66]

There are, thus, a number of CARF decisions suggesting conduit company arrangements can be set aside for tax purposes unless there is a valid business purpose[67] or external factors such as participation of independent parties or genuine economic risks point towards the nontax legitimacy of the arrangements.[68] This new

60. *See*, e.g., Administrative Council of Administrative Appeals, Judgment No. 1301-000.711, decided on 19 October 2011; and Administrative Council of Administrative Appeals, Judgment No. 1201-00.548, decided on 3 August 2011.
61. *See* Administrative Council of Administrative Appeals, Judgment No. 1102-000.875, decided on 12 June 2013.
62. *See* Administrative Council of Administrative Appeals, Judgment No. 1201-001.438, decided on 7 June 2016.
63. *See*, e.g., Administrative Council of Administrative Appeals, Judgment No. 1301-002.047, decided on 8 June 2016.
64. Administrative Council of Administrative Appeals, Judgment No. 1401-001.534, decided on 3 February 2016.
65. Softening as well the importance of the temporal element, *see* Marcos Shigueo Takata, "Empresa-veículo e a amortização fiscal do ágio: há um problema real?" ("Conduit Company and goodwill amortization: is there a real problem?", in Roberto Quiroga Mosquera & Alexsandro Broedel Lopes (eds), *Controvérsias jurídico-contábeis (aproximações e distanciamentos)*, vol. 5 (São Paulo: Dialética, 2014): 235.
66. Administrative Council of Administrative Appeals, Judgment No. 1201-001.438, decided on 7 June 2016.
67. *See* Administrative Council of Administrative Appeals, Judgment No. 1201-001.364, decided on 1 March 2016; and Administrative Council of Administrative Appeals, Judgment No. 1102-000.982, decided on 4 December 2013.
68. *See* Administrative Council of Administrative Appeals, Judgment No. 1401-001.534, decided on 3 February 2016.

"substance over form" approach has not been consistently applied in CARF decisions, however. In some cases, the CARF has ruled in favor of taxpayers provided transactions that may have been tax motivated comply with the strict letter of the law,[69] and in other times has gone so far as to assert business purpose analysis is irrelevant since taxpayers should be allowed to make any arrangements as they see fit.[70]

Separately, in July 2015, piggybacking Action 12 of the OECD G20 BEPS Project, the government introduced to the Congress legislation that arguably was an attempt to foster a general anti-avoidance doctrine via disclosure requirements that could only have been relevant if the doctrine existed.[71] Provisional Measure No. 685 (MP No. 685/2015),[72] would have established an obligation for taxpayers to disclose transactions that resulted in the elimination, reduction or deferral of taxes if: (i) the transaction cannot be justified independently of its tax outcome; (ii) the adopted form would not be usual for the intended transaction, or when the contract contained clauses that resulted in effects different from a typical contract; or (iii) the transaction fell with a list of impugned transactions to be made by the Federal Revenue Secretariat ("RFB"). The attempt was unsuccessful when the Congress rejected the proposed legislation, citing, among other reasons, the absence of definitions for expressions in the law such as "aggressive tax planning," "relevant reasons other than tax reasons," and "usual form."

§3.05 INTERPRETATION OF TAX TREATIES

[A] Introduction

Although Brazil signed its first tax treaties in the 1960s, the country's tax treaty network is rather small relative to that of the other so-called BRIC group countries, each of which has around 80 treaties.

Brazil is currently a party to 31 tax treaties,[73] most of which were concluded during the 1970s and the 1980s as a part of the country's development agenda. It is not

69. *See* Administrative Council of Administrative Appeals, Judgment No. 1101-000.835, decided on 5 December 2012.

70. *See*, e.g., Administrative Council of Administrative Appeals, Judgment No. 1201-001.245, decided on 12 January 2016.

71. *See* Ricardo Lodi Ribeiro, O dever de comunicar à Fazenda Pública o planejamento fiscal no Brasil ("The obligation to disclose tax planning to Tax Authorities in Brazil"), in *Revista Dialética de Direito Tributário*, (São Paulo, n. 242, 2015): 101.

72. For further analysis of the incompatibility between the MP No. 685/2015 and Action 12 of the OECD G20 BEPS Project, *see* Luís Eduardo Schoueri & Ricardo André Galendi Jr., Transparência Fiscal e Reciprocidade nas Perspectivas Interna e Internacional, in Valdir de Oliveira Rocha (ed.). *Grandes Questões Atuais do Direito Tributário*, vol. 19 (São Paulo: Dialética, 2015); 252–254.

73. The following list indicates the current Brazilian tax treaty partners, as well as the date of signature of the respective treaty, from the earliest to the most recent: Japan (24 January 1967); France (10 September 1971); Belgium (23 June 972; partially renegotiated on 20 November 2002); Denmark (27 August 1974); Spain (14 November 1974); Sweden (25 April 1975); Austria (24 May 1975); Italy (3 October 1978); Luxembourg (8 November 1978); Argentina (17 May 1980); Norway (21 August 1980); Ecuador (26 May 1983); Philippines (29 September 1983);

clear whether policymakers are aware that the decrease in the pace of concluding tax treaties in the last decades may be related to the country's movement from a traditional capital importer to a capital exporter with many of Brazil's multinationals investing abroad. At the same time, it is clear that foreign investors in Brazil face great uncertainty as a result of misconceptions and misinterpretations surrounding the existing treaties.

Brazilian courts hardly deal with tax treaties. As will be seen, CARF has issued some decisions. Only a few cases have reached the Superior Court of Justice or Federal Supreme Court. Before 1988, the latter had broader jurisdiction than constitutional matters and this may explain some decisions issued by it; after 1988, the Federal Supreme Court is limited to decide on constitutional issues only. But since one could claim that by not applying a treaty, tax authorities would be disregarding the Constitutional issue concerning to the prevalence of International Law before internal law, one could find a way to bring treaty cases to that Court.

Moreover, the scholarly debates often found in foreign judicial decisions on tax treaties[74] have found no counterparts in Brazilian decisions on tax treaties. When Brazilian courts are required to interpret the provisions of a tax treaty, their rulings are often not consistent with international practice. Symptomatic of this scenario is that relevant documents such as the Vienna Convention on the Law of Treaties (VCLT) and the Commentaries, Guidelines and Reports of the OECD and the UN are frequently not taken into account by the courts.

[B] The Vienna Convention on the Law of Treaties

Despite being recognized worldwide as bedrock for the interpretation and application of treaties, the VCLT was only ratified by Brazil in 2009.[75] That may explain why, as of yet, Brazilian judges seem unprepared to resort to the provisions of the Convention when facing tax treaties, in spite of the fact that doctrine has always recognized immediate application of the Convention as consuetudinary law. As a result, important cases involving tax treaty interpretation (such as the *Copesul* case, *Falcão* case and *Volvo 1* case)[76] were decided by the Superior Court of Justice without any regard to the Convention.

Canada (4 June 1984); Hungary (20 June 1986); Czech Republic and Slovakia (26 August 1986); India (26 April 1988); Korea (7 March 1989); Netherlands (8 March 1990); China (5 August 1991); Finland (2 April 1996); Portugal (16 May 2000); Chile (3 April 2001); Ukraine (16 January 2002); Israel (12 December 2002); Mexico (25 September 2003); South Africa (8 November 2003); Peru (17 February 2006); Trinidad and Tobago (23 July 2008); and Turkey (16 December 2010).

74. For instance, no relevant case law may be found on the adoption of ambulatory or static interpretation vis-à-vis the wording of Art. 3(2), as well as no reference may be found as to whether Brazilian Courts and tax authorities accept the "OECD New Approach" towards qualification conflicts.
75. The VCLT was approved by the Brazilian Congress on 17 July 2009 (Legislative Decree-law No. 496) and its ratification instrument was deposited with the Secretary-General of the United Nations on 25 September 2009. It became mandatory within the country as from 14 December 2009, when it was enacted by Decree-law No. 7.030.
76. Superior Court of Justice, Appeals No. 1.161.467/RS, 882.785/RS and 457.228/PR, respectively.

It is noteworthy, however, that in a still pending case, the so-called *Volvo 2*-case concerning the application of the 1975 Brazil-Sweden tax treaty (thus prior to VCLT enforcement worldwide), and the Federal Supreme Court did recognize a constitutional issue. In an already published opinion a Justice expressly referred to Article 27 of the VCLT – which would have "codified principles already required as international custom" – as to deny the possibility of treaty override under Brazilian law. This opinion indicates that the Justices may be ready, after all, to address the Convention when interpreting a tax treaty.[77]

[C] The OECD Commentaries

Similar to the case of the VCLT, it is unusual for Brazilian courts to refer to the OECD Commentaries when interpreting a tax treaty. A relevant exception may be found in a decision of CARF in the *Eagle I*-case.[78]

In referred case, upon the question whether profits derived from the application of Brazilian CFC rules would be subject to Article 7 or 10 of the Brazil-Spain treaty, reference was explicitly made to the OECD Commentaries with the argument that they would be "useful as a tool to help in the interpretation" insofar as "most treaties signed by Brazil follow the Model."[79] Interestingly enough, reference was made to the Commentaries themselves – transcribing the passage in which they assign their own "great assistance in the application and interpretation of the conventions and, in particular, in the settlement of any disputes" – rather than to the VCLT or any further observation as support for their relevance. The same considerations with respect to the Commentaries were addressed upon the judgment of the *Eagle II* case,[80] but on that occasion said opinion did not prevail.[81]

[D] Income from the Supply of Technical Services

Perhaps the most relevant case of (mis)interpretation of tax treaties by Brazilian courts concerns the qualification of income derived from the supply of technical services.

Although it is widely accepted by scholars and practitioners of international tax that Article 7 "forms the core of the treaty regime,"[82] as "the largest portion of income derived from international economic activities falls"[83] within this provision, Brazilian treaty practice tends to extend the scope of Article 12 which, due to the broad wording

77. Supreme Court, Appeal No. 460.320/PR, pending for judgment, Justice Gilmar Mendes Opinion.
78. Administrative Council of Administrative Appeals, Judgment No. 101-95.802, decided on 19 October .2006.
79. *Supra*, Justice Sandra Faroni, reporting.
80. Administrative Council of Administrative Appeals, Judgment No. 101-97.070, decided on 17 December .2008.
81. Though not due to her considerations regarding the interpretation of the treaty in light of the Commentaries, but rather to a mistaken understanding adopted by the majority of judges whereby CFC rules would apply straight to second tier CFCs so as to deny the application of Brazil-Spain tax treaty.
82. *See* Jonathan Schwarz, *Schwarz on tax treaties* (Surrey: Wolter Kluwer, 2009): 137.
83. *See* Klaus Vogel, *Double taxation conventions* (London: Kluwer Law, 1996): 399.

adopted in Brazilian treaties, could be deemed to be the real core of the treaty. Accordingly, on the one hand, technical services fall within the scope of Article 12 of Brazilian tax treaties, and, on the other hand, tax authorities were of the mistaken position that, in the very few cases this income would not fall therein (namely income from services in which no technology is transferred, as it would supposedly lie outside the ambit of Article 12), the income should be covered by Article 21, which, deviating from the OECD Model, enables the concurrent taxation of "other income" at source.

Whilst lower courts upheld the odd understanding that Article 7 only applies to "profits" - i.e., global revenues minus global expenses of a company - and not to single items of income, such as the remuneration for services - the Superior Court of Justice correctly settled the matter in the *Copesul* case,[84] where it concluded that the remuneration derived from technical services should fall under the provisions of Article 7 whenever this was not included within Article 12 by the treaty.

There is no doubt that the conclusion eventually adopted by the Court is consistent with international practice and the approach suggested by the OECD,[85] as well as with the position adopted by the majority of Brazilian scholars.[86] The judges did not address, however, the question of whether the concept of "profit" was sufficiently defined in the treaty itself, without the need of guidance by reference to domestic law. Interestingly, the provision of Article 7(4) indicates that the profit comprises several "items of income," which may or may not be separately dealt with in a specific Article of the Model.[87] Ignoring that the treaty itself would reject the position sustained by the tax authorities, the Court resorted to Brazilian internal law in order to determine the meaning of "profits" under Article 7 without clarifying on what basis it did so. Effectively, no reference was made at all to the general *renvoi* clause of Article 3(2) of the treaties concerned, so as to inquire whether the term "profits" would or not be

84. *Supra* note 61.
85. The Commentaries to the Model Convention of which, when distinguishing the know-how contracts (to which Art. 12 is applicable) of contracts in which the service is not followed by any technology transfer, recognizes about the former that "this type of contract thus differs from contracts for the provision of services, in which one of the parties undertakes to use the customary skills of his calling to execute work himself for the other party. Payments made under the latter contracts generally fall under Article 7." *See* OECD, *Model Tax Convention on Income and on Capital - Condensed Version* (OECD: Paris, 2010): para. 11.2 of the Commentaries to Art. 7.
86. *See* Alberto Xavier, *Direito tributário internacional do Brasil* (*Brazilian International Tax Law*), (Rio de Janeiro: Forense, 2004): 695; Gerd W. Rothmann, "Problemas de qualificação na aplicação das convenções contra a bitributação internacional" (Qualification Problems in the Application of Tax Treaties), in *Revista dialética de direito tributário*, No. 76 (São Paulo: Dialética, 2002); Sérgio A. Rocha, "O Ato Declaratório n. 1/2000 e a ilegalidade da obrigação de retenção do imposto de renda na fonte" (The Declaratory Act n. 1/2000 and the illegality of the obligation of withholding income tax at source), in *Revista dialética de direito tributário*, No. 58 (São Paulo: Dialética, 2000); Daniel V. Bellan, "Algumas considerações sobre a tributação dos royalties pagos a beneficiários residentes ou domiciliados no exterior" (Some Considerations on the Taxation of Royalties Paid to Beneficiaries Resident or Domiciled Abroad), in Heleno Tôrres (ed.), *Direito tributário internacional aplicado* (São Paulo: Quartier Latin, 2003).
87. The provision states that "where profits include items of income which are dealt with separately in other Articles of this Convention, then the provisions of those Articles shall not be affected by the provisions of this Article."

defined therein or, moreover, whether their context, as this is set by the VCLT, would require otherwise.

When taking as a premise that technical services which are not followed by a technology transfer were not included within the scope of Article 12 of the tax treaties, the Court ignores a relevant debate on the issue. Although "technical assistance and technical services" were part of the Brazilian treaty policy within the ambit of this Article,[88] no clarification on the meaning of these activities is to be found in the treaties.

Whilst one may understand, as the Superior Court seems to have, that technical services should always be ancillary and attached to know-how contracts while "pure" services would be those in which the technical knowledge of the service supplier is simply applied (and not transferred),[89] the fact is that a clear definition of "technical services" may not be found in Brazilian tax law, which applies the expression indiscriminately in what has been called "terminological Babel."[90]

In this sense, the issue is not as simple as the Court's opinion may suggest, and it is rather surprising that the judges remained unaware of the enormous implications of its judgment, because should it have concluded that technical services without technology transfer fall within the scope of Article 12, the Court would have effectively blocked the application of Article 7 to these services.[91]

When judging the *Copesul* case, the Superior Court of Justice missed the opportunity of clearly ascertaining the conditions under which a service may be deemed to be included within the scope of Article 12, and thus be taxable at source in Brazil, regardless of the presence of a PE in the country of a nonresident service supplier. Following a formal opinion rendered by the Attorney General of the National Treasury after the judgment of the *Copesul* case, the Revenue Service reviewed its previous understanding and took the position that technical services, whether followed by technology transfer or not, should fall under Article 12 or 14 of the applicable treaty. Where Article 21 is no longer considered, future litigation concerning the (broad) scope of Articles 12 and 14 is expected.

In summary, if the very conclusion achieved by the Superior Court of Justice in the judgment of the *Copesul* case meets the legitimate interests of the taxpayers and is in line with both the foreign and Brazilian scholars' understanding of the matter, the reasoning developed by the Court indicates the scenario faced by Brazilian Judiciary, where tax treaty issues start to reach courts which are unfamiliar with the structure of a tax treaty and the rational characteristic to its interpretation.

---

88. The exceptions are the treaties concluded with Japan, Sweden, France, Austria and Finland.
89. *See* Alberto Xavier, *supra* note 86, at 515.
90. *See* Gabriel Francisco Leonardos, "O imposto de renda de fonte sobre os pagamentos ao exterior por serviços técnicos – análise de um caso de renúncia fiscal do Brasil" (The Withholding Income Tax on the Payments Remitted Abroad for Technical Services – Analysis of a Case of Tax Waiver of Brazil), in *Revista dialética de direito tributário*, No. 40 (São Paulo: Dialética, 1999): 34.
91. In this respect, it is interesting to note that the Revenue Service Interpretative Declaratory Act No. 27/04, intended to clarify this issue within the ambit of the treaty between Brazil and Spain, rules that "it shall be included in the concept of royalties, for the purposes of application of this Convention, all technical services or technical assistance, regardless of whether they imply or not in the transfer of technology."

§3.06 CONCLUSIONS

A peculiarity of Brazilian federalism is the rigid allocation in the Constitution of jurisdiction to impose taxes and tax revenues. The boundaries between types of tax in the Constitution are not precise but instead rely on sometimes ambiguous historical terms. The complementary law defines the taxes in terms of taxable event, tax base and taxable person, preventing jurisdictional conflicts and thus avoiding simultaneous taxation of a singular taxable event by multiple jurisdictions.

The role of the courts in coordinating the taxes among the federal subdivisions is evident in cases in which the judges interpret the Constitution along with the provisions of the complementary law. By establishing the scope and the meaning of the provisions of the Constitution and of the complementary laws, the courts play a relevant role in determining the boundaries of each of the subdivisions' tax jurisdiction.

Until the mid-2000s, decisions by the CARF on tax planning tended to respect legal form and allow private law concepts to prevail. Despite the absence of a GAAR in Brazilian domestic legislation, the judges are now likely to make reference to "substance over form" and "business form" approaches, which lack clear legal grounds within Brazilian legislation.

Whilst relevant and comprehensive case law has already been handed down by the Supreme Court on the interpretation of the Constitution for purposes of tax coordination within the federation, Brazilian courts are not yet familiar with the interpretation of tax treaties as outlined by the international practice. Insofar as judges, generally, are not prepared to consult sources such as the OECD or UN Commentaries, or scholars' writings on treaty law, as is the practice in most other countries, it comes as no surprise that considerable weight is given by courts to the views and opinions of the tax authorities.

CHAPTER 4

Legal Interpretation of Tax Law: Canada

Kim Brooks

§4.01 INTRODUCTION

This chapter is designed to lay the ground for comparative study into legal interpretation in tax law. To that end, its goal is primarily descriptive. It is designed to address the kinds of factors that might support a comparative analysis of Canada's approach to legal interpretation. Presumably, similarities and differences among countries might be identified and explained based on a set of factors, including the structure of government, the design of adjudication mechanisms (both administrative and judicial), the dominant philosophies of language, the historic practices of interpretation, the importance of legislative purpose and the extent to which external aids are relied upon, and the overarching norms of grammar and their interaction with legislative drafting.

The chapter proceeds in nine parts. Section §4.02 describes the structure of Canadian government and the formal process for resolving tax disputes. Section §4.03 turns to an overview of the approach to legal interpretation, focusing largely on Canada's Supreme Court's approach in recent years. Section §4.04 explores more specific dilemmas of legal interpretation including how courts view the interpretation of tax laws compared to other legislative instruments, how tax law interacts with common law concepts, and how tax law and tax accounting are connected. Section §4.05 examines Canada's use of interpretive aids, highlighting the role played by parliamentary documents, administrative guidance, and secondary materials and materials from other jurisdictions. Section §4.06 reviews the use of interpretive conventions. Section §4.07 reflects on the impact of the general anti-avoidance rule (GAAR) on interpretive approaches. Sections §4.08 and §4.09 offer brief reflections on variations in the interpretation of the goods and services tax (GST) and the interpretation of tax treaties. Section §4.10 concludes.

§4.02 CANADA'S TAX SYSTEM

[A] Federal System Informs the Legislative Framework

Canada's federal state, with ten provinces and three territories, informs the design of its tax system. Constitutionally, the federal government is able to raise revenue through any mode of taxation and the provinces are limited to methods of direct taxation.[1] However, constitutional interpretation by the (UK) Privy Council, at the time Canada's final Court of Appeal, in an interpretation quite at odds with the conventional view of economists, found that a sales tax (and by analogy the view would extend to a GST or value added tax (VAT)) was a direct tax if stated separately from the tax-exclusive sale price and collected directly from the consumer at the time of sale.[2] Responsibility for tax matters is divided within the federal government, with the Department of Finance responsible for tax policy, the Canada Revenue Agency responsible for tax administration, and the Department of Justice responsible for tax litigation.

Canada's legislative tax framework includes laws at the federal and provincial levels, and specific taxing legislation as well as legislation that compels particular interpretive approaches. The two primary sources of federal taxing legislation are the *Income Tax Act* and the *Excise Tax Act*.[3] Subsidiary legislation, for example, the *Income Tax Regulations*,[4] support those primary legislative sources. Provinces have also enacted tax legislation, much of which piggy-backs from the federal legislation, and municipalities impose property taxes. Each of Canada's provinces has passed an *Interpretation Act*, and Canada has a national *Interpretation Act*.[5] The provincial Acts apply for the purposes of provincial laws, including the various provincial tax laws, and the federal Act applies for the purposes of federal enactments, including the *Income Tax Act* and the *Excise Tax Act*.

The *Interpretation Act* has several helpful provisions for those seeking to interpret tax legislation, including detailed provisions on time limits and the calculations of days and times of day.[6] Perhaps the most commonly referred to section is section 12, which provides, '[e]very enactment is deemed remedial, and shall be given such fair, large and liberal construction and interpretation as best ensures the attainment of its objects.'[7]

Supplementing Canada's domestic rules on international taxation, Canada has entered into approximately 95 double taxation treaties[8] and approximately 22 tax

1. *Constitution Act, 1867* (UK), 30 & 31 Vict, c 3, ss 91(3), 92(2), 92(9), reprinted in RSC 1985, Appendix II, No 5.
2. *Atlantic Smoke Shops Ltd. v. Conlon* [1943] A.C. 550.
3. *Income Tax Act*, RSC 1985, c 1 (5th Supp); *Excise Tax Act*, RSC 1985, c E-15.
4. *Income Tax Regulations*, CRC, c 945.
5. *Interpretation Act*, RSC 1985, c I-21.
6. *Interpretation Act*, RSC 1985, c I-21, ss 26–30.
7. *Interpretation Act*, RSC 1985, c I-21, s. 12.
8. Department of Finance Canada, *Tax Treaties: In Force*, https://www.fin.gc.ca/treaties-conventions/in_force--eng.asp.

information exchange agreements (with more under negotiation),[9] and has ratified the Convention on Mutual Administrative Assistance on Tax Matters.[10] Canada has an *Income Tax Conventions Interpretation Act*,[11] which applies to assist in interpreting conventions or agreements between Canada and another state on taxation of income. That Convention includes a number of definition sections (e.g., defines pensions),[12] as well as some provisions that supplement treaty provisions (e.g., a provision that provides additional guidance on the profits to be attributed to a permanent establishment),[13] and some provisions that arguably alter the effect of a treaty (e.g., a provision that deems a trust to be exclusively resident in Canada under certain conditions).[14] The Convention also requires that an ambulatory approach be used in interpreting tax treaties.[15]

All Canadian law is subordinate to the Canadian Constitution. In addition to the constitutional provisions that allocate taxing jurisdiction between the federal and provincial governments, the Charter's equality provisions and its search and seizure restrictions have featured in adjudications of the constitutionality of particular tax provisions or government actions.[16]

[B] Design of Adjudication Framework

The Canada Revenue Agency has responsibility for tax administration. The Agency drafts a variety of interpretive documents that assist supporting taxpayer compliance, including tax folios, circulars, rulings, and letter opinions.

If a taxpayer disputes a Canada Revenue Agency assessment, the adjudication process begins with an administrative appeal. If a dispute cannot be resolved in the appeals branch, then the taxpayer appeals to the court system. Canadian tax cases are usually decided first by the Tax Court of Canada, which since 1991 has had exclusive original jurisdiction over tax appeals from the administrative process.[17] The Tax Court

9. Department of Finance Canada, *Tax Information Exchange Agreements*, http://www.fin.gc.ca/treaties-conventions/tieaaerf-eng.asp.
10. Convention on Mutual Administrative Assistance on Tax Matters, (4 Apr. 1995), ETS No 127.
11. *Income Tax Conventions Interpretation Act*, RSC 1985, c I-4.
12. *Income Tax Conventions Interpretation Act*, RSC 1985, c I-4, s. 5.
13. *Income Tax Conventions Interpretation Act*, RSC 1985, c I-4, s. 4.
14. *Income Tax Conventions Interpretation Act*, RSC 1985, c I-4, s. 4.3.
15. *Income Tax Conventions Interpretation Act*, RSC 1985, c I-4, s. 3.
16. *See* e.g., *Symes v. Canada*, [1993] 4 SCR 695, [1993] SCJ No 131 (where the court considered whether the equality provision, s. 15, compelled the court to allow the deduction of child care expenses and determined it did not), *Thibaudeau v. Canada*, [1995] 2 SCR 627, [1995] SCJ No 42 (where the court considered whether an *Income Tax Act* provision requiring the respondent to include childcare alimony amounts in her taxable income infringed s. 15, and determined that it did not), *R v. Jarvis*, 2002 SCC 73, [2002] 3 SCR 757 (where the court considered whether the taxpayer's liberty interest under s. 7 was triggered by the introduction of statutorily compelled information at trial. The court determined that while the taxpayer's liberty interest under s. 7 was engaged, s. 7 does not prevent the use of statutorily compelled information in all contexts).
17. For a history of the Tax Court of Canada, *see* Ian MacGregor et al., *The Development of the Tax Court of Canada*, 58 (Supp) Can Tax J 87 (2010). Note that some matters, for example, challenges to the Minister's exercise of discretion, continue to be heard by the Federal Court Trial Division. *Federal Courts Act*, RSC 1985, c F-7, ss 18–18.1.

can hear cases under its general procedure, or where the amount in dispute is small, taxpayers can elect to proceed under an informal process. Decisions from the Tax Court can be appealed on errors of law to the Federal Court of Appeal (FCA). Parties must seek leave to appeal to the Supreme Court of Canada (SCC) from the FCA, and only a few tax cases are heard by the Supreme Court each year.

§4.03 TAX INTERPRETATION: THE UNDERLYING THEORY OF INTERPRETATION REFLECTED BY TAX DECISIONS AT THE SUPREME COURT OF CANADA

Since the Supreme Court serves as Canada's highest court, and since courts in Canada follow the principle of *stare decisis*, its approach to legal interpretation should be emblematic of the approach in Canada more generally. Like most common law jurisdictions, Canadian courts vacillate in both their articulated approach to statutory interpretation and the approach reflected in court decisions themselves. The standard Canadian textbooks on statutory interpretation tend to distinguish approaches on a spectrum, from 'original meaning' approaches (which are generally not common in Canada) or ordinary meaning approaches (more common) on one end of the spectrum, to purposive or consequential approaches at the other end of the spectrum.[18]

The idea behind ascribing the ordinary meaning of a provision is that a meaning can be attributed to the provision based on competent readers' understanding of how words might be understood in a narrow context. A judge seeking to understand a provision's ordinary meaning may take judicial notice of facts, may look at references like dictionaries (whether general, technical, or legal), and may rely on their knowledge.

In contrast, purposive, pragmatic, or consequential approaches tend to acknowledge the role of law in a broader economic, political, and social context.[19] Approaches on this end of the spectrum are more likely to take into account the fact that a judge's reading of law is necessarily part of a larger set of circumstances – a set of circumstances with consequences. For example, one reading might be more likely to promote tax avoidance activities than another; or one reading may be more likely to result in particular incentives being effective (or ineffective).

Ruth Sullivan, formerly a professor at the University of Ottawa's faculty of law and co-author of Canada's leading text on statutory interpretation, has labelled the more pragmatic approach the 'words-in-total context' approach. Her explanation of the

18. *See* e.g., Ruth Sullivan, *Statutory Interpretation in the Supreme Court of Canada*, 30 Ottawa L Rev 175 (1999); Randal N. Graham, *Statutory Interpretation: Theory and Practice* (1st ed., Toronto: Emond Montgomery Publications 2001).
19. There are differences among these approaches, *see* e.g., Neil Brooks, *The Appropriate Role of Courts in Interpreting GST Legislation: Reflections on the Canadian Experience*, 6 Australian GST J 1 at 11 (2006). However, since judges themselves rarely articulate with precision their interpretive approach, in describing what happens in decisions themselves, there is less need to offer anything other than a taxonomy that clusters decisions within two broad categories: those that adhere to a more plain or ordinary meaning approach and those that adhere to a more pragmatic or consequentialist approach.

method is, 'after taking into account all relevant and admissible considerations, the court must adopt an interpretation that is appropriate. An appropriate interpretation is one that can be justified in terms of (a) its plausibility, that is, its compliance with the legislative text; (b) its efficacy, that is, its promotion of legislative intent; and (c) its acceptability, that is, the outcome complies with legal norms; it is reasonable and just.'[20]

This chapter, which reviews the recent SCC tax jurisprudence, does not claim that the court's description of its approach to statutory interpretation is accurate. In other words, a court may claim to apply a words-in-total-context or textual, contextual, and purposive approach, but looking carefully at the decision, it may seem that the court has adopted a plain meaning or literal approach. Given the brevity of the chapter, I have focused on providing the court's own assessment of its approach, with only modest comments on whether that approach seems to be reflected in the decisions it has rendered.

Additionally, this chapter does not accept that the framework generally adopted by courts to describe their work is a sensible one. Instead, the author is convinced by the approach advocated by scholars who argue that judges ought to take a pragmatic, policy-oriented approach to statutory interpretation.[21] That argument is not pursued in this chapter, although the chapter occasionally raises questions about the sensibility of particular interpretive stances.

Sullivan's approach seems imminently sensible; yet, it has not received substantial endorsement by Canadian courts. Prior to 1984, a strict construction approach dominated the SCC's decisions. The Court's decision in *Stubart* offered a change in course.[22] Justice Estey, writing for the majority, claimed, 'the role of the tax statute in the community changed, as we have seen, and the application of strict construction to it receded. Courts today apply to this statute the plain meaning rule, but in a substantive sense so that if a taxpayer is within the spirit of the charge, he may be held liable.'[23] In *Stubart*, the Supreme Court endorsed a modern rule; namely, that 'the words of an Act are to be read in their entire context and in their grammatical and ordinary sense harmoniously with the scheme of the Act, the object of the Act, and the intention of Parliament.'[24] Justice Estey further elaborated on the Supreme Court's move away from strict interpretation in *Canada v. Golden*, where he affirmed:

> [i]n the construction of taxation statutes the law is not confined to a literal and virtually meaningless interpretation of the Act where the words will support on a broader construction a conclusion which is workable and in harmony with the evident purposes of the Act in question. Strict construction in the historic sense no longer finds a place in the canons of interpretation applicable to taxation statutes

20. Ruth Sullivan, *Sullivan and Driedger on the Construction of Statutes*, 3 (4th ed, Markham: Butterworths 2002).
21. Ruth Sullivan, *Statutory Interpretation in the Supreme Court of Canada*, 30 Ottawa L Rev 175 (1999); Neil Brooks, *The Responsibility of Judges in Interpreting Tax Legislation*, in Graeme S. Cooper, *Tax Avoidance and the Rule of Law*, 93 (Amsterdam: IBFD publications 1997).
22. *Stubart Investments Limited v. Canada*, [1984] 1 SCR 536, [1984] SCJ No 25.
23. *Stubart* at 578.
24. *Stubart Investments Limited v. Canada*, [1984] 1 SCR 536 at para. 316, [1984] SCJ No 25 citing E.A. Driedger, *Construction of Statutes*, (2nd ed, Toronto: Butterworths 1983) at 87.

> in an era such as the present, where taxation serves many purposes in addition to the old and traditional object of raising the cost of government from a somewhat unenthusiastic public.[25]

If *Stubart* signalled a change in direction, it was not a consistently adopted one. In two signature articles published in 1999, David Duff, a law professor at the University of British Columbia, explored the approach to statutory interpretation adopted by Canadian courts in tax cases.[26] In his work, Duff characterizes interpretive approaches taken in tax decisions as reflecting a spectrum, from strict to plain meaning to purposive to words-in-total context. He concludes that in the 15 years following *Stubart*, the Supreme Court vacillated in its articulated approach to statutory interpretation.[27] However, in Duff's 2007 article reviewing the contributions of then-retired Justice Iacobucci, he tracks the story of a Court that has returned in a committed way to its earlier days - days marked by a textual approach, uninterested in an assessment of purpose where the words of the statute were perceived to be clear or, regardless of the legislative wording, by the consequences of the interpretation.[28]

That pendulum swing has been maintained. *Canada Trustco*, decided by the SCC, is generally referred to as the source of the accepted approach to statutory interpretation in tax cases. In that decision, Chief Justice McLachlin and Justice Major affirmed that the words of an Act are to be read in their entire context and further stated:

25. *Canada v. Golden*, [1986] 1 SCR 209 at 214–215, [1986] SCJ No 5. The recognition that tax legislation does more than raise funds was repeated in *Québec (Communauté urbaine) v. Corp. Notre-Dame de Bon-Secours*, [1994] 3 SCR 3 at 16, where Justice Gonthier observes that tax legislation 'is also used for social and economic purposes.'
26. David G. Duff, *Interpreting the Income Tax Act – Part I: Interpretative Doctrines*, 47 Can Tax J 464 (1999); David G. Duff, *Interpreting the Income Tax Act – Part II: Toward a Pragmatic Approach*, 47 Can Tax J 741 (1999).
27. He concludes, just to provide some illustrative cases, that the Supreme Court endorsed a purposive approach in *Québec (Communauté urbaine) v. Corp. Notre-Dame de Bon-Secours*, [1994] 3 SCR 3, a plain meaning approach in *Canada v. Antosko*, [1994] 2 SCR 312, and a words-in-total-context approach in *Alberta (Treasury Branches) v. Canada (Minister of National Revenue – M.N.R.)*, [1996] 1 SCR 963, [1996] SCJ No 45.
28. *See* David G. Duff, *Justice Iacobucci and the 'Golden and Straight Metwand' of Canadian Tax Law*, 57 U Toronto LJ 525 at 567 (2007). For illustrations of decisions that reiterate the Supreme Court's willingness to adhere to a text-driven (or literal) approach of the interpretation of the *Income Tax Act*, *see* e.g., *Canada v. Antosko*, [1994] 2 SCR 312 at 326–327 where Justice Iacobucci states, '[w]hile it is true that the courts must view discrete sections of the *Income Tax Act* in light of the other provisions of the Act and of the purpose of the legislation, and that they must analyze a given transaction in the context of economic and commercial reality, such techniques cannot alter the result where the words of the statute are clear and plain and where the legal and practical effect of the transaction is undisputed.'; *Friesen v. Canada*, [1995] 3 SCR 103 at 113, [1995] SCJ No 71, where Justice Major notes that, '[i]n interpreting sections of the *Income Tax Act*, the correct approach, as set out by Estey J. In *Stubart Investments Ltd. v. Canada*.... Is to apply the plain meaning rule.' And that 'the clear language of the *Income Tax Act* takes precedence over a court's view of the object and purpose of a provision' (Major J at 136); and *65302 British Columbia Ltd. v. Canada*, [1999] 3 SCR 804 where Justice Iacobucci summarized at 50–51, '[t]his court has on many occasions endorsed Driedger's statement of the modern principle of statutory construction...This rule is no different for tax statutes ... However this court has also often been cautious in utilizing tools of statutory interpretation in order to stray from unambiguous statutory language'.

> [t]he interpretation of a statutory provision must be made according to a textual, contextual and purposive analysis to find a meaning that is harmonious with the Act as a whole. When the words of a provision are precise and unequivocal, the ordinary meaning of the words plays a dominant role in the interpretive process. On the other hand, where the words can support more than one reasonable meaning, the ordinary meaning of the words plays a lesser role. The relative effects of ordinary meaning, context and purpose on the interpretive process may vary, but in all cases the court must seek to read the provisions of an Act as a harmonious whole.[29]

Canada Trustco was a general anti-avoidance case; however, the interpretive approach expressed by the Court in it was quickly adopted into 'regular' tax cases. In the year following *Trustco*, the Court rendered *Placer Dome Canada Ltd. v. Ontario*.[30] In a decision authored by Justice LeBel, the Court endorsed its reasoning in *Trustco* and emphasized again its willingness to retreat from purpose, claiming, 'a provision [that] admits to no ambiguity in its meaning or in its application to the facts...must simply be applied.'[31]

Despite what at least at the outset might have appeared to be a relatively broadly framed approach that encouraged a 'textual, contextual and purposive' analysis,[32] the Court (and lower courts) continue to rely on approaches that seem aligned with a strict interpretation, and they regularly rely on *Canada Trustco's* tolerance for the 'ordinary meaning' approach where the words 'are precise and unequivocal'.[33]

Perhaps the Supreme Court's adherence to a formalist approach to statutory interpretation is explained in part by their perception that the detailed nature of such tax law implies a level of clarity and precision. Justice Rothstein, who authored many of the Supreme Court's tax judgments following *Trustco*, has noted, 'because of the degree of precision and detailed characteristics of many tax provisions, an emphasis has often been placed on textual interpretation where taxation statutes are concerned.'[34]

For example, in *Shell*, the court claimed that the provision it was being asked to interpret was 'clear and unambiguous', and it ignored the economic realities of the taxpayer's transactions.[35] The Supreme Court has also suggested that where the language of a section is clear, the court cannot look to the provision's purpose to 'create an unexpressed exception to clear language'.[36] The Supreme Court's view has been that the 'clear language' of the Act should prevail even if there is obvious tax avoidance at play, stating, '[c]ourts should not be quick to embellish the provisions of the Act in

29. *Canada Trustco Mortgage Co. v. Canada*, 2005 SCC 54 at para. 10, [2005] 2 SCR 601.
30. *Placer Dome Canada Ltd. v. Ontario (Minister of Finance)*, 2006 SCC 20, [2006] 1 SCR 715.
31. *Placer Dome* at para. 23.
32. For an optimistic read of the potential of *Canada Trustco see* e.g., Jinyan Li & David Piccolo, *Reviving the Modern Rule in the Interpretation of Tax Statutes: Baby Steps Taken in Canada Trustco, Mathew, Placer Dome and Imperial Oil*, 38 Sup Ct L Rev 519 (2007).
33. *Canada Trustco Mortgage Co. v. Canada*, 2005 SCC 54 at para. 10, [2005] 2 SCR 601.
34. *A.Y.S.A. Amateur Youth Soccer Association v. CRA*, 2007 SCC 42 at para. 16.
35. *Shell Canada Ltd. v. Canada*, [1999] 3 SCR 622 at 642, [1999] SCJ No 30.
36. *Placer Dome Canada Ltd. v. Ontario (Minister of Finance)*, 2006 SCC 20 at para. 23, [2006] 1 SCR 715.

respect to concerns about tax avoidance when it is open to Parliament to be precise and specific with respect to any mischief to be prevented.'[37]

The SCC's commitment to formalism has continued (and perhaps even intensified) in more recent decisions. For example, in *Canada v. Craig*, the Court adhered to a plain meaning approach in interpreting the phrase 'combination of farming and some other source of income'; in *Fundy Settlement v. Canada*, it resolved the matter of how a residency of a trust should be determined simply by analogy to the treatment of corporations; and in *Envision Credit Union v. Canada*, the majority judgment commences with the Duke of Westminster mantra, even though its role in resolving the case is unclear.[38] Therefore, despite the Supreme Court's 1984 decision in *Stubart*, which seemed to point toward a more nuanced and thoughtful approach to statutory interpretation, most tax cases in the SCC have adhered to a plain meaning approach that ignores the consequences of the court's analysis.[39]

§4.04 CANADA'S APPROACH TO THE RESOLUTION OF COMMON DILEMMAS OF LEGAL INTERPRETATION IN THE CONTEXT OF TAX LAW

Canada has grappled with many of the same issues as other jurisdictions who inherited early British tax jurisprudence, with the interaction of tax legislation with common law and tax legislation and administrative guidelines, and with the relationship between tax and accounting principles. These common dilemmas are reviewed in this part.

[A] The Special Nature of Tax Law: The Legacy of the Early British Case Law

The underlying theory of statutory interpretation suggests that the exercise of statutory interpretation should not be different for tax law than other areas of statutory law, with the major caveat that where a court adopts a pragmatic or consequentialist approach, it would be expected that the court would take steps to understand that unique

37. *Ludco Enterprises Ltd. v. Canada*, 2001 SCC 62 at para. 39, [2001] 2 SCR 1082.
38. *Canada v. Craig*, 2012 SCC 43, [2012] 2 SCR 489; *Fundy Settlement v. Canada*, 2012 SCC 14, [2012] 1 SCR 520; *Envision Credit Union v. Canada*, 2013 SCC 48, [2013] 3 SCR 191; Neil Brooks & Kim Brooks, *The Supreme Court's 2012 Tax Cases: Formalism Trumps Pragmatism and Good Sense*, 64 Sup Ct L Rev 267 (2014); Neil Brooks & Kim Brooks, *The Supreme Court's 2013 Tax Cases: Side-Stepping the Interesting, Important and Difficult Issues*, 68 Sup Ct L Rev 335 (2015).
39. This is the perception of most academic commentators. *See* e.g., Tamara Larre, *Supreme Court of Canada Tax Judgements of Justice LeBel*, 70 Sup Ct L Rev (2015) (Larre notes that the Supreme Court has returned to a more textually-driven approach to statutory interpretation, although she paints Justice LeBel as somewhat of an outlier to that direction); David G. Duff, *supra* note 28, p. 541 ('By the time [Justice Iacobucci] left the [Supreme] Court on 30 June 2004, the Supreme Court had moved sharply away from the purposive and substantive approach that it had adopted from the late 1970s to the early 1990s, toward an emphasis on the text of the relevant statutory provision and the legal form of transactions and relationships that more closely resembled the Anglo-Canadian approach to tax statutes.').

purposes and design of the legislation they seek to interpret, as well as the consequences of their alternative interpretations. However, perhaps oddly given the general adherence to a plain meaning approach, commentators and courts often distinguish tax law interpretation from 'other' statutory interpretation exercises.[40]

Courts have justified distinguishing interpretive approaches in tax law from other statutes as a result of three related views. First, some judges hold the view that where the law is ambiguous, it should be interpreted in favour of the taxpayer.[41] This version of a strict construction approach stems from the view that taxing statutes are harsh interventions by the state into the private lives of taxpayers and where the court is unable to make a clear determination about the law in dispute, the taxpayer should be given the benefit of the doubt.[42]

Relatedly, in some early cases, Canadian courts adopted the view that where a benefit provision embedded in tax law is ambiguous, it should be interpreted narrowly and in favour of the government.[43] The presumption rested on the idea that exemptions to tax law are presumably narrow (since the only purpose of the law is to collect revenue), and therefore a strict construction of benefit provisions is appropriate.[44]

40. *See* e.g., Chapter 7 of Randal N. Graham, *Statutory Interpretation: Theory and Practice* (1st ed., Toronto: Emond Montgomery Publications 2001).
41. This approach continues to be endorsed by the Supreme Court. For example, in *Placer Dome Canada Ltd. v. Ontario (Minister of Finance)*, 2006 SCC 20 at para. 24, [2006] 1 SCR 715 LeBel J states, '[a]lthough there is a residual presumption in favour of the taxpayer, it is residual only and applies in the exceptional case where application of the ordinary principles of interpretation does not resolve the issue... Any doubt about the meaning of a taxation statute must be reasonable, and no recourse to the presumption lies unless the usual rules of interpretation have been applied, to no avail, in an attempt to discern the meaning of the provision at issue.' For an illustration, *see Canada v. Fries*, [1990] 2 SCR 1322 at 1323, [1990] SCJ No 109 where the Supreme Court applied the interpretive principle that ambiguities should be resolved in favour the taxpayer, in holding that strike pay should be exempt from taxation. ('The benefit of the doubt must go to the taxpayers.')
42. *See* e.g., *Québec (Communauté urbaine) v. Corp. Notre-Dame de Bon-Secours*, [1994] 3 SCR 3 at 14. 'The rule was based on the fact that, like penal legislation, tax legislation imposes a burden on individuals and accordingly no one should be made subject to it unless the wording of the Act so provides in a clear and precise manner'.
43. As stated in *Notre-Dame* at 18, 'I should like to stress that it is no longer possible to apply automatically the rule that any tax exemption should be strictly construed.'
44. The classic example of this approach is *Witthuhn v. MNR* (1957), 17 Tax ABC 33, 57 DTC 174. In that decision, the Tax Review Board disallowed a medical expense deduction for a taxpayer whose wife could sit for a few hours each day in a rocking chair on the grounds that she was not 'necessarily confined by reason of illness, injury or affliction to a bed or wheelchair' as required by then-section 27(1)(c)(vi). In coming to this conclusion, W.S. Fisher, reasoned, '[i]t is not for this Board or for the Courts to attempt to give a very broad interpretation to the legislation as enacted by Parliament when the language used is quite clear and explicit, as to do so would be to enter upon the field of legislation.... However much one may consider that, in equity, a taxpayer should be entitled to a deduction in circumstances such as those present in this appeal, nevertheless if those circumstances do not coincide with the strict wording of the legislation, this Board has no jurisdiction to extend the provisions of the statute by granting the deduction claimed.' (at para. 7) *See also Spillet v. MNR*, [1967] Tax ABC 807 at para. 4, where Roland St-Onge confirms that the medical expense deduction provision was 'an exemption provision allowing deductions from the taxpayer's income where taxation is the rule. Consequently, that section should be construed strictly in favour of the Minister.'

Finally, courts have incorporated the House of Lords' decision in *Inland Revenue Commissioners v. Duke of Westminster*[45] into Canadian jurisprudence, particularly Lord Tomlin's oft-quoted statement that, '[e]very man is entitled if he can order his affairs so that the tax attaching under the appropriate Acts is less than it otherwise would be. If he succeeds in ordering them so as to secure this result then, however unappreciative the Commissioners of Inland Revenue or his fellow taxpayers may be of his ingenuity, he cannot be compelled to pay an increased tax.'[46] The importation of *Duke of Westminster* into Canadian tax law has led to resistance to recharacterizing transactions to ensure that economic income is subject to tax by some judges. The case is marshalled in aid of an interpretive position that looks to a transaction's form over its substance.[47]

Although there has been at least some movement away from these early views, as discussed above, the perception that the *Income Tax Act* is detailed and complex seems to inspire judges to read it more textually than other types of legislation. The result of that disposition is that even outside of the three related views expressed above, judges have taken a more general approach to distinguishing tax law from other areas of statutory interpretation. This sentiment is reflected in Justice Iacobucci's remarks in *65302 British Columbia*, where he claims that advocating for a textual approach to 'clear language and ...detailed provision[s]... is not an endorsement of a literalist approach to statutory interpretation, but a recognition that in applying the principles of interpretation to the Act, attention must be paid to the fact that the Act is one of the most detailed, complex, and comprehensive statutes in our legislative inventory and courts should be reluctant to embrace unexpressed notions of policy or principle in the guise of statutory interpretation.'[48]

As noted above, without delving too far into a normative view about how judges ought to interpret tax law, there is a justification to suggest that tax laws ought to be interpreted different from other laws; namely, tax law has a different fundamental objective. The primary objective of tax law is to tax the economic income of taxpayers fairly. An additional objective is often to provide persons with incentives (i.e., tax expenditures) to behave in particular ways. To that end, one could imagine that judges could sensibly distinguish tax laws from other types of laws in interpreting it;[49] however, it is not common to see a Canadian court recognize the fundamental purpose

45. *Duke of Westminster v. Commissioners of Inland Revenue*, [1936] AC 1, [1935] All ER Rep 259.
46. *Duke of Westminster v. Commissioners of Inland Revenue*, [1936] AC 1 at paras 19–20, [1935] All ER Rep 259.
47. *See* e.g., *Antosko, supra* note 27.
48. *65302 British Columbia Ltd v. Canada*, [1999] 3 SCR 804 at para. 51. *See also Inco Ltd v. Canada*, 2004 TCC 373 at para. 16 where the Tax Court of Canada claims, '...the plain meaning approach of itself is not a total rejection of purposive interpretation but is simply a recognition that object and purpose can play only a limited role in the interpretation of a statute that is as precise and detailed as the Act.' *Inco* was affirmed by the Federal Court of Appeal in *Inco Ltd v. Canada*, 2005 FCA 44, [2005] 1 CTC 367.
49. For example, almost no cases identify the provision subject to scrutiny as a tax expenditure, even though that would presumably be helpful in understanding the provision's role and purpose. But *see Symes v. Canada*, [1993] 4 SCR 695 at para. 109, [1993] SCJ No 131.

of tax laws in articulating their approach to understanding the statute and applying it to a given factual context.

[B] The Interaction Between Tax Legislation and Common Law

A second common dilemma in the design of tax laws is the degree to which the statute should be drafted to rely on judicial innovation and decision-making. In terms of the tax legislation itself, Canada's Supreme Court has pronounced that there is no judge-made tax law.[50] Despite that claim, there are common law rules that have been developed and are applied regularly in Canadian tax law. For example, there is no statutory provision that articulates a method for distinguishing capital from current expenses or business from personal expenses.[51] The methods for distinguishing those kinds of payments have evolved on a case-by-case basis over time.

Similarly, in some cases the words used in the law deliberately delegate interpretive scope to the courts. For example, employees are taxed on the value of all 'benefits'.[52] As a result, the courts have routinely been asked whether particular employee receipts constitute benefits that should be valued and subject to tax.[53] As an additional illustration, charitable organizations receive a number of tax benefits. 'Charitable organization' is not defined.[54] To understand the scope of the charitable purpose rules, the courts have turned to the common law jurisprudence on what constitutes a charity.[55]

The reliance on private law reflected in giving meaning to 'charitable organization' is not unique. Canadian courts regularly rely on the private law to support the interpretation of tax law.[56] In *Will-Kare Paving & Contracting*, Justice Major observes that, 'reference must be given to the broader commercial law to give meaning to words that, outside of the Act, are well-defined.'[57] In many decisions, for example, in *Wiebe Door Services Ltd. v. MNR*, one of the leading cases on the characterization of workers

50. In *Stewart v. Canada*, 2002 SCC 46 at para. 4, [2002] 2 SCR 645, Iacobucci J and Bastarache J, found that the reasonable expectation of profit test could not be upheld as it was contrary to 'the principle that courts should avoid judicial innovation and rule-making in tax law'.
51. *See* e.g., *Friesen, supra* note 28 at 115, where Justice Major notes, '[t]he concept of an adventure in the nature of trade is a judicial creation designed to determine which purchase and sale transactions are of a business nature and which are of a capital nature.' *See also Johns-Manville Canada Inc. v. Canada*, [1985] 2 SCR 46.
52. *Income Tax Act*, RSC 1985, c 1 (5th Supp) s. 6(1)(a).
53. *See* e.g., *Lowe v. Canada*, [1996] 2 CTC 33, 96 DTC 6226, where the Federal Court of Appeal reviews secondary material in assessing the purpose of the taxation of employee benefits and grapples with the evolution of the case law on what constitutes a 'benefit' for tax purposes when an employee receives an employer-provided trip.
54. *Income Tax Act*, RSC 1985, c 1 (5th Supp) s. 149.1(1) 'charitable purposes'.
55. *See* e.g., *Positive Action Against Pornography v. MNR*, [1988] 2 FC 340, [1988] 2 FCJ 134.
56. *See* e.g., *Agence du Revenu du Quebec v. Service Environmentaux AES Inc.*, 2013 SCC 65 at para. 45, 'tax law applies to transactions governed by, and the nature and legal consequences of which are determined by reference to, the common law or the civil law.'
57. *Will-Kare Paving & Contracting*, 2000 SCC 36 at para. 31, [2000] 1 SCR 915.

as employees or independent contractors, the court explored provincial private law in detail before giving meaning to the word 'employee'.[58]

[C] The Role of Administrative Guidance

The Canada Revenue Agency offers extensive administrative guidance, through the publication of information circulars, tax folios, advance rulings, and technical interpretations. Courts in Canada are not bound by that guidance, although they will sometimes look to information circulars and interpretation bulletins.[59] In *Nowegijick*, the SCC held that 'administrative policy and interpretation are not determinative but are entitled to weight and can be an "important factor" in case of doubt about the meaning of legislation'.[60] In that case, the Court relied on a Canada Revenue Agency interpretation bulletin, which supported the view that the taxpayer's income was tax-exempt under the federal *Indian Act*. This seems like an appropriate approach given the expertise and experience administrative agencies have in working, daily, with tax legislation.

The Supreme Court has offered some cautions, though, about the ability to administrative guidance to be useful where the legislation is ambiguous. In *Placer Dome Canada Ltd. v. Ontario (Minister of Finance)*,[61] the Court addressed the fact that the Canada Revenue Agency had changed its view on its interpretation of a particular provision. Justice LeBel observed that, '[i]t is well established that in resolving doubt about the meaning of a tax provision, the administrative practice and interpretation adopted by the Minister, while not determinative, are important factors to be weighed.' Nevertheless, given the context, Justice LeBel concluded that, '[a]lthough administrative practice can be an "important factor" in case of doubt about the meaning of legislation, it is not determinative. In a case such as the present one where a statutory provision admits of more than one possible meaning, the Minister, having decided that its former interpretation was incorrect, is not precluded from changing its practice.'[62]

[D] The Role of Accounting Principles

Stated generally, while Canadian concepts are informed by accounting principles, those principles are not fast and ready rules. A reader interested in the interaction between tax law and accounting and timing issues more generally in the Canadian

58. [1986] 2 CTC 200 (FCA).
59. *See* e.g., *Friesen, supra* note 28 at 122, *Schwartz v. Canada*, [1996] 1 SCR 254, [1996] SCJ No 1 at 272–276.
60. *Nowegijick v. R*, [1983] 1 SCR 29 at para. 28, [1983] SCJ No 5 (SCC). *See also Lowe, supra* note 53 at para. 18, '[p]aragraph 6(1)(a) is cast in broad and somewhat vague language. I am, accordingly, satisfied that this is a proper case for having some regard to the Department of National Revenue's own interpretations in construing paragraph 6(1)(a) even though they are non-binding.'
61. 2006 SCC 20, [2006] 1 SCR 715.
62. *Placer Dome Canada Ltd. v. Ontario (Minister of Finance)*, 2006 SCC 20 at para. 40, [2006] 1 SCR 715.

context can do no better than to order *Timing and Income Taxation: The Principles of Income Measurement for Tax Purposes*.[63] There are only a small number of instances where the language of the *Income Tax Act* itself relies on or refers to accounting principles. The phrase 'generally accepted accounting principles' (GAAP) is used in a few places, although not defined. There are some express references to GAAP in a few of the highly technical timing rules. Otherwise, the use of and reliance upon generally accepted accounted principles is informed by case law and Revenue Agency interpretations.

In *Symes*, a case about whether childcare expenses could be deducted as business expenses, the Supreme Court explored the relationship between GAAP and the meaning of profit in the *Income Tax Act*. Justice Iacobucci concludes that '[a]ny reference to G.A.A.P. connotes a degree of control by professional accountants which is inconsistent with a *legal* test for "profit" under section 9(1). Further, whereas an accountant questioning the propriety of a deduction may be motivated by a desire to present an appropriately conservative picture of current profitability, the *Act* is motivated by a different purpose: the raising of public revenues.'[64] Later, in *Canderel*, Iacobucci J. elaborates that, 'while GAAP may more often than not parallel the well-accepted business principles recognized by the law, there may be occasions on which they differ, and on such occasions the latter must prevail'.[65] As a result, Canadian courts rely on 'well-established business principles', adjusted by specific rules in the *Income Tax Act*, to come to 'an accurate picture' of a taxpayers' profit.[66]

In other cases, accounting principles play little role. For example, courts and the Canada Revenue Agency have concluded that accounting principles do not assist in characterizing payments as on current or capital account or in distinguishing regular income from capital gains income.[67]

§4.05 INTERPRETIVE AIDS

Canadian judges, like those in many jurisdictions, retain an interest in discerning 'legislative intent' as part of their examination of the meaning of ambiguous provisions. Additionally, in some cases, like in the interpretation of the GAAR, the courts have decided they need to expressly discern the purpose of the rules and in doing so, they resort to parliamentary and other documents as interpretive aids.

63. Brian Arnold et al., *Timing and Income Taxation: The Principles of Income Measurement for Tax Purposes*, (2nd ed, Canadian Tax Foundation 2015). This brief section draws liberally from Chapters 2 and 3.
64. *Symes*, *supra* note 16 at 723.
65. *Canderel Ltd. v. Canada*, [1998] 1 SCR 147 at para. 37, [1998] SCJ No 13.
66. *Canderel Ltd. v. Canada*, [1998] 1 SCR 147 at para. 53, [1998] SCJ No 13.
67. *See* e.g., CRA document no. 2010-0355871I7 (21 Apr. 2010).

[A] The Role of Legislative Intent and Parliamentary Documents

Earlier in Canadian judicial history, courts were unwilling to rely on extrinsic evidence as part of an examination of the legislative intent behind a statutory provision. That era has come to an end and Canadian courts are now quite willing to consider a variety of extrinsic documents.[68] Reviewing the legislative history is common.[69] Extrinsic materials include almost anything that can be connected to the particular legislation in issue, including white papers,[70] budgets,[71] speeches by the Minister of Finance,[72] technical notes,[73] briefs, background reports, legislative debates,[74] press releases, and other materials prepared for the public. For example, the FCA accepted that parliamentary history could be used to show, indirectly, the legislative intent in *Lor-Wes*

---

68. The exclusionary rule disappeared gradually in Canada and was dismissed altogether in *Rizzo & Rizzo Shoes Ltd. (Re)*, [1998] 1 SCR 27, [1998] SCJ No 2. There are, however, some decisions that suggest that recourse to extrinsic materials is not necessary where the provisions admit of no ambiguity. *See* e.g., *Rooke v. Canada*, 2002 FCA 393.
69. *See* e.g., *Canada v. Golden*, [1986] 1 SCR 209, [1986] SCJ No 5, where the Supreme Court reviewed earlier versions of the legislative provision in question (s. 68) to assess the legislature's purpose in its design.
70. In *R v. Redpath Industries Ltd*, [1984] DTC 6349 (Quebec S.C.) the court referred to the Carter Commission Report and a Finance White Paper in reviewing the purpose of the foreign affiliate rules.
71. In *Canterra Energy Ltd. v. Canada* (1986), [1987] 1 CTC 89 (FCA) the Court provided that budget documents are admissible but may not be given much weight because the provisions may change between the date of the budget and the enactment of the legislation. (At the Tax Court of Canada, Justice Reed concludes that (at para. 13), '[i]n this case, the Minister's statement has relevance generally to the issues involved and is admissible. It carries little weight, however, as to whether or not regulation 1207(2) (a) (ii) can result in a negative amount. The lack of weight flows from the fact that it carries no details with respect to the treatment to be accorded June 1976 to April 1977 expenses. Even if it had the weight such detail might carry would be questionable because of the ever-present possibility that the details of implementation could change between the date of announcement of the program and the date of issuance of the regulation. Indeed, in this case the Minister's statement indicated that only costs incurred between March 31, 1977 and April 1, 1980 would be eligible for the frontier exploration allowance. The regulation when finally promulgated took into account expenses incurred between June 1976 and April 1977 as well. Thus, while the Minister's statement has relevance generally to the issues in this case it cannot settle the very point in issue.' On appeal to the Federal Court of Appeal (at para. 25), Justice Urie declined to opine on the weight to be given to budget documents, stating, '[s]ince the learned Trial Judge gave little or no weight to the contents of a budget document referred to by counsel for the Respondent at trial, counsel for the Appellant, at the hearing in this Court, abandoned his attack on the propriety of referring to such documents. Not having had the benefit of argument from either counsel on this ground of attack, I refrain from any comment thereon.'
72. *See* e.g., *Canada v. Morrissey*, 89 DTC 5080 (FCA) where Justice Mahoney looked to the statements made by the Minister of Finance at the introduction of legislation limiting the deductibility of hobby farming losses.
73. *See* e.g., *Silicon Graphics Ltd v. Canada*, 2002 FCA 260 at para. 50 where Justice Sexton states that 'Technical Notes are not binding on the courts, but they are entitled to consideration.'
74. For a discussion of the Supreme Court's use of Hansard, *see* John James Magyar, *The Evolution of Hansard Use at the Supreme Court of Canada: A Comparative Study in Statutory Interpretation*, 33(3) Stat L Rev 363 (2012). *See also Canada (National Revenue) v. Thompson*, 2016 SCC 21, where the Court relies on legislative history (Hansard) for evidence of the legislature's intention around the privilege afforded to accounting records, and *Will-Kare Paving & Contracting Ltd v. Canada*, 2000 SCC 37.

Contracting Ltd. v. Canada.[75] The taxpayer had attempted to claim an investment tax credit, which had to be for property 'to be used by…[the taxpayer] in Canada primarily for …logging.'[76] In determining that the taxpayer was entitled to the investment tax credit, McGuigan J. relied on the statement of the Minister of Finance at the time the provision was introduced, noting that 'Hansard may be used, like the report of a commission of enquiry, in order to expose and examine the mischief, evil or condition to which the Legislature was directing its attention'.[77]

Courts will also have regard for the structure of the tax law and the various internal elements of its design.[78] For example, the Court addressed marginal notes in *Imperial Oil Ltd. v. Canada; Inco Ltd. v. Canada,*[79] Justice LeBel claiming that, '[a]lthough marginal notes are not entirely devoid of usefulness, their value is limited for a court that must address a serious problem of statutory interpretation. I would be loath to rely on one for that purpose and will return to the text of the statute itself, after considering some additional interpretive arguments raised by the litigants.' Courts also attend to headings; for example, in *Canadian Pacific Ltd v. A.G. (Can.)* the Supreme Court notes that titles are 'an integral part of the Act.'[80]

[B] The Role of Secondary Materials and Materials from Other Jurisdictions

Canadian courts have commonly turned to secondary materials and are occasionally influenced by court decisions from other jurisdictions. Neither of these types of sources is binding. For example, in *Stubart*, the Supreme Court looked to decisions in United States, Australia, and the United Kingdom to trace trends in the role for a business purpose text.[81] In *65302 British Columbia Ltd. v. Canada*, [1999] 3 SCR 804, the Court relied on tax articles by academics, including Richard Krever, textbooks on income tax law, and text books on statutory interpretation.[82]

75. *Lor-Wes Contracting Ltd. v. Canada*, [1985] FCJ No 178, [1986] 1 FC 346 (FCA). In *Lor-Wes*, the Federal Court of Appeal looked to the budget statement announcing the introduction of the investment tax credit as evidence of parliament's intention in the design of that provision.
76. *Income Tax Act*, RSC 1985, c 1 (5th Supp) s. 127(9) 'qualified property'.
77. *Lor-Wes Contracting v. Canada*, [1985] FCJ No 178 at 355, [1986] 1 FC 346 (FCA). *See also Symes v. Canada*, [1993] 4 SCR 695 at 749–750, [1993] SCJ No 131, where the Supreme Court relied on a federal government white paper in reasoning through whether childcare expenses could be deducted as business expenses.
78. *See Interpretation Act*, RSC 1985, c I-21 s. 14 ('Marginal notes and references to former enactments that appear after the end of a section or other division in an enactment form no part of the enactment, but are inserted for convenience of reference only.')
79. 2006 SCC 46 at para. 57, [2006] 2 SCR 447.
80. *Canadian Pacific Ltd v. AG (Can)*, [1986] 1 SCR 678 at para. 8. *See also AEL Microtel Ltd. v. Canada*, [1984] CTC 387 at para. 75 (FC), where the Court reasoned that the 'title serves the like purpose of a preamble. They are a key to open minds of the makers of the Act and the mischiefs they intend to redress.'
81. *See Stubart, supra* note 22 at 552–564.
82. *65302 British Columbia Ltd. v. Canada*, [1999] 3 SCR 804.

§4.06 INTERPRETIVE CONVENTIONS

Canada, like most jurisdictions, elevates some practices associated with reading legislation to quasi-rule status.

[A] Two Official Languages and Two Legal Systems

Canada is a bijural and bilingual country, which has ramifications for statutory interpretation. The Canadian Constitution requires that legislation be printed and published in French and English.[83] Each version (French and English) of federal legislation is considered equally authentic, and discrepancies must be resolved in a way that makes the two versions compatible.[84] This approach is often referred to as the shared meaning rule, and for a time it was ensconced in legislation.[85] The rule can be rebutted, however, where the shared meaning is inappropriate in the light of the legislative purpose, policy concerns, and external evidence.

In *Canada v. Compagnie Immobilière BCN*,[86] the SCC determined that the French and English drafts of a tax regulation could not be interpreted in a fashion that supported a shared meaning. The case turned on the difference between the English phrase 'has been disposed of' and the French phrase 'ont été aliénés'. The Court was required to decide whether extinguishing a lease and demolishing a building fit within either of those phrases. The Supreme Court decided that the English phrase was broader in its meaning and should be adopted over the narrower French wording in order to better promote the intention of the legislation.[87]

In addition to operating in two languages, Canada's bijural nature has consequences for statutory interpretation. In the main, the drafting of federal legislation must accommodate both common and civil law concepts.[88] This can be accomplished by using common law terms in the English draft and civil law terms in the French draft, although that approach is imperfect because in theory the English version should be equally applicable inside and outside of Quebec as should the French version. Alternatively, the drafter may look for a term that will address both the civil and common law realities.

83. *Constitution Act, 1867* (UK), 30 & 31 Vict., c 3, s. 133 reprinted in RSC 1985, Appendix II, No 5; *Constitution Act, 1982*, s. 18, being Schedule B to the *Canada Act 1982* (UK), 1982, c 11.
84. *See Reference Re Manitoba Language Rights*, [1985] 1 SCR 721 at 774–775, [1985] SCJ No 36; s. 18 of the *Constitution Act, 1982*.
85. *Official Languages Act*, RSC 1970, c O-2, repealed in 1988 S.C. 1988, c 38, s. 110.
86. *Canada v. Compagnie Immobilière BCN*, [1979] 1 SCR 865.
87. *See also Savage* where the Supreme Court reviewed the French version of para. 56(1)(n) of the *Income Tax Act* (which taxes prizes in some circumstances) to confirm that their conclusion based on the English wording that the prize received by Mrs. Savage should be taxable was similarly supported by the French version.
88. Canada's *Interpretation Act* requires that '[b]oth the common law and the civil law are equally authoritative and recognized sources of the law of property and civil rights in Canada and, unless otherwise provided by law, if in interpreting an enactment it is necessary to refer to a province's rules, principles or concepts forming part of the law of property and civil rights, reference must be made to the rules, principles and concepts in force in the province at the time the enactment is being applied.' Section 8.1.

In 1995, the Department of Justice adopted a policy on legislative bijuralism.[89] That policy committed the Department to reflecting common and civil law concepts in legislation. The Federal government subsequently passed three federal law-civil law harmonization acts.[90] They also passed the *Income Tax Amendments Act, 2000*,[91] which in Part 2 addresses harmonization of the *Income Tax Act* and the *Excise Tax Act* with the *Civil Code of Quebec*. That amendment attempted to better align the English and French versions of Canada's tax laws by ensuring the concepts relied upon were comparable for civil and common law purposes. For example, in each instance where the legislation relied on the concept of a mortgage, the concept of hypothec was introduced.

The Supreme Court considered two tax cases in 2016 that required it to grapple with the interaction between the civil and common law.[92] In *Jean Coutu Group (PJC) Inc v. Canada (AG)*,[93] and *Canada (AG) v. Fairmont Hotels Inc*,[94] the issue before the court was the circumstances in which the remedy of rectification should be available to the taxpayers. Justice Wagar accepted that the remedy of rectification under Quebec civil law and in equity have different origins. Nevertheless, he reasoned that, 'the natural convergence in principles and outcomes…is generally desirable, particularly in the tax context. Taxpayers in both Quebec and the common law provinces are subject to the same federal taxation system. They could expect to encounter similar results when they seek to amend documents that express their agreement and lead to unintended tax consequences.'[95]

[B] Maxims of Word Usage

Canadian courts rely on a set of maxims familiar to common law jurisdictions. Some commentators and Canadian courts have approached the use of maxims with scepticism, worried that their use violates the principle of adopting a 'fair, large and liberal' construction as demanded by Interpretation Acts. However, a more sensible approach seems to be to see maxims as 'point[ing] us to local inferences' and where those inferences are 'quite sensible' the maximum may be useful in assisting the reader to

89. The policy provides, 'it is imperative that the four Canadian legal audiences (Francophone civil lawyers, Francophone common law lawyers, Anglophone civil law lawyers and Anglophone common law lawyers) may, on the one hand, read federal statutes and regulations in the official language of their choice and, on the other, be able to find in them terminology and wording that are respectful of the concepts, notions and institutions proper to the legal system (civil law or common law) of their province or territory'. Department of Justice, *Policies and Directives*, http://www.justice.gc.ca/eng/csj-sjc/harmonization/bijurilex/policies-politiques.html.
90. Department of Justice, *Harmonization Acts and Related Information*, http://www.justice.gc.ca/eng/csj-sjc/harmonization/bijurilex/harmonization-loisdharmonisation.html.
91. *Income Tax Amendments Act*, SC 2001, c 17.
92. Other courts have also considered the alignment between the civil and common law. *See* e.g., *French v. Canada*, 2016 FCA 64.
93. 2016 SCC 55.
94. 2016 SCC 56.
95. *See Jean Coutu*, *supra* note 93 at para. 52.

come to a logical conclusion about an appropriate interpretation of the provision in question.[96]

As a starting place, Canadian courts will commonly rely on all manner of dictionaries to give meaning to words used in a provision.[97] They will also look at the meaning given to words in other areas of law.[98] They additionally rely on a cluster of familiar maxims of word usage, including: the associated words rule (*noscitur a sociis*), which suggests that the courts can interpret a word in the light of the other words in the related list;[99] the limited class rule (*ejusdem generis*), which compels the reader to interpret a general term in a list in the light of the words with which it is connected in a list; and the implied exclusion rule (*expressio unius est exclusion alterius*), which suggests that if legislation omits a particular word or phrase, when something similar is included, then that omission must have been intentional and therefore was meant to be excluded.[100] If the same words are used multiple times in a particular statute, the general view is that they should be interpreted to mean the same thing and if different words are used the assumption is that the legislature must have meant something different.[101]

Finally, the orthodox view is that every word must be given meaning, so if there are interpretations that require 'reading out' some of the words in a provision, those

96. *See* Randal N. Graham, *Statutory Interpretation: Theory and Practice*, 112, (1st ed., Toronto: Emond Montgomery Publications 2001).
97. *See also Interpretation Act*, RSC 1985, c I-21, s. 15 which provides that '[d]efinitions or rules of interpretation in an enactment apply to all the provisions of the enactment, including the provisions that contain those definitions or rules of interpretation' and that '[w]here an enactment contains an interpretation section or provision, it shall be read and construed (a) as being applicable only if a contrary intention does not appear; and (b) as being applicable to all other enactments relating to the same subject-matter unless a contrary intention appears.' As an illustration, *see Canada v. Savage*, [1983] 2 SCR 428 at 443, where the Court relies on the *Shorter Oxford Dictionary*, the *Funk and Wagnalls Standard College Dictionary*, and *Black's Law Dictionary*.
98. *See*, e.g., *Will-Kare Paving & Contracting Ltd. v. Canada*, 2000 SCC 36, [2000] 1 SCR 915 where the court relied on the common law meaning of the word 'sale'.
99. *See* e.g., *Canada v. Savage*, [1983] 2 SCR 428 at 443 (where the Supreme Court interpreted the word 'prize' in the light of the list of other payments (scholarship, fellowships, and bursaries) subjected to tax under para. 56(1)(n) of the Income Tax Act. 'The word "prize" is surrounded in the Income Tax Act by words which give it colour and meaning and content.')
100. *See* e.g., *65302 British Columbia Ltd v. Canada*, [1999] 3 SCR 804 where the Supreme Court reasoned that because the legislature had explicitly included an express provision to deny the deduction of illegal bribes, but had not expressly denied the deduction of fines and penalties, fines and penalties must have been intended to be deductible; *Hickman Motors Ltd v. Canada*, [1997] 2 SCR 336 at para. 80 ('In view of the above, in the absence of any other indication, I would hesitate to read any time period requirement into the Regulation, since, on the one hand, there is no clear legislation to that effect, and, on the other hand, the legislator is in the best position to determine such requirements. Had Parliament intended such time restrictions to apply to CCA, it would have said so – *expressio unius est exclusio alterius*.... Therefore, under Regulation 1102(1)(c), the property does not have to produce revenue during a specified minimum period').
101. *See* e.g., *Schwartz, supra* note 59 at 298. ('It is a well-established principle of interpretation that words used by Parliament are deemed to have the same meaning throughout the same statute.')

interpretations are to be avoided.[102] Similarly, courts have suggested that statutes should not be interpreted in a way that requires 'reading in' additional words. For example, in *Friesen*, Justice Major, writing for the majority of the Supreme Court reasoned:

> It is a basic principle of statutory interpretation that the court should not accept an interpretation which requires the insertion of extra wording where there is another acceptable interpretation which does not require any additional wording. Reading extra words into a statutory definition is even less acceptable when the phrases which must be read in appear in several other definitions in the same statute. If Parliament had intended to require that property must be relevant to the computation of income in a particular year in order to be inventory in that year, it would have added the necessary phraseology to make that clear.[103]

None of these maxims are 'rules' that must be followed and courts, including the Supreme Court, regularly appear to rely on them primarily to support an approach they have already decided to take.[104]

[C] Maxims Based on Conventions of Grammar

Canadian drafters, administrators, and courts rely on conventions of grammar. For example, in statutory definitions, the word 'includes' indicates that the definition is non-exhaustive, while 'means' indicates the definition is intended to be exhaustive. Shall is considered imperative and may is permissive.[105] 'And' is generally considered to be used in its joint construction (rather than joint and several, although context may suggest that and is used joint and severally) and 'or' is always disjunctive, although it may be mutually exclusive or inclusive, again depending on context.

[D] Maxims Based on Overlap

Canadian courts have a variety of mechanisms for addressing issues that arise where it appears that two provisions may result in conflicting results. In the main, if it is

102. *See* e.g., *Canada v. Golden*, [1986] 1 SCR 209, [1986] SCJ No 5 where Justice Estey, in the majority, sought to determine whether the expression 'something else' could refer to something other than property in the context of an allocation of purchase price under s. 68. Justice Estey relied on the view that all of the words of the section must be given meaning, reasoning that, '[w]hile "any property" can reasonably be understood as particular (any piece of property as opposed to any other piece of property) or general (any property as opposed to any thing which is not property), this potential ambiguity is resolved with reference to the other words of the section, which must all be given meaning' (at para. 4) *See also Canada (National Revenue) v. Thompson*, 2016 SCC 21 at para. 32 where the Court held that '[i]t is presumed that the legislature avoids superfluous or meaningless words, that it does not pointlessly repeat itself or speak in vain.'
103. *Friesen v. Canada*, [1995] 3 SCR 103 at para. 27, [1995] SCJ No 71.
104. *See*, e.g., our discussion of the Craig decision in Neil Brooks & Kim Brooks, *The Supreme Court's 2012 Tax Cases: Formalism Trumps Pragmatism and Good Sense*, 64 Sup Ct L Rev 267 at 272 (2014).
105. *See Interpretation Act*, RSC 1985, c I-21, s. 11 'The expression "shall" is to be construed as imperative and the expression "may" as permissive.'

possible to find a way to read the two provisions harmoniously, so that they can both apply, courts will do so. This approach aligns with the myth that the legislature has designed a coherent regulatory regime. Alternatively, a court may decide that one provision (or set of provisions) is designed to exhaustively cover the particular circumstances that have arisen. In those cases, courts have concluded that the 'exhaustive' provisions apply to the exclusion of the other arguably applicable provisions.[106]

Finally, where there are no obvious strategies to reduce the conflict, courts will determine that one set of provisions should be adhered to at the expense of the other. There are expressed paramountcy rules that provide illustrations of this general practice. For example, the implied exclusion rule (*specialia generalibus non derogant*) suggests that the more specific provisions apply to the exclusion of the more general provision.[107] As another illustration, courts may decide that subsequent legislation was intended to repeal earlier legislation and so they will apply the more recent provision. Statutory rules may be considered to be paramount over regulations (delegated legislation), given that their authority is derived from the legislature.

§4.07 THE GAAR

In part because of the reluctance of the judiciary to squarely address tax avoidance schemes through a robust and purposive or consequential interpretation of Canada's tax laws,[108] Canada enacted a GAAR in 1988.[109] The rule requires three conditions be satisfied: (1) the taxpayer must derive a tax benefit; (2) the taxpayer must engage in the

106. *See* e.g., *Symes v. Canada*, [1993] 4 SCR 695 at 750, [1993] SCJ No 131 where the Supreme Court of Canada held that the provisions designed to govern the deductibility of childcare expenses constituted a 'complete code' to the exclusion of the Act's more general provisions on the deduction of business expenses. (As concluded by Justice Iacobucci '...a straightforward approach to statutory interpretation has led me to conclude that the *Act* intends to address child care expenses, and does so in fact, entirely within s. 63.' *See also Schwartz, supra* note 59 at 293 where Justice La Forest held that a payment that fell outside the specific provisions that applied to retiring allowances could not then be included under the general charging provision (section 3). ('Parliament adopted a specific solution to a specific problem that resulted from a number of rulings by the courts respecting the taxability of payments similar to the one received by the appellant. ... To do otherwise [to allow the amount to be taxable although it fell outside the specific provisions] would defeat Parliament's intention by approving an analytical approach inconsistent with the basic principles of interpretation.')
107. *See*, for example, *Husky Oil Ltd v. Canada*, 2010 FCA 125 where Justice Sharlow held that the more specific amalgamation provisions in para. 87(4) should apply to the exclusion of the more general rule in s. 69(4).
108. *See* e.g., *Shell, supra* note 35 at pp. 641–642 where then Justice McLachlin offers, '[t]his Court has repeatedly held that courts must be sensitive to the economic realities of a particular transaction, rather than being bound to what first appears to be its legal form. ... But there are at least two *caveats* to this rule. First, this Court has never held that the economic realities of a situation can be used to recharacterize a taxpayer's *bona fide* legal relationships. ... Second, it is well established in this Court's tax jurisprudence that a search inquiry for either the "economic realities" of a particular transaction or the general object and spirit of the provision at issue can never supplant a court's duty to apply an unambiguous provision of the Act to the taxpayer's transaction.'
109. *Income Tax Act*, RSC 1985, c 1 (5th Supp) s. 245.

transaction primarily to obtain that benefit; and (3) the result of the transaction is an abuse or misuse of tax legislation.

Four GAAR cases have been heard by the Supreme Court.[110] Canadian courts take the position that the GAAR requires a variation to the approach to statutory interpretation. The Supreme Court, in a decision authored by McLachlin CJ and Major J, distinguished the interpretive approach in GAAR cases from other interpretive exercises:

> The *Income Tax Act* remains an instrument dominated by explicit provisions dictating specific consequences, inviting a largely textual interpretation. Onto this compendium of detailed stipulations, Parliament has engrafted quite a different sort of provision, the GAAR. This is a broadly drafted provision, intended to negate arrangements that would be permissible under a literal interpretation of other provisions of the *Income Tax Act*, on the basis that they amount to abusive tax avoidance. To the extent that the GAAR constitutes a 'provision to the contrary' as discussed in Shell..., the Duke of Westminster principle and the emphasis on textual interpretation may be attenuated. Ultimately, as affirmed in *Shell*, '[t]he courts' role is to interpret and apply the *Act* as it was adopted by Parliament'... The court must to the extent possible contemporaneously give effect to both the GAAR and the other provisions of the *Income Tax Act* relevant to a particular transaction.[111]

As summarized for the Court by Rothstein J in *Copthorne*, in the context of the GAAR, the 'textual, contextual and purposive' is used not to determine what the words in the legislation mean, but rather to determine the object, spirit or purpose of the provision:

> The object, spirit or purpose can be identified by applying the same interpretive approach employed by this Court in all questions of statutory interpretation – a 'unified textual, contextual and purposive approach'... While the approach is the same as in all statutory interpretation, the analysis seeks to determine a different aspect of the statute than in other cases. In a traditional statutory interpretation approach the court applies the textual, contextual and purposive analysis to determine what the words of the statute mean. In a GAAR analysis the textual, contextual and purposive analysis is employed to determine the object, spirit or purpose of a provision. Here the meaning of the words of the statute may be clear enough. The search is for the rationale that underlies the words that may not be capture by the bare meaning of the words themselves. However, determining the rationale of the relevant provisions of the Act should not be conflated with a value judgment of what is right or wrong nor with theories about what tax law ought to be or ought to do.[112]

For those who would hope that Canadian courts might be persuaded to adopt a pragmatic or consequentialist approach to statutory interpretation, the Supreme Court's view of GAAR has been disappointing. If the Court had adopted an approach

110. *Canada Trustco Mortgage Co. v. Canada*, 2005 SCC 54, [2005] 2 SCR 601; *Copthorne Holdings Ltd. v. Canada*, 2011 SCC 63, [2011] 3 SCR 721; *Lipson v. Canada*, 2009 SCC 1, [2009] 1 SCR 3; *Mathew v. Canada*, 2005 SCC 55, [2005] 2 SCR 643.
111. *Canada Trustco Mortgage Co. v. Canada*, 2005 SCC 54 at para. 10, [2005] 2 SCR 601.
112. *Copthorne Holdings Ltd. v. Canada*, 2011 SCC 63 at para. 70, [2011] 3 SCR 721.

that looked to the consequences of its interpretations at the outset, GAAR may not have been necessary. Or, the Court may have seen the enactment of GAAR as a signal to start to read all of the provisions in the Act with more attention to the consequences of alternative interpretations. Instead, as reflected in the brief description above, the GAAR has become a relatively limited tool to address only very obvious tax abuse.

§4.08 GST INTERPRETATION

Canada enacted the GST in 1991.[113] Since that time, there have been a couple thousand cases decided by the Tax Court of Canada and the FCA, and only two have been granted leave to appeal by the SCC. In 2009, the Court rendered a decision in *United Parcel Service Canada Ltd.* and in 2012 it released its decision in *City of Calgary*.[114] In *UPS* the Court held that a customs broker was entitled to a rebate for a GST overpayment. In *Calgary*, the Court was charged with deciding whether there was a single or multiple supplies (public transit services and transit facilities services) in the provision of the City of Calgary's transit services. The Court identified a list of factors (like whether the alleged separate supply is an integral part of the overall supply) for distinguishing separate from multiple supplies; but, since the case, like *UPS*, did not turn on statutory interpretation, the Court offered no reflections on how GST legislation should be interpreted in Canada.[115]

Nothing appears to distinguish judges' reasoning about how to interpret the GST legislation from their reasoning about how to interpret income tax legislation. The same resort to formalist and plain meaning reasoning prevails. The courts remain concerned with certainty,[116] rely on elements of the statute's design, and fail to expressly address the consequences of their interpretations. It may be the case that lower courts in both income tax and GST matters are more likely to adopt a consequentialist or pragmatic approach to resolving tax cases, even if they do not do so explicitly.[117]

113. For an article on the role of courts in its interpretation, *see* Neil Brooks, *supra* note 19.
114. *United Parcel Service Canada Ltd. v. Canada*, 2009 SCC 20, [2009] 1 SCR 657; *Calgary (City) v. Canada*, 2012 SCC 20, [2012] 1 SCR 689.
115. *United Parcel Service Canada Ltd. v. Canada*, 2009 SCC 20, [2009] 1 SCR 657; *Calgary (City) v. Canada*, 2012 SCC 20, [2012] 1 SCR 689.
116. *See* e.g., *High-Crest Enterprises Ltd. v. Canada*, 2015 TCC 230 at para. 82, where Justice Owen states, 'a reasonable degree of certainty in the scope of the definition is to be preferred over an unworkably broad interpretation that accepts any degree of purpose on the part of the grantor or organization. Such an interpretation is also consonant with the general proposition that certainty, predictability and fairness are the preferred outcome in the interpretation of tax law.'
117. Nevertheless, in a 2006 article, Neil Brooks argues that in many GST cases the courts adopt a consequentialist approach; that is, the judge either explicitly or implicitly decides the interpretive issue with a view to the results of his or her interpretation. Neil Brooks, *supra* note 19 at 15–18. For example, as he illustrates, the Canadian GST exempts 'food and drink for human consumption' but requires GST be charged on 'carbonated beverages'. The aim of the exclusion is to ensure that tax is not charged on necessities. Carbonated beverages, like other similar categories of consumable food and drink products, are not included in the exempt category because they are not considered necessities. When the Federal Court of Appeal had to decide whether GST should be imposed on carbonated water, it correctly held that the GST should be imposed since carbonated water was a carbonated beverage. This result is correct because

§4.09 TREATY INTERPRETATION

For international treaties to be given force of law in Canada they must be enacted domestically (through implementing legislation) or incorporated by reference.[118] Almost all of Canada's bilateral tax treaties follow the OECD Model closely, although some draw from UN Model variations. In contrast to Canada's other treaties, its treaty with the United States has substantial deviations. In terms of additional interpretive guidance, as noted above, Canada has an *Income Tax Conventions Interpretation Act* and is a signatory to the Vienna Convention on the Law of Treaties.

The dominant case on treaty interpretation in Canada continues to be *Crown Forest.*[119] In *Crown Forest*, the SCC addressed several, sometimes contentious, aspects of treaty interpretation:

- the terms of the treaty should be considered in the light of their object and purpose;
- the OECD model and commentary have high persuasive value in interpreting treaties;
- in some cases, the UN Model may assist in inferring the intention of treaty negotiators;
- cases from other jurisdictions may offer useful guidance;
- secondary material (e.g., articles by academics) may offer useful guidance; and
- expert evidence is allowed to assist the court to understand foreign law.

Subsequent cases have offered additional observations about the appropriate interpretation of tax treaties. For example, in *Prévost Car Inc. v. Canada*, the FCA noted that later commentaries may be relied upon where 'they represent a fair interpretation of the words of the Model Convention and do not conflict with Commentaries in existence at the time a specific treaty was entered and when, of course, neither treaty party had registered an objection to the new Commentaries.'[120]

§4.10 SUMMARY

Each country undoubtedly takes its own approach to the legal interpretation of tax laws; nevertheless, elements that inform their approach can be discerned. The division of the constitutional jurisdiction to tax in Canada means both federal and provincial laws must be consulted, and the bijural and bilingual nature of the country inform efforts to read federal legislation harmoniously, no matter where the taxpayer's

carbonated water is a luxury, or non-necessary, form of food or drink. However, while reaching the right result, the Federal Court of Appeal belaboured the decision by reviewing a variety of dictionary definitions of beverage and by contemplating how a server in a restaurant might ask a customer what he or she would like to consume as a 'beverage' (at 15–16).

118. For a discussion of how tax treaties are implemented in Canada, *see* Allison Christians, *While Parliament Sleeps: Tax Treaty Practice in Canada*, 10 J. Parl. & Political L 15 (2016).
119. *Crown Forest Industries Ltd. v. Canada*, [1995] SCJ No 56, 125 DLR (4th) 485.
120. *Prévost Car Inc. v. Canada*, [2009] FCJ No 241 at paras 10–11, 176 ACWS (3d) 278.

activities occur. The Supreme Court has endorsed a words-in-total-context or purposive approach, yet, a review of recent decisions suggest that the Court continues to rely heavily on the plain meaning approach and defers to a view of taxation borrowed from the early twentieth century in the UK. The type of tax imposed does not appear to have a significant effect on the court's approach to interpretation.

CHAPTER 5

Legal Interpretation of Tax Law: China

Dongmei Qiu

§5.01 INTRODUCTION

As some commentators have sharply pointed out, to understand the interpretation of tax law in China, the first and foremost question to explore is not the methodology but the allocation of interpretative powers.[1] Standing out as one of the characteristics that differentiates Chinese tax law from many others is the fact that interpretation of Chinese tax law is a responsibility distributed among legislature, judiciary and administrative organs, and one that is closely intertwined with legislative activities. The status quo, as commonly recognized in academia, is that the interpretation of tax law in China is mainly carried out by administrative entities, especially the State Administration of Taxation (SAT) and the Ministry of Finance (MoF), with the judiciary and the legislature playing very limited roles.

For those reasons, the structure in this report may be very different from other chapters. After a brief overview (§5.02) on the existing law on the legal interpretation, §5.03 depicts the tax system in China with a special emphasis on the legislation of tax law and the historical background of the devolution of legislative powers. Based on the statistical analysis of tax judicial cases during 1998 and 2014, §5.04 tries to explore reasons behind the paucity of tax litigation from cultural, legislative, institutional and political perspectives. Section §5.05 explores the role of administrative organs in the interpretation of tax law in China, illustrating how they act as the leading force in shaping new directions for tax law and interpretation. After the question on who is interpreting tax law is adequately addressed, §5.06 and §5.07 move to the core issue on how tax law is interpreted in real life. Section §5.06 provides general remarks on four

1. Wu Jingsong, *Reflection on Tax Administrative Interpretation in China* (in Chinese), 3 Taxation Research 69 (2010); Hu Yuhong, *Principles and Techniques of Law* (in Chinese) (China University of Political Science and Law Press: 2002), p. 45.

issues, namely the interrelation between judicial interpretation and administrative interpretation, the interrelation between the SAT and local tax agencies on the interpretation of tax law, the interpretation of double tax treaties and the interpretation of anti-avoidance rules. Section §5.07 examines four concrete examples including judicial cases and administrative rulings as illustrations. The last part provides a brief summary.

§5.02 RULES ON LEGAL INTERPRETATION IN GENERAL

In China, the Constitution provides little guidance on matters of legal interpretation except for a brief mention of the power of the Standing Committee of the National People's Congress (SCNPC) to interpret the Constitution and statutes.[2] While there is no single law on the interpretation of legislation, the existing scheme of legal interpretation is mainly based on the '1981 Resolution' adopted at the meeting of the SCNPC.[3] Based on this Resolution, the interpretative powers of law in China are distributed to the legislature, judiciary and the executive organs. The two highest judicial organs, the Supreme People's Court and the Supreme People's Procuratorate,[4] have the powers, respectively, to interpret questions involving the specific application of laws from the court trials and the procuratorial work. For the questions involving the specific application of laws unrelated to judicial or procuratorial work, the State Council, the highest executive body in China, shall provide interpretation. Above all, the SCNPC has the power to interpret statutes through making additional stipulations whenever there are loopholes in existing statutes or contradictory interpretations given by the Supreme People's Court and the Supreme People's Procuratorate.

2. Article 67(1) and (4), Constitution of the People's Republic of China, adopted at the Fifth Session of the Fifth National People's Congress on 4 December 1982, and the latest revision is on 10 March 2004.
3. Resolution on the Provision of an Improved Interpretation of Law, adopted in the 19th Meeting of the Standing Committee of the Fifth NPC, May 1981.
4. The Supreme People's Procuratorate is the highest agency at the national level responsible for both prosecution and investigation in China. It is mainly responsible for supervising regional procuratorates and special procuratorates to perform legal supervision by law and protecting the unified and proper enforcement of State laws. The Supreme People's Procuratorate has to report its work to the NPC and its Standing Committee, to whom it is responsible, and accept their supervision. According to the Constitution and statutes, the Supreme People's Procuratorate is primarily in charge of tasks, including: (1) leading the procuratorial work of regional and special procuratorates at all levels; (2) accepting and hearing cases of corruption, bribery, tort to citizen's democratic rights and misconduct in office, and placing them on file for investigation and prosecution; (3) performing legal supervision of the judicial process of courts and investigation of criminal cases; (4) deciding arrest and prosecution concerning severe criminal cases; (5) performing legal supervision of the trying of criminal cases; (6) lodging protests against effective but wrong judgments and rulings made by various courts to the Supreme People's Court according to law; (7) exercising legal supervision of activities conducted in prisons and reform through labour institutions; (8) providing legal explanations of the application of laws in practical procuratorial works; (9) formulating regulations and by laws concerning procuratorial works; (10) leading and administrating public procurators according to law; (11) organizing and guiding the education and training of officials with the procuratorial departments; (12) sponsoring negotiations with foreign procuratorial departments; and (13) developing judicial assistance.

While the 1981 Resolution was meant to draw a clear delineation on the interpretative powers among different organs, it failed to do so due to the inherent ambiguities and contradictions.[5] More fundamentally, the infirmities of this Resolution was inevitable considering the following fact: in China, all the government organs, including legislature, judiciary and the executive, are subordinate to the leadership of the Communist Party, and the law is expected to cope with the changing policies of the Party from time to time.[6] To achieve this purpose, the interpretation of law needs to retain a high degree of flexibility so that the law can be changed swiftly to adapt to the varying political situations.[7]

This flexibility comes at a cost with frustrating consequences: the overlap of interpretative powers among different organs, the lack of standardized usage of titles and the obscurity in legal effects of interpretive rules, and the lack of transparency in the interpretative process.[8] Many of these problems penetrate into the interpretation of tax law[9] except one: in the tax field, the overlap of interpretative powers among the legislature, judiciary and the execution rarely occurs. It has been widely acknowledged that it is the executive bodies, namely the State Council and its ministries, typically represented by the SAT and the MoF, that have been playing the leading and predominant role in the interpretation of China's tax law. In terms of legislative interpretation, although the Law on Legislation provides for the exclusive power to the SCNPC to interpret statutes,[10] in practice, there are almost no interpretations passed by the SCNPC on tax statutes. Meanwhile, the judiciary has been playing a marginal role in the resolution of tax disputes, and cases are few in which judges render interpretation on the application of tax provisions.

§5.03 TAX SYSTEM IN CHINA

The 1994 tax reform laid the foundations of the current tax regime in China. During that reform, the power of tax legislation was exclusively reserved for the central government, leaving local governments little room to make tax rules.[11] Local governments, in this context, refer to governments on four different levels: province, municipality, county and township. Their budgetary needs are met through revenue sharing with the

5. Kong Xiaohong, *Legal Interpretation in China*, 6(2) Connecticut Journal of International Law, 491, 497 (1991); Zhou Yongkun, *The Conflict between Legal Interpretation and Government in Accordance with a System of Law* (in Chinese), 27 Modern Law Science 3, 5 (2006).
6. Mo Zhang, *The Socialist Legal System with Chinese Characteristics: China's Discourse for the Rule of Law and a Bitter Experience*, 24(1) Temple International & Comparative Law Journal, 1 (2010).
7. Kong Xiaohong, *supra* note 5 at 492.
8. Wei Shengqiang, *We Need a Uniform Legal Interpretation Law* (in Chinese), 1 Legal Science 32, 33–34 (2007).
9. *See* e.g., Wu Jingsong, *supra* note 1; Sun Jianbo, *Research on Tax Law Interpretation* (in Chinese) (Law Press: 2006), pp. 239–259.
10. Article 45, Law on Legislation (2000, revised by the NPC in 2015).
11. State Council, Decision Regarding the Implementation of the Tax Sharing System of Fiscal Management, Guofa [1993] 85, 15 December 1993. For more detailed discussions on this State Council directive and the allocation of taxing powers between central government and the local governments, *see*: Wei Cui, *Fiscal Federalism in Chinese Taxation*, 3(3) World Tax Journal, 455 (2011).

central government. Under this tax sharing scheme, taxes are categorized into three types: central, local and shared taxes. Central taxes were those 'necessary for protecting national interest and implementing macroeconomic control' including import value added tax (VAT), excise tax, tax on vehicle purchases, stamp duty[12] and customs duty. Local taxes were those 'suitable for local administration' covering real estate tax, urban land-use tax, occupation tax on cultivated land, business tax, VAT on land, vehicle and vessel tax and deed tax. Revenue from major taxes directly linked to economic development, such as the VAT, income tax on enterprise and individuals and resource tax, is shared between the central and local governments. In May 2016, when business tax was fully integrated into the VAT, the sharing ratio of VAT between the central government and local governments was changed from 75:25 to 50:50.[13] To coordinate this tax sharing system, a bifurcated system of tax administration was established: state tax bureaus are responsible for the central and shared taxes, and local tax bureaus assume responsibility for the collection of local taxes.

Currently, there are 18 types of taxes in total. Although indirect taxes such as the VAT, a turnover tax on services and an excise tax yield most of the tax revenue, in recent years there has been an increasing focus by the state and taxpayers on the growing importance of direct taxes, particularly the enterprise income tax. The following chart provides a list of the major taxes and their contribution to total revenue income in 2016, which amounts to CNY 13.04 trillion (around USD 1.90 trillion).[14]

Domestic VAT (including business tax integrated into the VAT)	31.23%
Domestic excise	7.84%
VAT and excise on import	9.8%
Enterprise income tax	22.13%
Individual income tax	7.74%
Real estate tax	1.70%
Stamp duty	1.69%
VAT on land	3.23%
Urban land-use tax	1.73%
Customs duty	2.00%

The framework of tax law in China stands as a pyramid with three tiers: on the top are five statutes legislated by the National People's Congress (NPC) and its standing

12. Based on the decision made by the State Council on 31 December 2015, the stamp duty which used to be shared between the central and the local governments at the ratio of 97:3 was changed to central tax from 1 January 2016.
13. State Council, Notice on the Transitional Plan on Adjusting the Distribution of the Value-Added Tax Revenue between the Central Government and the Local Governments after the Comprehensive Promotion of the Pilot Program of Replacing Business Tax with Value-Added Tax, *Guofa* No. 26 [2016], issuance date: 29 April 2016, effective from 1 May 2016.
14. The statistics are based on the information published by the Ministry of Finance. *See* http://gks.mof.gov.cn/zhengfuxinxi/tongjishuju/201701/t20170123_2526014.html, visited on 24 January 2017.

committee, namely the Law on the Administration of Tax Collection, Individual Income Tax Law, Enterprise Income Tax Law (EITL), the Vehicle and Vessel Tax Law and the Environmental Protection Tax Law. A common feature of these statutes is that they are short in length and concise in content.[15] They normally contain the broad principles of fundamental tax matters and leave the detailed provisions to be dealt with by implementation regulations.

On the second-tier are the regulations issued by the State Council, which number more than 20. Under the Law on Legislation, the State Council is empowered to adopt administrative regulations, rules and measure to carry out laws enacted by the NPC and its standing committee. The NPC or its standing committee also delegates some of their legislative powers to the State Council. The State Council has used this delegated power to introduce most of the taxes in China, including the VAT, business tax, excise tax and customs duty.[16] They also set out the implementation rules for the existing tax statutes.[17]

The bottom of the pyramid is the ministerial regulations issued by the SAT and the MoF at the number of more than 50. The 'ministerial rules', according to the Law on Legislation, refer to rules that meet four criteria: (1) enacted by the SAT to implement the tax statutes, or administrative regulations, decisions and orders of the State Council; (2) passed by a ministerial session or a committee of the SAT; (3) promulgated by the head of the SAT in the form of an order; and (4) published in a timely manner in the Bulletin of the State Council or of the SAT and nationwide via circulated newspapers.[18] In addition to these formal instruments, there is a vast body of more than three thousand informal tax ruling issued by the SAT and the MoF. These rules are not accorded the status of law. Previously, many of them were classified as internal, and were restricted to use and circulation within tax agencies. But they do provide important guidance to taxpayers and tax agencies. Due to their practical importance and the increasing requirement placed by rule of law principles, most such rules are now publicly available.

Why is the power to design and interpret tax law so highly centralized in the hands of the State Council and its ministries? The historical reasons may be traced back to the delegation of legislative powers in the mid-1980s. In the early 1980s, one of the

15. For instance, there are only 15 articles in the Individual Income Tax Law, 60 articles in the Enterprise Income Tax Law, and 13 articles in the Vehicle and Vessel Tax Law. The longest statute is the Law on the Administration of Tax Collection with 94 articles.
16. *See* e.g., Interim Regulations on the Value-added Tax, promulgated by Order No. 134 of the State Council on 13 December 1993 and adopted on 5 November 2008; Interim Regulations on Business Tax, promulgated by the Order of the State Council No. 136 on 13 December 1993 and adopted on 5 November 2008; Tentative Regulations on Consumption Tax, promulgated by the Order of the State Council No. 135 on 13 December 1993 and adopted on 5 November 2008.
17. *See* e.g., Implementing Regulations of the Law on Enterprise Income Tax, Order of the State Council [2007] No. 512, promulgated on 6 December 2007; Implementing Regulations of the Individual Income Tax Law, promulgated on 28 January 1994 in accordance with the Order No. 142 of the State Council and most recently revised on 19 July 2011; Implementing Regulations of the Vehicle and Vessel Tax Law, adopted on 23 November 2011 and came into effect on 1 January 2012.
18. Articles 74–77, Law on Legislation, promulgated under the Order of the President [2000] No. 31 on 15 March 2000, effective on 1 July 2000.

daunting and urgent tasks facing the Chinese government was to build a legal system from scratch to meet the changing policies in the economic transition. This was a big void that could not be filled quickly. Given the limited competence of the legislature, the SCNPC made sweeping delegations of legislative powers to the State Council, and in the tax fields, the delegation was based on two directives.[19] Under the 1985 Directive, the SCNPC gave blanket permission to the State Council to make rules or regulations regarding all tax issues relating to 'reform of the economic system and opening to foreign countries'. In practice, the broad legislative powers enjoyed by the State Council were re-delegated to its ministries to make detailed tax rules. The devolution of legislative powers as such, however, was designed for transitional and experimental purposes.

In recent years, there has been increasingly less tolerance for this 'tax law vacuum', and in legal circles the call has risen for the legislature to reclaim its legislative powers in tax areas.[20] In March 2013, during the 12th Meeting of the NPC, a delegate's motion asking for the power of tax legislation, currently retained by the State Council, to be returned to the NPC and its Standing Committee (SCNPC) drew nation-wide attention. In November 2013, the principle of 'taxation by legislation' (*shuishoufading*) appeared, for the first time, in the report of third Plenum of the 18th Congress of the China's Communist Party (CCP). Subsequently, the 'taxation by legislation' principle was incorporated into the Outline of the 13th Five Year Plan for the National Economic and Social Development issued on 16 March 2016. The will of the people and the mission of the top leadership appear to converge.

The revision of the Legislation Law is a critical test as to how this 'agreed principle' is going to be put into practice. In the revised Legislation Law approved by the NPC on 15 March 2015, Article 8(6) provides 'institution of tax, tax rate, tax administration and other fundamental tax affairs' shall be governed by the law only. The explicit listing of the three core elements of taxation, compared with the vague wording in the old Law (i.e., tax issues), adds more clarity as to those areas where any entities – other than the legislative body – shall not trespass. In terms of taxation by legislation, this represents a significant change, and paves the way for a series of upcoming legislative activities in the tax field.

In October 2016, the draft laws on the Tobacco Leaf Tax and on the Vessel Tonnage Tax were publicized by the MoF, the SAT and Customs, respectively, to solicit opinions. In January 2017, another draft law on the Occupation Tax on Cultivated Land was released by the MoF and the SAT to solicit public comments. In due course, these three pieces of draft laws will be sent to the SCNPC for deliberation, and replace the

---

19. Decision of the NPC Standing Committee to Authorize the State Council to Reform the System of Industrial and Commercial Taxes and Issue Relevant Draft Tax Regulations for Trial Application (issued on 18 September 1984 and repealed on 27 June 2009); Decision of the NPC on Authorizing the State Council to Formulate Interim Provisions or Regulations Concerning Economic Structural Reform and Open Policy (10 April 1985). For the historical background of these two decisions, *see* Liu Xin & Wang Lingguang, *Statutory Taxation and Legislation Reservation* (in Chinese), 3 Administrative Law Review 81 (2008).
20. *See* e.g., Jianwen Liu, How the Tax Legislative Powers may be Returned to the NPC (in Chinese), Economic Information Daily, 27 March 2013; Mingsheng Yuan, The Legality Crisis of the Tax Administrative Crisis and the Solution (in Chinese), 1 Studies in Law and Business 52–57 (2010).

existing SC regulations. On 25 December 2016, a new tax was introduced in China based on the Environmental Protection Tax Law promulgated by the SCNPC, which takes effect from 1 January 2018.

§5.04 JUDICIARY INTERPRETATION: A WEAK ROLE IN THE INTERPRETATION OF TAX LAW

In China, there is no specialized tax court. Disputes launched by taxpayers against tax authorities are brought to the administrative chambers (*xingzheng shenpan ting*) of the civil court. The paucity of tax litigation (explained below) may well explain why there is still no tax court or tax chamber in China's court system. On the other hand, the absence of a specialized adjudicative body may help explain why some of the barriers to taxpayers appealing adverse interpretations have been difficult to overcome.

Table 4.1 Administrative Adjudication in the First Trial (1998–2014)[21]

Year	*Cases Accepted*	*Cases Settled*[22]	*Different Approaches Tax Cases Were Settled*					
Affirmation of Administrative Decisions	*Revocation of Administrative Ruling*	*Dismissal of the Lawsuit*	*Withdrawal of the Lawsuit*	*Administrative Compensation*	*Others*			
2014	398	389	40	34	34	137	0	144
2013	362	393	30	15	40	198	1	109
2012	436	384	25	17	22	191	0	129
2011	405	399	21	9	25	225	0	29
2010	398	402	31	14	26	245	2	84
2009	293	343	56	13	30	161	0	83
2008	334	286	61	17	33	115	1	59
2007	306	310	73	12	42	108	2	73
2006	359	356	41	27	34	173	1	80
2005	828	815	69	26	107	572	8	46
2004	1,032	1,041	124	70	88	338	5	416
2003	803	816	126	60	90	225	3	312

21. The statistic in this table for the years is based on China's Statistic Book and the website of the National Bureau of Statistics in China: http://www.stats.gov.cn/tjsj/ndsj/.
22. The number of cases settled in one year may include cases that had been accepted before that year.

Year	*Cases Accepted*	*Cases Settled*[22]	*Different Approaches Tax Cases Were Settled*					
Affirmation of Administrative Decisions	*Revocation of Administrative Ruling*	*Dismissal of the Lawsuit*	*Withdrawal of the Lawsuit*	*Administrative Compensation*	*Others*			
2002	1,496	1,482	91	73	125	733	7	453
2001	1,237	1,270	159	71	147	515	82	296
2000	2,055	2,025	157	183	164	1,200	54	267
1999	1,804	1,930	273	195	135	1,150	129	48
1998	2,069	1,939	96	123	140	1,466	33	81
Total	**14,615**	**14,580**	**1,473**	959	**1,282**	**7,752**	**328**	**2,709**

The total number of tax cases from 1998 to 2014 nationwide was 14,615 according to China's Statistic Yearbooks. At the turn of the century, there was a notable increase of tax litigation, which quickly changed to a steady decrease in the last decade. Where the number of courts at all levels total more than 3,500,[23] and only 398 tax disputes have been brought before the courts in 2014, almost one of 10 courts in China receives only one tax dispute in the whole year. Of these cases, more than half were settled as taxpayers withdrew the lawsuits. Moreover, of the remaining cases, actually adjudicated by the courts, the majority centre on tax procedures rather than substantive tax rules. Against the background of sharply increasing tax revenue and the growing awareness of the taxpayers' rights, the question arises what are the obstacles that hinder taxpayers in China from resorting to judicial appeals to resolve tax disputes and, consequently, lead to the weak voice of the courts in the interpretation of tax law? The underlying causes have been analysed in some scholarly writings[24] and are summarized below under four headings: cultural barriers, legislative obstacles, political or institutional hindrance, and the understatement of the verdicts.

[A] Cultural Barriers

The first tax case in China occurred in Henan Province in 1988 as a taxpayer claimed that the tax authorities' decision concerning the identification of taxpayers was wrong. The appellate court upheld the taxpayer's claim, and the verdict was published in the gazette of the Supreme People's Court. This case had a significant impact on the tax administration nationwide which prompted the promulgation of the administrative review regulation[25] in October 1989 with the intent to avoid another defeat of tax agencies in judicial proceedings.

In 1990, the administrative litigation law was enacted. However, the new rules did not inspire ordinary citizens to discard their usual timidity with respect to litigation against the government administration. This timidity should be understood in the context of the Chinese legal tradition rooted in Confucianism. Over a history of several thousand years, a highly centralized government headed by the emperor with absolute power ruled the country by means of a highly developed bureaucracy. Under the Confucian teaching, the primary obligation of every Chinese person is to fulfil the duties assigned to him or her according to the citizen's social status and to be submissive to the emperor unconditionally. The basis of the relationship between

23. *See* the website of the Supreme People's Court: http://www.court.gov.cn/jgsz/rmfyjj/, visited on 22 July 2013.
24. Wei Cui, *Does Judicial Independence Matter? A Study of the Determinants of Administrative Litigation in an Authoritarian Regime*, https://papers.ssrn.com/sol3/papers.cfm?abstract_id=2707436, August 2015.
25. Shi Xuecheng, *Resolution Mechanism on Tax Administrative Dispute* (in Chinese), PhD dissertation submitted to Southwestern University of Finance and Economics in 2010, downloaded from http://www.cnki.com.cn.

officials and ordinary citizens is not founded on 'rights' but instead on 'obligations'.[26] Meanwhile, the governors were perceived to be the protectors of their citizens like the father to the son, whose authority could hardly be challenged. Quite often, the governors took on multiple roles as judge, tax collector, decree-maker and general administrator. When the governor acted as a judge in disputes between citizens, the restoration of a harmonious relationship was held to be the overriding goal above other considerations.[27]

Against this background, the core values underpinning the establishment of administrative litigation in developed western countries are severally missing in China. Such values include the respect for private rights, checks and balances between the public powers and the belief in the rule of law.[28] Even today, the influence of this cultural heritage can be commonly found in tax practice. For example, under the impact of the notion of 'respecting officials as teachers' (*yi li wei shi*), taxpayers tend to consult tax authorities, rather than tax lawyers, before drafting tax planning schemes or making inquiries as to the meaning of a specific tax term. When disputes arise, taxpayers prefer to settle problems with tax authorities in private and through negotiations to maintain the long-term and cooperative relationship, instead of 'tearing down the face' and fighting for a temporary victory in court. In the small likelihood that a tax dispute enters into court proceedings, judges are inclined to avoid adjudication and facilitate the reconciliation through mediation or other informal processes. When judges are interpreting the law, the rules spelled out by the tax administration, even though in an informal way and subject to questions on the legality, are given more weight than they deserve.

[B] Legislative Obstacles

One legislative obstacle inhibiting the pursuit of tax appeals through the courts was created by the old administrative litigation law (1990–2014) that limits the scope of courts' jurisdiction to the examination of 'the validity of specific administrative conduct'.[29] As a result, courts cannot hear cases brought by citizens against 'abstract administrative conduct', namely administrative rules, regulations, decisions or orders with general binding force formulated and announced by administrative organs.[30]

26. William C. Jones, 'Trying to Understand the Current Chinese Legal System', in C. Stephen Hsu (ed.), *Understanding China's Legal System: Essays in Honor of Jerome A. Cohen* (New York: New York University Press, 2003), pp. 7–46.
27. Mo Zhang, *supra* note 6.
28. Yang Haikun & Zhu Zhongyi, *Investigation into the Stagnancy of the Administrative Litigation* (in Chinese), 4 Administrative Law Review 70 (1999).
29. According to Art. 2 of the Administrative Litigation Law (before 2014), where citizens and legal persons or other organizations which consider those specific acts of administrative authorities or their personnel have infringed their lawful interests, they have the right to bring the litigation to the court. NPC, Administrative Litigation Law, promulgated on 4 April 1989 and effective as of 1 October 1990.
30. *See* e.g., Art. 12 of Administrative Litigation Law; Supreme People's Court, Interpretations of Certain Issues in the Implementation of the Administrative Litigation Law, Art. 3, Fashi No. 8 [2000], promulgated on 8 March 2000 and effective on 10 March 2000.

When the court finds a tax rule invalid, it can either ignore it in the application of law in a specific case or report to the Supreme People's Court, which may then refer the matter to the State Council; but the court cannot invalidate it. This law barrier, however, was removed with the revision of the Administrative Litigation Law in 2014.[31] Under Article 2 of this revised law, the scope of the courts' jurisdiction has been broadened to cover any 'administrative action' taken by an administrative agency or any employee which infringes upon the legitimate rights and interests of the citizens. The authority of courts to review the legitimacy of administrative rulings is further reinforced by Article 53, which provides that 'a citizen, a legal person or any organization may concurrently file a request to review the regulatory document along with filing a complaint against the administrative action, if such a regulatory document developed by the administrative organs, based on which the alleged administrative actions was taken, is deemed illegal.' Nonetheless, the scope of courts' impact is still subject to certain restrictions. Under the existing rules, it is the validity, rather than the reasonableness, of the administrative conduct or the regulatory document that may come under review by the court.[32] As tax legislation in China is often drafted in a brief context using broad language and where the tax authorities have wide discretion in the implementation of tax rules, a wide range of tax administrative conduct cannot be corrected in judicial proceedings, even if in breach of the principles of proportionality, appropriateness or necessity, as long as it is not illegitimate. In other words, only conduct that is quite clearly *ultra vires* can be corrected.

Another legislative impediment to appeals arises from Article 88 of the Law on Tax Administration which sets two conditions precedent for persons seeking to appeal for tax disputes[33] other than those arising from sanction decisions or enforcement measures by tax authorities. First, prior to commencing an appeal the taxpayer must pay or remit the tax and the overdue fine according to the decision made by the tax authority, or provide an appropriate guaranty; and second, the taxpayer must exhaust all administrative review procedures. The possibility of a judicial remedy becomes available only after the administrative review panel has reached a final decision to which the taxpayer objects.[34] The journey of taxpayers to pursue judicial remedies is

31. SCNPC, Administrative Litigation Law, President Order 15 [2014], revised on 1 November 2014, effective from 1 October 1990.
32. According to Art. 56 of Fashi No. 8 [2008], when the plaintiff brought to the court specific administrative conduct which is legitimate but subject to the question of the reasonableness, the court shall reject the lawsuit.
33. According to Art. 100 of the Implementation Rules of the Law on the Administration of Tax Collection, the 'dispute over tax payment' (*nashuizhengyi*) as mentioned in Art. 88 of the Law on the Administration of Tax Collection refers to the dispute arising from the taxpayer, tax withholding agent or tax payment guarantor over such specific administrative acts by tax authorities as determining the subject of tax payment, target of tax collection, scope of tax collection, tax reduction and exemption, tax refund, applicable tax rate, base of tax assessment, stages of tax payment, period and place of tax payment, and means of tax levying.
34. The rational to make the administrative review a prerequisite for judicial proceedings is based on the assumptions that tax authorities would be at a better position to evaluate the tax-related administrative acts. It is conducive to the continuity and uniformity of decision-making process by tax authorities, whereas the caseload of the court can be effectively reduced. *See* Gu Guoxian, *Reflection and Perfection of the Existing Tax Litigation Mechanism* (in Chinese), 11(2) Journal of

not only long and thorny, but also economically costly. It is anticipated that this status quo is likely to change along with the ongoing and systematic revision of the Law on Tax Administration.[35] There exists unanimous consensus among academia and practitioners that Article 88 of the existing law should be revised to facilitate taxpayers' access to judicial remedies.

[C] Political or Institutional Hindrance

According to unofficial statistics,[36] the ratio of taxpayers who win their lawsuits against tax authorities in the past years ranges between 30% and 50%. This figure by itself does not suggest that the courts are strongly biased in the adjudication of tax disputes, but it cannot extinguish doubt on the issue of partiality of the courts. These doubts and questions primarily stem from two concerns: one is the possible political interference exerted by the local governments or the party on the judges in the pending cases, and the other is the general lack of capability of the judges to render professional and neutral decisions on tax matters. The former issue is a broad and complex topic beyond the scope of this chapter.[37] The latter issue is a pressing problem, which has received increasing attention especially from educators in the tax field.[38]

The existing curriculum of law schools at most universities marginalizes tax law by offering it only as an optional course. It is not surprising that most law graduates admitted to the courts have little or no knowledge on tax law, let alone taxation theories. The lack of sufficient tax knowledge has a number of negative impacts: judges who are uncertain of their competence in handling tax issues are inclined to accept the opinions of the tax authorities as authoritative, and in some extreme cases, even consult tax authorities at a higher level for suggestions before making decisions. Although the existing law grants judges the discretion to review the validity of the regulations issued by the SAT and MoF before applying them in a specific case, it is not uncommon in practice for judges to automatically take the informal tax rules issued by the SAT and MoF as the applicable legal basis without analysing whether such rules are *ultra vires* or in conflict with the laws and regulations of a higher authority. In this situation, the court's role as a source of neutral and independent viewpoints is severely limited.

Taxation College of Yangzhou University 37 (2006); Wang Hongmao, *An Analysis on the Defect in China's Tax Administrative Procedural System* (in Chinese), 290 Taxation Research 63-67 (2009).

35. The latest version of the Law on Tax Administration has been published by the State Council in January 2015 for public solicitation.
36. Wei Cui, *Foreign Administrative Law and International Taxation: A Case Study of Treaty Implementation in China*, 64(1) Administrative Law Review, 191, 217 (2012).
37. Shen Fujun, *Relationship between the Courts and Administrative Organs from the Perspective of Administrative Litigation* (in Chinese), 4 Legal Science 34-38 (2010).
38. *See* e.g., Li Jin, *Teaching Taxation Law in China*, 62(5) Bulletin for International Taxation 183 (2008).

[D] Understatement of the Verdicts

The writing of court judgments is a subject that has received scant attention in China. A commentator who carried out research on this subject once drew the conclusion that most verdicts written by judges in China are dry and empty as the deductive process and the logical analysis are left unstated and the application of the law is reduced to the mere mention of the name of the law and the provisions.[39] This observation echoes the conclusion of the author in reading dozens of tax judgments, which seems to follow a monotonous pattern on most occasions. This formula-based presentation partly explains the lack of development of any serious case law tradition in China and the continuing lack of consideration of precedents. This may also partly be explained by the traditional notion that the restoration of harmonious relationship is a more important goal than the stringent compliance with the law. In terms of relationships, there is a presumption that certain things are 'unspeakable' and cannot be fully articulated by words or sorted out by logic.[40] For these reasons, a judge would tend to keep the writing of the verdicts concise and abstract, and place more emphasis on reconciliation, which will not be mentioned in the written verdicts.

§5.05 ADMINISTRATIVE INTERPRETATION: THE LEADING FORCE IN TAX LAW INTERPRETATION AND POLICY DEVELOPMENT

In China, the marginal role of the legislature and the weak impact of the judiciary give way to the near monopoly status enjoyed by administrative organs in the interpretation of tax law.[41] The administrative organs in this context refer to the State Council and four of its ministries, namely the SAT, MoF, General Administration of Customs (GAC) and Customs Tariff Policy Commission (CTPC).[42] As the GAC and CTPC are specifically responsible for the formulation and development of tax rules related to customs, the SAT and MoF have been delegated with the responsibility to interpret tax laws in a wide range except for the customs.

At the level of the State Council, the interpretation on tax law is generally pronounced in two ways: one is to promulgate the implementation rules of tax statutes by setting out detailed operational rules. Given the brevity of the existing tax statutes as well as their excessive generality and vagueness in content, these implementation rules are often regarded as an extension of the legislative activities, rather than mere interpretation. The other way that the State Council makes interpretation is to interpret

39. Wei Shengqiang, *Some Thoughts on How to Improve China's Court Decisions* (in Chinese), 5 Science of Law 72, 75 (2012).
40. Ji Weidong, *Truth in the Law Interpretation* (Part II) (in Chinese), 1 Peking University Law Journal 1, 10–11 (1999).
41. Ye Jinyu, *Justification and Operation Guarantee of Interpretation Power of SAT* (in Chinese), 6 The Jurist 112–125 (2016).
42. For the powers of the Customs Tariff Commission on the law interpretation, *see* State Council Notices concerning the Power of Notice of the Customs Tariff Commission of the State Council to Interpret the Regulation of on Import and Export Duties, *Shuiweihui* [2004] No. 10, 5 July 2004.

administration regulations when clarification or supplementary provisions to such regulations are needed, or when ministries or governments at the provincial level encounter difficulties in giving interpretation or bring up different interpretations regarding the specific applications of administrative regulations in the course of tax administration.[43] In practice, the interpretation falling under the latter category is very rare.[44]

Given the limited role played by the State Council, the predominant task to interpret tax law actually falls upon the shoulders of two ministries, the SAT and the MoF, which are responsible for drafting tax statutes and implementation rules, providing ministerial regulations on tax issues and providing interpretation of the existing tax law.[45] In the absence of effective legislative guidance and judicial checks, the high centralization of powers with the SAT and the MoF – to legislate, interpret and administer tax law – is likely to lead to arbitrariness and disorder in rule-making. In terms of interpretation, the problems are manifested in multifaceted ways:

- The interpretative work undertaken by the SAT and/or the MoF is so closely interwoven with their legislative powers that the line between the two is very blurry.
- Examples of *ultra vires* or inconsistent interpretations that which deprive taxpayers of the rights under the higher laws are rampant.[46] Very few of such questionable interpretations are brought for review before the higher authorities.
- The interpretative norms which affect the rights and obligations of taxpayers are primarily issued in the form of informal rules which raises serious doubts on their legal effect.
- The lack of transparency in the formulation of tax rules is commonplace, and the implementation is usually procrastinated by the transmission of rules on paper from the top to bottom and impeded by the non-disclosure mechanism.
- Ultimately, taxpayers are put at a vulnerable and disadvantageous position facing the frequent and non-transparent changes of tax rules without effective channels to challenge the legality of such rules.

A reform process has commenced, not in an abrupt way, but using a progressive and piecemeal approach to bring gradual and visible adjustments to the existing tax system. The process of reform has taken place within the wider setting of a restructure of administrative law in China at the turn of the century which was driven by a

43. General office of State Council, Notice on the Power and Procedures on the Interpretation of Administrative Regulations, *Guobanfa* [1999] No. 43, 10 May 1999.
44. One example is *Guobanhan* No. 23 [2004] in which the general office of the State Council responded to the SAT's inquiry concerning the interpretation of the term 'collection and management' in Art. 5 under the Interim Regulations on the Urban Maintenance and Construction Tax.
45. For the missions and tasks of the SAT and the MoF, more detailed information can be accessed through their websites respectively: http://www.chinatax.gov.cn and http://www.mof.gov.cn.
46. *See* e.g., Cai Qiaoping, *Issues of Reduction in Effectiveness of China's Tax Law* (in Chinese), Finance and Tax Law Review, (2), Law Press, (2002).

combination of objectives: the needs of the market economy, the integration into the globalized world and the pursuit of the rule of law. The hallmark of this administrative law reform is the decision promulgated by the State Council in 1999 entitled the 'Comprehensive Promotion of the Administration in accordance with Law'.[47] In the following decade, the State Council provided a series of regulations, policy statements and implementation outlines to translate the abstract notion of 'administration in accordance with law' into concrete measures and actions, such as regulating procedures on the enactment of administrative regulations and rules, establishing the review system to check the legitimacy of existing administrative regulations and rules, designing rules to curb the arbitrary use of administrative discretion, providing channels for governmental information access and building up the accountability system for officials.[48] A general theme under this movement is to rein in the bureaucracy and give more weight to the protection of individual rights.

The SAT, following the lead of the State Council, has initiated some reform of tax processes. This reform has been carried out from the top to the bottom since 2000, and, in recent years, at an accelerated rate as the SAT has increased the pace to bring forward new regulations, rules or internal documents on tax procedural rules and make frequent revisions on the old rules. Within the past years, the efforts made by the SAT and its accomplishments are rather impressive. The new measure on tax normative rules (SAT order No. 20, 2010[49]) was promulgated in the form of the ministerial regulation to replace a previous set of rules applicable to the issuance of informal tax rules. A new regulation on tax administrative review (SAT order No. 21, 2010[50]) was issued with twice as many provisions as found in the predecessor regulation. The rules on the standardization of tax official documents (*Guoshuifa* No. 92, 2012[51]) provide greater detail than the previous rules. Official guidance was provided to curb the abusive use of administrative discretion (*Guoshuifa* No. 65, 2012[52]). Quite a few regulations and rules have also been issued regarding the protection of taxpayers'

47. State Council, Comprehensive Promotion of the Administration in accordance with Law, promulgated on 15 March 1999. This official document was issued in echo to the amendment of the Constitution in March 1999 which provides in Art. 5 that China shall pursue the administration in accordance with law.
48. For relevant regulations and the comments, *see* Shen Kui, *Administrative Self-regulation and Rule of Administrative Law: A Preliminary Investigation* (in Chinese), 3 Administrative Law Research, 12–17 (2011).
49. The comparison of SAT Order No. 20 [2010] and its predecessor, *Guoshuifa* [2005] No 201 can be read in Wei Cui, *What is the 'Law' in Chinese Tax Administration?*, 19(1) Asia Pacific Law Review, 73, 86 (2011). *See*, SAT, Administrative Measures for Formulating Normative Documents in Taxation (for Trial Implementation), *Guoshuifa* No 201[2005], effective on 1 March 2006 and repealed on 1 July 2010; SAT, the Administrative Measures for Formulating Normative Documents in Taxation, Order No. 20, promulgated on 10 February 2010 and effective on 1 July 2010.
50. SAT, Rules on Taxation Administrative Review, Order No. 21, promulgated on 10 February 2010 and effective on 1 April 2010.
51. SAT, Notice on the Standards of Official Documents in National Tax Administrative Organs, *Guoshuifa* No. 92 [2012], promulgated on 10 October 2012.
52. SAT, Guidance on Regulating Tax Administrative Discretion, *Guoshuifa* No. 65 [2012], promulgated on 3 July 2012.

interest and redefining the role of tax administration as part of an attempt to strike a balance between governmental efficiency and respect for the individual rights.[53]

Against this setting, the rules on how the tax administration is to interpret the tax law are gradually taking shape. To get a sound grasp, this process requires the coherent reading of the provisions scattered across a series of administrative regulations and rules, especially those issued recently by the SAT. In general, the SAT's interpretive powers are exercised in two scenarios: first to interpret tax-related administrative regulations enacted by the State Council or when the interpretation concerns the specific application of the administrative regulations.[54] Alternatively, the SAT may interpret the 'tax normative rules' it has enacted itself. The 'normative rules' are defined in SAT order No. 20 [2010] as the rules bearing the following three features: (1) made and promulgated by tax agencies at and above the county level; (2) which prescribe the rights and obligations of taxpayers, withholding agents and other parties against whom tax administrative actions may be taken; and (3) have general binding force and are applicable repeatedly within the jurisdiction of the tax agency.

The interpretation of the tax law made by the SAT is generally pronounced under three forms: bulletin (*gonggao*), opinion (*yijian*) and reply (*pifu*). A bulletin is used to announce important or legal matters to domestic and abroad on tax issues and is promulgated in public. An opinion is used to convey the opinions of tax authorities on important tax matters under the format of the letter (*han*). A common feature of bulletins and opinions is that both of them are normative rules and have general binding force and can be applied repeatedly. In contrast, a reply does not constitute a normative rule. It is used to address a specific inquiry from local tax authorities arising from a certain situation and theoretically has effect only in that particular case.[55]

When an interpretation is pronounced in the form of a bulletin or an opinion, the enactment shall comply with the procedures under the SAT order No. 20, 2010 which requires the solicitation of public opinions in the drafting process,[56] prohibits the retrospective effects of rules in principle and introduces the triple reviewing mechanism on the legitimacy of the rules.[57] The reviews may be conducted by the legal department of the rule-enactment agency in the drafting process, by the tax agency at a higher level when the rules are submitted for record, and also by the party against whom tax administrative actions are taken. In the latter scenario, a taxpayer who finds the interpretation made by tax administration in the form of bulletin or opinion inconsistent with the existing tax statutes, administrative regulations, ministerial

53. *See* e.g., SAT, Bulletin on the Rights and Obligations of Taxpayers, Bulletin No. 1 [2009], promulgated on 6 November 2009; SAT, Several Opinions on Strengthening the Protection of Taxpayers' Rights, *Shuizongfa* No. 15 [2013], promulgated on 9 February 2013; SAT, Notice on the transition of the functions (of tax administration) and improvements of service, *Shuizongfa* No. 74 [2013], promulgated on 12 July 2013.
54. General office of State Council, Notice on the Power and Procedures on the Interpretation of Administrative Regulations, *Guobanfa* [1999] No. 43, 10 May 1999.
55. *See* e.g., SAT Official Reply of the State Administration of Taxation to Issues Concerning Levying of Land Appreciation Tax on Above-ground Structures, *Guoshuihan* No. 347 [2010], promulgated on 26 July 2010.
56. Article 37, SAT order No. 20 [2010].
57. Articles 22 and 32, SAT order No. 20 [2010].

regulations or other superior rules, may apply to the rules-enacting tax authority or tax authority at a higher level to make a review on the legitimacy of such rules without entering into administrative review procedures or administrative litigation.

While much of the impetus behind the recent evolution in the interpretative rule of tax law arises from the self-regulatory movement within governments, especially the central government, the involvement of legal professionals, non-government entities and ordinary citizens should not be overlooked. One of the outstanding examples is the 'Foundations Incident' in 2009. In that case, 24 foundations collaborated to submit publicized letters to the State Council to request a review on the legality of two notices issued by the SAT and the MoF. One pivotal issue in this incident was whether the interpretation of the expression 'qualified non-government organizations (NGO)' under the EITL given by the MoF and the SAT was contrary to the EITL and its implementation rules.[58] Though this incident did not trigger the revision of these two notices, it was noted as 'one of the top ten events signaling the civilization development' in China in 2009. Another event that involves the participation of citizens in the interpretation of tax law took place in 2012. In October of that year, the SAT instituted an administrative review panel according to the Rules on Taxation Administrative Review. This panel was authorized to participate in the review proceedings and provide suggestions for settlement when the cases involve major and difficult tax issues. Out of the 24 members, one third of the panel comprises tax experts from academia, accounting firms and law firms.[59] While it still waits to be seen how this institutional arrangement will impact on the neutrality and fairness of administrative review proceedings with regard to the application and interpretation of tax law, the gesture of openness the SAT has shown represents a positive signal: the interpretation of tax law exercised by tax administrations in China is no longer an unconstrained power, and it is and will be subject to the increasing supervision from outsiders.

§5.06 INTERPRETATION OF TAX LAW IN PRACTICE: A PRELUDE

This part and the following part are closely interlinked as both try to depict how tax laws are interpreted in real life. While the following part (§5.07) provides four concrete examples including administrative rulings and courts judgments, this part serves as a prelude and provides introductory remarks on some key aspects that underlie the interpretative activities of tax law in China.

---

58. Regarding this incident, a discussion forum was hosted in the journal of 'Tax law and Case Review' which included the opinions and comments from tax experts. *See*: Xiong Wei et al., *Discussion Forum on 'The Meaning and Inspiration of the Questioning Raised by Taxpayers on the Legality of the Tax Normative Rules'* (in Chinese), 1 Tax Law and Case Review, Law Press, 1–22 (2010).
59. For the name list of the review panel to the SAT, *see* http://www.gov.cn/gzdt/2012-10/29/content_2253321.htm, visited on 25 July 2013.

[A] Interrelation Between Judicial Interpretation and Administrative Interpretation

Before the Law of Administrative Litigation was revised in 2014, courts had no power to strike down tax administrative rules that are inconsistent with the higher legislation. They could only submit the questionable ministerial regulation to the Supreme People's Court which, in turn, could refer the case to the State Council. It is the State Council that had the final say on the legality of the ministerial regulations and their interpretation. To date, there appear to be no precedents in which the Supreme People's Court has brought a tax administrative rule to the State Council for review even though scholars have identified the inconsistency of rules as a serious problem plaguing the tax legislation in China.[60] There have been a few cases in which courts have denied the validity of informal tax rules of the SAT and rendered decisions without making reference to such rules. The *PanAmSat* case[61] in 2002 is an example. In this case, the High Court in Beijing disregarded two SAT informal rules regarding the characterization of income arising from the lease of satellites and directly applied the tax statute and the tax treaty as the legal basis for its decision. In the rare cases where courts exercised limited judicial review, the general shortage of tax expertise among the judges has surfaced as an issue and hampered the courts' ability to provide constructive opinions to refine the interpretation of tax law.[62]

Although the Supreme People's Court has been actively involved in the interpretation of law in many areas such as procedural law, civil law, criminal law and administrative law through issuing numerous judicial interpretations or guidance, it plays a negligible role in the interpretation of tax law. This fact may be attributable to the paucity of tax litigation working in conjunction with the general reluctance of the judiciary to interfere with the administration. Although there are few judicial interpretations by the Supreme People's Court on tax matters, conflicts with administrative interpretations arise from time to time. One example is *fashui* No. 9 [2012].[63] In the reply to an inquiry from the High Court in Qinghai, the Supreme People's Court opined that the interest arising from the overdue tax payment owed by a bankrupt company fell under the category of 'fines imposed by administrative organs upon the bankrupt

60. *See* e.g., Cai Qiaoping, *supra* note 47; Zhang Xuebo, *Research on Legitimacy of Tax Administrative Document* (in Chinese), 10 Journal of South East University of Political Science and Law 3 (2008).

61. *PanAmSat International Systems, Inc. v. Second Department in the External Substation of the Beijing State Tax Bureau* (decision in the first instance (2001) 168) entered by the First Intermediate People's Court of Beijing on 20 December 2001); *PanAmSat International Systems, Inc. v. Second Department in the External Substation of the Beijing State Tax Bureau* (decision on appeal (*Gaoxingzhongzi* (2002) 24) entered by the Higher People's Court of Beijing on 20 December 2002).

62. The decision of PanAmSat case has been subject to questioning with regard to the interpretation of the provisions under the US-China tax treaty. *See* e.g., Chen Yanzhong, *Interpretation Issues of International Tax Treaties: A Preliminary Study* (Science Press: 2010), p. 4.

63. Supreme People's Court, Official Reply on Whether to Accept the Lawsuits Lodged by the Tax Authorities to Determine Their Creditor's Rights to the Late Fees of Tax Arrears Incurred by Bankrupt Enterprises, *Fashi* No. 9 [2012], promulgated on 26 June 2012, effective on 12 July 2012.

enterprise'[64] and thus would be considered an ordinary claim which did not enjoy priority in the bankruptcy compensation regime. This view stands in contrast to the opinions of the SAT in *Guoshuihan* No. 1084 [2008].[65] In this document, a reply to the inquiry of the Guangdong State Tax Bureau, the SAT held that interest arising from an overdue tax payment differs from fines both in the tax administration and payment sequence, and thus shall be treated as the equivalent of a 'tax payment' and given a compensation priority.[66] While both the Supreme People's Court and the SAT claimed to base their interpretation on the Law on the Administration of Tax Collection, they did not give detailed reasoning of their interpretative process, leaving observers to puzzle as to how opposite interpretations can derive from the same legal text. The contradiction between judicial interpretation and administrative interpretation as such is unresolved under the existing law. It not only brings confusion to taxpayers, but also increases the risks of tax agencies being challenged in court proceedings.

[B] Interrelation Between the SAT and Local Tax Agencies on the Interpretation of Tax Law

After the 1994 fiscal reform, the bifurcated system of tax administration was established in China which included state tax bureaus and local tax bureaus. Local tax agencies, in this context, refer to state tax bureaus and local tax bureaus at the provincial, municipal and county levels. They have much of the day-to-day responsibility for tax administration in China and are subordinate to the tax policy and technical guidance set out by the SAT.

The SAT has ruled that for tax normative rules, interpretation power exclusively belongs to the agency which enacted the rules.[67] In theory, therefore, local tax agencies cannot interpret the rules enacted by the SAT but merely apply them. In practice, of course, the application and interpretation of the law is inextricably intertwined, and it is difficult to ensure local tax agencies only follow SAT rules rather than exercise some creativity in applying general rules to particular transactions. In practice, two approaches have been taken to curtail the discretion of local tax agencies. On the one hand, the SAT endeavours to make the meaning of the rules more self-evident and easier to implement through several new strategies. For example, to clarify the meaning of a term used in the law or subordinate documents, the SAT provides both a descriptive definition and a list of factors to be considered when applying the definition

64. According to the Supreme People's Court, the 'fines and other relevant expenses imposed by administrative or judicial organs upon the bankrupt enterprise' are precluded from the scope of the bankruptcy claim. Supreme People's Court, Provisions on Issues Concerning the Hearing of Enterprise Bankruptcy Cases, *Fashi* No. 23 [2002], Art. 61(1), promulgated on 30 July 2002, effective on 1 September 2002.
65. SAT, Reply to whether tax compensation priority includes fines, *Guoshuihan* No. 1084 [2008], promulgated on 31 December 2008.
66. According to Art. 45 of the Law on Administration of the Tax Collection, unless otherwise provided, tax levied by tax authorities shall have priority over unsecured creditors' claims. If a defaulting taxpayer is fined or is subject to confiscation for his illegal income, tax levying shall take priority over the fine and confiscation.
67. Article 20 of the SAT order No. 20 [2010].

so local tax authorities can make an overall analysis based on the facts of each case.[68] In addition, selective rulings prepared by local agencies are published by the SAT as the examples for other agencies to follow.[69] Also, the drafting department of the SAT issues a commentary explaining the background, aims and key points of the new rules.[70] On the other hand, local tax agencies are directed to consult the SAT for instructions and guidance (*qingshi*) whenever they encounter uncertainties and ambiguities in the application of the SAT rules in a specific case. This mechanism of consultation for instructions, in essence an endorsement by the SAT of interpretative actions taken by local agencies, is widely used because it removes the risk of local tax agencies being found to have made mistakes and provides a defence in case of a possible court challenge.

However, local tax agencies are not puppets. Although the SAT has exerted increasing influence and supervision on local agencies regarding the application of tax law, there are vast areas out of its reach. The majority of tax rulings that are neither reported to the upper offices nor disclosed to the public are kept confidential between taxpayers and agencies. The non-transparency of the bargaining process, the complicated considerations in respect of relationships and the limited appreciation by tax officials of rule of law principles cast serious doubt on the implementation of tax rules in practice. The public dissemination of rulings reinforces these concerns. Ruling reports are one-sided stories told by agencies and presented in the China Taxation News, the newspaper published by the SAT. They usually contain a brief description on facts and a large body of text depicting actions taken by agencies to capture tax revenue. Meanwhile, the legal reasoning of the agency's decision, the taxpayers' propositions and the negotiation process are simply left out or played down. It occurs from time to time that the decisions of tax agencies clearly deviate from the literal meaning of tax rules or constitute interpretative activities prohibited by the SAT rules. Such problems cannot be rectified until the SAT takes notice and issues new circulars to give clarifications.

[C] Interpretation of Double Tax Treaties

The first tax treaty China concluded was with Japan in 1983. Today the treaty network of China has rapidly expanded and includes tax treaties with 102 countries and tax arrangements with Macau, Hong Kong and Taiwan.[71] Since 2008, the application of tax treaties emerged as a more significant subject than ever as the generous preferential tax treatments granted to companies with significant foreign ownership have disappeared

68. SAT, Guidance on Regulating Tax Administrative Discretion, *Guoshuifa* No. 65 [2012], promulgated on 3 July 2012.
69. SAT, Guidance on Regulating Tax Administrative Discretion, *Guoshuifa* No. 65 [2012], promulgated on 3 July 2012.
70. SAT, Several Opinions on Strengthening the Protection of Taxpayers' Rights, *Shuizongfa* No. 15 [2013], promulgated on 9 February 2013. It is noted that for the SAT normative tax rules issued after April 2012, they are often promulgated in company with the official commentary.
71. For the list of tax treaties China has entered into, as of July 2017, *see* http://www.chinatax.gov.cn/n810341/n810770/index.html, visited on 5 July 2017.

with the replacement of separate EITLs for foreign-owned and domestically-owned companies by a single EITL for all companies. In spite of the increasing importance of tax treaties, in practice, they are rarely interpreted by Chinese courts. To date, there have been a handful of reported cases which involve the application of tax treaties, including the *PanAmSat* (2002) and *Weihai* (2010).[72] Interpretation of tax treaties thus largely rests with the SAT.

A review of the SAT's rules on tax treaties over three decades reveals noteworthy dynamic changes in the approach taken by the SAT. The interpretation approach taken by the SAT on tax treaties has progressed from a scattered and fragmented approach to a systematic and comprehensive approach. Before 2008, most of the treaty-related interpretations issued by the SAT were aimed at addressing a certain provision in one specific tax treaty or tackled the application of a treaty provision to one particular case. The increasing significance of tax treaties after the consolidation of the domestic and foreign-owned company income tax laws into a single company income tax law in 2008 and the growing expertise of tax officials prompted SAT in 2010 to provide an overall guide to the interpretation of tax treaties. The resulting circular set out a detailed interpretation of every single provision in the China-Singapore tax treaty, and the guidance can be used to interpret other treaties concluded by China when the same provisions are included. However, the Singapore-China treaty interpretation circular, circular No. 75 [2010], is not the final word to all the issues arising from treaty interpretation. Driven by the emergence of various transaction and business models, the SAT continues to refine the issues of treaty interpretation based on a piecemeal and progressive approach. For instance, during the period from 2009 to 2013, SAT issued three circulars to define the meaning of the treaty term 'beneficial owner' (*see* §5.07[C]). A bulletin issued in 2013 provides additional rules in addition to circular No. 75 [2010] concerning the recognition of a permanent establishment arising from the cross-border secondment of personnel by non-resident companies (*see* §5.07[D]).[73] To fully appreciate the Chinese position on the application of tax treaties to capital gains derived by non-residents from the disposition of shares in a Chinese company, one needs to review a set of SAT circulars issued since 2009.[74]

The commentary to the OECD Model serves as an important reference for China to develop the interpretation on tax treaties. Since the 1990s, the SAT has prepared translations of the commentary and kept close watch over every revision made by the OECD. Meanwhile, as a non-member observer state of the OECD, China has engaged in

72. *See supra* note 23.
73. Bulletin No. 19 [2013].
74. *See* e.g., SAT, Tax Issues for Equity Transfers by Non-China Tax Resident Enterprises, *Guoshuihan* No. 698 [2009], promulgated on 15 December 2009, effective on 1 January 2008; SAT, Interpretation Notes on the Double Tax Agreement Concluded between China and Singapore, *Guoshuifa* No. 75 [2010], promulgated on 26 July 2010. SAT, Announcement on Several Issues Concerning the Administration of Income Tax on Non-Resident Enterprises, Bulletin [2011] No. 24, promulgated on 28 March 2011, effective on 1 April 2011; SAT, Announcement on Issues Concerning Capital Gains Provision under the Tax Treaties, Bulletin [2012] No. 59, promulgated and effective on 31 December 2012; SAT, Announcement on Several Issues concerning the Enterprise Income Tax on Income from the Indirect Transfer of Assets by Non-Resident Enterprises, Bulletin No. 7 [2015], issued and effective on 3 February 2015.

various discussions on the revision work of the commentary.[75] It is not surprising that many interpretative rules made by the SAT on tax treaties bear a striking resemblance to the content in the OECD commentary. However, the SAT does not merely transplant or import the rules. The status of China as a non-OECD Member State also leaves room for the SAT to design the interpretative rules with their own characteristics. On some occasions, the SAT brings in innovative elements to make the treaty terms more easy to implement for Chinese tax agencies, and on other occasions, it takes a view different from the OECD commentary to maintain its adherence to the protection of the source state interest (*see* §5.07[A]).

In addition to the influence of the international organizations like the OECD on SAT interpretations, the SAT is willing to enter into dialogues with tax professionals and treaty partners when shaping its interpretations of tax treaties. For example, the interpretation of revision of the treaty term on 'beneficial ownership' involves a close interaction with the Inland Revenue Department (IRD) in Hong Kong[76] and tax professionals in accounting firms or legal firms.

[D] Interpretation of Anti-avoidance Rules

In the VAT area, the anti-avoidance rule is quite simple. Article 7 of the Interim Regulations of the VAT provides that tax agencies may adjust the sales price when the price used by the taxpayer in the sales of goods or taxable services is obviously low without reasonable justification. Instructions on how to adjust sale prices (the equivalent of arm's length pricing in western tax terminology) are provided for in Article 16 of the Implementation Rules to the Interim Regulations.[77] The practice shows that, in the VAT area, it is criminal acts like the forging of VAT invoices or tax fraud rather than tax avoidance schemes that have received more attention from the tax administration.[78]

In the area of income tax, anti-avoidance rules are more complete, and the basic legal framework took form in chapter six of the EITL titled as 'the special tax adjustment'. This chapter introduces not only specific anti-avoidance rules such as thin capitalization rules, controlled foreign company rules and transfer pricing rules, but also provides the general anti-avoidance rules (GAAR). While the provisions under the EITL provides only a skeleton of anti-avoidance rules, the flesh is filled in by the

75. Li Jinyan, *The Great Fiscal Wall of China: Tax Treaties and Their Role in Defining and Defending China's Tax Base*, 66(9) Bulletin for International Taxation 452 (2012).
76. In SAT circular No. 165 [2013], it is explicitly mentioned that the guidance formulated by the SAT is based on the consultation with the IRD. It is reported that the promulgation of bulletin No. 30 [2009] is also under the impact from the IRD. *See* Gao Yang, *Review of the Recent Development on Hong Kong Tax Regime* (in Chinese), 11 International Taxation 57 (2012).
77. According to Art. 16 of the Implementation Rules to the Interim Regulations, tax authorities may make adjustments to the sales amount by reference to the benchmarks in the following order: (1) the average price of taxable activities of the same type conducted by the taxpayer in the most recent period; (2) the average price of taxable activities of the same type conducted by other taxpayers in the most recent period; (3) the composite assessable value.
78. Yang Xiaoqiang, *The Anti-Avoidance Rules in VAT*, submitted to the Fifth Ph.D. Forum on the Finance and Tax Law in China in Wuhan University, 5 May 2013.

Implementation Rules of the EITL and a series of rules made by the SAT. The SAT rules are expansive and can be illustrated as follows: circular No. 2[2009][79] contains 118 provisions that spell out the detailed rules to implement the special tax adjustment; circular No. 121[2008][80] provides rules on interest deduction under thin capitalization rules; circular No. 601[2009],[81] bulletin No. 30[2012][82] and circular 165[2013][83] form an integral part to define the term 'beneficial ownership'; circular No. 13[2012][84] and circular No. 16[2012][85] lay down the procedural rules for tax agencies on handling the special tax adjustment. Apart from the above, anti-avoidance rules are scattered in provisions of other tax rules. For example, under Article 10 of circular No. 59[2009],[86] transactions involving asset or equities within 12 months prior to or after a reorganization can be treated as one single transaction based on the substance over form principle.

This list goes on and on, and sends a strong message that tax agencies in China no longer harbour any tolerance for tax avoidance schemes. A fierce battle is now being waged against aggressive tax planning. The statistics show that in 2016 tax revenue collected by tax agencies through applying anti-avoidance measures reached CNY 61 billion (around USD 8.87 billion), which is 133 times the revenue raised from combating tax avoidance in 2005. Notwithstanding this success, there are serious concerns in terms of the legality of anti-avoidance rules, because the courts in China are not involved in their formulation and implementation. The anti-avoidance rules are likely interpreted and implemented by the various tax administrations in a manner strongly biased against taxpayers. Without effective constraints, the legitimate right of taxpayers to minimize the tax burden could be easily overlooked, and the autonomy of taxpayers in structuring their business schemes could be severely limited by the interference of those organs of public power. Such problems will be exacerbated when tax agencies are pressed to meet the tax quota assigned by the upper agencies and see anti-avoidance measures as effective ways to collect revenue, or when the revenue deriving from anti-avoidance is considered as a benchmark to evaluate the competence of tax administration.

---

79. SAT, Circular on the Implementing Measures for Special Tax Adjustments (Trial Implementation), *Guoshuifa* [2009] No. 2, promulgated on 8 January 2009, effective on 1 January 2008.
80. SAT and MoF, Circular on Tax Policy Issues Relating to Deduction of Interest Paid by Enterprises to Affiliated Parties, *Caishui* No. 121 [2008], promulgated and effective on 23 September 2008.
81. SAT, Notice on How to Understand and Determine the 'Beneficial Owners' in Tax Treaties, Circular No. 601 [2009], promulgated and effective on 27 October 2009.
82. SAT, Bulletin on the Recognition of Beneficial Owners in Tax Treaties, Bulletin No. 30 [2012], promulgated and effective on 29 June 2012.
83. SAT, Opinions on the Cases Involving Beneficial Ownership Raised by Hubei, Other Provinces and Cities concerning the Dividend Provision under the Tax Arrangement between the Mainland and Hong Kong, *Guoshuihan* No. 165 [2013], promulgated and effective on 12 April 2013.
84. SAT, Notice on the Internal Implementation Regulations on Special Tax Adjustments, *Guoshuifa* No. 13 [2012], promulgated on 10 February 2012, effective on 1 March 2012.
85. SAT, 'Notice on the Procedural Guidelines for Joint Review of Significant Special Tax Adjustments Cases (Trial)', *Guoshuifa* No. 16 [2012], promulgated on 16 February 2012, effective on 1 March 2012.
86. MoF and SAT, Notice on Enterprise Income Tax Treatment of Enterprise Reorganizations, *Caishui* No. 59 [2009], promulgated on 30 April 2009, effective on 1 January 2008.

Among the anti-avoidance rules, the GAAR is especially vulnerable to misinterpretation and abusive use. There are two reasons for this: the abstract meaning; and the interchangeable use with the doctrine of 'substance over form'. The GAAR in China was incorporated into the EITL which provides, in Article 47, that when the companies arrange transactions without reasonable business objectives to reduce taxable income, tax agencies are entitled to make readjustments in a reasonable manner. As the existing rules do not adequately explain the meaning of 'lack of reasonable business objectives',[87] the result is that, in practice, tax agencies tend to take a simplistic approach and assume that this is the case whenever taxpayers derive tax benefits. In their approach, tax agencies do not render much analysis nor do they appear to give much weight to arguments that the primary objective of a certain transaction is business-oriented, and tax savings are only ancillary in purpose. The SAT did set down a procedural requirement in Article 97 of circular No. 2 [2009] with the intent to curb the misuse of the GAAR. This provision requires local tax agencies to report cases involving the use of the GAAR to the SAT for approval. However, this safety valve has had very limited effect in reality, since tax agencies can easily apply the 'substance over form' doctrine to thwart business structures of taxpayers instead of relying on the GAAR provision. The doctrine of 'substance over form' is not codified in tax statutes, but appears from time to time in the SAT rules with a vague meaning and little guidance on application.[88] To clarify the application of the GAAR, in December 2014 the SAT issued Bulletin 32 [2014] which spells out the key features of tax avoidance, readjustment methods and the procedures of the GAAR investigation.[89]

§5.07 INTERPRETATION OF TAX LAW IN PRACTICE

This section provides four examples of the interpretation of tax law in China. The first, *Weihai*, is a judicial case involving the interpretation of a tax treaty in November 2010. While its verdict is not publicly accessible, information on the decision is available from the SAT's official notice on the case.[90] The second is a tax ruling made by Chongqing State Tax Bureau in 2011, which recharacterized service income as dividends, alleged based on a 'substance over form' doctrine. The third example concerns three interpretative rules made by the SAT during 2009 and 2013 on the

87. In para. 39 of SAT circular No. 159 [2008], three elements are provided to identify a 'transaction for lacking the reasonable commercial purpose', namely an artificial scheme, tax benefits and the primary purpose of the transaction to reap tax benefits. But the meaning for each element was not elaborated. According to Art. 120 of the Implementation Rules to the EITL, 'lack of reasonable business objectives' is generally described as taxpayers having a primary purpose to reduce, waive or postpone tax payments.
88. Article 93 of circular No. 2 [2009] provides a list of factors for tax agencies to discern the substance of a transaction, but this provision concerns the procedural requirements and is of little guidance to the application.
89. SAT, Measures for the Administration of General Anti-Tax Avoidance, Bulletin 32 [2014], issued on 2 December 2014, effective on 1 January 2015.
90. SAT, International Transport Cases Involved in the Implementation of Tax Treaties by the Office of the State Administration of Taxation in Shandong Province, *Guoshuibanfa* [2011] No. 34, promulgated on 21 March 2011.

interpretation of 'beneficial ownership' under treaties. The last example derives from a ruling made by Jiangsu tax bureau in 2010 concerning a permanent establishment arising from cross-border secondment as well as the evolutionary interpretation made by the SAT on this subject.

[A] *Weihai* (November 2010)

The *Weihai* case involved a Korean company, which entered into a time charter contract with a Chinese company in October 2009. Under the contract, the Korean company leased a ship to the Chinese company in Weihai for half a year, bore the costs of wages and remuneration of the entire crew, and correspondingly, received a rental fee from the Chinese company. The Korean company applied for an exemption from taxation in China for this rental income which it categorized as 'profits from the operation of international traffic' under the China-Korea tax treaty and thus subject to exclusive taxation in Korea.

However, the tax authority held different views based on the following reasoning: according to the SAT's circular 241 [1998], an informal tax rule to address inquiries, the 'profits from the operation of international traffic' under tax treaties are defined as the income of enterprises from their passenger or cargo transport services with vessels or airplanes, including the income from carrying out activities affiliated to international transport businesses. In other words, only if a company conducts business in transportation of passengers or cargo, income derived from the time-charter may be deemed as 'affiliated to income from international transport businesses' and falls under the category of 'profits from the operation of international traffic'. In this case, although the Korean company was competent to carry out business of international transportation based on the qualification certificate, both its registration certificate and the financial statement show that its actual business activities were restricted to the ship rental, albeit complete with operating crew, and not including transportation of passengers or cargoes in its own capacity as ship operator. On this basis, the tax authority contended that the income of the Korean company was subject to the provision of royalties under the China-Korea tax treaty which covers payments received as a consideration for the use of, or the right to use, industrial, commercial and scientific equipment, and is liable to withholding tax at 10% of gross income in China.

It is reported that the decision-making process of the tax agency in the *Weihai case* involved close collaboration with the upper authorities at the municipal and provincial levels, and received guidance from the SAT. The Korean company, after losing its administrative appeal, brought the dispute to the district court, which upheld the administrative decision.

The central issue at dispute was whether the rental income from the wet lease, i.e., leasing a ship on charter fully equipped, crewed and supplied, should be classified as profits from the operation of international traffic, or as royalties. At this point, the SAT took a stance different from the OECD: the OECD provides in the relevant Commentary that profits obtained by the wet lease of ships must be treated like the profits from the carriages of passengers or cargo,[91] whereas the SAT holds that both the income from wet lease and bare lease of ships by themselves does not constitute profits from the operation of international traffic, but simply are activities affiliated to the international transportation. The SAT's view was reiterated in circular No. 75 [2010], which set forth the view that a marine shipping company will derive profits from operation of international traffic only if its main business is international marine transportation business by ship and the affiliated business is of a supporting and incidental nature. To determine whether the activities are of an affiliated nature, the main business of the company shall be examined based on the company's industrial and commercial registration, vouchers and relevant materials. The percentage of income from the affiliated activities among the gross income from the international transportation business shall then be calculated. In principle, income from affiliated business shall not exceed 10% of the gross income within an accounting year.[92]

As China is a non-OECD member, the SAT's deviation from the OECD commentary in the interpretation should not trigger the issue of breaching international treaties. But the real problem is whether the unilateral interpretation given by the SAT conforms to the literal meaning of the treaty text or reflects the genuine intention of the parties at the conclusion of treaties. If not, this interpretative act would constitute the treaty override. The problems began to draw attention from several scholars in China in recent years. It may take some time, however, for the SAT to address and constrain its interpretative powers to comply with international obligations.

Another issue posed by this case concerns the consultation mechanism. While the tax authority to *Weihai* case involved the upper agencies and even the top echelon during the decision-making process, the local decision was actually the 'final say' in the administrative system. Under the existing law, taxpayers are required to first pursue administrative review proceedings before launching tax litigation. However, it is difficult to see the logic of allowing local tax authority to consult before reaching a final local level decision and then requiring taxpayers to seek an administrative review from the agency making a 'final' decision before commencing tax litigation.

[B] Recharacterization of Service Income as Dividends[93]

In 2011, the Chongqing State Tax Bureau made a ruling involving a Hong Kong company that received a service payment from a Chinese company. This Chinese company built a low-carbon waterway navigation and hydropower junction project in Chongqing. Under the Clean Development Mechanism (CDM) in the Kyoto Protocol, the Chinese company has a right to sell the certificated emissions reductions (CERs)

91. Paragraph 5, Art. 8, OECD Commentary (2010).
92. SAT, Interpretation Notes on the Double Tax Agreement Concluded between China and Singapore, circular No. 75 [2010], issuance date: 26 July 2010.
93. International Tax Administration of Chongqing State Tax Bureau, Case study of the CERs project, http://wenku.baidu.com/view/a788ec2cb4daa58da0114aab.html, visited on 17 May 2013; Alex Duan, *Income from Sale of Carbon Credits Is Taxable Dividend, Chinese Tax Authority Says*, Worldwide Tax Daily, 16 November 2011.

from the project to enterprises in developed countries. Due to technological requirements in the CDM, the Chinese company contracted with a Hong Kong company that was responsible for the development of the CDM project and for contact with potential buyers overseas for sale of the CERs. Under the contract, the Hong Kong company was to receive a portion of the sales income as remuneration.

In June 2008, the Chinese company made its first deal and sold the CERs to Mitsubishi Corporation in Japan. The first payment was made by the Mitsubishi Corporation in 2011 to the Chinese company at the amount of EUR 948,000 (CNY 8.81 million). Soon after the payment, the Chinese company applied to the tax bureau for clearance for remittance to the Hong Kong company (the transfer of funds abroad requires tax bureau authorization).[94] In the application package, the Hong Kong company provided a workload chart showing that it had spent approximately 400 accumulated workdays on the CDM project – 41.25% of the time in China and 58.75% of the time outside of China. The Hong Kong company asserted that this presence was insufficient to constitute a permanent establishment[95] and thus the service income it derived from the contract should not be taxed in China.

But this argument was not accepted by the tax agency that conducted a factual investigation in the matter. It found that, under the contract, the Hong Kong company took on all the preparatory work of the project, including the identification and design of the project, papers writing, seeking potential buyers and application for governmental approval inside and outside China, and bore all the expenses arising there from. The profits from the sales of the CERs, after the deduction of the expenses, were divided between the Hong Kong company and the Chinese company at the ratio of 35:65.

Based on the factual analysis, the tax bureau made reference to the provisions of 'dividends' under the mainland China-Hong Kong tax arrangement and raised the question how to categorize the income. In the arrangement, dividends are defined as income from shares or other rights, not being debt-claims, participating in profits, as well as income from other corporate rights, which is subject to the same taxation treatment as income from shares under the laws of the jurisdiction where the company making the distribution is a resident. The tax agency invoked the substance over form

---

94. Based on *Guoshuihan* [2008] No. 219, when a domestic entity makes the payment for services abroad at the designated banks at the amount of more than USD 50,000, this entity shall file a report with the tax authority. Within seven days after the report, the domestic entity is obliged to file the tax return or make explanations to the tax authority on tax matters of the transaction. The payment for services may arise from transactions of transportation, tourism, communication, building and erection, labour contracting, insurance, financial services, computer and information service, usage of proprietary rights and franchise, physical culture and entertainment service and other commercial service and government services, etc. *See* SAT, Issues Concerning the Imposition and Administration of Tax on External Payments for Services, *Guoshuihan* [2008] No. 219, promulgated and effective on 6 March 2008.
95. Under Art. 5(3)(2) of the tax arrangement between Hong Kong and the mainland China, to constitute the permanent establishment, the furnishing of services by an enterprise of one jurisdiction directly or through employees or other personnel engaged by the enterprise for such purpose, but only if activities of that nature continue (for the same or a connected project) in the other jurisdiction for a period or periods aggregating more than six months within any twelve-month period. In this case, it seems that the presence of the Hong Kong company in mainland China did not reach the time threshold.

doctrine, reasoning that the Hong Kong Company shared risk in the investment of the CDM projects, as it would have borne all the loss had the project failed, and, therefore, it derived income from the project in the nature of dividends, rather than as a service payment. While the negotiation process was completely hidden from the reported news, what was told is that the Hong Kong company ultimately accepted the decision of the tax agency and paid withholding tax on the income at the amount of CNY 302,000 (approximately USD 47,600).

This ruling seems to be premised on a presumption that any party, even when not holding a share in a company, as long as it partakes in the risks and profits of the company, would be deemed to be a shareholder of the company, and thus the income derived shall be categorized as dividends. While the plain text on the definition of 'dividends' under the mainland China-Hong Kong tax arrangement provides little support to this rational, the second sentence of the provision allows the scope of dividends to include 'income from other corporate rights which is subjected to the same taxation treatment as income from shares under the laws of the jurisdiction where the company making the distribution is a resident'. Therefore, it is necessary to examine whether such a recharacterization of income can find a legal basis in the tax law of Mainland China. In this regard, paragraph 3 of the provision on dividends in circular No. 75[2010] seems to be relevant. This paragraph was drafted to make a distinction between dividends and interest, and according to it, when it is hard to distinguish dividends and interest, the doctrine of 'substance over form' shall apply. In general, the income from debt claims shall not be considered as dividends, but if the creditor bears risks of the debtor company, interest may be recharacterized as dividends. To illustrate, a list of five factors is provided for tax agencies to ascertain whether the creditor did bear risks of the debtor company, and includes elements such as the creditor is entitled to the profits of the debtor company; the payment of interest depends on the profitability of the debtor company, etc.

If this paragraph of circular No. 75[2010] was indeed the basis for the analysis of the tax agency in Chongqing, the ensuing question is whether the SAT intended the criteria developed to distinguish interest from dividends to be used for recharacterising other income (including business income from a contract that allocates risk to both parties to the transaction) as dividends. Furthermore, while very little information was disclosed on the underlying rationale of tax agency, except for the mere mention of 'substance over form' doctrine, this reaffirms the concern that this doctrine, without being properly delimited, can be used by local tax agencies as a potent weapon to thwart the tax effectiveness of apparently legitimately planned business structures of taxpayers.

[C] Who Is the 'Beneficial Owner' under Tax Treaties?

Beneficial ownership is a concept under tax treaties to determine whether the recipient in one contracting state, deriving dividends, interest and royalties from a payer in the other contracting state, is eligible to treaty benefits. In recent years, this term has attracted increasing attention in the international tax community, and China is not an exception. In 2009, in response to the prevailing tax planning schemes that were perceived by tax authorities to be treaty shopping following the promulgation of the EITL, the SAT issued circular No. 601[2009] to shed light on the meaning on beneficial ownership. According to this circular, beneficial owners are defined as 'persons who have the right to own or dispose of the relevant income or an associated right and property'. Two types of entities are precluded from the scope of this definition, namely agents and conduit companies. On top of that, a list of seven adverse factors is provided as a benchmark for tax authorities to ascertain the beneficial ownership. These include a lack of substantial business operations or assets on the part of the recipient of the income, very limited assets, the size of the recipient company or the number of personnel being incompatible with the amount of income and an extremely low-tax burden in the other contracting state. In general, the interpretation made in circular No. 601[2009] is a hybrid one. On the one hand, it echoes the views in common law countries that the fundamental element of this concept shall be based on the ownership rights of the recipient with regard to income, and borrows the wording of the interpretative principles adopted in the OECD commentaries. On the other hand, it brings in certain innovative elements to enhance the administrative implementability for local tax officials, such as the list of negative factors, and the introduction of the 'substance-over-form' doctrine and substantive business requirements.

After circular No. 601[2009] was implemented, a series of administrative rulings were reported by tax agencies in which taxpayers were denied treaty benefits as a consequence of being disqualified as beneficial owners.[96] One common feature of these rulings is that tax agencies rarely address beneficial ownership from the perspective of the rights of the recipient towards the income, but place almost exclusive emphasis on the business substance of the company that received the dividends. The concept of beneficial ownership was, thus, used by tax agencies rather like the GAAR.

To address this problem, a second circular was issued by the SAT in June 2012, i.e., bulletin No. 30[2012]. The bulletin reiterates that the determination of beneficial ownership shall rest on the recipient's right to the income and emphasizes that the adverse factors listed in paragraph 2 of circular No. 601[2009] should be considered on a comprehensive basis and the existence of any single factor should not be sufficient to deny beneficial ownership. Again, the 'substance-over-form' doctrine was highlighted as an important benchmark for tax agencies to analyse particular cases. Moreover, the bulletin provides guidance for the scenario where an agent is involved, provides a 'safe-harbour rule' to simplify the administrative process,[97] and delimits the interpretative powers of local tax bureaus to reduce inconsistency in practice.

96. For the tax rulings and the analysis, *see* Qiu Dongmei, *The Concept of Beneficial Ownership in Chinas Tax Treaties – The Current State of Play*, 67(2) Bulletin for International Taxation 593 (2013).

97. Under bulletin No. 30 [2012], privileged treatment is granted to the recipients of income that meet certain economic requirements so as to be exempt from examination with regard to beneficial ownership. This safe-harbour rule applies in the following two scenarios: (1) where the recipient of income is a listed company resident in the other contracting state and (2) where the recipient of income is a resident of other contracting state and is wholly, directly or indirectly, owned by a listed company, which is a resident of that state. No enterprise residing

Even so, the interpretations given by the SAT did not end the confusion and questions in practice. In April 2013, to respond to inquiries from seven provincial or municipal tax bureaus as to whether the Hong Kong companies in question should be considered as beneficial owners of dividends under the Mainland China-Hong Kong Tax Arrangement, the SAT published the third circular on the meaning of beneficial ownership, i.e., circular No. 165[2013]. This circular, issued in the form of an opinion, has general binding force and can be used repeatedly by tax agencies. It serves as a supplement to its predecessors by pronouncing more detailed rules to the list of negative factors in circular No. 601[2009], the measures to discern the rights of a recipient on the income and the safe-harbour rules in bulletin No. 30[2012]. A noticeable theme under this new circular is to grant more protection to the rights of non-residents to enjoy treaty benefits since it explicitly states under each of its seven provisions what shall *not* be construed as negative factors in the determination of beneficial ownership or what shall *not* be considered as sufficient evidence to disqualify taxpayers as beneficial owners. For example, it provides that, if a recipient of the income does not distribute dividends to enterprises that are residents of another state, this recipient would not be caught by the first negative factor in circular No. 601[2009].[98] Next, the single fact that the recipient has no other investment project or other types of business activities except for holding a single investment project does not suffice to deny this recipient recognition as a beneficial owner, and other factors shall be taken in to account. Along with these changes, tax agencies are required to provide more solid evidence to ascertain the rights of non-residents with respect to the income, and cannot frustrate the application for beneficial ownership by counting on one or two facts and simply using the abstract doctrine of 'substance over form'.

[D] Permanent Establishment Arising from Cross-Border Secondment

Due to the significant drop in fiscal revenue resulting from the global economic downturn, the SAT issued a series of circulars[99] in 2009 to strengthen tax administration on non-residents. One type of transactions that came under close monitoring was the cross-border service rendered by non-resident companies to Chinese companies through the secondment of personnel. Under this arrangement, the non-resident

---

in a third jurisdiction should be interposed between the listed company and the recipient company. Dividends derived by the recipient should also arise from shares held by the listed company.

98. Under para. 2 of circular No. 601 [2009], the first negative factor is that the recipient must distribute all or the majority, for example, 60% or more, of the income to a resident of a third jurisdiction within a specified period, for example, 12 months.

99. *See* e.g., SAT, Notice on the Specific Measures to Strengthen Tax Collection and Administration, *Guoshuifa* No. 114 [2009], promulgated and effective on 27 July 2009; SAT, Notice on the Administrative Measures for the Assessment and Collection of Income Tax against Non-resident Enterprises, *Guoshuifa* No. 19 [2009], promulgated and effective on 20 February 2009; SAT, Circular of the International Taxation Department of the State Administration of Taxation on the Investigation of the Collections of Enterprise Income Tax on Foreign Entities for Their Provision of Services to Chinese Enterprises through Secondment of Personnel, *Jibianhan* No. 103 [2009], promulgated and effective on 2 July 2009.

company ('the dispatching company') dispatches its employees to serve in a Chinese company ('the receiving company') as senior executives or technicians, The Chinese company then pays the secondment fee or other fee of this nature to the non-resident company. From the perspective of income tax, a pivotal issue is whether the activities of the non-resident company in China have constituted the establishment or site, or the permanent establishment if the tax treaty is applicable. If yes, the non-resident company would be liable to income tax in China for the profits deriving from such an establishment. A key point hence is to distinguish who is the real employer of the seconded employee, the non-resident dispatching company or the Chinese receiving company. If it is the former, as long as the presence of seconded employee in China reached the threshold under the domestic law and tax treaties, the non-resident company would be considered to have permanent establishment in China.

In 2010, the tax bureau of Suzhou Industrial Park, in response to the SAT's general policy, carried out an industry-oriented investigation and one of the targeted sectors was the hotel business. A local hotel, which contracted with an international hotel management group in the Netherlands ('Dutch group'), drew their attention. Under the contract, the Dutch group was exclusively responsible for the management of this Chinese hotel whereas the Chinese hotel paid the Dutch group a management fee at the amount of 2% of business profits plus 5% of the gross operating profits. The management fee was paid to a Hong Kong bank account on a monthly basis.

The Dutch group argued that this management fee was not subject to income tax in China since it had no permanent establishment in China. The tax bureau launched a factual investigation and found that three senior executives of the hotel, including the general manager, were from Hong Kong. Under the management contract, the Dutch group could appoint certain senior executives of the hotel subordinate to itself, and the general manager was to represent the Dutch group at monthly meetings of the hotel.

To ascertain the real employer of these Hong Kong employees, tax officials examined the records of the hotel on the payment of foreign exchange and found that the monthly payments made by the hotel to the Dutch group exceeds the management fee and covered the insurance premium of the Hong Kong employees paid abroad. Furthermore, the records which the hotel filed with the local exit-entry administration bureau and the bureau of labour and social security show that these Hong Kong employees were employed by the Dutch group to handle the management affairs in the hotel. As further disclosed by tax authorities, the Dutch group ultimately admitted the existence of the employment contract with these three Hong Kong employees. Relying on the SAT circular No. 19[2009], the tax agency required the Dutch group to register as a permanent establishment in China, pay tax on the profits deriving therefrom and also pay the overdue tax.

This ruling was pioneering as it predates the SAT's guidance in circular No. 75[2010] which, for the first time, touches upon the permanent establishment issue arising from cross-border secondment. In circular No. 75[2010], the situations are depicted as to whether the parent company of a contracting state, by sending its employees to the subsidiary of the other contracting state, could create a permanent establishment in the other contracting state. The delineation line, according to this circular, rests upon a responsibility and risk analysis, that is, which company has the authority to instruct the employee(s) and which company bears responsibilities or risk for the results produced by the employee's work. In addition, the circular provides a list of four factors[100] to illustrate when the employee would be considered to perform duties for the parent company.

But circular No. 75[2010] has its limitations in dealing with the permanent establishment issue in cross-border secondment since it does not cover scenarios where the dispatching company and the receiving company have no parent-subsidiary relationship. It was not until the SAT issued bulletin No. 19[2013] in April 2013 that this gap was filled. In general, bulletin No. 19[2013] is a continuation of the principles set forth in circular No. 75[2010], and beyond that, it takes a step further by expanding the list of considerations to include five factors, extending the exceptional clause to situations when the dispatched employees are executing the shareholder's right of the dispatching company as well as clarifying documentation requirement in the tax assessment.[101]

According to the official commentary issued by the general office of the SAT along with the promulgation of bulletin No. 19[2013], if it can be substantiated that the non-resident dispatching company bears the risk and responsibility of the dispatched employee, as long as any one of the five factors is met, the dispatched employee would be considered to constitute a permanent establishment of the non-resident dispatching company. The five factors are as follows:

(i) The Chinese receiving company pays the non-resident dispatching company management fees or makes payments in the nature of service fees.
(ii) The payment to the non-resident dispatching company from the Chinese receiving company exceeds the dispatched employee's wages, salaries, social security contributions and other expenses borne by the non-resident dispatching company.
(iii) The non-resident dispatching company does not pass on all the related payments made by the Chinese receiving company to the dispatched employee; instead, the non-resident dispatching company retains a portion of such payments.
(iv) The dispatched employee's wages and salaries borne by the non-resident dispatching company are not fully subject to the individual income tax in China.
(v) The non-resident dispatching company may decide number, qualification, remuneration and working locations of the dispatched employees in China.

100. According to circular No. 75 [2010], the four factors include the following: (1) overseas parent company can instruct the work of seconded employees and assume the relevant responsibilities and risks resulting from their work; (2) number of seconded employees, as well as their qualification are determined by the overseas parent company; (3) salary of seconded employees is borne by the overseas parent company; and (4) overseas parent company derives profits from secondment of such employees.

101. For detailed description on bulletin No. 19 [2013], *see* Ernst & Young, *SAT Further Regulates Cross-border Secondment Arrangement*, Issue No. 2013003, 30 May 2013, http://www.ey.com/Publication/vwLUAssets/CTIN2013003_en/$FILE/CTIN2013003ENG.pdf, visited on 22 July 2013.

Based on the official commentary, if dispatched employees' wages and salaries borne by the non-resident dispatching company are fully subject to the individual income tax in China, this may be sufficient evidence to disprove that the non-resident dispatching company has an establishment or permanent establishment in China.

The *Suzhou* ruling and the evolutionary development of the SAT rules exhibit the dynamic changes of tax law interpretation in China. The SAT is driven by the practical need to pronounce rules to address various types of transactions. As the tax rules multiply and grow in complexity, to master a certain tax subject requires not only the reading of a set of tax rules and official commentaries that come hand in hand, but also, keeping an eye open for possible new rules to come.

§5.08 A BRIEF SUMMARY

The unique feature in the interpretation of tax law in China, as this research shows, is that administrative organs have been enjoying the near monopoly status in interpreting rules. Problems arise due to the centralization of powers and the lack of effective check, such as *ultra vires* interpretation, inconsistencies among the interpretative rules and the conflict with international norms. Judiciary has been and may continue to remain feeble in the tax field in the years to come especially when the cultural bondage, legal barriers and institutional hindrance remain in place.

Even so, there is still hope that interpretation of tax law in China will move forward following its own path, so as to adhere closer to basic principles of law which require predictability, transparency and legitimacy. This glimmer of hope derives from the following observations: tax legislation powers have been gradually restored to the hand of the legislative body; the state council and its ministries, subject to intrinsic regulatory constraints and the external supervision, are taking visible actions to rein in their own powers to enact and interpret the law; the SAT, following the domestic call to 'administrate according to the law', has begun to shift more consideration to the rights of taxpayers, reconsider the roles of tax agencies and put serious efforts into prevent the abusive use of authorities by tax agencies. The removal of some legislative obstacles for taxpayers to seek judicial remedies implies that courts may play an increasingly important role in tax disputes in the years to come. Externally, the integration of China into the international tax community requires the government to be more attentive to international norms and practices in other countries. Some modest but significant steps are now being taken. There is still a long way to go, but as Lao Tzu has wisely advised, every journey begins with a single step.

CHAPTER 6

Legal Interpretation of Tax Law: The European Union

Robert F. van Brederode & Gerard Meussen

§6.01 INTRODUCTION*

The relationship between European Union law (further: Union law), formerly referred to as Community law, and the national laws of its Member States is complicated. The treaties establishing the European Communities[1] and later the European Union have created a law system sui generis with its own terminology and underlying legal

* In the first edition of this book, the chapter on the European Union was co-authored by Tom O' Shea.

1. Treaty of 25 March 1957 establishing the European Economic Community, 298 UNTS 11 (entered into force 1 January 1958); treaty of 18 April 1951, establishing the European Coal and Steel Community, 261 UNTS 167 (entered into force as of 23 July 1952); Treaty of 25 March 1957, establishing the EURATOM, 298 UNTS 167 (entered into force on 1 January 1958). Together EURATOM, ECSC, and the EEC are the founding treaties of European integration as amended by later treaties. The ECSC expired on 23 July 2002, and since then the coal and steel sectors are incorporated within the legal scope of the EEC Treaty. The Maastricht Treaty of 1992 (OJ C191 of 29 July 1992) changed the name EEC to EC for the simple reason that the Community, beyond mere economic policy, is concerned with social, cultural and environmental policies. It also established the European Union (EU). The terminology may be confusing, especially to the non-European reader. It is important to realise that EC and EURATOM, with their common structures and institutions remain totally in place. The EU comprises the totality of the relations between the Member States, but is not a separate legal entity. The EU, therefore, is in essence a combination of supranational and intergovernmental power, but in the political sense only. Following the rejection of the proposed European Constitution in French and Dutch referendums in 2005, the Member States signed the Treaty of Lisbon on 13 December 2007, which retains much of the content of the rejected Constitution. It amends both the Treaty on European Union and the Treaty establishing the European Community, which is renamed Treaty on the Functioning of the European Union (TFEU).

principles.[2] Union law is the common internal law in the Member States rather than a law between the states as would be the case with traditional international law. Beyond the mere creation of mutual rights and duties between the states, as under traditional international law, it regulates the relation between the EU and its subjects, including both the Member States and private and legal persons, and between these subjects amongst themselves.[3] As a distinctive legal order, Union law regulates the powers, rights and obligations of the Union and its subjects and provides for the procedures required for determining, adjudicating and sanctioning of infringements of the law.[4] Union law is not common law or civil law; therefore, legal principles and precedents developed under common or civil law have no direct bearing on Union law.[5] Even if the same legal terminology is used, there exists no pertinence that the meaning would be the same.[6] According to established case law of the Court of Justice of the European Union (ECJ), Union law has priority over the national laws of the Member States.[7] Primacy of Union law arises from the treaty itself, because without it realisation of the objectives of the EU, in particular the establishment of an internal market, would be illusory.[8] When a country accedes to membership of the EU, it voluntarily limits its sovereign rights in favour of the Union it has decided to join. The Union only has the competences conferred on it by the Treaties, either exclusively or shared with the Member States. In the area of taxation, insofar as it affects intra-EU cross-border trade, competence is shared with preemption,[9] i.e., when and to the extent the Union exercises its competence, the Member States lose their individual competence.

Where in interstate legal transactions interpretation of the agreement is a matter for the contracting parties, the actions of the contracting parties of the EU and their subjects is supervised by the ECJ. National courts operate within and can rely on and refer to their national legal tradition, but that was not the case at the European level. The ECJ had to create such a legal order from the texts of the treaties and by reference to general principles of law, such as good faith, legal certainty, equality, legitimate

2. *See*, e.g., ECJ, 5 February 1963, Case 26/62, *Van Gend & Loos v. Administratie der Belastingen*, [1963] ECR 3; ECJ, 15 July 1964, Case 6/64, *Flaminio Costa v. E.N.E.L*, [1964] ECR 1194; ECJ, 19 November 1991, Joined Cases C-6/90 and C-9/90, *Andrea Francovich and Danila Bonifaci and others v. Italy*, [1991] ECR I-5357.
3. *See*, P.J.G Kapteyn, A.M. McDonnell, K.J.M. Mortelmans and C.W.A. Timmermans (eds), *The Law of the European Union and the European Communities*, 4th rev. edn (The Netherlands: Wolters Kluwer, 2008), Chapter II, especially pp. 71 et seq.
4. ECJ, 13 November 1964, Joined Cases 90/63 and 91/63, *Commission v. Luxembourg and Belgium*, [1964] ECR 1217.
5. ECJ, 14 January 1982, Case 64/81, *Nicolaus Corman & Fils SA v. Hauptzollamt Gronau*, [1982] ECR 13.
6. ECJ, 1 February 1977, Case 51/76, *Verbond van Nederlandse Ondernemingen v. Inspecteur der invoerrechten en accijnzen*, [1977] ECR 113.
7. First formulated in *Costa v. E.N.E.L*, *supra* note 2.
8. The supremacy of EC law is a cornerstone principle of Community law, but it is not provided for by the treaties. A Declaration attached to the Lisbon treaty provides, however, that 'in accordance with the settled case-law of the ECJ, the treaties and the law adopted by the EU on the basis of the treaties have primacy over the law of member states, under the conditions laid down by the said case-law'. Although it is not legally binding this Declaration represents the Member States' recognition of the ECJ case law on primacy of Community law.
9. The competence in the field of taxation is based on Art. 4(2)(a) TFEU.

expectations, proportionality[10] and abuse of rights.[11] These principles are derived either directly from the treaties or found to be common to the legal systems of the Member States.

There exists also a cooperative relationship between Union law and the laws of the Member States. Union law may refer to national law;[12] national law may supplement Union rules[13] or serve to implement them. The Union system of law affects the law of the Member States to the extent of the legal instrument applied to shape EU policy. The most important legal instruments are regulations and directives. A regulation is directly applicable in every Member State, i.e., it does not require any action by the national legislature, and can convey rights to and impose obligations on the Member States, their bodies and on individuals.[14] A directive, however, is only binding on each Member State as to the result to be achieved, but leaves to the national authorities the choice of form and methods.[15]

Member States are required to loyally cooperate with Union law, a principle derived by the ECJ from Article 10 of the EC treaty (now Article 4 TFEU), and which includes the legal obligation for the states to pay damages for losses incurred by individuals as a result of the non-compliance of a state with Union law.[16]

Private parties may invoke directly effective provisions of Union law before their national courts, also in cases where national rules conflict with or deviate from Union law. In the latter case, national courts must refrain from applying these national legal measures. The national courts are entrusted with the legal protection of citizens under Union law[17] and legal actions taken in this respect must follow national legal procedures and national rules on court jurisdiction. In this sense, national courts also act as Union courts. As a general rule, a litigant who wishes to invoke Union law must approach a national court. There exists no direct access to the ECJ for private parties in respect of Union law based on regulations and directives. The impact of Union law on

10. Later included in the EC Treaty through Art. 5 (now Art. 5 TFEU) and therewith generally applicable to Community action. *See also* Protocol No 2 TFEU.
11. *See*, T. Tridimas, *The General Principles of EU Law*, 2nd edn. Oxford EC Law Library (Oxford: Oxford University Press, 2006) and H.G. Schermers and D. Waelbroeck, *Judicial Protection in the European Communities*, 6th edn (Deventer: Kluwer Law International, 2001).
12. For instance, the nationality requirement plays an important role in determining who benefits from the freedom of establishment or the free movement of employees; and national law determines who is eligible to plead before the ECJ, *see* Art. 19, Statute of the Court of Justice.
13. Decisions of the ECJ, for example, are implemented in accordance with the procedures applicable in the various Member States, *see* Art. 299 TFEU (formerly Art. 256 of the EEC Treaty).
14. Article 288, 2nd para. TFEU (formerly Art. 249(2) EC).
15. Article 288, 3rd para. TFEU (formerly Art. 249(2) EC). Forms and methods, however, should be chosen in such a way that the stated result or objective of a certain provision in the Directive is also in fact achieved, *see* ECJ, 8 April 1976, Case 48/75, *Jean Noël Royer*, [1976] ECR 497, para. 75; and ECJ, 23 November 1977, Case 38/77, *Enka v. Inspecteur der invoerrechten en accijnzen*, [1977] ECR 2203, para. 11.
16. *Francovich, supra* note 2.
17. On the basis of Art. 10 EC, later Art. 4(3) EU. *See also*, ECJ, 16 December 1976, Case 33/76, *Rewe-Zentralfinanz eG and Rewe-Zentral AG v. Landwirtschaftskammer für das Saarland*, [1976] ECR 198, para. 5.

the national systems of law is, therefore, first and foremost in the hands of the national courts.

The ECJ is not placed above the national courts; they have distinct jurisdictions, but cooperate where Union law overlaps national law. Judicial cooperation is a key element in assessing the extent to which Union law affects national law or, from a different perspective, in measuring the effectiveness of Union law. This aspect is dealt with in §6.03 of this chapter. Another determining factor of Union law effectiveness is the method of interpretation used by the courts when called to explain Union law. Methods of interpretation are covered in §6.04 with focus solely on tax case law. Apart from the research subject of this book, the choice of tax case law would be a natural one, because taxation, and in particular indirect taxes, play a crucial role in realising the internal market as will be explained in §5.02. When discussing the methods of interpretation, we will focus on the guidance provided by the ECJ in this respect and then examine a limited number of cases in respect of value added tax (VAT) and Direct Tax respectively. A separate section (§6.05) is devoted to the doctrine of abuse of law as it is applied in combating tax fraud and evasion. Summary and conclusions are found in the final section.

§6.02 THE ESSENTIAL ROLE OF TAXATION IN REALISING THE INTERNAL MARKET

The most important tool used to realise the political and economic objectives of the EU is the establishment of a common or internal market. The common market has internal and external components. Externally, its aim is to create equal treatment of foreign trade among the Member States. This had been realised by the introduction of a common customs tariff. Internally, the aim is the creation of a single economic area, including all Member States, establishing free competition among businesses regardless of their location or nationality.

The foundations for the internal component are laid down with the formulation of the four freedoms, that is, the free movement of persons, services, goods and capital.[18] The free movement of goods implies the abolishment of existing and prevention of future trade barriers. This is partly realised by founding the internal market on a customs union. A customs union[19] implies the establishment of a common outer tariff, replacing the preceding tariffs of each individual state and preventing the diversion of trade,[20] and the abolition of internal import and export duties among the Member States.

The founding states realised that differences between the states in indirect tax systems could be the route to distortion of competition. They feared that the abolition

18. Article 26(2) TFEU, jo. Arts 28 and 29 (free movement of goods) and Arts 45 et seq. (free movement of persons, services and capital) TFEU (formerly Arts 14(2), 23, 24 and 39 EC).
19. Articles 25–31 EC.
20. If internal customs duties are abolished but Member States were to maintain their individual rates for trade with third countries, in reality products would be imported into the state with the lowest duties and then forwarded to the state of destination, effectively avoiding the higher rates applied by the latter state.

of internal customs tariffs, required to constitute the customs union, would simply trigger replacement by discriminatory border tax adjustments (BTA) for other indirect taxes. One of the problems at the time was that all of the founding Member States, with the exception of France, had a turnover tax, levied at each stage of the supply chain from manufacturer to final consumer. Under the assumption of the forward shifting of taxes, exact calculation of the domestic tax burden on a certain product cannot be accommodated under a turnover tax system because the tax actually incurred will depend on the length of the supply chain and the level of vertical integration.[21] As a result, it is equally impossible to determine the tax rate to be levied on importation or to be rebated on exportation in order to create a level playing field of competition. It was clear to all involved that BTAs based on estimations were in violation of the principles of neutrality and fair competition, and would be a threat to the realisation of the internal market. Harmonisation of the general sales tax systems would be required to avoid tariff manipulation at the border in an effort to create competitive advantages for domestic traders.[22] The choice was eventually made to replace the existing turnover taxes with a non-cumulative sales tax system, the VAT, that allows exact calculations of BTA.[23] A VAT is also levied on the sales that occur at each stage of the supply chain, but the difference from a turnover tax is that a credit is given for the tax incurred on business procurement. Therefore, under this system, tax accumulation or pyramiding is prevented and the domestic tax burden will always be equivalent to the price times the statutory rate.[24] As a result, exact BTAs are possible to ensure that exported goods are effectively untaxed and imported goods are taxed at the exact same level as domestically produced goods.

Clearly, indirect tax plays a vital role in assuring the proper functioning of the internal market, especially the free movement of goods, by creating a neutral environment, i.e., a level playing field, for competition. For that reason, harmonisation initially concentrated on indirect tax.

The harmonisation of indirect taxes is specifically provided for in the Treaties,[25] and it has been quite extensive, but there is no corresponding provision for direct taxes. Harmonisation of direct tax is, therefore, based on the general harmonisation provision

21. Turnover or gross receipt taxes (GRT) are still applied, particularly in the US at the sub-national level of government. For a concise treatise on the legal and economic complexities of GRTs in the US, *see* Robert F. van Brederode, *The Re-emergence of Gross Receipt Taxes in the US*, 19 (3) Int'l VAT Monitor, 182–191 (2008); and John L. Mikesell, *Gross Receipt Taxes in State Government Finances: A Review of Their History and Performance*. Background Paper, no. 53 (Washington, DC: Tax Foundation, January 2007).
22. Indeed, in practice the Member States displayed a continuous tendency to employ BTAs as protectionist measures; *see* Walter Hahn, *Steuerpolitische Willensbildungsprozeße in der Europäischen Gemeinschaft: das Beispiel der Umsatzsteuer-Harmonisierung* [*Tax Policy Process in the European Community: The Example of VAT Harmonization*] (Frankfurt am Main, 1988), at 88.
23. For an overview of the history of the tax harmonisation in the EU, *see*, Robert F. van Brederode, *Systems of General Sales Taxation: Theory, Policy and Practice* (Alphen aan den Rijn: Wolters Kluwer, Series in International Taxation 33, 2009), Ch. 10.2.4.
24. For a comparison of the different sales tax systems, especially retail sales tax, GRT and VAT, *see* Robert F. van Brederode, *supra*, Ch. 3.
25. *See* Art. 113 TFEU, formerly Art. 99 EC.

contained in Article 115 TFEU.[26] However, as this is an area of shared competence, the Union is restricted in its legislative actions by the principles of subsidiarity and proportionality. The former requires for Union action that the objectives sought cannot be sufficiently achieved through action of the Member States and can be better achieved at the EU level. The latter requires that Union action does not exceed the boundaries of what is needed to achieve the objectives of the Treaties.

To date, only four direct tax directives have been adopted: the Parent-Subsidiary Directive on intra-group cross-border dividends, the Tax Merger Directive on the tax consequences of cross-border mergers, the Interest and Royalty Directive on the intra-group cross-border payments of interest and royalties, and the Savings Directive on taxation of interest on savings in other Member States.[27] In addition, there are directives in the area of mutual assistance and recovery of taxes. The limited scope of direct tax harmonisation leaves more autonomy to the Member States. However, as parties to the Treaties, they have to exercise their competence in compliance with Union law. In particular, they must observe in their legislative efforts the rights of free movement granted to tax payers.

The tax law of the EU is, generally, laid down in the legal format of directives, which need to be implemented into national law.[28] Directives are binding as to their result but the Member States are free in their choice of form and means. Economic distortions may still occur where Member States deviate from the principles of the directives, or where the Member States apply, in law or practice, different interpretations of the same rules. In those instances, the proper functioning of the common market will depend on the judiciary, charged with guarding the integrity of Union law, i.e., the cooperation between the national courts and the ECJ as well as the guidance given by the latter to the former in how Union law should be understood and interpreted.

§6.03 COOPERATION BETWEEN NATIONAL COURTS AND ECJ

[A] Function of Preliminary Rulings

The cooperative relationship between the national courts with respect to their role as Union courts and the ECJ hinges upon Article 267 TFEU (formerly Article 234 EC), which provides the national courts with the eligibility or obligation to raise, and the ECJ with the jurisdiction to answer, preliminary questions on the validity and interpretation of Union law, including tax directives.

The text of Article 267 is as follows:

> The Court of Justice shall have jurisdiction to give preliminary rulings concerning:
>
> (a) The interpretation of the Treaties;

26. Formerly Art. 94 EC.
27. For a comprehensive overview, *see* Ben J.M. Terra and Peter J. Wattel, *European Tax Law*, 6th edn (Deventer: Wolters Kluwer, 2012), Chs 9, 10, 13 and 14 respectively.
28. The only exception is Customs Law, which is based on Regulations.

(b) The validity and interpretation of acts of the institutions, bodies, offices or agencies of the Union;

Where such a question is raised before any court or tribunal of a Member State, that court or tribunal may, if it considers that a decision on the question is necessary to enable it to give judgment, request the Court of Justice to give a ruling thereon.

Where any such question is raised in a case pending before a court or tribunal of a Member State against whose decisions there is no judicial remedy under national law, that court or tribunal shall bring the matter before the Court of Justice.

(...)

The purpose of this provision is to ensure correct and uniform application of Union law in all Member States. In the words of the ECJ: '(...) for the preservation of the Community character of law established by the Treaty and (...) ensuring that in all circumstances this law is the same in all states of the Community.'[29] It is important to realise that, each within its own jurisdiction, ECJ and national courts cooperate to achieve this objective.

The national courts have the authority and right, and if it is a court of last instance it is obliged, to ask preliminary questions if an issue of interpretation or validity of EU law is raised before it either by the parties or by the national court itself ex officio. If so, a national court will suspend proceedings and notify the ECJ of the decision to refer the matter.[30]

A preliminary ruling is binding on the national court hearing the case.[31] That does not mean that a national court is excluded from raising more preliminary questions in the same case. If new facts arise, or the application of the first reference leads to complications or a totally new issue emerges, a new reference for a preliminary ruling may be due.[32] The preliminary ruling given by the ECJ in a certain case has 'authority of interpretation'[33] for all courts other than the one that raised the question.

The functions of the ECJ and the national courts are distinct: the first is limited to the interpretation of Union law and to deciding whether actions by the Union or its institutions are valid, the latter have to apply Union law (as interpreted and explained by the ECJ) to the facts of the case. For example, the ECJ does not have the competence to opine on whether certain national laws are incompatible with Union law, but will provide the referring court with sufficient interpretation to enable it to make such a decision. This functional separation between interpretation and application is not as

29. ECJ, 16 January 1974, Case 166/73, *Rheinmühlen-Düsseldorf v. Einfuhr- und Vorratsstelle für Getreide und Futtermittel* (II), [1974] ECR 33, para. 2.
30. Article 23, Statute of the Court of Justice.
31. ECJ, 24 June 1969, Case 29/68, *Milch- Fett und Eierkontor GmbH v. Hauptzollamt Saarbrücken*, [1969] ECR 165, para. 2.
32. For an example of multiple references in the same case, *see* ECJ, 12 December 2006, Case C-446/04, *Test Claimants in the FII Group Litigation*, [2006] ECR I-11753; ECJ, 12 November 2012, Case C-35/11, *Test Claimants in the FII Group Litigation 2*, ECLI:EU:C:2012:707; and ECJ, 12 December 2013, Case C-362/12, *Test Claimants in the FII Group Litigation 3*, ECLI-:EU:C:2013:834, *see* AG Opinion of 5 September 2013.
33. ECJ, 27 March 1963, Joined Cases 28/62 and 30/62, *Da Costa en Schaake NV et al. v. Nederlandse Belastingadministratie*, [1963] ECR 11.

strict in practice as it may be in theory, simply because the ECJ renders it ruling on the interpretation of Union law within the context of the facts of the referred case. The facts and circumstances may be so specific that the preliminary ruling given by the ECJ cannot be generally applied.[34]

The ECJ can only deal with issues that are brought before it, usually by a preliminary ruling request procedure or by an infringement action initiated by the European Commission. The obligation and entitlement of national courts under Article 267 to refer questions is, therefore, a crucial element of the effectiveness of Union law. In itself, questions related to the interpretation of Article 267, which article of course is also part of Union law, are subject to the oversight of the ECJ.

From the perspective of progressing harmonisation the collaboration between national courts and the ECJ is crucial. The relationship is also delicate given the dichotomy between national autonomy and centralism. In a recent case, the UK Supreme Court took the unprecedented step of ignoring the ECJ's preliminary ruling on grounds that its judgment was based upon an incomplete evaluation of the facts of the case and failed to reflect the legal arguments made before it, because the referring court[35] had not clearly presented the central issues and related facts.[36] The Supreme Court explained that where the ECJ is charged with interpreting Union law, the national courts must evaluate the facts of the case and the application of Union law to those facts following the preliminary reference. As stated before, one cannot make a surgical divide between interpretation and application. Regardless of the underlying merits of the case, preliminary rulings are binding on the referring court[37] and by ignoring the ECJ's ruling the UK will have violated Union law, exposing it to infringement procedures. Moreover, it has created a precedent, which (unintentionally) invites courts of other Member States to ignore ECJ rulings that are considered unfavourable. Instead, the UK Supreme Court should have posed new preliminary questions to the ECJ presenting the complete set of facts, since a national court is not excluded from re-addressing the ECJ in the same case.

---

34. *See*, e.g., ECJ, 11 June 2009, Case C-572/07, *RLRE Tellmer Property s.r.o. v. Finanní editelství v. Ústí nad Labem*, [2009] ECR I-4983 where the Court was called to decide whether cleaning services had to be treated as a single bundled service with the letting of a residential building (exempt from VAT) or as an independent service (taxed). The Court concluded that it was an independent service but this conclusion was based on the fact that the service was separately invoiced and the tenants were in the position to acquire the cleaning services from a third party supplier. The weight of these specific facts on the outcome of the case should prevent the conclusion that ancillary services, as a general rule, should be unbundled from the principle leasing service for VAT purposes.
35. The House of Lords, the predecessor of the UK Supreme Court.
36. UK Supreme Court, 13 March 2013, *HMRC v. Aimia Coalition Loyalty UK Limited*, [2013] UKSC 15. For an extensive commentary on the case, *see* Geoffrey Morse and Rita de la Feria, *HMRC v Aimia Coalition Loyalty UK Ltd (UKSC): A Question Too Far?* 3 BTR, 287–298 (2013).
37. *See supra* note 31.

[B] Conditions for Preliminary Ruling Request

Article 267 provides any national court with the right to refer a question to the ECJ, but mandates a reference by the court of last resort. According to the ECJ this has to be understood as the highest court in the case and not necessarily as the highest court in the national hierarchy,[38] which is an important distinction because not all issues can be escalated in all jurisdictions to the highest hierarchical court.

In the highly acclaimed *CILFIT*-case the ECJ took the opportunity to provide further guidance to the national courts in regard of their obligations under Article 267 (then Article 234 EC).[39] An Italian Court of Appeals had raised the question whether the obligation to consult the ECJ was absolute. The ECJ pointed out that the obligation to refer preliminary questions of Union law is not absolute. If it were, individual persons would have been given direct access to the ECJ. The ECJ then explained the parameters of the obligation to consult. It held that a national court of last resort is obliged to consult the ECJ, unless:

- the issue of Community (Union) law raised has no direct bearing on the outcome of the underlying case;
- the question raised relates to a point of law on which the ECJ has ruled earlier (acte éclairé doctrine);
- there is no reasonable doubt about the answers to the question raised (acte clair doctrine).

Since the obligation to consult the ECJ is expressly postulated, it is assumed that the above is an exhaustive summary of exceptions. Moreover, the exceptions appear in a fixed order, which must be followed by the national courts.

[1] Relevance

The first exception basically asks a national court to consider whether a decision on Union law is required to enable it to render judgment. If that is not the case, the national court is under no obligation to refer. Without this condition, the absurd situation would emerge of addressing the ECJ with questions the answer to which have no bearing on the solution of the case that the referring court is hearing. The relevance of the question is a precondition for the right, respectively the obligation to refer to the ECJ.[40] In principle, the assessment of the relevance of a question is the prerogative of the national court. The national court needs to decide whether a preliminary ruling on the interpretation of Union law is needed and the ECJ, in accordance with its distinct role and jurisdiction, will neither question nor criticise the grounds of the referring court's assessment. In other words, relevance is presumed.[41] Having that said, the

38. *Costa v. E.N.E.L, supra* note 2.
39. ECJ, 6 October 1982, Case 283/81, *Srl CILFIT et al. v. Ministry of Health*, [1982] ECR 3415.
40. P.J.G. Kapteyn et al., *supra* note 3, at 496.
41. ECJ, 5 December 2006, Joint Cases C-94/04, *Frederico Cipola v. Rosaria Fazari* and C-202/04, *Stefano Macrino and Claudia Capodarte v. Roberto Meloni*, [2006] ECR I-11421, para. 25.

ECJ's role under Article 267 is linked to the resolution of a dispute and, therefore, it does not accept jurisdiction where the questions raised are not connected to a real dispute, but are general or hypothetical in nature.[42] Other than that the ECJ cannot refuse to hear a case.

[2] Acte Eclairé

If the question raised is, indeed, relevant for the outcome of the case, the national court should determine whether it is exonerated from asking preliminary questions under the second exception. It would be unsubstantial to approach the ECJ with questions the Court has already answered in earlier cases. It is essential to establish whether in these earlier cases the questions relate to the same point of law and, therefore, already, have been clarified. The questions do not have to be strictly identical, nor is it required that the previous rulings were given in Article 267 proceedings.[43] Nevertheless, a national court is always entitled to bring a matter before the ECJ if it believes the latter may redefine legal principles or reconsider earlier rulings.[44] Another reason to address the ECJ with a request for a preliminary ruling on matters raised earlier arises when the facts or rules involved are slightly different than in previous preliminary ruling requests, or when uncertainty exists as to the proper interpretation of these earlier rulings. The *Tellmer*-case[45] referred to earlier in this section is a good example. The language of the proceedings that has force of law is the language of the court requesting a preliminary ruling. In this case that was the Czech language. Commentators using translations disagreed on whether the ruling had only relevance for the particular case (the translation referring to 'the tenants') or had general application (the translation referring to 'tenants'). This disagreement cannot be resolved without a further reference to the ECJ because the language of the proceedings, Czech, does not know the definite particle and cannot, therefore, offer any solution in the matter.

[3] Acte Clair

The last exceptions offered by the ECJ is generally known as the 'acte claire' doctrine.[46] In the words of the Court 'the correct application of Community law may be so evident that no reasonable doubt can exist as to the manner in which the question raised must

42. *See*, e.g., ECJ, 16 December 1981, Case 244/80, *Foglia v. Novello*, [1981] ECR 3045; ECJ, 22 November 1978, Case 93/78, *Mattheus v. Doego Fruchtimport und Tiefkühlkost eG*, [1978] ECR 2203; and ECJ, 12 June 2003, Case C-112/00, *Eugen Schmidberger, Internationale Transporte und Planzüge v. Republik Österreich*, [2003] ECR I-5659, especially paras 30–33 that provide an overview of relevant case law.
43. *CILFIT, supra* note 39, para. 14.
44. *CILFIT, supra* note 39, para. 15. Therefore, the same question may be referred as, for example for tax law in ECJ, 6 March 2007, Case C-292/04, *Meilicke*, [2007] ECR I-01835, following ECJ 7 September 2004, Case C-319/02, *Petri Manninen*, [2004] ECR I-7477.
45. *Supra* note 34.
46. The acte clair theory was developed in France by the judiciary to offset the power granted to the executive branch of government to interpret international treaties.

be resolved.'[47] This exception appears to have the charm of being obvious and pragmatic. There seems to be no rationale to mandate referral of questions to which the answer is clear. On the other hand, this exception bears the risk of being used by national courts to maintain their autonomy and even to set aside case law of the ECJ with which they do not agree. This risk is not just hypothetical as demonstrated by the infamous *Cohn-Bendit* case, in which the French Conseil d'Etat, despite settled case law of the ECJ, disallowed an individual to challenge an administrative decision, which conflicted with a directive.[48] Perhaps cautious for this reason,[49] the ECJ attached an absolute condition to the application of the acte clair doctrine. Before coming to the conclusion that the answer to a question of Union law is obvious, the national court must be convinced that the matter would be 'equally obvious to the courts of the other Member States and to the ECJ'.[50] While making this assessment, a national court must take into account that all 24 language versions of Union law have equal authenticity and, as a consequence, a comparison of the different versions will be required for its interpretation.[51] In addition, a national court must realise that the nature of Union law is unique in its context and concepts and, therefore, needs to be interpreted separately from national rules.[52] These caveats clearly serve the purpose to press on the national courts how delicate their role is in realising uniform interpretation of Union law and

47. *CILFIT, supra* note 39, para. 16.
48. Conseil d'Etat of 22 December 1978, in *Ministre de l'intérieur v. Cohn-Bendit*, [1978] *Recueil Lebon* 524, also published in [1979] CMLR 701. Cohn-Bendit is a German national who was deported from France as one of the leaders of the 1968 student revolt in Paris. Several years later he sought to return to pursue a job opportunity, but the government refused to rescind the deportation order, which refusal Cohn-Bendit challenged on the grounds of infringement of Directive 64/221/EEC of 25 February 1964 on the coordination of special measures concerning the movement and residence of foreign nationals which are justified on grounds of public policy, public security or public health, [1964] OJ, 056, 850. The lower court (Tribunal Administratif) decided to refer preliminary questions to the ECJ regarding the interpretation of said directive. By doing so, the Tribunal implicitly recognised the principle of direct effect of a directive. On appeal, the Conseil d'Etat overturned the decision and disallowed the reference.
49. It took until 1989 before the Conseil d'Etat changed course, *see* Conseil d'Etat, 3 February 1989, *Compagnie Alitalia*, [1989] *Recueil Lebon* 44, and 20 October 1989, *Nicolo*, [1989] *Recueil Lebon* 190. For further reading *see*, for example, Lionel Neville Brown, John Bell and Jean-Michel Galabert, *French Administrative Law*, 5th edn (Oxford University Press, 1998): 284, 285; Trevor C. Hartley, *The Foundations of European Community Law: An Introduction to the Constitutional and Administrative Law of the European Community*, 6th edn (Oxford: Oxford University Press, 2007), 250 et seq.; Philippe Manin, 'The Nicolo case of the Conseil d'Etat: French Constitutional Law and the Supreme Administrative Court's Acceptance of the Primacy of Community Law over Subsequent National Statute Law', *CMLR* 499 (1991); and Andrew Oppenheimer (ed.), *The Relationship Between European Community Law and National Law: The Cases*, Vol. 2 (Cambridge: Cambridge University Press, 2003), 195 et seq. In Germany, the Bundesfinanzhof was as reluctant in accepting the direct effect of provisions of the Sixth VAT Directive, until the intervention by the Bundesverfaßungsgericht (Constitutional Court), 8 April 1987, case 2 BvR 687/85, [1988] 3 *CMLR* 1. For further reading *see*, for example, Cecile Brokelind (ed.), *Towards a Homogeneous EC Direct Tax Law: An Assessment of the Member States* (Amsterdam: IBFD, 2007), 31 et seq.; and Henry G. Schermers and Denis F. Waelbroeck, *Judicial Protection in the European Communities* (Deventer: Wolters Kluwer, 1992), 133 et seq.; Andrew Oppenheimer, *supra*, 232 et seq.
50. *CILFIT, supra* note 39, para. 17.
51. *CILFIT, supra* note 39, para. 18.
52. *CILFIT, supra* note 39, paras 19 and 20.

how careful they have to be when making the decision not to refer a question to the ECJ. An example of a national court applying the acte clair doctrine is a Netherlands case where the Supreme Court had to decide, among other issues, whether the sale of the single immoveable property could be regarded in terms of the directive as a (non-taxable) 'totality of assets' in the meaning of Article 5(8) of the Sixth Directive[53] (now Article 19 of Directive 2006/112[54]). In the view of the Supreme Court that was not the case, and it added there '[could not] reasonably be room for doubt' on the subject.[55] Evidently, from the choice of words, the Supreme Court believed that the 'acte claire' doctrine applied in this case and it did not follow a recommendation to ask preliminary questions. No explanation was given, however, as to why this was such a clear case,[56] which is unfortunate given the conditions introduced by the ECJ for the use of the acte clair doctrine.

§6.04 INTERPRETATION OF EU TAX LAW

[A] General Approach of ECJ and Sources

The ECJ is charged with ensuring that the law is observed in the interpretation and application of the treaty.[57] Above the task of supervising the actions of all Member States and their organs, this includes the task of developing the EU legal order. National courts operate within the context of legal principles and concepts, collectively constituting a national legal tradition. Such a tradition did not exist at the supranational level with the inception of the EU. However, such a legal tradition is essential for the administration of justice, because legal questions cannot be resolved exclusively on the basis of the text of the treaties. For that purpose, the ECJ built a framework for the interpretation of treaty law, which would support the acceptance of said law and the interpretation given, because it is founded on general principles of law, such as legal certainty, equality, good faith, proportionality, non-discrimination and abuse of rights.[58] Basically, the ECJ fills lacunas in Union law by applying general principles of law, either directly derived from Union law itself or found in the legal traditions of the Member States, thus creating unwritten Union law. In essence, the ECJ applies

53. Sixth Directive (77/388/EEC) of 17 May 1977, [1977] OJ, L 145.
54. Directive 2006/112/EC of 28 November 2006, [2006] OJ, L 347/1.
55. Translation by author.
56. I assume the Court was guided by the use of the plural form: a single immoveable property cannot be a totality of assets, or in other language versions 'une universalité de biens' and 'ein Gesämtvermögen'.
57. Article 220 EEC.
58. *See* P.J.G. Kapteyn et al., *supra* note 3, at 421 et seq.; and more specifically Henry G. Schermers and Denis Waelbroeck, *Judicial Protection in the European Communities*, 6th edn (Deventer: Kluwer Law International, 2001). On interpretation methods, *see also*: Gordon Slynn, *The Court of Justice of the European Communities*, 33 I.C.L.Q., 409–429 (1984); Joxerramon Bengoetxea, *The Legal Reasoning of the European Court of Justice* (Oxford: Oxford University Press, 1993); Nial Fennelly, 'Legal Interpretation at the European Court of Justice', 20 (3) *Fordham International Law Journal*, 656–879 (1996); Miguel P. Maduro, 'Interpreting European Law: Judicial Adjudication in a Context of Constitutional Pluralism', 1 (2) *European Journal of Legal Studies*, 1–21 (2007).

comparative law techniques in its exercise of finding law. But many principles are also derived from the treaties themselves. Good examples are the principle of loyal cooperation and the principle of state liability for losses caused by state infringements of Union law, both originally based on Article 10 of the EC treaty (now Article 4 TFEU). State liability is particularly dealt with in §6.04[B].

Where all EU languages are equally authentic, linguistic comparison is a practical requirement when searching for a common meaning, but not an easy one especially for national courts, which are, unlike the ECJ, deprived of professional linguistic support.[59] In many instances linguistic ambiguity triggers a teleological solution; however, also when the textual meaning is clear the ECJ may refer to the purpose and context of a legal provision to support its reasoning.[60] As mentioned before, EU law has its own terminology and concepts. To understand and explain terms in the tax Directives, reference can be made to their meaning in other EU Directives (as further discussed in §6.04[C]). When interpreting EU law, the ECJ takes a teleological approach, i.e., it considers 'the general scheme;[61] the spirit, wording, the system and objectives;[62] and context'[63] of Treaties and tax law Directives. In doing so, the Court may make use of a wide range of sources, including the purpose and objectives contained in the treaties and tax Directives, legislative history, such as proposals by the European Commission.[64] Teleological interpretation by the ECJ takes place at two, connected levels. The Court does not limit itself to identifying the purpose of individual legal rules, but does so within the context of the purpose of the EU legal order. In other words, relevant is not just the purpose of specific rules that needs to be interpreted but also the purpose of the legal context in which those rules exist.[65]

[B] Application of European Legal Principles

There are many legal principles derived by the ECJ either from the treaties or from the legal traditions of the Member States, but two principles are particularly relevant to our purpose, namely the principle of equivalence and the principle of effectiveness, in

59. *See* on this subject, e.g., Lawrence M. Solan, 'The Interpretation of Multilingual Statutes by the European Court of Justice', 34 (2) *Brooklyn Journal of International Law*, 277–301 (2009); Mattias Derlén, *Multilingual Interpretation of European Union Law* (Alphen aan den Rijn: Kluwer Law International, 2009); and Gerd Toscani, 'Translation and Law – The Multilingual Context of the European Union Institutions', 30 *International Journal of Legal Information*: 288–307 (2002).
60. For an example related to VAT, *see* ECJ, 15 March 1989, Case 51/88, *Knut Hamann v. Finanzamt Hamburg-Eimsbüttel*, [1989] ECR 767.
61. *Van Gend en Loos*, *supra* note 2, para. B2.
62. ECH, 21 February 1973, Case 6/72, *Europemballage Corp. & Continental Can Co. v. Commission*, [1973] ECR 215, para. 22.
63. ECJ, 17 November 1983, Case 292/82, *Merck v. Hauptzollamt Hamburg-Jonas*, [1983] ECR I-3781, para. 12.
64. Including cases where that proposal has been rejected, *see* ECJ, 28 March 1996, Case C-468/93, *Gemeente Emmen*, [1996] ECR I-1756, para. 21; and proposals not yet adopted, *see* e.g., ECJ, 11 July 1996, Case C-25/95, *Otte v. Germany*, [1996] ECR I-3745.
65. *See*, Miguel Maduro, *supra* note 58 at 5; and Mitchel Lasser, *Judicial Deliberations. A Comparative Analysis of Judicial Transparency and Legitimacy* (Oxford: Oxford University Press, 2004), at 359, who describes it as 'teleological and meta-teleological reasoning'.

connection with the obligation of Member States under Article 10 of the EC treaty (Article 4 TFEU) to cooperate with Union law. Although it is true that the national courts are required to interpret national law as far as possible in conformity with Union law, the extent to which Union law can be enforced depends on the legal remedies provided for under national law and the conditions under which they can be applied. In this sense, Union law piggybacks national law. Since the national legal systems are considerably divergent in the remedies they provide, the uniform application of Union law is at risk and, as a result, the direct effect and primacy of Union law may be negatively affected. The ECJ, however, has explained that there are minimum conditions for the Member States to fulfil their obligation to ensure compliance with Union law under Article 10 EC (Article 4 TFEU). The principle of equivalence, as an application of the non-discrimination principle[66] in the specific area of procedural rules and conditions, basically requires that rules for protecting Union rights cannot be less favourable than those governing domestic actions.[67] As a consequence of the cooperative judiciary system of the EU, the task to ensure that the principle of equivalence is, indeed, honoured and upheld rests with the national courts, being solely acquainted with their national procedural rules and, therefore, equipped to make such a judgment.[68]

According to the ECJ, the principle of effective judicial control reflects 'a general principle of law stemming from the constitutional traditions common to the Member States'[69] and Member States have the obligation under Article 10 EC (Article 4 TFEU) to ensure judicial protection of an individual's right under Union law.[70] This means that the national courts must interpret the procedural rules governing actions brought before them in such a manner as to attain this objective,[71] which may entail setting aside national legal rules when required to ensure the effectiveness of the protection.[72] The principles of equivalence and effectiveness interact where the latter sets parameters for exercising the former. Unacceptable is, thus, the situation where equivalence

66. Article 18 TFEU (formerly Art. 12 of the EC treaty).
67. First established in the *Rewe* case, *supra* note 17 and confirmed in ECJ, 16 December 1976, Case 45/76, *Comet v. Productschap voor Siergewassen*, [1976] ECR 2043; ECJ, 5 March 1980, Case 265/78, *Ferwerda v. Productschap voor Vee en Vlees*, [1980] ECR 617 and ECJ, 10 July 1997, Case C-261/95, *Rosalba Palmisani v. Instituto nazionale della previdenza sociale (INPS)*, [1997] ECR I-4025.
68. Subject, however, to the Commission's right to challenge the national courts findings on grounds of breach of EU Law.
69. ECJ, 13 March 2007, Case C-432/05, *Unibet (London) Ltd, Unibet (International) Ltd v. Justitiekanslern*, [2007] ECR I-2271, para. 37. This principle is found in Arts 6 and 13 of the European Convention for the Protection of Human Rights and Fundamental Freedoms (Rome, 4 November 1950, Council of Europe, European Treaty Series, No. 5), and in Art. 47 of the Charter of fundamental rights of the European Union (Nice 7 December 2000, [2000] OJ, C364/1) and, as such, is recognised as a fundamental right.
70. *Unibet, supra* note 69, para. 38.
71. *Unibet, supra* note 69, para. 44.
72. *See*, ECJ, 28 June 1978, Case 70/77, *Simmenthal SpA v. Amministrazione delle finanze dello Stato (Simmenthal I)*, [1978] ECR 1453 and ECJ, 19 June 1990, Case C-213/89, *The Queen v. Secretary of State for Transport, ex parte Factortame (Factortame I)*, [1990] ECR I-2433.

exists *de iure* but is rendered impotent de facto, in other words, where the exercise of the rights is made virtually impossible or excessively difficult.[73]

The *Francovich* case[74] introduced the doctrine of state liability enabling individuals to obtain reparation when their rights are violated by a breach of Union law for which a Member State can be held responsible.[75] According to the ECJ, the reparation by the Member State is essential when it has not implemented a Directive in due time and consequently the individuals are unable to enforce their rights granted by Union law before the national courts. The ECJ founded its decision on two arguments. First, it concluded that such a liability was inherent to the system of the (then) EC treaty and, second, the Court derived the liability from the obligation to cooperate of Article 10 EC (Article 4 TFEU). The principle was further developed in subsequent cases. In *Brasserie du Pêcheur*,[76] the ECJ has made clear that the principle of state liability applies to all breaches of Union law regardless which organ of the State was responsible for the breach, even if that is the legislature or a national court.[77] It has stressed 'Since the Treaty contains no provision expressly and specifically governing the consequences of breaches of Community law by Member States, it is for the Court, in pursuance of the task conferred on it by Article 164 EC[78] of ensuring that in the interpretation and application of the Treaty the law is observed, to rule on such a question (...).' In the *Dillenkofer* case,[79] the ECJ further developed the conditions for state liability, when it held that 'Failure to take any measure to transpose a directive in order to achieve the result it prescribes within the period laid down for that purpose constitutes per se a serious breach of Community law and consequently gives rise to a right of reparation for individuals suffering injury if the result prescribed by the directive entails the grant to individuals of rights whose content is identifiable and a causal link exists between the breach of the State's obligation and the loss and damage suffered.'[80]

The activist approach of the ECJ tightens national autonomy and sovereignty and some Member States have argued that a general right to compensation under Union law is not inherent and could only be created by national legislation. Interestingly,

73. *See* for more detailed treatise, Paul P. Craig and Gráinne De Búrca, *EU Law: Text, Cases, and Materials* (Oxford: Oxford University Press, 2007), 309 et seq.; P.J.G. Kapteyn et al., *supra* note 3, at 545 et seq.; and Margot Horspool and Matthew Humphreys, *European Union Law*, 4th edn (Oxford: Oxford University Press, 2006), 202 et seq.
74. *Francovich, supra* note 2.
75. *See* in more detail, Paul P. Craig and Gráinne De Búrca, *supra* note 73, 328 et seq.; P.J.G. Kapteyn et al., *supra* note 3, at 556 et seq.; Roy Davis, *Liability in Damages for a Breach of Community Law: Some Reflection on the Question of Who to Sue and the Concept of 'the State'*, 31 ELRev, 69 (2006).
76. ECJ, 5 March 1996, Joined Cases C-46/93 and C-48/93, *Brasserie du Pêcheur SA v. Bundesrepublik Deutschland* and *The Queen v. Secretary of State for Transport, ex parte: Factortame Ltd and others (Factortame III)*, [1996] ECR I-1029, paras 31–32.
77. ECJ, 30 September 2003, Case C-224/01, *Gerhard Köbler v. Republik Österreich*, [2003] ECR I-10239 and ECJ, 13 June 2006, Case C-173/03, *Traghetti del Mediterraneo SpA v. Republica italiana*, [2006] ECR I-5177.
78. Now Art. 180 TFEU.
79. ECJ, 8 October 1996, Joined Cases C-178/94, C-179/94, C-188/94, C-189/94 and C-190/94, *Erich Dillenkofer, et al. v. Bundesrepublik Deutschland*, [1996] ECR I-4845.
80. *Dillenkofer, supra*, para. 27.

however, the Treaty of Lisbon[81] inserted the following provision into Article 19(1) TEU: '(...) Member States shall provide remedies sufficient to ensure effective legal protection in the fields covered by Union law.' It appears that the Lisbon Treaty codifies the ECJ's principles of effectiveness and equivalence.

Although the Lisbon Treaty has not created general rules on state liability it could be argued that it also codifies the principles developed in the *Francovich* case.

The question remains how this works out in the area of tax law. When national tax law in its wording, or through application or interpretation violates Union law, the state is liable for damages, which translates into the obligation to pay interest. The question is how the interest must be calculated. In 2001 the ECJ ruled that the UK tax provisions concerning payment of advanced corporation tax as it affected subsidiary companies whose parent company was outside the UK contravened Article 43 (then Article 52) of the EC treaty, the provisions of which are now found in Article 49 TFEU.[82] Subsequently, Sempra Metals Ltd (formerly Metallgesellschaft Ltd) filed suit to recover restitution in terms of interest in respect of the tax paid prematurely. The House of Lords realised that Community law requires that a remedy be offered in domestic law.

Under English law, a claimant can recover damages for losses caused by breach of contract or a tort with the exception of claims for interest losses.[83] However, in 1952 it was recognised that loss due to late payment might be recoverable if it constituted special damage.[84] It seems illogical to allow the recovery of special and not of general damages for loss of the use of money. Simple interest is available under statute and both simple and compound interest can be awarded in equity. However, where equity is invoked in aid of the common law the reverse is true, because the court in the past believed not to be authorised to do so or it would usurp the function of the legislature (Parliament).[85]

This claim in the case was made for restitution, i.e., a claim for the time value of money by which Revenue was unjustly enriched. The House of Lords changed direction by recognising the possibility of rewarding compound interest under the restitutionary remedy at common law. Since the law of restitution is the law of gain-based recovery, the enrichment needs to be valued from the perspective of the enrichee, in other words, the interest rate appropriate for the defendant's circumstances need to be applied, i.e., the interest rate at which the government could borrow in the market at the relevant times, which, along with any other type of commercial borrowing, is calculated at rate of interest that is compounded.[86] This was a corporate tax case and it does not surprise that the subsequent question was raised whether

81. Treaty of Lisbon amending the Treaty on European Union and the Treaty establishing the European Community, signed in Lisbon, 13 December 2007, [2007] OJ, 17 December 2007, No. C306/1.
82. ECJ, 8 March 2001, Joined Cases C-397/98 and C-410/98, *Metallgesellschaft Ltd and others, Hoechst AG and Hoechst UK Ltd v. Commissioners of Inland Revenue*, [2001] ECR I-1727.
83. *London, Chatham and Dover Railway Co v. South Eastern Railway Co.*, [1893] AC 429.
84. *Trans Trust SPRL v. Danubian Trading Co Ltd.*, [1952] 2 QB 297.
85. *Westdeutsche Landesbank Girozentrale v. Islington London Borough Council*, [1996] AC 669.
86. *Sempra Metals Limited v. Commissioners of Inland Revenue and another*, [2007] UKHL 34.

compound interest can also be rewarded in cases of overpayment of VAT, notwithstanding a provision in the UK statutory law that precludes the award of compound interest.[87]

The chance to find out came in 2012 when the UK High Court, Chancery Division, referred a preliminary question on that issue to the ECJ. This case also demonstrates the dynamics of the referral process and how the responsibilities in administrating justice are balanced between national courts and the ECJ.

Littlewoods Retail Limited[88] carried on catalogue-based home shopping businesses. Those businesses involved Littlewoods distributing catalogues and selling the goods shown in those catalogues through networks of persons known as 'agents.' The agents earned commission on sales made by or through them, which might be taken in cash, applied in respect of past purchases made by the agents themselves or (at an enhanced rate) applied towards future purchases. These commissions were mistakenly treated as consideration for services provided by the agents to Littlewoods, where they should have been treated as a discount against the consideration for past purchases (if taken in cash or applied in respect of those purchases) or future purchases (if applied at the enhanced rate towards future purchases). Littlewoods therefore overpaid VAT in respect of certain supplies because the taxable amount of goods supplied by it was mistakenly taken to be greater than it was. These overpaid sums were, according to the referring court, not lawfully due under both national and EU law. Littlewoods was reimbursed for the overpaid VAT and also received simple interest pursuant to and calculated in accordance with the relevant UK statutory provisions.

Subsequently, Littlewoods filed claims for compound interest. Of course, effectiveness is the primary underlying legal principle for the claim, since the UK High Court had established a violation of Union law. Through the principle of equivalence, the *Sempra*-ruling comes into play as grounds for awarding compound interest for VAT, because rules for protecting Union rights cannot be less favourable than those governing domestic actions. In essence, the referring court asked whether it was in accordance with Union law for national law only to offer simple interest on amounts of VAT overpaid by reason of non-compliance with Union law, or whether payment of compound interest was required. With reference to earlier cases, the ECJ stated that it is indeed an obligation for Member States to provide restitution with interest amounts of tax levied in breach of EU law. However, there is no EU legislation that governs the method of interest calculation. Therefore, in absence of such EU legislation, it is for each Member State to determine whether the principal sum must bear simple interest, compound interest or another type of interest with the caveat that such determination must be in compliance with the principles of effectiveness and equivalence.[89] The ECJ then refers the case back to the UK High Court to rule within the guidelines provided.

87. Section 78, VAT Act 1994. Interest is computed by reference to s. 197 of the Finance Act 1996 and the Air Passenger Duty and Other Indirect Taxes (Interest Rate) Regulations 1998. Rates are fixed by a formula referable to the average base lending rates of six clearing banks, which is called the 'reference rate'. The interest rate applicable under s. 78 is the reference rate minus 1%.

88. ECJ, 19 July 2012, Case C-591/10, *Littlewoods Retail Ltd and Others v. Her Majesty's Commissioners for Revenue and Customs*, ECLI:EU:C:2012:478.

89. *Supra* note 88, paras 27 and 34.

As to the principle of effectiveness, it is interesting that the ECJ notes that the amount of simple interest received by Littlewoods exceeds by more than 23% that of the principal sum,[90] echoing remarks by Advocate-General Trstenjak in her Opinion, but not explicitly concurring with her conclusion that this interest payment *'readily complies with the principle of effectiveness'* in this case.[91]

As to the principle of equivalence, the ECJ held that there is no obligation for a Member State to make the most favourable cause of action in domestic law pertaining to tax available to the taxpayer, but only those causes of action which pertain to claims based on infringements of national law having a similar purpose and similar essential characteristics to claims based on infringements of EU law.[92]

The ECJ abstains from providing an explicit answer as to whether the payment of compound interest is required under the principle of equivalence in relation to overpayments of VAT where such a remedy is available for overpayments of corporate income tax, claiming that national courts are better equipped to make that judgment as they have 'direct knowledge of the procedural rules governing restitution actions against the State'.[93] However, in a recent UK Supreme Court case, the judges could not find consensus on the remedies that are required to be made available under the principle of equivalence and, thus, on what type of interest would be adequate and filed a further reference to the ECJ.[94]

[C] Transplanted Categories

To explain terminology used in tax directives, the ECJ at times refers to definitions of the same terms as used in other directives. A good example is the *Card Protection Plan*-case where the ECJ, called to define insurance services for VAT purposes, referred to the meaning and definition in other Directives:

> (…) the essentials of an insurance transaction are, as generally understood, that the insurer undertakes, in return for prior payment of a premium, to provide the insured, in the event of materialisation of the risk covered, with the service agreed when the contract was concluded. It is not essential that the service the insurer has undertaken to provide in the event of loss consists in the payment of a sum of money, as that service may also take the form of the provision of assistance in cash or in kind of the type listed in the annex Directive 73/239 as amended by Directive

90. *Supra* note 88, para. 30.
91. Opinion Advocate General Trstenjak of 12 January 2012, Case C-591/10, ECLI:EU:C:2012:9, para. 37. The reasoning is not convincing. The absolute amount of interest relative to the principal sum bears no relevance in determining compliance with the principle of effectiveness, because the sum of interest correlates directly to the period of time over which the principal sum has been outstanding, in this case from 1973–2004, i.e., for 31 years. In other words, the amount of interest being greater than the principal sum in not *ipso facto* proof that the interest rewarded is adequate compensation for the delay in repayment of the principal sum. If the absolute amount of interest would be a factor, then simple interest would be acceptable for long outstanding debt and compound interest may possibly become the norm for short outstanding debt, a result that is arbitrary in nature and seems to violate the principle of equal treatment.
92. *Supra* note 88, para. 31.
93. *Supra* note 88, para. 31.
94. *Test Claimants in the FII Group Litigation v. HMRC*, [2012] UKSC 19.

> 84/641. There is no reason for the interpretation of the term 'insurance' to differ according to whether it appears in the directive on insurance or in the Sixth Directive.[95]

Another example, in the area of direct tax, is the *Punch Graphix*-case.[96] At issue was whether profits realised by a Belgian printing company upon a merger by acquisition where it absorbed assets of two subsidiary companies could be treated as liquidation proceeds in terms of Article 4(1) of the Parent-Subsidiary Directive. Where the Parent-Subsidiary Directive did not contain a definition of liquidation, the ECJ noted that the Merger Directive did contain a definition of a merger that referred to liquidation. The Court explained that even though the definition of merger appears in the merger directive and not in the Parent-Subsidiary directive, that 'does not prevent that definition from being taken into account for the purposes of the interpretation of the concept of "liquidation" within the meaning of Article 4(1) of [the Parent-Subsidiary Directive]'.[97]

[D] Conforming Interpretation

When interpreting national law, a national court must take into account the provisions of Union law of which the national law is the reflection. Directives are binding as to the result, and the obligation to implement a Directive and to achieve its objective or result binds all authorities of a state, including the judiciary. The ECJ formulated this principle for the first time in *Von Colson and Kamann*.[98] This principle has direct consequences for the method of interpretation to be used by national courts. In applying national law, and in particular those provisions of national law implementing a Directive, national courts must interpret such laws in light of the wording and purpose of the Directive in order to achieve the result referred to in the third paragraph of Article 189(249) EC.[99] To that end, national courts, making full use of the freedom of judgment granted to them by their national laws, must interpret and apply laws adopted to implement a Directive in consistency with the requirements of Union law.[100]

English law, for example, recognises the principle that the wording of a law adopted after signature of a treaty and relating to an international obligation of the national state under the treaty should be interpreted as having been intended to comply rather than to conflict with such an obligation.[101] Perhaps influenced by the approach in his home country, Advocate-General Sir Gordon Slynn endorsed the above legal

95. ECJ, 25 February 1999, Case C-349/96, *Card Protection Plan Ltd.*, [1999] ECR I-973, paras 17 and 18.
96. ECJ, 18 October 2012, Case C-371/11, *Punch Graphix Prepress Belgium*, ECLI:EU:C:2012:647.
97. *Punch Graphix, supra*, para. 35.
98. ECJ, 10 April 1984, Case 14/83, *Von Colson and Kamann v. Land Nordrhein-Westphalen*, [1984] ECR 1891.
99. *Von Colson and Kamann, supra*, para. 26. Confirmed in ECJ, 13 November 1990, Case C-106/89, *Marleasing v. Comercial Internacional de Alimentación*, [1990] ECR I-4135.
100. *Von Colson and Kamann, supra* note 98, para. 28.
101. Lord Diplock in *Garland v. British Railways Engineering Limited*, [1983] 2AC 751,771.

principle in his opinion to the ECJ in the *Marshall* case.[102] However, he expressly limited the scope of this principle to provisions of national law adopted after the treaty or the individual directives had entered into force. In his view, applying the principle of interpretation in conformity or consistency with the treaty or directives to national law adopted prior to such time would go too far. The duty of interpretation in consistency or conformity with Union law is inherent in the system of the EC, EU and TFEU treaties, because it enables national courts to ensure the effectiveness of Union law, thus fulfilling the obligations of the Member States under Article 10 EC (Article 4 TFEU).[103] To that extent, it is irrelevant whether the national law has been adopted *ex ante* or *ex post* of Union law.[104] Conformity interpretation, however, is not absolute. First, it is limited by general principles of law, such as legal certainty and fundamental rights, such as fair trial.[105] Second, interpretation in conformity with a directive is only possible insofar as the national provision provides sufficient latitude to do so.[106] Third, national provisions cannot be interpreted *contra legem*.[107]

Conformity interpretation is of course a matter for national courts and as such beyond the scope of this chapter. As an illustration, we will further examine two national court cases, one in the area of VAT and the other in the area of corporate income tax. In the *Hong Kong* case[108] the question arose whether a trade organisation, which supplies services free of charge, is a taxable person entitled to recover the VAT it incurred on its procurement. The Hong Kong Trade Development Council is an organisation charged with promoting trade between Hong Kong and other countries. From its Amsterdam offices, it provides free of charge information and advice about Hong Kong and about trade opportunities with Hong Kong. The Council is funded by a fixed annual grant from the Hong Kong government. The ECJ had ruled that activities free of charge do not constitute transactions of a taxable person under the provisions of the second VAT Directive. However, that did not fully resolve the case for the referring court, since the text of the Directive and the text of the Netherlands VAT Act were distinctively different.

The concept of taxable person is defined in Article 7 of the Dutch VAT Act as follows:[109]

---

102. ECJ, 26 January 1986, Case 152/84, *Marshall v. Southampton and South-West Hampshire Area Health Authority*, [1986] ECR 723.
103. ECJ, 5 October 2004, Joint Cases C-397-403/01, *Bernhard Pfeiffer et al. v. Deutsches Rotes Kreuz Kreisverband Waldshut eV*, [2004] ECR I-8835, para. 114.
104. ECJ, 4 July 2006, Case C-212/04, *Konstantinos Adeneler et al. v. Ellinikos Organismos Galaktos (ELOG)*, [2006] ECR I-6057.
105. ECJ, 16 June 2005, Case C-105/03, *Maria Pupino*, [2005] ECR I-5285, paras 58–60.
106. In the words of the ECJ 'as far as possible', *see* Case C-397-403/01, *Pfeiffer*, *supra* note 103, para. 113.
107. *Konstantinos Adeneler*, *supra* note 104, para. 110.
108. Hoge Raad, 6 October 1982, Case 20260, *Hong Kong Trade Development Council*, [1982] BNB 312.
109. Translation by the author. Dutch text:

    (1) Ondernemer is ieder die een bedrijf zelfstandig uitoefent.
    (2) Waar in deze wet wordt gesproken van bedrijf, wordt daaronder mede verstaan:
        a. beroep;
        b. exploitatie van een vermogensbestanddeel om er duurzaam opbrengst uit te verkrijgen.

(1) Entrepreneur is everyone who independently conducts a business.
(2) A business includes: a) a profession
b) the exploitation of a capital good for the purpose of generating regular income.
(...)

In comparison, the Directive defines a taxable person as:[110]

> 'Taxable person' means any person who independently and habitually engages in transactions pertaining to the activities of producers, traders or persons providing services, whether or not for gain.

The Netherlands Supreme Court deemed the concept of entrepreneur within the meaning of Article 7 of the VAT Act, notwithstanding the substantial difference in wording and formulation, to be equal to the concept of taxable person in de Second Directive.

The other example is the British *Vodafone 2*-case.[111] Vodafone was challenging an assessment to tax on the profits of its wholly-owned Luxembourg resident subsidiary under the CFC rules. This subsidiary was the intermediate holding company and provided finance to a group of European subsidiaries. HMRC contended that the interest income earned by the Luxembourg subsidiary on this finance should be apportioned to Vodafone under the CFC rules as none of the exemptions, narrowing its scope, applied. The High Court agreed with Vodafone that the UK CFC rules were contrary to EC law because they restricted the freedom of establishment. However, the Court of Appeal restricted the application of the CFC rules by interpreting them as if there were a new additional exception, applying retroactively, for companies actually established in another Member State and carrying on genuine economic activities. In reaching this view, the Court of Appeal held that in construing UK domestic law consistently with European law, the courts are not constrained by conventional rules of construction, will be permitted to depart from the strict and literal words in the relevant legislation, and may impute words into that legislation that are necessary to comply with EU law. The Court walks a fine line between interpretation and legislation, but it concludes that introducing a new exception does not substantially depart from the fundamental features of the CFC rules and constitutes, therefore, interpretation.

---

(3) (...).

110. Article 4 of the Second Directive (*infra* note 113). Compare also Art. 9 of Directive 2006/112 (*supra* note 54) and Art. 4 the Sixth Directive (*supra* note 53). 'Taxable person means any person who independently and habitually engages in transactions pertaining to the activities of producers, traders or persons providing services, whether or not for gain.'
111. *Vodafone 2 v. HMRC*, [2009] EWCA Civ 446 (22 May 2009).

[E] Case Law on VAT

[1] General Remarks

Apart from the legal principles developed by the ECJ for Union law in general, there exist economic principles that dominate VAT. All taxes rely on economic assumptions such as tax incidence, of course, but for the purpose of EU-VAT, the economic principles on which it is based take precedence over legal provisions. The priority of economic principles or purpose over legal format is the direct result of the manner in which VAT has been introduced in the EU in 1967. Two directives were enacted, the First VAT Directive[112] defining the purpose and principle workings of the system where the Second Directive[113] providing the legal format and modalities through which the envisioned system should be realised. The First Directive, therefore, relates to the Second Directive as an explanatory memorandum; and the Second Directive is merely the legal vehicle to deliver the economic structure laid out in the First Directive. From this perspective, the ECJ considers the legal provisions not only to be subordinate but also to be subservient to the conceptual structure of the tax. Where, and to the extent, the legal provisions are insufficient to achieve the purpose of the tax the ECJ will correct them through teleological interpretation as will be demonstrated in §6.04[E][3] and §6.04[E][4]. This approach contrasts starkly with especially the tradition found in the Common law countries, Ireland and the UK, where literal interpretation of statutory wording is the dominant rule for tax law, unless the result would lead to an absurdity, i.e., the application of literal meaning would clearly defeat the purposes of the Act.[114] Because VAT is based on European law, the Common or Civil law traditions of jurisprudence in tax law are not per se relevant. But that does not mean that literal interpretation never has a place, because under the principle of legal certainty, which is of particular importance in taxation matters, taxable persons, tax authorities and Member States need to rely on the clear and precise wording of the relevant Union law.[115] In *Commission v. Ireland*, for example, the Advocate-General and the ECJ agreed with the defendant that the VAT grouping provision should be interpreted on the basis of its wording thus allowing non-taxable persons to be part of a VAT group.[116]

---

112. First (VAT) Directive (67/227/EEC) of 11 April 1967, [1967] OJ, L 71/1301. It was repealed when Directive 2006/112 (*see supra* note 54) entered into force on 1 January 2007, but the first three paragraphs of Art. 2, First Directive were reproduced in Art. 1(2) of Directive 2006/112.
113. Second (VAT) Directive (67/228/EEC) of 11 April 1967, [1967] OJ, L 71/1303, replaced by the Sixth Directive (*see supra* note 53) on 1 January 1978 and subsequently, by Directive 2006/112 (*see supra* note 54) on 1 January 2007.
114. House of Lords, 13 December 1978, *Jones v. Wrotham Park Settled Estates and another*, [1980] AC 74, 105.
115. ECJ, 15 July 2010, Case C-582/08, *Commission v. United Kingdom*, [2010] ECR I-7195, paras 49–51.
116. ECJ, 9 April 2013, Case C-85/11, *Commission v. Ireland*, ECLI:EU:C:2013:217. Opinion A-G Jääskinen, 27 November 2012. ECLI:EU:C:2012:753. The ECJ rejected the Commission's view that literal interpretation would run counter to the objectives and purposes of the provision.

National VAT law has to be compliant with EU-VAT law and the national courts need to follow the guidance of the ECJ in interpreting their national law as earlier explained in §6.03[A].

The principles of VAT have to be understood and interpreted against the stated purpose of the EU, i.e., the creation of an internal market and the supportive role that indirect tax is to fulfil in that respect, as explained in §6.02. The preamble to the First Directive makes a clear reference to the common market, which '(...) presupposes the prior application in Member States of legislation concerning turnover taxes that will not distort conditions of competition or hinder the free movement of goods and services (...).' Further down it is explained that '(...) (s)uch a system of value added tax achieves the highest degree of simplicity and of neutrality when the tax is levied in as general a manner as possible and when its scope covers all stages of production and distribution and the provision of services. (...)'

The VAT system is then defined in more detail in Article 2 of the First Directive:

> The principle of the common system of value added tax involves the application to goods and services of a general tax on consumption exactly proportional to the price of the goods and services, whatever the number of transactions which take place in the production and distribution process before the stage at which tax is charged.
>
> On each transaction, value added tax, calculated on the price of goods or services at the rate applicable to such goods or services, shall be chargeable after deduction of the amount of value added tax borne directly by the various cost components.
>
> The common system of value added tax shall be applied up to and including the retail trade stage.

The main features of the tax emerging from this definition is an all stage tax (see paragraph 3) on consumption (thus not on production) that has a general application and should therefore include, at least in principle, all goods and services, and does not pyramid (see paragraph 1), which is realised by providing a credit for VAT paid on all costs (see paragraph 2).

The principle of neutrality, introduced in the preamble, often operates in tandem with the general principles of equal treatment and non-discrimination. That should not come as a surprise, because the principle of neutrality is, to an extent, the embodiment of equality and non-discrimination for VAT purposes. Similar goods or services should bear the same tax burden regardless of the length of their respective supply chain otherwise economic distortions would arise, frustrating the free movement of goods and services within the common market. Neutrality and especially the prohibition of tax accumulation and the right to offset tax incurred on procurement from tax due on sales are central in the jurisprudence of the ECJ. In §6.04[E][4] we will discuss several Court rulings demonstrating the application of the principle of neutrality.

[2] Strict or Restricted Scope Interpretation

It is established case law that the scope of VAT exemptions is subject to strict interpretation. Where the VAT is designed to be a general tax on private consumption including, at least conceptually, all supplies of goods and services, exemptions clearly derogate from the principal rule, and as such this approach is rational. In fact, that is the exact motivation of the Court of Justice. Exemptions[117] 'are to be interpreted strictly since they constitute exceptions to the general principle that turnover tax is to be levied on all services supplied for consideration by a taxable person'.[118]

In an infringement procedure against Italy, the ECJ held that the exemption of medical care in the exercise of the medical and paramedical professions[119] does not include veterinary services, because all language versions of the Directive, except the English and Italian ones, expressly limit the exemption to care administered to persons and, therefore, care provided to animals is not covered by the exemption.[120] In *Bulthuis-Griffioen*[121] the Court ruled that a daycare centre operated by a *natural person* could not share in the exemption for the supply by organisations, i.e., *legal persons*, of social and welfare services.[122]

In relation to the exemption for medical care, the Court held that it does not apply to medical services consisting, not in the provision of care to persons by diagnosing and treating a disease or any other health disorder, but in establishing the genetic affinity of individuals through biological tests.[123] In addition, medical advice provided by a doctor to a court of law to establish the eligibility for disability pension of a claimant is not exempt because, although the performance of that service solicits the medical skills of the provider and may involve activities which are typical of the medical profession, the principal purpose of the service is not the protection, including the maintenance or restoration, of the health of the person to whom the report relates.[124]

Subsequently, the Court was called to determine whether the services of a stem cell bank consisting of the collection of umbilical cord blood, the testing and processing of that blood, and the storage of stem cells contained in it, for future therapeutic use were covered by the medical care exemption. The Court was somewhat ambivalent in its judgment. First it stated that these services 'do not appear to have as their direct purpose any actual diagnosis, treatment or cure of diseases or health disorders, or any actual protection, maintenance or restoration of health'. Indeed, the future use for medical treatment is not a given. As the Court noted, 'The services are intended only to ensure that a particular resource will be available for medical treatment in the uncertain event that treatment becomes necessary (...).' Realising that appearances are not necessarily facts, it continued with the caveat that the exemption may, however,

117. *See* Arts 132, 135 and 136 of Directive 2006/112.
118. ECJ, 15 June 1989, Case C-348/87 *Stichting Uitvoering Financiële Acties*, [1989] ECR 1737, para. 13.
119. At the time laid down in Art. 13A (1) (c) of the Sixth Directive; now in Art. 132(1)(c) Directive 2006/112.
120. ECJ, 24 May 1988, Case C-122/87, *Commission v. Italy*, [1988] ECR 2685, para. 9.
121. ECJ, 11 August 1995, Case C-453/93, *W. Bulthuis-Griffioen*, [1995] ECR I-2341.
122. Article 13A (l) (g) of the Sixth Directive; now Art. 132 (1) (g) of Directive 2006/112.
123. ECJ, 14 September 2000, Case C-384/98, *D. v. W.*, [2000] ECR I-6795.
124. ECJ, 20 November 2003, Case C-212/01, *Unterpertinger*, [2003] ERC I-13859, para. 43.

apply but only if the referring court would conclude that 'the analysis of umbilical cord blood is actually intended to enable a medical diagnosis to be made (...)'.[125]

In another case[126] the ECJ was requested to explain the scope of the exemption for services by certain non-profit organisations to their members.[127] The Institute of the Motor Industry is a voluntary association of persons working in the retail sector of the motor industry and it claimed to qualify as an exempt trade union under Union law. The national court considered that the Institute would not qualify as a trade union under the ordinary meaning of the expression used in the English version of the Directive, but also noted that the term used in the French and other language version would allow for a broader scope of definition. First, the ECJ explains how different language version must be used and balanced when interpreting tax law. The wording used in one language version of a provision cannot serve as the sole basis for the interpretation of that provision, or be made to override the other language versions in that regard. Such an approach would be incompatible with the requirement of the uniform application of Union law. In the event of divergence between the language versions, the provision in question must be interpreted by reference to the purpose and general scheme of the rules of which it forms a part.[128] Next the Court points out that the context of the exemption is vital for the interpretation, in this case that the exemptions listed in Article 13A of the Sixth Directive refer to activities performed in the public interest. This then leads to the conclusion that a non-profit-making organisation which aims to promote the interests of its members cannot, where that object is not put into practice by defending and representing the collective interests of its members vis-à-vis the relevant decision-makers, be regarded as having objects of a trade-union nature within the meaning of Article 13A(1)(l) of the Sixth Directive.[129]

The ECJ takes the text of VAT legislation as a starting point when interpreting exemptions, comparing, when required, the text in several or all languages versions to obtain clarity of their meaning. Because exemptions are exceptions to the main rule of general taxability, they must be interpreted strictly, i.e., as limited in both subjective scope (the service provider) and objective scope (type of service). 'Nevertheless', in the Courts own words, 'the interpretation of (...) terms must be consistent with the objectives pursued by those exemptions and comply with the requirements of the principle of fiscal neutrality inherent in the common system of VAT. Thus, the requirement of strict interpretation does not mean that the terms used to specify the exemptions (...) should be construed in such a way as to deprive the exemptions of their intended effect.'[130] It appears that the ECJ follows an approach somewhat analogous to the doctrine of literal interpretation under Common Law that prevails

125. ECJ, 10 June 2010, Case C-86/09, *Future Health Technologies*, [2010] ERC I-5215, paras 43, 44, 45 and 47.
126. ECJ, 12 November 1998, Case C-149/97, *Institute of the Motor Industry*, [1998] ECR I-7053.
127. Article 13A (1) (l) of the Sixth Directive; now Article 132 (1) (l) of Directive 2006/112.
128. *Institute of the Motor Industry*, *supra* note 126, para. 16. This is settled case law, *see also* ECJ, 27 March 1990, Case C-372/88 *Milk Marketing Board v. Cricket St Thomas*, [1990] ECR I-1345, paras 18 and 19.
129. *Institute of the Motor Industry*, *supra* note 126, para. 19.
130. *Future Health Technologies*, *supra* note 125, para. 30.

unless the result would be absurd (see §6.04[E][1]). A strict interpretation of exemptions that would distort the very rationale of the exemption in question would by any measure constitute an absurdity.

A good example of the nuanced approach of the ECJ applied to the main rule of strict interpretation of exemptions can be found in *Commission v. France*, where it held that the medical and hospital care exemption should not be 'construed unduly strictly (...), since the exemption is designed to ensure that the benefits (...) are not hindered by the increased costs if such care that would follow if they were subject to VAT'.[131]

The restrictive interpretation is often founded on the purpose of a legislative provision, such as the therapeutic aim of the medical care exemption. '(...) The exemption is designed to facilitate the protection of human health, which includes diagnosis and examination for the purpose of ascertaining whether a person is suffering from a medical condition with a view to treating it if that is possible. It does not include diagnosis and examination if done for some other purpose, such as that of determining the premium payable on an insurance policy.'[132] Medical practitioners are not exempt, but the provision of medical care. Also, the meaning of the term 'medical care' is narrower than the activity of the medical profession in general.

[3] Teleological Interpretation: General

A good first example of the approach taken by the ECJ is its ruling on a preliminary question posed by the Netherlands Supreme Court in the *Hong Kong* case,[133] earlier discussed in §6.04[D]. The question was whether an organisation that provided services free of charge constituted a taxable person under the Second VAT directive, eligible for a credit of VAT paid on its procurement. The ECJ noted that the text of the Second Directive did not provide any clarity as to this point and then follows a reasoning based on the purpose of the directive. It starts its reasoning by noting that VAT is applied up to and including the retail stage and is calculated on the price of goods and services, but that tax incurred on inputs is deducted. It then notes that tax is no longer deductible when the chain of transactions reaches the final consumer. Finally, the ECJ concludes that when services are provided free of charge no tax can be due since there exists no basis of assessment (price). 'In such circumstances the person providing services must be assimilated to a final consumer because he is at the final stage of the production and distribution chain.'[134]

In another Dutch case[135] the ECJ was called again to judge eligibility of input-VAT credit, this time in relation to activities in the preparatory phase of a business. Mr and Mrs Rompelman acquired future title to two units, zoned as commercial, in premises

131. ECJ, 11 January 2001, Case C-76/99, *Commission v. France*, [2001] ECR I-249, paras 21 and 23.
132. ECJ, 20 November 2003, Case C-307/01, Peter *d'Ambrumenil, Dispute Resolution Services Ltd*, [2003] ECR I-13989, para. 23.
133. ECJ, 1 April 1982, Case 89/81, *Staatssecretaris van Financiën v. Hong Kong Trade Development Council*, [1982] ECR 1277.
134. *Hong Kong, supra*, para. 10.
135. ECJ, 14 February 1985, Case 268/83, *D.A. Rompelman and E.A. Rompelman-Van Deelen v. Minister van Financiën*, [1985] ECR 655.

under construction, which would be leased (subject to VAT) to traders. They sought to recover the VAT charged on the instalment payments, which Revenue declined on the ground that the actual exploitation of the units had not yet commenced. Since the outcome of the case hinged on the interpretation of the term 'exploitation' in the definition article of the directive, reference for a preliminary ruling was made. The text of Article 4 of the Sixth VAT Directive (then in force) is as follows:

1. 'Taxable person' shall mean any person who independently carries out in any place any economic activity specified in paragraph 2, whatever the purpose or results of that activity.
2. The economic activities referred to in paragraph 1 shall comprise all activities of producers, traders and persons supplying services including mining and agricultural activities and activities of the professions. The exploitation of tangible or intangible property for the purpose of obtaining income therefrom on a continuing basis shall also be considered an economic activity.

After explaining the background and purpose of the VAT system, the ECJ considered that economic activities might consist in several consecutive transactions. Therefore, 'preparatory acts, such as the acquisition of assets (...) which form part of those transactions must themselves be treated as constituting economic activity'. The ECJ then motivates its decision by referring to the neutrality principle. 'The principle that VAT should be neutral as regards the tax burden on a business requires that the first investment expenditure incurred for the purposes of and with the view to commencing a business must be regarded as an economic activity.' Otherwise a trader would not be able to recover VAT on his costs, which would, in the words of the Court, 'create an arbitrary distinction between investment expenditure incurred before the actual exploitation of immovable property and expenditure incurred during exploitation'.[136]

A subsequent matter arose in the *INZO* case.[137] INZO commissioned a profitability study with a view to developing a seawater desalination process. On the basis of this study, it decided to abandon the project and, as a result, INZO never actually made any supply to anyone. It shall be clear that INZO qualified as a taxable person on the basis of the earlier *Rompelman* ruling. However, the business never reached the operational phase and was in fact terminated in its infancy. The question was raised whether INZO's status as taxable person could be revoked retrospectively, with loss of the right to recover input-VAT, when it became clear that INZO would never make any supplies.

The ECJ rejected this approach on the grounds that retrospective change of status would infringe the general principle of legal certainty. In addition, the neutrality principle would be breached, because a difference in tax burden would be created between those who are and those who are not successful in launching their businesses. A problem is posed by the text of Article 17 of the sixth VAT directive[138] that regulated the right to deduct input-VAT at the time of the proceedings, because it limits the

136. *Rompelman, supra* note 135, para. 23.
137. ECJ, 29 February 1996, Case C-110/94, *Intercommunale voor Zeewaterontzilting (INZO) v. Belgian State*, [1996] ECR I-857.
138. Now Art. 168 of Directive 2006/112.

deduction of VAT to inputs 'used for the purposes of his taxable transactions'. Where in *Rompelman*, the taxable activities occurred at a later point in time, in INZO there were no taxable transactions at all. The ECJ found a solution to do justice to the economic principles of VAT by reading 'his taxable transactions' as a reference to transactions intended at the time the input tax was incurred. As demonstrated, the ECJ is remarkable 'activist' in interpreting the VAT law in such a manner that it fulfils its economic objections.

As discussed above, the ECJ develops unwritten Union law on the basis of general principles of law or economic principles in matters of taxation, when there is a lacuna in the design of, for example, a directive. An example of such a lacuna can be found in *Securento*,[139] which deals with the attribution of input VAT when the recipient of the inputs, on the one hand, makes both taxable and exempt supplies (economic activities) and, on the other hand, also has a separate activity which does not amount to a business (non-economic activities).

The solution for this situation seems obvious. Input-VAT directly related to taxable output should be recoverable, input-VAT related to exempt sales and non-business activities should not be recoverable, and the tax on general inputs, which cannot be directly allocated, should be recoverable pro rata, i.e., on the basis of apportionment. However, although the Directive offers an apportionment mechanism for mixed use, the wording of the text is inaccurate in that it apparently has missed to anticipate the possibility of non-business activities. The text of the directive, as relevant, reads as follows:

1. The proportion deductible (...) shall be made up of a fraction having:
   - as numerator, the total amount, exclusive of value added tax, of turnover per year attributable to transactions in respect of which value added tax is deductible – (...),
   - as denominator, the total amount, exclusive of value added tax, of turnover per year attributable to transactions included in the numerator and to transactions in respect of which VAT is not deductible.[140]

The above rules cover exclusively expenditure related to economic activities with a distinction between taxable economic activities that give rise to the right to deduct and exempt economic activities that do not give such a right. Arguably, under a literal interpretation of this provision, input-tax attributable to the non-economic activities would be recoverable. The ECJ points out that the rules governing deduction are intended to provide complete relief to a trader for VAT paid in the course of economic activities. Overhead inputs can only give rise to VAT recovery if, and to the extent, they directly relate to taxable output.[141] Where the Directive does not contain the guidance necessary to make correct calculation of the proportion of tax that is recoverable, the

139. ECJ, 13 March 2008, Case C-437/06, *Securenta Göttinger Immobilienanlagen und Vermögens-management AG v. Finanzamt Göttingen*, [2008] ECR I-1597.
140. Article 19 of the Sixth Directive and Art. 174 of Directive 2006/112.
141. *Securenta, supra* note 139, para. 27.

Member States 'are required to exercise that power, having regard to the aims and broad logic of the Directive'.[142]

Again we can conclude that the ECJ takes the purpose of the VAT system as the foundation for its reasoning. Where the directive is incomplete, the Member States (through its judiciary) are required to fill the lacuna in a manner that ensures the effectiveness of Union law.

Another area where the application of VAT required the intervention of the ECJ is the practice of promotion sales using different types of coupons.[143] Boots is a national retail chain in the UK that tried to increase its sales volume through a promotion scheme involving coupons printed on the packaging of certain products. Customers, buying these products, received these coupons free of charge. The bearer of such a coupon was entitled to a price reduction equal to the nominal value indicated on the coupon upon the subsequent purchase of the same of certain other products indicated on the coupon. Boots accounted for VAT on the discounted price. Revenue, however, was of the opinion that VAT was due also on the value of the surrendered coupon. Central in this case was the interpretation of the concept of taxable amount as found in the VAT directive, the text of which is as follows:

> (...) everything which constitutes the consideration which has been or is to be obtained by the supplier from the purchaser, the customer or a third party (...)[144]
>
> The taxable amount shall not include:
>
> (...)
>
> b. price discounts and rebates allowed to the customer and accounted for at the time of supply;[145]
>
> (...)

According to the ECJ discounts and rebates 'constitute a reduction of the price at which an article is lawfully offered to the customer, since the seller agrees to forego the sum presented by the rebate in order precisely to induce the customer to buy the article'.[146] The exclusion of discounts and rebates is only an application of the definition of taxable amount, which, as the Court has explained in earlier cases,[147] is the consideration actually received.[148] The ECJ did not accept the argument, made by

142. *Securenta, supra* note 139, para. 35.
143. In the meantime, legislative measures have been taken to address the VAT treatment of discount vouchers, which will enter into force on 1 January 2019, *see* Council Directive (EU) 2016/1065 of 27 June 2016 amending Directive 2006/112/EC as regards the treatment of vouchers, OJ L 177 (1 July 2016). It is out of the scope and beyond the purpose of this chapter to discuss the content of the new rules; *see* however, Jeroen Bijl, *The European Union's New VAT Rules for Vouchers: The Emperor's New Clothes?* (27) 6 Int'l VAT Monitor, 407–410 (2016).
144. Article 11 A (1)(a) of the Sixth Directive (*see supra* note 53), in effect at the time of the proceedings, and Art. 73 of Directive 2006/112 (*see supra* note 54).
145. Article 11 A (2) of the Sixth Directive (*see supra* note 53) and Art. 79 of Directive 2006/112 (*see supra* note 54).
146. ECJ, 27 March 1990, Case C-126/88, *Boots Company plc v. Commissioners of Customs and Excise,* [1990] ECR I-1235, para. 18.
147. ECJ, 23 November 1988, Case 230/87, *Naturally Yours Cosmetics Limited v. Commissioners of Customs and Excise,* [1988] ECR 6365.
148. *Boots, supra* note 146, para. 19.

the United Kingdom in the proceedings, that the coupon represented value to Boots and should, for that reason, be included in the taxable amount.[149] The coupon only incorporated the obligation of Boots to allow the bearer, in exchange for it, a price reduction.[150]

The ECJ takes this much further in *Elida Gibbs*.[151] The focus in this case is not on the retailer but on the position of the manufacturer. Again, a coupon is printed on the wrapping of certain goods entitling the consumer to a discount on subsequent purchases. There are two variations, either the coupon is presented to the retailer for an immediate discount of the retail price and, subsequently the retailer is reimbursed by the manufacturer; or the customer pays full retail price, mails the coupon to the manufacturer and receives a rebate from the manufacturer. Under both scenarios, the retailer receives the full retail price. Where the manufacturer pays part of the price to the retailer, this constitutes a third party payment, covered by the main definition rule of the VAT directives. The question arising in the *Elida Gibbs* case was whether the manufacturer could reduce the taxable amount of its sale to the wholesaler or retailer[152] with the rebate, which was paid out to the final consumer. *Elida Gibbs* was of the opinion that this rebate should be considered as a retroactive discount of its own sales price. The distinction with the *Boots* case will be clear: Boots gave a discount to its own customer; the manufacturer gives a discount to the final customer of another business downstream the supply chain. Normally, a downstream supply of goods should be matched with an upstream flow of payments; and rebates take place between subsequent stages of the supply chain. In this case, however, the rebate, like the knight in chess, skipped one or two stages. This fact pattern is difficult to compromise with the literal wording of the relevant provisions of the Directive, reason for Advocate-General Fennelly to advise that the taxable amount of the manufacturer should not be adjusted. Excluded from the taxable amount are discounts given to one's customer, but the customer of the manufacturer, the wholesaler or retailer, did not receive a discount; the discount was given, downstream the supply chain, to the final consumer who did not directly procure the product from the manufacturer. In addition, under the second scenario, the discount was not accounted for at the time of the supply as required by the directive's provision, but paid out later at the time that the coupon was surrendered to the manufacturer. In the view of the Advocate General, a direct link is needed between the reduction and the relevant taxable transaction. Where the Directive contains no mechanism for the manufacturer's taxable amount to be reduced by reference to its payments to the consumers, the payments by the manufacturer to the

149. The coupon is a bearer note that does have a monetary value to consumers, but it is difficult to understand how it could have monetary value for Boots once the coupon has been surrendered, since the obligation and entitlement embodied by the coupon, which offset each other, are now in the same hand.

150. *Boots*, *supra* note 146, para. 21.

151. ECJ, 24 October 1996, Case C-317/94, *Elida Gibbs Ltd. v. Commissioners of Customs and Excise*, [1996] ECR I-5339.

152. Elida Gibbs sold sometimes directly to the retailer and sometimes through a wholesaler, but this makes no difference for the principle of the case.

consumers have to be regarded as simply an arrangement under which the manufacturer met part of the consumer's cost of acquiring the goods without any further tax implications.

The ECJ, however, approached the problem from the perspective of the purpose of the EU VAT system. VAT is supposed to be a tax on final consumption and, by intention, businesses should not carry any burden of the tax since they only operate as collectors of the tax and not as actual taxpayer. The Court describes the principles of the tax and the consequences derived from them as follows:

> The basic principle of the VAT system is that it is intended to tax only the final consumer. Consequently, the taxable amount serving as a basis for the VAT to be collected by the tax authorities cannot exceed the consideration actually paid by the final consumer which is the basis for calculating the VAT ultimately borne by him.[153]
>
> (...)
>
> It follows that, having regard in each case to the machinery of the VAT system, its operation and the role of the intermediaries, the tax authorities may not in any circumstances charge an amount exceeding the tax paid by the final consumer.[154]

Notwithstanding the above formulation of the principles, the Court still needed to somehow reconcile these principles with the mechanics of the tax as laid down in the directive. The ECJ first acknowledges that the provisions regarding price reductions refer 'to the normal case of contractual relations entered into directly between two contracting parties, which are modified subsequently'. This observation, however, did not pose a serious hurdle for the Court to arrive at the desired result. In the same paragraph it continues: 'the fact remains, however, that the provision is an expression of the principle, emphasised above, that the position of taxable persons must be neutral.' Apparently, in the view of the ECJ, the provisions of the directive are not in violation of the neutrality principle but embody it. It therefore follows that, 'in order to ensure observance of the principle of neutrality', account should be taken of rebates, which miss out a link in the contractual chain. 'Otherwise, the tax authorities would receive by way of VAT a sum greater than that actually paid by the final consumer, at the expense of the taxable person.'[155]

This case clearly demonstrates that in the view of the ECJ the economic principles of the VAT should take precedence over legal provisions. The provisions of the VAT directive serve to realise certain economic outcomes. If and where, due to imperfections in their design, they are unable to deliver the economic requirements of VAT, the Member States and their judiciary, nevertheless, need to ensure that these results are realised by improving the failing mechanism.[156]

---

153. *Elida Gibbs, supra* note 151, para. 19.
154. *Elida Gibbs, supra* note 151, para. 24.
155. *Elida Gibbs, supra* note 151, para. 31.
156. However, the ECJ does not always follow this approach. A good example of where the ECJ preferred to elevate legal over economic relations is ECJ, 18 July 2007, Case C-277/05, *Société thermale d'Eugénie-les-Bains v. Ministère de L'Economie, des Finances et de L'Industrie*, [2007] ECR I-6415. Customers paid a reservation fee or deposit when booking a room. The deposits

[4] *Teleological Interpretation: Neutrality Principle*

As indicated before, it is an explicit economic objective of EU-VAT not to distort conditions of competition and the optimum allocation of resources. This is often referred to as the principle of neutrality, which is the expression of the equal treatment principle for the purpose of VAT. Under the neutrality principle, the tax burden on the final consumer should not depend on the level of integration of the manufacturing and supply chain (vertical neutrality); and the tax should not discriminate between taxpayers in comparable positions (horizontal neutrality). Neutrality is the overriding principle of EU-VAT in that it may have primacy over other principles, especially the principle of strict interpretation.[157] For this reason, it seems appropriate to take a closer look at this method of interpretation, as a species of teleological interpretation, and in particular as it has been applied to exemptions.

An appropriate starting point is a case where the Court explained the circumstances under which the principle of fiscal neutrality was not infringed:

> (...) in introducing and maintaining in force a VAT rate of 2.1% solely for reimbursable medical products, the French legislation (...) does not infringe the principle of fiscal neutrality. Reimbursable and non-reimbursable medical products are not similar products in competition with each other (...). Once included in the list of reimbursable products, a medical product will, vis-à-vis a non-reimbursable medical product, have a decisive advantage for the final consumer (...). Consequently it is not the lower rate of VAT which provides the reason for his decision to purchase.[158]

Two criteria are decisive here for determining whether products are in competition: the (non) similarity of the products, and the perception of the buyer.

In *Gregg*[159] the ECJ ruled that a recognised nursing home run in the form of a partnership, notwithstanding that a partnership is not a legal person under domestic law, can be an 'establishment' or 'organisation' within the meaning of the medical and welfare exemption provisions of the Directive. The Court reasons as follows:

> The terms 'establishment' and 'organisation' are in principle sufficiently broad to include natural persons as well. It may be added that none of the language versions (...) include the term 'legal person', which would have been clear and unambiguous, instead of the abovementioned terms. (...)
>
> It is true that the terms 'establishment' and 'organisation' suggest the existence of an individualised entity performing a particular function. Those conditions are, however, satisfied not only by legal persons but also by one or more natural persons running a business.

---

received by the company were deducted from the amount subsequently paid for accommodation or retained by the company in cases where customers cancelled their reservations. The court found that the retained deposits were not subject to VAT as they constituted a mere cancellation fee compensating for the loss of business.

157. Christian Amand, *VAT for Public Entities and Charities – Should the Sixth Directive Be Renegotiated?*, (19) 6 Int'l VAT Monitor, 433–443 (2006).
158. ECJ, 3 May 2001, Case C-481/98, *Commission v. France*, [2001] ECR I-3369, paras 25 and 27.
159. ECJ, 7 September 1999, Case C-216/97, *Jennifer and Mervyn Gregg*, [1999] ECR I-4947.

> That interpretation, to the effect that the terms 'establishment' and 'organisation' do not refer only to legal persons, is, in particular, consistent with the principle of fiscal neutrality inherent in the common system of VAT and in compliance with which the exemptions (...) must be applied (...).[160]

The Directive provides the Member States with the option to subject exemptions to conditions. In *L.u.P* the Court explained that where national law has made conditions for the recognition of private institutions as exempt organisations, these conditions must be the same for all these institutions to comply with the principle of fiscal neutrality.[161] It was further explained in *Ines Zimmermann*, that national legislation may not lay down materially different conditions for profit-making entities and non-profit making legal persons as this would constitute a violation of the principle of fiscal neutrality.[162]

The question was raised whether national legislation could condition the exemption for private non-profit sports organisations[163] on charging membership fees that would not exceed a threshold specified in national VAT law. The Court notices, 'to apply such a criterion may result, first, in a non-profit making body being excluded from the benefit of the exemption provided for by the provision and, secondly, in a profit-making body being able to benefit from it'. The States are not permitted to introduce conditions that alter the scope of the exemption.[164] In this particular case, the national legislation had gone too far in that it opened the exemption to for-profit organisations (contrary to the clear text of the Directive's provision), while at the same time distorting competition between non-profit sports organisations, providing similar services to their members.

EU VAT law also exempts '(...) cultural services and goods closely linked thereto supplied by bodies governed by public law or by other cultural bodies recognised by the Member State concerned.'[165] In *Hoffmann*[166] the question was raised whether three soloists, performing for the audience together but contracting individually with the impresario, can constitute a 'body' and as such share in the exemption. Making a reference to the *Gregg*-case, the ECJ explains that:

> In particular, such performers may, in the same way as a cultural group, carry on their activity professionally, semi-professionally or on an amateur basis and do so either on a profit-making basis, or without payment or, as the case may be, on an expenses-only basis. In those various cases, even if the performer supplies his services entirely by his own means, and whatever the legal form he has chosen for his activity, he appears as an individualised entity carrying on a cultural activity, in the same way as a cultural group.

160. *Gregg, supra*, paras 17, 18, and 19.
161. ECJ, 8 June 2006, Case C-106/05, *L.u.P., GmbH v. Finanzamt Bochum-Mitte*, [2006] ECR I-5123, para. 50.
162. ECJ, 15 November 2012, Case C-174/11, *Finanzamt Steglitz v. Ines Zimmermann*, ECLI-:EU:C:2012:716, para. 58.
163. Article 13A (1) (m) of the Sixth Directive, respectively Art. 132 (1) (m) of Directive 2006/112.
164. ECJ, 7 May 1998, Case C-124/96, *Commission v. Spain*, [1998] ECR I-2501, paras 17–21.
165. Article 13A (1) (n) of the Sixth Directive, respectively Art. 132 (1) (n) of Directive 2006/112.
166. ECJ, 3 April 2003, Case C-144/00, *Matthias Hoffmann*, [2003] ECR I-2921.

> Consequently, the principle of fiscal neutrality requires that individual performers, as long as their services are recognised as cultural, may be regarded, like cultural groups, as bodies similar to public-law bodies supplying certain cultural services (...).[167]

Fiscal neutrality played a decisive role in a number of cases, all related to gambling activities.[168] In *Fischer* the Court ruled that a Member State may not impose VAT on the unlawful operation of roulette, when the corresponding activity carried out by a licensed public casino is exempt.

> (...) the principle of fiscal neutrality precludes a generalised distinction from being drawn in the levying of VAT between unlawful and lawful transactions. It follows that Member States cannot reserve the exemption solely to lawful games of chance.[169]

In *Linneweber* the Court rejected different VAT treatment between public gambling and private gambling, the former being exempt and the latter taxable, stating that the identity of the supplier is irrelevant for the purposes of the VAT gambling exemption. The Court pointed out that although the Member States have retained authority to formulate conditions and limitations of that exemption, they must do so while respecting the neutrality principle, which precludes treating similar goods and supplies of services, which are thus in competition with each other, differently for VAT purposes. The identity of the operators of games and the legal form by means of which they exercise their activities are, as a rule, irrelevant in assessing whether products or services supplied are comparable.[170]

In *Rank Group* the Court had opportunity to explain how the concept of competition needs to be approached within the context of the principle of fiscal neutrality. The Court held that a distinction between different classes of bingo machines and different classes of slot machines was not acceptable where the services were comparable from the point of view of the customer and met the same need of the customer.

> (...) the similar nature of two supplies of services entails the consequence that they are in competition with each other. Accordingly, the actual existence of competition between two supplies of services does not constitute an independent and additional condition for infringement of the principle of fiscal neutrality if the supplies in question are identical or similar from the point of view of the consumer and meet the same needs of the consumer (...).[171]

167. *Hoffmann, supra*, paras 26 and 27.
168. Article 13B (f) of the Sixth Directive, respectively Art. 135 (1) (i) of Directive 2006/112.
169. ECJ, 11 June 1998, Case C-283/95, *Karlheinz Fischer v. Finanzamt Donaueschingen*, [1998] ECR I-3369, para. 28.
170. ECJ, 17 February 2005, Joint Cases C-453/02 and C-462/02, *Edith Linneweber v. Finanzamt Gladbeck and Savvas Akritidis v. Finanzamt Herne-West*, [2005] ECR I-1131, paras 23, 24, 25 and 29.
171. ECJ, 10 November 2011, Joined Cases C-259/10 and C-260/10, *The Rank Group plc*, [2011] ECR I-10947, paras 3, 34 and 36.

That the perspective of the customer is taken as the decisive factor appears adequate for a general consumption tax. 'Consumer needs' and 'consumer point of view' are not to be taken as separate criterions formulated by the ECJ for determining whether different treatment is allowed. Rather, in our view, customer needs are just a specification of the customer's perspective to product comparability.

The criteria in *Rank* applied to VAT are not new or surprising where the same reasoning has been applied for other indirect taxes (excise taxes) levied at different rates for domestic and imported products respectively. According to its case law, domestic and imported products are 'similar' according to the ECJ when they 'have similar characteristics and meet the same needs from the point of view of consumers'.[172] The idea is not to examine whether products are identical but to determine 'their similar and comparable use'.[173] As a consequence, it is the social and economic use of the product that dictates its similarity with other products. Consideration must be given to the context of consumption and the consumer's attitude, because products are qualified as similar if consumers perceive them as such.[174]

Prima facie it may seem that the application of the neutrality principle leads to a broadening of the scope of an exemption, which would contradict the ECJ's starting point of strict interpretation. However, that is an optical illusion. In our opinion, the ECJ has created a system of 'checks and balances' as to the interpretation of exemptions. Strict interpretation is checked (two-dimensionally) by the purpose and objectives of the exemptions themselves, which cannot be distorted or altered through the means of interpretation. Strict interpretation is further limited in space (three-dimensionally) through the overriding demands of fiscal neutrality, i.e., equal treatment. In the words of the ECJ:

> (...) the terms used to specify the exemptions (...) are to be interpreted strictly. Nevertheless, the interpretation of those terms must be consistent with the objectives underlying the exemptions and must comply with the requirements of the principle of fiscal neutrality inherent in the common system of VAT. Accordingly, the requirement of strict interpretation does not mean that the terms used to specify the exemptions (...) must be construed in such a way as to deprive the exemptions of their intended effects. (...)[175]

However, the principle of neutrality is also subject to limitations in its application.

> [the] principle [of fiscal neutrality] cannot extend the scope of an exemption in the absence of clear wording to that effect. That principle is not a rule of primary law which can condition the validity of an exemption, but a principle of interpretation,

172. ECJ, 17 February 1976, Case C-45/75, *Rewe-Zentrale des Lebensmittel-Großhandels GmbH v. Hauptzollamt Landau/Pfalz*, [1976] ECR 181. The same formulation was used in *Rank, supra*, para. 44.
173. ECJ, 27 February 1980, Case C-168/78 *Commission v. France*, [1980] ECR 347, para. 5; ECJ, 4 March 1986, Case C-106/84, *Commission v. Denmark*, [1986] ECR 833, para. 12 and ECJ, 11 August 1995, Joint Cases C-367/93 to C-377/93, *F.G. Roders and Others v. Inspecteur der Invoerrechten en Accijnzen*, [1995] ECR I-2229, para. 27.
174. *See*, for example, ECJ, 18 April 1991, Case C-230/89 *Commission v. Greece*, [1991] ECR I-1909.
175. *Ines Zimmermann*, *supra* note 162, paras 22.

to be applied concurrently with the principle of strict interpretation of exemptions.[176]

[F] Case Law on Corporate Income Tax

[1] General Remarks

Where in the area of indirect tax a high degree of harmonisation has been reached, leaving little tax sovereignty to the Member States, the opposite is true for direct taxes. Union law provides no legal basis for determining priority between Member States applying overlapping rules of tax jurisdiction. Therefore, in the area of direct taxation, the Member States have a considerable amount of discretion.

In the famous *Schempp*[177] judgment, the Court ruled that the EC Treaty (now TFEU) offers no guarantee to a citizen of the Union that transferring his activities to a Member State other than that in which he previously resided will be neutral as regards taxation. Given the disparities in the tax legislation of the Member States, such a transfer may be to the citizen's advantage in terms of taxation or not, according to circumstances.

However, Member States must exercise their legislative discretion in consistency with Union law.[178] The large extent of autonomy that Member States have retained, naturally limits the oversight role of the ECJ in the area of direct taxation.[179] The case law on indirect tax is concerned with the implementation of EU rules by the Member States, i.e., whether the national implementation measures are in line with the rules and regulations at EU level. For direct tax the ECJ has to find the correct balance between the sovereignty and legitimate interests of the individual Member State, embodied in its unharmonised domestic tax law, and the interest of the internal market, in particular the Treaty Freedoms (see §6.02), which have direct effect. Furthermore, a Member State's autonomy finds restriction in the boundaries set by the general principles of Union law, particularly the principles of equivalence and effectiveness (see §6.04[B]). In that respect, it must be noted that the ECJ has competence to interpret EU law but not to interpret national law. In addition, between all Member

176. ECJ, 19 July 2012, Case C-44/11, *Deutsche Bank*, ECLI:EU:C:2012:484, para. 45. Similar wording is used in *Ines Zimmermann, supra* note 162, para. 50.
177. ECJ, 12 July 2005, Case C-403/03, *Egon Schempp v. Finanzamt München V*, [2005] ECR I-06421. In this case, the German tax authorities refused a German resident national an income tax deduction for maintenance payments made to a former spouse, who had moved her residency to Austria, where such a deduction would have been allowed had the spouse remained a resident of Germany. However, the difference in treatment was a direct result of the divergence between the income tax systems in Germany and Austria, in that only the former considered such maintenance payments as taxable income of the spouse. *See also* ECJ 15 July 2004, Case C-365/02, *Lindfors*, ECLI:EU:C:2004:449.
178. ECJ, 14 February 1995, Case C-279/93, *Finanzamt Köln-Altstadt v. Roland Schumacker*, [1995] ECR I-225, para. 21.
179. For an overview of the role of the ECJ in realising direct tax harmonisation, *see* Joachim Englisch, *Tax Coordination between Member States in the EU – Role of the ECJ*, in Michael Lang et al. (eds), Horizontal Tax Coordination (Amsterdam: IBFD, 2012), 3–50.

States exists an extensive bilateral network of tax treaties based on the OECD Model Double Taxation Convention. All this makes the ECJ's task challenging and complex. Because Union law provides no guidance to prioritise nexus factors the ECJ has accepted that infringements of the fundamental freedoms must be accepted where they result from the interaction of two different national tax systems.[180] Prevention of double taxation[181] is, in essence, left to the discretion of the Member States.[182] Judicial scrutiny is reserved for different treatment of non-residents or of foreign-source income within a single jurisdiction.

The first step in the balancing act of the ECJ lies in determining whether a national measure that restricts the exercise of the Treaty Freedoms is nevertheless justified because it serves an overriding purpose or reason of public interest. If so, the national measure needs to be tested against the requirements of the principle of proportionality, in that such a measure may not restrict the Freedoms more than required to realise that purpose of public interest.[183]

The so-called rule of reason plays a crucial role in the ECJ's evaluation of national direct tax legislations.[184] It seeks to strike a balance between national (tax) sovereignty and the requirements of the EU internal market. In *Dassonville* the ECJ developed a formula of extensive interpretation of the guarantees on free movement of goods where it ruled that 'all trading rules enacted by Member States which are capable of hindering, directly or indirectly, actually or potentially, intra-Community trade are to be considered as measures having an effect equivalent to quantitative restrictions' (which are prohibited) unless the national measures are reasonable[185] This left little room to manoeuvre for individual Member States, but in *Cassis de Dijon* the Court provided relief in creating an exception to these guarantees where a Member State was protecting a legitimate national interest. The Court reasoned:

> (...) obstacles to movement within the community resulting from disparities between the national laws (...) must be accepted in so far as those provisions may

180. In fact, the Court accepts all nexus factors currently in use in international tax law to determine tax jurisdiction as compatible to Union law. Worldwide taxation by the residence state was accepted in ECJ, 15 April 2010, Case C-96/08, *CIBA*, [2010] ECR I-2911; source state taxation was accepted in ECJ, 21 January 2010, Case C-311/08, *Société de Gestion Industrielle (SGI)*, [2010] ECR I-487; nationality taxation in ECJ, 23 February 2006, Case C-513/03, *Van Hilten-van der Heijden*, [2006] ECR I-1957; and territoriality taxation in ECJ, 15 May 2008, Case C-414/06, *Lidl Belgium*, [2008] ECR I-3601.
181. There are two types of double taxation – economic and juridical. Economic double taxation may be caused by the rules of a single Member State. If it is and if that Member State provides for relief domestically, then it may also have to provide relief cross-border. *See Manninen*, *supra* note 44, for example, among others. However, juridical double taxation is caused by the interaction between the rules of two States. Thus, in *Damseaux*, *infra* note 180 and ECJ, 14 November 2006, Case C-513/04 *Mark Kerckhaert and Bernadette Morres v. Belgische Staat*, [2006] ECR I-10967 the ECJ was unable to insist that one State solve this problem since it amounted to a disparity rather than a restriction.
182. ECJ, 16 July 2009, Case C-128/08, *Jacques Damseaux v. Belgium*, [2009] ECR I-6823 and ECJ, 12 February 2009, Case C-67/08, *Margarete Block v. Finanzamt Kaufbeuren*, [2009] ECR I-883.
183. *See*, for example, ECJ, 21 February 2013, Case C-123/11, *A Oy*, ECLI:EU:C:2013:84.
184. For an overview, *see* Ben J.M. Terra and Peter J. Wattel, *supra* note 27, s. 3.2.2, 59 et seq.
185. ECJ, 11 July 1974, Case 8/74, *Procureur du Roy v. Benoît and Gustave Dassonville*, [1974] ECR 837, para. 5.

> be recognised as being necessary in order to satisfy mandatory requirements relating in particular to the effectiveness of fiscal supervision, the protection of public health, the fairness of commercial transactions and the defence of the consumer.[186]

This so-called rule of reason has subsequently been extended to all fundamental freedoms.[187] Since the 1990s, the rule of reason has also attained considerable significance in the area of non-harmonised taxation, where the unwritten public policy reasons accepted by the Court are far more relevant than those explicitly mentioned in the Treaty. Thus, in *Marks & Spencer,* the ECJ upheld the argument of the UK that the need to ensure balance in the allocation of taxing rights between the Member States was such a general interest.[188] At issue was cross-border loss relief. In particular, the question was raised whether the UK could deny Marks & Spencer deducting from its taxable profits in the UK losses incurred by its subsidiaries established in Belgium, Germany and France despite group relief being available under UK law to resident companies. The ECJ addressed the question in the context of whether such provisions constitute a restriction on the freedom of establishment.[189] The Court concludes that the absence of group relief to domestic parent companies for the losses of their foreign subsidiaries when available for the losses of their domestic subsidiaries hinders the exercise by that parent company of its freedom of establishment by deterring it from setting up subsidiaries in other Member States.[190] Then the Court finds a reason of public interest based on the territoriality principle as a justification of the different treatment of resident and non-resident taxpayers.

In the context of that argument, the Court accepted three justification factors, namely (1) a balanced allocation of the taxing power between Member States; (2) the prevention of taxpayers using losses twice and (3) the prevention of tax avoidance through loss tax-planning.[191] The Court concluded that this justification did not meet

186. ECJ, 20 February 1979, Case 120/78, *Rewe-Zentrale AG v. Bundesmonopolverwaltung für Branntwein (Cassis de Dijon)* [1979] ECR 649, para. 8.
187. *See,* for example, ECJ, 30 November 1995, Case C-55/94, *Gebhard,* [1995] ECR I-4165, para. 37. The 'rule of reason' does not apply in discriminatory situations. This is made very clear in *Commission v. Spain (Lotteries)* and *Gebhard* and numerous other cases where the *Gebhard* formula was applied. National rules which are discriminatory on grounds of nationality may only be justified by provisions contained in the Treaty such as public policy, public security and public health. Note that public health does not apply to free movement of capital and that freedom also contains its own special derogations. Other national rules, which are indirectly discriminatory (*Biehl, Ritter-Coulais, O'Flynn v. Adjudication Officer*), or which constitute a restriction on the exercise of the freedoms, may be justified by a general interest reason. *See* ECJ, 6 October 2009, Case C-153/08, *Commission of the European Communities v. Kingdom of Spain ('Lotteries'),* [2009] ECR I-09735; ECJ, 8 May 1990, Case C-175/88, *Klaus Biehl v. Administration des contributions du grand-duché de Luxembourg,* [1990] ECR I-01779; ECJ, 21 February 2006, Case C-152/03, *Hans-Jürgen Ritter-Coulais and Monique Ritter-Coulais v. Finanzamt Germersheim,* [2006] ECR I-01711 and ECJ, 23 May 1996, Case C-237/94, *John O'Flynn v. Adjudication Officer,* [1996] ECR I-02617.
188. ECJ, 13 December 2005, Case C-446/03, *Marks & Spencer,* [2005] ECR I-10837. For an in-depth analysis of this case, *see* Tom O'Shea, *Marks and Spencer v. Halsey (HM Inspector of Taxes): Restriction, Justification and Proportionality,* 15 (2) EC Tax Review, 66–82 (2006).
189. *See* Arts 43 and 48 EC, respectively Arts 49 and 54 TFEU.
190. *Marks & Spencer, supra* note 188, paras 32–34.
191. *Marks & Spencer, supra* note 188, paras 44–50.

the principle of proportionality in situations where the parent company could demonstrate that there was 'no possibility'[192] of getting their losses relieved in the Member State of the subsidiary. The ECJ has also accepted other general interest justifications such as the need to ensure the coherence of the tax system;[193] the need to prevent the risk of tax avoidance;[194] the need to ensure the effective collection of tax[195] and the need to preserve the effectiveness of fiscal supervision.[196]

The ECJ is extremely consistent in its approach in the direct tax arena[197] and its approach in the direct tax field is no different from that adopted in its internal market jurisprudence more generally. This consistency becomes apparent when analysing the Court's direct tax cases through the application of the national treatment principle from both a host Member State (§6.04[F][2]) and an origin Member State (§6.04[F][3]) perspective.

[2] Freedom of Establishment and Host Member States

The first corporate income tax case is known as *Commission v. France ('Avoir Fiscal')* or simply, *Avoir Fiscal.*[198] This was an infringement proceeding brought by the European Commission against France. The Commission argued that France taxed dividends paid by French companies to French parent companies more favourably than similar dividends paid to branches in France of companies resident in other Member States. Thus, the French tax rules in question deterred such foreign companies from holding shares in French companies through their French branches because they were denied the tax credits in question.

Under the French tax rules, when dividends were distributed by a French resident company a tax credit ('avoir fiscal') equivalent to half the corporation tax paid by the dividend paying company was granted to recipients of the dividends. The tax credit

192. *Marks & Spencer, supra* note 188, para. 55.

193. *See* ECJ, 28 January 1992, Case C-204/90, *Hans-Martin Bachmann v. Belgian State,* [1990] ECR I-00249 and ECJ, 23 October 2008, Case C-157/07, *Finanzamt für Körperschaften III in Berlin v. Krankenheim Ruhesitz am Wannsee-Seniorenheimstatt GmbH,* [2008] ECR I-08061.

194. *See* ECJ, 16 July 1998, Case C-264/96, *Imperial Chemical Industries plc (ICI) v. Kenneth Hall Colmer* (Her Majesty's Inspector of Taxes), [1998] ECR I-04695 and *Marks & Spencer, supra* note 188.

195. *See* ECJ, 3 October 2006, Case C-290/04, *FKP Scorpio Konzertproduktionen GmbH v. Finanzamt Hamburg-Eimsbüttel,* [2006] ECR I-09461.

196. *See* ECJ, 15 May 1997, Case C-250/95, *Futura Participations SA and Singer v. Administration des contributions,* [1997] ECR I-02471.

197. *See* Tom O'Shea, *EU Tax Law and Double Tax Conventions* (London: Avoir Fiscal Limited, 2008), and Tom O'Shea, *European Tax Controversies: A British-Dutch Debate: Back to Basics and Is the ECJ Consistent?,* 1 WTJ, 100–127 (2013). For a different, and highly critical, view on the ECJ, *see* for example, E.C.C.M. Kemmeren, *Double Tax Conventions on Income and Capital and the EU: Past, Present and Future,* 21 (3) EC Tax Rev., 157–177 (2012); P.J. Wattel, *Exit Taxation in the EU/EEA Before and After National Grid Indus,* Tax Notes Int'l, 30 January 2012, 371. Also *see* Michael J. Graetz and Alvin C. Warren Jr., *Dividend Taxation in Europe: When the ECJ Makes Tax Policy,* 44 CMLR, 1577–1623 (2007); claiming that the ECJ is undermining the fiscal autonomy of the Member States and that its approach to income tax issues is incoherent.

198. ECJ, 28 January 1986, Case 270/83, *Commission of the European Communities v. French Republic ('Avoir Fiscal'),* [1986] ECR 273. *See* Tom O'Shea, *From Avoir Fiscal to Marks & Spencer,* 41 Tax Notes International, 587–612 (2006).

could be set off against the tax payable by the recipient of the dividends and constituted income of that person. However, the benefit of the tax credit was restricted to persons who had their habitual residence or registered office in France or who were resident outside France but benefited from a double tax convention whereby the tax credit was granted. Consequently, these tax credits were denied to companies from other Member States which established themselves in France via a French branch since branches did not create a 'resident' entity in France.

The Commission argued that such French tax rules were incompatible with the freedom of establishment which allowed companies of other Member States to establish branches, agencies or subsidiaries in France. This entitled such companies to 'national treatment' in France, namely, no less favourable tax treatment than French companies in a comparable situation.

[a] Comparability

The *Avoir Fiscal* case was the first decision in the direct tax field, concerning a host Member State situation and a national tax rule, where the ECJ had to consider whether foreign companies with branches in France were in a comparable situation to local French companies. In other words, whether, from a host Member State perspective, the French tax rules at issue constituted a restriction on the exercise of the freedom of establishment or whether they discriminated on grounds of nationality against companies from Member States other than France which had established branches in France.

The ECJ decided the comparability issue in a fairly straightforward way. The Court observed that for the purpose of determining income liable to corporate income tax, the French tax rules did not distinguish between local companies and foreign companies with a branch in France. Both were taxed in a similar way on profits earned in France. Since both were taxed in the same way as regards profits, both should receive the same tax advantages. In other words, there was no objective difference in their situations to justify a difference in treatment.

The Court highlighted that since the rules at issue 'place companies whose registered office is in France and branches and agencies situated in France of companies whose registered office is abroad on the same footing for the purposes of taxing their profits, those rules, cannot, without giving rise to discrimination, treat them differently in regard to the grant of an advantage related to taxation, such as shareholders' tax credits. By treating the two forms of establishment in the same way for the purposes of taxing their profits, the French legislature has in fact admitted that there is no objective difference between their positions in regard to the detailed rules and conditions relating to that taxation which could justify different treatment.'[199]

199. *Avoir Fiscal*, *supra* note 198, para. 20.

Thus, when two situations are comparable, the national tax system should treat them equally.[200] Therefore, if tax credits are granted to local companies, then they should also be granted to companies from other Member States, which have exercised the freedom of establishment in France through the creation of branches there.

[b] Objective Justification and General Interest Justifications

In its jurisprudence, whenever the ECJ determines that the situations at issue in a case are comparable, the Member State is given an opportunity to demonstrate a) whether there is an objective justification for the different treatment in the case at hand and b) whether there are general interest justifications at stake, which might justify the national rules in question. In such instances, the ECJ is balancing the right of the Member State to retain its tax rule with the right of the taxpayer to exercise a fundamental freedom right guaranteed by the Treaty.

In *Avoir Fiscal*, France argued that its rules were justified because (i) residents and non-residents were not in a comparable situation. Although the Court has accepted that this is generally the case,[201] *Avoir Fiscal* is an example of a situation where the ECJ determined that residents and non-residents could be in a comparable situation. Hence, a non-resident (such as a company with a branch in France) might have to receive no less favourable tax treatment in France because it was entitled to national treatment in France under the freedom of establishment provisions of the Treaty of Rome.

France also argued that branches received certain advantages, which companies resident in France did not receive. The Court rejected this argument, pointing out that even if such advantages existed they cannot justify a breach of the national treatment principle guaranteed by the freedom of establishment. The Court noted that the freedom of establishment prohibited 'all discrimination, even if only of a limited nature'.[202]

The ECJ also rejected the French argument that companies from other Member States could avoid the tax credits' problem in relation to branches by simply setting up a subsidiary in France. The Court explained that this could not justify the different treatment since the freedom of establishment 'expressly leaves traders free to choose the appropriate legal form in which to pursue their activities in another Member

200. Equally means that the cross-border situation should be treated no less favourably than the purely domestic situation. This means that the cross-border situation may also be treated more favourably than the domestic situation. This 'reverse discrimination' is accepted by the ECJ under the current scheme of the Treaties. For examples in the Court's direct tax jurisprudence, *see*, *Van Hilten*, *supra* note 180, and *Bouanich*, *infra* note 241. In *Van Hilten*, the Dutch inheritance tax rules at issue could treat Dutch nationals worse than nationals of other Member States resident in the Netherlands. In *Bouanich*, it was clear that taxation under the French-Swedish Double Tax Convention could be more favourable (15%) than under the Swedish domestic rules (30%) where the investment was made.

201. For an explanation, *see Schumacker*, *supra* note 178, paras 31–34. For an analysis of this case, *see* Tom O'Shea, *European Tax Controversies: Quis Custodies Ipsos Custodes?*, 1 ECTJ 39–98 (2011/12).

202. *Avoir Fiscal*, *supra* note 198, para. 21.

State'.[203] In other words, a company could choose to establish via a branch, an agency or a subsidiary according to its preference.

France also argued that the difference in tax treatment was the result of differences in national tax systems in the absence of harmonised rules at the Community level, consequently, the rules were necessary to combat the risk of tax evasion This argument was also rejected by the ECJ which stated that 'the EEC Treaty does not permit any derogation from the fundamental principle of freedom of establishment on such a ground'. In other words, where a national rule discriminates on grounds of nationality, the only derogations permitted are those contained in provisions of the Treaty, in this case, the freedom of establishment. A general interest justification such as the need to prevent the risk of tax evasion or tax avoidance cannot justify a rule that is discriminatory on grounds of nationality, which in relation to companies relates to the seat of the company.[204]

France also argued, unsuccessfully, that double tax conventions caused the different tax treatment in question, pointing out that it had granted the tax credits to foreign companies when the same tax advantage was reciprocally agreed in a double tax convention. In response, the Court underlined that the rights conferred by the freedom of establishment 'are unconditional and a Member State cannot make respect for them subject to the contents of an agreement concluded with another Member State. In particular, that article does not permit those rights to be made subject to a condition of reciprocity imposed for the purpose of obtaining corresponding advantages in other Member States.'[205]

The Court in *Avoir Fiscal* therefore established the parameters of the national treatment test from a host State perspective. Two years later, in *Daily Mail,*[206] the ECJ determined that the freedom of establishment also applied from an origin Member State perspective. In coming to this conclusion, the ECJ interpreted the wording of the freedom of establishment in the broadest possible way.

[3] Freedom of Establishment and Origin Member States

The first corporate income tax case involving an origin Member State situation was *Daily Mail*, even though in the judgment itself, the Court determined that the freedom of establishment was not engaged. In *Daily Mail*, the Court interpreted the freedom of establishment provision of the Treaty in a very broad way, highlighting that even though 'those provisions are directed mainly to ensuring that foreign nationals and companies are treated in the host Member State in the same was as nationals of that State, they also prohibit the Member State of origin from hindering the establishment

203. *Avoir Fiscal, supra* note 198, para. 22.
204. For a clear explanation of this concept by the ECJ *see* ECJ, 6 October 2009, Case C-153/08, *Commission v. Spain ("'Lotteries"')*, [2009] ECR I-9735, paras 36–38.
205. *Avoir Fiscal, supra* note 198, para. 26.
206. ECJ, 27 September 1988, Case 81/87, *The Queen v. H. M. Treasury and Commissioners of Inland Revenue, ex parte Daily Mail and General Trust plc.*, [1988] ECR 05483.

in another Member State of one of its nationals or of a company incorporated under its legislation which comes within the definition contained in Article 58'.[207]

This broad interpretation of the freedom of establishment was necessary since otherwise, as the ECJ pointed out, the rights guaranteed by the freedom of establishment 'would be rendered meaningless if the Member State of origin could prohibit undertakings from leaving in order to establish themselves in another Member State'.[208] The Court explained that in the case of a company, 'the right of establishment is generally exercised by the setting-up of agencies, branches or subsidiaries'. The Court noted that a company 'may also exercise its right of establishment by taking part in the incorporation of a company in another Member State'.[209]

In subsequent cases, the ECJ continued applying this broad interpretation to the concept of freedom of establishment, holding in *Cartesio*[210] that the freedom establishment applied to conversion situations when an origin State entity moved its registered office to another Member State which had company rules which allowed re-domiciliation. The Court observed that 'the situation where the seat of a company incorporated under the law of one Member State is transferred to another Member State with no change as regards the law which governs that company falls to be distinguished from the situation where a company governed by the law of one Member State moves to another Member State with an attendant change as regards the national law applicable, since in the latter situation the company is converted into a form of company which is governed by the law of the Member State to which it has moved'.[211] The Court commented that such a barrier to the actual conversion of a company 'without prior winding-up or liquidation, into a company governed by the law of the Member State to which it wishes to relocate constitutes a restriction on the freedom of establishment of the company concerned which, unless it serves overriding requirements in the public interest, is prohibited under Article 43 EC'.[212]

In *SEVIC*,[213] the ECJ determined that the freedom of establishment applied to a cross-border merger situation. The Court noted 'the right of establishment covers all measures which permit or even merely facilitate access to another Member State and the pursuit of an economic activity in that State by allowing the persons concerned to participate in the economic life of the country effectively and under the same conditions as national operators'.[214] The Court went on to explain that cross-border merger operations 'like other company transformation operations, respond to the needs for cooperation and consolidation between companies established in different Member States. They constitute particular methods of exercise of the freedom of establishment, important for the proper functioning of the internal market, and are

207. *Daily Mail, supra* note 206, para. 16. Art. 58 EEC became Art. 48 EC and is now Art. 54 TFEU.
208. *Daily Mail, supra* note 206, para. 16.
209. *Daily Mail, supra* note 206, para. 17.
210. ECJ, 16 December 2008, Case C-210/06, *Cartesio Oktató és Szolgáltató bt.*, [2008] ECR I-9641. For an analysis of this case, *see* Tom O'Shea, *Cartesio: Moving a Company's Seat Now Easier in the EU*, 47 Tax Notes International, 394–397 (2009).
211. *Cartesio, supra* note 210, para. 111.
212. *Cartesio, supra* note 210, para. 113.
213. ECJ, 13 December 2005, Case C-411/03, *SEVIC Systems AG*, [2005] ECR I-10805.
214. *SEVIC supra*, para. 18.

therefore amongst those economic activities in respect of which Member States are required to comply with the freedom of establishment laid down by Article 43 EC'.[215]

It is clear from this jurisprudence that EU law continues to evolve through the interpretation of EU law concepts, such as the *freedom of establishment*, by the ECJ. This development of EU law is driven by the cases which come before the ECJ for decision, whether by way of the preliminary ruling procedure or by way of infringement proceedings brought by the European Commission against Member States. If national tax rules fail to comply with EU law, the Member States are obliged[216] to ensure that they alter their tax systems so that they fully comply with EU law. The Court therefore plays a key 'negative integration' role under the scheme contained in the EU Treaties through its interpretation of EU law.

[4] Strict or Restricted Scope Interpretation

As to VAT (see §5.04[E][2]) it is established case law that the scope of exemptions is subject to strict interpretation, because they are exceptions to the general principle underlying that tax. In the area of direct tax, the ECJ follows a similar path as demonstrated by the *Manninen*-case.[217] The Treaty on the European Union introduced full liberalisation of capital movements and of payments both intra-EU and with third countries.[218] Article 65(1)(a) and (b) TFEU contains restrictions to the free movement of capital where it allows differential tax treatment by Member States of resident and non-resident taxpayers and between domestic and foreign-source investment income. However, these measures cannot constitute arbitrary discrimination or a disguised restriction on the free movement of capital and payments, according to Article 65(3) TFEU. Under Finnish law, the recipient of dividend is granted a corporation tax credit in respect of a dividend paid by a domestic share company, but not in respect of dividend income he paid by a foreign company. Mr Manninen receives dividends from a Swedish company. The purpose of the tax credit is to prevent the double taxation of company profits distributed to shareholders by setting off the corporation tax due from the company distributing dividends against the income tax due from the shareholder. Since the tax credit applies only to dividends paid by Finnish companies, that legislation disadvantages those receiving dividends from companies established in other Member States. Thus, the tax legislation has the effect of deterring residents of Finland from investing in companies resident in other Member States or, from the opposite perspective, it restricts the abilities of foreign companies to raise capital in Finland. In that sense, the ECJ concludes that the law restricts the free movement of capital.[219] Union law appears to allow such restriction, given the text of Article 65(1)(a) TFEU. However, the ECJ explains:

---

215. *SEVIC*, *supra* note 213, para. 19.
216. Article 4(3) TEU provides that 'The Member States shall take any appropriate measure, general or particular, to ensure fulfilment of the obligations arising out of the Treaties or resulting from the acts of the institutions of the Union.'
217. *Supra* note 44. *See* Ben J.M. Terra and Peter J. Wattel, *supra* note 27, at 31.
218. *See* Art. 63 TFEU (formerly Art. 56 EC).
219. *Manninen*, *supra* note 44, paras 20–24.

> (...) it should be noted that [this] Article (...), which, as a derogation from the fundamental principle of the free movement of capital, must be interpreted strictly, cannot be interpreted as meaning that any tax legislation making a distinction between taxpayers by reference to the place where they invest their capital is automatically compatible with the Treaty.[220]

Where the Treaty in Article 63 TFEU prohibits all restrictions on the free movement of capital, Article 65(1) (a) provides some room for the Member States in the realm of taxation. However, they are limited in exercising this authority by the boundaries set in the third paragraph said article, and by the strict interpretation applied by the ECJ to their remaining authority:

> A distinction must (...) be made between unequal treatment which is permitted (...) and arbitrary discrimination which is prohibited (...). In that respect, the case-law shows that, for national tax legislation like that at issue (...) to be (...) regarded as compatible with the Treaty provisions on the free movement of capital, the difference in treatment must concern situations which are not objectively comparable or be justified by overriding reasons in the general interest, such as the need to safeguard the coherence of the tax system (...). In order to be justified, moreover, the difference in treatment between different categories of dividends must not go beyond what is necessary in order to attain the objective of the legislation.[221]

Given the wording of the above paragraph, it has been suggested that the ECJ treats Article 65(1)(a) and (3) as a codification of its own 'rule of reason' applied to the area of capital movement, therewith retaining all limits on fiscal sovereignty of the Member States imposed by its case law on other fundamental treaty freedoms.[222]

[5] OECD Model Treaty Standards as Source of Interpretation

[a] Introduction

To date, there exists no model VAT convention that provides standards to be used in bilateral treaties.[223] However, in the area of direct tax all Member States have an extensive global network of bilateral treaties to prevent double taxation and, although all based on the OECD model treaty, none is identical and important differences remain. Do provisions of existing treaties between Member States play a role in determining whether national law is inconsistent with Union law? In other words, if prima facie a national tax provision is in violation of Union law, can an overriding reason of public interest be found in a bilateral tax treaty? Indeed, on several occasions

220. *Manninen, supra* note 44, para. 28.
221. *Manninen, supra* note 44, para. 29.
222. Ben J.M. Terra and Peter J. Wattel, *supra* note 27, at 31 and 32.
223. In the past, double taxation of VAT was not perceived as a problem, but that has changed with the on-going proliferation of VAT and the intensifying of cross-border trade in services. *See* on this subject, Thomas Ecker, *A VAT/GST Model Convention*, Doctoral Series 25 (Amsterdam: IBFD, 2013). Recently, the OECD has published International VAT/GST Guidelines for public comments, which may indicate a movement in the direction of a model treaty.

the ECJ has used OECD or tax treaty standards to determine whether an allocation of taxing rights was balanced and, thus, should be preserved as an overriding public interest.[224] In particular, the Court has repeatedly held that Member States should not be forced to forego revenue to which they are entitled based on internationally accepted substantiations of the territoriality principle (*see also* §6.04[F][1]) both for personal and corporate income tax.[225] According to Englisch[226] the territoriality principle is particularly important as regards three types of national tax rules. The first is loss consolidation regimes that disallow cross-border loss relief (see §6.04[F][1]).[227] The second is exit taxes aimed at the taxation of accrued but yet unrealised capital gains when the taxing power is at risk to be lost.[228] And the third is tax rules aimed at preventing certain types of profit shifting and related tax evasion strategies.[229]

In a recent case, the ECJ found that it was compatible with EU law (Articles 56 and 58 EC, now Articles 63 and 65 TFEU) for a Member State to deny a tax payer to offset capital losses from the sale of real estate in France against Finnish capital gains from the sale of shares on the basis of the bilateral double taxation treaty between those two countries, notwithstanding that the tax payer would be eligible to offset those losses had the real estate been located in Finland.[230]

The application of OECD standards may have a negative effect on the progress of direct tax harmonisation where Member States may seek to enhance their autonomy by finding OECD approval for certain policies and practices.[231]

The next section looks at the interaction between the rules contained in the double tax conventions of the Member States with EU law. These rules play an important role in the regulatory framework for tax in the EU in the absence of harmonised tax rules at the EU level.[232]

---

224. *Schumacker, supra* note 178; ECJ, 12 May 1998, Case C-336/96, *Mr and Mrs Robert Gilly v. Directeur des Services Fiscaux du Bas-Rhin,* [1998] ECR I-2793; *Van Hilten-van der Heijden, supra* note 180, para. 48; ECJ, 7 September 2006, Case C-470/04, *N* [2006] ECR I-7409; ECJ, 8 November 2007, Case C-379/05, *Amurta SGPS v. Inspecteur van de Belastingdienst Amsterdam,* [2007] ECR I-9569; ECJ, 15 May 2008, Case C-414/06, *Lidl Belgium,* [2008] ECR I-3601.
225. For example, ECJ, 29 March 2007, Case C-347/04, *Rewe-Zentralfinanz,* [2007] ECR I-2647, para. 42; ECJ, 18 July 2007, Case C-231/05, *Oy AA,* [2007] ECR I-6373, para. 54; ECJ, 18 June 2009, Case C-303/07, *Aberdeen Property Fininvest Alpha,* [2009] ECR I-5145, para. 66.2.
226. Joachim Englisch, *supra* note 179, at 17.
227. *See*, for example, *Marks & Spencer, supra* note 188, para. 46; and *Lidl Belgium, supra* note 224, paras 31 et seq.
228. *See*, for example, ECJ, 7 September 2006, Case C-470/04, *N* [2006] ECR I-7409, para. 46; ECJ, 29 November 2011, Case C-371/10, *National Grid Indus,* [2011] ECR I-12273, para. 46; ECJ, 12 July 2012, Case C-269/09, *Commission v. Spain,* ECLI:EU:C:2012:439, para. 78.
229. *See*, for example, ECJ, 12 September 2006, Case C-196/04, *Cadbury Schweppes,* [2006] ECR I-7995, paras 55 et seq.; ECJ, 23 April 2008, Case C-201/05, *CFC and Divided GLO,* [2008] I-2875, para. 77 (CFC regime); ECJ, 13 March 2007, Case C-524/04, *Thin Cap GLO,* [2007] ECR I-2107, paras 74 et seq.; ECJ, 17 January 2008, Case C-105/07, *Lammers & Van Cleeff,* [2008] ECR I-173, para. 28 (thin capitalisation); ECJ, 21 January 2010, Case C-311/08, *SGI,* [2010] ECR I-487, para. 60 (transfer pricing).
230. ECJ 7 November 2013, Case C-322/11, *K,* ECLI:EU:C:2013:716.
231. Joachim Englisch, *supra* note 179, at 18.
232. For a detailed discussion of the regulatory framework for tax in the EU *see* Tom O'Shea, 'EU Tax Regulatory Framework', 955 *The Tax Journal,* 21–24 (2008).

[b] *The Interaction Between Double Tax Conventions and EU Law*

[i] General Remarks

Double tax conventions concluded by the Member States must also comply with EU law, subject to an exception contained in Article 307 EC.[233] This is clear from the Court's *Gottardo* judgment where the ECJ stated that 'when giving effect to commitments assumed under international agreements, be it an agreement between Member States or an agreement between a Member State and one or more non-member countries, Member States are required, subject to the provisions of Article 307 EC, to comply with the obligations that Community law imposes on them. The fact that non-member countries, for their part, are not obliged to comply with any Community-law obligation is of no relevance in this respect'.[234]

The Article 307 EC exception relates to double tax conventions and international agreements (so-called prior agreements or pre-Community agreements) concluded by a Member State before it joined the EU. Such agreements are binding contracts under international law. Since such prior agreements may contain provisions which are incompatible with EU law, Article 307 EC provides that the Member State is obliged to either amend such agreements or terminate them to ensure full compliance with EU law.[235]

Double tax conventions are necessary since few rules exist at the EU level to deal with overlapping tax jurisdiction. There is the Parent Subsidiary Directive which deals with cross-border dividend payments between associated companies and permanent establishments, the Interest and Royalties Directive which concerns certain cross-border interest and royalty payments and the Arbitration Convention which relates certain transfer pricing disputes involving EU companies. Other than these legislative instruments, double tax conventions are necessary to assist with the regulation of double taxation issues within the EU and internationally whenever an EU Member State is involved. Consequently, in the absence of EU law rules, double tax conventions between two EU Member States and between an EU Member State and a Third Country exist and form part of the regulatory framework for taxation in the EU.

Double tax conventions entered into by EU Member States are obliged to comply with EU law. Accordingly, in an EU law environment, issues may arise concerning EU

233. Article 307 EC is now Art. 351 TFEU.

234. ECJ, 15 January 2002, Case C-55/00, *Elide Gottardo v. Istituto nazionale della previdenza sociale (INPS)*, [2002] ECR I-0413, para. 33.

235. To date, no double tax conventions have been challenged under Art. 307 EC (Art. 351 TFEU). However, there have been ECJ decisions concerning the compatibility of bilateral investment treaties with free movement of capital. *See* ECJ, 3 March 2009, Case C-205/06, *Commission v. Austria (Bilateral Investment Treaties)*, [2009] ECR I-01301; ECJ, 19 November 2009, Case C-118/07, *Commission v. Finland (Bilateral Investment Treaties)*, [2009] ECR I-10889, and ECJ, 3 March 2009, Case C-249/06, *Commission v. Sweden (Bilateral Investment Treaties)*, [2009] ECR I-01301.

law which do not exist outside the EU's regulatory framework. One example of such a problem is seen in the Court's *Saint-Gobain* judgment.[236]

[ii] The National Treatment Principle

In *Saint-Gobain*, a French company exercised its freedom of establishment and created a branch in Germany. This branch was refused certain tax advantages concerning the receipt of foreign dividends, which were granted to Germany resident companies. Since Saint-Gobain was a French company with a branch located in Germany, it did not qualify for such tax advantages. However, the company argued that it was entitled to national treatment in Germany along the lines of the *Avoir Fiscal* judgment discussed above.

The ECJ noted that the refusal to grant to tax concessions in question to the permanent establishment in Germany of Saint-Gobain made it 'less attractive for those companies to have inter-corporate holdings through German branches (...), which thus restricts the freedom to choose the most appropriate legal form for the pursuit of activities in another Member State'.[237] The Court dismissed the German arguments that the French company with the branch in Germany was not in a comparable situation to a resident company, highlighting that both were liable to tax on dividends received in Germany.

Similarly, the Court rejected the German argument that the realm of double tax conventions was outside the scope of Community competence. The Court pointed out that although the Member States remained competent to enter into double tax conventions as far as 'the exercise of the power of taxation so allocated is concerned, the Member States nevertheless may not disregard Community rules. According to the settled case-law of the Court, although direct taxation is a matter for the Member States, they must nevertheless exercise their taxation powers consistently with Community law'.[238] The Court explained that in the case of 'a double-taxation treaty concluded between a Member State and a non-member country, the national treatment principle requires the Member State which is party to the treaty to grant to permanent establishments of non-resident companies the advantages provided for by that treaty on the same conditions as those which apply to resident companies'.[239] This means that Germany was obliged to ensure that the French company with the branch in Germany received no less favourable tax treatment than a German resident company. The Court's interpretation of the national treatment principle did not impact on the third country's situation under its double tax convention with Germany. Accordingly, in *Saint-Gobain*, for instance, the United States of America (USA) was not obliged to reduce its withholding taxes on the USA dividends paid to the branch of the French

236. ECR, 21 September 1991, Case C-307/97, *Compagnie de Saint-Gobain v. Finanzamt Aachen-Innenstadt*, [1999] ECR I-6161.
237. *Saint-Gobain*, *supra*, para. 42.
238. *Saint-Gobain*, *supra* note 236, para. 57.
239. *Saint-Gobain*, *supra* note 236, para. 58.

company located in Germany; this was a matter for Germany to deal with to ensure national treatment was received by *Saint-Gobain*.[240]

[iii] Reverse Discrimination

Interestingly, the ECJ has interpreted the fundamental freedoms in a way that allows for better treatment of foreign nationals than own nationals. This is clear from judgments like *Bouanich*[241] and *Van Hilten*,[242] both direct tax cases.

In *Bouanich*, The ECJ scrutinised Swedish rules concerning the repurchase of shares in a Swedish company by a French investor (Bouanich). If a Swedish investor made the same investment in the shares of the Swedish company and had those shares repurchased, that investor would be treated as receiving a capital gain taxed in Sweden at the rate of 30% with a deduction for the acquisition cost of the shares whereas Bouanich was treated as receiving a deemed dividend taxed at the reduced rate of 15% under the Swedish-French Double Tax Convention with a deduction for the nominal value of the shares. Bouanich complained that these Swedish rules infringed her free movement of capital rights.

The ECJ noted that Bouanich was in a comparable situation to a Swedish resident investor even though she was a non-resident since her acquisition costs were the same as a resident investor in relation to the taxation of the profits made on the repurchase of the shares by the Swedish company. The ECJ explained 'the cost of acquisition is directly linked to the payment made on the occasion of a share repurchase so that, in this regard, residents and non-residents are in a comparable situation'.[243] The Court went on to conclude that it was a matter for the Swedish referring court 'to determine in the proceedings before it whether the fact that non-resident shareholders are permitted to deduct the nominal value and are liable to a maximum tax rate of 15% amounts to treatment that is no less favourable than that afforded to resident shareholders, who have the right to deduct the cost of acquisition and are taxed at a rate of 30%'.[244]

The significance of the ECJ's ruling should be noted. If the tax treatment under the double tax convention is less favourable than national treatment in Sweden, then Bouanich is entitled to claim national treatment because the Court determined that she was in a comparable situation to a Swedish resident investor. However, if the tax treatment under the double tax convention is better than national treatment, clearly, Bouanich is entitled to benefit from this more favourable tax treatment. This means that the ECJ may allow a 'reverse discrimination' to occur in that it is possible under the double tax convention for a non-resident investor to be treated better for tax purposes than a resident investor.

240. For the United Kingdom's response to *Saint-Gobain*, *see* http://www.hmrc.gov.uk/manuals/intmanual/INTM168340.htm (last visited 12 August 2013).
241. ECJ, 19 January 2006, Case C-265/04, *Margaretha Bouanich v. Skatteverket*, [2006] ECR I-923.
242. *Van Hilten*, *supra* note 180.
243. *Bouanich*, *supra* note 241, para. 40.
244. *Bouanich*, *supra* note 241, para. 55.

This interpretation of EU law was also applied in *Van Hilten*, in a case relating to Dutch inheritance tax rules which were upheld by the ECJ as being in keeping with the free movement of capital. Those rules imposed a trailing tax for 10 years on Dutch nationals who left the Netherlands and who died within 10 years of emigration. The Heirs of Van Hilten challenged these rules on the grounds that they restricted the free movement of capital but the Court held that since the Netherlands applied similar tax rules for all Dutch nationals whether they died in the Netherlands or elsewhere, there was no restriction on the free movement of capital. The Court pointed out 'such distinctions, for the purposes of allocating powers of taxation, cannot be regarded as constituting discrimination prohibited by Article 73b of the Treaty. They flow, in the absence of any unifying or harmonising measures adopted in the Community context, from the Member States' power to define, by treaty or unilaterally, the criteria for allocating their powers of taxation.'[245] Accordingly, the Dutch tax rules at issue treated Dutch nationals less favourably than Dutch residents from other Member States who left the Netherlands and died within 10 years of emigration. In the latter situation, the Dutch tax rules did not apply.

The *Van Hilten* case demonstrates that 'reverse discrimination' is acceptable to the ECJ given the right set of circumstances and when the national treatment principle also applies from an origin Member State perspective, the correct comparator involves two origin Member State nationals one of which is exercising a fundamental freedom or EU citizenship right.

[c] Neutralisation

The fundamental freedoms require equal treatment of residents and non-residents and of domestic-sourced and foreign-sourced income subject to the Court's comments in *ACT IV GLO* on the different obligations of source and resident Member States for the elimination of double taxation.[246] Justification for certain national tax treatment can be found in the 'rule of reason' previously discussed. In addition, the ECJ accepts discrimination that restrictions may be neutralised by the rules contained in a double tax convention. This is clear since the Court's *Bouanich* judgment. Such is a practical approach that makes good sense from an end-result perspective, because in such circumstances the restrictive treatment is effectively erased. This demonstrates that the rules contained in the double tax conventions of the Member States have to be taken into consideration when assessing whether a restriction on the exercise of a fundamental freedom has taken place because the double tax convention may have healed, neutralised or removed the restriction in question. See *Amurta* as an example where the approach is highlighted by the Court, but where the tax convention in question

245. *Van Hilten, supra* note 180, para. 47.
246. ECJ, 12 December 2006, Case C-374/04, *Test Claimants in Class IV of the ACT Group Litigation v. Commissioners of Inland Revenue* ("'*ACT IV GLO*"'), [2006] ECR I-11673, para. 65. The Court makes it clear in para. 68 that once 'a Member State, unilaterally or by a convention, imposes a charge to income tax not only on resident shareholders but also on non-resident shareholders in respect of dividends which they receive from a resident company, the position of those non-resident shareholders becomes comparable to that of resident shareholders.'

failed to remove the restriction in question.[247] The approach by the ECJ is factual in the sense that a neutralised taxpayer position must be actually achieved. In *Denkavit France* the French withholding tax on outbound dividends, which constituted a restriction on the freedom of establishment, was creditable under the tax treaty with the Netherlands; however, where the latter exempted participation dividends received by parent companies there was in effect no corporation tax against which to credit the withholding tax. As a result, no relief from the restriction was achieved and the withholding tax rules of France as the source state were held to be incompatible with Union law.[248] The same line of reasoning concerning the issue of neutralisation can also be seen in the joined cases C-10/14, C-14/14, and C-17/14.[249]

§6.05 ABUSE OF LAW IN THE EU

The ECJ has also been active in the tax avoidance field, developing its own interpretation as to what constitutes *tax avoidance*.[250] Thus, in paragraph 26 of *ICI*,[251] the Court determined that tax avoidance equated to wholly artificial arrangements, set up to circumvent the United Kingdom's tax legislation. The Court confirmed this approach in later cases.[252]

In *Halifax*, a landmark case concerning tax avoidance in the VAT field, the Court outlined that a general anti-abuse principle existed in EU law prohibiting 'transactions carried out not in the context of normal commercial operations, but solely for the purpose of wrongfully obtaining advantages provided for by Community law'.[253] However, the Court explained 'a trader's choice between exempt transactions and taxable transactions may be based on a range of factors, including tax considerations relating to the VAT system... [and that] ...taxpayers may choose to structure their business so as to limit their tax liability'.[254]

The Court went on to formulate a two-pronged test for abuse, stating that an abusive practice could exist only if, first, the transactions concerned 'result in the accrual of a tax advantage the grant of which would be contrary to the purpose of those

247. *Amurta*, *supra* note 224. This conclusion was confirmed in relation to inheritance tax in ECJ, 11 September 2008, Case C-43/07, *Arens-Sikkens*, [2008] ECR I-6887.
248. ECJ, 14 December 2006, Case C-170/05, *Denkavit France*, [2006] ECR I-11949. For a detailed analysis of the *Denkavit Internationaal* and *ACT IV GLO* cases, *see* Tom O'Shea, *Dividend Taxation Post-Manninen: Shifting Sands or Solid Foundations?*, (2007) 45 Tax Notes International, 887–918.
249. ECJ, 17 September 2015, *J. B. G. T. Miljoen*, Case C-10/14, *X*, Case C-14/14 and *Société Générale SA*, Case C-17/14 *v. Staatssecretaris van Financiën*, ECLI:EU:C:2015:608.
250. For a detailed discussion of the Court's view of *tax avoidance*, *see* Tom O'Shea, *CFC Reforms in the UK – Some EU Law Comments*, 13 (1) ECTJ 65-89 (2012–2013); *see also*, Robert F. van Brederode, *Third Party Risks and Liabilities in Case of VAT Fraud in the EU*, 34 (1) Int'l Tax J, 31–39 (2008).
251. *Supra* note 194.
252. *See Marks & Spencer*, *supra* note 188 and *SGI*, *supra* note 180, for instance.
253. ECJ, 21 February 2006, Case C-255/02, *Halifax Plc et al. v. Commissioners of Customs & Excise*, [2006] ECR I-01609, para. 69.
254. *Halifax*, *supra* note 253, para. 73.

provisions'.[255] And second, that 'it must also be apparent from a number of objective factors that the essential aim of the transactions concerned is to obtain a tax advantage... the prohibition of abuse is not relevant where the economic activity carried out may have some explanation other than the mere attainment of tax advantages'.[256] The Court's emphasis is on 'normal commercial operations'[257] and 'the real substance and significance of the transactions concerned'. The Court's guidance to the national court highlighted that 'it may take account of the purely artificial nature of those transactions and the links of a legal, economic and/or personal nature between the operators involved in the scheme for reduction of the tax burden'.[258]

The Court's reasoning in *Halifax* was followed in the later *RBS Deutschland*[259] judgment also concerning VAT and in *Cadbury Schweppes*,[260] a direct tax case. In *RBS Deutschland*, the Court noted that 'the characteristics of the transactions at issue in the main proceedings and the nature of the relations between the companies that carried out those transactions contain nothing to suggest an artificial arrangement that does not reflect economic reality and the sole aim of which is to obtain a tax advantage.'[261] The Court also pointed out that 'taxable persons are generally free to choose the organisational structures and the form of transactions which they consider to be most appropriate for their economic activities and for the purposes of limiting their tax burdens'.[262]

In *Cadbury Schweppes*, the Court applied the same two-pronged test for abuse in the direct tax field in relation to the United Kingdom's controlled foreign company rules. The Court ruled 'nationals of a Member State cannot attempt, under cover of the rights created by the Treaty, improperly to circumvent their national legislation. They must not improperly or fraudulently take advantage of provisions of Community law'.[263] However, the Court went on to hold that 'the fact that a Community national, whether a natural or a legal person, sought to profit from tax advantages in force in a Member State other than his State of residence cannot in itself deprive him of the right to rely on the provisions of the Treaty'.[264] The Court pointed out 'the fact that the company was established in a Member State for the purpose of benefiting from more favourable legislation does not in itself suffice to constitute abuse of that freedom'.[265]

The Court went on to explain that 'any advantage resulting from the low taxation to which a subsidiary established in a Member State other than the one in which the parent company was incorporated is subject cannot by itself authorise that Member

255. *Halifax, supra* note 253, para. 74.
256. *Halifax, supra* note 253, para. 75.
257. *Halifax, supra* note 253, para. 80.
258. *Halifax, supra* note 253, para. 81.
259. ECJ, 22 December 2010, Case C-277/09, *The Commissioners for Her Majesty's Revenue & Customs v. RBS Deutschland Holdings GmbH*, [2010] ECR I-13805.
260. *Cadbury Schweppes, supra* note 229.
261. *RBS Deutschland, supra* note 259, para. 51.
262. *RBS Deutschland, supra* note 259, para. 53.
263. *Cadbury Schweppes, supra* note 229, para. 35.
264. *Cadbury Schweppes, supra* note 229, para. 36.
265. *Cadbury Schweppes, supra* note 229, para. 37.

State to offset that advantage by less favourable tax treatment of the parent company'.[266] Furthermore, the Court highlighted that 'the mere fact that a resident company establishes a secondary establishment, such as a subsidiary, in another Member State cannot set up a general presumption of tax evasion and justify a measure which compromises the exercise of a fundamental freedom guaranteed by the Treaty'.[267]

However, the Court stressed that controlled foreign company rules could be justified where they related to 'wholly artificial arrangements aimed at circumventing the application of the legislation of the Member State concerned'.[268] The Court explained that 'in order for a restriction on the freedom of establishment to be justified on the ground of prevention of abusive practices, the specific objective of such a restriction must be to prevent conduct involving the creation of wholly artificial arrangements which do not reflect economic reality, with a view to escaping the tax normally due on the profits generated by activities carried out on national territory'.[269] This type of conduct was sufficient to 'undermine the right of the Member States to exercise their tax jurisdiction in relation to the activities carried out in their territory and thus to jeopardise a balanced allocation between Member States of the power to impose taxes'.[270] Therefore, the Court had to investigate whether the restriction on the freedom of establishment could be justified by the need to prevent loss to its taxable base owing to the existence of wholly artificial arrangements.

The ECJ determined, first, that controlled foreign company rules prevented the national tax base from being eroded by wholly artificial arrangements. Next, the Court had to assess whether the CFC rules in question were in keeping with the principle of proportionality. The Court confirmed that 'the fact that none of the exceptions provided for by the legislation on CFCs applies and that the intention to obtain tax relief prompted the incorporation of the CFC and the conclusion of the transactions between the latter and the resident company does not suffice to conclude that there is a wholly artificial arrangement intended solely to escape that tax'.[271]

The Court then went on to apply its *Halifax* test for abuse, pointing out that in order to find that there is such an arrangement 'there must be, in addition to a subjective element consisting in the intention to obtain a tax advantage, objective circumstances showing that, despite formal observance of the conditions laid down by Community law, the objective pursued by freedom of establishment, as set out in paragraphs 54 and 55 of this judgment, has not been achieved'.[272] In other words, there must be a subjective and an objective analysis of the situation at hand.

The Court explained that 'in order for the legislation on CFCs to comply with Community law, the taxation provided for by that legislation must be excluded where, despite the existence of tax motives, the incorporation of a CFC reflects economic

266. *Cadbury Schweppes*, *supra* note 229, para. 49.
267. *Cadbury Schweppes*, *supra* note 229, para. 50.
268. *Cadbury Schweppes*, *supra* note 229, para. 51.
269. *Cadbury Schweppes*, *supra* note 229, para. 55.
270. *Cadbury Schweppes*, *supra* note 229, para. 56.
271. *Cadbury Schweppes*, *supra* note 229, para. 63.
272. *Cadbury Schweppes*, *supra* note 229, para. 64.

reality'.[273] The Court stressed that there must be 'an actual establishment intended to carry on genuine economic activities in the host Member State'.[274] And, for this establishment to reflect economic reality, the Court determined that 'that finding must be based on objective factors which are ascertainable by third parties with regard, in particular, to the extent to which the CFC physically exists in terms of premises, staff and equipment'.[275] The Court concluded that the resident company, 'which is best placed for that purpose, must be given an opportunity to produce evidence that the CFC is actually established and that its activities are genuine'.[276] In the subsequent *Thin Cap GLO*[277] and *SGI*[278] cases, concerning thin capitalisation and transfer pricing rules respectively, the Court applied similar reasoning in determining whether national anti-abuse rules were compatible with the freedom of establishment. This was confirmed in later ECJ decisions[279] where the Court stated:

> 'According to settled case-law of the Court, where rules are predicated on an assessment of objective and verifiable elements making it possible to identify the existence of a wholly artificial arrangement entered into for tax reasons alone, they may be regarded as not going beyond what is necessary to prevent tax evasion and tax avoidance, if, on each occasion on which the existence of such an arrangement cannot be ruled out, those rules give the taxpayer an opportunity, without subjecting him to undue administrative constraints, to provide evidence of any commercial justification that there may have been for that transaction.'

The ECJ has thus adopted a simple approach in relation to national anti-abuse rules. Such may be justified on grounds of preventing the risk of tax avoidance where they specifically target 'wholly artificial arrangements designed to circumvent the legislation of the Member State concerned'.[280] But they may also be justified where they are 'not specifically designed to exclude from the tax advantage it confers such purely artificial arrangements - devoid of economic reality, created with the aim of escaping the tax normally due on the profits generated by activities carried out on national territory.'[281] The Court noted that such rules 'may nevertheless be regarded as justified by the objective of preventing tax avoidance, taken together with that of preserving the balanced allocation of the power to impose taxes between the Member States.'[282]

To sum up, Member States may retain their national anti-abuse rules such as CFC, Thin cap and Transfer pricing rules, but such national rules must comply with EU law, in particular, the freedom of establishment. The Court's interpretation of the

273. *Cadbury Schweppes, supra* note 229, para. 65.
274. *Cadbury Schweppes, supra* note 229, para. 66.
275. *Cadbury Schweppes, supra* note 229, para. 67.
276. *Cadbury Schweppes, supra* note 229, para. 70.
277. *Thin Cap GLO, supra* note 229.
278. *SGI, supra* note 180.
279. ECJ, 13 November 2014, Case C-112/14, *Commission v. United Kingdom of Great Britain and Northern Ireland*, ECLI:EU:C:2014:2369, para. 27 and ECJ, 3 October 2013, Case C-282/12, *Itelcar – Automóveis de Aluguer Lda v. Fazenda Pública*, ECLI:EU:C:2013:629, para. 37.
280. *SGI, supra* note 180, para. 65.
281. *SGI, supra* note 180, para. 66.
282. *SGI, supra* note 180, para. 66.

concept of tax avoidance is very important in this respect and is not as wide as might be expected because of the principle of proportionality. National anti-abuse rules are seen as restrictions on the freedom of establishment unless justified and proportionate. This means the Member States may only maintain such rules in situations where wholly artificial arrangements designed to circumvent the national tax system exist and the taxpayer has been given the opportunity to produce evidence that no such wholly artificial arrangement exists.

§6.06 CONCLUSIONS AND FINAL REMARKS

Although they share some features, the EU is not a federation of states but a single market. Apart from the ECJ, which functions to an extent as the Supreme Court for Union law, there is no separate lower court system comparable to for example federal district and appeal courts in the US. In fact, the national courts fulfil a double role where they are also charged with the application and interpretation of Union law. Cooperation between the ECJ and the national courts is imperative for the effectiveness of Union law. The tool provided in the treaty to accomplish this is the right and obligation of the national courts to address the ECJ with preliminary questions regarding Union law and the jurisdiction of the latter to answer those questions. The obligation to address the ECJ is not absolute. There is no reason to ask preliminary questions if the point of law is either clear or has been clarified in earlier rulings of the ECJ, but the national courts should not draw that conclusion lightly.

It can be anticipated that the national courts hold different views where their starting point in legal reasoning originates in distinct legal traditions. Common methods of interpretation are necessary to ensure uniform and equal administration of justice under Union law. The ECJ is remarkably proactive in its interpretation of Union law and is in fact the motor behind the European integration. Although the word 'activist' is somewhat charged and the Court has been criticised for this approach, it seems to make sense within the EU context.[283] However, this interpretative role has

283. On the 'activism' of the ECJ, *see* e.g., Eric Stein, *Lawyers, Judges and the Making of a Transnational Constitution*, 75 (1) American J Int'l L, 1–27 (1981); Mauro Cappelletti, *The Law-Making Power of the Judges and Its Limits: A Comparative Analysis*, 8 Monash University Law Review, 15–67 (1981–1982); Mauro Cappelletti, *Is the European Court of Justice Running Wild?*, 12 European Law Review, 3–17 (1987); Hjalte Rasmussen, *Between Self-restraint and Activism: A Judicial Policy for the European Court*, 13 European Law Review, 28–38 (1988); Fernand Schockweiler, *La Cour de justice des Communautés européennes dépasse-t-elle les limites de ses attributions?*, 18 Journal des Tribunaux, Droit Européen, 73–80 (1995); Patrick Neill, *The European Court of Justice: A Case Study in Judicial Activism*, 218, Intergovernmental Conference, Minutes of Evidence, House of Lords 1996; Takis Tridimas, *The European Court of Justice and Judicial Activism*, 21 European Law Review, 199–210 (1996); David Edward, *Judicial Activism – Myth or Reality?*, in David Campbell and Meropi Voyatzi (eds), *Legal Reasoning and Judicial Interpretation of European Law* (Essays in Honour of Lord Mackenzie-Stuart) (Gosport: Trenton Publishing, 1996), 29–67; D. Keeleng, *In Praise of Judicial Activism, but What Does It Mean? And Has the European Court of Justice Ever Practiced It?*, in Curti Gialdino (ed.), *Scritti in Onore di G.F. Mancini* (Milano: Giuffré, 1998), 505–536; Oreste Pollicino, *Legal Reasoning of the Court of Justice in the Context of the Principle of Equality between Judicial Activism and Self Restraint*, 5 (3) German Law Journal, 283–317 (2004); Henri

been given to it by the TFEU. Consequently, concepts such as the 'freedom of establishment' continue to evolve. In that sense, the Court is merely fulfilling its function as the main interpreter of the meaning of EU law. It is important to realise that the ECJ has to operate within a context deprived of a legal tradition and, therefore, has to develop its own 'European' tradition. That provides the ECJ with significant room to move, unprecedented from the perspective of courts of last resort operating within established traditions.

The question however remains whether the ECJ does not go too far in shaping the TFEU Treaty freedoms in cases of direct taxation, given the fact that direct taxes are hardly harmonised at the EU level. This is particular manifest when the ECJ develops doctrines as it did, for example, in the *Schumacker* and *Marcks & Spencer* cases, that continue to have a huge financial impact on the direct tax regimes of all the 28 Member States. The ECJ's notion of discrimination in direct tax cases is not free from criticism but, in general, it can be said that its case law has had a significant harmonising effect on the direct tax regimes of the Member States. It is, therefore, generally acknowledged that the case law of the ECJ has impacted the direct tax systems of the Member States far more substantially than the few direct tax directives that have been adopted in the past. And that is a remarkable achievement in itself.

In the field of taxation, as demonstrated by several VAT cases, the ECJ, generally, does not accept a legalistic approach. Its reasoning is based on the purpose and economic objectives of the tax. Where the mechanics of a VAT directive fail to deliver the intended result, the Court has shown no hesitation in interpreting the text in a manner that is consistent with the purpose of the tax. Teleological interpretation is clearly the dominant methodology applied by the ECJ in VAT cases. However, the court also applies a restrictive interpretation, particularly when provisions of EU law constitute exceptions to the main rules, such as VAT exemptions or, for direct tax, when derogations are involved.

A detailed study of the Court's case law since 1986 reveals the consistency of the ECJ, which is not a tax court. Rather, the ECJ may be described in the direct tax field as an 'internal market' Court because most of its jurisprudence involves a national tax rule, which interacts with a fundamental freedom or EU citizenship right. The national tax rule will either be in an origin Member State setting or in a host State environment. Understanding whether a host or origin state situation is at play assists immensely in understanding how to analyse the case at hand; how to compute the correct comparator; whether discrimination on grounds of nationality exists; whether indirect discrimination is possibly at stake or whether a restriction analysis is the correct approach.

In many respects, the ECJ functions like a common law court. Past cases have a huge significance for current cases. This is evident from both its direct tax and VAT jurisprudence. The Court's case law is extremely consistent but continues to evolve so that new issues continue to arise in the cases which come before the Court. Moreover, it is apparent from the Court's tax jurisprudence that the Court rarely overrules its

---

de Waele, *The Role of the European Court of Justice in the Integration Process: Contemporary and Normative Assessment*, 6 (1) Hanse Law Review, 3-26 (2010).

previous judgments. Instead, it sometimes distinguishes a previous line of cases and before heading off in a slightly different direction.[284]

The Court regularly uses paragraphs from previous judgments and inserts them, often verbatim, into current judgments.[285] Thus, in the direct tax cases for example, near the start of every judgment, the Court will highlight that 'Although, as Community law stands at present, direct taxation does not as such fall within the purview of the Community, the powers retained by the Member States must nevertheless be exercised consistently with Community law'.[286]

The Court will also link current statements in judgments to previous cases and provide references to previous case law and relevant paragraphs.

Therefore, it may be said that the Court places great relevance on its previous case law and it has built up a considerable jurisprudence concerning direct taxes (over 280 judgments between 1960 and 2016 and VAT (over 750 judgments until 2016), but there is no principle of *stare decisis*[287] in operation even though in practice the ECJ generally follows its previous rulings.

284. *See*, for example, ECJ, 24 November 1993, Joined Cases C-267/91 and C-268/91, *Criminal proceedings against Bernard Keck and Daniel Mithouard* (Keck), [1993] ECR I-06097 and ECJ, 25 July 2008, Case C-127/08, *Blaise Baheten Metock and Others v. Minister for Justice, Equality and Law Reform*, [2008] ECR I-06241.
285. This practice relates to the fact that each paragraph of a judgment of the ECJ has to be voted upon and agreed by all the judges. There are no dissenting opinions in the judgments of the ECJ just a single judgment in each case.
286. *Schumacker*, *supra* note 178, para. 21.
287. *Stare decisis* is a legal principle by which courts are obliged to respect the precedent established by prior decisions. A precedent is a principle or rule established in an earlier case that is either binding on or persuasive for a court when deciding subsequent cases with similar issues or facts. *See*, for example, *Machado v. Fontes* (1897) 2 QB 231; *Young v. Bristol Aeroplane Co. Ltd.* (1944) 1 KB 718 and *Boys v. Chaplin*, [1968] 2 WLR 328. For some of the literature on this topic, *see* P.R. Beaumont, *Indirect Effect of Directives and Stare Decisis*, 55 (3) S.L.G., 77–78 (1987); Peter W. Edge, *Decisions of the Judicial Committee of the Privy Council in Other Jurisdictions: Limits of Stare Decisis in Commonwealth Jurisdictions*, 20 (2) C.L.B., 720–727 (1994); Michael Littlewood, *The Privy Council, the Source of Income and Stare Decisis*, 2 B.T.R., 121–145 (2004); T. Prime and G. Scanlan, *Stare Decisis and the Court of Appeal; Judicial Confusion and Judicial Reform?*, C.J.Q., 212–227 (2004); Anne Scully-Hill and Hans Mahncke, *The Emergence of the Doctrine of Stare Decisis in the World Trade Organization Dispute Settlement System*, 36 (2) Legal I.E.I., 133–156 (2009); Frank Emmert, *Stare Decisis: A Universally Misunderstood Idea*, 6 (2) Leg., 207–227 (2012) and David P. Boyle, *Circumstances in Which Stare Decisis Applies*, 31 (5) I.L.T., 68–69 (2013).

CHAPTER 7
Legal Interpretation of Tax Law: France

Thomas Dubut

Whereas the importance of legal interpretation is generally acknowledged in the literature, its precise meaning and functions vary among jurisdictions, but also among branches of law. The legal interpretation of tax law in France indeed raises issues not replicated in other branches of law, while at the same time reflecting the main features of legal interpretation in the French legal order.

This chapter is structured as follows. The introduction briefly explains the French legal system, with a special emphasis on the place of tax law (§7.01). The meaning and functions of legal interpretation in the French legal theory will then be explained with a view to assessing their concrete implications for tax law (§7.02), also in light of the fact that the French tax legislation contains almost no interpretation rules or definitions (§7.03). Against this background, it will then be possible to focus on the main principles and methods used in the legal interpretation of tax law by the tax administration (§7.04) and the French courts (§7.05). A special section will be dedicated to the legal interpretation of VAT law, which has been largely harmonized at the EU level and should be thus interpreted according to the principles and methods of EU law, which are not necessarily the same as the principles and methods applied to the other fields of tax law in France (§7.06). Some tentative conclusions will be drawn in the final section (§7.07).

§7.01 INTRODUCTORY REMARKS ON THE FRENCH LEGAL SYSTEM

[A] The Continental Character of the French Legal System

As most of the European legal orders, the French legal system is a continental, civil law one: France follows the civil law tradition, according to which the rules of law are basically written and codified.[1] Whereas this does not exclude the existence of non-written rules of law, in particular customary law, it is generally accepted that any non-written rules can only be applied insofar as a written rule of law contains a reference to this end.[2] The French civil law code, for instance, does contain several references to customs to supplement its provisions;[3] by contrast, it is not accepted that non-written rules can override written rules (*contra legem* customary law).[4]

Against this background, and contrary to what happens in the common law jurisdictions, the case law of the courts is not in principle a source of law, as there is no 'rule of precedent' in the French legal order.[5] It is generally accepted that the judgments apply the rules of law in a given case and do not create generally applicable rules.[6] However, the influence of the judgments of the French Supreme Courts shall not be undermined: there is an undeniable trend of the lower courts to follow the interpretation of the law of the Supreme Courts in cases other than the one that gave rise to the interpretation, although in principle they have no legal obligation to do so. This has been one of the most disputed issues in French legal theory over the course of the last two decades, as is explained further below in §7.02.

[B] The Dual System of Courts in France

Another basic feature of the French legal order is the so-called 'dual system of courts'. According to this system, there are two separate orders of courts, the judicial order that deals with civil and criminal law cases and the administrative order that deals with cases against the public administration. The Court of Cassation (*Court de Cassation*) is the Supreme Court of the judicial order, whereas the Council of State (*Conseil d'Etat*) is the Supreme Court of the administrative order.

Historically, the existence of a specific judge to deal with cases involving the public administration was seen as a privilege, as it was intended to preserve the administration and the government from the ordinary courts. However, nowadays the independence of the administrative judge is undisputable. This is due to the prestige of the Council of State, but also to the recognition of the constitutional value of the principle of independence of the administrative judge.[7] A specific court, the Tribunal of Conflicts (*Tribunal des conflits*), has been established to resolve cases of positive or negative conflict between the two orders of courts.[8] The Tribunal of Conflicts has an

1. René David, *French Law – Its Structure, Sources, and Methodology*, Baton Rouge: Louisiana State University Press, 1972, p. 9.
2. *See* Bernard Stirn, *La place de la coutume internationale en droit public français*, 12 The Law and Practice of International Courts and Tribunals: 267–271 (2013).
3. *See*, for examples, Art. 2279 or 1135 of the Civil Code.
4. CE, 6 June 1997, No. 148683, *Aquarone* (which dealt with international customary law), Rec. Lebon, 206.
5. Some French academics do not agree on this point. *See* mainly: Philippe Jestaz, *Les sources du droit*, 2nd ed., Paris: Dalloz, 2015, p. 11.
6. This is clearly stated in Art. 5 of the French Civil Code.
7. Conseil constitutionnel, No. 80.119 DC, 22 July 1980, décision Validation d'actes administratifs.
8. Lionel Neville Brown, John Bell & Jean-Michel Galabert, *French Administrative Law*, 5th ed., Oxford-New York: Clarendon Press-Oxford University Press, 1998, p. 149.

important role in tax matters, as some tax disputes belong to the judicial order and some other to the administrative order and the allocation is not always obvious.

An important feature of the French jurisdictional system is that both French Supreme Courts can be requested to provide guidance to the lower courts belonging to their order on the interpretation of the law, when these are dealing with a case presenting specific legal complexity.[9] In this case, the Court of Cassation and the Council of State respectively are issuing opinions (*avis*), which, despite the fact that they are not legally binding upon lower courts, undoubtedly have a harmonizing effect on French case law. It should be highlighted however that the opinions issued by the French Supreme Courts exclusively concern the interpretation of general rules and not the legal qualification of the facts of the case, which is in the remit of the lower courts.[10]

[C] The Judicial Review of Legislation Enacted by the Parliament in France

Another important element of the French system is the existence of a separate Court entrusted with the judicial review of legislation enacted by Parliament, the Constitutional Council (*Conseil constitutionnel*). According to the French Constitution, the French Constitutional Council has the exclusive competence to assess the compatibility of laws enacted by Parliament and, as a consequence of the 'constitutional block' doctrine, all international treaties signed by France.[11] Traditionally, in France, judicial review of laws enacted by the Parliament could only be exercised before their entry into force. In case the Constitutional Council concluded that one or more of the provisions of the draft laws were unconstitutional, they could not enter into force at all (*a priori* review).[12]

However, recent reform of the French constitutional adjudication system[13] empowered the ordinary courts, both of the judicial and of the administrative order, to submit an application for a preliminary ruling (prejudicial question) on the conformity of an enacted legislative provision with the Constitution (*a posteriori* review), if one of the parties in an ongoing case alleges that this provision is not compatible with the 'rights and freedoms that the Constitution guarantees'. The application for a preliminary ruling is submitted to the Supreme Courts, i.e., the Court of Cassation and the

9. *See* Arts 1031-1 to 1031-7 of the new Code of civil procedure; Arts 706-64 to 706-70 of the Code of criminal procedure; Arts L. 441-1 à L. 441-4 and R. 151-1 of the Code of the judicial organization; and finally Art. L. 113-1 of the Code of Administrative Justice.
10. Vincent Dussart, *Les avis contentieux du Conseil d'Etat en matière fiscal*, 210 Les Petites affiches: 3–12 (20 October 2004).
11. The French 'Constitutional block' (*bloc de constitutionnalité*) includes not only the Constitution of 1958, but also the other texts referred to in its preamble: The Declaration of the Rights of Man and Citizen of 1789, the preamble of the Constitution of 1946 (which adds a number of 'social rights', as well as the equality of males and females), The Charter for the Environment of 2004 (http://www.conseil-constitutionnel.fr/conseil-constitutionnel/english/constitution/constitution-of-4-october-1958.25742.html).
12. Michel Troper, 'Constitutional Law', in Etienne Picard & George A. Bermann (eds), *Introduction to French Law*, The Netherlands: Kluwer Law International, 2008, pp. 30 et seq.
13. Constitutional Law No 2008-724 of 23 July 2008 that introduced Art. 61-1 in the Constitution.

Council of State respectively, which take the final decision to submit it or not to the Constitutional Council. This procedure is called 'question prioritaire de constitutionnalité' (QPC)[14] and has been implemented since 1 March 2010.[15]

The French Constitutional Council has an important role in tax matters because, according to the French Constitution, only a law enacted by Parliament can contain rules on tax base, tax rates and tax recovery.[16] As mentioned above, the judicial review of laws enacted by Parliament belongs to the exclusive competence of the Constitutional Council, which indeed regularly reviews tax legislation and has developed a considerable body of case law.[17] As a matter of fact, according to recent statistics, the vast majority of prejudicial questions submitted to the Constitutional Court by the Council of State stems from disputes in tax matters.[18]

By contrast, contrary to other Constitutional Courts in Europe, such as the German *Bundesverfassungsgericht*, the French Constitutional Council is not empowered to review a general rule unless the measure has been enacted by Parliament. Thus, for instance, the judicial review of ministerial decrees or administrative orders belongs to the administrative courts and in particular the Council of State.

Although, in principle, judicial review of legislation results either in the validation or in validation of one or more provisions, it has also an important interpretative function. In fact, in the same way as other constitutional Courts in Europe,[19] the French Constitutional Council often accepts the compatibility of a provision with the rules and principles of the 'constitutional block', the doctrine adopted by the French Constitutional Council that permits review of laws subject to the provisions in the Constitution and broader principles set out in the Constitution. This is made through a so-called declaration of conformity to the Constitution subject to a reservation of interpretation (*constitutionalité sous reserve d'interprétation*).[20] In practical terms, such a reservation puts an obligation upon the authorities entrusted with the application of the law to interpret it in a specific way. Although the technique of reservation of interpretation is not specific to tax law, but is generally applied by the French Constitutional Council, some specific illustrations can also be found regarding tax rules. Some concrete examples are presented below under §7.05[E].

---

14. Otto Pfersmann, Concrete Review as Indirect Constitutional Complaint in French Constitutional Law: A Comparative Perspective, 6(2) European Constitutional Law Review: 223–248 (June 2010). *See also* Sophie Boyron, *The Constitution of France: A Contextual Analysis*, Oxford: Hart Publishing, 2012, pp. 154 et seq.
15. From March 2010 to June 2016, this procedure had a real success and, despite the filtering of two Supreme Courts, more than 500 QPCs have been submitted to the CC. (http://www.conseil-constitutionnel.fr/conseil-constitutionnel/francais/nouveaux-cahiers-du-conseil/cahier-n-54/bilan-statistique-au-30-septembre-2016.148598.html)
16. This is the so-called principle of legality of taxes guaranteed in Art. 34 of the French Constitution of 1958.
17. Loic Philip, *Droit fiscal constitutionnel: Evolution d'une jurisprudence*, Paris: Economica, 2014.
18. Conseil d'Etat, *Rapport Public 2016*, Paris: La documentation française, 2016. *See also*: Marc Guillaume, *La question prioritaire de constitutionnalité et le droit fiscal*, 14 Revue de droit fiscal (7 April 2011).
19. For instance, the German or the Italian Constitutional Courts.
20. *See* Alexandre Viala, *Les réserves d'interprétation dans la jurisprudence du Conseil constitutionnel*, Paris: LGDJ, 1999.

[D] The Place of Tax Law in the French Legal and Jurisdictional Order

Against this background, it is hardly surprising that the French Tax Law is not only written, but also largely codified. The main tax rules are indeed codified in two documents, the General Code of Taxes (*Code general des impôts – CGI*) and the Book of Tax procedures (*Livre des procédures fiscales – LPF*). The CGI covers direct and indirect taxes, i.e., income tax, corporate tax, VAT, registration fees and local taxes, and has around 2,000 articles, whereas the LPF contains the rules that apply to tax audits, tax disputes and tax recovery.[21]

Tax law makes part of the French public law and more precisely of administrative law, and tax disputes are in principle within the remit of administrative courts and ultimately of the Council of State. However, there are also tax disputes that are in the remit of the judicial order. By contrast, there are no specific tax courts, as in other civil law[22] and in common law countries.[23] The allocation of competences between the two jurisdictional orders in tax matters is the result of an historic, progressive shaping, which is today reflected in the LPF.

More precisely, although in principle the disputes related to the tax base belong to the administrative courts, the ordinary/judicial courts are competent for disputes related to the tax base of registration fees and other fees applied in case of transmission of property,[24] but also for disputes related to the tax base of the wealth tax (*ISF*). This exception is due to the fact that according to the French 'constitutional block', the ordinary/judicial judge is the guardian of the private property;[25] as a result, disputes for taxes that concern private property of the taxpayer should also fall within the remit of the competence of the ordinary/judicial courts and not of the administrative judge. Similarly, actions for the annulment of tax recovery proceedings[26] as well as damage claims against the public administration for illegal actions (including in the field of taxation) fall within the jurisdiction of the judicial courts. In any case, the allocation of competences between the two orders of courts in tax matters is complex and has given rise to several decisions of the Tribunal of Conflicts; the tax administration has even issued guidance in this respect.[27]

21. However, the codification of the tax rules does not prejudge in no way a better readability of the tax legislation. To date the Tax Code (CGI and LPF) dates from 1950s and has never been subject to a recodification.
22. For instance, in Italy or Portugal.
23. This is the case in many Anglo-Saxon countries, e.g., the United States, Canada, South Africa, New Zealand or Australia.
24. Article 199 LPF.
25. CC, Decision no 89-256 DC of 25 July 1989.
26. Article 281 LPF.
27. BOI-CTX-ADM-10-10-10-20120912.

§7.02 MEANING AND FUNCTIONS OF LEGAL INTERPRETATION IN FRENCH LEGAL THEORY

[A] The French Debate on Interpretation

Interpretation has been one of the main topics discussed in French Legal Theory over the last decade. A passionate debate is indeed still ongoing in France on the specific meaning of legal interpretation and the normative basis for Court judgments, in particular those of the Supreme Courts, i.e., the Court of Cassation, the Council of State and the Constitutional Court. This debate was initiated by an important faction within French Legal Theory, according to which legal texts have no objective meaning but instead are gateways for judges to interpret and determine their meaning. In doing so, the judge – or at least the supreme judge – is thus legally free to decide, as the judgment is not subject to any further appeal. This school of thought belongs to Legal Realism and is known as 'Realistic Theory of Interpretation' (*théorie réaliste de l'interprétation*).[28]

Although there is no appeal against the judgments of the Supreme Courts, the realistic theory of interpretation acknowledges that their decision-making is not entirely free. Contrary to the traditional positivist conception, however, the constraint does not arise from the meaning of the applicable legal rules – in other words decision-making is not framed by the interpretation of the text – but rather from sociological or political factors, including the obligation to provide a convincing explanation or rationale to the forum of public opinion.[29]

Although, currently, the 'realistic theory of interpretation' is very influential in French legal theory, in particular in constitutional law, its premises are not unanimously accepted. Ultimately, this theory goes against the written, civil law character of the French legal order and would allocate to the Supreme Courts the power to decide on the content of general rules irrespective of the wording of the texts. Although there might be cases in which the Supreme Courts have indeed taken decisions incompatible with the rules in place, the weakness of the realistic theory consists of trying to provide a conceptual justification for these cases and even allocating a general power to the judge to transgress the rules enacted by the legislators. Another important group of French legal theorists takes the position that the realistic theory fails to distinguish conceptually different operations and their legal consequences, if any.[30]

28. Michel Troper. *La théorie du droit, le droit, l'Etat*, Paris: PUF, 2001, pp. 69–84.
29. Michel Troper, Véronique Champeil-Desplats & Christophe Grzegorczyk (eds), *Théorie des contraintes juridiques*, Bruxelles-Paris: Bruylant-LGDJ, 2005.
30. *See* mainly Otto Pfersmann, *Contre le néo-réalisme juridique. Pour un débat sur l'interprétation*, Revue française de droit constitutionnel: 279–334 (2002), but also Etienne Picard, 'Contre la Théorie réaliste de l'interprétation juridique', in Gilles Darcy, Véronique Labrot & Mathieu Doat (eds), *L'office du juge*, Paris: Les colloques du Sénat, 2006, pp. 42 et seq.

[B] The Various Meanings of the Term 'Legal Interpretation'

It is indeed necessary to identify the different meanings of the term 'interpretation' in law and specify the meaning that will be adopted in this chapter. Interpretation may refer at least to the followings two distinct operations:

(i) The *intellectual operation* by which the meaning of a text is determined.
(ii) The *normative operation* by which a specific decision is made in a given case on the basis of generally applicable rules.

Although the two operations are often closely connected in the rationale for judgments and administrative decisions, they are conceptually distinct: the legal interpretation as intellectual operation does not exclusively belong to the institutions empowered to apply the rules of law with authority (which are mainly the courts and the administration), but is a central part of the work of all legal practitioners and academics. Conversely, although the application of the rules in a specific case - often called in the French literature 'qualification' of facts, might require the interpretation of general rules, this is not always the case. As a result, the reasoning behind a judgment or of an administrative decision might or might not include the interpretation of the relevant texts, even in a civil law system like the French one. This is usually the case when the meaning of the text is deemed to be clear and the reasoning behind the decision focuses on the application of law to specific fact situations, in other words in subsuming an individual situation to the general, abstract rules.

In this chapter, the term 'legal interpretation' is used for the interpretation of tax rules by actors empowered to apply these rules to concrete cases, in particular the tax administration and the judge. The analysis is limited to the intellectual operation of determining the precise meaning of a legal text intended to set a generally applicable, abstract rule and clearly distinguish this operation from the normative operation by which the rule is applied in a specific case with legal authority. The later operation consists in the creation of an individual/specific decision, in other words an individual rule, and in this sense it is a normative operation and not an intellectual one.

The courts and the tax administration need to proceed to the legal interpretation of the tax rules in place before taking an individual decision at least in the following cases: when the text of the legislation contains general, abstract terms; when there is no explicit rule for a given situation; and, when two rules are contradicting each other. The analysis of legal interpretation of tax law will precisely focus on the methods used by the tax administration and the courts when a rule is drafted in such a way that its application in a given case requires its interpretation as an intellectual operation of determining the meaning of a text.

The general analysis that follows mainly takes into account the legal interpretation of tax rules on income, corporate, property taxes and registration fees. The VAT law has been mostly harmonized in the EU and the drafting and interpretation of national legislation presents several specificities, as it has to comply with binding EU rules and legal interpretation of the Court of Justice of the EU. A special paragraph will be dedicated to this topic.

§7.03 THE ABSENCE OF INTERPRETATION RULES IN FRENCH TAX LAW

Although it is extensively written and codified, one of the most surprising features of French tax law is the absence of any rules on interpretation. Contrary to the case with other French Codes, the CGI does not contain definitions of recurrent terms, such as the term 'tax' or the term 'permanent establishment' for domestic purposes (*entreprise exploitée en France*). Similarly, there are no explicit interpretation rules referring to common interpretation methods, namely literal interpretation, historic interpretation, contextual interpretation, teleological interpretation, living interpretation, etc.

On the other hand, the Civil Code contains a general principal, applicable to all the branches of French law, according to which the judge cannot refuse to render judgment in a given case on the grounds that the law is silent, unclear or insufficient.[31] In France, the denial of justice is a criminal offence.[32] At the same time it constitutes a violation of the right to a fair trial guaranteed by Article 6 §1 of the European Convention of Human Rights. It follows that the judge is obliged to interpret and apply the law, even when its provisions are unclear or contradictory and even when there are no specific interpretation rules to provide guidance.

By contrast, interpretation rules can be found in other branches of French law and in particular in the civil code, which contains extensive rules on the interpretation of contracts.[33] However, these rules do not apply to tax matters.

§7.04 LEGAL INTERPRETATION OF TAX LAW BY THE FRENCH TAX ADMINISTRATION

[A] The Role of the 'Administrative Doctrine'

At first sight it might appear surprising that a concrete analysis of legal interpretation of tax law in France commences with a look at the interpretation provided by the tax administration. However, the so-called 'administrative doctrine', in other words the interpretation of tax rules by the tax administration, plays a very important role, both in terms of quality and in terms of quantity.

It is generally accepted that the French tax law, although extensively written and codified, is poorly drafted and structured.[34] As already mentioned, the CGI contains around 2,000 provisions enacted by Parliament, many of which are frequently modified by the annual fiscal law (*Loi de Finances*). The draft version of these provisions is prepared by the French tax administration and the measures are then (re)shaped and adapted during the ordinary legislative procedure, where the necessary expertise and

31. Article 4 of the French Civil Code.
32. Article 434-7-16 of the French Penal Code.
33. Articles 1188–1192 of the French Civil code.
34. *See* Michel Taly, *Le code général des impôts, Elephant Man juridique*, 4(151) Pouvoirs: 87–97 (2014); Olivier Fouquet, *Améliorer la sécurité juridique des relations entre l'administration fiscale et les contribuables: une nouvelle approche*, Rapport au ministre du Budget, Paris: La Documentation Française, June 2008, pp. 10 et seq.

technical background is often lacking,[35] before insertion into the CGI. The general lack of technical expertise among legislators negatively affects the readability and intelligibility of the CGI as a whole. The intelligibility and transparency of the law is a constitutional requirement as a consequence of the 'constitutional block' doctrine, the French Constitutional Court has consequently invalidated several tax provisions on the grounds that they were too complicated and thus not compatible with this requirement.[36] As a matter of fact, without the interpretation of these texts by the tax administration, taxpayers and their counsels would have difficulty comprehending the tax law.

The French tax administration has made significant efforts to remedy this situation and provide guidance. More significantly, it is editing an annually updated handbook[37] gathering the main provisions of the CGI as applied by its agents, as well as several guidance documents (tax circulars, instructions or memos). In addition, since 2009, several draft guidance documents are subject to online public consultation for comments before their adoption. Contrary to the French tax legislation, the quality of the French 'tax doctrine' is generally acknowledged, as the different guidance documents edited by the French tax administration are usually very informative and easy to read and to understand.

Moreover, these guidance documents are easily accessible to everyone: they are regrouped in the so-called 'basic documentation' (*Documentation de base*) and are regularly published in a dedicated database.[38] In quantitative terms, on average, the French tax administration publishes around 200 new guidance documents/instructions per year, and the total volume of them in 2012 was estimated at more than 40,000 pages.[39]

[B] The Main Orientations of the 'Administrative Doctrine'

Generally speaking, the interpretation of tax rules by the French tax administration is protective of the taxpayers and often less rigid than a purely formal reading of the texts would suggest. Although this is an observation and not a binding principle, i.e., an obligation for the tax administration, it is generally verified in practice. For instance, there have been cases where the guidance of the tax administration provided some additional deadline for the submission of tax returns.[40] In other cases, the doctrine of the French tax administration has put in place procedures of pre-consultation intended

35. Cour des Comptes, *Les relations de l'administration fiscale avec les particuliers et les entreprises*, Rapport public thématique, February 2012, p. 82; Michel Taly, *Les coulisses de la politique fiscale*, Paris: PUF, 2016, pp. 75 et seq.
36. CC, QPC no 2012-298 of 8 March 2013; CC, QPC no 2013-351 of 25 October 2013; CC, QPC no 2010-28, 17 September 2010.
37. *Précis de fiscalité* 2017, available on the tax administration website (https://www.impots.gouv.fr/portail/www2/precis/precis.html).
38. Bulletin Officiel des Finances Publiques-Impôts: http://bofip.impots.gouv.fr/bofip/1-PGP.html.
39. Jocelyn Pierre, Mettre en ligne du droit: l'expérience BOFIP-Impôts, des réponses informatiques à des questions juridiques, Revue générale du droit on line, 2013, no10887 (www.revuegeneraledudroit.eu/?p = 10887).
40. Instruction 13 K-2-06, 3 March 2006.

to provide taxpayers with legal certainty as to the tax treatment of a specific operation or transaction.[41]

There are of course also cases in which the tax administration has put in place favourable rules regarding the tax base or tax recovery, which should in principle be adopted through a law enacted by Parliament, as prescribed in Article 34 of the French Constitution of 1958. Although a guidance document containing such rules is in principle unconstitutional and would be invalidated by the administrative judge,[42] it is in most of the cases formally inserted in a law enacted by Parliament at a later stage.[43]

[C] The Legal Effects of the 'Administrative Doctrine'

The most important feature of the French 'administrative doctrine' is its binding character, explicitly foreseen in Article L. 80 A LPF, and equivalent to the doctrine of justified expectations applied in other jurisdictions. According to this provision, the French administration is bound by its own interpretation of the tax rules. More precisely, this provision covers two different situations: on the one hand, it precludes a (supplementary) tax reassessment, if the initial tax assessment was in line with the established 'administrative doctrine' at the time and, on the other hand, it precludes any tax assessment (even a primary one) if it goes against published 'administrative doctrine'. The purpose of this provision is to protect the taxpayer who has followed the 'administrative doctrine' to go through a tax (re)assessment in case the interpretation of the tax administration has in the meantime changed or has been declared illegal and annulled by the courts. It goes without saying that the binding character of the 'administrative doctrine' can only be invoked in favour of the taxpayer; the tax administration cannot use Article L. 80 A LPF against the taxpayer.

The provision of Article L. 80 A LPF is intended to enhance legal certainty and is strictly interpreted by the Council of State. Consistent with this approach, the protection afforded by Article L. 80 A LPF only extends to interpretations included in guidance documents edited by the tax administration (i.e., signed by the Minister or the Director of the Ministry of Finances) and does not extend to interpretations provided by other branches of the French administration. When the provision is used by a taxpayer as a shield against reassessment in respect of a prior tax period, any document of the tax administration, including documents provided only to the taxpayer, can be taken into account to establish the 'administrative doctrine' at the time the initial tax assessment was made. In the case of an initial assessment, taxpayers must show that the guidance documents have been published. Publication includes posting in the BOFiP-Impôt database on the webpage of the French Directorate General for Public Finances (DGFIP) or even in the Official Journal of the French Republic (for instance, the Ministerial Responses given to Parliamentary Questions). The Council of State does

41. As for the advance pricing agreement procedure or the specific ruling for the valuation of a business in case of its donation.
42. CE, 18 December 2002, No. 233618, *Mme Duvignères*, Rec. Lebon 463.
43. For example, the advance pricing agreement procedure was introduced by Art. L. 80 B, 7° of the LPF and the 'valuation of business' ruling by Art. L. 18 of the LPF.

not accept the interpretation given in the handbook of the French tax administration[44] or the explanations included in the tax returns[45] as elements to be taken into account to establish the administrative doctrine.

Furthermore, the interpretation of tax rules by the tax administration as provided in the various guidance documents should be strictly, in other words literally, interpreted. In practical terms, this implies that the situation of the taxpayer should be exactly the one described in the 'administrative doctrine' to benefit from the protection contained in Article L. 80 A of the LPF. By contrast, the other generally accepted methods of interpretation such as *per analogiam* or *a contrario* and *a fortiori* argumentation should be excluded. This is called in French legal literature the 'principle of literal interpretation of the administrative doctrine'.[46]

It should be noted here that under French tax law, taxpayers may seek the equivalent of a private ruling for their specific situation prior to entering into arrangements that may yield tax outcomes.[47] The advice tendered will be binding on the tax administration, provided that the taxpayer has followed it and has acted in good faith. As already explained, however, this process does not constitute legal interpretation in the strict sense of the word, as it does not concern the interpretation of rules, but rather their application in a given case through an assessment of the facts.

§7.05 LEGAL INTERPRETATION OF TAX LAW BY THE JUDGE

[A] The French Debate over the 'Autonomy of Tax Law'

An ongoing debate in France concerns the 'autonomy of tax law' or the question whether interpretation of tax law by the courts follows the same methods as applied to the other areas of law such as administrative law, or presents different, tax law-specific, features.[48]

The starting point of this debate is the observation that, although the tax legislation often uses the same terms as other branches of law, the tax administration and the courts do not necessarily adopt the same definition of these terms. For instance, the French tax law uses the term 'company' or 'immovable property', but the meaning of these terms is not necessarily the same as the one provided in company law or in civil

44. CE, No. 38.607, 13 December 1989, *Le Prestre*, RJF 2/90, 199.
45. CE, 12 January 1987, no 40.686.
46. Laurence Vapaille, *La doctrine administrative fiscale*, Paris: L'Harmattan, 2000, pp. 199 et seq.
47. Article L. 80 B of the LPF provides for a general advance ruling (*rescrit*) procedure (1°), which has been complemented by specific rulings that may be asked by the taxpayer: – on the eligibility regarding some specific tax incentives or regimes, such as the exceptional depreciation for specified equipments and a corporate tax exemption for new businesses (2°), the R&D tax credit (3° & 3°bis), the innovative start-up businesses tax regime (4°) and the competitiveness cluster tax regime (5°); – on the qualification as a French permanent establishment (6°) and as business income (8°); – but also on an agreed intra-firm transfer pricing policy (7°). Moreover, an advance ruling may be asked: – on the valuation of a business in case of its donation (Art. L. 18 of the LPF); and on the abuse of law (*abus de droit*) character of an operation (Art. L. 64B of the LPF).
48. Maurice Cozian & Louis Trotabas, *Propos désobligeants sur une 'tarte à la crème': l'autonomie et le réalisme du droit fiscal'*, 13 Droit fiscal: 100125 (31 March 1999).

law. The same may also apply to the definition of abstract terms, such as 'customary present'. While tax courts take into account the property of the donor to assess whether a present should be deemed customary or not, civil judges base their decision generally on the revenues of the donor.

It should not be concluded however that this is a general principle. In many cases the tax legislation specifically refers to the provisions of other areas of law (transplanted categories).[49] In other cases, courts use definitions found in other disciplines of law.[50] In both situations the concept of the autonomy of tax law lacks support in practice. More generally, it is accepted that when the tax law borrows concepts and terms from other branches of law, these concepts and terms should be defined in the same way. This is often the case in VAT law, which contains various references to civil law concepts, such as the one of 'price.'[51] In the same way, when determining the different deductible expenses, the judge tries to follow as close as possible the definition of accounting legislation.[52]

Against this background, it is more appropriate to speak not of the autonomy, but rather of the specificity of tax law, which requires a case-by-case analysis to assess whether a definition used in another branch of law would be appropriate for the purposes of the application of particular provisions of tax law. In this respect, the French academic literature speaks of the 'principle of independence of legislations'.[53]

The clearest illustration of the independence of different branches of law is found in the separation of criminal and tax law.[54] A good example is given by the tax treatment of illicit revenues, i.e., revenues generated through illegal activities as prescribed in criminal law. As a matter of fact, despite their illicit character, these revenues are fully taken into account for tax purposes in France.[55] On the grounds of the independence of criminal and tax law, the tax administration had formerly adopted a policy of assessing taxpayers on the basis of evidence that was afterwards declared null and void by the criminal judge. However, the Constitutional Council has now put an end to this administrative practice.[56]

[B] The Strict Interpretation of the Tax Rules by the Courts

The fact that the tax law is not autonomous does not necessarily imply that the interpretation of tax law by the French courts does not present some specific features. However, in contrast with governing legislation in many other areas of law,[57] tax legislation does not contain explicit interpretation principles. Courts have filled the

49. *See* for instance Art. 206 CGI who refers to the Labour Code.
50. CE, 31 March 1978, No. 01.683, *Richard*, Rec. Lebon 168.
51. CE, 14 December 1979, No. 11.798, *Comité de propagande de la banane*, RJF 1/80, 99.
52. CE, 2 June 2006, No. 266.997, *Sté Lever Faberge*, RJF 8-9/2006, 995.
53. Martin Collet. *Droit fiscal*, 6th ed., Paris: PUF, 2017, no 177 et seq.
54. Florence Deboissy, *Retour sur un principe controversé: l'indépendance des procédures pénale et fiscale*, 51–52 Droit fiscal: Etude no 692 (2014).
55. CE, No. 97.719, 5 May 1976, *Mlle X*, RJF 7-8/76, 326.
56. Constitutional Council, judgment 2013-679 DC, 4 December 2013, cons. 33.
57. For instance, the French civil code contains rules on the interpretation of agreements (*conventions*). *See* Arts 1156–1164 of the French Civil Code.

gap, and the interpretation principles can only be understood by systematic reading of the case law. This is a very difficult exercise in France, as the French courts, and in particular the Council of State, are very laconic and explanations of the rationale for judgments is generally limited to a few lines.[58]

As a result of this laconism, in France, the rationale for judgments of the Council of State, which is the main supreme forum for tax matters, never explicitly refers to elements such as the explanatory memorandum prepared for the introduction of the law (*exposé des motifs*), administrative doctrine or rulings, other case law as a precedent, judgments of foreign courts or legislative debates. Although French judges take these elements into account when deliberating,[59] and the Council of State has, for instance, a specific comparative law unit tasked to provide an analysis of each case from a comparative law perspective, they do not explicitly figure in the explanation of the rationale for judgments, which have the form of a classical, short syllogism. Some indications of the basic principles underpinning a specific judgment of the Council of State can be found in the conclusions of the *Rapporteur public,*[60] in the event the judgment follows these conclusions, which are deprived of legal value though.

The most important feature of the legal interpretation of tax law is the principle of strict interpretation of tax law. This principle has been explicitly formulated both in case law[61] and administrative doctrine[62] and is closely related to the constitutional principle of legality, according to which only a law enacted by Parliament can contain rules on tax base, tax rate and tax recovery. In this sense, the principle of strict interpretation aims also at preserving the competence of the legislature. This implies, on the one hand, that the role of analogy interpretation of tax law should be limited and, on the other hand, that the will of the legislator, as expressed during the preparation of the text (the *travaux préparatoires*) should be given priority. However, as already said, in France, the text of the judgment of the Council of State never contains a reference to the *travaux préparatoires*, but these are often thoroughly considered in the conclusions of the *Rapporteur public.*[63]

Some more specific principles of the legal interpretation of tax law by the courts are also closely linked with general principle of strict interpretation. This is the case for instance with the principle of 'strict interpretation of rules establishing tax privileges',

58. Pierre Brunet, *Le style déductif du Conseil d'État et la ligne de partage des mots*, 3(91) Droit et Société: 545–561 (2015).
59. For instance, the Council of State has a specific legal service putting together all these elements before the deliberation, including a comparative law team, who is putting together information on foreign judgments.
60. The 'rapporteur public' is an independent member of the Council of State who, during the court session, sums up the case and the relevant case law and submits its own proposal as for settling the case.
61. Court of Cassation, 15 February 1943, *Société française des câbles télégraphiques*, Sirey 1944, I, 53. *See*: Philippe Marchessou, 'Réflexions contemporaines sur l'interprétation des textes fiscaux', in *Mélanges Paul Amselek*. Bruxelles: Bruylant, 2005, pp. 551 et seq.; Julien Guez, 'L'interprétation jurisprudentielle en droit fiscal doit-elle être spécifique? Retour sur le principe d'interprétation stricte en droit fiscal', in *L'année fiscale*, Paris: PUF, 2004, pp. 139 et seq.
62. BOI-CTX-DG-20-10-10, No. 270.
63. Conclusions Séners on CE, 4 August 2006, No. 285.201, *Sté Kaufman & Broad Participations*, RJF 11/06, 1330.

as these rules are derogatory,[64] the principle of strict interpretation of tax treaties,[65] and the principle of non-interference of the tax administration in the management of an enterprise.[66]

The principle of strict interpretation is contrasting with the attitude of the courts in general administrative law matters, where in the absence of extensive codification of the applicable rules, the case law has progressively extracted a set of general principles and rules that the administration should comply with. The most famous category is the 'general principles of law' (*principes généraux du droit*) that case law has shaped throughout the years.[67] In this sense, and given that the administrative judge is often a tax judge as well, the principle of strict interpretation is a genuine specificity of the French tax law.

[C] The Cases of Creative Interpretation

The principle of strict interpretation implies that the judge should apply the tax rules literally, taking eventually into account the will of the legislator. This should in principle exclude any creative or constructive interpretation going beyond the letter of the text.

Part of the academic literature indeed refuses to acknowledge the existence of a principle of strict interpretation, by quoting some cases of 'creative interpretation' by the courts.[68] However, most of these cases are not real cases of creative interpretation, but cases in which the legislators have implicitly entrusted a (more or less extended) margin of appreciation to the tax administration and to the tax courts by using general, abstract terms, subject as such to several different interpretations. It follows that the tax administration and the courts are free to define these terms and even to change their interpretation to make it evolve over time, without any change of the text.[69]

One of the most eloquent examples, in this respect, is the General Anti-avoidance Rule, known in France as the 'abuse of law' (*abus de droit*) rule.[70] This provision refers both to fictitious acts and to acts that try to benefit from a literal application of tax rules against the objectives set by their authors and empowers the tax administration to put these acts aside or requalify them. It is obvious that the principle of strict or literal interpretation cannot apply in this case, as the legislator explicitly empowered the

64. CE, 27 July 2009, No. 312.165, *Mme Dubosqu*, RJF 12/09, 1102.
65. CE, 6 May 1996, No. 154.217, *SA Quartz d'Alsace*, RJF 6/98, 731.
66. CE, 27 July 1984, No. 34.588, *SA Renfort Service*, RJF 10/84, 564.
67. Etienne Picard & Georges A. Bermann, 'Administrative Law', in Etienne Picard & George A. Bermann (eds), *Introduction to French Law*, The Netherlands: Kluwer Law International, 2008, pp. 76–78.
68. Christophe De La Mardière, 'Le pouvoir créateur du juge de l'impôt', in *Archives de philosophie du droit – La création du droit par le juge*, t. 50: 229 et seq. (2007).
69. CE, 14 February 2001, No. 189.572, *Boniface*, RJF 5/01, 614 (concerning 'the *usual* stock exchange operations').
70. Article 64 LPF. For an overview of the French GAAR, *see* Thomas Dubut, 'France', in Michael Lang, Jeffrey Owens, Pasquale Pistone, Alexander Rust, Josef Schuch & Claus Staringer (eds), *General Anti-Avoidance Rules (GAARs) – A Key Element of Tax Systems in the Post-BEPS Tax World?* Amsterdam: IBFD, 2016, pp. 275–297.

judge to depart from a purely literal application of the texts and subsequently appreciate the facts concerned.

In France, the most frequently quoted principle of creative interpretation by the tax courts is the concept of 'abnormal act of management' (*acte anormal de gestion*), developed by the court for the purpose of extending the list of non-deductible expenditures beyond the letter of the CGI.[71] Although this concept is not an explicit legislative creation, it can be perceived as an application of the general principle of the 'abuse of law' rule, which empowers the tax administration and the courts to set aside fictitious operations or operations merely intended to decrease the tax base by benefiting from a literal application of the rules. An arrangement that seeks to create the appearance of a real, deductible expenditure, whereas in fact it only decreases the tax base without satisfying any real business purpose, is precisely what constitutes an abnormal act of management.

The principle of strict interpretation of the text does not exclude however the applicability of some general, non-written principles of administrative law in tax matters. This is the case in particular with the principle of the rights of defence.[72] These 'general principles of law' supplement the tax legislation and can override rules adopted by the tax administration, but cannot dismiss the application of rules enacted by Parliament.

[D] The So-called Economic Reasoning in Tax Case Law

Another specificity of legal interpretation of tax rules by the courts often highlighted in academic literature is the so-called economic reasoning in tax case law,[73] according to which tax rules cannot be interpreted merely on the basis of legal arguments, but an economic analysis is often required.

The links between taxation and economy are of course undeniable, as taxes ultimately concern economic operations. However, the economic reasoning in the case law of the French courts concerns the qualification of the facts and not the interpretation of tax rules. The most frequent example is the application by the Council of State of Article 1448 CGI, according to which the so-called professional tax shall be established on the basis of the '*contributing capacity* of the taxpayers'. The term 'contributing capacity' is an abstract term, the use of which gives some margin of appreciation to the tax administration and to the courts to further define it and thus determine its precise scope.

The definition of the term 'contributing capacity' for the application of Article 1448 CGI in the case law of the Council of State refers to the assets *under the control* of the taxpayer,[74] a purely legal definition. It is true that when determining the assets of the taxpayer in a given case, the Council of State does not merely take into account the

71. Daniel Gutmann, *Droit fiscal des affaires*, 7th ed., Paris: Montchrétien, 2016, no 630 et seq.
72. CE, 2 July 2003, No. 233944, *Guth*, RJF 10/03, 1110.
73. Bernard Plagnet, 'Le raisonnement économique dans la jurisprudence fiscale', in *Études en l'honneur de Loïc Philip*, Paris: Economica, 2005, pp. 529 et seq.
74. CE, 19 April 2000, No. 172003, *SA Fabricauto-Essarauto*, RJF 5/00, 631.

property rights as established in law, but also examines who has the exploitation of the assets in practical terms. In doing so, the Council of State does not interpret tax rules in an economic way, but appreciates facts independent of their legal denominations in other areas of law. In this sense, the 'economic reasoning in tax case law' is just another illustration of the principle of independence of laws, according to which the tax administration and the tax courts are not bound by the definitions provided in other branches of law and the qualifications made by other courts.

[E] The So-called 'Neutralizing Interpretation'

Another important feature of French case law is the so-called 'neutralizing interpretation', which is based on the assumption that legal provisions conform to provisions and norms of higher order. The application of this interpretative technique is not limited to constitutional provisions. When reviewing the provisions enacted by the administration, the Council of State often also presumes their compatibility with binding international law and agreements.

Although this is not a feature unique to the interpretation of tax law, tax law offers some very eloquent examples. For instance, in a recent judgment, the French Constitutional Council admitted that the cumulative application of criminal and administrative sanctions is not contrary to the constitutional principle of *ne bis in idem*, which prohibits a defendant from being prosecuted repeatedly for the same offence, but clarified that no criminal sanctions can be applied if in final determination it is concluded that no tax deficiency exists.[75] Similarly, the Constitutional Council accepted the compatibility with the Constitution of a tax provision, which imposed retroactively specific high revenues, but explicitly excluded revenues that had been subject to withholding taxes from the scope of this retroactive application.[76] In both cases, the Constitutional Council restricted the interpretation of the provisions concerned to ensure compliance with the Constitution. Both the Council of State and the Court of Cassation have accepted that they are bound by the restrictions on interpretation established by the Constitutional Council.[77]

The case law of the Council of State also presents several cases of neutralizing interpretation, intended to ensure that the application of a tax law provision would not result in a violation of higher principles of the legal order. For instance, the Council of State had concluded that when the tax base is based on tax returns, the tax administration cannot proceed with a reassessment without having invited the taxpayer to present his observations, otherwise it would infringe on the taxpayer's rights to defence.[78] In this specific case, the LPF explicitly excluded the application of some

75. CC, 24 June 2016, No. 2016-545 QPC and No. 2016-546 QPC. *See* Daniel Gutmann, *Sanctions fiscales et Constitution*, 33 Nouveaux Cahiers du Conseil constitutionnel: 41 et seq. (October 2011).
76. CC, 5 December 2014, No. 2014-435 QPC.
77. CE, 11 March 1994, No. 115052, *SA 'La Cinq'*, Rec. Lebon 118; Court of Cassation, Civ. 2e, 28 June 1995, No. 94-50.002, *Préfet de la région Midi-Pyrénées c/ Bechta*, Bulletin 1995 II No. 221, 127.
78. CE, 5 June 2002, No. 219840, *Simoens*, RJF 8-9/02, 934.

procedural guarantees for this specific reassessment and a part of the doctrine even considered that this is a case of *contra legem* reasoning and not simply neutralizing interpretation.[79]

EU law may also have a neutralizing effect on the interpretation of domestic tax law and double tax treaty provisions, which should be in line with EU requirements and in particular with the fundamental freedoms.[80]

[F] The Interpretation of Double Tax Treaties by the French Courts

The interpretation of double tax treaties by the French courts presents some specificities, given that there are concrete interpretation rules both in general international law and in the text of many double tax treaties.

In this context it is noteworthy that until 1990 the French Courts refused to interpret the clauses of international treaties, as this was considered to be in the remit of the Ministry of Foreign affairs. Although the administration remains free to interpret these clauses, the Council of State finally accepted that it is no longer bound by the interpretation given by the Minister of Foreign affairs.[81]

The main rules applicable for the interpretation of international treaties are included in the Vienna Convention on the law of treaties (VCLT) of 23 May 1969.[82] Although France has not signed this Convention because of its opposition to the concept of *ius cogens*,[83] it is generally accepted that the provisions on the interpretation of treaties reflect customary international law and are binding upon all States including France, irrespective of the signing of the VCLT. The Council of State has indeed reflected on the rules of interpretation of the Vienna Convention in tax matters[84] and has even accepted that the same term might be used with a different meaning in two articles of the same convention taking into account the objectives of each provision, but also the fact that the English version uses two different terms, in line with Articles 31 and 33 of the Vienna Convention.[85]

The most important rule of interpretation included in double tax treaties is the clause included in Article 3§2 of the OECD Model Tax Convention (MTC),[86] according to which any term not explicitly defined in the treaty should be defined according to the domestic law, the definitions of tax law prevailing over the definitions of other branches of law. The French Council of State applies this principle even for the

79. Stéphane Austry, *QPC fiscale et effets de la décision dans le temps*, 33 Nouveaux Cahiers du Conseil constitutionnel (October 2011).
80. Daniel Gutmann, *Tax Treaty Interpretation in France, the Relevance of EC Law*, 10(4) EC Tax Review: 204 (2001).
81. CE, 29 June 1990, No. 78.519, *Gisti*, RJF 9/90, 1096.
82. Articles 31, 32 and 33 VCLT.
83. *See* Jean Combacau & Serge Sur, *Droit International Public*, 12th ed., Paris: LGDJ, 2016, pp. 49 et seq.
84. CE, 17 December 2003, No. 239677, *Heskes*, RJF 3/03, 249.
85. CE, 27 July 2012, No 337656, *M. Regazzacci*, RJF 11/12, 1012.
86. *OECD Model Tax Convention on Income and on Capital*, Paris: OECD, 2015.

interpretation of double tax treaties that do not contain a clause equivalent to Article 3§2 of the OECD MTC.[87]

In addition, the French conception of how a definition should be understood is often quite restrictive and requires the existence of a synthetic definition. For instance, the Council of State concluded that the double tax treaty between France and the Netherlands did not contain any definition of dividends, despite the existence of a quite long enumeration of different forms of dividends[88] and thus made use of domestic law definitions. The Council of State also accepted that the domestic law definition could be found not only in the written, codified legislation, but also in case law.

For the rest, as already mentioned above, the French courts follow the principle of literal interpretation of double tax treaties, in line with Article 31 of the VCLT. This interpretation is based on the *ordinary meaning* of terms used within their specific *context.*[89] The predominance of literal interpretation of double tax treaties is also partly due to the fact that the *travaux préparatoires* of double tax treaties remain secret and are thus inaccessible to the judge. The comparison with the provisions of the OECD and UN MTCs and their commentaries can partially fill in this gap. However, the French Council of State does not accept the ambulatory interpretation of treaty provisions and only takes into account the commentaries anterior to the signing of the treaty, if relevant;[90] the commentaries published after the signing of the tax treaty concerned don't have any legal value for the French judge[91] and can only eventually deploy some persuasive power for its reasoning.[92]

This does not imply however that the interpretation of tax treaties does not evolve over time. In a very interesting case regarding the interpretation of Article 22§2 d) of the tax treaty between France and Brazil, the tax administration initially considered this provision to be a genuine tax sparing clause (and more precisely a matching credit), which gives rise to a tax credit irrespective of whether the tax was effectively paid in Brazil,[93] but later reversed its position and concluded that no tax credit could be given if no tax had been levied in Brazil.[94] Although the tax administration is of course free to reconsider its interpretation of tax rules, the new interpretation was not

87. CE, 22 May 1992, No. 63266, *SPA Raffaella,* RJF 7/92, 960.
88. CE, 13 October 1999, No. 190083, *SA Banque française de l'Orient,* RJF 12/99, 1587.
89. For more examples, *see*: Philippe Martin, *L'interprétation des conventions fiscales internationales*, 24 Droit fiscal (13 June 2013). *See also*: Thomas Dubut, Modélisation des normes et normativité des modèles. Le caractère normatif ambivalent du Modèle de Convention fiscale concernant le revenu et la fortune de l'OCDE en droit international public, 1 Revue belge de droit international: 212–239 (2009); Daniel Gutmann, 'Tax Treaty Interpretation in France', in Michael Lang (ed.), *Tax Treaty Interpretation*, The Netherlands: Kluwer Law International, 2001, pp. 95–117.
90. CE, 27 July 2001, No. 215124, *SA Golay Buchel France,* RJF 11/01, 1428.
91. CE, 30 December 2003, No. 233894, *Andritz,* RJF 2/04, 238.
92. For more details, *see*: Thomas Dubut, *Les Commentaires du Modèle de Convention fiscale de l'OCDE et l'interprétation des conventions bilatérales contre la double imposition. Contribution à l'étude de la normativité sans efficacité en droit international public,* 34(3) Revue de la recherche juridique - Droit prospectif: 1449–1472 (2009).
93. Instruction 8 December 1972: BOI 14 B-17-72; Dr. fisc. 1973; no 1-2, instr. 4054.
94. Instruction 5 December 1997: BOI 14 A-7-97; Dr. fisc. 1998; no 3, instr. 11904.

supported by the wording of the treaty and the discussions in Parliament during its ratification.[95] However, the Council of State validated the new interpretation.[96]

Another noteworthy principle for the interpretation of double tax treaties by the Council of State is the so-called 'neutralizing interpretation', which provides for the interpretation of provisions of a treaty in a manner that is consistent with the higher rules and in particular the rules and principles of the 'constitutional block'.[97] This principle is also used with regards to VAT law, in line with the requirement of EU legislation and case law.

§7.06 LEGAL INTERPRETATION OF VAT LAW

Since 1967[98] the European Union has been issuing VAT directives that the Member States have to transpose into their national law with a view to harmonizing VAT law across the EU. As a result, the main provisions of the French VAT system are determined by the EU directives and in particular by the Sixth Directive and its successor, the so-called VAT Directive. The Sixth Directive was first adopted by the Council on 17 May 1977.[99] It has been modified several times, but remains the pillar of EU VAT law.

The VAT Directives and their subsequent amendments have been transposed into the French legal system through laws enacted by Parliament as prescribed by the French Constitution of 1958. From a formal point of view, these laws have the same legal value and are subject to the same judicial review as all other French laws enacted by Parliament. However, their interpretation by the administration and the courts presents some specificities that should be highlighted here.

First and foremost, according to the French Council of State, the transposition laws have to be interpreted in the light of the text of the Directive.[100] The use of the text of the directive in order to interpret the text of the transposition law is called in the French literature 'justiciability of interpretation' (*invocabilité d'intérpretation*), as it results in recognizing some legal effects to the directive, which cannot in principle be directly invoked by private persons, if it has not been transposed into domestic law.

In VAT matters, the use of the directives for the interpretation of domestic law provisions is even more significant that extensive guidance on their meaning and application is provided at the EU level. First of all, in line with Article 398 of the VAT directive, a VAT Committee was established to promote the uniform application of the provisions of this directive across EU Member States. Member States have to consult the VAT Committee before they make use in their national legislation of options provided to them by that directive. The VAT Committee also examines questions

95. Guy Gest, *L'affaire des crédits d'impôt brésiliens, ou les limites de l'interprétation littérale des Conventions fiscales*, 50(69) Droit fiscal (14 December 2006).
96. CE, 26 July 2006, No. 284930, *Sté Natexis Banques Populaires*, RJF 11/06, 1421.
97. CE, 3 July 1996, No. 169219, *Koné*, Rec, Lebon 255.
98. Directive 67/228/CEE.
99. Directive 77/388/CEE.
100. CE, 22 December 1989, No. 86113, *Min. du Budget c/ Cercle militaire mixte de la caserne Mortier*, Rec. Lebon, 260.

concerning the application of EU VAT provisions raised by the Commission or a Member State. As a result of the discussion, the VAT Committee may agree guidelines on specific matters. The VAT Committee cannot take legally binding decisions, as it is in principle an advisory Committee. However, under Article 397 of the VAT Directive, the Council can, upon proposal by the Commission, adopt by unanimity measures necessary to implement the directive. On that basis, some guidelines agreed by the VAT Committee have been transformed into binding implementing measures. These measures, which are directly applicable without requiring transposition into national law, can be found in the VAT Implementing Regulation.[101]

The European Commission also issues VAT guidelines. These guidelines are explanatory notes and other documents intended to provide practical and informal guidance about how particular provisions of EU VAT law should be applied. They are not legally binding, but are published on the website of the Directorate General for Taxation and Customs.[102]

The most significant aspect of the 'justificiability of interpretation' is that it enables the French courts to take into account the case law of the European Court of Justice and its methods of interpretation. The academic literature has indeed identified several cases in which the interpretation of the Council of State has evolved in line with case law of the Court of Justice in VAT matters.[103] Furthermore, although in principle the judgments of the French Council of State do not quote other judgments (of the same or other jurisdictions), in VAT there have been cases in which a reference to a judgment of the European Court of Justice is explicitly included in the 'visas'.[104]

In addition, the Council of State does not hesitate to submit prejudicial questions to the European Court of Justice to inquire about the compatibility of domestic law rules with EU legislation, even when the conclusion seems obvious. A part of the academic literature is suggesting that this is a conscious choice intended to oblige the European Court to take a decision that will apply across the EU, contrary to a decision of the French Council of State which would only be binding to the French tax authorities. The ultimate goal would be to ensure the uniform application of VAT law rules and thus provide a level playing field among all Member States.[105]

§7.07 CONCLUSION

The legal interpretation of tax law in France clearly reflects some of the main features of the French legal order, while it presents at the same time some specificities linked to the fact that, contrary to general administrative law, tax law is extensively codified. French tax rules are mainly included in tax laws enacted by Parliament, which are complex and difficult to access. The French tax administration and the French Courts

101. Council Implementing Regulation (EU) No. 282/2011.
102. https://ec.europa.eu/taxation_customs/business/vat/commission-guidelines_en.
103. Martin Collet, *Le juge fiscal français et le contentieux TVA*, 128 Revue française de finances publiques: 125 et seq. (2014).
104. CE, 1 July 2009, No. 295689, *SARL Alain Palanchon*, RJF 10/09, 822, which mentions explicitly the ECJ Teleos judgment (Case C-409/04).
105. Martin Collet, *supra* note 103.

have contributed significantly to making tax law understandable and accessible to taxpayers, striking a difficult balance between the need to respect the competence of the legislature as prescribed by the French Constitution and the rights of the tax payers guaranteed by the 'constitutional block' as well as European and International law.

To this end, several often opposing interpretation methods are being applied, ranging from the principle of strict interpretation of tax law to that of interpretation in line with higher norms of the legal order, intended to ensure the appropriate solution on a case-by-case basis. As a result, the interpretation of tax law in France is generally strict, without, however, excluding potential evolutions over time. It remains to be seen whether this French approach of interpretation could remain in place in case of a further harmonization of tax law at the EU level.

CHAPTER 8

Legal Interpretation of Tax Law: Germany

Caroline Heber & Christian Sternberg

§8.01 INTRODUCTION

As is the case with the other countries on the European continent, Germany has a civil law system, which is based on statutes (rather than precedent), and the role of the courts is to apply this law. The courts in general do not create law and binding doctrine of *stare-decisis* is unknown in German law.[1] The German legal system consists of a hierarchy of interrelated laws. Acts passed by the Parliament have to adhere to the German Constitution. Since Germany is a Member State of the European Union, parliamentary acts also have to conform with primary and secondary European Law. Due to the hierarchy, inferior statutory law has to be interpreted by the courts so it does not contradict with superior law provisions.

Judicial approaches to the interpretation of tax law in Germany include four distinct but complementing methods of interpretation, generally referred to as the four canons of Savigny: an initial approach that looks at the words of a provision, a broader approach that looks at the wider broader structure of the statute, a third approach that bases the interpretation of a section on the historical background of the provision, and the fourth approach that seeks to elaborate upon the function of a particular provision in the tax law.

The general approaches to interpreting tax laws are complemented through the application of specific doctrines related to developing the law further, reviewed in the third section of this chapter. The fourth section considers the impact of economic equivalent views and anti-abuse rules while the fifth section looks at the impact of German constitutional law and European Union law on tax law interpretation. Finally,

1. One important exception, however, is the binding nature of decisions of the Federal Constitutional Court in Germany, *see* s. 31 of the Federal Constitutional Court Act (Gesetz über das Bundesverfassungsgericht, BVerfGG).

the sixth section considers some special rules that apply to interpretation of international tax measures.

§8.02 THE CANON OF INTERPRETATION RULES

Only in rare cases will the mere wording of the legal provisions apply directly and unambiguously to the facts of a case and determine the correct application of the law; instead, in most cases the provisions have to be interpreted in order to give the provision the most appropriate meaning in the context of the case at hand. The question then arises of what constitutes a proper interpretation and application of the law.[2] This question is not limited to tax laws but is of a general nature. In Germany, there exists general consensus that the methods to be used for proper interpretation and application of the law should not differ between the different areas of the law. As a result, interpretation and application of tax laws is in general not different from the application of the law in any other area.

The question of proper interpretation of the law has been debated for decades in academia and practice. The disputes mainly arise from different or opposing philosophical approaches to understanding law. Should statutes be interpreted literally or based on their so-called *telos*? How may the *telos* of a statute be determined? Is it based on the legislative intent as declared in explanatory memorandums and in Parliament debates or on the purpose that the statute fulfils in the overall legal framework? For legal practice, the courts have found consensus as to which factors should be taken into account for interpreting and applying the law; whereas these issues remain subject to debate in academia and, in particular, in legal philosophy and legal theory.

Despite this, the so-called 'jurisprudence of evaluations' (*Wertungsjurisprudenz*) has reached a general consensus that statutes resolve a competition of interests and necessarily incorporate a value-based judgment that determines which interest shall prevail in certain circumstances.[3] The jurisprudence of evaluations finds its roots in the so-called 'jurisprudence of interests' (*Interessenjurisprudenz*), which also argues that statutes solve a competition of interests.[4] However, the proponents of the jurisprudence of evaluations criticize those supporting the jurisprudence of interests for their assumption that the value-based judgment in itself is an interest.[5]

Irrespective of these differences, the words used in a statute have the function of expressing this judgment. Thus, statutory interpretation should be based on this

2. Karl Larenz, *Methodenlehre der Rechtswissenschaft* (*Legal Methodology*) (Berlin: Springer-Verlag, 6th edn, 1991), pp. 312 et seq.; Joachim Lang, 'General Rules of Statute Interpretation in Germany', in Klaus Vogel (ed.), *Interpretation of Tax Law and Treaties and Transfer Pricing in Japan and Germany* (The Hague: Kluwer Law International, 1998), p. 62.
3. Franz Bydlinski, *Juristische Methodenlehre und Rechtsbegriff* (*Legal Methodology and the Concept of Law*) (Vienna: Springer-Verlag, 2nd edn, 1991), pp. 124 et seq., 270 et seq.; Joachim Lang, *supra* note 2, pp. 60 et seq.
4. Philipp Heck, 'Begriffsjurisprudenz und Interessenjurisprudenz', in Günter Ellscheid and Winfried Hassemer, *Interessenjurisprudenz* (Darmstadt: Wissenschaftliche Buchgesellschaft, 1974), pp. 88 et seq.
5. Karl Larenz, *supra* note 2 at pp. 119 et seq., Franz Bydlinski, *supra* note 3 at pp. 123 et seq.

judgment and the *telos* of a provision instead of on a literal interpretation.[6] However, in legal theory and legal philosophy it is highly disputed how this *telos* should be construed. Some authors argue in favour of a historical interpretation: the *telos* of a provision is determined by the legislator at the time when it enacts the provision. In this sense, it is subjective as it refers to the intention of the legislator. Others are of the opinion that a provision should be interpreted with respect to its purpose and the function it fulfils in the legal framework. Such an objective approach tries to disentangle intentions of the legislator and the purpose of a provision as expressed by the wording. In Germany, both methods play an important role. Irrespective of this debate, certain methods of statutory interpretation have evolved and even in academia *general* consensus on these methods has been reached.[7]

For many decades, the Federal Constitutional Court has held that statutory interpretation must be based on the purpose of a provision instead of a literal or historical interpretation. The interpretation and application should be governed by the function of a provision in the legal framework as expressed in its wording. According to the Federal Constitutional Court, a provision has to be interpreted with respect to its own intention or in different terms according to the objective intention of the legislator as it is contained in the provision.[8]

To achieve this outcome, an interpretation shall be based on an analysis of the wording, system, evolution of the provision and its function in the legal framework or, put differently, its overall purpose. This basically reflects the canon of interpretation rules as proposed by Savigny.[9] The wording of a provision sets the boundaries of statutory interpretation. Within these boundaries, an interpretation based on the provision's purpose will prevail. This purpose is determined applying the so-called 'external system', using a systematic analysis, and the so-called 'internal system', using a purposive analysis. The legislative intent as analysed by the evolutionary approach may be used for giving guidance on the purpose of a particular provision. However, if this purpose is not reflected in the wording, it will not prevail in legal interpretation.[10]

---

6. Joachim Lang, *supra* note 2 at p. 63.
7. Wolfgang Schön, 'Interpretation of Tax Statutes', in Klaus Vogel (ed.), *Interpretation of Tax Law and Treaties and Transfer Pricing in Japan and Germany* (The Hague: Kluwer Law International, 1998), p. 70; Karl Larenz, *supra* note 2 at pp. 316 et seq.
8. 1 BVerfGE 299, 312 (BVerfG 1952); 11 BVerfGE 126, 132 (BVerfG 1960); 105 BVerfGE 135, 157 (BVerfG 2002); Joachim Lang, *supra* note 2 at p. 64; Karl Larenz, *supra* note 2 at pp. 312 et seq.; Joachim Englisch, 'Rechtsanwendung im Steuerrecht' ('Application of the Law in Taxation'), in Klaus Tipke et al. (eds), *Steuerrecht* (*Tax Law*) (Cologne: Dr. Otto Schmidt Verlag, 22nd edn, 2015), § 5 paras 49, 51 et seq.; Klaus-Dieter Drüen, '§ 4 AO' ('Sect. 4 General Tax Code'), in Klaus Tipke and Heinrich Wilhelm Kruse (eds), *AO/FGO* (*General Tax Code / Code on the Procedure of Tax Courts*) (Cologne: Dr. Otto Schmidt Verlag, loose-leaf, 2016), paras 231 et seq., 235 et seq.
9. Karl Larenz, *supra* note 2 at pp. 319 et seq.
10. *See* in particular the decisions of the Federal Constitutional Court, 1 BVerfGE 299, 312 (BVerfG 1952); 6 BVerfGE 55, 71 et seq. (BVerfG 1957); 8 BVerfGE 274, 306 (BVerfG 1958); 10 BVerfGE 234, 243 (BVerfG 1959); 11 BVerfGE 126, 132 (BVerfG 1960); 41 BVerfGE 291, 309 (BVerfG 1976); 47 BVerfGE 109, 126 (BVerfG 1978); 62 BVerfGE 1, 44 (BVerfG 1983); 105 BVerfGE 135, 157 (BVerfG 2002). Furthermore, note *inter alia* 2014 BStBl II 135 (BFH 2013); 2014 BStBl II 58 (BFH 2013); 2013 BStBl II 785 (BFH 2012); 2011 BStBl II 277 (BFH 2010); 1987 BStBl II 670 (BFH 1987); 1974 BStBl II 572 (BFH 1974).

[A] The Wording of a Provision

Although statutes are not interpreted literally, the wording of a statute plays a crucial role. The words are used to express a value-based judgment, solving a competition of interests, which has to be applied in particular cases. Thus, the wording of a statute is the starting point for any interpretation of a provision and marks the boundaries of statutory interpretation. This is the dividing line between legal interpretation and development of the law by judicial interpretation.[11]

The meaning of a word is in many cases ambiguous. If the understanding is unambiguous and the facts of a case are clearly covered by the wording, the case may be subsumed under the so-called conceptual core (*Begriffskern*) of a provision. It contains all unambiguous possible meanings of a word. The conceptual periphery (*Begriffshof*), on the other hand, contains all interpretations of a word according to which the facts of case may, but do not necessarily have to, be subsumed.[12]

In any case, the interpretation should coincide with the purpose of the law. However, if a case can clearly be subsumed under the conceptual core of the wording used in the provision, the provision may under no circumstances be interpreted differently. At the same time, the application of the provision may not be in line with its own purpose; this contradicts the very aim of statutory interpretation, which is to apply a provision according to its purpose. Still, the wording of a statute marks the boundaries of interpretation and any interpretation must not contradict the wording. Excluding a case that can clearly be subsumed under the conceptual core from the scope of the provision, would neglect the clear wording of a provision. In Germany, such an approach is not assumed to be part of statutory interpretation but of developing the law further by judicial interpretation; in this particular case, the question of applying a teleological reduction would arise.[13] At the same time, if the facts of a case cannot be subsumed under the conceptual periphery of a provision, it cannot be applied by means of interpretation but by analogy only.[14] In other words, based on the *telos* of the law, a teleological reduction carves out from the legal understanding of the word certain unambiguous meanings belonging to its conceptual core, whereas an analogy extends the legal understanding of a word to cases that cannot be subsumed under the wording even with respect to its conceptual periphery.

Example:

According to sections 19, and 8 subsection 2, and 6 subsection 1 number 4 of the German Income Tax Act, the value of private use of a motor vehicle that is used for business purposes is taxable income to the employee. The income is calculated by taking 1% of the catalogue price of the motor vehicle.

---

11. Franz Bydlinski, *supra* note 3 at pp. 441, 467 et seq.; Karl Larenz, *supra* note 2 at pp. 322, 343.
12. Franz Bydlinski, *supra* note 3 at pp. 118, 437 et seq.; Karl Larenz, *supra* note 2 at pp. 320 et seq.; 1985 BStBl II 151 (BFH 1984).
13. *See* §8.03[B] and 1998 BStBl II 208 (BFH 1997); 1975 BStBl II 12 (BFH 1974); 1974 BStBl II 572 (BFH 1974); 1964 BStBl III 188 (BFH 1964).
14. *See* §8.03[A] and *inter alia* 2005 BStBl II 756 (BFH 2005); 2000 BStBl II 438 (BFH 2000).

A car can be subsumed under the term 'motor vehicle', being unambiguously part of the conceptual core of the term 'motor vehicle'. Doubts arise with respect to mobile homes, lorries or motorized bicycles (mopeds). All these may but do not necessarily have to be characterized as a 'motor vehicle'. As a result, these understandings belong to the conceptual periphery of the term.

[B] Statutory System

The interpretation of one single provision that is part of a statute shall consider the system of the statute and the position of the provisions in the statute. In particular, this method analyses the structure of the statute, the order of the provisions and the relations between them. This approach establishes the external system of a statute and its internal provisions.[15]

The external system of a statute derives from its sections, subsections, paragraphs, and so on. Headings used for the provisions and structural elements like sections also need to be considered.[16] These elements will in general illustrate the function a provision has in the legal framework as the external system will generally be based on the internal system of the provisions. However, important exceptions apply. The structure of a statute may be the result of historical reasons and developments. In these cases, the external system does not necessarily build on the internal system of the provisions contained in a statute. Instead, historical perspectives and developments govern the structure of a statute in a manner that does not reflect accurately the statute's internal system. Nevertheless, the internal system is decisive for the application of a provision to a particular case.[17]

Notwithstanding any discrepancy between the structure of a statute based on history and its intended internal structure, logic can usually provide an accurate guide to the relationship between provisions. For example, based on the wording and order of a statute, a provision may be understood as covering a general case. Provisions following a general provision will ordinarily deal with certain special cases. In general, each provision should logically deal with discrete issues; it could not be logical for one provision to be interpreted so broadly that it covers the territory of another, rendering one redundant.[18]

15. Karl Larenz, *supra* note 2 at pp. 326 et seq.; 437 et seq.; Franz Bydlinski, *supra* note 3 at pp. 442 et seq.
16. Franz Bydlinski, *supra* note 3 at pp. 443 et seq.; Joachim Englisch, *supra* note 8 at § 5 para. 64.
17. 1974 BStBl II 572 (BFH 1974); Karl Larenz, *supra* note 2 at p. 327; Joachim Lang, *supra* note 2 at p. 65; Klaus Tipke, *Die Steuerrechtsordnung* (*The Tax System)*,Volume III (Cologne: Dr. Otto Schmidt Verlag, 2nd edn, 2012), p. 1613.
18. Franz Bydlinski, *supra* note 3 at pp. 443 et seq.

[C] Purpose of a Provision

[1] Historical Interpretation: Legislative Intent

A historical interpretation tries to determine the intention and rationale of the legislature for enacting a particular provision. This is not a simple or straightforward exercise as the legislature consists of the German Parliament and in many cases the German Federal Assembly with hundreds of members holding differing political views.[19] Moreover, many tax statutes are prepared by the Federal Ministry of Finance including technical papers and explanatory memorandums. Thus, determining the legislative intent is not an unambiguous operation. Nevertheless, in most instances the legislative intent can be determined.

A historical interpretation has to consider the whole evolutionary history of a provision and a statute as well as subsequent developments.

The material to be taken into account includes parliamentary debates and explanatory memorandums. As far as the wordings of the statute and former draft proposals match, explanatory memorandums of the draft proposals prepared by ministries play an important role.[20]

As far as tax law is concerned, the statutes are rather old and many provisions as well as the structure of the statute stem from the early twentieth century. Notably, the wording of some provisions has not been changed since then. For a historical analysis, it is important to take into account the materials from the early twentieth century as these illustrate the original structure and historical meaning of certain provisions even if the provision has subsequently been changed. However, a historical analysis then needs to take into account changes in the use of terms as well as economic and social contexts when analysing historical materials and the wording of particular provisions.[21]

For subsequent changes of a provision, one should, first of all, use all the material mentioned before that is used to analyse the historical meaning of the original provision. However, changes illustrate clearly existing deficiencies in the law that the legislator wants to correct. These deficiencies may have been revealed by courts and academics beforehand. Thus, court cases and academic literature may be of importance by evaluating the legislative intent as well.[22] As the statute is used to correct mistakes in the law, one should also include the wording of the old provision to construe the intention of the change.

19. Henning Tappe, *Die Begründung von Steuergesetzen* (*The Justification of Tax Laws*) (Habilitations thesis: Münster, 2012), pp. 265 et seq.; Karl Larenz, *supra* note 2 at p. 318; Joachim Englisch, *supra* note 8 at § 5 para. 50.
20. Joachim Englisch, *supra* note 8 at § 5 paras 60 et seq.; Karl Larenz, *supra* note 2 at pp. 330 et seq.; Franz Bydlinski, *supra* note 3 at pp. 449 et seq.
21. 1974 BStBl II 572 (BFH 1974); Karl Larenz, *supra* note 2 at pp. 351 et seq.
22. 1984 BStBl II 327 (BFH 1984); Joachim Englisch, *supra* note 8 at § 5 para. 61; Franz Bydlinski, *supra* note 3 at p. 453.

[2] *Purpose of a Statute*

The purpose of a provision within the legal framework is decisive for the interpretation and application of the law. As has been mentioned before, provisions have to accord to superior legal determinants; in Germany, the Constitution and the doctrine of adequacy play a major role.[23]

[a] *Purpose of Tax Laws*

Tax laws shall be interpreted with respect to their own function. In Germany, tax laws are primarily viewed as a vehicle to levy taxes in a just manner.[24] However, the prevailing view rejects such an approach for purposes of interpretation, because the interest to levy taxes is always in favour of the exchequer und thus not suitable for a balanced interpretation of the tax laws even if the equality dimension is emphasized.[25]

For that reason, according to the prevailing view in Germany, tax laws should be interpreted from a more narrow purposive perspective, i.e., based on the purpose of each provision within the statute containing it. This emphasizes the function of a single provision in the overall tax law and in particular the function it has in determining the tax liability.[26] For example, public companies are taxed according to the income gained in a particular tax year irrespective of how this income is distributed among the shareholders. If a controlling shareholder is employed by the company and paid a remuneration exceeding the arm's length value, section 8, subsection 3, sentence 2 of the Corporate Income Tax Act treats the excessive remuneration as a profit distribution and the company is unable to deduct the cost of excessive remuneration as a business expense. The purpose of this provision, therefore, is to prevent a company from reducing its taxable income by way of hidden profit distributions and to assure that the full business income is subject to corporate income tax.

23. Cf. to this effect 13 BVerfGE 318 (BVerfG 1962); 2007 BStBl II 47 (BFH 2006); 1992 BStBl II 720 (BFH 1992); 1992 BStBl II 241 (BFH 1991); 1984 BStBl II 327 (BFH 1984); Karl Larenz, *supra* note 2 at pp. 333 et seq., 339 et seq.
24. Klaus Vogel, 'Grundzüge des Finanzrechts des Grundgesetzes' ('Constitutional Foundation of the Fiscal Law'), in Josef Isensee & Paul Kirchhof (eds), *Handbuch des Staatsrechts* (*Compendium of the German Constitutional Law*), Volume IV (Heidelberg: C.F. Müller, 2nd edn, 1999), § 87 para. 71; Henning Tappe, *supra* note 19 at p. 162.
25. Klaus Vogel, *supra* note 24 at § 87 para. 71; Wolfgang Schön, *supra* note 7 at p. 73. However, the Great Chamber of the *Federal Fiscal Court* inferred this argument once, cf. 1984 BStBl II 751 (BFH 1984).
26. 2007 BStBl II 714 (BFH 2007); 2007 BStBl II 47 (BFH 2006); 1995 BStBl II 586 (BFH 1995); 1992 BStBl II 720 (BFH 1992); 1984 BStBl II 160 (BFH 1983); 1970 BStBl II 310 (BFH 1969); Wolfgang Schön, *supra* note 7 at p. 73; Wolfgang Schön, 'Gestaltungsfreiheit und Belastungsgleichheit als Grundlagen des Steuerrechts' ('Freedom of Design and Equal Sharing of the Tax Burden as the Main Features of Tax Law'), in Rainer Hüttemann (ed.), *Gestaltungsfreiheit und Gestaltungsmissbrauch im Steuerrecht* (*Freedom of Design and Abuse of Law in Tax Law*), DStJG, Vol. 33 (Cologne: Dr. Otto Schmidt Verlag, 2010), pp. 50 et seq. and Klaus-Dieter Drüen, *supra* note 8 at paras 277 et seq. with further references.

Separately, taxes may be used to influence, i.e., to (dis)incentivise economic behaviour. In those cases, a tax provision must be interpreted from the perspective of realizing this objective efficiently.[27]

[b] *Tax Law in the Overall Legal Framework and Transplanted Categories*

Tax laws will often use the same words also utilized in other areas of law, such as contract law, corporate law or partnership law. This raises the question as to what extent the interpretation of these transplanted terminologies in tax acts has to coincide with the meaning given to them in these other areas of the law. Further, the question arises to what extent tax laws have to be interpreted in line with value-judgments of private law.

The relationship between tax law and private law is still under debate in Germany. At one end of the spectrum, proponents argue either based on the presumption that tax laws are an annex to private law or based on the principle of legal certainty that the legal framework should be coherent and legal terminologies used in different areas of the law should be interpreted in the same manner.[28] A more cautious approach, based on the principle of legal certainty, is that transplanted legal categories are presumed to have the same meaning in tax law, unless the contrary has been established.[29] At the other end of the spectrum are those who argue the general function of tax laws is very different from the function of private law and any term used in tax law should in general be interpreted in a way that furthers the purpose of the tax law as it uses the term, even if that differs from the private law meaning.[30] Notably, if a provision is interpreted narrowly with reference to private law terminology, the issue of developing the law further by judicial interpretation will arise more frequently. In contrast, the same results might be achieved through an interpretation of the provision independent of the private law meaning. If this approach is taken, the question of whether judicial interpretation to develop the law further is necessary does not arise.

The Federal Constitutional Court initially adopted a strict view that interpretation of some transplanted terms in tax laws should follow their meaning in private law. According to the court, tax laws and private law are closely related in areas where tax laws refer directly to the legal form of behaviour. In these circumstances, in the absence of sound rationales, the legislature is presumed not to intend a different meaning where it has adopted terms used in another legal category.[31] The Court

27. 1995 BStBl II 586 (BFH 1995); 1992 BStBl II 241 (BFH 1991); 1973 BStBl II 182 (BFH 1972); 1972 BStBl II 75 (BFH 1971); 1970 BStBl II 597 (BFH 1970).
28. Kurt Jacob Ball-Kaduri, *Steuerrecht und Privatrecht* (*Tax Law and Private Law*) (Mannheim: Bensheimer, 1924); *see also* Johanna Hey, 'Einführung zum EStG' ('Introduction to the Individual Income Tax Code'), in Carl Herrmann et al. (eds), *Einkommensteuer- und Körperschaftsteuergesetz* (*Individual and Corporate Income Tax Code*) (Cologne: Dr. Otto Schmidt Verlag, loose-leaf, 2016), paras 910 et seq. for further references. *See also* Klaus Tipke, *Die Steuerrechtsordnung* (*The Tax System*), Volume I (Cologne: Dr. Otto Schmidt Verlag, 2nd edn, 2000), pp. 49 et seq. for further details.
29. Wolfgang Schön, *supra* note 7 at p. 71.
30. Klaus Tipke, *Die Steuerrechtsordnung*, *supra* note 17 at pp. 50, 57 et seq.
31. 13 BVerfGE 331 (BVerfG 1961).

subsequently clarified this position, indicating courts may interpret tax laws differently than private laws. The relationship between taxation and private law is not of such a kind that it is required of tax laws to adopt private law meanings in every case. Consequently, it is important to determine, in a first step, whether or not tax laws attach the tax liability to any particular private law entities or concepts.[32] Finally, in 1991, the court appeared to reverse itself completely in terms of the initial approach, deciding that even in cases of transplanted terminology, tax laws should be interpreted independently, because tax laws and private law are distinct areas of the legal framework, both having their own purposes; neither of them has a superior standing in the legal framework.[33]

The Federal Fiscal Court adopted this approach of interpreting transplanted terminology. In the first step, the court elaborates whether transplanted terminology used in tax law is meant to be linked to a particular private law entity or concept; if this is the case, the private law meaning will be adopted for interpreting the tax law.[34] Otherwise, the transplanted terminology is interpreted in a manner based on the policy underlying tax law, independently of its meaning in private law.[35] This approach is illustrated by the Federal Fiscal Court on the tax treatment of joint stakeholders in an undivided estate. In German estate law, stakeholders in an undivided estate are distinct from partners where jointly held entitlements arise as a result of partnership law. The economic interests of the two groups of persons are similar, however. The Federal Fiscal Court concluded the partnership measures in the German Income Tax Act also include joint stakeholders in an undivided estate because of their similar nature, although, the German Income Tax Act uses the term 'partnership' and despite the fact that there is clear difference between stakeholders and partners in partnership law and estate law, respectively.[36]

[c] Economic Approach

The Imperial Order on Levies enacted in 1919 stated in section 4 that any interpretation of tax laws should bear in mind the purpose and economic relevance of a provision and the facts of the case. This provision remained in force until 1977 and formed the basis

32. 26 BVerfGE 327 (BVerfG 1969).
33. 1992 BStBl II 212 (BVerfG 1991).
34. *See inter alia* BFH IV R 35/13 (BFH 2016); 2015 BStBl II 545 (BFH 2015); 2015 HFR 1062 (BFH 2015); 2015 BStBl II 483 (BFH 2014); 2013 BStBl 231 (BFH 2012); 2011 BStBl II 367 (BFH 2010); 2007 BStBl II 608 (BFH 2007); 1985 BStBl II 339 (BFH 1985); 1984 BStBl II 751 (BFH 1984). *See also* 2016 HFR 924 (BFH 2016); 2016 BFH/NV 65 (BFH 2015); 2006 BStBl II 661 (BFH 2006); 2004 BStBl II 607 (BFH 2004); 1985 BStBl II 309 (BFH 1985).
35. *See inter alia* 254 BFHE 371 (BFH 2016); 254 BFHE 283 (BFH 2016); 254 BFHE 246 (BFH 2016); 254 BFHE 164 (BFH 2016); 252 BFHE 17 (BFH 2015); 2015 BStBl II 567 (BFH 2015); 2007 BStBl II 893 (BFH 2007); 2001 BFH/NV 1457 (BFH 2001); 1999 BStBl II 168 (1998); 1996 BStBl II 232 (BFH 1995); 1984 BStBl II 751 (BFH 1984).
36. 1984 BStBl II 751 (BFH 1984); 1983 BStBl II 299 (BFH 1982); 1977 BStBl II 201 (BFH 1976); 1971 BStBl II 87 (BFH 1970).

for what is known as the economic approach to statutory interpretation.[37] Today, the economic approach is not considered a distinct method of statutory interpretation of tax laws. Instead, the economic approach is seen as being an element of the process of construing the function of a provision.

Tax laws generally impose tax on the consequences of some economic behaviour. An economic analysis of the outcome of behaviour would ensure the appropriate tax provision applied to it, whatever structure was used to achieve the outcome. For example, the consequences of a not commonly used contract law structure could be subsumed under a tax provision designed for the more commonly used structure if the unusual structure yielded the same economic result as the commonly employed structure covered by the tax provision. Thus, the economic approach is also a means to tackle tax avoidance schemes subject to any limitation in the wording of the statute and consideration of the overall function of the tax provision.[38]

[d] Argument for a Contrary Treatment

As soon as the internal system of the tax law is established, the system may be used as the foundation for developing an *argumentum e contrario*, meaning an argument based on the contrary. The *argumentum e contrario* can only be established if the law provides a specific provision that is meant to be exhaustive. An *argumentum e contrario* has two limbs. First, it is an argument according to which a provision is interpreted narrowly and does not cover a case because one or more other provisions, which have a similar purpose, do not address the factual scenario of the case at hand. Second, it is an argument according to which the existence of conditions attached to one element of the rule or set of rules governing an issue are assumed not to extend to a second element of the rule or set of rules if the conditions are explicitly mentioned in relation to the first element and omitted from the second. The *argumentum e contrario* has been applied extensively.[39] Its operation is illustrated in a recent decision of the Federal Fiscal Court concerning the conditions required for a group of companies to establish a fiscal unity under the German income tax regime. A fiscal unity is a unified

37. However, the proper interpretation of this provision was disputed. Some stated that the economic approach required considering the facts of a case from an economic perspective in line with substance-over-form doctrines known in other countries. Others interpreted the provision in a way according to which the provision should be interpreted with respect to its economic relevance. *See also* Cf. Klaus-Dieter Drüen, *supra* note 8 at paras 320 et seq.; Wolfgang Schön, *supra* note 7 at p. 72.
38. Cf. also Klaus-Dieter Drüen, *supra* note 8 at paras 320 et seq.; Wolfgang Schön, *supra* note 7 at p. 72; Wolfgang Schön, 'Legalität, Gestaltungsfreiheit und Belastungsgleichheit als Grundlage des Steuerrechts' ('Legality Principle, Freedom of Legal Arrangements and Equal Sharing of the Tax Burden as the Main Features of Tax Law'), in Rainer Hüttemann (ed.), *Gestaltungsfreiheit und Gestaltungsmissbrauch im Steuerrecht* (*Freedom of Design and Abuse of Law in Tax Law*), DStJG, Vol. 33 (Cologne: Dr. Otto Schmidt Verlag, 2010), pp. 29, 50; Henning Tappe, *supra* note 19, p. 171.
39. 2014 BStBl II 168 (BFH 2013); 243 BFHE 51 (BFH 2013); 2013 BStBl II 1048 (BFH 2013); 2012 BStBl II 254 (BFH 2011); 2011 BStBl II 506 (BFH 2010); 2004 BFH/NV 182 (BFH 2003); 2003 BStBl II 646 (BFH 2002); 1996 BStBl II 28 (BFH 1995); 1996 BFH/NV 464 (BFH 1995); 1991 BStBl II 413 (BFH 1990); 1988 BStBl II 782 (BFH 1988); 1988 BStBl II 180 (BFH 1987); 1984 BStBl II 809.

fiscal regime between a controlling company and lower tier companies it controls. The law states that a fiscal unit can only be established with respect to a particular fiscal year if the companies are fiscally integrated from the beginning of that year and that the controlling company has carried on the business. The German tax authority had argued that the carried-on-business requirement should be understood as to require the company to have carried on its business from the beginning of the controlled company's fiscal year, in line with the condition related to fiscal integration. The Federal Fiscal Court decided this further condition for the carried-on-business requirement was not supported by the law. Since the provision that spelt out the requirements for a fiscal unity contained a limitation only with respect to the fiscal unity's financial integration requirement, it found *e contrario* the limitation did not apply to the business activity requirement.[40]

§8.03 FURTHER DEVELOPMENT OF THE LAW BY JUDICIAL INTERPRETATION

The German Constitution embraces the principle of separation of powers and accordingly Germany has three separate and distinct branches: legislature, executive and judiciary.[41] These branches should control each other, and each is strictly prohibited from appropriating functions of one of the other branches.[42] Thus, the judiciary and executive can only act within the boundaries of the written law[43] as enacted by the legislature. In this context, the question arises whether a judge is entitled to further develop the law in a way that necessarily goes beyond a mere interpretation of the legislative provisions. It could be argued that such a development of the law is not in line with the principle of the separation of powers, because it would be the judiciary that creates law instead of the legislature. However, since such a strict separation of the powers is both impractical and unfeasible,[44] the Federal Constitutional Court characterized the filling of a gap in the law as a traditional task of a judge.[45] Legal constructs and concepts that derive not from the written law but rather form the case law of the Federal Fiscal Court, such as the concept of separate business assets[46] and the company

40. 2014 BStBl II 272 (BFH 2013).
41. Article 20 subs. 2 of the German Constitution.
42. Bernd Grzesdzick, 'Art. 20 GG', in Theodor Maunz & Günter Dürig (eds), *Grundgesetz Kommentar* (*Commentary on the German Constitutional Law*) (Munich: Beck-Verlag, loose-leaf, 2016), paras 4 et seq.
43. Article 20 subs. 3 of the German Constitution.
44. 34 BVerfGE 269 (BVerfG 1973).
45. 3 BVerfGE 225 (BVerfG 1953); for defining a gap in the law *see* Claus-Wilhelm Canaris, *Die Feststellung von Lücken im Gesetz* (*The Finding of Gaps in the Law*) (Berlin: Duncker und Humblot Verlag, 2nd edn, 1983).
46. The German term is Sonderbetriebsvermögen and is divided in Sonderbetriebsvermögen I and Sonderbetriebsvermögen II. The first mentioned term covers all assets that are owned by the partners of a partnership but are used for the activities of the partnership. If assets are allocated to this sphere (Sonderbetriebsvermögen I) they are within the tax net, and thus the selling of these assets may trigger income tax; 26 BVerfGE 327 (BVerfG 1969); The term Sonderbetriebsvermögen II covers all assets that are necessary for holding the shares in the partnership, from

split,[47] are developed within the constitutional boundaries, according to the Federal Constitutional Court.

While judges are entitled to develop the law further in some circumstances,[48] they must do so respecting the general principles of law such as the principle of equal treatment and the protection of legitimate expectations.[49] The mechanisms that judges can use to develop the law further are discussed below.

[A] Analogy

The instrument of analogy (*argumentum a simile*) applies in circumstances where the facts of a case are not covered by one or more legal provisions but are substantially similar to those falling within their scope. The mechanism of analogy achieves a necessary equal treatment of substantially similar scenarios where not all are explicitly addressed by the law. The conclusion by analogy can be drawn either with respect to a single legal provision or with respect to a set of legal provisions.[50]

Up to the early 1980s, analogical interpretation in tax matters was not accepted in legal practice for reasons similar to the prohibition of analogy in criminal law matters (*nulla poena sine crime*), laid down in Article 103 subsection 2 of the German Constitution.[51] However, in more recent time, the Federal Fiscal Court generally acknowledged the application of the analogy mechanism both to the advantage and disadvantage of the taxpayer.[52] The question of whether the application of analogy in

the partners' point of view (e.g., bank credit) 1991 BStBl II 800 (BFH 1991); 1993 NJW 2734 (BVerfG 1992); *see* for more details Claudia Sparrer, *Sonderbetriebsvermögen* (Berlin: LIT Verlag, 2007), 27 et seq.

47. The German term is Betriebsaufspaltung and this concept corresponds to the Sonderbetriebsvermögen in the field of companies limited by shares; 69 BVerfGE 188 (BVerfG 1985); for a critical review *see* Brigitte Knobbe-Keuk, 'Die Betriebsaufspaltung – ein "Rechtsinstitut"?', in Franz Hörstmann et al. (eds), *Steuerberater-Jahrbuch 1980/81* (Cologne: Verlag Dr. Otto Schmidt, 1981), 335.
48. For the question of the justification of a further development of the law contra legem *see* Wolfgang Spindler, 'Richterliche Rechtsfortbildung und Rechtssicherheit' ('Further Development of the Law by Judges and Legal Certainty'), in Hanno Kube et al. (eds), *Leitgedanken des Rechts* II (Heidelberg: C. F. Müller, 2013), 1789, 1792.
49. 34 BVerfGE 269 (BVerfG 1973); 1979 NJW 305 (BVerfG 1978), the judge is not entitled to limit rights which are provided by the law according to a constitutional interpretation; 69 BVerfGE 315 (BVerfG 1985) the judge is not entitled to further develop the law according to his/her own policy considerations if there is no gap in the law.
50. Joachim Englisch, *supra* note 8 at § 5 para. 80.
51. *See* for a general analysis Klaus Tipke, *Die Steuerrechtsordnung* (*The Tax System*), Vol. I (Cologne: Dr. Otto Schmidt Verlag, 2nd edn, 2000), p. 198; Joachim Englisch, *supra* note 8 at § 5 para. 81; Rainer Barth, *Richterliche Rechtsfortbildung im Steuerrecht* (*Development of the Law by Judges*) (Berlin: Duncker und Humblot Verlag, 1996), pp. 405 et seq.
52. To the advantage of the taxpayer: 2009 BStBl II 587 (BFH 2009); 2012 BStBl II 74 (BFH 2011), the analogous use of § 15(4) of the German Value Added Tax Code for the allocation of the input VAT in cases where the goods are used both for economic and non-economic purposes. The court was mainly driven by the principle of neutrality within the European VAT system; to the disadvantage of the taxpayer: 1984 BStBl II 221 (BFH 1984); for the general justification of the application of analogy to the disadvantage of the taxpayer: 2007 BStBl II 621 (BFH 2007);

tax matters is permitted can only be answered with respect to the principle of separation of powers and the rule of law.[53]

[B] Teleological Reduction and Extension

Teleological reduction and extension is another form of filling an unintended gap in the law. Teleological reduction should apply in cases where the wording of the legislation is too broad, leading to a situation where a provision appears to cover scenarios that were not intended to be regulated.[54] The counterpart to this mechanism is represented by teleological extension in cases where the wording of the provision is too narrow and does not cover all scenarios that were intended to be regulated.[55] Teleological extension is distinguished from the analogy mechanism (*see* §8.03[A]) that is also used to extend the operation of a statutory provision. In cases where the teleological extension is applied, the gap in the law is filled by applying general legal principles and thereby broadening the scope of an existing legal provision.[56] If, however, the mechanism of analogy is used, an existing legal provision is applied to a scenario that is not covered by the wording of this provision.[57]

Neither teleological extension nor reduction may be applied to alter the policy effect of a law if the underlying policy objective is misguided. Both teleological extension and teleological reduction may only be applied if the interpretation of a provision would lead to results that are either absurd,[58] contrary to the economic logic,[59] or not intended by the legislator.[60]

The German Federal Court has applied the teleological reduction not only to the advantage of the taxpayer but also to the disadvantage of the taxpayer.[61] The question of whether such an approach is constitutional needs to be answered on the basis of the same criteria used to determine this for the mechanism of analogy; thus, the legal

Wolfgang Schön, 'Legalität, Gestaltungsfreiheit und Belastungsgleichheit als Grundlage des Steuerrechts', *supra* note 38, pp. 29, 51 et seq.; Wolfgang Spindler, *supra* note 48 at 1789, 1793 et seq.

53. Section §8.03[C].
54. 1992 BStBl II 786 (BFH 1992); 2002 BStBl II 793 (BFH 2001); 2002 BStBl II 753 (BFH 2002); 2006 BStBl II 776 (BFH 2006); 88 BVerfGE 145 (BVerfG 1993); *see also* Franz Bydlinski, *Grundzüge der juristischen Methodenlehre* (*Outline of the Legal Methodology*) (Vienna: Facultas-Verlag, 2nd edn, 2012), pp. 90 et seq.
55. 2012 BStBl II 312 (BFH 2011); 237 BFHE 106 (BFH 2012); 2013 BStBl II 665 (BFH 2013); 2010 BStBl II 971 (BFH 2010), extension of s. 6 subs. 5 of the German Tax Code to the transfer of joint total assets of sister companies with identical participations; Joachim Englisch, *supra* note 8 at § 5 para. 86.
56. Joachim Englisch, *supra* note 8 at § 5 para. 86; Franz Bydlinski, *supra* note 3 at pp. 481 et seq.
57. The German Federal Fiscal Court is characterizing both, the teleological extension and the mechanism of analogy, as separate and distinct mechanism, 2010 BStBl II 873 (BFH 2010); 2013 DB 1155 (BFH 2013).
58. 2007 BStBl II 893 (BFH 2007); 2003 BStBl II 798 (BFH 2003).
59. 1998 BStBl II 131 (BFH 1997).
60. 2012 BStBl II 312 (BFH 2011); 237 BFHE 106 (BFH 2012); 2013 BStBl II 665 (BFH 2013).
61. 2006 BStBl II 776 (BFH 2006).

admissibility has to be examined with respect to the rule of law and the principle of separation of powers.[62]

[C] The Rule of Law and the Principle of Separation of Powers

Whether the further development of the law through judicial interpretation is constitutional needs to be answered from the perspective of the rule of law and the principle of separation of powers. Despite the fact that the Federal Constitutional Court generally accepts that a judge can further develop the law,[63] the dissenting opinion in a recent case outlined the limits of the further development of the law by judicial interpretation.[64]

While the judgment of the Federal Constitutional Court concerned criminal law, the findings of the court relating to the further development of the law through judicial interpretation have a general application. Thus, as far as tax law is concerned, the further development of the law is methodically possible. According to the Federal Fiscal Court, the entitlement to a further development of the law does not depend on whether or not it is to the advantage of the taxpayer. However, in the literature it is argued that from the point of view of the rule of law, it does make a difference if the tax burden increases or decreases through the application of the law *praeter legem*.[65]

A recent case of the Federal Fiscal Court appears to restrict the application of the mechanism of analogy. Even though the use of an analogy mechanism would have been for the advantage of the taxpayer and the mechanism of analogy would have achieved an equal treatment of two comparable situations as required by the principle of equal treatment, the Federal Fiscal Court refused to do so. The court viewed the tax provision to be exhaustive in the circumstances of the case.[66]

§8.04 TAX PLANNING, ECONOMIC APPROACH AND GENERAL ANTI-ABUSE RULES

Tax Planning plays a crucial role in the modern tax world. Individuals as well as corporations try to reduce their tax burdens by restructuring their affairs. The tax administration, in turn, tries to counter taxpayers' actions by applying the tax provisions to the economic result of transactions rather than their nominal legal form and if necessary by applying the general anti-abuse rule contained in section 42 of the German General Tax Act, which provides for the determination of tax liability disregarding the effect of tax avoidance schemes.

62. Section §8.03[C].
63. 34 BVerfGE 269 (BVerfG 1973); 71 BVerfGE 354 (BVerfG 1986).
64. 122 BVerfGE 248 (BVerfG 2009).
65. Wolfgang Schön, 'Legalität, Gestaltungsfreiheit und Belastungsgleichheit als Grundlage des Steuerrechts', *supra* note 38 at pp. 29, 54.
66. 2013 BStBl II 1004 (BFH 2013) para. 27. It may be necessary to note that the court put the question of whether the national provision that includes a differentiation before the German Constitutional Court. Thus, the court was not applying the mechanism of analogy by subsequently accepting a differentiation that may be unconstitutional.

The Federal Fiscal Court has consistently held that taxpayers may structure their economic affairs as they wish, regardless of whether this leads to a reduction of the overall tax burden. Tax reduction in itself is not sufficient ground to characterize a structure as an illegitimate tax avoidance scheme.[67] Whether a structure is considered as illegitimate tax avoidance depends on its abusive nature. Section 42 of the German General Tax Act prohibits 'abusing legal options for tax planning schemes'. Since 2008, section 42 of the German General Tax Act has defined the concept of abuse; it is 'deemed to exist, where an inappropriate legal option is selected, which, in comparison with an appropriate option, leads to tax advantages unintended by law for the taxpayer or a third party. This shall not apply where the taxpayer provides evidence of non-tax reasons for the selected option which is relevant when viewed from an overall perspective.'

Up to now, the German courts have not addressed the issue whether the newly included definition of the concept of abuse results in a different scope of application.[68] According to the case law to section 42 of the German General Tax Act before implementing an abuse definition, the Federal Fiscal Court considered an abuse in cases where the legal structure is inappropriate from the perspective of the economic aim to be achieved and where the structure is solely aimed at lowering the tax burden. The legal structure may comprise several distinct steps undertaken by the same taxpayer or by different persons acting on the basis of a specific relationship. The intermediate steps taken as such may reduce the overall tax burden, but would be subject to a different tax treatment resulting in a higher tax burden if not viewed distinctly but altogether. These intermediary steps can be disregarded if the steps are part of an overall planning structure that will, only if taken together, reflect properly the economic scenario under scrutiny according to the tax provisions in question.[69]

67. 243 BFHE 376 (BFH 2013); 2013 BStBl II 934 (BFH 2013); 196 BFHE 128 (BFH 2001); 1996 BStBl II 158 (BFH 1995); 1988 BStBl II 942 (BFH 1988); 1983 BStBl II 272 (BFH 1982); 1964 BStBl III 667 (BFH 1964).
68. In 238 BFHE 344 (BFH 2012), the first chamber mentioned that the definition of abuse in s. 42 of the General Tax Code corresponds to the current approach of the courts, whereas the judge at the Federal Fiscal Court Michael Wendt, '§ 42 AO vor dem Hintergrund der Rechtsprechung' ('Section 42 of the General Tax Code in Light of the Case Law'), in Rainer Hüttemann (ed.), *Gestaltungsfreiheit und Gestaltungsmissbrauch im Steuerrecht* (*Freedom of Design and Abuse of Law in Tax Law*), DStJG, Vol. 33 (Cologne: Dr. Otto Schmidt Verlag, 2010), pp. 136 et seq. opposes this view. *See also* Klaus-Dieter Drüen, 'Vor § 42' ('Sect. 42', in Klaus Tipke & Heinrich Wilhelm Kruse (eds), *AO/FGO* (*General Tax Code / Code on the Procedure of Tax Courts*) (Cologne: Dr. Otto Schmidt Verlag, loose-leaf, 2016), para. 37 with further references and an analysis of the new provision. *See also* Wolfgang Schön, 'Legalität, Gestaltungsfreiheit und Belastungsgleichheit als Grundlage des Steuerrechts', *supra* note 38 at pp. 29, 59 et seq.; Joachim Englisch, *supra* note 8 at § 5 paras 126 et seq.
69. 2013 BStBl II 1021 (BFH 2013); 2013 BStBl II 934 (BFH 2013); 2013 BFH/NV 1094 (BFH 2013); 2006 BStBl II 359 (BFH 2005); 2001 BStBl II 101 (BFH 2000); 1998 BStBl II 667 (BFH 1998); 1996 BStBl. II 443 (BFH 1996); 1991 BStBl II 327 (BFH 1990). *See also* Wolfgang Spindler, *Der 'Gesamtplan' in der Rechtsprechung des BFH* (*Overall Planning Structures and the Federal Fiscal Court's Case Law*), DStR, 1 (2005); Guido Förster, 'Die Gesamtplanrechtsprechung im Steuerrecht' (The Case Law on Overall Planning Structures in the Tax Law), in Dieter Carlé et al. (eds), *Festschrift for Klaus Korn* (Bonn-Berlin: Stollfuß Verlag, 2005), pp. 3 et seq. and Michael Tanzer, 'Der Gesamtplan im Rahmen steuerlicher Tatbestände' ('Overall Planning Structures and Tax Provisions'), in Rainer Hüttemann (ed.), *Gestaltungsfreiheit und Gestaltungsmissbrauch im*

However, a legal structure must not be considered abusive or intermediate steps must not be taken together if there are substantial non-tax reasons for choosing the structure. In particular, how the taxpayer structures its economic behaviour is not under scrutiny. The courts will only consider the legal structure. Whether a legal structure is inappropriate is determined with reference to the typical legal structure assumed by the legislator. According to this reference case, the legal structure chosen is inappropriate if it is artificial, unusual, impractical, etc. viewed with respect to the overall facts of the case. Moreover, based on the purpose of the possibly circumvented provision, the legal structure must result in an unintended reduction of the tax burden. Thus, the courts will not take into account whether the way in which the economic behaviour is structured is appropriate. Taxpayers may also infer further non-tax reasons for a particular structure that are not economic in nature. These motives, however, have to be substantial with respect to the legal structure in question to exclude the case from the scope of section 42 of the German General Tax Act.[70]

The legal consequences of applying section 42 of the German General Tax Act are debated in the literature. There is general agreement that according to section 42 of the German General Tax Act the tax is levied irrespective of the tax avoidance scheme. Some authors state that the tax provision that shall cover the behaviour is applied by means of analogy, required by section 42 of the German General Tax Act. Thus, the legal consequence requires applying circumvented tax provision by way of analogy.[71] Others argue that section 42 of the German General Tax Act assumes an appropriate factual scenario for the facts of the case that in a second step is subsumed under the circumvented tax provision.[72]

Moreover, it is also debated whether tax avoidance issues may be solved completely by matters of interpretation.[73] In our opinion, this is not the case. The scope for an economic interpretation of tax provisions is limited. First, any interpretation has to be in line with the wording of the provision. Second, many tax provisions directly refer to private law and public economic law terminology to cover certain behaviour. These references may not be ignored and, therefore, they limit the possibilities to tackle tax avoidance schemes. In particular, when a provision refers to a fundamental concept of private law like corporations or partnerships, an interpretation may not disregard a

---

Steuerrecht (*Freedom of Design and Abuse of Law in Tax Law*), DStJG, Vol. 33 (Cologne: Dr. Otto Schmidt Verlag, 2010), pp. 189 et seq.

70. 2014 BFH/NV 297 (BFH 2013); 2013 BFH/NV 1094 (BFH 2013); 2013 BFH/NV 193 (BFH 2012); 2012 BStBl II 638 (BFH 2012); 238 BFHE 344 (BFH 2012); 2006 BStBl II 359 (BFH 2005); 196 BFHE 128 (BFH 2001); 1996 BStBl II 158 (BFH 1995); 1991 BFH/NV 432 (BFH 1989); 1988 BStBl II 942 (BFH 1988); 1983 BStBl II 272 (BFH 1982); 1964 BStBl III 667 (BFH 1964); Klaus-Dieter Drüen, 'Vor § 42', *supra* note 68 at paras 17 et seq. and Klaus-Dieter Drüen, '§ 42 AO' ('Sect. 42 General Tax Code'), in Klaus Tipke & Heinrich Wilhelm Kruse (eds), *AO/FGO* (*General Tax Code / Code on the Procedure of Tax Courts*) (Cologne: Dr. Otto Schmidt Verlag, loose-leaf, 2016), paras 33 et seq.
71. *See* Klaus-Dieter Drüen, '§ 42 AO', *supra* note 70 at paras 9 et seq. with further references.
72. Wolfgang Schön, *supra* note 7 at p. 77; Joachim Englisch, *supra* note 8 at § 5 para. 134; Henning Tappe, *supra* note 19 at p. 172.
73. So-called *Innentheorie*, cf. *inter alia* Heinrich Weber-Grellet, *Steuern im modernen Verfassungsstaat* (*Taxes in the Modern State*) (Cologne: Dr. Otto Schmidt Verlag, 2001), pp. 222 et seq.; Klaus Tipke, *Die Steuerrechtsordnung*, *supra* note 17 at pp. 1667 et seq.

corporation simply because it is assumed to be an intermediate company merely created for tax reasons.[74]

Example-Case I[75]

Parents decide to give one of their houses to their child. The house had been purchased nine years before the donation occurred and since then it had been used for renting purposes. At the same time, the child made a gift to his parents of EUR 500,000, which was the estimated value of the real estate received from the parents.

According to section 22 subsection 1 number 2 and section 23 subsection 1 number 1 of the German Income Tax Act, profit on the sale of real estate is taxable if the property was acquired not more than 10 years before the sale and was not used as personal accommodation. In the example, it is questionable whether the real estate has actually been sold by the parents. Formally, both the real estate and the money were donated (even though it may be considered a sale from a private law perspective). From an economic perspective, however, the EUR 500,000 was directly related to the transfer of property and thus economically a sale occurred. Consequently, a purposive interpretation of the provisions in question covers the facts of the case. Furthermore, such an interpretation does neither contradict any other purpose of the provision nor its wording. In summary, this avoidance structure will be covered by an economically based purposive interpretation of the provisions in question.

Example-Case II[76]

Both A and B decide to buy identical houses. Both houses are located next to each other in the same street. At the very same day, both conclude a rental contract. A becomes the landlord of B and B becomes the landlord of A. In their income tax statements, both declare the rental earnings as well as expenses relating to the income; these exceed the earnings and reduce the overall tax burden of A and B.

Rental income, including losses from rental activities, will be taken into account in the tax base, if they result from a taxable rental activity (sections 2 and 21 subsection 1 number 1 of the Income Tax Act). Both A and B engage in a rental activity; the contracts concluded are performed. Accordingly, A and B are allowed to deduct expenses from their earnings. By means of interpretation, the activity cannot be excluded from the scope of these provisions. As a matter of fact, from the perspective of the provisions, the houses are rented out. Whether or not they would have acquired the other house otherwise is of no importance.

However, the example-case II might be covered by section 42 of the German General Tax Act. Then, the abusive scheme would be neglected resulting in the tax burden normally due. If A and B had acquired their respective houses for their own personal accommodation, they would not be able to deduct any expenses and their

74. In particular, cf. Wolfgang Schön, 'Gestaltungsfreiheit und Belastungsgleichheit als Grundlagen des Steuerrechts', *supra* note 26 at pp. 50 et seq.
75. This example is based on a decision of the Federal Fiscal Court, *see* 2006 BStBl II 359 (BFH 2005).
76. This example is taken from a Federal Fiscal Court decision, cf. 1991 BStBl II 904 (BFH 1991).

overall tax burden would not be reduced. Buying the house of a neighbour and renting the houses to each other is an inappropriate structure since the aim of the parties was to obtain a house for their own living purposes. This structure results in an unintended tax advantage as A and B may not deduct expenses with respect to their own personal accommodation. Furthermore, they do not have any substantial non-tax reasons for choosing this structure. Thus, the structure will be considered abusive.

§8.05 INTERPRETATION IN THE LIGHT OF CONSTITUTIONAL LAW AND EUROPEAN UNION LAW

[A] Constitutional Law

The German law system is hierarchically structured. The German Constitution represents the highest level in the German law system and thus, every provision of inferior law has to comply with the constitution. The interpretation according to the constitution can be characterized as one limb of the purposive interpretation. It tries to achieve conformity with superior rules of law.

Generally, the interpretation in accordance with constitutional law will be applied in cases where the application of the various other methods of interpretation (*see* §8.02) leads to results that are not all in line with constitutional law. Non-complying interpretation methods must be ignored, and priority is given to those interpretation methods providing constitutional results.[77] It can generally be contended that legislative bodies will be compliant with the constitution and do not want to infringe it. Despite this, the interpretation of provisions in accordance with the constitution can only go as far as the interpretation remains within the widest possible sense of the wording of the provision (*lex-lata*-boundary).[78]

Thus, this interpretation method cannot function as a correction mechanism if a provision of law contradicts constitutional law. In such cases, legal mechanisms, such as invalidity, non-application or invalidation of the existing and unconstitutional provision, must be applied.[79] The power to declare a provision to be unconstitutional and to invalidate it lies with the Federal Constitutional Court.[80]

[B] Interpretation of German Tax Law in Conformity with European Union Directives

New methodological issues arose due to the overlap between national and European law. Since the Union law enjoys priority over conflicting national law,[81] national law has to be interpreted in the light of and in accordance with European law regardless of

77. 68 BVerfGE 337 (BVerfG 1984); 88 BVerfGE 203 (BVerfG 1993); 112 BVerfGE 164 (BVerfG 2005).
78. 72 BVerfGE 278 (BVerfG 1986); 88 BVerfGE 203 (BVerfG 1993); Franz Bydlinski, *Grundzüge der juristischen Methodenlehre, supra* note 54 at pp. 54 and 108 et seq.
79. Franz Bydlinski, *Grundzüge der juristischen Methodenlehre, supra* note 54 at p. 55.
80. Article 100 of the German Constitution.
81. *See* Chapter 6 of this volume; ECJ, 17 December 1970, Case 11/70, *Internationale Handelsgesellschaft*, [1970] ECR 1125; 2010 BFHE 231, 360 (BFH 2010); 2014 NJW 576 (BGH 2013); *see also* Walter Frenz, *Europarecht* (*European Law*) (Berlin: Springer-Verlag, 2011), para. 124.

whether European law is of a primary or secondary source. The general principles of a conforming interpretation are illustrated in Chapter 6 of this volume;[82] thus, the authors will only discuss special issues for the interpretation of German tax law.

The fact that national courts are required to interpret national law in accordance with the wording and purpose of a directive, has been beyond debate since the Court of Justice of the European Union (ECJ) cases *von Colson and Kamann*,[83] and *Harz.*[84] The Federal Constitutional Court also highlighted that not only the legislator is required to enforce Union law, also the courts are required to do so.[85] National courts must interpret national law provisions that transpose European Union law in a way that best reflects the intention of the European Union drafters. Thus, they are required to use only those national interpretation methods leading to results that are in conformity with Union law.[86]

A question that has been debated extensively in German academic literature whether courts are also required to develop further the law for achieving conformity with Union law. The German methodology strictly distinguishes between further developments of the law by judges and administrative authorities and the interpretation of provisions of law.[87] Despite this, the ECJ does not methodologically distinguish between these two instruments; the court is generally referring to the term '*interprétation*' in accordance with the French methodological tradition.[88] The broad understanding of the ECJ of the term interpretation led to a discussion in German academia whether judges and, if so, to what extent and when, are required to further develop national law in order to apply national legislation in conformity with the directive.[89]

The ECJ ruled in a number of cases that the principle that national law must be applied in conformity with European Union law 'requires national courts to do whatever lies within their jurisdiction, taking the whole body of domestic law into

82. *See* §6.04[D] for further details.
83. ECJ, 10 April 1984, Case 14/83, *Sabine von Colson and Elisabeth Kamann v. Land Nordrhein-Westfalen*, [1984] ECR 1891, para. 26.
84. ECJ, 10 April 1984, Case 79/83, *Dorit Harz v. Deutsche Tradax GmbH*, [1984] ECR 1921 (ECJ 1984), para. 26.
85. 1988 NJW 1459 (BVerfG 1987).
86. 1988 NJW 1459 (BVerfG 1987).
87. Clemens Höpfner & Bernd Rüthers, *Grundlagen einer Europäischen Methodenlehre* (*Fundamentals for an European Methodology*), Archiv für die civilistischePraxis, 1, 4 (2009); Franz Bydlinski, *Grundzüge der juristischen Methodenlehre*, *supra* note 54 at pp. 54 and 76 et seq.
88. Jörg Neuner, 'Die Rechtsfortbildung' ('The Further Development of the Law') in Karl Riesenhuber (ed.), *Europäische Methodenlehre* (*European Methodology*) (Berlin: De Gruyter Verlag, 3rd edn, 2015), § 12 para. 2; Stefan Vogenauer, *Eine gemeineuropäische Methodenlehre des Rechts – Plädoyer und Programm* (*A Uniform European Methodology – Pleading and Program*), Zeitschrift für Europäisches Privatrecht, 234, 248 (2005).
89. Nils Grosche, *Rechtsfortbildung und Unionsrecht* (*Development of Law and Law of the European Union*) (Tübingen: Mohr Siebeck, 2011), p. 80 with detailed references in footnote 18; Wulf-Henning Roth & Christian Jopen, 'Die richtlinienkonforme Auslegung' ('The Interpretation in Conformity with Directives'), in Karl Riesenhuber (ed.), *Europäische Methodenlehre* (*European Methodology*) (Berlin: De Gruyter Verlag, 3rd edn, 2015), § 13 paras 48 et seq.; Kathrin Kroll-Ludwigs & Markus Ludwigs, *Die richtlinienkonforme Rechtsfortbildung im Gesamtsystem der Richtlinienwirkung* (*The Further Development of the Law in Conformity with Directives in Light of the System of the Effects of the Directive*), Zeitschrift für das juristische Studium, 7, 8 et seq. (2009).

consideration and applying the interpretative methods recognised by domestic law, with a view to ensuring that the directive in question is fully effective and achieving an outcome consistent with the objective pursued by it'.[90] This wide-ranging principle is, however, limited by general principles of law, like legal certainty and non-retroactivity,[91] and, importantly, the principle that national law must be interpreted in conformity with European Union law 'cannot serve as the basis for an interpretation of national law *contra legem*' (emphasis added).[92]

German legal methodology does not only cover the interpretation of legal provisions but also the further development of the law in cases where a gap in the law needs to be filled.[93] Since judges and administrative authorities are required to use every instrument that lies within their jurisdiction to ensure the efficacy of the directive, the principle that national law must be interpreted in conformity with European Union law may only be satisfied insofar as judges and administrative authorities are also entitled to further develop national law within the existing limits according to national law.

If authorities that apply the law are required to further develop the existing law in order to comply with the directive, they must not act *contra legem*.[94] The authorities would, however, act *contra legem* if the outcome of the further development of the law contradicted the intention of the legislator established by a purposive interpretation. In cases where the legislator amends the national legislation to comply with the directive, it is questionable whether the intention of the legislator is limited to the will to transpose the directive. If this were the case, the further development of the law, in order to comply with the directive, would effectively have no limitation. Every future interpretation of the directive by the ECJ would be applicable regardless of the wording of the provision(s) used by the national legislator, because the initial intention of the legislator is *only* to transform the directive *correctly*.[95] On the other hand, it is also possible to simply characterize the will of the legislator to amend the national legislation to comply with the directive as the *motivation* to take action. In this regard, the will to comply with the directive does not say anything about the aim of the legislator in respect of the content of the legislation.[96] There are strong voices in

90. ECJ, 24 July 2006, Case C-212/04, *Konstantinos Adeneler and Others v. Ellinikos Organismos Galaktos*, [2006] ECR I-6057, para. 111; ECJ, 15 April 2008, Case C-268/06, *Impact v. Minister for Agriculture and Food and Others*, [2008] ECR I-2483, para. 101; *see also* ECJ, 5 October 2004, Cases C-397/01 to 403/01, *Bernhard Pfeiffer and others*, [2004] ECR I-8835, paras 115, 116 and 118.
91. ECJ, 8 October 1987, Case 80/86, *Kolpinghuis Nijmegen BV*, [1987] ECR 3969, para. 13; ECJ, 16 June 2005, Case C-105/03, *Maria Pupino*, [2005] ECR I-5285, para. 44; *Konstantinos Adeneler, supra* note 90, para. 110; *Impact, supra* note 90, para. 100.
92. *Pupino, supra* note 91, para. 47; *Konstantinos Adeneler, supra* note 90, para. 110; *Impact, supra* note 90, para. 100.
93. *See* §8.03.
94. *See* note 90, *see also* Jörg Neuner, *Die Rechtsfindung contra legem* (*The Finding of Justice Contra Legem*) (Munich: C.H. Beck Verlag, 2nd edn, 2005).
95. Günter Hirsch, *Auf dem Weg zum Richterstaat?* (*On the Way to a State Where Judges Impose the Law?*), JZ, 853, 857 (2008).
96. Wolfgang Schön, *Die Auslegung europäischen Steuerrechts* (*The Interpretation of European Tax Law*) (Cologne: Otto Schmidt Verlag, 1993), p. 37; Markus Lutter, *Die Auslegung angeglichenen Rechts* (*The Interpretation of Aligned Legislation*), JZ, 593, 596 (1992); *see also* Christine

academia that do not want to limit the intention of the legislator to the mere will to transpose the directive; this may only be the motivation of the legislator to take action. The *telos* of the legislation needs to be differentiated from the mere *causa* and, thus, the fact that the legislator amends national provisions to comply with the directive does not say anything about the *telos*. However, if the legislator expressly states a wish to transpose a Union directive into national law, the intention of the legislator plays a role when examining the *telos* of these provisions.[97]

The German Federal Court of Justice had to deal with this issue in the *Quelle* case.[98] This case concerned the application of private law provisions; however, the main findings of this case are also applicable to tax law cases. According to a preliminary ruling initiated by the German Federal Court, the ECJ ruled that Article 3 of the Consumer Sales Directive prescribes that a consumer is not required to pay any compensation if goods that are not in conformity have to be replaced.[99] However, the German national provisions that were in place at that time[100] entitled the seller, in cases where goods are replaced, to a payment by way of compensation for the benefits from the use of the goods until their replacement with new goods.[101] The German Federal Court of Justice tried to interpret the national provisions in accordance with Union law. The court argued on the basis that the legislator's intention was to transpose the directive correctly. If the legislator had already known that the directive denies the seller's entitlement to a compensation payment, the legislator would have amended the national provisions in a different way.[102] The court concluded that an unintended gap in the law exists, which justifies the further development of the law. The gap in the law existed because the legislator expressly stated in the explanatory memorandum that the seller is entitled to a compensation payment in cases where the seller has to replace a good that is not in conformity; on the other hand, however, the legislator wanted to transpose the directive into national law correctly and both aims are conflicting according to the ECJ case law. The court filled this gap by way of a teleological reduction.[103]

In a recent VAT-case the Federal Fiscal Court ruled in the same way as the German Federal Court of Justice did. The court argued that courts and other bodies applying the law are entitled to fill the gap in the law that exists due to the fact that the legislator wanted to transpose the directive into national law correctly and the wrong assumption of the legislator that this provision is in conformity with the directive.[104]

Osterloh-Konrad, *'Quelle' und die Folgen: kein Nutzungsersatz bei Ersatzlieferung* (*'Quelle' and the consequences: No compensation payment for replacement*), CR, 545, 546 et seq. (2008).

97. 19 BverfGK 89 (BVerfG 2011).
98. ECJ, 17 April 2008, Case C-404/06, *Quelle AG v. Bundeseverband der Verbraucherzentralen und Verbraucherverbände*, [2008] ECR I-2685.
99. *Quelle*, *supra* note 98, para. 43.
100. Section 439 subs. 4 in a conjunct reading with s. 346 subs. 1 of the German Civil Code (*Bürgerliches Gesetzbuch*).
101. *Quelle*, *supra* note 98, para. 14.
102. 179 BGHZ 27 (BGH 2008).
103. *See* §8.03[B].
104. 243 BFHE 8 (BFH 2013), para. 26.

§8.06 SPECIAL RULES FOR INTERNATIONAL TAX LAW

[A] Dualism

Germany follows a dualistic approach and thus, differentiates between international and national law.[105] Accordingly, all international treaties have to be transposed into national law in accordance with Article 59 subsection 2 of the German Constitution. Only general rules of international law shall be part of the German federal law without explicit transformation, Article 25 of the German Constitution. Despite the fact that international treaties have to be transposed into national law, they do not lose their character as international law. The international standards for interpreting international agreements still have to apply.[106]

[B] Principles for the Interpretation of International Agreements

[1] General Observations

In Germany, any tax treaty is considered to coordinate the taxing rights of the contracting states by limiting their right to apply their own domestic tax laws in regard to cross-border transactions.[107] Therefore, there is always a link between national tax law and international agreements that are signed in order to avoid double taxation among the contracting states. Further, these tax treaties often refer to the meaning of the terms under specific domestic law when defining the term within the treaty[108] or where no definition in the treaty exists the terms shall, 'unless the context otherwise requires, have the meaning that it has at the time under the law of the state [applying the tax treaty] for the purpose of the taxes to which the (...) [tax treaty applies]'.[109] This close relationship between national tax law and tax treaty law leads to the problem that national authorities interpret tax treaty law solely in accordance with their understanding of the national tax law. However, these tax treaties are international agreements between two (or more) states and thus, they are not solely imposed by the national legislator. This emphasizes the fact that the meaning of a term, phrase or provision used in the treaty cannot be fleshed out solely by referring to the understanding of this term, phrase of provision under national law – the meaning both contracting states

105. For example, 111 BVerfGE 307 (BVerfG 2004), para. 34.
106. *See* for a detailed analysis of the case law of the German Federal Fiscal Court (*Bundesfinanzhof*) regarding the interpretation of tax treaties with respect to international standards on the interpretation of international agreements Michael Lang et al., *Die Auslegung von Doppelbesteuerungsabkommen in der Rechtsprechung des Bundesfinanzhofs* (*The Interpretation of Double Tax Treaties according to the Case Law of the German Federal Fiscal Court*) (Vienna: Linde Verlag, 1998).
107. Moris Lehner, 'Interpretation of Tax Treaties According to German Theory and Practice', in Klaus Vogel (ed.), *Interpretation of Tax Law and Treaties and Transfer Pricing in Japan and Germany* (The Hague: Kluwer Law International, 1998), p. 91.
108. For example, residence or dividends.
109. Article 3 subs. 2 of the OECD MC.

objectively wanted to agree on is the essential parameter for the interpretation.[110] Thus, the Federal Fiscal Court accepts that a term used in domestic law as well as in the tax treaties does not necessarily have to be interpreted in the same way.[111] Only if the tax treaty cannot be interpreted autonomously, e.g., parts of the treaty are explicitly linked to national law, the national interpretation methods and the national understanding of specific terms should be taken into account to determine the meaning of the treaty provisions.[112]

[2] Vienna Convention on the Law of Treaties

Since tax treaties are international agreements, their creation, consequences and interpretation are determined by the rules of the Vienna Convention on the Law of Treaties (VCLT).[113] As far as the interpretation of the tax treaty is concerned, Articles 31 through 33 of the VCLT are the relevant provisions. They are of a general nature and do not provide any specific interpretation rules for tax treaties.

According to these provisions, the *ordinary meaning* of the *terms* used in the tax treaty is of primary importance. The Federal Fiscal Court accepts the need for a literal interpretation of tax treaties and, thus, the court did not allow an interpretation against the clear wording of the provisions of these agreements.[114] The meaning of the terms used in the treaties is essential for its interpretation but not only with respect to its meaning within that particular provision but within the treaty as a whole. Thus, the systematic interpretation of treaty terms plays an extended role.[115]

According to Article 31 subsection 1 of the VCLT, a teleological interpretation is generally acknowledged. The aim of avoiding double taxation and double non-taxation was not accepted as the *object and purpose* of the treaty by the early case law of the Federal Fiscal Court.[116] Despite this, in more recent judgments the court argued that tax treaties aim at avoiding double taxation and double non-taxation; however, the court used the teleological approach to confirm the results of the other interpretation methods only.[117]

The intention of the contracting states is only essential insofar as it has been expressed in the text of the treaty (Article 31 subsection 4 of the VCLT). Even the

110. *See*, for example, Helmut Debatin, *Doppelbesteuerungsabkommen und innerstaatliches Recht (Double Tax Treaties and National Law)*, 23 DStR, Beihefter, 1, 5 (1992).
111. 254 BFHE 365 (BFH 2016); 2014 BStBl II 875 (BFH 2014); 2009 BStBl II 758 (BFH 2006); 2009 BStBl II 356 (BFH 2007); 2003 BStBl II 631 (BFH 2002); 1995 BStBl II 683 (BFH 1995); 1991 BStBl II 444 (BFH 1991); 1988 BStBl II 574 (BFH 1988); 1986 BStBl II 659 (BFH 1986); 1986 BStBl II 4 (BFH 1985); 1979 BStBl II 527 (BFH 1979).
112. Helmut Debatin, *supra* note 110 at 6.
113. Klaus Vogel & Alexander Rust, 'Introduction', in Ekkehart Reimer & Alexander Rust (eds), Klaus Vogel on *Double Taxation Conventions*, Volume I (Alphen aan den Rijn: Kluwer Law International, 4th edn, 2015), para. 32.
114. 1965 BStBl III 258 (BFH 1965); *see* for more details Ekkehart Reimer, 'Tax Treaty Interpretation in Germany' in Michael Lang, *Tax Treaty Interpretation* (Vienna: Linde Verlag, 2001), 119, 124 et seq.
115. 2013 DB 2657 (BFH 2013).
116. Ekkehart Reimer, *supra* note 114 at 126.
117. For example, 1994 BStBl II 508 (BFH 1994); *see also* Ekkehart Reimer, *supra* note 114 at 127.

purpose mentioned in Article 31 of the VCLT is not equivalent to the subjective intention of the parties; it refers to 'the goal of the treaty as reflected objectively by the treaty as a whole'.[118] Therefore, the importance of the subjective intention of the parties is considered minor by interpreting tax treaties.

[3] OECD Materials

Among OECD Member States there is some form of *soft obligation* to apply the OECD Model Convention (OECD MC) unless the state has entered original reservations or unless material reasons for not applying the OECD MC are given.[119] The Commentary to the OECD MC is also of particular importance. The OECD Commentary provides guidance on how to interpret and understand specific terms, phrases or provisions within the OECD MC. The logic of taking into account the OECD Commentary seems questionable, given the prescription of Articles 31 through 33 of the VCLT for strict textual interpretation. The Federal Fiscal Court nevertheless generally refers to the OECD Commentary in its findings.[120] However, the court has not expressly stated why the OECD Commentary can be used as a source of interpretation from the point of view of the VCLT.[121]

Since the OECD Commentary is constantly modified, it is questionable whether changes and amendments to the OECD Commentary should influence the interpretation of tax treaties signed before these changes or amendments have been approved by the OECD Member States. In earlier cases, the Federal Fiscal Court used the OECD Commentary in its current version without addressing this issue.[122] However, in recent time, the court has ruled that a dynamic interpretation of the tax treaties should not be adopted, leading to the conclusion that there should be no consideration of a version of the OECD Commentary that was not in place when the treaty was signed.[123]

Despite this, Germany might however, follow the intention of the OECD to interpret tax treaties in a more dynamic way. The tax treaty with Austria signed in 2000 includes a provision in the protocol allowing a dynamic interpretation by using the OECD Commentary in the current version.[124]

118. Klaus Vogel & Alexander Rust, *supra* note 113, para. 82.
119. Klaus Vogel & Alexander Rust, *supra* note 113, para. 101.
120. 1987 BStBl II 171 (BFH 1986); 1999 BStBl II 207 (BFH 1988); 1992 BStBl II 937 (BFH 1992); the BFH even referred to the OECD Commentary where the other country is not a country of the OECD 1994 BStBl II 218 (BFH 1993).
121. Arne Schnitger, *Die Einbeziehung des OECD-Kommentars in die Rechtsprechung des BFH (Taking into Account the OECD Commentary in the Light of the Case Law of the German Federal Fiscal Court)*, (IStR, 402 (2002).
122. 1998 BStBl II 21 (BFH 1997).
123. 253 BFHE 52 (BFH 2015); 2014 BStBl II 791 (BFH 2014); 2014 BStBl II 721 (BFH 2014); 2012 BStBl II 106 (BFH 2011); 234 BFHE 63 (BFH 2011); 2011 BStBl II 156 (BFH 2010).
124. 2002 BGBl II 12.

[C] Treaty Override

Section 2 of the German General Tax Act mandates the primary application of international law that was transposed into national law over other national tax law provisions. This provision does, however, not lay down an absolute priority of provisions that have their roots in international law over other national tax law provisions. Thus, section 2 of the German General Tax Act does not establish a hierarchy between different tax law provisions.[125] Generally, national law provisions transforming international tax law agreements into national law and other tax law provisions have the same hierarchical level, in other words one is not inferior to the other. If there is a conflict between these provisions, the more specific law provision shall have priority over the more general one (*lex specialis derogat leges generales*). The more specific provision shall take precedence over the more general provision even if the general one has been passed by the parliament later than the more specific provision (*lex specialis prior derogat legi generali posteriori*).[126] Leaving aside the question whether provisions transposing international tax law agreements into national law can be characterized as *leges speciales*, national tax law provisions can explicitly state that they have priority over international tax law agreements and their national transposing provisions. If a national law provision that is provided with priority over the provision transposing international agreements into domestic law conflicts with the later one, the national law will override international tax agreements. In 2015, the German Constitutional Court ruled on constitutional issues of a treaty override.[127] The case concerned the constitutionality of section 50d, subsection 8, sentence 1 of the German Income Tax Act as amended by the German Annual Tax Act 2003.[128] This provision applies to income from employment that shall be taxable in the source state, according to the tax treaty signed between Germany and the source country. Germany as the state of residence will only exempt this income from tax if the taxpayer furnishes proof of the taxation of this income in the source state. The German Constitutional Court came to the conclusion that the national legislator is not bound by the law transposing the treaty. If the legislator were obliged not to touch on old legislation, the fundamental principle of democracy would be infringed. Even though the German constitution highly respects the international legal order, the legislator is free to enact a law that contradicts international treaties. Moreover, the impact of both the principle of *pacta sunt servanda* and the rule of law do not require a different outcome.

125. Alexander Rust & Ekkehart Reimer, *Treaty Override im deutschen Internationalen Steuerrecht* (*Treaty Override in German International Tax Law*), IStR, 843, 844 (2005).
126. For determining the general and the specific rule *see* Karl Larenz, *supra* note 2 at p. 251.
127. BVerfG 2 BvL 1/12 (2015).
128. 236 BFHE 304 (BFH 2012).

§8.07 FINAL REMARKS

The traditional German interpretation methods have been adjusted to meet the requirements under European Union law. Interpretation methods such as the interpretation of national law in conformity with the directives or primary Union law (European treaties) are necessary to grant European Union law the required priority. This approach is part of the requirement of a purposive interpretation of statutory law in accordance with superior law provisions and the need to establish a constant and coherent legal framework. The purpose of a provision governing its interpretation is identified by considering how a particular provision solves a specific competition of interest. Since the requirements of superior provisions must be met, these provisions give specific guidance for determining the purpose. Although a purposive interpretation of the law is required, different methods may be used to achieve this goal. Within the boundaries of the wording of the provision, the system of the statute and the development of the provisions over time, including the intention of the legislator expressed in technical papers, explanatory memorandums and parliamentary debates, can be exploited to elaborate the purpose of a particular provision.

Tax planning raises methodological problems in tax law. Tax planning and tax abuse specifically aim at circumventing the tax law to reduce the tax burden. Tackling these issues by means of an economic interpretation requires a careful application of the methodology as an interpretation is limited by the wording and overall purpose of a provision. That is why a general anti-avoidance rule had to be included in the law to tackle abusive behaviour. Nevertheless, this raises concerns on how to interpret these properly since their interpretation must not be unlimited.

CHAPTER 9

Legal Interpretation of Tax Law: Hong Kong

*Wilson Chow**

§9.01 INTRODUCTION AND BACKGROUND

Three themes introduce this chapter, and they inform us why legal interpretation of taxation law in Hong Kong has evolved in the way it has. They are historical development (which explains the reliance placed by Hong Kong courts on precedents from comparable common law jurisdictions and illustrates that, in different periods of Hong Kong's legal history, different approaches to statutory interpretation have evolved), simplicity and stability (which explains why Hong Kong 'tax law' in many key areas is found in case law, rather than statutory intervention; which supports the comparatively recent adoption by the courts of a practical and purposive approach to statutory interpretation; and which, as we will see, has not been inimical to the interests of the Revenue) and low taxation rates (which, in part, explains the antipathy apparent in the courts to 'tax avoidance' transactions and which, in turn, reinforces the purposive approach).

[A] The Taxation System in Hong Kong[1]

Income tax is a relatively recent fiscal impost in Hong Kong. It was first enacted by the *War Revenue Ordinance*[2] to 'impose War taxes and regulate the collection thereof'.

*. In the first edition this chapter was prepared by Andrew Halkyard.
1. *See* generally, Michael Littlewood, *Taxation without Representation: The History of Hong Kong's Troublingly Successful Tax System* (Hong Kong: Hong Kong University Press, 2010), a significant part of which is distilled in an article by him bearing the same name British Tax Review 212 (2002).
2. Ordinance No. 13 of 1940.

This Ordinance was based upon Addington's *Income Tax Act 1803*,[3] which introduced the concept of a schedular tax system, as distinct from a general income tax, in the United Kingdom (UK). It also incorporated key features of the *Model Colonial Territories Income Tax Ordinance 1922*,[4] including exemption for offshore income and sharply distinguishing between items of revenue and capital (for both income and expenditure). This had the effect of importing large rafts of Commonwealth case law (initially mainly from the UK) on these topics into Hong Kong, from which local courts historically placed reliance.[5] They continue to do so – although it is only fair to note that Hong Kong has an independent and vibrant judiciary led by a respected Court of Final Appeal (CFA) which, partly by virtue of its ability to enrol non-permanent judges from other common law jurisdictions, has attracted jurists of the highest calibre.

The *War Revenue Ordinance's* brief life ended on Christmas day in 1941. Its successor appeared on 3 May 1947 when the *Inland Revenue Ordinance* (IRO) was enacted to 'impose a Tax on Earnings and Profits'.[6] Despite many technical amendments to the IRO since 1947, Hong Kong's taxation legislation today remains broadly similar in form and content to the 1940 Ordinance. The main features of that legislation are: low proportional tax rates, a jurisdiction to tax depending almost entirely upon the concept of source, tax imposed on only three types of income (from employment, land and buildings, and profits from a trade, profession or business), no capital gains tax, no tax on dividends or investment income (including interest on bank deposits), a very limited system of withholding taxes, and the absence of a broadly based indirect tax (such as Value Added Tax or a Goods and Services Tax).[7]

[B] Relations Between the Central and Sub-central Government in Terms of Taxing Power, Tax Collection and Revenue Sharing

Since the resumption of sovereignty on 1 July 1997, Hong Kong has enjoyed a special status under Article 31 of the Constitution of the People's Republic of China (PRC) as a Special Administrative Region ('HKSAR'). Apart from the promise of a high degree of autonomy for the HKSAR, the *Basic Law of the HKSAR* ('*Basic Law*')[8] also provides that the laws previously in force in Hong Kong, including the common law, rules of equity, ordinances and subordinate legislation, shall be maintained except for any that violate the *Basic Law* itself and subject to any amendment by the Hong Kong legislature. Article 108 of the *Basic Law* provides unambiguously that 'Hong Kong shall practice an

3. 43 Geo. III. c. 122.
4. Contained in the *Report of the Inter-Departmental Committee on Income Tax in Colonies Not Possessing Responsible Government* (London: HMSO, 1922).
5. A good example involves the meaning of 'plant' for the purposes of granting depreciation allowances – the leading case in Hong Kong is still the classic UK decision concerning a horse: *Yarmouth v. France* (1887) 19 QBD 647.
6. Ordinance No. 20 of 1947.
7. *See* further, Andrew Halkyard & Stephen Phua, *Taxation of Income in Singapore and Hong Kong*, Sing. J.L.S. 1, 3–5 (2007).
8. Contained in, and *see* generally, Yash Ghai, *Hong Kong's New Constitutional Order: The Resumption of Chinese Sovereignty and the Basic Law*, 2nd edn. (Hong Kong: Hong Kong University Press, 1999).

independent taxation system'. Article 106 goes on to state that the Central People's Government is prohibited from levying taxation in Hong Kong. In addition, the independence of the judiciary is protected by Article 85 of the *Basic Law*. Thus, the decisions of Hong Kong courts are not subject to appeal to, or supervision by, any other court in the PRC. The combined effect of all these provisions has meant that, in theory and in practice, the key features of Hong Kong's income taxation system, including simplicity and stability and low tax rates, have been maintained post-1997.

[C] The Role of the Doctrine of Precedent for the Courts When Interpreting Tax Law

As a common law jurisdiction, the doctrine of precedent is enshrined in Hong Kong. Thus, decisions of superior courts bind lower courts on matters *pari materia*. A nuanced and adept use of precedent and discrimination in rejecting either overly narrow or overly expansive interpretations of earlier cases and statutory wording are indicative of a sophisticated judicial system. It is pleasing to note that Hong Kong courts have displayed these attributes. Perhaps the best example supporting this conclusion is the way they have, by and large, made sense from a minefield of difficult conceptual issues relating to the source of profits – which has historically been viewed as a facts and circumstances test and which thus has the potential to be applied in a very eclectic manner.[9] As one commentator has observed:

> *[One] lesson that Hong Kong seems to offer is that a legislature might avoid considerable complexity by placing greater trust in judges. The complexity of most countries' tax laws is very largely due to the perceived need to provide for every conceivable case and to spell out the rules in advance, so that taxpayers can make commercial decisions with reasonable certainty of the tax consequences to follow. Hong Kong's legislature, however, has promulgated rules of a very general nature and left it to the courts to interpret them so that the system works. That has meant, most importantly, that it has fallen to the courts to interpret the legislation so as to accord with three basic norms. First, taxation must be in accordance with the law. It must not be, or appear to be, arbitrary or capricious. Second, the courts must not give the tax system a broader scope than the legislature intended, or, at least, they must not appear to do so. And, third, the courts must interpret the law so as not to permit excessive erosion of the government's revenues. Hong Kong's courts seem to have succeeded on all three counts. That, in turn, has been possible only because the legislature produced a statute capable of sustaining a workable interpretation. The best example is the one I have emphasized – that Hong Kong profits tax is imposed only on profits 'arising in or derived from Hong Kong.' The courts have determined what those words mean and have developed a meaning that is adequately principled, adequately respectful of taxpayers' rights, and adequately protective of the government's revenues.*[10] (emphasis added)

9. *See* further, Andrew Halkyard & Stephen Phua, *Taxation of Income in Singapore and Hong Kong*, Sing. J.L.S, 1, 8–9 (2007).
10. Michael Littlewood, *How Simple Can Tax Law Be? The Instructive Case of Hong Kong*, 38 Tax Notes Int'l 689, 701–702 (2005).

[D] No Value Added Tax / Goods and Services Tax in Hong Kong

Unlike most jurisdictions, Hong Kong has not enacted any broadly based indirect tax such as VAT or GST. The focus in this chapter is therefore, with one exception,[11] exclusively on the legal interpretation of the IRO which, as noted above, only taxes income from employment, income from land and buildings and profits from a trade, profession, or business carried on in Hong Kong.

[E] Double Tax Agreements

Hong Kong has, particularly since 2010, concluded a moderate number of comprehensive Double Tax Agreements (DTAs) – 35 as at November 2016. To date, no court in Hong Kong has interpreted the terms of any of its DTAs. However, in interpreting and applying the provisions of its DTA with the PRC (Mainland China), Hong Kong's Inland Revenue Department (IRD) has stated that it will refer to the Vienna Convention on the Law of Treaties (1969), the Commentaries on the relevant Articles of the Model Tax Conventions of the OECD and the United Nations, as well as to the principles of interpretation of taxation law used in Hong Kong.[12] There is no reason to suggest that Hong Kong would take any other approach in interpreting its other DTAs.

§9.02 DOMESTIC RULES FOR INTERPRETING TAX LAW

[A] Historical Perspective

The key principles relating to statutory interpretation of tax law in Hong Kong were initially derived from older UK case law. They reflect a distinctly literal approach, namely: (1) tax is payable if, and only if, the strict wording of the statute is satisfied irrespective of what appears to be the spirit or intention of the statute (*Partington v. Attorney General*[13]); (2) when interpreting the wording of a statute it is necessary to look fairly at the language used and construe the wording according to its natural significance (*Cape Brandy Syndicate v. IRC*[14]); (3) the principle of strict or literal construction applies even though the result seems anomalous or unjust and irrespective of whether it operates for or against the Revenue since 'there is no equity about a

11. The one other major tax imposed in Hong Kong is stamp duty (estate duty was abolished in 2005). This is imposed on various conveyancing documents relating to immovable property in Hong Kong and contract notes and instruments of transfer relating to Hong Kong stock: *see* Stamp Duty Ordinance (LHK, Cap. 117). Interestingly, this tax gave rise to a highly instructive decision of Hong Kong's highest court, the CFA, which unambiguously adopted a purposive approach to statutory interpretation to deny an exemption for an instrument which was created under a complex, yet obvious, tax avoidance arrangement: *see CSR v. Arrowtown Assets Ltd* [2004] 1 HKLRD 77 (discussed in detail at s. §9.03[A] below).
12. *See* Departmental and Interpretation and Practice Notes No. 44, para. 4, available at www.ird.gov.hk/eng/ppr/dip.htm (last accessed, 15 November 2016).
13. (1869) LR 4 HL 100.
14. (1921) 12 TC 358.

tax',[15] but (4) where there is an ambiguity, a more lenient interpretation should be given in favour of the taxpayer (*D'Avigdor-Goldsmid v. IRC*[16]).

The principles were summarised by the Privy Council (which prior to 1 July 1997 was Hong Kong's highest court) in *Mangin v. IRC*:[17]

> *First, the words are to be given their ordinary meaning. They are not to be given some other meaning simply because their object is to frustrate legitimate tax avoidance devices. ... Moral precepts are not applicable to the interpretation of revenue statutes.*
>
> *Secondly, [here the words of Rowlatt J. in the Cape Brandy Syndicate case quoted above were specifically approved].*
>
> *Thirdly, the object of the construction of a statute being to ascertain the will of the legislature it may be presumed that neither injustice nor absurdity was intended. If therefore a literal interpretation would produce such a result, and the language admits of an interpretation which would avoid it, then such an interpretation may be adopted.*
>
> *Fourthly, the history of an enactment and the reasons which led to its being passed may be used as an aid to its construction.*

These principles were adopted by Hong Kong courts in various tax cases including *CIR v. Chan Tin-chu*[18] and *Asia Television Ltd v. CIR.*[19] Interestingly, in the latter case Mortimer J. acknowledged (in terms similar to the third and fourth principles set out in *Mangin v. IRC*) that it may be necessary to give words a meaning other than their ordinary meaning because of the history of the legislation or if the ordinary meaning of the words produces an absurdly unjust result or produces simple absurdity in the legislation.[20] In hindsight, this acknowledgment prefaced the arrival of a more holistic, purposive approach to statutory interpretation in Hong Kong.

[B] The Modern Approach

In modern times, the search for the correct interpretation of a statutory provision still generally begins - but does not necessarily end - with consideration of the plain meaning of the words used in the statute. Indeed, it has always been the case in Hong Kong that where the meaning of the statutory words is unclear or ambiguous, it is permissible to seek assistance by considering the remedial purpose of the legislation

---

15. *Cape Brandy Syndicate v. IRC* (1921) 12 TC 358 at p. 366 per Rowlatt J. The full text of this well-known dictum is as follows: 'In taxation you have to look simply at what is clearly said. There is no equity about a tax; there is no room for any intendment; you read nothing in; you imply nothing, but you look fairly at what is said and at what is said clearly and that is the tax.'
16. [1953] AC 347.
17. [1971] AC 739 at 746.
18. (1966) 1 HKTC 284 at 292.
19. (1987) 2 HKTC 198 at 206-207.
20. *See* further, Law Reform Commission of Hong Kong Report, *Extrinsic Materials as an Aid to Statutory Interpretation* (March 1997), available at www.hkreform.gov.hk/en/docs/rstatutory-e.pdf (last accessed, 15 November 2016). Paragraphs 6.85-6.87 of the Report deals specifically with interpretation of taxation legislation.

and its context to construe those words so as to ensure the attainment of the object of the legislation.[21,22]

In contrast to the approach referred to in §9.02[A] above, we will see below that in more recent cases Hong Kong courts have stressed that they are not hamstrung by a literal interpretation when construing legislation. In short, they have held that it is important to consider the context, the scheme of the legislation (or statutory framework) and its purposes in a holistic way and that it is not permissible to attribute a meaning which does not accord with the legislative intent properly understood. This conclusion should come as no surprise. Not only does it accord with the terms of section 19 of the *Interpretation and General Clauses Ordinance*,[23] but the change in approach was signalled at least several years earlier by the House of Lords in *IRC v. McGuckian*,[24] where Lord Steyn stressed, albeit in a tax avoidance context, that all taxation legislation must be interpreted in a 'purposive' manner and that pure literalism should be rejected.

This development received the unqualified support of Hong Kong's CFA in *Shiu Wing Ltd v. Commissioner of Estate Duty*[25] (an estate duty case) and *CSR v. Arrowtown Assets Ltd*[26] (a stamp duty case). Both cases accepted that *IRC v. McGuckian*, and the *Ramsay*[27] and *Furniss v. Dawson*[28] line of cases on which it relied, formulated a

21. Specifically, s. 19 of the *Interpretation and General Clauses Ordinance* (LHK, Cap. 1) states: 'An Ordinance shall be deemed to be remedial and shall receive such fair, large and liberal construction and interpretation as will best ensure the attainment of the object of the Ordinance according to its true intent, meaning and spirit.' In the past, Hong Kong courts have given s. 19 limited attention (*see* Peter Wesley-Smith, *Literal or Liberal: The Notorious Section 19*, 12 HKLJ 203 (1982)) – but this is not the case today.
22. The purposive approach to statutory interpretation now ascendant in Hong Kong was accompanied by the courts paying more attention to the prescriptive terms of s. 19. *See*, e.g., *Foo Ying v. Commissioner of Estate Duty* [1989] 2 HKLR 376 (a decision upheld by the Court of Appeal, albeit on more general grounds of statutory interpretation: (1990) 3 HKTC 372). A further illustration is *CIR v. Loganathan* [2000] 1 HKLRD 914 where Cheung J., referring to s. 19, undertook a detailed analysis to ascertain the intent of the legislature in relation to the power of the Commissioner to 'personally' assess penalty tax: *held* – the assessment of penalty tax must be made personally by a public officer holding the rank for the time being of Commissioner and was not simply reserved to the person permanently holding the substantive rank of Commissioner.
23. *See supra* note 21.
24. [1997] 1 WLR 991 at pp. 999–1000. This development did not come 'out of the blue' – indeed, Lord Steyn acknowledged that 'the intellectual breakthrough' came in 1981 in *Ramsay's* case where Lord Wilberforce re-examined the principle of statutory construction that a subject is only to be taxed upon clear words by asking 'What are clear words?' and answered that 'The court is not confined to a literal interpretation but should consider the context and scheme of the relevant Act as a whole, and its purpose may, indeed should, be regarded.' In Lord Steyn's view, this speech marked the rejection by the House of Lords of pure literalism in interpreting tax statutes.
25. [2000] 3 HKLRD 76.
26. [2004] 1 HKLRD 77, discussed in detail in s. §9.03[A] below. *See* further, *Lam Soon Trademark Ltd v. CIR* (2006) 9 HKCFAR 391 at para. 20, a profits tax case.
27. [1982] AC 300.
28. [1984] AC 474.

purposive approach to statutory construction. In *HKSAR v. Lam Kwong Wai*[29] Mason NPJ explained the change in approach as follows:

> *The modern approach to statutory interpretation insists that context and purpose be considered in the first instance, especially in the case of general words, and not merely at some later stage when ambiguity may be thought to arise.*

The context of the statutory provision should be taken in its widest sense.[30] In other words, the relevant provisions of the legislation should be read together and in the context of the whole statute as a purposive unity in its appropriate legal and social setting. It is then necessary to identify the interpretative considerations involved and, if they conflict, to weigh and balance them.[31]

[C] The Tax Avoidance Context

As a result of its straightforward tax system and low tax rates, Hong Kong does not offer the same incentives for tax avoidance schemes as do many other tax systems. Prior to the 1980s, where the question of tax avoidance arose, cases had been decided in accordance with the principle established in *IRC v. Duke of Westminster*.[32] This principle built upon the premise that every person has the right to take every legal step he or she wishes to minimise his or her tax liability. In the event, where there was a genuine transaction which created legal rights and obligations, form prevailed over substance.[33] This approach probably reflected a commonly held view that taxation was a compulsory appropriation of income that belongs to the individual and should be contrived to take out of his or her pocket as little as possible.[34]

29. (2006) 9 HKCFAR 574 at 606. Other CFA decisions outside the taxation arena have enshrined the purposive approach in Hong Kong: *see*, e.g., *Medical Council of Hong Kong v. Chow Siu Shek* (2000) 3 HKCFAR 144, *Town Planning Board v. Society for the Protection of the Harbour* (2004) 7 HKCFAR 1 and *Ho Choi Wan v. Hong Kong Housing Authority* [2005] 4 HKLRD 706. Although concerned with the interpretation of the *Basic Law*, reference should also be made to the CFA's decision in *Director of Immigration v. Chong Fung Yuen* (2001) 4 HKCFAR 211 at 223–225, which discusses the common law approach to statutory interpretation in Hong Kong.
30. *HKSAR v. Cheung Kwun Yin* (2009) 12 HKCFAR 568 at paras 11–14.
31. *Medical Council of Hong Kong v. Chow Siu Shek* (2000) 3 HKCFAR 144 at 154. In no event, however, can a court attribute to a statutory provision a meaning which the language of the statute, understood in the light of its context and the statutory purpose, is incapable of bearing: *see HKSAR v. Lam Kwong Wai* (2006) 9 HKCFAR 574, per Mason NPJ at 606, *China Field Ltd v. Appeal Tribunal (Buildings) (No. 2)* (2009) 12 HKCFAR 342, per Bokhary PJ at para. 36 and *HKSAR v. Fugro Geotechnical Services Ltd* (2014) 17 HKCFAR 755, per Fok PJ at para. 22.
32. [1936] AC 1.
33. The best Hong Kong example of this approach is *CIR v. Howe* (1977) 1 HKTC 936. The case involved a Hong Kong author who assigned copyright of his works to a Panamanian company in which he was the controlling shareholder in consideration of a capital sum (tax free) and a very small salary (attracting minimal, if any, tax). The royalties earned by the company would have been non-taxable on the grounds that they were sourced outside Hong Kong: *held* – the scheme to avoid Hong Kong tax was effective and not 'artificial or fictitious' for the purposes of Hong Kong's first, and very simple, general anti-avoidance provision.
34. Such sentiments are often attributed to Adam Smith's canons of taxation. It is however instructive to quote the full sentence on which this view is based: 'Every tax ought to be so

As indicated above, the influence and reliance upon the *Duke of Westminster* 'doctrine' changed after the decisions of the House of Lords in *Ramsay* and *Furniss v. Dawson*. Indeed, the *Duke of Westminster* is generally only cited in Hong Kong today as a somewhat disparaging illustration of how tax law remained remarkably resistant to the new non-formalist methods of interpretation and how it was mistakenly left behind as some island of literal interpretation.[35]

Although the *Ramsay* and *Furniss v. Dawson* line of cases has now been interpreted as formulating a broad purposive approach to statutory interpretation *and* a realistic approach to the analysis of the facts, its genesis is found in the fight to combat tax avoidance. In this context it can operate in a swingeing fashion. This conclusion will be illustrated in §9.03[A] below when we analyse the CFA decision in *Arrowtown Assets Ltd v. CSR*. Before doing so, it is relevant and useful to trace the development, parameters, and effect of the *Ramsay* approach:

(1) *Ramsay* involved a highly artificial tax avoidance scheme which had no commercial or lasting effect on the taxpayer, was self-cancelling and was held to be ineffective.
(2) *Furniss v. Dawson* took *Ramsay* a stage further by extending its ambit to a genuine commercial transaction, which was not self-cancelling, where the end result was achieved by means of a composite linear transaction into which there had been inserted one or more steps having no business purpose apart from the avoidance of tax. In the event, the inserted steps (but not the end result) could be disregarded in determining the tax consequences of the commercial transaction.
(3) In *Shiu Wing*[36] the CFA concluded that the *Ramsay* approach was part of Hong Kong law and had general application to revenue legislation. Delivering the leading judgment, Mason NPJ stated:

> *This element of the Ramsay principle may be expressed by stating that where there is a single pre-ordained, composite transaction intended to be carried out in its entirety, the court is not compelled for tax purposes to ignore its composite character and to break it up into its individual constituent steps so that the statute is then applied to those steps separately. If the purpose of the intermediate steps in the*

contrived as both to take out and keep out of the pockets of the people as little as possible, *over and above what it brings into the public treasury of the state.*' (*The Wealth of Nations* Book 5, Chap. 2 [emphasis added]).

35. *See, e.g., CSR v. Arrowtown Assets Ltd* [2004] 1 HKLRD 77, per Ribeiro PJ at para. 32 (compare Lord Millett NPJ at para. 114). The *Duke of Westminster* was also cited by the CFA in *Ngai Lik Electronics Co. Ltd v. CIR* (2009) 12 HKCFAR 296, per Ribeiro PJ at para. 99, to illustrate the conclusion that confining the court to the legal form of a transaction has no place in interpreting the main general anti-avoidance provision in the IRO, s. 61A. On this basis, although not yet specifically referenced in local judgments, Hong Kong courts would doubtless support the regimen of the High Court of Australia decision in *FCT v. Spotless Services Ltd* (1996) 186 CLR 404 which concluded that general anti-avoidance provisions (such as s. 61A) should not be emasculated by reference to the earlier restrictive decisions, such as the *Duke of Westminster*, which are redolent of 'the muffled echoes of old arguments'.
36. [2000] 3 HKLRD 76.

composite transaction was fiscal they may be disregarded. The composite transaction may then have consequences which bring it within a charging provision of the statute.

(4) In *Shiu Wing* Litton PJ was prepared to accept that *Ramsay* enjoined the court 'to look to substance rather than to form'.

(5) It is important to reiterate that the *Ramsay* approach is not authority for disregarding or rearranging the end result of a transaction. Rather, it is authority for the proposition that once the inserted tax avoidance steps are disregarded, the tax statute must be applied to the end result of the actual transaction (or 'real transaction')[37] and, in this regard, it is not possible under *Ramsay* to reconstitute the entire transaction by giving it a different character to its true character. Lord Millett (a non-permanent judge of the CFA) reinforced this conclusion by commenting, albeit in an extrajudicial capacity, that:

The question in every case is whether what the taxpayer did was within the intendment of the [statute] ... The Ramsay principle does not permit the Court to recharacterise the facts. It requires the Court to apply the statute to what the taxpayer has actually done.[38]

(6) The *Ramsay* approach does not depend on whether the relevant Act contains a general anti-avoidance provision[39] (GAAR), such as that found in section 61A of the IRO. Thus, in combating perceived cases of 'tax avoidance', the IRD in Hong Kong has relied upon the totality of the following approaches: (a) adopting a purposive interpretation of the substantive statutory provision; (b) using the *Ramsay* line of cases as an aid to statutory interpretation; *and* (c) in the event that these arguments are unsuccessful, relying upon the GAAR to counter the tax benefit claimed.[40]

---

37. In *MacNiven v. Westmoreland Investments Ltd* [2001] STC 237, Lord Nicholls puts it this way: '[The cases following *Ramsay*] cannot be understood as laying down factual prerequisites which must exist before the court may apply the purposive, *Ramsay* approach to the interpretation of a taxing statute. ... The need to consider a document or transaction in its proper context, and the need to adopt a purposive approach when construing taxation legislation, are principles of general application.'
38. *Ramsay Comes to Hong Kong*, 31 HKLJ 20 (2001).
39. *IRC v. McGuckian* [1997] 1 WLR 991, per Lord Cooke at 1005. *See* generally, Andrew Halkyard, *Common Law and Tax Avoidance: Back to the Future?*, 14 *Revenue Law Journal* 19 (2004).
40. *See*, e.g., *CIR v. HIT Finance Ltd*, a case involving a claim to deduct interest paid under a circular series of loan transactions entered into to finance an intra-group transfer of assets. Under the law as it then was, a potential mismatch was created since the interest ultimately received by the group's offshore finance company was non-taxable as being sourced outside Hong Kong. The Court of Appeal (HCIA 15/2005) rejected the Commissioner's arguments, which were based in part upon the application of *Ramsay* as an aid to interpret the general deductibility provision (s. 16(1) of the IRO). Although, on appeal, the CFA ((2007) 10 HKCFAR 717) agreed that the interest expense qualified for deduction under s. 16(1), it nonetheless concluded that the circular flow and immediate repayment of the borrowed funds to the sole non-associated party, an interposed

(7) In the event, it is beyond doubt that courts in Hong Kong are prepared to strike down tax avoidance schemes which rely for their success on a strictly literal interpretation of legislation. As shown in (6) above, the IRD's anti-avoidance arsenal is extensive.

[D] What External Sources Can a Court Consider When Interpreting Legislation?

The modern approach to statutory interpretation adopted in Hong Kong of purposive construction and engaging with the strictures of section 19 of the *Interpretation and General Clauses Ordinance* does not, of itself, provide practical guidance as to how to achieve that interpretation. Where the meaning of statutory wording is clear, the courts generally give effect to the natural and ordinary meaning of the words used, although §9.02[B] above shows that the context or purpose of the legislation may point to a different meaning. In this regard, the purpose of a statutory provision may be evident from: (1) the provision itself considered in a holistic way; (2) a Law Reform Commission report (where the legislation implements a recommendation of the report); (3) explanations given by a Minister or Secretary when introducing the Bill and possibly speeches made on the Bill by the lawmakers in the Legislative Council (Hong Kong's lawmaking body); or (4) the Explanatory Memorandum to the Bill.[41]

However, whether we can use these external sources to ascertain the *meaning* of the legislative wording, as was suggested by the landmark decision of the House of Lords in *Pepper v. Hart*,[42] is a fundamentally different question. Although courts in Hong Kong have applied *Pepper v. Hart* on isolated occasions on the assumption that it applies,[43] they have kept open the question whether and the extent to which the decision applies in Hong Kong. They have opined that when this question arises for

---

bank, showed that the transaction was entered into for the sole or dominant purpose of the taxpayer obtaining a tax benefit in the form of an interest deduction. It followed that the benefit could be countered by applying the GAAR.

41. *See PCCW-HK Telephone Ltd v. Telecommunications Authority* [2005] 3 HKLRD 235 and *Director of Lands v. Yin Shuen Enterprises Ltd* (2003) 6 HKCFAR 1. The Court of Appeal in *Ho Kwok Tai v. CSD* (2016) CACV 52/2016, by way of obiter, considered the statement in the Financial Secretary's blog in the internet to be of no assistance in arriving at the true construction of the relevant statutory provision in the Stamp Duty Ordinance (LHK, Cap 117) at issue in that case.
42. [1992] 3 WLR 1032. The headnote provides a good summary of the decision: 'Subject to any question of Parliamentary privilege, the rule excluding reference to Parliamentary material as an aid to statutory construction should be relaxed so as to permit such reference where (a) legislation was ambiguous or obscure or led to absurdity, (b) the material relied upon consisted of one or more statements by a minister or other promoter of the Bill together if necessary with such other Parliamentary material as was necessary to understand such statements and their effect and (c) the statements relied upon were clear.'
43. *See*, e.g., *Hong Kong Clays & Kaolin Co Ltd v. Director of Lands* [1999] 1 HKLRD 527 and *Commissioner of Rating & Valuation v. Agrila Ltd* [2001] 2 HKLRD 36. For a historical and comparative review of relevant authorities, *see* Law Reform Commission of Hong Kong Report, *Extrinsic Materials as an Aid to Statutory Interpretation* (March 1997), available at www.hkreform.gov.hk/en/docs/rstatutory-e.pdf (last accessed, 15 November 2016).

consideration the practical as well as the conceptual and constitutional implications involved in the Hong Kong context would need to be considered.[44]

The scepticism apparent in the preceding paragraph reflects the CFA's decision in *PCCW-HK Telephone Ltd v. Telecommunications Authority*[45] where Bokhary PJ held:

> *It has been clear at least since the decision of the Full Court in* Elson-Vernon Knitters Ltd v Sino-Indo-American Spinners Ltd *[1972] HKLR 468 that the Objects and Reasons or Explanatory Memorandum annexed to a Bill is admissible for the purpose of ascertaining the mischief which the proposed statute was intended to remedy. Explanations given by Ministers when introducing a Bill are also admissible for that purpose. But to treat ministerial statements about the meaning and effect of proposed legislation as reflecting the will of the legislature would go beyond using such statements to ascertain the mischief against which a statute is aimed. Lord Millett NPJ, with whom the other members of this Court agreed, said this in* Director of Lands v Yin Shuen Enterprises Ltd *(2003) 6 HKCFAR 1 at p. 15 F–H:*
>
> *'Such evidence is admissible for a limited purpose only, to enable the Court to understand the factual context in which the statute was enacted and the mischief at which it was aimed. This is not the same as treating the statements of the executive about the meaning and effect of the statutory language as reflecting the will of the legislature. Within the permissible limits, however, the admissible evidence is not confined to the Explanatory Memorandum of Objects and Reasons, but must logically extend to explanations given by Ministers when introducing the Bill.'*[46]

[E] Principles of Commercial Accounting

Throughout the past decade, there has been a heated debate in Hong Kong on the impact of generally accepted accounting principles in determining 'profits' for the purpose of assessing profits tax under the IRO. The genesis for this debate was the CFA decision in *CIR v. Secan Ltd.*[47] In *Secan* interest paid by a property developer on a loan used to finance a development for resale was, in accordance with generally accepted accounting principles, included in the value of trading stock as at year end instead of being immediately expensed in the developer's profit and loss account. Notwithstanding this accounting treatment, the developer sought to deduct the interest expense in the year it was paid. The attempt failed. The CFA held that no 'outgoing' was 'incurred' under the general deduction provisions of section 16(1) of the IRO, since the payment of interest was not recorded in the profit and loss account and such accounting treatment was not prohibited by any provision of the IRO. This is a clear example of accounting records impacting upon day-to-day interpretation issues, and seemingly

44. *See HKSAR v. Cheung Kwun Yin* (2009) 12 HKCFAR 568 per Li CJ.
45. [2005] 3 HKLRD 235.
46. This dictum was applied by the Court of Appeal in *Moulin Global Eyecare Trading Ltd (in liquidation) v. CIR* [2012] 2 HKLRD 911 at paras 31–32: *held* – extrinsic materials can only be used for a limited purpose, namely, to enable the court to understand the factual context in which the statute was enacted and the mischief at which the statute was aimed and not for the purpose of construing the words of the statute itself; and followed in *Good Mark Industrial Limited v. CIR* [2015] 2 HKLRD 16 and most recently in *Ho Kwok Tai v. CSD* (2016) CACV 52/2016.
47. (2000) 3 HKCFAR 411.

goes well beyond the traditionally held view that net profits computed in accordance with generally accepted accounting principles is simply the starting point for measuring taxable ('assessable') profits. In the event, it was hardly surprising that commentators argued that *Secan* placed the importance of accounting records in determining assessable profits on an even higher plane than previously thought.

Recently, however, in *CIR v. Nice Cheer Investment Ltd*[48] the CFA revisited, and reiterated, the principle that reliance on principles of commercial accounting to determine assessable profits must be in conformity with the provisions of the IRO. Specifically, the court decided that unrealised gains arising from an accounting adjustment revaluing 'trading investments' at year end were not liable to profits tax. Lord Millett NPJ, on behalf of the court, held that the appeal raised a matter of statutory interpretation, not accounting practice and that whilst the *amount* of any profits is a question of fact, what constitutes 'profits' for the purposes of the IRO and whether any disputed amount represents 'assessable profits' are questions of law to be determined by the court. Lord Millett concluded by stating that whilst general principles of commercial accounting were not irrelevant to the question before the court, their assistance is limited since those principles are always subject to the overriding requirement of conformity with the IRO, not merely with the express words of the statute, but also with the way in which they have been judicially interpreted.[49]

[F] Legislative Mistakes

Where there has been a failure to amend legislation correctly and an obvious mistake has been made, courts in Hong Kong have held that they should not attempt to provide a meaning where in fact there is none[50] or rectify a statutory omission.[51] It is not entirely clear in these cases whether the courts considered that the legislative intent was known and, indeed, whether this would have made any difference to their outcome. Nonetheless, it is still fair comment that, to date, Hong Kong courts have not said that they have discretion to read the law as if the mistake had not been made.

[G] The Effect of the Bill of Rights Ordinance on Statutory Interpretation

There is one instance in Hong Kong where the provisions of non-tax legislation can affect the meaning of words in taxation law. That exception refers to the operation of the *Hong Kong Bill of Rights Ordinance* ('BORO'),[52] which may result in a legislative provision being read down (or struck down) to the extent that it violates the human rights protections contained in that ordinance. To date, two court decisions have

48. (2013) 16 HKCFAR 813.
49. *Supra.*, at paras 13, 15-16 and 33–35.
50. *Leung Shee-wing v. CIR* (1989) 3 HKTC 209 at 222.
51. *CIR v. Chan Tin-chu* (1966) 1 HKTC 284 where, following a retrospective amendment restricting the number of tax officials who could issue assessments, the court refused to rectify the legislature's omission to validate assessments made during the transitional period between the start of the year of assessment and the date the legislation was passed.
52. LHK, Cap. 383.

declared that taxation provisions violated the BORO, namely, the 'stop order' provision preventing persons with outstanding tax liabilities from leaving Hong Kong[53] and the mandatory requirement to pay stamp duty in dispute before an appeal against the imposition of duty.[54] In both cases, the impugned legislation pre-dated the enactment of the BORO, and the offending provisions were struck down (although they were later amended so as to be compliant with the BORO).[55]

Although challenges have not yet been mounted before the courts, other possible areas where taxation provisions may be inconsistent with the BORO include the burden of proof placed upon taxpayers in challenging penalty tax assessments and, for the purpose of granting personal allowances to a married couple, the discrimination in restricting the interpretation of 'marriage' and 'married person' to the union between a male and a female.

[H] Transplanted Categories

In many countries, interpretation of income tax law reveals so-called transplanted categories. This means that courts will draw upon definitions in other areas of law when interpreting words in the income tax law. In Hong Kong there are no explicit examples of this occurring. However, there are two implicit examples. The first relates to the definition of 'employment', which has been interpreted by using the tests developed for tort law purposes in order to determine liability to salaries tax.[56] The second relates to the meaning of 'use' of a trademark in Hong Kong, which has been

53. *See CIR v. Lee Lai-ping* [1993] HKPLR 141.
54. *See Harvest Sheen Ltd v. Collector of Stamp Revenue* (1997) 4 HKTC 750.
55. For the sake of completeness, reference should also be made to the effect of the *Basic Law* - in particular Art. 39 which implements, or arguably gives constitutional effect to the implementation of, the International Covenant on Civil and Political Rights as applied to Hong Kong through the BORO. The position is a little unclear but ultimately this seems to be an issue of constitutional interpretation. In any event, to the extent that legislation (including tax legislation) is inconsistent with the *Basic Law*, it will be unconstitutional. Various unsuccessful challenges to the validity of other provisions in the IRO have been attempted, including those restricting access to the court: *see*, e.g., when defending an action to recover disputed tax under s. 75 (*CIR v. Nam Tai Trading Co. Ltd* (2009) DCTC 4250/2008 and *CIR v. Shelcore Hong Kong Limited* (2011) DCTC 5209/2009), and the limitations of the case stated procedure in an appeal from a decision of the Board of Review under s. 69 (*Lee Yee Shing v. Board of Review and CIR* [2012] 2 HKLRD 981; but note that the case stated procedure has, since 1 April 2016, been replaced by an appeal directly to the Court of First Instance with leave on a question of law). In *Wong Chak Sin v. CSD* (2016) DCSA 19/2014, the appellant sought to challenge the constitutionality of amendments to the Stamp Duty Ordinance (LHK, Cap 117) in the absence of an exemption originally included in the proposed Bill which was subsequently removed on recommendation by the Bills Committee as violating Arts 6 and 105 of the Basic Law but failed in light of the Court of Appeal decision in *Weson Investment Ltd v. CIR* [2007] 2 HKLRD 567.
56. The distinction is relevant because income from 'employment' is liable to salaries tax under s. 8(1) of the IRO, whereas the profits of an independent contractor are liable to profits tax, which results in a much more benevolent deduction regime applying. The leading case in Hong Kong is the CFA decision in *Poon Chau Nam v. Yim Siu Cheng* [2007] 1 HKLRD 951, which involved a claim for worker's compensation.

interpreted by reference to the territorial nature of the relevant rights conferred under trademark law in order to determine liability to profits tax.[57]

[I] Administrative Concessions

For Hong Kong taxation purposes, how significant is the role played by administrative concessions? Specifically, if the result of a strict interpretation of law is capricious or unfair, does the IRD resolve the unfairness by administrative practice or granting an extra-statutory concession? The answer is clear – extra-statutory concessions are rarely granted and, indeed, the IRD has no explicit statutory authority to do so.[58] It follows that any interpretative role they may have in Hong Kong is very limited.

[J] IRD Interpretation and Practice Notes

To properly understand Hong Kong's taxation system, it would be a serious mistake to underestimate the significance and pervading influence of the IRD's Departmental Interpretation & Practice Notes (DIPNs). They are critically important for taxation advisers and taxpayers generally, and it is fair comment (not least for the reason that litigation in Hong Kong tends to be extremely expensive) that DIPNs are, at best, soft law and, at worst, de facto legislation (although, to be fair, there is no evidence that the IRD has abused its powers to enlarge its assessment powers by publishing expansive interpretations).[59]

In short, DIPNs provide much needed detail for taxpayers faced with interpreting and applying legislation which, as we saw in §9.01[A] and §9.01[C] above, in many key areas (e.g., source of profits and source of employment income) is drafted in quite general terms. Taxpayers crave certainty in their tax affairs. Thus, it should come as no surprise that the DIPNs play a particularly important yet sensitive role in Hong Kong's taxation system. Assessments based upon interpretations contained in the DIPNs can be challenged through the normal objection and appeals procedures. They do not however bind, and should not be uncritically relied upon by, the courts.[60]

---

57. The issue involved the interpretation of the withholding tax provision applying to royalty payments under s. 15(1)(b) of the IRO: *see CIR v. Emerson Radio Corp* (1999) 2 HKCFAR 501.
58. *See* generally, Andrew Halkyard, 'Revenue Law Discretions and the Rule of Law in Hong Kong', in *The Delicate Balance: Tax, Discretion and the Rule of Law*, eds. Chris Evans, Judith Freedman & Richard Krever (Amsterdam: IBFD, 2011), at 201–222. Contrast the position in the UK: *see* Judith Freedman & John Vella, 'HMRC's Management of the UK Tax System: The Boundaries of Legitimate Discretion' (same volume) at 102–108 and *Current Note*, BTR 385 (2006), which trace the development of the law in the UK governing the power of the Revenue Commissioners to grant extra-statutory concessions.
59. *See* Andrew Halkyard, 'Revenue Law Discretions and the Rule of Law in Hong Kong', in *The Delicate Balance: Tax, Discretion and the Rule of Law*, eds. Chris Evans, Judith Freedman & Richard Krever (Amsterdam: IBFD, 2011), at 215–216.
60. *See CIR v. Datatronic Ltd* [2009] 4 HKLRD 675 where the Court of Appeal firmly indicated that the decision of the lower court was wrongly premised upon applying a DIPN. At para. 19 the court stated: 'With respect, whether profits tax is payable is governed by s. 14. Profits tax is payable in respect of profits which arose in or were derived from Hong Kong. If under s. 14 no profits tax is payable DIPN 21 is irrelevant.'

In view of the disclaimer in each DIPN that it is 'not binding' on the IRD, that it is directed to all taxpayers, and that the Commissioner cannot fetter himself in the exercise of his statutory duties, it is doubtful whether a taxpayer to whom the terms of a DIPN were not applied could mount a challenge against an assessment on this ground alone. However, a relatively modern and developing doctrine of substantive legitimate expectation, which the CFA has stated forms part of Hong Kong's administrative law,[61] may provide some hope that a failure to honour a legitimate expectation of a substantive outcome or benefit set out in a DIPN might result in such unfairness as to amount to an abuse of power justifying intervention by the court. It should be appreciated however that taxpayers are seldom successful in judicial review applications on these grounds - and the trite, but often true, epithet of the need for 'an exceptional case' is well justified in this area.[62]

[K] Judicial Precedents and Judgments of Foreign (Commonwealth) Courts

As stated in §9.01[3] above, Hong Kong, a common law jurisdiction, adopts the doctrine of precedent. Thus, decisions of superior courts bind lower courts on matters *pari materia*. Strictly speaking, the doctrine does not cover judgments delivered by other superior common law courts (such as the Supreme Court of the UK or the High Court of Australia). This is so notwithstanding that Hong Kong's income tax law was derived from the *Model Colonial Territories Income Tax Ordinance 1922*[63] which has been interpreted by courts from numerous Commonwealth countries. However, the jurisprudential legacy of this Model is considerable and some of its key provisions (e.g., dealing with the source of employment income, source of profits, and the capital / revenue dichotomy) have been the interpreted by a variety of Commonwealth courts (including the UK, Australia, South Africa and India), the decisions of which have been relied upon and applied by Hong Kong courts on numerous occasions.

The use of UK case law in Hong Kong was considered by the Privy Council in *Glynn v. CIR*[64] which held that it was logical and sensible that 'expressions employed in British legislation and authorities on the meaning of such expressions are of assistance in construing identical expressions in Hong Kong legislation with the same subject matter.' This statement should be equally applicable to legislation and relevant authorities from other Commonwealth jurisdictions.

In *A Solicitor v. Law Society of Hong Kong*,[65] the CFA held that: (1) Privy Council[66] decisions on appeal from Hong Kong continue to be binding in Hong Kong (except on

61. *See Ng Siu Tung v. Director of Immigration* (2002) 5 HKCFAR 1.
62. Compare, Judith Freedman & John Vella, 'HMRC's Management of the UK Tax System: The Boundaries of Legitimate Discretion', in *The Delicate Balance: Tax, Discretion and the Rule of Law*, eds. Chris Evans, Judith Freedman & Richard Krever (Amsterdam: IBFD, 2011), at 102–108.
63. *See* s. §9.01[A] above.
64. [1990] 2 WLR 633 at 639.
65. [2008] 2 HKLRD 576.
66. Prior to 1 July 1997, the Privy Council was Hong Kong's highest court.

the CFA itself) after 1 July 1997; and (2) Privy Council decisions on non-Hong Kong appeals and House of Lords (now known as the Supreme Court) decisions are not binding in Hong Kong after 1 July 1997, although Hong Kong courts are entitled to pay appropriate respect to those decisions and to other relevant decisions from other Commonwealth countries.

§9.03 WHAT DO THE COURTS ACTUALLY DO?

Section 9.02 of this chapter stated the general principles – but it is equally illuminating to see what the courts actually do when faced with contemporary statutory interpretation problems. The analysis that follows does not purport to cover all modern case law on interpreting tax statutes in Hong Kong (since much of this has been referenced above). Instead, we will seek to demonstrate interpretation methodology by discussing a selection of court cases which aim to illustrate: (a) the anti-avoidance context; (b) the difficulties in applying the purposive approach; and (c) the problems of balancing and choosing between competing considerations.

[A] The Tax Avoidance Context in a Nutshell: The Instructive Case of *Arrowtown*

It was shown in §9.02[C] above that (1) tax avoidance activity is not looked upon favourably by the courts in Hong Kong today and (2) in this context, the application of the *Ramsay* line of cases can operate in a swingeing fashion. No better illustration of these conclusions is found than in the CFA decision of *CSR v. Arrowtown Assets Ltd.*[67]

Arrowtown involved a complex avoidance arrangement to take advantage of a stamp duty exemption for transfers between 'associated companies' provided by section 45 of the *Stamp Duty Ordinance*.[68] The facts were complex. In short however, the share structure of the assignee (Arrowtown) of the underlying landed property was, prior to the assignment, flooded by worthless 'B' class shares. The original 'A' class shares, which held all substantive rights to voting, dividends, and return upon liquidation, were then transferred to the 'new owner' while the existing shareholder (the assignor) continued to hold the 'B' class shares. The sole purpose for issuing the 'B' class shares was to provide literal compliance with the exemption which prescribed that the assignor beneficially owned, directly or indirectly, a minimum 90% of the 'issued share capital' of the assignee.

On its face, the exemption applied since the 90% threshold did not discriminate between different classes of shares – the provision was simply a copy of an old UK provision which, without embellishment, referred to beneficial ownership of the assignee's 'issued share capital'. What the legislature actually intended a very long time ago, when it copied an even older UK provision, is problematic at best. Yet, without apparent difficulty, the CFA simply stated that the legislature could never have

67. [2004] 1 HKLRD 77.
68. LHK, Cap. 117.

intended that the 'B' class shares should fall within the meaning of 'issued share capital' for the purposes of the exemption 'even if the literal requirements for exemption were complied with'. The contrast with the *Duke of Westminster* 'doctrine' could hardly be clearer. Notwithstanding these comments, and bearing in mind the general way in which many important provisions of the IRO are drafted (see §9.01[A] and §9.01[C] above), such an approach is entirely consistent with the well-known dictum of Judge Learned Hand in *Gilbert v. Commissioner of Inland Revenue*[69] which, interestingly, was quoted by Lord Wilberforce in *Ramsay* and referred to by Mason NPJ in *Shiu Wing*:[70]

> *It is a corollary of the universally accepted canon of interpretation that the literal meaning of the words in a statute is seldom, if ever, the conclusive measure of its scope. Except in rare instances statutes are written in general terms and do not undertake to specify all the occasions they are meant to cover; and their 'interpretation' demands the projection of their expressed purpose upon occasions, not present in the minds of those who enacted them. The Income Tax Act imposes liabilities upon taxpayers based upon their financial transactions ... If, however, the taxpayer enters into a transaction that does not appreciably affect his beneficial interest except to reduce his tax, the law will disregard it; for we cannot suppose it was part of the Act to provide an escape from the liabilities it sought to impose.*

In conclusion, it would perhaps be over-reaching to suggest that courts in Hong Kong are hostile to perceived cases of tax avoidance. But *Arrowtown* clearly illustrates where their sympathies lie and, in terms of statutory interpretation, provides little comfort to the more aggressive tax planner.

[B] Unfairness and the Difficulties in Applying the Purposive Approach: *Braitrim*[71]

Braitrim, a Hong Kong company, carried on a business of supplying and selling plastic garment hangers. The hangers were manufactured by two unrelated companies in Mainland China using moulds belonging to and provided by Braitrim on a no-cost basis.[72] Braitrim's profits were fully liable to profits tax in Hong Kong. It claimed a deduction for the cost of the moulds under section 16G of the IRO on the basis that they were plant and machinery which qualified as 'prescribed fixed assets'. The IRD disallowed the deduction and contended that the moulds were 'excluded fixed assets', which were defined by section 16G(6) to mean '[prescribed] fixed assets in which any person holds rights as a lessee under a lease'.

69. 248 F.2d 399 (1957).
70. [2002] 3 HKLRD 76 at pp. 99–100.
71. *Braitrim (Far East) Ltd v. CIR* (2012) CACV 45/2012. A succinct explanation of the background to, and business model adopted in, this case is provided by Yun & Chan, *Hong Kong: No Deduction for Manufacturing Assets Used in China, Court Says, Tax Notes International* 148–150 (14 January 2013).
72. Presumably the economic cost of providing the moulds would be reflected in the purchase price paid for the hangers.

If the commonly understood meaning of the word 'lease' applied, the moulds were not 'excluded fixed assets' since patently there was no lease entered into between Braitrim and the Mainland companies. Indeed, this was common ground between the parties. However, the word 'lease' was separately defined in the general definition section 2(1) to include 'any arrangement under which a right to use the machinery or plan is granted by the owner of the machinery or plant to another person'. If this definition applied to section 16G(6), then the moulds were 'excluded fixed assets' since they were the subject of an arrangement under which a right to use the moulds was granted by Braitrim to the Mainland companies. Section 2(1) provides that the definitions enacted in it apply 'unless the context otherwise requires'.

In the event, the Court of Appeal agreed with the Commissioner that the word 'lease' appearing in section 16G(6) was intended to be understood in the sense required by the extended definition. Even though this definition was originally enacted for anti-avoidance purposes (to counter tax avoidance arrangements involving leveraged leases of assets used wholly or principally outside Hong Kong), the main reason for the court's conclusion was that the legislative history showed that the definition was removed from the anti-avoidance provision (section 39E) and re-enacted in section 2(1) at the same time that section 16G was enacted. It followed, in the court's view, that the extended definition of lease was intended to apply to section 16G as well as to section 39E and that the context of the IRO did not dictate a contrary result.

What is the effect of this decision? Simply put it means that the deduction provided by section 16G is limited to taxpayers who purchase plant and machinery and use it themselves, but not to those who permit others to use them under some other arrangement, irrespective of whether there is any avoidance connotation (apparently there was no such connotation in *Braitrim*). On its face this seems unfair (the company's profits were fully taxable, yet no deduction was allowed for the cost of its manufacturing plant), the decision is far reaching (most factories of Hong Kong manufacturers are now located in Mainland China and operated by a Chinese entity), surely this is not a result that the legislators would have contemplated if they had fully considered the case (as stated above, the definition of lease was initially enacted as part of a suite of anti-avoidance measures and contract manufacturing arrangements in Mainland China, which have not been suggested to be tax motivated, have increased exponentially since that time) and, indeed, it took the IRD several years after the definition was enacted to start denying depreciation allowances for the cost of manufacturing assets owned by Hong Kong companies but used by another party outside Hong Kong on a no-cost basis.

What role did the purposive approach play in this decision? Even though the court attempted to embark upon a holistic remedial and mischief approach, and considered whether for the purposes of section 16G the meaning of 'lease' should be interpreted in a wider legal and social sense (as indicated above, this was rejected because, relying on the legislative history, the court decided that the intent of the statutory wording was clear), reliance on legislative materials would not have changed the result. The reason is that the materials referred to by the court, namely, the Explanatory Memorandum and the Statement of the Secretary moving the Bill, simply threw no light on whether the re-enacted definition should apply outside an anti-avoidance context.

The reality is that the legislators probably did not consider the full ramifications of what they had enacted.[73] A statutory interpretation then prevailed which, while justifiable, looks unfair, was detrimental to the taxpayer, and would not look out of place in pre-1990s jurisprudence. It might be countered that the result reflects the long-held view that the courts will not rectify a legislative omission (see §9.02[F] above). Even so, the decision in *Braitrim* is a far cry from the swingeing result and judicial reasoning so obviously apparent in the anti-avoidance context of *Arrowtown*.

[C] The Problems of Balancing and Choosing Between Competing Considerations: *Turner Entertainment Networks*[74]

This case concerned the interpretation of section 15(1)(a), (b) and (ba) of the IRO, which provides:

> For the purposes of this Ordinance, the sums described in the following paragraphs shall be deemed to be receipts arising in or derived from Hong Kong from a trade, profession or business carried on in Hong Kong –
>
> (a) sums, not otherwise chargeable to tax under this Part, received by or accrued to a person *from the exhibition or use in Hong Kong of cinematograph or television film or tape, any sound recording, or any advertising material connected with such film, tape or recording*;

73. *Ho Kwok Tai v. CSD* (2016) CACV 52/2016 may serve as another example. The Court of Appeal effectively held, in overturning the lower court's decision ((2016) HCAL 49/2015), that while Hong Kong Permanent Residents (HKPRs) who have disposed of all their residential properties *before* acquiring a new residential property would be charged the lower ad valorem stamp duty rates (under section 29BB, Stamp Duty Ordinance (LHK, Cap 117)), a HKPR would be denied of the refund (under section 29DF) in case he or she needs to dispose of more than one residential property *after* acquiring the new property. In other words, his or her original property must be his or her sole residential property. In arriving at this conclusion, the court considered that the correct approach in considering whether the refund provision should apply is to look at the existing properties individually rather than collectively. Accordingly, had one (or another) of the existing properties been disposed of prior to the acquisition of the new property, the applicable instrument for acquiring the new property would still have been chargeable with stamp duty with the enhanced scale of rates in view of the fact that he was the owner of some other residential property on the date of acquiring the new property (para. 40). In this regard, the court found support from the time limit for applying for the refund as in the event that the applicant was the beneficial owner of more than one residential property which he disposed of after acquiring the new property, there could be more than one date under which the 'original property' is transferred or divested and in such a case, there would be impracticability in determining the precise timeframe for the applicant to apply for refund (para. 43). Furthermore, the court considered the definition of 'original property', in both English ('another property') and in Chinese ('另一物業') and held that it cannot refer to more than one property and, therefore, the general interpretative aid laid down in section 7(1) of the Interpretation and General Clauses Ordinance (Cap 1) (namely, 'Words and expressions in singular include the plural and words and expressions in the plural include the singular') should not have been applied to the interpretation of the expression because a contrary intention does appear from the context of the provision (paras 41–42, 44).
74. *Turner Entertainment Networks Asia, Inc v. CIR* (2012) HCIA 4/2010 and on appeal [2015] 3 HKLRD 295.

(b) sums, not otherwise chargeable to tax under this Part, received by or accrued to a person for the use of or right to use in Hong Kong any patent, design, trademark, copyright material, secret process or formula or other property of a similar nature, or for imparting or undertaking to impart knowledge directly or indirectly connected with the use in Hong Kong of any such patent, design, trademark, copyright material, secret process or formula or other property;

(ba) sums, not otherwise chargeable to tax under this Part, received by or accrued to a person for the use of or right to use outside Hong Kong any patent, design, trademark, copyright material, secret process or formula or other property of a similar nature, or for imparting or undertaking to impart knowledge directly or indirectly connected with the use outside Hong Kong of any such patent, design, trademark, copyright material, secret process or formula or other property, which are deductible in ascertaining the assessable profits of a person under this Part.

The text in italics shows the sole differences between paragraphs (b) and (ba). They are clearly related. Both paragraphs should be contrasted with the underlined text of paragraph (a) which, on its face, looks like a standalone provision.

Under licence agreements, Turner Entertainment obtained the right to exhibit a series of Chinese language television programmes to be screened in Taiwan. In consideration for the licences, the company was obliged to pay a licence fee to an associated offshore company. The IRD took the view that the licence fee was liable to profits tax and chargeable to the licensor (the payee) by way of an assessment raised on Turner Entertainment (the payor). At its core, the issue in dispute was straight forward – does the licence fee simply fall to be considered under section 15(1)(a) (in which case it would not be liable to profits tax since it was not a sum received 'from the exhibition or use *in* Hong Kong of ... television film') or was it permissible to also consider section 15(1)(ba) (in which case it would be liable to profits tax on the basis that, more generally, it was a sum received 'for the use of or right to use *outside* Hong Kong any ... copyright material ... or other property of a similar nature ... *which was deductible in ascertaining the assessable profits of a person*').

As highlighted in italics above, apart from the last part of section 15(1)(ba) (which deems certain deductible payments to be liable to profits tax in the hands of the recipient), the language of section 15(1)(ba) tracks that of section 15(1)(b) word for word – except for changing the phrase 'in Hong Kong' to 'outside Hong Kong'.[75] By way of contrast, apart from the first line, the wording of section 15(1)(a) is totally different. In short, the wording of section 15(1)(a), which was enacted at the same time as section 15(1)(b), was not mirrored in anything like the same way that section 15(1)(ba) mirrored section 15(1)(b). A strong argument could thus be made that any sum paid for the use or exhibition of a 'television film' should be interpreted simply by reference to

75. It is not in dispute that the genesis for enacting s. 15(1)(ba) was to counter the effects of the decision in *CIR v. Emerson Radio Corp* (1999) 2 HKCFAR 501 which, it should be noted, exposed the territorial limitations of s. 15(1)(b). Indeed, as the judge stated in *Turner Entertainment* (2012) HCIA 4/2010 at para. 31: 'In short, s. 15(1)(ba) provided a geographic extension of the deeming provision under s. 15(1)(b).'

section 15(1)(a) since this was the specific and only provision dealing explicitly with payments arising from the exploitation of films.

The judge at first instance did not agree. Instead, he concluded that:[76]

> *Each of the paragraphs in section 15(1) is a deeming provision introduced to deal with an individual tax issue, and there is no central theme to the section. Because the various paragraphs were intended to deal with different situations, they need not necessarily be mutually exclusive.*

What then is (1) the separate situation (or mischief) to which section 15(1)(a) is directed and (2) what, if any, independent meaning can be given to that paragraph if television film and cinematographic rights fall within the meaning of 'copyright material' or 'other property of a similar nature' within section 15(1)(b) and (ba)? Unfortunately, the judge did not clarify the first question and the answer to the second question appears to be 'none at all' (with the possible exception of deeming payments made for related advertising material as taxable). Although the judge considered the legislative history (which showed that section 15(1)(a) and (b) were enacted at the same time) and the Explanatory Memorandum when section 15(1)(ba) was enacted (which, whilst hardly conclusive of the issue in dispute, was nonetheless 'apparently introduced in response to the judgment of the CFA in *CIR v. Emerson Radio Corp*' [which, as indicated above, dealt solely with the interpretation of section 15(1)(b)]), he concluded by stating that section 15(1)(ba), by referring to 'or other property of a similar nature', is indicative of an intention to apply this deeming provision to *all* forms of intellectual property.[77] With respect, this seems a half-hearted attempt at purposive interpretation. Given the obvious similarity between the wording of section 15(1)(b) and (ba) and their sharp contrast with the wording of section 15(1)(a), if one goal of legislative drafting in the taxation area is to promote reasonable certainty of tax treatment for those reading the relevant provision, the result reached in *Turner Entertainment* clearly gives pause for concern.

Confusingly, the judge proceeded to support his conclusion by stating that the last part of section 15(1)(ba), which refers to sums 'which are deductible [for profits tax purposes]', is consistent with Hong Kong's source jurisdiction to tax because 'where a Hong Kong business is said to have incurred royalty expenses in producing its Hong Kong sourced profits, the intellectual property concerned must have been used in Hong Kong, so that the royalty income for the use of intellectual property should be taxable in Hong Kong'.[78] This leap in logic is, with respect, not justified - either in its

76. (2012) HCIA 4/2010 at para. 69, which was essentially agreed by the Court of Appeal (*see* [2015] 3 HKLRD 295 at paras 25-27).
77. (2012) HCIA 4/2010 at paras 30-31, 34-35 and 53. Similarly, the Court of Appeal ([2015] 3 HKLRD 295) concluded that payments for the grant of rights to exhibit television programmes outside Hong Kong were chargeable under s. 15(1)(ba) as being for the use or right to use 'copyright material', even though payments for the right to exhibit or use television films could also fall within the subject matter covered by ss 15(1)(a) and (b) although in this case neither s. 15(1)(a) nor (b) applied since such payments were not for the use of the relevant rights in Hong Kong.
78. (2012) HCIA 4/2010 at para. 58. This point, however, was not dealt with by the Court of Appeal. Nevertheless, the court might not have done better. Apart from what has been stated in note 77

conclusion or by reference to section 15(1)(ba) which is predicated upon the relevant intellectual property being used 'outside Hong Kong'. The judge does not mention that all the profits of Turner Entertainment (including the Taiwan distribution fees) *were* offered for assessment and liable to profits tax in Hong Kong. Thus, there was no mismatch between the deductibility of the payment to the offshore licensor and the taxability of the related receipts. The liability to profits tax of the licensor is, of course, an entirely separate matter.

§9.04 CONCLUSIONS

In §9.02 above, we have seen that the traditional 'rules' for statutory interpretation should more accurately be described as 'approaches' or 'guides'; that these may conflict in a particular case; and, as a result, in different periods of Hong Kong's legal history greater or lesser emphasis has been placed on one approach rather than another.[79] We have also seen in §9.02[A] and §9.02[B] above that the modern trend of statutory interpretation of taxation legislation in Hong Kong has shifted from a literal to a purposive approach. Of course, this does not mean that the ordinary meaning of the words used is ignored;[80] but where there is no obvious meaning the emphasis now is on a contextual approach designed to identify the purpose of a statute and to give effect to it.[81]

---

above, the court rejected the appellant's other arguments that: (a) the concepts of 'use' and 'right to use' within s. 15(1)(b) must necessarily be determined by applying intellectual property law concepts. In this regard, the court concluded that 'the fact that sections 15(1)(b) and (ba) cover a variety of forms of intellectual property is, in itself, a factor that militates against the adoption of technical and limited meanings of use in relation to each, since that would require the same single word, in the same provision, to be given different meaning or content in relation to different forms of intellectual property listed in the same provision' (para. 16). Although this quote relates specifically to s. 15(1)(b) and (ba), the words 'use' and 'right to use' are also contained in s. 15(1)(a); and (b) the word 'use' excludes the exhibition of cinematograph or television film or tape. The court held that 'There is no reason why "use" should not include "exhibition" where that is how a particular form of intellectual property might be deployed by someone other than the copyright holder in consideration of the payment of a fee to the copyright holder' (para. 22). As to the difference between sums 'from' (s. 15(1)(a)) and sums 'for' (s. 15(1)(b) and (ba)) the relevant use of the various forms of intellectual property, the Court of Appeal stated: 'Section 15(1)(a) thus more naturally relates to a situation in which the owner of the film or sound recording is involved... in the exhibition or other use of it, whereas section 15(1)(b) and (ba) relate to a situation where he is not, or at least where the use is by another, or the right to use it is conferred on another' (para. 26). As a result: 'Section 15(1)(a) refers to the "exhibition or use" of the "media works" it mentions. This would seem to require the actual exhibition or use of such "media works", and that the sums be generated from the exhibition or use itself, rather than from a licensing arrangement under which payment is made by someone other than the owner for the use of (or the right to use) the "media works" in question. Thus under section 15(1)(b) and (ba), fees would be assessable even if the licensee did not exhibit the "media works" or use the intellectual property the right to use which was the consideration for the fees' (para. 27).

79. Compare, Law Commission Report, *The Interpretation of Statutes* (1969) HC 256 at 14.
80. The UK Supreme Court in *Grays Timber Products Ltd v. HMRC* [2010] UKSC 4 at para. 37 put it thus: '[although] the principle that tax was to be charged only by clear words might be less potent than it was ... it is still relevant to the interpretation of taxing statutes.'
81. *See* further, *IRC v. McGuckian* [1997] 1 WLR 991, per Lord Steyn at 999.

In practice, court decisions rarely fall squarely in either camp. Thus, in §9.03 above we examined how Hong Kong courts actually apply those approaches in contemporary cases. We discovered that while they appear antipathetic to perceived cases of tax avoidance (§9.03[A]), the purposive approach does have its limitations, the most important being the difficulty of determining the mischief to which legislation is directed and the often inconclusive nature of the legislative materials considered by the courts (§9.03[B] and §9.03[C]).[82] We also found that, even whilst attempting to embark upon a purposive approach (albeit that this was fairly muted in the case of *Turner Entertainment*), the courts have struggled with balancing competing considerations including whether an anti-avoidance focus or, indeed, unfairness were intended by the law makers (§9.03[B]) and whether it is desirable to interpret legislation in a way which promotes good drafting and reasonable certainty of tax treatment (§9.03[C]). Interestingly, in all of the cases analysed, the decisions were not inimical to the interests of the Revenue. Without wishing to end on too pessimistic a note, this seems to indicate that the IRD would be happy with the current status quo in interpreting taxation legislation in Hong Kong and that taxpayers need a strong and clear case to succeed in any dispute.[83]

82. Compare, Judith Freedman, *Interpreting Tax Statutes: Tax Avoidance and the Intention of Parliament*, 123 LQR 53 (2007) who states: 'Statutory interpretation may be the process of discovering parliamentary intention, but this intention, never a straightforward concept, is especially difficult to ascertain in tax legislation, where complex legal concepts are often used to achieve economic ends.'

83. Since my early years as a young tax appeals officer, I have never forgotten the sage words of the head of the Appeals Branch. They went like this: 'It's tough being a tax man. In considering the merits of any appeal, we always need to look for and apply the statutory intent. But if a taxpayer's case falls within the wording of the statute, then he is entitled to succeed.' Outside the tax avoidance context (and I recognise the difficulties inherent in this carve-out) I have always thought that this was the right approach. But I will charge the reader to query whether those sentiments are ascendant in today's fiscal environment.

CHAPTER 10
Legal Interpretation of Tax Law: Italy

Carlo Garbarino

§10.01 INTRODUCTION

[A] Definitional Concepts About Interpretation in the Italian Tax System

A few definitional concepts are required at the outset about interpretation in the Italian tax system to clearly define the scope of this chapter. The first remark is that the Italian legal culture is permeated by legal positivism, i.e., the idea that the legal system is a complete and consistent set of rules that are posited and organized in a hierarchical structure. As a result, deference is afforded to the 'letter of law', particularly that of general statutory norms, with scant attention to case law (this is also due to the fact that Italy is not a common law system).[1]

So 'interpretation' is meant here to be the *attribution of a meaning to the text of posited norms*, rather than the development of broad policies. There is also a specific tax reason for the predominance of this concept of interpretation: the Italian tax system is a sub-set of the legal system that mainly includes statutory rules that require interpretive techniques for their application. Thus the concept of 'interpretation' that is considered here includes the analysis of interpretive techniques that are actually used to apply tax laws, rather than a hermeneutic concept of 'interpretation' as a general view of the law as a social engineering tool.[2]

1. On legal positivism in Italy *see* for example: Norberto Bobbio, *Giusnaturalismo e positivismo giuridico* (Milano: Edizioni di Comunità, 1965); Norberto Bobbio, *Positivismo giuridico* (Torino: Giappichelli, 1979); Uberto Scarpelli, *Cos'è il positivismo giuridico* (Milano, 1965); Mario Jori (ed.), *Legal Positivism* (Aldershot: Dartmouth: The International Library of Jurisprudence, 1992).
2. The term 'interpretation' in American neo-constitutionalism and generally in the Anglo-Saxon legal tradition is often used with a wider, and more vague, meaning; *see* for example Ronald Dworkin, *Law's Empire* (Cambridge: Harvard University Press, 1986). That approach to 'interpretation' is not used in this chapter.

The second remark points at the fact that the old conception according to which the interpreter 'reveals' the actual, unique and pre-existing meaning of the norm[3] is not currently practiced by jurists in Italy, be they practitioners or academics. Based on major doctrinal contributions in the 1970s, a distinction is made between the 'text' of a rule in natural prescriptive language and the 'meaning' of that rule, being understood that such a 'meaning' is one of many potentially available outcomes of diversified competing interpretive strategies.[4] So different 'players' or 'actors' are able to employ competitive 'interpretative strategies' of a single rule (or set of rules) and the actual meaning of that rule or rules is the outcome of a law-in-action process (*see infra* §10.01[B]).

In conclusion there is no single or unique 'true norm' to be revealed but rather different 'norms' that are the result of different interpretive strategies of the same normative text. If that is true, then, in Italy currently there is no prevailing interpretive canon for tax laws such as the canon '*in dubio contra fiscum*' advocated by the liberal tradition of the Nineteenth century (if in doubt, select the interpretation not favourable to the Tax Authorities), or '*in dubio pro fisco*' (if in doubt, select the interpretation favourable to the Tax Authorities).[5]

This approach to tax interpretation, however, does not imply a full interpretive scepticism according to which interpretation can lead to any outcome: according to a well-established approach there is a framework of potential interpretations available, from which the interpreter can select one by using particular '*interpretive techniques*' based on clusters or arrangements of '*arguments*' that essentially advocate the persuasiveness of the interpretive outcome.[6] Therefore, the different types of tax interpretation – such as '*strict*' versus '*purposive*' interpretation, *see infra* §10.02 and §10.03 – will be viewed here by looking at the arguments and interpretive techniques actually used by agents in advocating these types of tax interpretation.

In the approach used in this chapter, the analysis of interpretive techniques and arguments does exclude however that agents – particularly judges – can also create (i.e., enact) so-called *implicit norms*[7] and *principles*[8] which are established through techniques of '*legal construction*', i.e., the ordering of ethical, societal, and other

3. The assumption of the pre-existence of the 'real' meaning of a norm has been developed by jurists during the Enlightenment on the basis of the idea that the law should and could be known. On that tradition *see* for example: Giovanni Tarello, *Diritto, enunciati, usi* (Bologna: Il Mulino, 1974), p. 108.
4. The distinction between the text of the rule and the meaning of the rule resulting from interpretation has been introduced by Vezio Crisafulli, 'Disposizione (e norma)', in *Enciclopedia del Diritto*, Vol. XIII (Milano: Giuffrè, 1964). *See also*: Riccardo Guastini, *Dalle fonti alle norme* (Torino: Giappichelli, 1992); Giovanni Tarello, *Studi sulla teoria generale dei precetti, I. Introduzione al linguaggio precettivi* (Milano, 1968) (estratto da *Annali Giurisprudenza Genova, I,* 1968), 459 et seq.; Giovanni Tarello, 'L'interpretazione della legge', in Antonio Cicu, Francesco Messineo and Luigi Mengoni (eds), *Trattato di diritto civile* (Milano: Giuffrè, 1980).
5. On these canons *see* for example Massimo S. Giannini, 'L'interpretazione e l'integrazione delle leggi tributarie' in (1941) I *Riv. Dir. Fin.*, 123.
6. On the framework of possible 7 available interpretations *see*, for example: Hans Kelsen, *Dottrina pura del diritto,* Transl. by M.G. Losano. (Torino: Einaudi, 1966), Chapter VIII, but also Herbert L.A. Hart, *The Concept of Law* (2nd edition, 1961, Oxford: Clarendon Press).
7. For a definition of implicit tax norms *see infra* s. §10.03[E].
8. For a definition of tax principles *see infra* s. §10.03[E].

axiological values to support legal solutions and outcomes, a process that does not amount to tax interpretation in the sense used here. For example, Italian judges have created a judicial concept of 'tax abuse' (*see infra* §10.04[C]), which is not the result of interpretation, but rather is the creation of a judicial norm by a set of non-interpretive arguments of legal construction. In other cases agents rely on axiological principles to enact new implicit norms that take the form of binding principles (*see* for example *infra* §10.03[E]). Again, in these cases, principles are judge-made norms created through legal construction.

This chapter illustrates the two polarities in current Italian tax law-in-action: '*strict interpretation*' (or 'literal interpretation') and '*purposive interpretation*'. Strict interpretation comprises a set of interpretive arguments that will be analysed in detail *infra* at §10.02 and has gained traction as a result of the liberal ideology that dominated civil law in the last part of the nineteenth century. According to that ideology taxes are an intrusion of Government into the sphere of private life and a limitation of personal liberty and infringement of property rights, so that tax laws should be interpreted conservatively according to the actual meaning of the words, and not purposively according to their spirit, rationale, or other extra-textual elements.

By contrast, '*purposive interpretation*' relies on elements other than the text of the norm, and is based on an array of different extra-textual factors, particularly when substance must prevail over form. It thus relies on a set of interpretive arguments that look at the spirit or rationale of tax laws (these arguments will be analysed in details *infra* §10.03). The approach also includes, in a very broad sense, techniques of legal construction in which agents enact implicit norms and binding principles without actually attributing the meaning to existing posited norms.

Purposive interpretation emerged for two reasons: (i) the need to address so-called hard cases, i.e., cases that cannot be solved through strict interpretation due to the increasing complexities of the tax system; and (ii) the need to counteract aggressive strategies of taxpayers exploiting the limitations of strict interpretation. This has resulted in a new brand of interpretive ideologies – particularly in governmental agencies – according to which individual positions of taxpayers can be 'compressed' by social policies, and this has ultimately created a problem of protection of constitutionally protected rights. Because of the increasing complexity of auditing techniques and the judicial activism of the Italian *Corte di Cassazione* (the '*Cassazione*'), a paradigm shift is currently under way in which the purposive interpretation is gradually predominating over the strict interpretation (*see infra* §10.04).

Scholars and practitioners assert that when the literal meaning of tax laws is clear, strict interpretation is adequate. Interpretation based on the meaning of the words in their connection therefore constitutes a sort of Golden Rule or first step in the process of interpretation and application of tax rules (*see infra* §10.02). However, strict interpretation may not be appropriate where the task is interpreting how the legislation is to be applied to complex or convoluted arrangements or where the law intends for social policy to prevail over individual rights.[9] In recent times, judges have turned to

9. Article 23 of the Italian Constitution, establishes that personal or patrimonial obligations can be imposed only on the basis of Law, but interpretive discretion is implicitly allowed.

the alternative approach of purposive interpretation in these cases to establish a set of guiding values or norms, in most cases not mentioned in the text (*see* for example *infra* §10.04[C]).

[B] Actor-Based Interpretative Approaches and Italian Tax Law in Action

Interpretation is developed and propounded by different agents or 'actors' within the Italian tax system, each of them advancing different interests and supporting different values. These actors are essentially the following: Tax Authorities, tax courts, tax scholars and tax practitioners. So, tax interpretation varies depending on the type of actor who propounds it, with the result that there is so-called authentic interpretation enacted by Tax Authorities, judicial interpretation developed by tax courts, doctrinal interpretation propounded by tax scholars, and practical interpretations advanced by tax practitioners.[10]

'*Authentic interpretation*' enacted by Tax Authorities can be explicitly found in interpretive regulations (*see infra* §10.05[B]), but encompasses also the positions taken by auditing offices on a case-by-case basis when motivating their tax assessments, when advancing their arguments in tax litigation, or when replying to specific questions posed by taxpayers in private letter rulings. Authentic interpretation is generally binding on a case-by-case basis unless overturned by a judge, but interpretive regulations are generally not binding (*see infra* §10.05[B]).

Authentic interpretation should be impartial, and this is imposed by Article 97 of the Constitution, which provides that public offices are organized according to the provisions of law, so as to ensure the 'efficiency and impartiality of administration'.[11] Unfortunately Tax Authorities de facto advance a specific set of strategic and practical interests - namely revenue raising - so that the interpretation propounded by them is almost invariably that which is more favourable to the Treasury. Tax Authorities however - differently from other actors - are bound by the principle of efficiency and impartiality of administration, imposed by Article 97 of the Italian Constitution, with the consequence that their interpretation should not be moulded to advance a practical interest. Unfortunately this approach has been accepted by part of the doctrine as advancing a so-called tax interest (so-called *interesse fiscale*[12]). The result is obfuscation of Government action.

Judicial interpretation developed by tax courts is generally binding on a case-by-case basis. Courts had traditionally taken an over-legalistic approach that downplayed purposive interpretation,[13] but recently have swiftly moved to a substantive approach and developed the doctrine of 'abuse of tax laws' (*see infra* §10.04[C]), that supports

10. This model applied to tax law is generally advanced by William Twining and David Miers, *Come fare cose con regole*. Transl. Carlo Garbarino (Milano: Giuffrè, 1990), 408.
11. Mauro Beghin, *Diritto Tributario*, (Torino: Giappicchelli, 2011), 47.
12. Pietro Boria, *L'interesse fiscale* (Torino: Giappichelli, 2002).
13. *See* for example: Giancarlo Zoppini, 'Prospettiva critica della giurisprudenza "antielusiva" della Corte di Cassazione (1969–1999)', (1999) 1 *Riv. dir. trib.*, 919; Mauro Beghin, *Diritto Tributario*, (Torino: Giappicchelli, 2011), p. 50.

the so-called tax interest (*'interesse fiscale'*), with the result taxpayers' rights have been significantly eroded.

Doctrinal interpretation is propounded by tax scholars in law review articles, papers, books, and other media and is not binding. *Practical interpretation* is advanced by tax practitioners either in legal briefs or in memoranda. Practical interpretation, like doctrinal interpretation, is not binding however, and unlike doctrinal interpretation, it is not generally available to the public. Practical interpretation is, essentially, a proposal to the judge to assign to a specific norm, and in the context of specific litigation, a specific meaning, so it does not purport to have a general impact. By contrast, doctrinal interpretation is, essentially, a reasoned proposal to assign to a specific norm, in general, a specific meaning, so it does purport to have a general impact. However, the current trend in Italy is that doctrinal and practical interpretations merge when arguments advanced by practitioners are published in law review articles, papers, books, and other media authored directly by practitioners or scholars.

To understand the structure of Italian tax law, one must analyse the complex relationship between the various types of interpretations advanced by different actors within the tax system. Tax law is a complex institutional process, not just the mere collection of validly enacted legislation.[14] The analysis of actor-based interpretations provides a dynamic approach to taxation and focuses on tax law as the result of the social activity of a group or a community institutionally involved in creating it. Thus the tax interpretation process can be seen as an arena in which different philosophical views compete, a view that belies the idea that tax law is unitary.

These groups, identified above, produce different kinds of texts: statutes, regulations, opinions, briefs, and articles, and they each have an archive (previously written documents) and a professionally tested style to transform old documents and produce new ones. These texts and documents, and the way in which they are produced, interrelated, re-used, and cited, become key features in understanding the structure and evolution of Italian tax law in action, which can therefore be understood as a set of interlocked documents used by the involved actors according to their respective interpretive strategies. Thus, one must look at the so-called operative rules, i.e., at the actual rules implemented by tax law in action as the result of actor-based interpretations.[15]

Within the Italian tax system there is often *competition* among actor-based interpretations, as these interpretations do not necessarily coincide in determining the operative tax rules. For example, guidelines of Tax Authorities may conflict with case law and scholarly opinions, or case law can generate conflicting trends. Also, the operative tax rules may not be uniform because one operative rule may be provided by case law, another by scholars, and yet another one by statutes, etc. As a result of

14. *See* for example on this approach: Rodolfo Sacco & Pier G. Monateri, 'Legal Formants', in Peter Newman (ed.), *The New Palgrave Dictionary of Economics and the Law* (London: Macmillan, 1998).
15. On 'operative rules' *see*: Carlo Garbarino, 'An Evolutionary Approach to Comparative Taxation: Methods and Agenda for Research' (2009) *Am. J. Comp. Law*, 677.

competition among different interpretive strategies, there is often an underlying dialectic process within the Italian tax system.

However, when different actor-based interpretations work together they contribute in defining an institutional cooperative arrangement that comes in two basic patterns: a 'top-down pattern' in which tax statutes are enacted and subsequently interpreted and implemented by administrative guidelines and/or case law as well as supported by the opinions of tax scholars; and a 'bottom-up pattern' in which administrative guidelines in conjunction with case law and opinions of legal scholars shape tax law in action with virtually no recourse to legislation.

Over the course of the last decade, Italian tax judges have begun to safeguard Government's interests rather than protecting taxpayers' rights, leading to a convergence pattern that exhibits the following features: (i) prevailing judicial interpretations are eventually adjudicated by the *Cassazione* against the scholarly positions and in favour of Tax Authorities; (ii) scholarly interpretations tend to converge as a reaction to the purposive approach taken by Tax Authorities; (iii) conflicts among interpretations advanced by lower courts are adjudicated by the *Cassazione* against the taxpayers; and (iv) the prevailing interpretation by Tax Authorities and prevailing judicial interpretation tend to converge.

This matrix of interactions has reversed a previous trend in which scholarly interpretations, generally opposed to interpretations advanced by Tax Authorities, influenced judicial interpretations. In that previous scenario of actor-based interpretation there was a tension between, on the one hand, scholarly and judicial interpretations aimed at protecting taxpayers' rights, and, on the other hand, interpretations advanced by Tax Authorities, in most cases advancing practical interests of tax offices.

[C] Complexity of Tax Laws and Its Impact on Interpretation

Several features of the Italian tax system have a contingent impact on interpretative techniques. First, tax laws are not collected in a systematic body of laws akin to, for example, the Internal Revenue Code in the US, or at least in line with the European experience of codification of laws. There are indeed collections of tax laws that bring together provisions relating to a specific area (such as income taxes, audits, litigation, and so on) that are denominated '*testi unici*' (consolidated texts). These consolidated texts, however, simply amount to a mere collection of existent provisions, which are re-numbered and divided by topic. There is no encompassing structure allowing for regular updates on the basis of a systematic arrangement.

The result is that Italian tax laws constitute a body of laws that is composed of many sub-systems that are not coordinated. For example, broad economic legislation may contain important tax rules, or, by contrast, a technical piece of legislation may introduce important tax changes, but those modifications are not included in the relevant consolidated texts.[16] This is a typical example of hypertrophic legislation that

16. Raffaello Braccini, 'Mutamenti nelle basi del diritto tributario: la crisi dell'idea di "sistema"', (1997) IV *Giur. It.*, 313.

creates a host of technical problems in the area of coordination and makes it quite difficult to identify general principles. Moreover, each individual tax has specific procedural rules (in terms of tax returns, audits, litigation, and so on), so that quite often there are conflicts of rules or gaps in the tax system.

In the absence of clearly articulated underlying principles and policies, deference is given to the text of the law to ensure proper technical application of a particular norm within its micro-system.[17] There is only one text denominated '*Statuto del contribuente*' (Charter of Rights of the Taxpayer, hereinafter the 'Tax Charter') that has a rather stable structure.[18] The Tax Charter enunciates principles of tax laws and can be modified by subsequent legislation only if such legislation expressly pinpoints the specific provisions to be modified. This is called the 'reinforced' nature of the Tax Charter.

A second feature of the Italian tax system that has a direct impact on interpretative techniques is its fast rate of change: legislative and regulatory bodies continuously enact new rules to adapt the tax system to new economic realities, contractual arrangements, and institutions. Moreover, in a continuous search for revenues, tax laws are continuously amended. Another cause of the continuous change of tax laws is the pernicious loop in which opportunistic taxpayers devise new aggressive tax strategies and Tax Authorities close the loopholes by enacting complex anti-avoidance rules. In tax matters the so-called sunset laws are also quite frequent, i.e., provisions that apply to specific situations which occur before a certain date, providing, for example, tax breaks, tax credits, step-up of assets. The impact of this situation is that interpretive techniques do not establish consistent trends, but rather haphazardly follow the pace of change.

A third feature of the Italian tax system that has a direct impact on interpretative techniques is a peculiar normative mechanism that is allowed by Article 76 of the Italian Constitution: the executive branch can enact law-decrees which are immediately effective, but which must be approved by Parliament within 60 days. Parliament usually approves law-decrees with amendments that in most cases are retroactive, thereby creating transitional complex in-period rules. By contrast, if law-decrees are not converted into law, many situations originally covered by them need to be regulated by ad hoc retroactive legislation. The impact of this situation on tax interpretation is that often retroactive statutory interpretive norms are enacted which are idiosyncratically geared to transition rules (*see infra* §10.05[A]).

A fourth feature of the Italian tax system that has a direct impact on interpretative techniques is that often tax laws imply the use of accounting, financial and economic concepts that are not defined by tax laws.[19] For example, the taxation of financial instruments requires a definition of the underlying transactions, and the taxation of business income requires the use of accounting principles, and so on. Furthermore tax rules often describe computations by using natural language rather than mathematical

17. *See* for example Corte cost., 3 March 1989, No. 84, in (1990) I(1) *Giur. It.*, 1379; Corte cost., 3 September 1995, No. 430, and Corte cost., 23 July 2002, No. 375, *ibid.*
18. Law, 27 July 2000, No. 212.
19. Giuseppe Melis, *L'interpretazione nel diritto tributario* (Padova: Cedam 2003).

symbols, and this makes them often unintelligible. The impact of this situation on tax interpretation is that non-tax concepts are 'imported' into the tax system and this creates a significant level of uncertainty.

The last feature of the Italian tax system that has a direct impact on interpretative techniques is the fact that there is no explicit tradition of statutory drafting. As a result tax statutes are drafted by teams originating from different governmental structures: for example a bill on the reform of corporate tax may originate from highest echelons of the Treasury, while a bill on value added tax (VAT) may originate from a concerted action of different lobbies. These variations in language and style do not help the interpreters in their task. Moreover when a new tax provision is enacted, it is very unlikely that such a provision enters an area that is still unregulated, and in most cases there is already an existing maze of norms. New provisions, therefore, are inserted into the existing normative web through additions, deletions, and substitutions. As a result, the interpreter is facing diachronically different sets of norms which complicate the application of norms to the facts at hand, often creating uncertainty.

The level of uncertainty of tax laws resulting from their complexity is so high that, as a result of an intense doctrinal debate, Article 10 of the Tax Charter provides that sanctions are not enforced when the violation of tax rules is the result of an 'objective situation of uncertainty as to the scope of a tax norm', clarifying that the occurrence of uncertainty is not limited to situations when litigation is pending.[20]

To mitigate interpretation problems Article 2 of the Tax Charter – titled 'Clarity and transparency of tax norms' – provides a set of drafting guidelines. First, tax statutes must expressly mention their topic and each provision must have a title that clarifies its normative and semantic content; this is to prevent so-called silent norms from slipping into the tax system undetected. Second, non-tax statutes cannot include tax norms; this is to prevent so-called intruded norms to emerge outside of the tax system. Third, links between tax norms must be clearly identified and also contain the topic of the linked norm; this is to prevent implicit links from substantially changing the normative content of a norm. Fourth a tax norm that modifies another tax norm must report the text of the modified norm.

§10.02 STRICT INTERPRETATION OF TAX LAWS

Strict interpretation naturally takes place within Italian tax culture based on the text of posited norms. Judges often use strict interpretation to justify their decisions about the application of tax laws.[21] It comprises a basic dyad of interpretive arguments, the so-called *a contrario* argument and the argument of the plain meaning of the text. The '*a contrario*' argument is an overarching implicit rationale, based on the Latin tenet '*ubi lex voluit dixit, ubi tacuit noluit*', which amounts to a counterfactual: if the legislator

20. *See also* Art. 8 D. lgs, 31 December 1992, No. 546. On this problem *see*: Maurizio Logozzo, *L'ignoranza della legge tributaria* (Milano: Giuffrè, 2002).
21. *See* for example: *Cass.*, 25 February 2009, No. 4501; *Cass.*, 6 February 2009, No. 2931. In general *see*: Giuseppe Melis, *L'Interpretazione nel Diritto Tributario*, (Padova: Cedam, 2003), pp. 61 et seq.

did not say something, then it clearly did not actually mean to say something (i.e., if legislator had wanted something, it would have said so). This basically amounts to a legal ideology postulating that there is a non-regulated space beyond the boundaries of the regulated 'normative space'.

The argument of the plain meaning of the text (*see infra* §10.02[A]) is not only based on common sense, but is also imposed by existing norms as a constraint on interpretation. It is often based on semantic links established by the interpreters, depending on whether the retained meaning is found within the tax system (internal links), or without the tax system (external links). Moreover, strict interpretation based on plain meaning relies on the attribution of a 'specialized meaning' to terms used in natural or legal language by the operation of stipulating definitions or conceptual transplants that occur between different areas of the Italian legal system (*see infra* §10.02[B]).

[A] The Plain Meaning of the Text

The current approach is that the interpreter can use all sorts of arguments, but also that there are a few 'constraints' on interpretation. The main constraint is of a historical nature: when in 1942 the Italian Civil Code was adopted, it also contained a set of very general rules - denominated '*Preleggi*' - that have traditionally served as general principles of the Italian legal system. Article 12 of *Preleggi*, in the matter of interpretation, provides that 'In applying the law one cannot attribute a meaning other that that is made evident by the proper meaning of the words according to their connections and by the intention of the legislator'. So, Article 12 establishes strict interpretation as the first step in the interpretation of legal norms in general, and this includes also tax norms.[22]

Article 12 of *Preleggi* embodies a definite trend within the Italian legal culture, i.e., the idea that the method of strict interpretation is the Golden Rule, the first step in the interpretive process, and it poses several constraints on the interpreter. The first constraint, introduced by Article 12 of *Preleggi*, on strict interpretation is that the interpreter of tax laws must rely on 'the proper meaning of the words'. Therefore, the interpreter must assume that such a meaning exists, even if there are doubts as to the actual meaning of those words used by the norm to be interpreted. So the first stage of tax interpretation is the analysis of the words, i.e., the literal analysis of the normative text.

The assumption of the existence of plain meaning implies a set of linguistic problems.[23] First, semantic problems must be solved, in the sense that an actual meaning must be found of each word or for fixed combination of words such as 'due process', 'ability to pay', and so on. Second, syntactic problems must be solved, in the sense that connections among words must be identified, as quite often there are

22. *See* for example Gaspare Falsitta, *Manuale di diritto tributario* (Padova: CEDAM, 2015), pp. 199-201.
23. *See* for example Alf Ross, *On Law and Justice*. Transl. by Margaret Dutton (London: Stevens & Sons, 1958), p. 103.

so-called syntactic ambiguities: for example, the connector 'or' in certain cases can be deemed to represent a disjunction, but in other cases can be deemed to represent a conjunction, and this is very relevant in tax rules that often set forth complex requirements for their application.

Another major problem in practicing strict interpretation is that tax legislation uses terms that have lay and technical meanings. In this respect, there are different situations for which guidelines have been developed by establishing semantic links. These links are of two types depending on whether the retained meaning is found within the tax system (*internal links*), or without the tax system (*external links*).

There is an internal link when the interpreted norm consists of words that acquire a 'specialized' meaning for the purpose of tax law. For example 'ability to pay' uses generic words but is not a generic concept, rather one that has been defined by the jurisprudence of the Constitutional Court. In these cases, an internal link between the interpreted norm and such a tax specialized meaning is established, so that the tax-legal meaning is retained.

By contrast, an external link occurs when the term used in the interpreted norm comes from ordinary language. In these cases, a link between the interpreted norm and the generic meaning of natural language is established, so that the current meaning of the term is adopted in tax law. For example, if the legislator refers to 'automobiles', than there is no doubt that the regular or common meaning should be used.

Another type of external link occurs when the term used by the interpreted norm comes from a technical language (such as that of accounting, finance, or technology). In these cases a link between the interpreted norm and that non-tax specialized meaning is established, so that such non-tax meaning is retained. For example, if the legislator refers a specific concept (such as EBITDA) by using a technical denomination, then such a specialized meaning should be used unless an express derogation is made (in which case the external concept acquires a tax meaning through a stipulating definition, *see* next section).

[B] Legislative Definitions and Conceptual Transplants

In many instances, the term used in the interpreted norm comes from natural or legal language but it acquires in tax law a 'specialized meaning' by operation of a stipulating definition provided by the law that is binding for the interpreter (so-called *legislative definitions*). Like semantic links, legislative definitions are of two types depending on whether the definition is found within the tax system (*internal definitions*), or without the tax system (*external definitions*).

Legislative internal definitions are widely used and create specialized frameworks for the use of terms. For example, 'permanent establishment' is not a generic or economic concept, but one that is defined by (domestic and treaty) tax law. The structure of these internal legislative definitions is often 'For the purposes of section so-and-so, the term "X" means "Y"'. As tax law is developing rapidly, there can be definitions of the same term in different areas of tax law. For example, the definition of 'business activities' is different for the purposes of income taxes and VAT (in most cases there are specialized legislative definitions). The cases in which a term is defined by explicit statutory language increased over time to make complex tax statutes more manageable for the interpreters.

The relevance of internal legislative definitions is threefold. First, they are binding, unlike academic definitions or jurisprudential definitions (in a civil law system such as that of Italy). Second, in addition to providing the meaning of a term, these definitions often also enucleate a legal concept or pre-determine a legal structure. For example, the concept of '*responsabile di imposta*' defined by tax laws is extensively meant to denote an agent or an intermediary who has a duty to report to Tax Authorities transactions carried out by third parties. Third, the binding nature of these definitions is generally retroactive, as they imply that from the very beginning a certain term or expression had a given meaning.

Legislative external definitions occur when there are definitions stipulated outside of tax law (i.e., in different areas of the Italian legal system), which is retained by tax law. Typically, there is a 'renvoi' by tax law to civil law, so that the civil law concept becomes a tax law concept through a legislative external definition. In practice, the tax legislator borrows the non-tax definition. This is often due to the fact that the non-tax concept usually predates the tax concept. For example, there is a definition of 'residence' of individuals in civil law and one in tax law, and tax law refers (with qualifications) to civil law to define tax residence. In other cases, concepts denoted by the same term in civil law and in tax law differ in their actual meaning. In these cases the tax meaning usually prevails, i.e., there is an internal legislative definition.

Another feature in the process of attributing meaning to the terms used in the interpreted norm is that the tax legislator often refers to legal concepts (rather than strict legislative definitions) that are established in other areas of the Italian legal system. For example, a tax statute may subject a certain legal act to tax, such as a 'sale', that is established by civil law. This is a 'meta-concept' that implies a transplant that occurs between two areas of the same legal system, because that contract, as defined by civil law as a 'sale' (its 'area of origin'), is then subject to tax on the basis of tax laws (its 'area of destination').

Quite often the issue is not just of attributing a meaning to a term, but it rather involves complex qualification and interpretation issues. In summary, the question is whether the interpreter: (i) is bound to keep the meaning the concept has in its 'area of origin'; or (ii) is allowed create a new meaning of the concept within tax law, i.e., the 'area of destination'. Commentators have taken opposite views: a functional approach and a formal approach.

The proponents of the functional approach essentially advocate the 'autonomy' of tax law from other areas of the legal system, and believe that interpreters can develop a specialized tax concept that differs from the concept found in other areas. According to this approach it is possible to adopt a so-called functional interpretation of tax laws, on the basis of which terms and concepts in tax law must be used and applied in their 'economic' sense.[24]

24. *See* for example Dino Jarach, 'La considerazione del contenuto economico nella interpretazione delle leggi d'imposta', (1937) *Riv. dir. fin.*, 56.

It is not exactly clear what this economic sense is, but it appears that it implies that the 'substance' of a transaction should prevail over its legal 'form'. For example if the taxable situation is a transfer of goods, tax law should essentially focus on the economic transfer (*price v. goods*), rather than on the formal legal qualification of the contract under civil law as an actual 'sale' ('*compravendita*'), as specifically regulated by the Civil Code, As a result, the formal transfer of the legal title may be irrelevant if the purchaser has acquired full economic control of the goods.[25]

By contrast, according to the formal approach it is not possible to adopt the 'functional interpretation' of tax laws, because the interpreter should stick to the proper legal meaning of terms and concepts in their 'area of origin', rather than to investigate the 'economic' nature of a legal arrangement. The consequence is that the proponents of this approach recommend that the tax treatment is entirely determined by the legal 'form' of the transaction. For example, a sale of goods (*compravendita*) occurs, and is taxable, only if there is a formal transfer of the legal title of the goods in accordance to civil law principles.

These two approaches have adopted extreme positions (one looking exclusively at substance, the other exclusively at form) but in their mainstream variations both approaches tend to converge to address a flexible view to strict tax interpretation. The functional approach advocates a non-formalistic interpretation of tax laws that carefully considers the genuine economic nature of the transactions by looking at the actual policies underlying the taxing norms. The formal approach, in turn, aims at restricting the exercise of discretionary powers by Tax Authorities by respecting the letter of the norm, rather than its substance. So while the functional approach aims at a practical application of tax rules based on the substance of legal transactions, the formal approach strives to ensure a predictable application of the law (in Italian this is generally denominated '*certezza del diritto*', i.e., certainty of law).

§10.03 DIFFERENT TYPES OF PURPOSIVE INTERPRETATION OF TAX LAWS

The mainstream position is that when strict interpretation fails, it is permissible to turn to purposive interpretation that takes into account an array of factors in addition to the literal text of the norm.[26] While there are an unlimited number of variations to purposive interpretation, examples fall into five broad schools: (i) intention-based interpretation, (ii) systemic interpretation, (iii) analogical interpretation, (iv) extensive interpretation; and (v) conforming interpretation.[27]

As mentioned *supra* at §10.01, 'purposive interpretation' is meant here also to include, in a very broad sense, certain techniques of legal construction in which agents

25. *See* for example Ezio Vanoni (1932), 'Natura ed interpretazione delle leggi tributarie', reprinted in F. Forte and C. Longobardi (eds), Ezio Vanoni, *Opere Giuridiche*, Vol. I (Milano: Giuffrè, 1961, 2002).
26. In general on purposive interpretation: Giuseppe Melis, *L'Interpretazione nel Diritto Tributario*, (Padova: Cedam, 2003), 163 et seq.
27. *See* for example Gaspare Falsitta, Manuale di diritto tributario (Padova: CEDAM, 2015), pp. 201/207.

enact implicit norms or binding principles without actually attributing the meaning to existing posited norms; this is analysed *infra* at §10.03[E] under the heading of tax construction based on implied norms and general principles. The next section, §10.04, will then look at a new breed of purposive interpretation techniques (mainly judge-made) based on the interpretive arguments of 'substance over form' in its various forms (anti-avoidance interpretation, substance over form in the application of the Italian general anti-avoidance rule (GAAR), and judicial approaches to the abuse of tax laws).

[A] Intention-Based and Systemic Interpretation

The interpretive criteria that look at the intention of the legislator are generally defined as 'subjective interpretation' and aim at identifying the purported 'intention' of the normative authority that issued the relevant norms. Subjective interpretation looks at an intentional meaning, and discounts the fact that such a legislator is a pluri-personal entity by advancing a 'conjecture' about the collective intention of such agents. The conjecture about the 'intention' of the legislator does not rely on the meaning of the 'text' but on several 'extra-textual' elements such as the *travaux preparatoires*, the policies that underlie the normative process, the political situation, and so on.

There is also a variant of the argument that actually looks at the intention of the tax 'law' in itself, i.e., at its underlying policies (what is often defined in Italy as '*ratio legis*'). In this variant the intention of the legislator boils down to the scope of the tax norms, and in some cases the interpreter selects the meaning that ensures that the purported scope of the tax norms is achieved.[28]

The other interpretive criteria that look at the systemic context should be distinguished from those that just look at the intention of the legislator, in the sense that intention-based interpretation becomes a part of a wider systemic interpretive strategy. These criteria essentially look at tax laws as a 'system', so they fully consider the 'systemic context' of tax law. The underpinning of this approach is the view of tax laws as a system that is: (i) *coherent* (in terms of values) because the norms can be referred to a set of coherent principles and values, (ii) (logically) *consistent* because there are no conflicts among tax norms, and (iii) *complete* because there are no gaps in the tax system.

Clearly tax laws do not have a natural quality of being a 'system' endowed by these three features, but the agents interpret and apply the norms to make them operate as a system. As a result, the systemic argument, when used to interpret one or more norms, also relies on a constellation of other norms and fragments of norms that are, in various degrees, connected with the norms to be interpreted. This systemic interpretation is basically carried out by putting together various norms (and their interpretation) to substantiate a coherent and systemic interpretive position. In practice the systemic interpretation requires that the norm that is interpreted should be placed

28. *See* for example: Giuseppe Melis, *L'Interpretazione nel Diritto Tributario*, (Padova: Cedam, 2003), pp. 301 et seq.

within the tax system as a whole, and particularly in the systemic web of connections between different areas of the tax system.[29]

There are two variants of this systemic argument: one based on the actual normative context (i.e., the disposition and structure of tax norms) and one based on policy arguments (i.e., the reasons that underlie tax norms). The variant of the systemic argument based on the normative context uses two sub-arguments: '*combinato disposto*' and '*terminological consistency*'. In the so-called *combinato disposto* several rules are combined to extract a single norm. For example when situation X is taxable under Norm A if requirements 1 and 2 are met, and the same situation X is taxable under Norm B if requirements 3 and 4 are met, then a norm C is extracted according to which situation X is taxable if requirements 1, 2, 3 and 4 are met. According to the argument of '*terminological consistency*', if Norm A1 has meaning X in sub-set Y of the tax systems, then same/similar Norm A2 in sub-set W of the tax systems should have the same meaning, unless there are specific reasons why the meaning should be different.

The variant of the systemic argument: based on policy arguments essentially applies principle or policy used in a sub-set Y to another sub-set W. For example, the principle of transparency of administrative action is applied in administrative-tax action as well. Scholars have also emphasized, within this policy-oriented variant of systemic interpretation, the relevance that should be given at what they call the '*rationale*' (in Italian the *ratio*, from Latin) of a certain tax. The '*rationale*' of a tax is the actual economic reason of that tax, or in other terms the underlying policy/ies that originated that tax.[30]

The canon of interpretation used in these cases is that an interpretive solution that promotes the achievement of those policy/ies should be preferred to one that conflicts with them. For example, the basic policy of VAT is to levy a tax on the economic fact constituted by the consumption of private individuals (final consumers), and therefore VAT is neutral on intermediary entities that are not final consumers. The consequence is that interpretive solutions that are in line with this neutrality principle should prevail over those that conflict with it. In this kind of analysis, the substance of the transactions as well as the 'intention' (i.e., the goal) of the law becomes relevant, so that policy oriented systemic interpretation is often hybridized with a moderate intention-based substance over form approach.

[B] Analogical Interpretation

Another cluster of purposive interpretive techniques of tax laws can be encompassed under the label of 'interpretation based on analogy' or 'analogical interpretation,' as in the Italian tax culture a significant debate revolves around the use of 'analogy' (*analogia*) in tax interpretation. The *raison d'*être of this debate is found in Article 12 of *Preleggi*, which provides that: 'if a case cannot be decided on the basis of a specific

29. Manlio Ingrosso, 'Diritto, sistema e giustizia tributaria', (1990) *Rass. trib.*, 183.
30. *Cass.*, 3 April 1990, No. 2702. On this issue *see*, for example: Maurizio Logozzo, 'Capacità contributiva ed interpretazione della legge tributaria', (1990) *Boll. trib.*, 1653.

norm, one has to look at norms that regulate similar situations or matters; if the case remains perplexed, then the decision is based on the general principles of the legal system'.

Analogical interpretation can take two forms based on slightly different techniques: '*analogia legis*' and '*analogia iuris*'. There is *analogia legis* when a case is decided on the basis of the norms that regulate similar situations or matters. The logical structure of *analogia legis* to fill a gap is the following: first, an assessment is made that situation A prima facie is not regulated; second, situation B regulated by norm X is found within the tax system; third, reasons are provided as to the fact that situation B is 'similar' to situation A; finally, norm X regulating situation B is applied to situation A, thereby filling the gap. This interpretative technique makes it possible to apply to the case at hand norms of the tax system on the basis of the similar functions of those other norms.

By contrast, there is *analogia iuris* when the case is decided on the basis of the general principles of the legal system. The logical structure of *analogia iuris* to fill a gap is the following: first, an assessment is made that situation A is prima facie not regulated; second, a principle Y regulating situations B, C, D within the tax system is found; third, reasons are provided as to the fact that situations B, C, and D are 'similar' to situation A; finally, principle Y regulating situations B, C, and D is applied to situation A, thereby filling the gap. This interpretative technique makes it possible to apply to the case at hand general principles of the legal system or of the tax system (these principles are not necessarily actual norms posited by the legislator).

Analogical interpretation is used within the tax system to fill so-called actual gaps ('*lacune tecniche*'), as opposed to 'apparent gaps' ('*lacune ideologiche*').[31] There is an actual gap when there is no norm that applies to a specific situation, while there is an apparent gap when a specific situation is 'external' to the scope of a norm. In practice, in the apparent gap case, if the norm did not include a specific situation within its scope, such a situation is not regulated (i.e., belongs to the unregulated normative space),[32] so there is no gap in the tax system.

So, there are actual gaps when situations are not regulated, and these gaps can be filled by recourse to analogical interpretation. This may occur when the tax legislator, for some reason, came short of regulating a specific situation, but there is a practical need to fill the gap. The following are examples of actual gaps of the tax system: a tax norm establishes a taxable situation such as a capital gain, but does not provide how to determine the amount of the capital gains;[33] a tax norm provides that recourse should be made to 'arm's length value', but does not provide how to determine such value; a tax norm provides that a tax return must be filed by a certain date, but does not provide the exact procedure.[34] In all these cases the interpreter can look at similar cases and matters. By contrast, there is an apparent gap when a certain situation is not explicitly regulated, and there is no need of analogical interpretation.

31. Norberto Bobbio, 'Lacune del diritto', in *Nov.mo dig. it.*, vol. IX (Torino: UTET, 1963), 423.
32. *See* for example Amedeo G. Conte, in *Digesto IV* (Discipline civilistiche) (Torino: UTET, 1988).
33. *See* for example Trib. Pen. Milano, 29 March 1999, in (1999) *Giur. it.*, 1543.
34. *Cass.*, 25 September 1996, No. 8456, in (1997) I(1) *Giur. it.*, 1055.

[C] Extensive Interpretation

There are also cases in which the interpreter has to identify the exact reach – i.e., the scope of application – of a tax norm, rather than to fill gaps in the tax system by recourse to analogical interpretation. In this respect, there are two conflicting approaches.

According to the first approach, situations that are not explicitly mentioned by Norm D but which are 'similar' to the situation that is included in norm D ('external situations') can be actually regulated by norm D if: (i) through analysis based on analogy those situations are sufficiently 'similar' to the core situations covered by norm; or (ii) the terms used in norm D can be semantically 'extended' to cover situations that prima facie are external. So, according to this approach, tax norms can be applied by using analogical or extensive interpretation to identify their scope of application.

Several arguments are used to support this approach: first, the 'principle of legality' of Article 23 of the Italian Constitution, according to which 'no obligations of a personal or a financial nature may be imposed on any person except by law', does not limit interpretive activities by agents; second, tax norms do cover a set of explicit core situations, but like other norms have an 'open texture' that is co-extensive with the use of natural language, so even situations that are not pre-defined in the text may be included in the scope of them when the text of the norm is properly interpreted.

According to the second opposite approach, a tax norm D must be interpreted on the basis of the meaning of its text using strict interpretation and situations that are not explicitly mentioned by Norm D but which are 'similar' to the situations that are included in norm D ('external situations'), are actually meant to be exempted. So in practice, according to this approach, analogical or extensive interpretation cannot be used to extend the scope of application of taxing norms.

Italian courts increasingly apply tax norms using analogical or extensive interpretation to identify their scope of application, particular in international tax matters, for example in determining where is the actual place of management and control of a company.[35]

Several arguments are used to support this position: first, the analogical or extensive application of tax norms would be prevented by the so-called principle of legality enshrined by Article 23 of the Italian Constitution;[36] second, tax norms cover so-called non-inclusive situations (*'norme a fatticpecie esclusiva'*), i.e., norms that are not based on principles but on detailed requirements;[37] third, situations beyond the scope of the norm are not evidence of an actual gap of the tax system, but rather evidence of an intent of not regulating those situations.

35. Cass. 7 February 2013, No. 2869, Comm. Trib. Regionale (Firenze) 18 gennaio 2008, No. 61; Cass. 23 February 2012, No. 7080; Cass. 30 October 2015, No. 43809 (Dolce & Gabbana case).
36. Antonio Berliri, *Principi di diritto tributario*, vol. I, (Milano: Giuffrè, 1967), 143.
37. Massimo S. Giannini, *L'interpretazione e l'integrazione delle leggi tributarie* (1941) I *Riv. Dir. Fin.*, 124.

The debate over the use of analogical or extensive interpretation of taxing norms has also spread to norms that provide exemptions and favourable treatments ('exemption norms'). According to the approach in favour of analogical or extensive interpretation, those norms may be extended beyond the scope that is revealed by using strict interpretation when it is proved that they are application of an overarching principle or policy,[38] while according to those against that type of interpretation, these exemption norms cannot be extended beyond the scope that is revealed by using strict interpretation.

[D] Conforming Interpretation

The so-called conforming interpretation ('*interpretazione adeguatrice*') is a creation of scholars and has a definite impact on the interpretive techniques of judges and administrative agencies. It requires a brief introduction concerning the concepts of '*substantial hierarchies*' and '*validity*' in the Italian tax system.

A substantial hierarchy[39] is one which occurs between two tax rules (R1 and R2) when a third validity rule establishes that the lower rule R2 is invalid if it does not meet certain validity requirements in respect to the validity rule. The two tax rules R1 and R2 are linked by a substantial hierarchy created by a third rule (the validity rule) which establishes the validity requirements (e.g., that R2 is invalid if it conflicts with R1).

Thus, a substantial hierarchy is a relation between a higher tax rule R1 and a lower tax rule R2 in which the lower rule R2 is subject to a certain *validity* requirements established by the validity rule. In these cases, one could say that the lower rule R2 is 'subject' to the higher rule R1 via the operation of the validity rule. Thus in a chain of substantial hierarchies (a chain of validity) in the Italian tax system, statutes are subject to constitutional rules, tax regulations are subject to tax statutes, decisions issued by tax agencies are subject to statutes and regulations, and so on. There are substantial hierarchies at each level of the tax system. For example, a statute may be 'subject' to another set of rules (those general rules that establish validity requirements, such as rules on equal treatment or due process of law, and so on).

Kelsen, for example, establishes the chain of validity concept on the so-called basic norm and traces back the validity of any norm to the validity of such a basic norm. He notes that an individual norm is *valid* as part of a definite legal order because it has been created in conformity with a statute; he adds 'this statute, finally, receives its *validity* from the constitution, since it has been established by the competent organ in the way the constitution prescribes. If we ask why the constitution is *valid*, perhaps we come upon an older constitution. Ultimately, we reach some constitution that is the

38. Salvatore La Rosa, 'Esenzioni ed agevolazioni tributarie', in *Enc. Giur. Treccani.*, vol. XIII (Roma: 1989), p. 423.
39. In addition to substantial hierarchies there are other types of hierarchies in the tax system, such as so-called structural hierarchies between norms enacted by different agents with normative powers, so-called logical hierarchies created by certain norms referring to other norms in various ways (such as norms abrogating other norms, legislative definitions, etc.), and 'axiological hierarchies' established by the interpreter between two or more norms through value-judgments (such as hierarchies of legal principles).

first historically and that was laid down by an individual usurper or by some kind of assembly (...). It is postulated that one ought to behave as the individual, or the individuals, who laid down the first constitution have ordained. This is the basic norm of the legal order under consideration.'[40]

Interpreters are agents operating within the Italian tax system who are bound by the constraints of the substantial hierarchies and the validity concept, with the result that a given interpreter - for example a tax administrative agency - will prioritize an interpretation of a norm that is in line with the validity constraints, i.e., the interpretive outcome that conforms with the higher tax rule, and in doing so it will develop a 'conforming interpretation', i.e., an interpretation that adapts the tax system to top-down values and principles that underlie the system itself.

For example, if a judge using different interpretive techniques comes up with several alternative possible interpretive outcomes of the same tax norm, she will select the specific interpretation that is consistent with the relevant constitutional norm. The rule of thumb here is that the interpreter must exclude the possible interpretations that conflict with the Constitution, because a statutory tax norm can be considered as unconstitutional only if there is just one available interpretation that is against the Constitution. Interpretations that are in line with the Constitution must be preserved.

The Constitutional Court safeguards this principle by not accepting cases in which the judges rely on an interpretation of the norm that is against the Constitution and ask the Constitutional Court to declare such a norm (in such an interpretation) as conflicting with the Constitution, when instead there are potential interpretations that are in line with the Constitution.[41] For example, the Constitutional Court has rejected a question that was raised in respect to Article 12(7) of the Tax Charter concerning tax audits, based on the claim that such a norm does *not* provide for the invalidity of a tax assessment that is notified irregularly. The Court stated that there was no need to discuss the constitutional validity of that norm because any assessment issued with a violation of notification procedure would be null and void anyway.[42] In another case, a judge raised an issue before the Constitutional Court claiming that a certain norm that did not allow for the suspension of collection, while such norm could in fact be interpreted as allowing such suspension, so the request was dismissed.[43]

The conforming interpretation also operates on the international plane so that three canons have been consistently developed: (i) domestic statutes should be interpreted in line with the EU Treaty; (ii) domestic statutes should be interpreted in line with tax treaties to prevent double taxation; (iii) tax treaties should be interpreted in line with the EU Treaty.[44] Conforming interpretation also percolates down in the lower echelons of the Italian tax system where two additional canons have been

40. Hans Kelsen, *General Theory of Law and State*, Transl. by Anders Wedberg (New York: Russell & Russell, 1961), 115, cited by Joseph Raz, *The Concept of a Legal System* (Oxford: Clarendon Press, 2003) at 97.
41. Corte cost., 12 March 1999, No. 84, in (1999) I(1) *Giur. It.*, 1999, 1565.
42. Corte cost., ordinance 24 July 2009, No. 244, in (2009) *Rass. trib.*, 1783; Corte cost., 10 March 2006, No. 244, in (2006) *Boll. trib.*, 637.
43. Corte cost., 17 June 2010, No. 217.
44. *Cass.*, 10 December 2002, No. 5768, in (2000) II *Riv. dir.trib.*, 2000, 312.

created: (i) tax regulations must be interpreted and applied consistently with the relevant statutory norms; (ii) when legislative powers are delegated by parliament to the executive branch of government, the norms issued by the latter must be interpreted in line with the delegating law.

[E] Tax Implied Norms and Tax Principles

As mentioned, 'purposive interpretation' includes not only the interpretive techniques discussed in the previous sections, §10.03[A] through §10.03[D], but also includes in a very broad sense, certain non-interpretive techniques of legal construction in which agents enact precepts that are *not* posited norms and that essentially take two forms: (i) binding '*principles*'; or (ii) '*implicit norms*'.

While tax norms are rules posed in a conditional form (such as If F, then G) and often are subject to multiple detailed requirements arranged in a complex structure [such as If F, and (F2 or F3) but not F4, then G], *tax principles* are rules that are *not* posed in a conditional form, but which rather: (i) have a 'foundational' nature; and (ii) are indeterminate in their scope. The 'foundational nature' of a tax principle is created by agents by developing an array of non-interpretative value-based arguments according to which, for example, tax neutrality, or ability to pay, or horizontal equity, or tax transparency, and so on, are the basis for the coherent application of other posited norms in terms of values.

The 'indeterminacy' of tax principles can take three forms. First, the scope of principles is not subject to requirements enumerated *ex ante* (e.g., 'tax neutrality should always be attained').[45] Second, principles are defeasible, in the sense that the list of derogations is open-ended (e.g., 'tax neutrality should always be attained, except in important circumstances').[46] Third, principles are vague, either because they are non-self-executing in so far as they require other norms to be applied, or because they express policies that can be applied in different / alternative ways (again the principle of tax neutrality is a good tax example of this aspect of principles).[47]

An *implicit tax norm* is a norm that is *not* the result of interpretation of a written normative text, rather it is enacted by an agent who relies on non-interpretive techniques, such as valid logical deduction, reasoning arguments which are not derived from logic (such as analogies and other persuasive or policy/political arguments), doctrinal assumptions, and so on. An implicit tax norm can also take the form of an implicit principle when it is derived from one or more other norms and principles. In practice implicit tax norms and principles cannot be found in a written text to be interpreted, but can be extracted by agents through legal construction techniques.

For decades legal positivism has prevailed in the Italian tax culture, and this led to a model in which the tax system included just 'posited norms', rather than tax

45. In contrast, requirements are determined *ex ante* for explicit tax norms.
46. Again, in contrast, explicit tax norms are not defeasible, in the sense that the list of derogations is limited and detailed.
47. Explicit tax norms, instead, are precise, either because they are not self-executing, or because there are no different or alternative modes of application.

principles and implicit tax norms. The general idea was that norms formulated and duly enacted belong to the tax system as a set of posited norms, while principles simply constitute policies that were beyond the boundaries of the tax system. The consequence was that principles and implicit norms could be used to understand the political and practical underpinning of tax norms but not to regulate conduct directly.

In the last few years however, tax principles and implicit tax norms have been integrated within the Italian tax system, and this is due to several factors: first, even the prevailing legal positivism has accepted the idea that policies and principles have a binding effect because they are a special type of norms; second, EU law very often uses principles and policies either in the Treaties establishing the EU or in the Directives and Regulations that are binding for the Member States, with the result that those principles and policies have become part of the Italian tax system; finally in many cases the Italian legislator enacts explicit norms that have the structure of principles and policies, rather than that of detailed rules of conduct.[48]

Quite often perplexed cases are now solved by recourse to principles. For example, tax procedures are regulated by Law No. 241 of 7 August 1990 that established general principles for all kinds of administrative procedures. These principles include the right that a dispute be decided by a judge, the right of the taxpayer to be heard, due process of law, the proportionality principle, and so on. Moreover the Charter of Taxpayers establishes an extended set of principles that protect the taxpayers vis-à-vis administrative and Tax Authorities. Case law has clarified that these principles constitute the ratification by the legislator of already existing constitutional principles.[49] The result is that not only the principles established by the Tax Charter are directly binding, but also that they can be used in interpreting and applying other norms.

Other principles have become of paramount importance in the interpretive process, and this is mainly due to the impact of scholarly ideas on best practices. For example general principles accepted in civil law to regulate economic obligations – such as the so-called *principio di buona fede* (principle of good faith),[50] and the right to be reimbursed – are generally applied in tax law. Other principles have been endogenously developed by tax law: for example if the taxpayer complies with guidelines provided by the Tax Authorities, such guidelines cannot be changed retroactively (so-called *tutela dell' affidamento*[51]), or domestic double juridical taxation is prohibited.[52]

48. *See* these examples of judicially-created principles: *Cass.*, Sezione V Civile, Sentenza, 18 January 2012, No. 634; *Cass.*, Sezione V Civile, Sentenza, 18 July 2013, No. 17673; *Cass.*, Sezione V Civile, Sentenza, 27 June 2011, No. 14071; *Cass.*, Sezione V Civile, Sentenza, 6 October 2011, No. 20450.
49. On the use of principles established by the Tax Charter in interpretation of tax laws *see* for example: *Cass.*, 10 December 2002, No. 17576, in (2003) I(1) *Giur. It.*, 2194; *Cass.*, 31 January 2011, No. 2221.
50. Francesco Benatti, 'Principio di buona fede ed obbligazione tributaria', (1986) 12 *Boll. trib.*, 94.
51. Eugenio Della Valle, 'Revirement ministeriale e buona fede nell'esercizio della funzione impositiva', (1995) I *Riv. dir.trib.*, 587.
52. Enrico Marello, 'Il divieto di doppia imposizione come principio generale del sistema tributario', (1997) 6 *Giur. cost.*, 4127.

§10.04 THE USE OF PURPOSIVE INTERPRETATION TO ADDRESS TAX AVOIDANCE

Like other countries, the Italian tax system adopts a tri-partite approach to the qualification of aggressive taxpayers' conduct: '*tax saving*' (or '*tax mitigation*'), '*tax avoidance*', and '*tax evasion*'. While conducts that lead to tax evasion are described in detail by the rules providing for administrative and criminal sanctions, the distinction between legitimate tax saving and tax avoidance is often blurred and, therefore, interpretive techniques and a quite pro-active judicial approach began in the last few years to operate interstitially among statutory definitions.

One can therefore distinguish three subsequent stages to the definitional problem of tax avoidance: the development of basic anti-avoidance interpretative techniques (*see infra* §10.04[A]), the evolution of interpretive arguments based on 'substance over form' in the application of the Italian GAAR (*see infra* §10.04[B]), and finally the emergence of judicial approaches to the so-called *abuse of tax laws* (*see infra* §10.04[C]). Only the first two stages directly involved interpretive techniques, while the third stage led to the establishment of a kind of ethical clause applied by judges.

[A] Basic Anti-avoidance Interpretation

Tax avoidance can be perpetrated through the actual bypassing by the taxpayer of a tax norm, which thus becomes the 'avoided norm'. Interpretive techniques of a purposive nature thus have been traditionally used in Italy to counteract tax avoidance, essentially by advocating that the 'avoided norm' has a wider scope than that envisaged by the taxpayer. This goal is achieved by relying on a purposive interpretation that specifically relies on both textual and extra-textual elements to broaden the scope of the 'avoided norm'.

When purposive interpretation relies on textual elements, it adopts a broad meaning of the terms used by the interpreted norm (the 'avoided norm'), for example if the norm establishes a list of taxable situations, each of them is semantically extended, so that the transaction carried out by the taxpayer is 'attracted' within the scope of the norm.

When anti-avoidance interpretation relies on extra-textual elements, it uses all sorts of substance over form approaches to advocate a more pervasive scope of the interpreted norm (the 'avoided norm'). For example, the norm is deemed to include also all transactions that are functionally similar to those explicitly covered by the avoided norm, so that the transaction carried out by the taxpayer is 'attracted' within the scope of the norm. Furthermore, according to the so-called functional interpretation (*see supra* §10.02[B]), the scope of the avoided norm can be found by looking at the 'economic' sense of the terms used by that norm.

The anti-avoidance interpretation can be used when the taxpayer carries out transactions that are not explicitly mentioned in the text embodying the norm (the 'avoided norm'), but that may be deemed to be included in that norm when recourse is made to the substance of the transaction. As a result interpretation has become a bone of contention when it is employed to deal with tax avoidance. There are two camps: the *legalistic approach* and *the substantive approach*.

The proponents of the legalistic approach claim that tax avoidance cannot be targeted by interpretive techniques because tax laws must be known *ex ante* and 'certain' and invoke the use of special anti-avoidance rules, while the proponents of the substantive approach believe that there is a trade-off between the value of '*ex ante* certainty' and a careful examination of the actual nature of an underlying transaction. It should be noted that the substantive approach is predominating because it forms part of the purposive interpretation methodology used by Tax Authorities and judges, along with a consideration of the intention of the legislator and the systemic context.

In conclusion, in respect to tax avoidance the legalistic approach and the substantive approach are both based on opposed legal values that are privileged by the interpreter, a kind of 'legal ideology', rather than on a norm imposed by the legislator, but in the current paradigm shift toward purposive interpretation, the traditional legalistic approach is now being predominated by the substantive approach.

[B] The Interpretive Argument Based on Substance over Form Established by the Italian GAAR

In many cases it has proved impossible to address tax avoidance by relying only on the kind of purposive interpretation described in the previous section. An example is when a transaction that actually perpetrates tax avoidance is remote from the scope of the avoided norm. Under the legalistic approach initially adopted in Italy, the strict interpretive techniques basically allowed all sorts of tax minimization strategies in so far as these respected the letter of the law. In a process of legal transplant,[53] however, Italy introduced in 1997 a sort of precursor of a standard GAAR (Article 37-*bis*, decree 600 of 1973, 'Article 37-*bis*').[54]

Article 37-*bis* had a complex structure which can be summarized as follows:

> a) Article 37-bis (1) stated the basic requirements of tax avoidance by providing that: 'Tax Authorities have the power to disregard for tax purposes acts, facts and legal arrangements, also in their functional connection, lacking a valid business purpose, aimed at by-passing rights and duties provided for by tax rules, and at obtaining tax reductions or tax reimbursements which would not be legally available';
>
> b) Article 37-bis (2) provided that 'Tax Authorities have the power to disallow tax benefits achieved through the acts, facts and legal arrangements mentioned at (1), by applying taxes in accordance with the tax rules which were thereby avoided';

53. On this process *see* for example: Carlo Garbarino, 'Comparative Taxation and Legal Theory: The Tax Design Case of the Transplant of General Anti-Avoidance Rules', (2010) 11(2) *Theoretical Inquiries in the L.* 764–790.
54. On the previous tax avoidance clause, *see*: Franco Paparella, 'Riflessioni in margine all'art. 10 della Legge 1990, No. 408, relativo alla ristrutturazione delle imprese', (1995) 6 *Dir. prat. trib.*, 1835.

c) Article 37-bis (3) provided that Article 37-bis (1) and (2) are applied upon the condition that, within the taxpayer's behaviour, one or more transactions expressly listed by same (3) are carried out;

d) Article 37-bis (4) – (8) provide procedural rules for assessments based on Article 37-bis.Article 37-bis constituted a sort of precursor to a standard GAAR, albeit a GAAR subject to an important limitation. While the broad definition of avoidance provided by § 1 of Art. 37-*bis* could potentially constitute a general anti-avoidance rule, § 3 of Art. 37-*bis* limits its application to the transactions explicitly listed in § 3. The restrictions reflect the traditional resistance of legislators to the adoption of a general statutory anti-avoidance clause. The application of the rule was limited by § 3 to specific transactions: corporate transformations; mergers, de-mergers; liquidations, contributions of assets in exchange for shares; transfers of business; transfers of receivables; and any transactions involving shares, quotas, notes and other securities.

In short, according to Article 37-*bis*, Tax Authorities have the power to disregard for tax purposes a broad range of transactions, provided that these transactions meet the requirements contemplated by same Article 37-*bis*. An interpretive argument has thus been established that takes the form of a multi-pronged test. When this argument is deployed, invoking Article 37-*bis*, tax avoidance is detected when the following requirements are met: (1) '*tax saving*'; (2) lack of '*valid business purpose*'; (3) existence of a '*purposive scheme*' aimed at '*by-passing of rights and duties*', or (4) existence of a '*purposive scheme*' aimed at '*obtaining tax reductions*'. These requirements are analysed in more detail below.

'*Tax saving*' is the mere reduction, either directly or indirectly, of the tax burden that would have arisen in a benchmark comparable situation in which the transactions being considered where not perpetrated. It is noted that the occurrence of a tax saving by itself does not constitute tax avoidance.

Whether a '*valid business purpose*' for a certain transaction exists is determined on the basis of a substantive analysis of the business and financial strategies of a firm.[55] With reference to the assessment of the valid business purpose, there are basically two interpretive arguments. In the *first argument*, if the tax saving is the only reason underlying a transaction, then it has no valid business purpose; these kind of transactions are '*tax-driven*' and imply tax avoidance. In the *second argument*, if the transaction has both a valid business purpose and a tax reason, then one has to assess the prevailing nature of the tax reason versus the business reason. For example, in structured finance transactions it is usually required that the transaction be '*pre-tax positive*'; i.e., that the gain of the transaction is not exclusively deriving from tax savings.[56]

The existence of a '*purposive scheme*' aimed at '*by-passing of rights and duties*' is the typical situation in which the taxpayer arranges his course of affairs in such a way to unduly avoid or prevent the application of the normal taxing rules (the '*tax duty*' or

55. *See* for example: Enrico Potito, 'Le "valide ragioni economiche" di cui all'art. 37 – bis del D.p.r. No. 600/1973: considerazioni di un economista d'azienda', (1999) 1 *Rassegna tributaria*, 63, and *Cass.*, case No. 1465, 21 January 2009.
56. Such an approach has however been criticized; *see* for example: Giuseppe Zizzo, *Ragioni economiche e scopi fiscali nella clausola antielusione*, (2008) 1 *Rassegna tributaria*, 170.

'*obligation*') provided for the normal course of action. The Government Report on Article 37-*bis* clarified that '*by-passing*' of tax rights *does not occur* when the taxpayer makes an election *which is expressly provided for by tax rules* among two alternative courses of action equally available, thereby achieving a tax reduction.[57] In such cases, the taxpayer has a right to choose among alternative tax treatments that are considered by the tax system as equally available and legally obtainable. This occurs, for example, when a tax relief is obtained as a result of an election or of the meeting of certain requirements.

The existence of a '*purposive scheme*' aimed at '*obtaining tax reductions*' is a situation in which the taxpayer arranges his course of affairs in such a way that any kind of tax benefit is obtained (the '*tax reductions*') which would not be available under the normal course of action.

Moreover there is a '*purposive scheme*' when the transaction conflicts with: (i) general principles of tax law; (ii) specific principles of a certain area of tax law; (iii) the function of tax rules; or (iv) the natural entitlement of tax positions. For example, a taxpayer may violate: (i) the general principles of tax law according to which one should not allocate income to other parties; or (ii) specific principles of a certain area of tax law such as the rule that if capital gains on participations are exempt, capital losses are not deductible; (iii) the function of tax rules, such as the function of jurisdictional links for taxing income sourced in Italy; or (iv) the natural entitlement of tax positions by allocating portions of income to related parties.

The Government Report on Article 37-*bis* clarified that a transaction is a purposive scheme when the taxpayer combines various arrangements, which per se are legitimate, in order to obtain a final result – a tax saving – which is *not* legitimate because it conflicts with tax principles, etc. (so-called *combination method*).

In conclusion, purposive scheme analysis becomes the final phase of a complex approach based on '*substance over form*', and this is the distinguishing feature of an interpretive argument whose essential structure is dictated by Article 37-*bis*. The interpreter retains broad discretionary power, which are, however, limited by the structure of the GAAR.

[C] Judicial Approaches to the Abuse of Tax Laws Leading to a GAAR

In a recent series of decisions the *Cassazione* introduced a new judicial anti-abuse principle, which operates beyond the scope of the Italian GAAR. According to this principle, transactions that have the exclusive goal of obtaining a tax benefit are deemed to constitute tax abuse. Therefore, the tax effects of such transactions can be disregarded by the Tax Authorities without the need to meet all the requirements set out by Article 37-*bis*.[58]

57. Circular. 19 December 1997, No. 320/E-III-6-1375, http://home.ilfisco.it/perl/fol.pl?cmd-doc=rimsel-prassi-004259-14938583-8c98fd1f124a08d78be0790cba1d9944-t-45329.
58. *See* for example *Cass.*, 4 April 2008, No. 8772; *Cass.*, 23 December 2008, Nos 30055, 30056 and 30057; *Cass.*, 21 January 2009, No. 1465.

In virtually all the cases, the arguments used by the *Cassazione* are based on a common structure which can be summarized as follows. There is no doubt that the taxpayer can freely choose to carry out his activities in the most effective way to reduce the tax burden, as the freedom to conduct private economic activities is expressly protected by Article 41 of the Italian Constitution. The limit to the exercise of such a freedom, which amounts to a legitimate 'use' of tax laws, is the inappropriate use of legal arrangements which amount to an abuse of law ('*abuso della forma giuridica*'). Such an abuse results from the selection of a particular legal arrangement whose exclusive goal is to obtain a tax reduction and, therefore, is an abuse of a fundamental right (the freedom to conduct private economic activities) provided for by the domestic legal system and community law.[59]

The judicial anti-abuse principle has been introduced in a system already endowed with a GAAR and innumerable specific anti-avoidance rules. The introduction of such a judge-made anti-abuse principle amounts to a significant departure from usual practice and blurs the distinction between avoidance and abuse.[60] This approach has been criticized and scholars argued that the discretionary powers granted to tax agencies and tax courts by the anti-abuse principle undermine the basic principle that tax laws be certain in their purpose and meaning in order to prevent a discretionary use of administrative powers by tax offices.[61]

The cases on the anti-abuse principle have been delivered by the *Cassazione* both in its appellate and in its nomophylactic function[62] and, therefore, their impact is particularly relevant.[63] In other cases the *Cassazione* has requested a decision from the Court of Justice of the European Union (ECJ) under the preliminary ruling procedure and thus seceded to the ECJ the decision on specific issues.[64]

In a series of cases decided in 2005, the *Cassazione* held that a contract used by the taxpayer to obtain an 'unlawful' reduction of taxes could be declared void and that the tax benefits resulting from such a contract could be disregarded. The judicial anti-abuse doctrine was developed further in 2008, when it was extended to cases in which the transaction amounted to an abuse of tax law rather than simply a violation of tax laws via the use of contractual arrangements. It is worth noting that while initially it was held that it was upon the taxpayer to prove that his behaviour was not of an abusive nature,[65] in the most recent cases it has been held that it is upon the Tax Authorities to prove that behaviour was abusive.[66]

59. *See* for example: *Cass.*, 4 April 2008, No. 8772.
60. Antonio Lovisolo, 'Abuso del diritto e clausola generale antielusiva alla ricerca di un principio', (2009) I *Riv. dir. trib.*, 89.
61. Gianni Marongiu, 'Abuso del diritto o abuso del potere?', (2009) 13 *Corr. trib.*, 1077.
62. The 'nomophylactic function', means that a special session ('*sessioni riunite*') has the function of dealing with conflicting decisions given by different chambers of the same *Cassazione*. In the exercise of this function, the court develops a unitary and coherent principle, which is particularly important in shaping tax law in action.
63. *Cass.*, ordinances No. 12301 and No. 12302, 24 May 2006 (direct taxes) remitting the case to *Cassazione* in special session, leading to *Cass.*, 23 December 2008, Nos 30055, 30056 and 30057.
64. *Cass.*, ordinance, 4 October 2006, No. 21371, remitting the case to ECJ, leading to C-425-06 (*Part Service*) case, February 21, 2008; ordinance, 21 December 2007, No. 26996.
65. *Cass.*, 21 April 2008, No. 10257.
66. *Cass.*, 17 October 2008, No. 25374.

In the cases involving the abuse of tax law, the *Cassazione* has expressly acknowledged that a principle of law was being created. After an initial reliance on EU law (*see* note 52), the *Cassazione* at the end of 2008[67] held that the anti-abuse principle is derived directly from the principle of ability to pay enshrined in Article 53 of the Italian Constitution.[68] According to the *Cassazione,* Article 53 of the Italian Constitution is the basic norm (or principle) from which all the statutory norms of the tax system are derived, including those attributing benefits to the taxpayers. As a consequence, taxpayers who gain a benefit from a misuse or abuse of tax legislation violate the ability to pay principle.[69]

Italian tax law implicitly acknowledged the principle rooted in EC law and in the ECJ concept of abuse of law that taxpayers cannot benefit from tax savings if they enter into transactions exclusively to achieve those tax savings.[70] The Supreme Court emphasized the significance of the introduction of such a GAAR for all fields of taxation.

The Supreme Court applied the ECJ's abuse of tax law rule not just in the field of EU-harmonized taxes, but also in relation to non-EU-harmonized taxes, on the basis of the argument that, according to the previous ECJ case-law, although direct taxation is a prerogative of the Member States, they shall nevertheless exercise it consistently with the fundamental principles of EC law.[71] As a consequence, a case law-based general anti-abuse rule was developed, in spite of the aversion of the Italian legislature towards the introduction of such a provision, as discussed above.

The Supreme Court has clarified the concept of abuse of law, stating that it presupposes *'manipulation'* and *'alteration'* of *'typical negotiated agreements'* through *'an unreasonable conduct under normal market conditions'* pursued *'only to achieve such tax result.'*[72] The evidential burden to show these conditions were present rests with the Tax Administration, *'while the taxpayer bears the burden to allege the existence of alternative or concurring economic reasons that may justify transactions to be structured in that way'*.[73]

67. *Cass.*, 23 December 2008, Nos 30055, 30056 and 30057.
68. Article 53 provides that 'all taxpayers must contribute to public expenditures in accordance with their ability to pay'.
69. *See also* in general: Gaspare Falsitta, 'L'interpretazione antielusiva della norma tributaria come clausola generale immanente al sistema e direttamente ricavabile dai principi costituzionali', (2009) *Corriere Giuridico,* 296; Raffaello Lupi and Dario Stevanato, 'Tecniche interpretative e pretesa immanenza di una norma generale antielusiva', (2009) 6 *Corr. trib.*, 403.
70. *See Cass.*, 5 May 2006, No. 10353; 29 September 2006, No. 21221: 13 October 2006, No. 22023; 4 May 2007, No. 10273. For comments on decision 29 September 2006, No. 21221, *see* S. Gianoncelli, 'Contrasto all'elusione fiscale in materia di imposte sui redditi e divieto comunitario di abuso del diritt'o, in *Giurisprudenza Italiana* (2008), 1297 et seq.
71. *See Cass.*, 4 April 2008 No. 8772 and 17 October 2008, No. 25374. *See also* Caterina Innamorato, 'An Unwritten Anti-abuse Principle in the Italian Tax System, European Taxation' 8 (2008), 449 et seq.; Francesco Pedrotti, Il principio giurisprudenziale comunitario di abuso del diritto come strumento di contrasto alle operazioni elusive domestiche: il caso del cd. Dividend stripping (o usufrutto azionario), in *Diritto e Pratica Tributaria Internazionale* 2 (2008), 1010 et seq.
72. Cass., 30 November 2012, No. 21390.
73. *Supra.*

The *Cassazione* further developed the concept of abuse of law in later decisions.[74]

To sum up, the Italian tax system was characterized by the simultaneous and ambiguous existence of two rules. On the one hand, a specific anti-avoidance rule contained in Article 37-*bis* sets forth cases of transactions that could be disregarded by the Tax Administration subject to Tax Administration ensuring the taxpayer had the right to be heard before the issuance of the assessment. On the other hand, a general principle of prohibition of abuse of tax legislation was created by the Supreme Court, but its distinguishing features, scope, and procedural safeguards were largely undefined with the result of often fragmented and uncoordinated action of local tax offices and lower tax courts.

This situation led the Italian Parliament to empower the Government to proceed to a review of the current anti-avoidance rules (Law No. 23/2014) with a view to unifying them in a codified general anti-abuse clause. According to the Parliamentary guidelines contained in Law No. 23/2014, any abusive conduct had to be defined as '*misuse of legal instruments suitable to achieving tax savings, even if such conduct is not in conflict with any specific rule*'. However, the Parliament's guidelines highlighted that taxpayers have a right to choose between two or more possible transactions which have the same commercial result but which produce different taxable amounts.

More specifically, according to the Parliament's guidelines, the future anti-abuse clause was to be based in the following principles: (a) for a transaction to be characterized as an abuse of tax laws, the purpose of obtaining a tax benefit should its prevailing reason; (b) there can be no abuse when one or more transactions are dictated by 'non-marginal non-tax reasons' (i.e., important business reasons).

With the recent enactment of Article 10-*bis* of the Delegated Decree No. 128/2015 ('*Provisions on legal certainty in relations between tax authorities and taxpayers*'), and the simultaneous repeal of Article 37-*bis*, the Italian Government has finally codified the rules on the so-called abuse of tax law and made it clear that the legislative concept of 'avoidance' and the judicial concept of 'abuse of law' have in fact the same meaning.

Article 10-*bis* of Delegated Decree No. 128/2015 is titled '*Abuse of law or anti-avoidance rules*' and largely inspired by the European Union recommendations. This new legislative concept of 'abuse of law or anti-avoidance' includes the features of transactions which can be disregarded by Tax Authorities following a mandatory procedure to be initiated by them aimed at granting the taxpayers' right to be heard before the issuance of an assessment.

The general concept of 'abuse of law or anti-avoidance' is set forth by § 1 of Article 10-*bis*, according to which 'one or more transactions devoid of any economic substance shall constitute abuse of law if, despite the formal observance of the tax rules, they essentially achieve undue tax benefits'. The term 'essentially' according to the initial interpretations means that the undue benefits need to be essential to the purpose of the transaction for the transaction to be abusive. In general, transactions can be classified as abusive if there is: (i) the lack of economic substance; (ii) the

74. *See* for example: *Cass.*, 27 February 2013, No. 4901; *Cass.*, 26 February 2014, No. 4604; *Cass.*, 25 November 2015, No. 24024; *Cass.*, 17 June 2016, No. 12548.

achievement of undue tax benefits; as well as (iii) the fact that the undue benefits are essential to the purpose of the transaction.

In addition to the general anti-abuse clause, Delegated Decree No. 128/2015 introduced a cooperative compliance programme. Such measure is in line with the OECD recommendations[75] and other jurisdictions' best practices[76] for the development of a renewed relationship between corporate taxpayers and Tax Authorities aimed at preventing tax avoidance at source.[77]

In continental law, principles are not just generic statements or policy guidelines, but are binding in respect to Tax Authorities and taxpayers as well. Thus the anti-abuse principle is binding, as it amounts to a general ethical clause aimed at identifying an abuse of tax law.[78] In summary, anti-abuse decisions rely on a tautological definition of abuse according to which the 'abuse' is the 'distorted' (as opposed to the un-distorted) use of tax laws. In spite of the fact that Italy does not have a common law system, the *ratio decidendi* of previous cases (basically the tautological definition of tax abuse) have been constantly followed in the last six years by other judges in subsequent cases. The most essential feature of such a clause is that it constitutes a kind of 'empty box'

---

75. OCSE, *Co-operative Compliance: A Framework. From Enhanced Relationship to Cooperative Compliance*, (2013) available at http://www.oecd-ilibrary.org/docserver/download/2313201e.pdf?expires=1414514965&id=id&accname=ocid177380&checksum=FCAB5DDBA80770F31CAD3655AFDBE1FC; OCSE, *Study into the Role of Tax Intermediaries*, (2008) available at http://www.oecd.org/tax/administration/39882938.pdf. *See also* Jeffrey Owens, The 'Enhanced Relationship': A Challenge for Revenue Bodies and Taxpayers, *European Taxation*, July 2008, p. 351.
76. In particular, Australia, the Netherlands, UK and the US have been the leading jurisdictions in developing cooperative compliance programmes. For the Australian programme, please *see* Australian Taxation Office for the Commonwealth of Australia, *Large business and tax compliance* (2014), available at https://www.ato.gov.au/uploadedFiles/Content/LB_I/downloads/BUSINESS16985LargebusinessandtaxCompliance.pdf; For the Dutch programme, please *see* The Netherlands Tax and Customs Administration, *Horizontal Monitoring within the medium to very large businesses segment*, 30 November 2010, pp. 7–8, reperibile alla pagina http://download.belastingdienst.nl/belastingdienst/docs/horizontal_monitoring_very_large_businesses_dv4061z1pleng.pdf; The Netherlands Tax and Customs Administration, Supervision Large Business in the Netherlands, (2013) available at http://download.belastingdienst.nl/belastingdienst/docs/supervision_large_business_in_netherlands_dv4231z1fdeng.pdf; The Netherlands Tax and Customs Administration, Guide to Horizontal Monitoring within the SME segment, (2012), available at http://download.belastingdienst.nl/belastingdienst/docs/guide_horiz_monit_dv4071z1pleng.pdf.; Committee Horizontal Monitoring Tax and Custom Administration, *Tax supervision - Made to measure. Flexible when possible, strict when necessary* (2012), reperibile alla pagina https://www.ifa.nl/Document/Publicaties/Enhanced%20Relationship%20Project/tax_supervision_made_to_measure_tz0151z1fdeng.pdf.; For the UK programme, please *see* HM Reenue & Customs, *The framework for a better relationship*, (2008), reperibile alla pagina www.hmrc.gov.uk/budget2008/supplementary.htm. For the US programme, please *see* Internal Revenue Service, *Internal Revenue Manual - 4.51.8 Compliance Assurance Process (CAP) Examinations*, reperibile alla pagina http://www.irs.gov/Businesses/Corporations/Compliance-Assurance-Process.
77. John Braithwaite, *Large Businesses and the Compliance Model*, in Valerie Braithwaite, *Taxing Democracy: Understanding Tax Avoidance and Evasion* (Burlington, VT: Ashgate, 2003), p. 177; Valerie Braithwaite, 'Responsive Regulation and Taxation', 29 *L. & Policy* 3 (2007); Kristina Murphy, 'Moving Towards a More Effective Model of Regulatory Enforcement in the Australian Tax Office', *British Tax Rev.* 603 (2004).
78. John Prebble & Zoë Prebble, 'Comparing the General Anti-avoidance Rule of Income Tax Law with the Civil Law Doctrine of Abuse of Law', (2008) 4 *Eur. Taxn*, 151.

in which, on a case-by-case basis, Tax Authorities and tax courts can include the most diverse transactions when they deem that these trespass the boundaries of the 'normal' (i.e., non-abusive) use of tax laws.

The anti-abuse principle has an 'open texture'[79] as it takes the form of a broad implicit norm that is applicable to a potentially unlimited range of situations. The consequence is that when an agent invokes the tax anti-abuse principle, she does not employ an interpretive technique aimed at finding the meaning of a norm like the anti-avoidance interpretation based on a multi-pronged test used to apply Article 37-*bis*, she enacts a singular ethical anti-abuse norm that is binding.

§10.05 INTERPRETIVE TAX NORMS AND GUIDELINES

[A] The Conundrum of Statutory Interpretive Norms

An interesting feature of the use of interpretive techniques in the Italian tax tradition is that the legislator often enacts norms - other than legislative definitions stipulating specialized tax meaning (*see supra* §10.02[B]) - that propound an interpretation of other norms. These are meta-norms (i.e., norms regulating norms), in which an 'interpretive norm' addresses an 'interpreted norm', and have a binding nature as to the actual interpretive outcome to be attributed by agents to the interpreted norm.

There are essentially two situations in which interpretive norms are enacted. In the first situation there are genuine interpretive norms, while in the second situation there are apparent interpretive norms. In the first situation (*genuine interpretive norms*) there are actual doubts as to the interpretation of a given norm, either due to poor drafting, or to opposing judicial views, or to a clash of the positions of judges and Tax Authorities, so that the legislator steps in with a preferred interpretation. This interpretation must be therefore preferred by the agents in applying the interpreted norm over other possible interpretations.

The outcome of genuine interpretive norms is threefold: (i) Tax Authorities will enforce the interpreted norm on the basis of the interpretive norms; (ii) judges will not be free to select among competing interpretations; and (iii) taxpayers will be able to rely on the interpreted norm.

Genuine interpretive norms have two distinguishing features. The first feature is that they do *not* abrogate the previous (interpreted) norm, with the result that in the tax system the old norm (interpreted norm) is maintained, and a new norm (the interpretive norm) is introduced, and thus the two norms co-exist.[80] The second feature is that genuine interpretive norms are retroactive (they do not provide for the future) as their goal is to establish the meaning of a previously enacted norm.[81]

The other situation (*apparent interpretive norms*) is that in which the legislator decides to issue a norm to trump judicial or administrative interpretations that conflict

79. This concept of 'open texture' or 'penumbra' has been coined by Herbert L.A. Hart, *The Concept of Law*, 2nd edition, (Oxford: Clarendon Press, 1961).
80. Corte cost., 4 April 1990, No. 155, in (1990) *Giur. cost.*, 952.
81. Corte cost., 25 July 1995, No. 376, in (1997) I *Foro. it.*, 346.

with the policies of the norms that were issued. For example, an interpretative statute provides that, *for the future*, a norm must be interpreted in a certain way. These norms abrogate the previous norms. It is not easy to identify apparent interpretive norms, but essentially they are innovative – abrogative norms which regulate anew the interests that are at stake in relation to a previous norm.[82] In certain cases the legislator explicitly abrogates the old norm and then enacts a new norm with embedded the new binding interpretation.

So apparent interpretive norms are in fact abrogating norms and, differently from genuine interpretive norms (which are always retroactive), they can either regulate situations that occur *after* their adoption, or regulate for situations arising in the future but that occurred *before* their adoption.

The typical situation when apparent interpretive norms are enacted is when the legislator decides to replace the existing text of a norm with a clearer and more complete new text: in this case the new norm regulates situations that occur *after* its enactment. Another case is when the legislator decides to replace the existing text of a norm with a clearer and more complete new text that is deemed to apply *ex tunc*: in this case the new norm regulates situations that occur *before* its enactment. In both cases these norms technically are *not* interpretive norms, but rather innovative-abrogating norms.

The problem is that agents and practitioners often consider these apparent interpretive norms (which are *not* retroactive norms) as genuine interpretive norms (which are retroactive), so that even in the case of innovative norms an issue is raised about whether the (alleged) interpretation operates retroactively. So, there are endless debates between two opposing positions. According to the first position, if the legislator has changed the norm, then it is impossible that the new interpretation of that norm be retroactive. By contrast, according to the second position, the fact that the legislator has changed the norm is clear evidence that its intention was that the new interpretation of that norm be fully retroactive.

The Tax Charter has tried to solve these problems and at Article 1 provides that 'interpretive norms can be enacted only in exceptional circumstances through a statute and explicitly defining the norms as introducing authentic interpretation'. The term 'authentic interpretation' is a term of art in Italian legal discourse, and it means an interpretation which is formally issued by the authority that enacted the interpreted norm and which is, therefore, evidence of the actual intention of the legislator (*see supra* §10.03[A]). Article 1 thus covers genuine retroactive interpretive norms and of course recognizes their existence within the legal system, but also limits the use of apparent interpretive norms. And yet the practice of apparent interpretive norms is pervasive because the legislator has an interest in qualifying as 'interpretive' a norm that in actuality is an innovative norm, so that the qualification of the norm is simply an obfuscation of its innovative nature.

The Constitutional Court has rarely addressed the improper use of apparent interpretive norms and basically allows the use of alleged 'authentic interpretation' as

82. Corte cost., 28 December 1990, No. 244, in (1990) *Giur. cost.*, 3284.

a means to change statutory tax law.[83] The Court has specifically noted that apparent interpretive norms do not impinge on the legitimate exercise of adjudicative jurisdiction by courts because the activity of the legislator – a substantive change of the interest at stake – is ontologically different from the activity of judges – the application of a general norm to a specific situation.[84]

The result is that apparent interpretive norms trump established judicial trends. For example courts have generally held that income from illegal activities cannot be taxed and the legislator has introduced a retroactive norm that explicitly taxes income from illegal activities, with the result that courts have adapted to this new binding principle.[85]

One important limit to interpretive norms is a general doctrine elaborated by the Constitutional Court, according to which these norms – including apparent interpretive norms – are unconstitutional if: (i) subject to current taxation an ability to pay that was manifested by the taxpayer in the past and which is not continuing in the present ('reasonableness test'); or (ii) conflict with other constitutionally protected rights of the taxpayers, such has the expectation that a norm on which taxpayers have genuinely relied in organizing their activities is not subsequently changed (this right is defined '*tutela dell'affidamento*'). The first test is based on the concept of 'ability to pay' enshrined in Article 53 of the Constitution, while the second is based on Article 10 of the Tax Charter. The Constitutional Court has also established another limit to interpretive norms, as it established that those norms are unconstitutional when specifically aimed at modifying the outcome of specific pending litigation.

[B] Non-statutory Interpretive Guidelines

Tax Authorities use interpretive guidelines when they enact regulations which advance specific interpretive solutions in respect to the application of tax statutes. These interpretive regulations take different forms as they may be issued as 'letter rulings' ('*note*'), interpretive rulings ('*risoluzioni*'), or interpretive guidelines ('*circolari*').

Interpretive regulations construe and explain the tax statutes and are descriptive in form, often including examples to illustrate the operation of the statutory provision. They are entitled to great weight, but they may be disregarded by a court if inconsistent with the statutory language or when there is no statutory basis to support the regulatory provision. In practice a court may reject the position of an interpretive regulation if the tax statute has a meaning that is clear, unambiguous, and in conflict with that interpretive regulation.

83. *See* for example: Corte cost., 10 December 1981, No. 18, in (1982) I(1) *Giur. it.*, 1982, 800; Corte cost., 25 July 1995, No. 376, in (1997) I *Foro. it.*, 346.
84. Corte cost., 23 December 1997, No. 432; Corte cost., 27 July 2000, No. 374.
85. *Cass.*, 10 December 2002, No. 5768, in (1995) I(1) *Giur. it.*, 2001.

Interpretive regulations express the position of the tax administration,[86] but are not binding for the judges or the taxpayers.[87] Therefore, interpretive regulations are guidelines which do not constitute tax norms in the strict sense, and they should be distinguished from interpretive norms. So when a statute may reasonably be construed to have any one of several alternative meanings, the selection of one such meaning in the regulation will not be conclusive in so far as one or more of the alternative interpretations advanced by the taxpayer are preferable in the view of the judge.

Interpretive regulations are important even if they are not legally binding for the judges or the taxpayers. First, interpretive regulations are the outcome of requests made by taxpayers, so they summarize which is the position of Tax Authorities. Second, interpretive regulations ensure that Tax Authorities take the same position across the board, preventing conflicting interpretations. Third, taxpayers can rely on the position of interpretive regulations, and if they are modified retroactively they are not binding because the bona fide behaviour of taxpayers is protected by the doctrine denominated '*tutela dell'affidamento*' developed by judges and explicitly affirmed by the Tax Charter. Fourth, often interpretive regulations amount to practical instructions on how to file the tax return or to follow procedures. Fifth, interpretive regulations are drafted by essentially the same offices which drafted the tax legislation that they explain, with the consequence that they clarify complex issues that involve technical interpretation; this is the reason why interpretive regulations are usually issued after the enactment of tax statutes.[88]

§10.06 INTERPRETATION OF TAX TREATIES

[A] Strict Versus Purposive Interpretation and Three Methods to Interpret Tax Treaties

It is possible to discern a tension in tax treaties cases that have been decided in Italy between strict interpretation and purposive interpretation. According to the former approach, treaty rules are interpreted on the basis of the ordinary meaning of terms, while according to the latter approach treaty rules are interpreted on the basis of the intention of the parties and the purpose/scope of the treaty.

A good example of this tension is a recent case which dealt with the issue whether the royalties subject to a maximum rate of withholding tax under Article 12 of the Italy-US tax treaty applied to payments made in respect of 'rights assimilated to copyrights' in the same way it applied to payments made in respect of copyrights. The issue to be decided was whether rights assimilated to copyrights was sufficiently similar to copyrights to be caught by the term 'all other cases' included in the list of

86. Interpretive regulations are not legally binding only for the tax offices; *see*, for example *Cass.*, 10 November 2000, No. 14619; *Cass.*, sez. Un., 2 November 2007, No. 23031.
87. *Cass.*, 6 August 2008, No. 21154.
88. Enrico Antonini, 'Norma di legge, standard giuridico ed interpretazione ministeriale', (1979) 1 *Riv. Dir. Fin.*, 425.

royalty types set out in the treaty.[89] As the treaty did not explicitly address the issue, the *Cassazione* turned first to domestic law to interpret the application of the treaty to these payments, relying on Article 3(2) of the treaty[90] which contains a 'general renvoi clause' (*see infra* §10.06[B]) whereby the meaning of a term not defined by the treaty must be found in the domestic laws of the source-country, i.e., Italy in this case.

The *Cassazione* observed that under Italian domestic law, 'rights assimilated to copyrights' would not be considered analogous to copyrights, unlike the case in some other jurisdictions. However, the *Cassazione* further observed that under a strict application of the renvoi approach, there could be a dual qualification of the payments under the laws of the two Contracting States (in that case Italy and the US) potentially leading to double taxation. To mitigate that problem the *Cassazione* adopted a purposive treaty interpretation and held that both 'copyrights' and 'rights assimilated to copyrights' were covered by Article 12(2) of the treaty.

In most of the cases about tax treaties, strict interpretation is the first step, an approach that conforms to Article 31(1) of the Vienna Convention on the Law of Treaties (VCLT), which stipulates that a treaty shall be interpreted in good faith in accordance with the ordinary meaning to be given to the terms of the treaty in their context and in the light of its object and purpose. In many cases strict interpretation of the tax treaties is in fact based on the idea that they are ordinary laws introduced in the Italian legal system by a special law denominated 'order of execution'. In several instances however when the strict approach did not solve issues, it has been acknowledged that it was possible to refer to extra-textual elements, and this is in accordance with the broader approach advocated by Articles 31(2) and (3)[91] and 32[92] of VCLT.

In conclusion, Articles 31 and 32 of VCLT constitute in Italy the basis for an integrated approach to interpretation of tax treaties, in which strict interpretation comes first and looks at the textual elements, while purposive interpretation looks at a broad context (i.e., supplementary means of interpretation) when strict interpretation

89. *Cass.*, 29 September 2006, No. 21220.
90. Article 3(2) provides that: 'As regards the application of this Convention by a Contracting State any term not defined therein shall, unless the context otherwise requires, have the meaning which it has under the law of that State concerning the taxes to which this Convention applies.'
91. Article 31, provides: '(1) A treaty shall be interpreted in good faith in accordance with the ordinary meaning to be given to the terms of the treaty in their "context" and in the light of its object and purpose. (2) The context for the purpose of the interpretation of a treaty shall comprise, in addition to the text, including its preamble and annexes; (a) any agreement relating to the treaty which was made between all the parties in connection with the conclusion of the treaty; (b) any instrument which was made by one or more parties in connection with the conclusion of the treaty and accepted by the other parties as an instrument related to the treaty. (3) There shall be taken into account, together with the context: (a) any subsequent agreement between the parties regarding the interpretation of the treaty or the application of its provisions; (b) any subsequent practice in the application of the treaty which establishes the agreement of the parties regarding its interpretation; (c) any relevant rules of international law applicable in the relations between the parties.'
92. Article 32 (titled 'Supplementary means of interpretation') provides that recourse may be had to supplementary means of interpretation, including the preparatory work of the treaty and the circumstances of its conclusion in order to confirm the meaning resulting from the application of Art. 31, or to determine the meaning when the interpretation according to Art. 31(a) leaves the meaning ambiguous or obscure; or (b) leads to a result which is manifestly absurd or unreasonable.

would yield a result inconsistent with the purpose of the treaty. Strict and purposive interpretations are, in turn, used in three approaches to treaty interpretation mandated by Article 3(2) of the OECD Model Convention,[93] reflected in Italian tax treaties: renvoi, contextual interpretation, and autonomous interpretation.

First, Article 3(2) points at 'any term not defined in the treaty' and clarifies that these terms have the meaning that they have under the law of that State for the purposes of the taxes to which the Convention applies, and this is the so-called *renvoi* method. Second, Article 3(2) points at 'terms that are defined in the treaty, but for which the context requires another interpretation', setting the stage for the so-called *contextual interpretation*. Third, Article 3(2) points at 'terms that are defined in the treaty', and for which the context does not requires another interpretation, leading to the so-called *autonomous interpretation*.

[B] Renvoi and Strict Interpretation of Tax Treaties

According to the first method mandated by Article 3(2) – the renvoi method – the 'terms not defined in the treaty' have the meaning that they have at that time under the tax laws of Italy for the purposes of the taxes to which the Convention applies.[94] Under this approach, the meaning under the applicable tax laws prevails over a meaning given to the term under other laws of that State.[95] Before the renvoi method can be applied, it must be determined if the term is defined not only in the basic treaty but also in the treaty's '*co-text*' comprising the text of the treaty itself together with the preamble, as well as Protocols made between all the parties in connection with the conclusion of the treaty and any instruments made in connection with the conclusion of the treaty, such a explicative notes made by one or more parties and accepted by the other parties as an instrument related to the treaty. In the Italian legal system these explicative notes take the form of circular letters issues by Tax Authorities, which provide an unilateral interpretation and do not necessarily lead to agreed-upon interpretation (*see infra* §10.06[C]).

93. Article 3(2) of the OECD Model Treaty provides that: 'As regards the application of the Convention at any time by a Contracting State, any term not defined therein shall, unless the context otherwise requires, have the meaning that it has at that time under the law of that State for the purposes of the taxes to which the Convention applies, any meaning under the applicable tax laws of that State prevailing over a meaning given to the term under other laws of that State.'
94. Judicial examples of the renvoi method are: *Cass.*, No. 6583, 22 March 2011; *Cass.* No. 1550/2012, 3 February 2012; *Cass.*, No. 7355/2012, 11 May 2012.
95. Paragraph 13.1 of the OECD Commentary to Art. 3 allows reference to domestic Italian tax and non-tax laws, and clarifies that for the purposes of Art. 3(2), the meaning of any term not defined in the Convention may be ascertained by reference to the meaning it has for the purpose of any relevant provision of the domestic law of a Contracting State, whether or not a tax law. Paragraph 13.1 of the OECD Commentary also clarifies that, where a term is defined differently for the purposes of different laws of a Contracting State, the meaning given to that term for purposes of the laws imposing the taxes to which the Convention applies shall prevail over all others, including those given for the purposes of other tax laws, as well as that States that are able to enter into MAPs (under Art. 25 and, in particular, § 3 thereof) that establish the meanings of terms not defined in the Convention should take those agreements into account in interpreting those terms.

A potential outcome of the renvoi method is the risk that the each of the parties to a treaty applying its domestic law definition of terms will adopt incompatible meanings leading to double taxation or double non-taxation. It may be possible to resolve the inconsistent interpretations using the mutual agreement procedure under Article 25 of the Model Convention (hereinafter 'MAP'). A second issue raised by the renvoi method is whether terms are to be interpreted using an ambulatory or static interpretation doctrine. Under the static interpretation approach, the ordinary meaning of a rule of treaty is attributed when the treaty is concluded. By contrast, the ambulatory interpretation approach adopts the current meaning of terms used in the treaty.

The main argument in favour of static interpretation is that the Contracting States are bound by the original provisions of the Treaty on the basis of the principle *pacta sunt servanda*, so that the stability of the meaning of treaty rules prevents any de facto modifications of the treaty.[96] For example the *Cassazione* has held in a permanent establishment case that no decisive relevance should be attributed to the 2005 modifications of the OECD Commentary on Article 5 of the OECD Model Convention.[97]

By contrast, there are several arguments in favour of ambulatory interpretation. First, when Contracting States adapt the original provisions through interpretation there is no need of specific treaty procedures. Second, a flexible approach to the meaning of the treaty provisions allows a de facto modification of the treaty that is consistent with economic and legal developments, an adjustment process that preserve ongoing contractual relations.

In practice the rule of thumb currently adopted in Italy is that if static interpretation fails, ambulatory interpretation is to be used.[98] However if the ambulatory interpretation adopted by Italy is not accepted also by the other Contracting State, recourse to the MAP is needed. In theory, if the Competent Authorities do not adopt a mutually agreed interpretation, each party might view the other has having made a de facto violation of the treaty potentially leading to termination of the treaty.

[C] Contextual and Autonomous Interpretation of Tax Treaties

Contextual interpretation is a widely accepted approach by practitioners and academics in Italy in respect to tax treaties. This contextual interpretation is based on Article 3(2), which refers to 'terms that are defined in the treaty, but for which the *context* requires another interpretation'.

Contextual interpretation has created two major problems. The first problem is identifying the elements of the 'context' that can be used if due respect is to be given to VCLT. The second problem lies in determining the exact role of the OECD Model

96. It has been pointed out that ambulatory interpretation would practically attribute to an international body, the OECD Fiscal Committee, the power to indirectly change a convention already ratified by the national parliaments and turned into a national law. *See* Stefano Guglielmi, 'Il caso Philip Morris nelle recenti modifiche al Commentario OCSE', (2006) *Fiscalità Internazionale*: 148-157.
97. *Cass.*, 17 April 2007, No. 13579 in (2007) 29 *Corriere tributario*, 2353.
98. Article 3(2) of OECD Model modified in 1995 adopted ambulatory interpretation.

Convention and the Commentary in such contextual interpretation. The former problem is discussed in this section, while the later problem will be addressed in the next section.

The review of current judicial approaches and best practices reveals that the 'context' in contextual interpretation has the broadest meaning and includes essentially all the elements beyond the mere text, as listed by Article 31(2) and (3) of VCLT. These elements will be grouped here under two headings: '*strict context*', as defined by Article 31(3), and '*broad context*' as defined by Article 32(1).

The 'strict context' (Article 31(3), VCLT) includes any subsequent agreement between the parties regarding the interpretation of the treaty or the application of its provisions; i.e., agreements resulting from MAPs, as well as any subsequent practice in the application of the treaty which establishes the agreement of the parties regarding its interpretation that can be drawn from such MAPs. It also includes any relevant rules of international law applicable in the relations between the parties.

The 'broad context' (Article 32(1), VCLT) includes supplementary means of interpretation, such as the preparatory work for the treaty including the minutes of the meetings of the tax delegations, as well as the circumstances of conclusion of the treaty.

Frequently in Italy, judges use the '*autonomous interpretation*' method set out in Article 3(2), which applies to terms that are defined in the treaty and used in a context does not requires another interpretation. Autonomous interpretation sometimes has been mixed with purposive interpretation, by pointing, for example, at the intentions of the Contracting States.[99] National judges have used autonomous interpretation to terms used in self-executing rules that can be applied without consideration of any other law. An example of a self-executing rule is Article 29 of the Italy-Switzerland treaty regulating the refund claims in respect of taxes withheld at source.[100]

When using autonomous interpretation, courts have made recourse to the full 'VCLT context' indicated by Articles 31 and 32 VCLT, and there was limited recourse to domestic laws. The wider treaty context, including the OECD Commentary may provide the treaty meaning of terms required for autonomous interpretation. Examples of this approach in Italy included cases involving permanent establishments (Article 5), interest (Article 11(3)), exemption or foreign tax credit for foreign-source income (Articles 23A and 23B), and non-discrimination (Article 24).

[D] The Role of the OECD Commentary in the Interpretation of Italian Tax Treaties

As mentioned above, the second problem of contextual interpretation of tax treaties is determining the exact role of the OECD Model Convention and the Commentary. Scholars have suggested the OECD Commentary may be used for two distinct purposes. The first is to set out solutions that can be used as policy guidelines for negotiators and

99. This is in line with Art. 31(4) of VCLT, which provides that a special meaning shall be given to a term if it is established that the parties so intended.
100. *Cass.*, 21 April 2001, No. 5927.

policy makers when concluding tax treaties for Italy. The second is a source of guidance the correct interpretation of actual tax treaties.

It is clear that although Italy has not formally endorsed or approved the OECD Commentary, Italian negotiators have drawn on the OECD Commentary concluding tax treaties.[101] The OECD Model Convention itself has been used as the basis for Italian treaties with both OECD Member countries and non-Member countries.

While the OECD Commentary has a policy impact on development of the Italian treaty network, it has no binding role in respect of treaty interpretation by courts in Italy or Competent Authorities. As paragraph 29 of the Introduction to the OECD Model Convention points out, the Commentaries are not legally binding international instruments. They can nevertheless be of great assistance in the application and interpretation of the treaties and, in particular, in the settlement of any disputes.

Italian tax scholars suggest that the OECD Commentary is binding only if one of five conditions are satisfied: (i) the position expressed by the OECD Commentary is evidence of international customary law; (ii) both Italy and the other Contracting State expressly refer to OECD Commentary in the treaty or annexed documents;[102] (iii) Italy has entered into a tax treaty with another OECD member with a text equal to the OECD Model and both Contracting States accept the OECD interpretation; (iv) there is proof that the OECD Commentary has been effectively used in the negotiation process in relation to the issue at stake; or (v) a term is not defined at all by domestic laws of both Contracting States but is unequivocally defined by the OECD Commentary.[103]

Italian courts have taken a somewhat different position, however. Even where judges acknowledge the non-binding nature of the OECD Commentary, they often invoke it as an interpretive authority. The practical result is that Italian courts, instead of following 'OECD orthodoxy', have genuinely created new interpretative positions by relying on the OECD Commentary as validation of their rulings. In effect, an OECD rationale is being used as the basis for a new, genuinely domestic, interpretation of treaty provisions. The *Cassazione* has directly referred to Article 7(3) of the 1977 OECD Model Convention in deciding a case concerning attribution of costs to the permanent establishment[104] and used both Article 5(7) of the OECD Model Convention and the related sections of the OECD Commentary when interpreting the definition of the permanent establishment under the so-called agency clause of the treaties in the *Philip Morris* case, a decision that was subsequently criticized by the OECD.[105]

101. *Cass.*, 2 February 2000, No. 1122.
102. For instance, the Protocol of the treaty with Mexico, provides that 'with reference to para. 4 of Art. 7 mentioned before, the Contracting States shall apply the provisions contained therein in accordance with their domestic laws and in the sense given to such paragraph in the Commentaries of the 1977 Model Convention drawn up by the OECD Committee on Fiscal Affairs'.
103. *See* generally, Carlo Garbarino, *Manuale di tassazione internazionale* (Deventer: Kluwer, 2008) pp. 202–206; Carlo Garbarino, 'Alcune considerazioni sulle Convenzioni per evitare le doppie imposizioni' (1989) *Dir. comm. internaz.*, 51; Giuseppe Melis, 'L'interpretazione delle convenzioni internazionali in materia di imposte sul reddito e sul patrimonio', (1995) *Rass. trib.*, 1966.
104. *See Cass.*, 1 August 2000, No. 10062, in (2002) II *Diritto e Pratica Tributaria*, 483.
105. *See Cass.*, 7 March 2002, No. 3368; *Cass.*, 25 May 2002, No. 7682.

The OECD Commentary or other OECD reports and documents constituting 'soft tax law' are often implemented in the Italian legal system by legislative measures or administrative guidelines that essentially transplant OECD policies. For example, Italian tax treaties often reproduce the exact wording of the clauses of the OECD Model, while Tax Authorities have implemented the OECD cost-sharing and transfer pricing policies in circulars and other documents.[106] This process, however, does not involve interpretation.

Another issue that has been addressed in Italian case law is the so-called parallel treaty interpretation, i.e., the extension of an interpretation of a treaty between Italy and State A to a separate treaty of Italy with State B. The OECD Commentary suggests the interpretation of one treaty can only be extended to another treaty if the second treaty adopts the same rule as the first treaty. An interesting application of this OECD guideline can be found in respect to certain refunds available on Italy to foreign recipients of dividends pursuant to the provisions of different treaties of Italy with EU partners. Since those treaties included provisions that essentially adopted the same wording and rationale, the *Cassazione* ruled that the provisions had the same meaning in all of Italy's tax treaties.

§10.07 VAT INTERPRETATION

VAT is a European tax, introduced in Italy in 1972 by means of a legislative decree (D.P.R. 26 October 1972, No. 633) which has been amended from time to time, particularly to reflect binding changes of EU VAT Directives. Because the Italian VAT is essentially an EU tax, the interpretive principles developed by the ECJ are also applied by Italian Tax Authorities and judges.

Income tax and VAT interpretive techniques in Italy tend to converge. This is due to a number of factors. The main two factors are of an institutional nature. First, VAT is administered by the same offices that audit taxpayers for income tax purposes and essentially by the same personnel. Second, VAT is truly a European tax devised to ensure the achievement of the common market and therefore, in its implementation in Italy, it differs from its predecessor, the turnover or gross receipts tax. As a result, there exists no traditional interpretation in relation to transaction-based taxes.[107]

A third factor that contributes to convergence of interpretive techniques is a technical one. VAT laws are self-contained, without incorporation of accounting concepts, so that most of concepts in the VAT such as supply, consideration, exempt supplies, zero-rated supplies, etc., have essentially been developed by attributing a specialized VAT meaning, applying the same techniques used for direct taxes, i.e., legislative definitions (*see supra* §10.02[B]).

There are many examples of this endogenous development of VAT concepts: services are deemed to be completed for VAT purposes when the price is paid or

106. *Agenzia Entrate*, Circular No. 32, 8 April 1980; *Agenzia Entrate*, Circular No. 271/E/1059/SP/97, 21 October 1997.

107. *Cass.*, pen., 1 February 1985, in (1985) I *Rass. Avv. Stato*, 346 has defined VAT on imports as a kind of import duty.

invoiced, and not when they are completed;[108] VAT is deducted for acquired goods and services that are 'related' to the business of the taxpayer and this concept differs from a merely accounting concept;[109] a VAT subject must exercise business activities effectively so that legal qualifications are not relevant by themselves.[110]

Generally speaking, there is no incorporation in VAT of the accounting concepts used in income taxes. This may lead to different practical results, but the interpretive techniques are exactly the same. For example, if a business entity receives a contribution from Government, it must recognize the payment as profit for income tax purposes even if there was no supply for VAT purposes, and so on.

One could however identify notable usages in the VAT area of standard interpretive techniques originally developed in connection with income taxes. For example, VAT is replete with concessions adopted to achieve a wide range of economic, social or political objectives and which are explicitly recognized, such as exempt supplies, lower than standard rate supplies, or zero-rated supplies.

In that respect, courts have developed a reverse-usage of the standard strict interpretation used in income taxes, which has revealed that the doctrine of strict interpretation operates differently depending on the type of tax norms that are involved (*see supra* §10.02[A]). If the norms *broaden* the private sphere of the taxpayer, providing a VAT exemption, or favourable treatment, then strict interpretation operates in favour of the Tax Authorities, essentially by preventing the extension of the scope of the VAT exemption norms. In practice, with VAT concessions, the *enumerated list* of non-taxable or exempt supplies cannot be broadened through interpretation (*see also* Chapter 6, §6.04[E][2]).

This strict interpretive technique is used conversely in income taxes to favour the taxpayer by preventing the extension of the scope of the base, limiting it to the *enumerated list* of taxable situations that cannot be generally broadened by interpretation (*see supra* §10.03[C]).

The convergence of standard interpretive techniques described in the previous sections of this chapter in relation to income taxes with VAT interpretive techniques has led to a situation in which there are no major notable differences in the approaches taken to interpretation of VAT laws in Italy vis-à-vis other taxation laws. Strict interpretation techniques have been extensively developed by VAT offices, and among the techniques of purposive interpretation the ones most applied in the area of VAT are conforming interpretation and interpretation based on general principles because of the top-down EU matrix of VAT.

A good example of conforming interpretation can be found in the decisions which justify VAT on imports from non-EU countries, as such VAT has the purpose to equate domestically produced and goods coming from EU countries to goods coming from non-EU countries.[111] Interpretation based on general principles has been applied in clarifying, on the basis of basic tenets of civil and public law, that the VAT charge

108. *Cass.*, 1 October 2010, No. 20527.
109. *Cass.*, 14 July 2004, No. 13056.
110. *Cass.*, 12 February 2007, No. 3022.
111. *See Cass.*, pen., 19 January 1994, in (1994) II *Foro. It.*, 408.

connects VAT-payers, while the obligation to remit VAT connects Tax Authorities and taxpayers, so that litigation concerning the VAT charge is competence of civil law courts.[112] Similarly the right to VAT reimbursement can be activated without the need to modify the invoices, if the substantial requirements are met.[113]

Purposive interpretation is used to address avoidance in VAT matters, and it should be noted that the EU impact on Italian judicial approaches to the abuse of tax laws (*see supra* §10.04[C]) has been pervasive. The pillar of the *Cassazione* in developing the anti-abuse principle was EU VAT law: the court initially stated that the anti-abuse principle was newly created law imposed by *Halifax plc and Others v. Commissioners of Customs & Excise*[114] and other cases decided by the ECJ in VAT matters,[115] and that this principle applies to all areas of tax law, from indirect taxes such as VAT or stamp duty to direct taxes such as personal or corporate income taxes.

112. *Cass.*, 28 October 1995, No. 11313, in (1996) I *Giur. It.*, 449.
113. *Cass.*, 13 March 2000, No. 2868, in (2000) I *Foro. It.*, 1465.
114. ECJ, 21 February 2006, Case C-255/02, [2006] ECR I-1609.
115. ECJ, 21 February 2006, Case C-223/03, *University of Huddersfield Higher Education Corporation v. Commissioners of Customs & Excise* [2006] ECR I-1751; ECJ, 21 February 2008, Case C-425-06, *Ministero dell'Economia e delle Finanze v. Part Service srl* [2008] ECR I-0897; ECJ, 14 February 1995, Case C-279/93, *Finanzamt Köln-Altstadt v. Schumacker* [1995] ECR I-0225; ECJ, 13 July 1993, Case C-330/91, *R v. IRC ex parte Commerzbank* [1993] ECR I-4017; ECJ, 15 May 1997, Case C-250/95, *Futura Participations SA v. Administrations des Contributions* [1997] ECR I-2471.

CHAPTER 11

Legal Interpretation of Tax Law: Japan

Yoshihiro Masui

§11.01 INTRODUCTION

This chapter highlights the contemporary trends in tax law interpretation in Japan. In general terms, Japan's Supreme Court takes a literal approach to tax statutory interpretation with due regard to the objective and purpose of the statutory provision. This applies with equal force to value added tax (VAT) and Income Tax Laws, as will be demonstrated in the following sections.

The next section first explains institutional background to various agents who are in charge of interpreting tax statutes (§11.02). The following sections discuss VAT cases (§11.03) and income tax cases (§11.04).[1] Each section is divided into subsections on treaty law interpretation and on domestic law interpretation. The last section briefly concludes (§11.05).

This chapter focuses on a few selected court decisions. They are well known and easily found in contemporary casebooks[2] used for teaching tax law at universities in Japan. An English translation project is underway for significant Supreme Court decisions reported in *Minshu* [Civil Case Reporter] and *Keishu* [Criminal Case Reporter]. English text of these court holdings is available on the website operated by the Supreme Court of Japan.[3]

---

1. Yoshihiro Masui, The Responsibility of Judges in Interpreting Tax Legislation: Japan's Experience, *Osgood Hall Law Journal* 52.2 (2015): 491–512 examines some of the court decisions discussed in §11.04[B] of this chapter.
2. Hiroshi Kaneko et al., *Casebook Sozeiho* [*Casebook Tax Law*] (Kobundo, 4th edition, 2013), Minoru Nakazato et al. (eds), *Sozei Hanrei Hyakusen* [*100 Cases in Tax Law*] (Yuhikaku, 6th edition, 2016), and Minoru Nakazato & Yoshihiro Masui (eds), *Sozeiho Hanrei Roppo* [*Tax Law: Principal Statutes, Regulations, and Cases*] (Yuhikaku, 3rd edition, 2017).
3. http://www.courts.go.jp/english/ (visited 29 August 2016). *See also*, http://www.asianlii.org/resources/232.html (ASIAN LII resources on Japan available in English, visited 13 August 2017).

§11.02 BACKGROUND

[A] Constitutional Background

Under the constitutional principle in Japan, taxation must be based on statutes created by the *Diet* (Japanese parliament).[4] A literal approach to the interpretation of tax statutes is derived from this constitutional principle, for two reasons: democracy and liberalism:

- *Democracy*. The *Diet* creates law because its representatives are elected by the people. Tax officers and judges must follow the literal meaning of the words chosen by the *Diet*. Otherwise they can in effect override the decisions of the legislature.
- *Liberalism*. Literal interpretation gives certainty to economic life of citizens. It precludes unforeseen consequences to private parties involved. Predetermined, clear rules are a foundation for the smooth working of a market economy.

Japan's Supreme Court has consistently made clear the following points:

- It is a constitutional requirement to clearly define in statutes: (i) legal conditions for taxation; and (ii) procedures for tax assessment and collection.[5]
- Article 84 of the Constitution is a declaration of the 'rule of law' principle for tax purposes. As such, requirements similar to (i) and (ii) above are imposed on public levies other than taxes.[6]
- Article 84 of the Constitution guarantees the protection of legal certainty in taxation. Retroactive application of an income tax provision disallowing loss utilization needs to be scrutinized. The judicial test for such constitutional review is whether the legislation is a reasonable restriction on the property rights involved.[7]

Against this constitutional background, Japanese commentators tend to emphasize a literal approach to interpreting tax statutes. If one looks more closely, however, judges facing real-world disputes often take into account the purpose and objective of tax provisions in question. As a result, they sometimes deviate from strict interpretation of the word used in the tax statutes. Because Japan does not have a general law on the interpretation of legislation, one needs to examine the real court cases to understand the dynamics of judges' interpretative enterprise.

4. Article 84 of the Japanese Constitution. *See*, Hiroshi Kaneko, The Principle of Statute-based Taxation in Japan, in Paul Kirchhof et al. (eds), *Staaten und Steuern, Festschrift für Klaus Vogel zum 70. Geburtstag*, 807 (Heidelberg: C.F. Müller, 2000).
5. Supreme Court, 27 March 1985, *Ohshima*, Minshu, Vol. 39, No. 2, 247.
6. Supreme Court, 1 March 2006, *Asahikawa National Insurance*, Minshu, Vol. 60, No. 2, 587.
7. Supreme Court, 30 September 2011, *Retroactivity*, Minshu, Vol. 65, No. 6, 2756.

[B] More Institutional Backgrounds

Before examining the court cases, it is necessary to explain some of the institutional backgrounds to the interpretation of tax statutes, particularly with regard to VAT and Income Tax Laws in Japan.[8]

[1] Accumulated Number of Court Cases

Japan's VAT was introduced only in 1988.[9] In contrast, Japan's income tax dates back to 1887. Compared with ample court decisions dealing with income tax, there is an insufficient number of VAT cases for an observer to determine whether a VAT-distinct interpretation method is emerging.

[2] Tax Mix

Japan is currently an income tax country. In 2016, income taxes, both individual and corporate, contributed more than 50% of the total national tax revenue. On the other hand, VAT generated nearly 22% of the national tax revenue with a modest single tax rate of 8% (6.3% for national government and 1.7% for local governments). VAT's share is likely to increase in the future as the VAT rate will be raised to 10% in October 2019.

[3] Federalism Aspects

Taxation at the local government level is streamlined as far as VAT and income taxes are concerned. VAT is collected by the National Tax Agency (NTA). Out of the 8% rate, 6.3% is allocated to national government and 1.7% to prefectures. Each prefecture receives its share of the VAT revenue according to a formula based on the sales amount. Within each prefecture, half of the VAT revenue, thus received, is divided among cities according to a formula based on population and on the number of employees. Similarly, local income taxes are a piggyback to national income taxes. The NTA collects individual and corporate income taxes. Local governments use the same information in the tax returns that are submitted to the NTA. This is possible because national and local income tax bases are almost identical.

---

8. This subsection is a brief summary of Japan's tax and legal system. An interested reader should read Hugh J. Ault & Brian Arnold. *Comparative Income Taxation: A Structural Analysis* (Alphen aan den Rijn: Kluwer, 3rd edition, 2010) at 93, Curtis J. Milhaupt et al., *The Japanese Legal System* (Foundation Press, 2nd edition, 2012), at 129, and Hiromitsu Ishi, *The Japanese Tax System* (Oxford: Oxford University Press, 3rd edition, 2001).
9. As early as in 1949, the Shoup Mission to Japan recommended an introduction of a VAT defined as a sum of profit, interest, rents, and payroll. The VAT system was legislated in 1950, but was repealed in 1954 without being implemented. *See*, Rita de la Feria & Richard Krever, 'Ending VAT Exemptions: Towards a *Post*-Modern VAT', in Rita de la Feria (ed.). *VAT Exemptions: Consequences and Design Alternatives* (Alphen aan den Rijn: Kluwer, 2013), at 3, footnote 2.

[4] *NTA's Interpretation*

The NTA is one of the most powerful law enforcement agencies in Japan. It has more than 55,000 staff. It needs a unified enforcement in order to avoid discrepancies among district offices and tax officials. Thus the NTA issues various interpretative circulars. Circulars are an organization-internal norm and are followed by tax officials. They do not legally bind judicial courts and private citizens. However, because circulars make clear the NTA's position, tax practitioners cannot neglect them. Often the interpretation taken in NTA's circulars guide everyday practice by tax accountants and corporate tax managers.

[5] *National Tax Tribunal*

Taxpayers for both VAT and income tax appeal to normal judicial courts when they are dissatisfied with the initial decisions of the National Tax Tribunal, a quasi-judicial body organized as an outer body of the NTA. During the fiscal year 2015, the National Tax Tribunal handled 2,098 cases. Taxpayers won 184 cases partially or totally. When the Tribunal makes a decision based on an interpretation different from NTA's circulars, it must make its case to the Commissioner of the NTA. The Commissioner's instruction for the Tribunal must be based on the decision of the National Tax Council, unless the Tribunal's interpretation approves the taxpayer's position and the Commissioner accepts such interpretation.

[6] *Judiciary*

Courts in Japan are streamlined across the nation. Tax litigation starts at the level of the District Court, moves to High Court, and finally goes to Supreme Court, if certiorari is granted. At each instance, generalist judges hear tax cases. In the metropolitan area, tax and other administrative law cases are centred in a few particular divisions of the Tokyo District Court. In the trial, the NTA is represented by legal staff of the Ministry of Justice. Disputes in respect of both VAT and income taxes are settled within this framework of national judicial system. During the fiscal year 2015, 125 tax assessment cases were decided at the District Court level. Taxpayers won 13 cases partially or totally.

[7] *Contrast with Other Areas of Law*

Judges' attitude towards interpretation varies from one area of law to another. Court cases dealing with contracts and torts, for example, demonstrate extensive use of purposive interpretation and analogies. Court cases in criminal law, on the other hand, tend to be stricter in interpreting the legal conditions and in evaluating evidence. Tax law interpretation in Japan can be said to hold the middle of the two, although it is somewhat closer to criminal law court practice compared with other branches of administrative law, such as zoning and environmental protection.

§11.03 INTERPRETATION OF VAT LAW

[A] International

Japan has no VAT treaties[10] comparable to income tax treaties governing substantive allocation of tax jurisdictions. Therefore, there are no court cases dealing with the interpretation of treaties specifically related to VAT.

Several provisions in Japan's bilateral income tax treaties do cover VAT, as well as income taxes. Examples include provisions on non-discrimination and information exchange. Japan also ratified the multilateral treaty on administrative assistance that also covers VAT. Therefore, VAT cases might arise in relation to such treaty provisions. However, this still remains a theoretical possibility.

[B] Domestic

[1] In General

As explained in §11.02[B], there are at present only a small number of court decisions dealing with VAT Law in Japan. Still, a few cases may be relevant for understanding the attitude of judges in interpreting VAT Law.

[2] VAT and Income Tax Compared

The following cases show the uniformity of interpretation between VAT and Income Tax Laws. One of the procedural requirements for claiming an input tax credit under Japan's VAT Law is to 'keep' one's books and receipts. In a case covering the fiscal year 1990 (the *Input tax credit* case), an individual businessman refused to show his books and receipts when he was audited. It was only later, in the litigation stage, that he produced his books and receipts. He argued that he had in fact secretly 'kept' his books and receipts so that the requirement for the input tax credit was fulfilled. The Supreme Court denied his claim, stating that a taxpayer must keep his books and receipts in such a manner as to be able to show to relevant tax officers when audited.[11] The court derived this interpretation from its reading of other provisions in the VAT Law. The court's reasoning therefore could be characterized as a sort of systematic interpretation.

Interestingly, the Supreme Court reached exactly the same conclusion in an income tax case (the *Blue return* case) dealing with the same wording in a procedural provision of the Income Tax Law.[12] The issue was again whether or not the taxpayer 'kept' his books and receipts. This was a condition necessary for the taxpayer to enjoy his privileged status accorded to so-called blue return filers. The Supreme Court in the

10. Thomas Ecker, *A VAT/GST Model Convention: Tax Treaties as Solution for Value Added Tax and Goods and Services Tax Double Taxation* (Amsterdam: IBFD, 2013).
11. Supreme Court, 16 December 2004, *Input tax credit*, Minshu, Vol. 58, No. 9, 2458.
12. Supreme Court, 10 March 2005, *Blue return*, Minshu, Vol. 59, No. 2, 379.

Blue return case interpreted the provision in the same manner as in *Input tax credit* case. From these two cases, one may state that Japan's Supreme Court does not differentiate its interpretative stance between VAT and income tax, at least on an issue concerning procedural requirements.

[3] Objective and Purpose of the Provision

The Supreme Court's interpretation on a more substantive issue in VAT Law interpretation, moreover, does not seem to be peculiar or unique to VAT Law. The court takes the same literal approach with due regard to the objective and purpose of the provision in question, as shown in the *Exemption threshold* case.[13] The registration threshold for VAT used to be quite high and was JPY 30 million when the dispute arose in 1995. The base amount for testing the threshold was defined as 'taxable sales amount' and was to be measured on an after-tax basis. A formerly exempt business had an actual sales amount of JPY 30.52 million in its previous fiscal years. It deducted the notional amount corresponding to the output tax amount (= 3% of the sales amount) and claimed that its exempt status should remain unchanged. Referring to the objectives and purpose of the threshold for exempting small businesses, the Supreme Court refused to deduct the notional VAT amount that was never paid in reality.

Of course, how one articulates the exact objective and purpose of the provision is the heart of the question. To illustrate this point, let us turn to a lower court decision (the *Lease termination* case) denying an input tax credit to a business corporation for its payment made to its lessees when a lease contract was terminated.[14] The reasoning of the Tokyo District Court was that no property was transferred because the right of the lessees was terminated. The court supported this reasoning by referring to the objective and purpose of input tax credit to avoid accumulation of taxes levied in multiple stages. According to the court, it was impossible in this case to conceive the next stage of the VAT transaction chain. The court further justified this VAT treatment which is different from the income tax treatment where capital gains tax captures various payments in consideration of termination of rights. This court decision had the result of affirming NTA's circular.

[4] Predecessor Indirect Tax Laws

When the VAT was introduced in 1988, it replaced the Commodity Tax, which was an indirect tax on the sale of goods that were specifically listed in the statute. The introduction of VAT meant an overhaul of the former Commodity Tax whose tax base was narrow and did not cover services.

13. Supreme Court, 1 February 2005, *Exemption threshold*, Minshu, Vol. 59, No. 2, 245.
14. Tokyo District Court, 8 August 1997, *Lease termination*, Gyoshu, Vol. 48, No. 7-8, 539.

Because it was a complete overhaul, many interpretative issues under the Commodity Tax Law simply disappeared under the new VAT Law. For example, an issue arose as to whether or not a formula-one racing car was a 'normal passenger automobile' which was specifically listed as one of the taxable items under the Commodity Tax Law. The Supreme Court held that a certain type of racing car fell in the category of 'normal passenger automobile'.[15] The court's reasoning expanded the ordinary meaning of the word 'normal' in order to arrive at the conclusion that the racing car in question was taxable. This reasoning was criticized by a dissenting opinion written by Justice Ozaki and supported by Justice Motohara. Such interpretative disagreement does not arise under the current VAT, because its tax base is broad and covers transfer of goods and provision of services almost without exception.

§11.04 INTERPRETATION OF INCOME TAX LAW

[A] International

[1] Glaxo *Case*

The single most important decision on the interpretation of income tax treaties in Japan is the *Glaxo* case.[16] In *Glaxo*, the Supreme Court upheld the compatibility of Japan's CFC rule with Article 7 (business profit clause) of the Japan-Singapore Income Tax Treaty. The court read the first sentence of Article 7 ('no taxation without a PE') in conjunction with the second sentence, and construed the first sentence as prohibiting a PE State from exercising its taxation right on an enterprise resident in another Contracting State. According to the court, Japan's application of its CFC rule was an exercise of its taxation right on Japan's domestic corporations and therefore was not prohibited or restricted by Article 7. The Commentary to the OECD Model Tax Convention was referred to as 'supplementary means of interpretation' set forth in Article 32 of the Vienna Convention on the Law of Treaties.[17] It did not distinguish Commentaries prior to or later than the ratification of the Japan-Singapore Income Tax Treaty.

The Supreme Court could have ended its discussion here, but went on to support the above conclusion by examining whether or not Japan's CFC rule would be compatible with the purpose and objective of the Treaty. The court found that the CFC rule contained various exemptions for genuine local business activities and that foreign tax credit was available in case the CFC rule was triggered. As Japan's CFC rule was reasonable as a whole, the court concluded, it did not impede Singapore's taxation right and was compatible with the purpose and objective of Japan-Singapore Income Tax Treaty.[18]

15. Supreme Court, 11 November 1997, *Racing Car*, Hanrei Jiho, No. 1654, 71.
16. Supreme Court, 29 October 2009, *Glaxo*, Minshu, Vol. 63, No. 8, 1881.
17. Vienna Convention on the Law of Treaties 1969, UNTS 1155, 331.
18. *See* the comments by Philip Baker and Toshio Miyatake in (2011) 12 International Tax Law Report 644.

The taxpayer's petition for certiorari cited several foreign court cases including *Schneider Electric*[19] decided by the French Conseil d'État.[20] The ruling of the Supreme Court, however, did not mention any of them. One may only speculate as to the reason for its silence. At least it is fair to state that Japan's courts almost never cite or refer to foreign court decisions in tax cases. This does not mean foreign court decisions played no role in the deliberation of *Glaxo* case. A case commentary written by the Supreme Court law clerk in charge of the case discussed the implication of *Schneider Electric* and suggested that it was doubtful it had relevance for the present case given the difference in tax systems and the wide range of opinions in the literature.[21]

[2] Other Treaty Cases

Other than the *Glaxo* case, there are only a few cases at the lower court level that deal with interpretation of income tax treaties. For example, the Tokyo High Court affirmed a corresponding downward adjustment by the NTA following the US primary adjustment in transfer pricing disputes in a period when Japan-US Income Tax Treaty lacked an explicit provision under its Article 9 for corresponding adjustment.[22] The court based its conclusion on the domestic law effect of mutual agreement between Japan's and US' competent authorities.

In another case, distributions from a Japanese operator to Dutch investors in a TK contract, a Commercial Law structure whose origin is German *stille Gesellschaft* (silent partnership), were held to be 'other income' under Japan-Netherlands Income Tax Treaty.[23] Accordingly, the Japanese government was precluded from imposing a withholding tax on the outgoing distribution. In addition, the operator was able to deduct the distributed amount from its corporate income tax base. On the receiving end, Dutch investors were not taxed either. NTA contended that such double non-taxation should not be permitted. The court simply replied that the matter should be left to renegotiation of the treaty.

[B] Domestic

[1] Literal/Teleological Interpretation

When interpreting tax statutes, Japan's Supreme Court examines the wording, as well as the objective and purpose of the provision. Thus a business corporation was held to be able to deduct an amount for the whole 'period' of its employment contract with its

19. Conseil d'Etat, 28 June 2002, Case No. 232276, *Schneider Electric*, RJF 10/02, no. 1080. For an analysis, *see*, e.g., Patrick Dibout, L'inapplicabilité de l'article 209 B du CGI face à la convention fiscale franco-suisse du 9 septembre 1966, (2002) 36 *Revue de Droit Fiscal*, 1133–1141.
20. The Conseil d'État is the Supreme Administrative Court for direct taxation and VAT matters in France.
21. Yukihito Okada, Case Commentary, (2011) 63 (7) *Hoso Jiho* [*Lawyers Association Journal*] 1731, 1748.
22. Tokyo High Court, 28 March 1996, *Corresponding Adjustment*, Hanrei Jiho, No. 1574, 57.
23. Tokyo High Court, 28 June 2007, *Guidant*, Hanrei Jiho, No. 1985, 23.

employees for income tax withholding purposes based on the literal reading of the term 'period' and on the legislative purpose of deduction in question.[24]

Sometimes the Supreme Court places more emphasis on the purpose of the legislation. When a business corporation had incurred the cost of life insurance premiums for its employees, such employees were held to be unable to deduct the amount of such premium at the later stage when they received their insurance proceeds.[25] The main reasoning of the court was its emphasis on the purpose of deduction to arrive at an accurate net income. The court went on to state that the phrase 'the amount paid for gaining the revenue' presupposed the same person earning income and making payments.

The literal approach combined with teleological reading of the statute also applies to various tax concessions in the Special Tax Measures Law (STML). STML is an exception to the Income Tax Law and contains various tax expenditures. An individual landowner was denied to utilize a special deduction for capital gains tax levied upon transfer of the land to local municipalities.[26] The court examined the purpose of the special deduction and found that the landowner had no real intention to build a building on his land and merely produced a paper application. As a result, the landowner received considerations not in a purchase 'based on' the specific provision of the Zoning Law referred to in the STML. The ruling is interesting in two respects. First, it did not start from the premise that tax expenditure provisions should be strictly interpreted. Second, it examined the purpose not only of STML, but also of Zoning Law, and found that the facts of this case did not fit in to the anticipated framework.

[2] Transplanted Category

The relationship between tax law and private law has been extensively discussed in Japanese literature.[27] One issue is whether or not a tax interpretation should follow private law interpretation when the tax statute 'borrows' concepts which are employed in private law (transplanted category).

Japan's Supreme Court takes the general position that uniform interpretation should prevail. Case law along this line developed in the early 1960s.[28] This basic stance was affirmed in the 1990s, when the court interpreted the meaning of the word 'spouse' as a partner in a legally valid marriage under the Civil Code.[29] The same attitude is found in a case where the term 'family member' was held to mean a family

24. Supreme Court, 2 March 2010, *Hostess Remuneration*, Minshu, Vol. 64, No. 2, 420.
25. Supreme Court, 13 January 2012, *Insurance Premium*, Minshu, Vol. 66, No. 1, 1.
26. Supreme Court, 13 April 2010, *Zoning*, Minshu, Vol. 64, No. 3, 791.
27. Yoshihiro Masui, 'Statutory Interpretation as a Process of Tax Law Making: the Case of Japan', in Klaus Vogel (ed.). *Interpretation of Tax Law and Treaties and Transfer Pricing in Japan and Germany* (Alphen aan den Rijn: Kluwer, 1998), 21, 28.
28. Supreme Court, 7 October 1960, *Suzuya Finance*, Minshu, Vol. 14, No. 12, 2420 for the term 'dividend'; Supreme Court, 27 October 1961, *Kangyo Keizai*, Minshu, Vol. 15, No. 9, 2357 for the term 'TK contract'.
29. Supreme Court, 9 September 1997, *Marital Deduction*, Shomu Geppo, Vol. 44, No. 6, 1009.

within the sense of the Civil Code for the purpose of dependent family deduction in Income Tax Law.[30]

As is often the case for any doctrine, there is an exception to uniform interpretation. The Supreme Court permits room for departures from uniform interpretation when the context of the tax provision so requires. The term 'gift' in a rollover of cost base provision was thus construed as not to include onerous gift that brings about an economic benefit to the donor.[31] The Supreme Court itself did not dwell upon the reasoning for departing from the definition of gift under the Civil Code that included both pure gifts and onerous gifts. However, it supported the lower court decision. That decision explained the structure of the Income Tax Law that the cost base of property in the hand of the donor is carried over to the donee when the taxation of capital gains/losses in the underlying property is deferred.

Thus the general attitude in favour of uniform interpretation has room for exceptions. It is not a categorical interpretative method. Its application is somewhat flexible. In spite of this flexibility, the uniform interpretation faces a number of challenges. For instance, the borrowed concept may lack a clear pre-determined content in private law. A lower court decision nevertheless tried to follow private law construction in a case where the meaning of 'body of group without legal personality' was disputed.[32] Interpretative issues become even more complex when legal concepts of foreign jurisdictions are involved. The proper entity classification of Delaware LPS for tax purposes was litigated in various lower courts with conflicting conclusions. The Supreme Court decided that the Delaware LPS was a 'corporation' under Japan's Income Tax Law.[33]

[3] Tax Avoidance: SAARs

Japan does not have a General Anti Avoidance Rule (GAAR) in its tax code. On the other hand, there are a number of Specific Anti-Avoidance Rules (SAARs). Some SAARs are quite extensive and give power to a tax director to recalculate the amount of corporate income tax if he/she finds that the amount of corporate income tax is 'unduly reduced'. Such SAARs apply to act or computation of a family company, to a corporate reorganization, and to a consolidated tax return.

When three or less shareholders hold more than 50% of the shares in a company, that company is defined as a 'family company'. Nearly 96% of corporations operating in Japan belong to this category. Therefore, the SAAR applicable to family companies covers most corporations and can hardly be called 'specific' as far as its coverage is concerned.

30. Supreme Court, 17 October 1991, *Dependent family*, Shomu Geppo, Vol. 36, No. 5, 911.
31. Supreme Court, 19 July 1988, *Onerous Gift*, Hanrei Jiho, No. 1290, 56.
32. Fukuoka High Court, 18 July 1990, *Mice scheme*, Hanrei Jiho, No. 1395, 34.
33. Supreme Court, 17 July 2015, *Delaware LPS*, Minshu, Vol. 69, No. 5, 1253. A Korean commentator took note of Japanese judicial developments, *see* Ji-Hyun Yoon, 'An End of a Journey or a New Beginning? – The 2012 Trilogy of Supreme Court Decisions on International Tax', (2013) 19 (3) *Asia-Pacific Tax Bulletin*, 190, 192.

For corporate income tax purposes the SAAR applicable to family companies dates back to 1923. The statutory language has been modified several times but has remained unchanged since 1950. The essential part of the current provision reads as follows:[34]

> Corporation Tax Law Article 132(1)
>
> In making determination or correction of a corporation tax regarding the corporations prescribed in the following, a tax director may compute the tax base or the net loss of corporation tax, or the amount of corporation tax, in accordance of his/her recognition, notwithstanding the act or computation by the corporation, when he/she finds that the said act or computation by the corporation, if respected, would result in an undue reduction of the burden of corporation tax (emphasis added).
>
> (i) family company which is a domestic corporation
> (ii) [translation omitted].

This provision has been constantly held to be constitutional in spite of its rather broad conditions for application. Interestingly, the SAAR for family companies exists only for individual income tax, corporate income tax, inheritance tax, and gift taxes, but not for VAT.

A number of court cases have dealt with the application of this provision. Most importantly, the court developed a general test for determining whether the act or computation resulted in an 'undue reduction' of the corporation tax. The general test was to inquire the reasonableness of an act and calculation of the family corporation as a pure economic actor.[35]

The legal effect of applying this provision is to recalculate the amount of income, deductions, and tax amount only for corporate income tax purposes. It does not extend to withholding taxes.[36] Nor does it modify the private law effect of underlying transactions.

Starting from the 1990s, the NTA began to apply the SAAR for family companies on individual income tax cases. A notable example is a case involving an interest-free loan exceeding JPY 345 billion from an individual shareholder to the family company that he owned.[37] The court affirmed NTA's application of the SAAR that created income to the shareholder on the theory that he should have received an adequate amount of interest in an arm's length setting. The conclusion was later confirmed by the Supreme Court.

In a recent case, the Supreme Court applied the SAAR to a corporate reorganization, disallowing the carryover of net operating losses of a merged company.[38] The Court interpreted the word 'unduly reduced' in Corporation Tax Law Article 132-2 as

34. Translation and emphasis by the author.
35. Supreme Court, 21 April 1978, *Korakuen Hotel*, Shomu Geppo, Vol. 24, No. 8, 1694, affirming the lower court decision.
36. Supreme Court, 14 December 1973, *Tsukamoto Shoji*, Shomu Geppo, Vol. 20, No. 6, 146.
37. Tokyo High Court, 31 May 1999, *Pachinko Heiwa*, Shomu Geppo, Vol. 51, No. 8, 2135.
38. Supreme Court, 29 February 2016, *Yahoo*, Hanrei Times No. 1424, 68. *See also* its accompanying case, Supreme Court, 29 February 2016, *IDCF*, Hanrei Times No. 1424, 83.

meaning the reduction of corporate tax burden with an 'abuse' of corporate reorganization provisions as a device for tax avoidance. The factors to consider in order to determine whether or not such 'abuse' exists would be: (1) the unreasonableness of act and computation in question; (2) the non-existence of reasonable business purpose and other relevant facts. The Court required both: (a) the intention to reduce the tax burden; and (b) the manner that deviates from the objective of the corporate reorganization provisions, in order for the SAAR to apply.

[4] Tax Avoidance: Judicial Activism

In response to corporate tax shelters that became a social issue in the early 2000s, the Supreme Court countered the practice in three consecutive cases. In the first, a foreign tax credit was disallowed as an 'abuse' of the system.[39] The court stated the policy objective of the foreign tax credit system and denied its application because the transaction deviated from the original purpose of the system. The court also noted that the transaction was incurring a loss on a pre-tax basis. The ruling could be read as teleological interpretation which is derived from the court's reading of the purpose of the provision. However, the usage of the term 'abuse' was rather new and created stirs among commentators.

In the second case, a depreciation deduction was disallowed to a corporate investor in a partnership structure that purchased film in a circular transaction.[40] The Court found that the partnership had, in substance, lost the right to exploit and to dispose of the film, that the partnership did not incur financial risks, and that the corporate investor did not have an interest in the business profits of the film production. The film in question was held not to be a 'depreciable asset' in the meaning of the Corporation Tax Law.

In the third case, value shifting from a domestic corporate shareholder to a foreign shareholder was disallowed.[41] The corporate shareholder had a wholly owned Netherlands subsidiary. The subsidiary issued new shares to another Netherlands corporate shareholder well below market price. As a result, the domestic shareholder suffered a dilution in the share value in the old stock. The dilution was intentional and was based on an agreement among the parties involved. The court applied the basic provision in income computation for gratuitous transfers by finding that there was a 'transaction' in this case.

[5] Common Sense

The Supreme Court took a common sense view in determining whether or not a commercial bank's bad-debt could be written off as a loss in its corporate income tax

39. Supreme Court, 19 December 2005, *Risona Bank*, Minshu, Vol. 59, No. 10, 2964.
40. Supreme Court, 24 January 2006, *Film Lease*, Minshu, Vol. 60, No. 1, 252.
41. Supreme Court, 24 January 2006, *Obunsha Holding*, Hanrei Jiho, No. 1923, 20.

computation.[42] The case arose in the middle of the financial crisis after the crash of the bubble economy in the early 1990s in Japan. The court stated that the corporation could deduct the bad-debt loss only when the whole amount of debt was unenforceable and that such unenforceability was objectively clear. The court emphasized that the test for such conditions must be 'examined globally according to a socially accepted idea'. The court produced a few factors for such examination: debtor's circumstances, creditor's circumstances, and economic environment. The examination is basically a question of fact-finding, but the overall resort to common sense paved the way to admitting the bank a deduction of bad-debt loss in the amount of JPY 376 billion.

[6] Estoppel

As mentioned in §11.02[A], the principle of statute-based taxation prevails in Japan. Tax officials have no discretion to reduce or increase the amount of tax liability that is dictated by statutes. Otherwise, there could be room for unequal treatment and, potentially, corruption. It follows that if a tax official makes an assessment based on an incorrect interpretation of statutes, the tax assessment must be corrected.

When a taxpayer relies on an incorrect interpretation or incorrect advice issued by tax officials, however, there arises a question whether taxpayer's reliance needs to be protected. The Supreme Court is naturally reluctant to endorse a wrong interpretation. However, the court hints at applying the doctrine of estoppel in limited circumstances.[43] The Supreme Court stated that at least the following factors must be fulfilled before its application may be considered: tax authority's issuance of its formal position, taxpayer's action based on a reliance on such formal position, economic damages produced by the tax assessment contrary to the issued formal position, and lack of responsibility on the part of the taxpayer. Under this holding, the scope for taxpayer remedy is rather narrow. However, it is significant that the Supreme Court mentioned the possibility that the taxpayer's reliance can be protected. The court doctrine formed the basis for the development of the Japanese version of advance ruling, which was formalized in 2001 and expanded in 2004.

§11.05 CONCLUSIONS

Several themes emerge from the foregoing:

- Japan's Supreme Court takes a literal approach to tax statutory interpretation with due regard to the objective and purpose of the provision.
- There is no striking difference in judges' interpretive attitudes between VAT and Income Tax Laws.
- Treaty case law is only beginning to emerge in Japan.

42. Supreme Court, 24 December 2004, *Industrial Bank of Japan*, Minshu, Vol. 58, No. 9, 2637.
43. Supreme Court, 30 October 1987, *Estoppel*, Hanrei Jiho, No. 1262, 91.

- Transplanted concept is interpreted uniformly with its original meaning, but the court is flexible to modify its meaning if the context so requires.
- Anti-avoidance rule for family companies in Japan is a broad provision, and the court developed a reasonableness test in its application.
- There has been recent judicial activism to counter corporate tax shelters.

CHAPTER 12

Legal Interpretation of Tax Law: Russian Federation

Danil V. Vinnitskiy

§12.01 INTRODUCTION

The Russian legal system belongs to the systems of continental law and, in the view of some historians and legal theorists, it possesses quite noticeable common features with the German legal system in particular.[1] However, the economy which existed in the USSR (based on the dominance of public property) also left significant traces and, in some aspects, still influences the legal system of modern Russia, although much of this influence has been removed in the course of modernization of legislation over the past two decades.

Interpretation is a key factor in any legal system as it is the vehicle by which law really affects society. In the tradition of legal systems belonging to the Romano-Germanic legal family, Russian law is based on major codified legislative acts, including a general part that contains the most abstract and important provisions. The Russian tax legislation is not an exception here; it is systemized into a single/codified act – the Tax Code of the Russian Federation. The Code consists of two parts, with first part containing general provisions and the second part dealing with the rules applicable to particular taxes. Each particular factual situation, which requires the application of an abstract legal norm, is unique. The application of abstract provisions to particular fact situations is only possible with careful interpretation of the relevant norm in light of the particular facts.

In the recent years, and more precisely since 2006,[2] one may see an increasing role for case law in the Russian legal system, especially in the area of tax law, which has

1. Victor D. Perevalov, *Theory of State and Law*, 2nd edn (Moscow: Urait, 2012), 366 C. 366.
2. *See* §12.04 of this chapter.

led to a decreasing role of the *pure* doctrinal interpretation of legal norms and principles and of the administrative interpretation as well. Consequently, judicial doctrines, more concrete in their content, are starting to develop and become a relatively independent object of interpretation which leads to new 'derivative' doctrines splitting off (even more concrete and designed to be applied in regard to quite a narrow category of disputes), etc.

From a practical perspective the interpretation activity in the Russian legal system is manifest at four levels. The highest level of interpretation takes place at the constitutional level, with interpretation provided by the Russian Constitutional Court viewed as a special kind of interpretation. By virtue of the status of the Constitutional Court, it is equal in its legal force to the Russian Constitution itself if the objects of interpretation are constitutional norms. If the objects of interpretation by the Russian Constitutional Court are the norms of 'usual' laws then, while the law being interpreted is in force, this interpretation is binding for all those who will apply the respective law.

A second level of interpretation is judicial interpretation apart from the interpretation provided by the Russian Federation (RF) Constitutional Court. This type of interpretation is the most important kind of interpretation for tax law as the majority of tax disputes are solved in the commercial courts and in the courts of general jurisdiction.

A third level of interpretation is administrative interpretation. Administrative interpretation as a form of official interpretation was very important from 1991 to 1999, during the period of the Russian post-soviet tax system but before the codification of tax legislation. Since 1 January 1999, acts of administrative interpretation provided by tax authorities are not binding for taxpayers and courts.

The fourth level of interpretation is doctrinal interpretation outside the actual tax dispute resolution process. This kind of interpretation indirectly influences, through the legal education system and academic discussions, the interpretation activity at the levels of constitutional jurisprudence, proceedings in the 'usual' courts and administrative practice. However, the peculiarity of the doctrinal interpretation in the Russian Federation is that it is strictly segmented according to the branches of law, with the constitutional law playing the role of the connecting environment.[3] The practical consequence of such segmentation is a principle that precludes the application of rules established in one branch of law to situations regulated by other branches of law.

In order to examine in more detail the issues of interpretation in Russian tax law it is necessary first to look at a number of general issues characterizing the Russian legal and tax systems generally, and in particular: (1) to review the system of tax authorities and their powers; (2) to consider the Russian system of courts and their respective jurisdictions; (3) to summarize the Russian system of taxation; and (4) to look at the system of principles underlying Russian tax law and interpretation rules.

3. Sergey S. Alekseyev, *General Theory of Law*, vol. 1 (Moscow: Yuridicheskaya literatura, 1981), 240–250 1981, C. 240–250).

§12.02 TAX AUTHORITIES, TAXATION AND JUDICIAL SYSTEM

[A] The Interpretative Power of the Tax Authorities

The organizational structure of the authorities imposing taxes in the Russian Federation is defined in a special federal law - the RF Tax Code (the first part of this Code has been in effect since 1 January 1999). According to Article 30(1) of the RF Tax Code, tax authorities form a single centralized system controlling compliance with tax laws, correct computation and payment of taxes to the Russian budgetary system. The organization of the tax authorities includes the central tax administration and its territorial subdivisions at the regional and municipal levels.[4] The central tax administration, known as the Federal Tax Service (FTS), is a federal body of state power. Its territorial subdivisions are therefore not subordinate to the RF regions and municipalities. Article 30(4) of the RF Tax Code provides that the tax authorities perform their functions and interact with the executive authorities of the RF regions and municipalities. However, 'interaction' in this context means only the coordination of activities.

The FTS may not lay down general rules for taxation (legal normative acts) but is obliged to strictly exercise the established tax rules in accordance with the procedures defined by the RF Tax Code.[5] With some exceptions,[6] only the FTS possesses the authority to levy all federal, regional and local (municipal) taxes in the RF.

While carrying out its quite broad powers, the FTS and its territorial subdivisions perform a great number of legally significant actions: inspections of taxpayers, the demanding and obtaining of documents, decisions on the recovery of taxes, interest and tax penalties, suspension of operations relating to accounts of the taxpayer, etc. According to Russian tax law, all these decisions and actions of the tax authorities may be appealed in the judicial or (and) administrative system. Some years ago, both kinds of remedies (judicial and administrative) could be used simultaneously but now pre-court procedure is obligatory in nearly all important tax disputes. In particular, if a taxpayer wishes to challenge the decision of a tax authority concerning tax sanctions, the taxpayer must first file an administrative complaint and only if and after it has been rejected (entirely or partly) is the taxpayer able to appeal to the court.[7] This rule has only been in effect since 1 January 2009 and is aimed at decreasing the great number of tax disputes with which Russian courts had to deal. Since the amendments of 2013 to the RF Tax Code came into force, the pre-court administrative procedure has been obligatory for nearly all important tax disputes.

4. The RF Government regulation of 30 September 2004 № 506 'On Federal Tax Service' (version of 20 March 2013) specified the powers of the tax authorities. Additionally, Order of the RF Ministry of Finance of 9 August 2005 № 101-n adopted the Act 'On territorial subdivisions of the RF Federal Tax Service' (version of 5 April 2012). However, now this Order has been replaced by Model regulation on 'On territorial subdivisions of the RF Federal Tax Service' (Order of the RF Ministry of Finance of 17 July 2014 № 61.
5. Articles 4, 31–32 of the RF Tax Code.
6. The powers of the RF Customs Service to levy VAT and excises on imports and the powers of some state authorities to impose levies of parafiscal character, for example, pension fund contributions.
7. Article 138(2) of the RF Tax Code.

When one considers interpretation of tax legislation by the tax authorities in Russia, it is important to take into account the special regime for recovery of taxes for natural persons (without the status of entrepreneur). In the case of natural persons, a court decision is needed in order to recover unpaid taxes, interest and sanctions. A tax authority has to apply to court within six months following the date on which its demand to pay a tax voluntarily was not met.[8] As a result, comprehensive judicial control over all decisions on tax recoveries concerning natural persons is exercised (irrespective of the citizenship, residence or domicile of the natural person). This approach is based on a decision by the RF Constitutional Court where it held that preliminary judicial control over the decisions of a tax authority is a necessary guarantee for natural persons from unjustified interference from tax authority control.[9]

[B] System of Courts and Their Interpretative Jurisdictions

Legal protection of taxpayers is quite a multi-faceted and urgent topic and there is probably no jurisdiction in the world where taxpayers' protection would be found wholly sufficient (for one reason or another). In particular, difficult issues arise when violations of taxpayers' rights are the result of conflicting interpretations of legal norms at different levels of legal regulations. In the Russian Federation, at least two classes of problems of this kind are evident. The first is when taxpayers' rights suffer due to conflicting interpretations of federal and regional laws, with one of the interpretations being more favourable for taxpayers than the other. The second class of problems arises when taxpayers' rights suffer due to conflicting interpretations of tax law norms (federal or regional) and constitutional legal regulations, particularly the RF Constitution.

It is interesting to see how these two categories of problems are dealt with in the Russian Federation. Of particular significance are the situations when the Russian legal system provides for the protection of taxpayers' rights in special courts (judicial bodies) and the preliminary ruling procedures can be applied.

The first set of problems, conflict between the interpretations of federal and regional tax legislation is quite rare in current Russian practice because, although establishing the main principles of taxation is a joint competence of the federal and regional governments within the RF,[10] in fact the Russian tax legislation is quite centralized, being based on the RF Tax Code. The regions of the Federation[11] may only regulate quite a narrow range of tax matters such as granting tax privileges and deferral

8. Article 48 of the RF Tax Code.
9. Decision of 17 December 1996 № 20-P examining the constitutionality of Art. 11(1) (2 and 3) of the RF Law of 24 June 1993 'On the Federal bodies of tax police'; in particular para. 4. The Russian Federation (RF) Law of 24 June 1993 'On the Federal bodies of tax police' was abolished but it is not relevant for the legal significance of the above-mentioned court decision as it was based directly on the interpretation of the RF Constitution.
10. Article 72 of the RF Constitution.
11. There are 85 regions of the Russian Federation; they are usually called 'subjects of the Russian Federation'.

with regard to the payment of tax (under certain conditions provided for by the RF Tax Code).

In case there are certain contradictions between the interpretations of regional and federal tax legislation that infringe taxpayers' rights, a taxpayer can go to an 'ordinary' court[12] to challenge the regional law. In addition, fourteen regions of the Russian Federation, in particular St.Petersburg and Sverdlovsk region, have special courts known as Charter Courts[13] that provide taxpayers with the additional possibility of challenging regional tax legislation on grounds of its conflict with the Charter[14] of the region. However, the preliminary ruling procedure is not applicable in the case of Charter challenge cases. If a taxpayer decides to challenge regional tax legislation in an 'ordinary' court, the court has no right to forward a request to the Charter Court even if it finds that the regional tax legislation contradicts the Charter of the given region. Thus, the jurisdiction of Charter Courts is not of an exceptional or imperative character.

Claims that taxpayers' rights have been violated by a conflict between tax legislation (federal or regional) and the RF Constitution (and the constitutional principles formulated in it) may only be pursued in the RF Constitutional Court, which has exclusive authority in this field. The Federal Constitutional Law provides that taxpayers may directly address the RF Constitutional Court, as well as 'ordinary' courts (which hear tax cases), if they have doubts whether the application of (federal or regional) tax law is in accordance with the RF Constitution.[15] An 'ordinary' court may forward a request to the RF Constitutional Court to rule on the constitutionality of tax measures at any stage of the procedure.[16] Once the issue has been forwarded, the proceedings in the 'ordinary' court will be suspended.

Article 3(3) of Federal Constitutional Law of 21 July 1994 № 1-FKZ 'On the RF Constitutional Court' specifies that 'with the purpose of protecting the constitutional order, the fundamental rights and freedoms and providing the supremacy and direct effect of the RF Constitution on the entire territory of the Russian Federation', the RF Constitutional Court, at the request of other courts, reviews 'the constitutionality of a law which is applied or has to be applied in a certain case'. However, the RF Constitutional Court deals only (and exclusively) with the legal matters. When carrying out constitutional proceedings, the RF Constitutional Court must refrain from establishing and examining the facts of the case to the extent of the competence of other courts or other authorities. Referrals are made to the RF Constitutional Court on the

12. By 'ordinary' courts we mean a court of general jurisdiction to which individuals have access and commercial courts that companies and businesses can address.
13. The term derives from the title of the main legal act that determines the status of the respective regions of the Federation – 'Charter'.
14. All Charters of the regions of the Federation include a rule that regional legislation must comply with federal legislation. Due to this clause, Charter Courts can in fact handle a wide range of matters, including the compliance of the regional legislation with federal legislation. However, the decisions of 'ordinary' courts in any case have priority in this field, on the basis of the jurisdiction provided for by the RF Constitution.
15. The Federal Constitutional Law of 21.07.1994 № 1-FKZ (amended 5 April 2013) 'On RF Constitutional Court'.
16. Article 101 of Law № 1-FKZ.

basis of 'the uncertainty which has been found in understanding the provisions of the RF Constitution'.[17]

It is not often that ordinary courts forward requests to the RF Constitutional Court. The number of direct applications by citizens is significantly greater. One of the important recent cases which was tried at court request is the RF Constitutional Court Decision of 14 July 2005 №9-P 'On the case of controlling the constitutionality of provisions of Article 113 of the RF Tax Code in connection with the complaint from G.A. Polyakova and the request from the Federal Commercial Court of Moscow district.' In this case the RF Constitutional Court decided to examine two independent cases together – the complaint from the individual and the court request – because they both concerned the same tax norm, which defines the time limitation for legal responsibility of a taxpayer.

Where the law[18] does not sufficiently specify the procedural details for dealing with a court request, the grounds on which the RF Constitutional Court may deny the request to hear a case are also not quite obvious. In particular, the RF Constitutional Court can decide that there is *no uncertainty* as to the meaning of the RF Constitution and that the tax law under challenge is quite in accordance with it. Such a decision can be adopted without open proceedings in which the taxpayer could participate.

As the RF Constitutional Court does not examine the facts of a case, even its affirmative decision only provides limited (constitutional) protection of taxpayers' rights because the 'ordinary' court has to decide the case on a broader account of facts and legal principles than presented to the RF Constitutional Court.[19] The RF Constitutional Court may disagree with the opinion expressed in the request of an 'ordinary' court and find the legal norm that is challenged to be in accordance with the RF Constitution. However, it may give a new interpretation which will be different from the one expressed in the 'ordinary' court's practice. In this situation the 'ordinary' courts will have to follow this new interpretation as it has a binding character for them.

A Decision of the RF Constitutional Court on an 'ordinary' court ruling request is not only binding for the requesting court and the taxpayer involved, but will have precedence for all other courts dealing with similar cases and even for the legislator. The latter may not override or repudiate the RF Constitutional Court position by adopting a new law with the same content as such a law would be initially invalid because of its conflict with the established interpretation of the RF Constitution.

17. Article 36 of Law № 1-FKZ.
18. Chapter XIII of Law № 1-FKZ.
19. Not all the legal norms relevant for the case will be checked by the RF Constitutional Court but only those which were pointed out in the 'ordinary' court request.

[C] Tax System and Principles

[1] General Overview of the Russian Tax System and Recent Trends in Tax Policy

The Russian tax system has undergone very important changes since 2000. During this period the second part of the Russian Federation Tax Code, each chapter of which is devoted to a certain tax, was developed and adopted. The second part of the RF Tax Code has replaced the un-systemized legislation of the 1990s, which was developed in quite a hurry and under conditions of permanent budget deficit and which, as a result, had many shortcomings, including those connected with legislative technique.

[a] Tax on Income of Natural Persons

In the post-2000 reforms, the primary changes in terms of the personal income tax were the lowering of tax rates and broadening of the tax base. A flat tax rate of 13% was adopted for most types of income derived by resident natural persons. However, a relative high rate of 30% for non-residents remained unchanged, as well as a high 35% rate for some irregular categories of income such as income from lottery winnings and grants received from affiliated persons. The introduction of a flat tax rate allowed abolishing the uniform procedure of filing tax returns, previously compulsory for everyone, and reducing compliance costs. The tax base was significantly broadened by abolishing some ineffective tax privileges and mainly by including into the tax base non-monetary incomes, that is payments in kind or as a 'material benefit' such as interest-free loans and written off debts.

[b] Tax on Profits of Organizations

The general principle of the reform, lowering the rates and broadening the tax base, also applied to the reform of the tax on profits of organizations. However, the tax rate was not reduced significantly, falling from 24% to 20% (with the possibility of further reduction of the latter at the regional level. At the same time, with the adoption in 2002 of the new 25th chapter of the Russian Federation Tax Code dealing with the tax on profits of organizations, all previous tax privileges were abolished. Among the other significant innovations was the introduction of an open list of deductions allowable when calculating taxable income.[20]

[c] Other Business Taxes

Some business taxes were introduced in the framework of special tax regimes established by Part II of the RF Tax Code. These include a simplified system of taxation,

20. Previously there was a closed list of expenses approved by the Russian Government Ruling № 552; evidently, that approach did not correspond to the realities of the market economy.

a single tax on presumed income, a single tax on agriculture producers, a fixed business tax for small business, and a single tax for production sharing agreement regimes.

[d] Value Added Tax

The adoption of the second part of the RF Tax Code (Chapter 21 'VAT') saw a significant improvement of the VAT system. In particular, collection rules in regard to different kinds of operations were specified, as well as the conditions of applying tax privileges, including the reduced rate of VAT (10%). On the whole, the general trend of the reform was to move the Russian VAT model closer to the VAT model applied in the European Union, Russia's main trade and economic partner. In regard to import and export of goods (including transportation and ancillary services) a concept of a '0% tax rate' was introduced and the detailed rules providing for the conditions of its application and VAT refund to exporters were established. Also, all the legislative powers connected with VAT regulation were transferred to the federal level exclusively and the previous regional sales tax was abolished in 2004.

[e] Excises

The legal regime for excises is provided for by Chapter 22 of the RF Tax Code, which replaced a previous special law. The production of alcohol, tobacco, fuel and cars remained subject to excise tax but the production of oil and natural gas was shifted to a specific tax on the extraction of natural resources in Chapter 26 of the Code. Similar as with VAT, the legal regime for excises in the Eurasian Economic Union / Customs Union (of the Russian Federation, the Republic of Kazakhstan, the Republic of Belarus, the Republic Kyrgyzstan and the Republic of Armenia) was regulated in detail through a system of special international multilateral tax treaties – *see* Article 72 of the Treaty on the Eurasian Economic Union of 29 May 2014 and Attachment № 18 to it.

[f] Recurrent Taxes on Capital

Within the framework of tax reform and the adoption of the second part of the RF Tax Code, Chapter 30 was included into the Code, dealing with taxation of property of organizations. This tax was given the status of a regional tax. However, a new tax on property owned by natural persons was introduced in 2015. It had previously been regulated by a 1991 that had proved problematic as a consequence of strong social resistance to the taxation of immovable property owned by natural persons should be based on the *market* value of the property. Moreover, the creation of a unified state cadastre of property has not yet been fully completed.

[g] Non-recurrent Taxes on Capital

The inheritance and gift tax on property was abolished in 2006. Under current law, inheritance of property is exempted from taxation, but gifts (unless between close relatives) are subject to personal income tax in accordance with Chapter 23 of the RF Tax Code.

[h] Compulsory Social Security Contributions Paid to Government

Social security contributions were traditionally held in extra-budgetary funds such as the pension fund and the compulsory medical and social insurance funds. The legal regime of their collection has changed three times in opposite directions since 2000. *First* they were shifted from the area of parafiscal contributions (levies earmarked for a specific purpose and paid to an authority separate from the National Tax Service) to the area of taxation. *After a short time*, the former collection regime was restored and contributions were withdrawn from the Russian tax system. As with personal income tax, the most important material changes are lower rates and broader tax base. In particular, a regressive scale of rates was introduced for taxing employers (contributions are computed in regard to payroll),[21] as well as the lump-sum tax for self-employed persons. In 2016, social security contributions were incorporated in Chapter 34 of the RF Tax Code again.

[i] Environmental Taxes

The Russian tax system includes no taxes specifically identified as environmental taxes. However, materially, some taxes actually perform this function including water tax (Chapter 25.2) and charges for the use of wildlife and aquatic biological resources (Chapter 25.1). In addition, parafiscal charges that depend on the level of pollution are imposed.

[j] Other Taxes

An important tax in terms of revenue generation is the tax on the extraction of natural resources.[22] Most natural resources are taxed on the basis of the cost or value of the resources extracted. The extraction taxes imposed on oil and natural gas are levied on the basis of the volume of extraction of these resources (Article 388 of the RF Tax Code). Other taxes introduced in Part II of the RF Tax Code include a municipal land tax, a regional transport tax and a regional gambling business tax.

A review of the Russian tax system reveals that there is no organizational or economic basis for segmentation of legal interpretation depending on the characteristics of a particular tax. Moreover, the Russian tax system is quite centralized and the

21. For instance, from 26% to 2% (before abolishing the single social tax per 1 January 2010).
22. Chapter 26 of the RF Tax Code.

main actors involved in tax law interpretation are all part of the federal level of government (the FTS, the RF Constitutional Court, commercial courts and courts of general jurisdictions, the RF Ministry of Finance, etc.).

[2] Principles of Russian Tax Law and Interpretation Rules

[a] General Constitutional Framework for Legal Interpretation by the Tax Authorities

Although the formulation of general principles of taxation is constitutionally a joint competence of the federation and RF regions,[23] according to the RF Constitutional Court insofar as the general principles of taxation are connected with securing the fundamental rights of individuals, they are within the competence of the federation.[24] This approach also reflects, according to the Court, one of the foundation stones of the RF constitutional system, the principle of a 'unified economic space'[25] which means, in particular, that within the limits of the territory of the Russian Federation any customs borders, charges, duties or any other obstacles to the free movement of goods, services or capital are strictly prohibited.[26] From a procedural perspective, the 'unified economic space' and, consequently, the unified tax system are secured by the single system of federal tax authorities – the FTS. The tax authorities as federal bodies under the RF Constitution are subordinate exclusively to the federal government.[27]

In a 2004 case, the RF Constitutional Court clearly formulated general constitutional parameters for the tax administration to observe when exercising its authority.[28] In this case, the provisions of the RF Tax Code on the time limits for tax inspections, including the inspections exercised by the superior tax authority (as a form of control of the activities of an inferior tax authority which held a previous inspection) were analysed. In its decision, the RF Constitutional Court stressed that in giving the authority to tax administration the legislator must ensure compliance with Articles 55, 8, 17, 34, and 35 of the RF Constitution. According to these provisions, a restriction of taxpayer constitutional rights is allowed when the following principles are respected and implemented: the principles of justice, adequacy, proportionality and the admissibility of restrictions in favour of the public interest which is evidently of constitutional value.

23. According to Art. 72(1) ('i') of the RF Constitution.
24. Foremost, and taking into account its structural links to other provisions of the RF Constitution, in its Decision of 21 March 1997 № 5-P 'On verifying the constitutionality of Arts 18(2) and 20 of the RF Law "On the fundamentals of the RF tax system".'
25. Article 8(1) of the RF Constitution.
26. Article 74(1) of the RF Constitution; Art. 3(4) of the RF Tax Code.
27. Articles 71('j'), 78(1) of the RF Constitution.
28. Decision of the RF Constitutional Court of 16 July 2004 № 14-P 'On verifying the constitutionality of Art. 89(2) of the RF Tax Code in connection with the complaints of A.D. Yegorov and N.V. Chuyev.'

[b] *Principle of Legality in Russian Tax Law*

The principle of legality is a key principle, directly derived from the RF Constitution. Normative legal rules must be applied in accordance with the procedures provided for by law, and in particular, by the RF Tax Code. The system of taxes and the general taxation principles in the RF are established by federal law.[29] In this context, as the RF Constitutional Court has stressed repeatedly, the activities of tax authorities must be exercised in accordance with general constitutional principles of organization and activities of all state executive authorities, including the principles of 'rule of law' and inadmissibility of arbitrary interference in the economic activities of the company (entrepreneur) being inspected. Court practice follows the principle of necessity of taxation and obligation to pay taxes. At the same time, the procedural requirements established by law are obligatory for tax authorities[30] and may not be ignored under the pretext of the constitutional significance of taxation.[31]

[c] *Principle of Determinacy in Russian Tax Law*

There have been a considerable number of court decisions, including RF Constitutional court decisions, which have held tax normative acts invalid because of violation of the principle of determinacy or certainty of legal regulation. An example is a 1999 decision of the RF Constitutional Court[32] in which the court found that the procedure of imposing sanctions on a taxpayer had not taken the degree of culpability into account and that the grounds for imposing different sanctions were not clearly identified.[33] According to the Court, uncertainty or indeterminacy as to the legal content of the provisions conflicts with the basic principles of law in regard to imposing public law sanctions.[34] The fundamental legal criteria of certainty or determinacy, clarity, non-ambiguity of a legal norm follows from the constitutional principle of equality,[35] as equality can only be implemented in the case of a uniform understanding and interpretation of a norm by all courts and executive authorities. Indeterminacy or uncertainty as to the content of a legal norm, in contrast, would lead to an unlimited discretion in its application and, consequently to the violation of the principles of equality and supremacy of law.

---

29. On the basis of Arts 72(1)(i) and 75(3) of the RF Constitution.
30. Articles 15, 18 of the RF Constitution.
31. *See* e.g., the Decision of the RF Constitutional Court of 1 December 1997.
32. Decision of the RF Constitutional Court of 15 July 1999 № 11-P 'On verifying the constitutionality of the RF Laws on the RF Tax Service', 'On the fundamentals of the RF tax system' and 'On the federal bodies of tax police'.
33. *See* e.g., Art. 13(1)(a) of the former RF Law 'On the fundamentals of the RF tax system'.
34. Earlier the criterion of determinacy of a legal norm as a constitutional requirement for the legislator was formulated in the Decision of the RF Constitutional Court of 25 April 1995 on a non-tax case 'On verifying the constitutionality of Article 54 of the RF Housing Code'.
35. Article 19(1) of the RF Constitution.

[d] *Principle of Equality and Proportionality in Russian Tax Law*

In a 2004 case, the RF Constitutional Court stressed the importance of the principle of equality when procedural rules are applied in tax matters.[36] This principle does not exclude differences in the legal treatment of taxpayers taking into account the objective differences in their actual circumstances, however. In particular, the RF Constitutional Court pointed out that the RF Tax Code provides for both a unified and differentiated approach to establishing time limits within which a tax inspection may be carried out. This dualistic approach is aimed at realizing equal treatment and equal legal protection for all taxpayers while allowing flexibility to the extent taxpayers' situations are demonstrably different.[37] Accordingly, the Court held that it is in accordance with the RF Constitution to differentiate between the time limits of tax inspections based on such criteria as the peculiarities of the tax regime to be applied, the scope of economic activity, etc. However, the differentiation must be justified and the criteria used to make the differentiation must be established in accordance with the principles of certainty, determinacy, clarity and non-ambiguity of a legal norm.

[e] *Presumption of Bona Fides and the Burden of Proof in Russian Tax Law*

An important constitutional guarantee in tax matters derived from Russian legal doctrine is that a taxpayer is not obliged to prove the lawfulness of his activities (operations); they are presumed to be lawful and his intentions are considered bone fide until proven otherwise.[38] This principle influences the distribution of the burden of proof in tax cases as it means the burden of proof lies primarily on the tax authorities, although, in accordance with the judicial procedural rules, a taxpayer is obliged to provide proof supporting the arguments which are used for the taxpayer's position.

[f] *Right of Appeal and Comprehensive Court Control*

As the RF Constitutional Court has repeatedly pointed out, the guarantee of judicial protection applies to all persons[39] and cannot be subject to any restrictions as it secures the actual implementation of all other constitutional rights and freedoms. According to the RF Constitutional Court, the state is responsible for the comprehensive implementation of the right of judicial protection, which must be fair, competent and effective. In the Decision of 16 July 2004 № 14-P, the Court held that it is not the original task of 'ordinary' courts to control the activities of tax authorities if they exercise those activities in the framework of their discretionary competence. However, 'to secure the

36. Paragraph 3 of the Decision of 16 July 2004 № 14-P, *supra* note 28.
37. *See* Art. 19 of the RF Constitution.
38. One of the important court decisions on this issue is the RF Constitutional Court Decision of 25 July 2001 № 138-O, taken at the request of the RF tax authorities to interpret the previous Decision of 12 October 1998. The Court stressed that according to the meaning of Art. 3(7) of the RF Tax Code and provisions of the RF Constitution the presumption of the bona fide of taxpayers exists in tax relations.
39. Article 46(1) and (2) of the RF Constitution.

balance of public and private interests' it is necessary for courts to verify the exercise of discretionary competence in case the activities of a tax authority infringe the fundamental rights of taxpayers in respect of activities such as inspections, the demanding and obtaining of documents, or assigning expert examination.

As follows from Articles 46(1), 52, 53 and 120 of the RF Constitution, a taxpayer must have a right to go to court in the case of the possible arbitrary exercise of discretionary competence of executive authorities including the tax authorities. Thus, the RF Constitutional Court proceeds from the principle of comprehensive judicial control and considers it necessary to also control the exercise of discretionary competence of tax authorities.

[g] Compensation for Damages Incurred as the Result of Unlawful Actions

Article 35 of the RF Tax Code provides for the possibility of compensation for damages incurred as the result of unlawful actions by the tax administration. Payment of compensatory damages is provided through the federal budget and the procedure is regulated by and based on general principles of tort law, including the principle of full compensation of damages. The order in which compensation is paid out is provided for by the RF Budget Code. In practice, claims by taxpayers for compensatory damages are quite rare. On the whole, the RF Tax Code clearly proceeds from the baseline that causing unlawful damages to a taxpayer is prohibited.[40] Abuse of power by a tax authority is also the violation of constitutional rules.[41]

§12.03 ADMINISTRATIVE INTERPRETATION IN RUSSIAN TAX LAW

[A] Individual Acts of Interpretation Issued by Tax Authorities

[1] General Overview

The complexity and the detailed character of tax legislation give great significance to the practice of interpretation by tax authorities and accordingly the tax legislation contains a number of provisions dealing with legal interpretation by tax authorities. Three particularly important sets of provisions are those establishing the right of a taxpayer to receive an 'act of interpretation' (tax ruling) and the obligations of some state authorities to issue it,[42] the provisions defining the legal nature of tax rulings and determining the powers of the state authorities to issue them,[43] and the provisions determining the legal consequences of compliance by a taxpayer with an 'act of interpretation' (tax ruling) that turned out to be wrong and inconsistent with tax legislation.[44] The importance of these provisions for practice may be illustrated by

40. Articles 35, 103 of the RF Tax Code.
41. *See*, the RF Constitutional Court Decision of 16 June 2004 № 14-P, *supra* note 28.
42. Articles 21(1)(1), 21(1)(2), 32(1)(4) and 31(1)(6) of the RF Tax Code.
43. Articles 4, 32(1)(5) and 34.2 of the RF Tax Code.
44. Articles 75(8) and 111(1)(3) of the RF Tax Code.

statistics on the involvement, by mid-year of 2013, of the Commercial Courts[45] in which taxpayers sought relief from penalties levied on the basis of an incorrect act of interpretation in tax rulings provided by tax authorities or the Ministry of Finance. In all, during thirteen years the rule was in force about 1,450 cases were heard at different levels of the Commercial Court system, illustrating the practical significance of the issue. The number of cases on the issue decreased in the period 2013–2016, reflecting a more consistent interpretation of tax issues by the tax administration and consequently greater stability and predictability in the assessment process.

[2] Legal Framework and Nature

Russian tax law does not establish a clear borderline between two different kinds of acts of administrative interpretation – private tax rulings (aimed at a single taxpayer) and general tax rulings (for any person). In this context, it is necessary to define the correlation between tax rulings as acts of interpretation and as sources of tax law. This issue is quite important in connection with the activity of the Ministry of Finance and tax authorities, as it is they who are authorized to officially interpret Russian tax legislation. Often state authorities give an abstract interpretation of a tax rule in their response to a taxpayer's ruling request. This reply may later be published (or put in an electronic database), thus potentially providing guidance to all taxpayers in the same or similar situation. The question arises of whether in such a situation tax rulings become normative, or remain an act of interpretation.

The RF Tax Code distinguishes clearly between acts of statutory regulation and legal rules produced by executive authorities. The former includes acts adopted by the Russian State Duma (Parliament), regional parliaments and by the representative bodies of municipalities (Article 1 of the RF Tax Code). The latter includes legal acts of executive authorities mentioned in Article 4 of the RF Tax Code.[46] It follows from the wording of this Article that normative legal acts may be issued by three executive authorities: the RF Government, the RF Ministry of Finance,[47] and the Federal Customs Service.[48] Article 4(2) of the RF Tax Code specifies that the FTS with its territorial subdivisions[49] may not issue normative legal acts on taxation. Thus, from the point of view of the RF Tax Code, the RF Ministry of Finance may, in principle, issue normative legal acts[50] but the FTS is not granted this power.

45. Commercial Courts of federal districts (which are 10 in Russia) are the cassation, i.e., the third court instance (after the first and appellate ones). Commercial Courts deal, in particular, with cases between tax authorities and taxpayers which have the status of an organization (legal entity) or an individual entrepreneur. Commercial Courts, as a rule, do not deal with cases involving individuals without the status of an individual entrepreneur.
46. The norm is effective in the version amended by the Federal law of 27 June 2006 № 137-FZ.
47. *See* §1 of the Regulation 'On the RF Ministry of Finance' adopted by the Decree of the RF Government of 30 June 2004 № 329 (version of 30 May 2007).
48. *See* §2 of the RF President Decree of 11 May 2006 № 473 (version of 24 September 2007).
49. Article 30 of the RF Tax Code.
50. The concept of normative legal act is mostly dogmatic, formulated by academics. However, courts have defined this concept too. Thus, according to §12 of the Ruling of the RF Supreme Court Plenum of 20 January 2003 № 2 'On certain issues which arose in connection with

The issuing of normative legal acts in the form of letters and telegrams is not allowed.[51] Structural subdivisions and territorial subdivisions of executive federal state authorities may not issue normative legal acts. However, a large majority of individual tax law interpretation acts of financial and tax authorities are given in the form of so-called letters and are issued on behalf of certain departments of the central administration of the RF Ministry of Finance or the FTS or on behalf of territorial subdivisions of these authorities. Consequently, according to the above-mentioned formal criteria, the interpretation acts of both the RF Ministry of Finance and the FTS should not be regarded of normative character.

There are inconsistent court decisions on this issue. The RF Supreme Court[52] refused to find letter rulings[53] invalid on grounds that it lacked jurisdiction to rule on this.[54] The Court argued that the letters challenged by the claimant are not normative legal acts as they do not establish legal norms and also did not undergo state registration in the RF Ministry of Justice, which is obligatory for such normative legal acts. Commercial Courts reached similar conclusions concerning letters of interpretation character issued by territorial tax authorities. For example, the Commercial Court of the East Siberian federal district held that letters of tax administration which contain tax law interpretations are of recommendation character, are not obligatory[55] and do not entail any legal consequences for taxpayers.[56] In contrast, the RF Supreme Commercial Court has a different point of view on the issue.[57] The Court has held that a letter ruling had features of a normative legal act. The Court considered that this letter is addressed to territorial tax administrations and aimed at establishing a uniform order of levying an income tax for individuals on daily allowances. As the RF Ministry of

adopting the RF Code of Civil Procedure', a normative legal act means an act issued in the established order by the authorized state body, municipal body or an official, establishing legal norms (norms of behaviour) which are (1) obligatory for some categories of persons; (2) designed to be applied repeatedly; and (3) are in force regardless of the fact whether a specific legal relationship provided for by the act arose or was terminated. A similar view may be found in §9 of the Ruling of the RF Supreme Court Plenum of 29 November 2007 №48 'On practice concerning the cases on issuing legal normative acts'.

51. *See* §2 of the Regulation 'On preparing normative legal acts of executive federal state bodies and their registration' adopted by the RF Government Decree of 13 August 1997 № 1009 (version of 27 March 2013).
52. In accordance with Art. 27(1)(2) of the RF Code of Civil Procedure, the RF Supreme Court as a Court of First Instance tried cases of challenging normative legal acts of different executive federal state bodies concerning the rights, freedoms and interests of individuals and organizations. Now the same provision has been provided for by Art. 2(1)(4) of Federal Constitutional Law of 5 February 2014 № 3-FKZ 'On the RF Supreme Court'.
53. Letter of the Department of Tax, Customs and Tariff Policy of the RF Ministry of Finance of 3 May 2005 № 03-05-01-05/54 and the letter of the RF Ministry of Finance of 11 July 2005 № 03-05-01-03/63 (these documents are not currently in force).
54. Decision of the RF Supreme Court of 27 December 2005 № GKPI05-1625.
55. Article 21(1)(11) of the RF Tax Code provides that taxpayers 'shall have the right to ... not fulfill unlawful legal acts and requirements of tax bodies, other competent bodies and their officials which do not correspond to the RF Tax Code or other federal laws'.
56. Decision of the Commercial Court of the East Siberian federal district of 1 July 2004 № A78-552/04-C2-28/74-Ф02-2381/04-C1.
57. Decision of the Presidium of the RF Supreme Commercial Court of 26 January 2005 № 16141/04 'On finding invalid the letter of the RF Ministry of Taxes and Charges 17 February 2004 № 04-2-06/127'.

Taxes and Charges (RF MTC)[58] instructs this order should be brought to the notice of the subordinate tax administrations and this distinguishes the given letter from the interpretation acts on some specific requests of taxpayers (private tax rulings). The letter in question was found inconsistent with the RF Tax Code and not effective as a legal normative act. It should be stressed that the challenged letter was adopted on 17 February 2004; on the date of its adopting the right of the RF MTC to issue normative legal acts within the framework of their competence was established by §11 of the Regulation 'On the RF Ministry of Taxes and Charges' approved by the RF Government Decree of 16 October 2000 №783.[59] However, this decision of the RF Supreme Commercial Court is still important in regard to legal acts of the RF Ministry of Finance.

The position of the RF Ministry of Finance is that the information on tax legislation and written interpretation acts on applying tax laws which taxpayers are entitled to obtain in accordance with Article 21(1) (1 and 2) of the RF Tax Code are not of normative character and, *mutatis mutandis*, taxpayers are not obliged to comply with its position.[60] Thus, the RF Ministry of Finance intention is to avoid giving its acts of tax law interpretation the force of normative legal acts.

[3] Subjective Scope and Objective Scope of a Tax Ruling

[a] Applicants Entitled to Obtain a Ruling

According to Article 21(1)(1) and 21(1)(2) of the RF Tax Code it is the *taxpayers* who are entitled to obtain tax law interpretation acts from tax and financial authorities. The concept of a taxpayer is defined in Article 19 of the RF Tax Code as organizations and individuals on whom tax liability is imposed in accordance with the Code. In addition, Article 11 of the RF Tax Code defines the concept of organization to include, in addition to Russian and foreign legal entities, branches and establishments of foreign legal entities, branches and establishments of international organizations, and foreign corporate formations without the status of legal entity but possessing civil legal capacity.

As a consequence, organizations that are not civil law subjects according to Russian civil law will still be entitled to independently realize their tax rights, including the right to obtain tax law interpretation rulings.

Article 21(3) of the RF Tax Code states that payers of state charges in general have the same rights as taxpayers. Consequently, the payers of state charges (e.g., State duty) will also be entitled to receive tax law interpretation rulings along with taxpayers.

Article 24 of the RF Tax Code includes the definition of the concept of another participant in the tax process – tax agent. Article 24(1) defines tax agents as persons on whom in accordance with the RF Tax Code the obligations to compute, withhold and transfer tax payments to the budget of the RF are imposed. By virtue of Article 24(2) of

58. The RF Ministry of Taxes and Charges was transformed into the Federal Tax Service of Russia.
59. This legal act became ineffective due to the issue of the RF Government Decree of 30 September 2004 №506.
60. Letter of 3 March 2006 №03-02-07/1-47.

the RF Tax Code, tax agents enjoy the same rights as taxpayers unless the RF Tax Code explicitly states otherwise. Also otherwise provided for by the RF Tax Code, tax agents, similar to taxpayers, are entitled to obtain tax law interpretation acts. This issue is of interest in respect to subjects that are not taxpayers in regard to taxes but retain the status of tax agent. For example, a subdivision of the FTS is not a taxpayer but would be recognized as a legal entity from the point of view of civil law and, because it has the status of a tax agent in respect of the individual income tax it withholds from its employees' salaries, it would be entitled to obtain a ruling.

[b] Issues for Which a Ruling May Be Requested

In accordance with Article 21(1) of the RF Tax Code taxpayers are entitled to obtain the information (also in written form) from the tax authorities where they are registered on existing taxes and charges, on statutory legislation on taxes and charges and normative acts adopted in accordance with them, on the order of computing and paying taxes and charges, on rights and obligations of taxpayers, and on the powers of tax authorities and their officials. Article 21(1)(1) entitles taxpayers to receive the forms of tax returns and the information on how to complete them. Thus, the RF Tax Code allows taxpayers to request any information concerning tax legislation both of general character and in regard to specific taxes. Taxpayers are not obliged to confirm whether they intend to apply the ruling request at any point in the future. It is therefore of no significance whether the taxpayer's ruling request relates to a present or a future transaction. However, the tax period to which a respective ruling of a competent authority refers may be quite relevant.

[4] Issuing Authorities: Tax and Financial Bodies

In accordance with Article 21(1) of the RF Tax Code, taxpayers are entitled to obtain necessary information on taxation in writing from the tax office of registration,[61] and written interpretation rulings from the RF Ministry of Finance on the application of RF tax legislation. A practical issue arises in determining which government entity should issue a tax ruling at the taxpayer's request. The RF Ministry of Finance believes that in *specific economic situations* a taxpayer should address the tax office with which the taxpayer is registered with specific questions on computing and paying taxes. At the same time, a taxpayer is entitled to a ruling from the RF Ministry of Finance (or from other financial authorities of RF Regions or municipalities) on abstract questions of applying tax legislation.[62]

Other letter rulings offer a slightly different model of allocating competence to issue tax law interpretation rulings. Tax offices have the obligation to provide copies of information contained in tax legislation and the normative legal acts adopted in

61. This taxpayer's right corresponds with the obligation of tax authorities to provide such information, *see* Art. 32(1)(4) of the RF Tax Code.
62. Letter of 21 September 2004 №03-02-07/39 (§1 and §2).

accordance with the legislation. In this model of division of responsibilities, *elementary questions* which do not require a legal opinion and interpretation of laws on taxation should be directed to the tax authority and questions which require the analysis and interpretation of tax legislation and a legal opinion should be directed to the RF Ministry of Finance.[63]

The uncertainty resulting from these differing views and the controversial position of the RF Ministry of Finance is not of essential significance, as it happens very seldom that a tax office would refuse to issue a ruling to a taxpayer and should a tax local office have any problems reaching a decision, it can request advice from the Central Administration of the FTS which in its turn can come to an agreement on the legal position with the RF Ministry of Finance.

With a system that authorizes both the RF Ministry of Finance and the FTS to issue tax rulings, the more urgent problem appears to be the potential for conflicting or contradictory opinions concerning the same or similar situations. Under Article 32(1)(5) of the RF Tax Code, tax authorities are obliged to follow guidance provided by rulings of the RF Ministry of Finance on applying tax legislation. Consequently, when collisions arise priority is given to the rulings issued by the RF Ministry of Finance. To reduce the occurrence of inconsistent rulings, a joint commission has been formed to coordinate the interaction between the RF Ministry of Finance and the FTS in regard to interpretation of tax legislation.[64]

[5] Protection Enjoyed by the Recipient of a Ruling (Act of Official Interpretation)

Article 111(1)(3)[65] of the RF Tax Code effectively makes tax rulings binding on the tax authority by exonerating a taxpayer from any wrong-doing and preventing the imposition of tax penalties if taxpayer has complied with directions in written rulings on computing and paying a tax (or on any other question of applying tax legislation) issued by a competent tax authority. Article 75(8) of the RF Tax Code similarly protects a taxpayer (and other persons placed on the same footing) from interest charges if an underpayment results from compliance with incorrect rulings.[66] The principle underlying these measures have a constitutional basis in the principle 'of maintaining trust of the citizens to law and the actions of the state'.[67] A ruling is effectively binding on the tax authority in respect of tax periods covered by the ruling, regardless of when the ruling itself has been issued. However, rulings are not binding on the tax authority if they are based on incomplete and incorrect information given to the authority by a taxpayer.

63. *See*, the letter of the Federal Tax Service of Russia of 26 January 2005 №III-6-01/58.
64. By Decree of the RF Ministry of Finance of 9 August 2005 № 102H (version of 17 July 2006).
65. The article is effective in the version amended by the Federal law of 27 August 2006 № 137-FZ.
66. An earlier version of Art. 75(8) of the RF Tax Code did not limit the possibility of levying interests on taxpayers who erred in their tax reporting due to compliance with an incorrect tax ruling.
67. *See*, for instance, the Decision of the RF Constitutional Court of 5 July 2005 № 246-O.

Officials authorized to sign rulings of the FTS are the Head of the Tax Service of Russia and the Head's deputies as well as heads of territory subdivisions of the Service and their deputies within their competence.[68] Officials authorized to express the position of the RF Ministry of Finance in written rulings on the issues of applying RF tax legislation are the RF Minister of Finance and Deputy Minister of Finance as well as the head and deputy head of the Department of Tax, Customs and Tariff Policy.[69] Only rulings signed by these persons represent the position of the RF Ministry of Finance in the sense of Article 111 and Article 75(8) of the RF Tax Code.

In addition to the letters of the RF Ministry of Finance and the FTS of Russia, the Commercial Courts quite often recognize in their case law four types of communication as official rulings that exempt taxpayers from tax penalties:

- decisions by a tax authority based on the results of a previous tax audit in which the computation of a tax in similar situations was accepted;[70]
- written directives of a superior state authority to an inferior one;[71]
- methodology recommendations on computing and paying a tax;[72]
- instructions on filling in tax returns.[73]

Articles and commentary in mass media, replies to questions given by officials in database on their face should not be considered as official rulings as they usually represent a personal opinion of an official of a certain state authority. However, case law is not consistent in this respect. Courts, at times, have protected taxpayers in receipt of information other than a technically compliant ruling. In one case, for example, a taxpayer claimed that he treated short-term loans as tax exempt services on the basis of a written opinion of the deputy head of the Department of Analysis and Methodology of Indirect Taxes of the RF Ministry of Finance published in a newspaper. The Court held that in this situation the taxpayer should not be subject to tax penalties in accordance with Article 111(1)(3) of the RF Tax Code.[74] In another case, heard by the Commercial Court of the North-Western federal district, for example, the taxpayer was unsuccessful in arguing that the opinion of the adviser of the FTS published in a database could serve as a ground for exemption from penalties according to Article 111(1)(3) of the RF Tax Code.[75]

68. RF Ministry of Finance, Letter of 13 January 2005 № 03-02-07/1-1.
69. Letter of the RF Ministry of Finance of 6 May 2005 № 03-02-07/1-116.
70. Decision of the Commercial Court of the North Western federal district of 4 March 2005 № A56-26746/04.
71. Decision of the Commercial Court of the Moscow federal district of 13 January (17 January) 2005 № KA-A41/12802-04.
72. Decision of the Commercial Court of the Volgo-Vyatskiy federal district of 23 December 2004 № A79-5685/2004-CK1-5372.
73. Decision of the Commercial Court of the West Siberian federal district of 22 December 2004 № A56-276/04.
74. Decision of the Commercial Court of the Volgo-Vyatskiy federal district of 10 November 2004 № A43-14279/2003-31-632.
75. Decision of the Commercial Court of the North-Western federal district of 22 March 2004 № A05-9051/03-20.

Rulings only protect taxpayers against imposing tax penalties and interests. They do not prevent the tax authority from computing and collecting underreported taxes from the taxpayer. The law does not specify any particular validity period for tax rulings. However, a systematic analysis of the RF Tax Code suggests that taxpayers complying with a tax ruling are protected until the underlying law interpreted by the ruling has been changed or until the ruling has been abolished, either directly or indirectly (i.e., by the issuing authority or a superior authority). Once a tax ruling has been found in violation of the law by a competent court, it ceases to provide taxpayer protection prospectively. Subsequent transactions are not covered by ruling protection.

§12.04 JURIDICAL INTERPRETATION IN RUSSIAN TAX LAW

[A] Introduction

It is evident that the application of the RF Tax Code to a large extent will depend on how the provisions of the RF Tax Code are interpreted by the courts, especially the RF Supreme Commercial Court of the Russian Federation prior to 8 August 2014 and its replacement body since then, a 30-judge Economic Collegium that is a part of an expanded RF Supreme Court. Judicial decisions, especially decisions of the former RF Supreme Commercial Court in the period 2006–2014, may be regarded as precedent, although Russian doctrinal texts will more often use the phrases 'legal position' or 'judicial doctrine' to describe a rule applicable in subsequent judicial acts. It was not unusual for judicial decisions, especially judicial decisions of the RF Supreme Commercial Court in the period 2006–2014, to *go beyond a literal interpretation of statutory norms and, basically, create new, derivative norms* – legal interpretations that are binding upon inferior courts.

Case law[76] has undergone very substantial changes in the last eight years.

[B] Judgments of the Courts as Acts of Interpretation and Sources of Law[77]

[1] Approaches of Academics and Practitioners

The role of case law and, in particular, decrees of the Presidium of the RF Supreme Commercial Court (RF SCC) and currently of the RF Supreme Court has been the subject of constant academic debate. Some authors consider it to be a special source of Russian law while others view it as an interpretative/derivative source. A third group

76. In this chapter, the term 'case law' is used to denote the totality of court precedents that contain applicable legal positions and judicial doctrines.
77. The author used for the preparation of this part of the article his previously presented expert opinions for courts and international arbitrage.

does not regard it as a source of law at all, although this group concedes it is of key importance in the resolution of individual legal cases.[78]

This debate has a long history. In the Soviet era, views were expressed (though not as often or universally as now) to the effect that 'judicial doctrine serves as an important source of Soviet law because the Supreme Courts of the Union and the Union republics publish bulletins of "model judgments" and verdicts in specific cases. Theoretically, the inferior courts are not bound by these judgments. In practice, however, every lawyer knows that if he refers in court to a ruling of the RF Supreme Court in a similar case, the court will decide his case in exactly the same way. However, leaving aside these de facto outcomes, the Plenums of the RF Supreme Court issue resolutions that provide theoretical explanations of the law, which, in effect, establish new legal norms'.[79]

Starting in the 1990s, under the new economic conditions and following the modernization of the legal system, these views became more and more widespread. For example, Professor V.P. Mozolin argued that '(...) the rulings and decrees/resolutions of the higher courts formulate general judicial doctrine as a source of law that stands alongside the legal consciousness and statutes (and other normative acts)'.[80] O.M. Sviridenko, President of the Central District Federal Commercial Court and formerly the President of the Moscow City Commercial Court, suggested that: '[b]ecause clarifications from the RF Supreme Court and the RF Supreme Commercial Court are binding upon judges we should concur with those academics who recognize the case law of the higher courts as a source of law. We think that vesting the courts with the law-making function will facilitate improvements to existing legislation.'[81]

Technical decisions issued by a panel of RF Supreme Commercial Court judges on whether cases should be passed on to the Presidium for consideration may also sometimes be treated as governing rules. The regulatory significance of rulings of the RF Supreme Commercial Court is evidenced by the fact that inferior courts regularly cite them in their judgments.

78. *See*: Vitaliy V. Sorokin, 'Judicial Practice as a Source of Law: For and Against', Sibirskiy yuridicheskiy vestnik, 2003, № 3; Sergey A. Notin, Judicial Practice within the System of Sources of Tax Law: EC and RF as Examples: Dissertation for Ph.D. in Law, 2003; Svetlana V. Miroshnik & Valeriy V. Raygorodskiy, 'Decisions of the RF Constitutional Court as a Source of Tax Law', Nalogi (newspaper), 2008, № 21; Anna A. Kopina, 'The Place of Judicial Practice within the System of Sources of Tax Law', Finansovoye pravo, 2008, № 12; Olga A. Tonenkova, 'Judicial Practice as a Source of Administrative Law', Administrativnoye pravo and protsess, 2010, № 2: 42-44; Arman Y. Mkrtumyan, 'Judicial Practice as a Source of Russian Law: Historical and Legal Aspects', Istoriya gosudarstva and prava, 2008, № 9; Elena M. Tsyganova, 'Judicial Practice as a Source of Law', Yuridicheskiy mir, 2006, № 2 and elsewhere.

79. Anatoliy A. Tille, *Socialist Comparative Jurisprudence*, (Moscow, 1975), 143.

80. Viktor P. Mozolin, 'Future Paths for Development of Civil Law', *Zhurnal rossiyskogo* prava, 2007, № 3.

81. Oleg M. Sviridenko, 'Judicial Practice - A Source of Russian Law?', Sovremennoye pravo, 2010, № 10: 64-65.

[2] The Legislative Basis for the Judicial Role

In the period 1993–2014 Article 127 of the RF Constitution established the RF SCC as the highest judicial authority in the resolution of economic disputes and other cases heard by the commercial courts and provided, in the procedural forms envisaged by federal law, judicial supervision of their activities and provides clarification of questions of case law. Since 8 August 2014, in accordance with Article 126 of the RF Constitution, the RF Supreme Court (RF SC) exercises the functions of the RF SCC. Article 23 of the Federal Constitutional Law (1996)[82] in effect reproduced the Article 127 of the RF Constitution; currently Article 19 provides the same in regard to the RF SC.

Article 16 of the Federal Constitutional Law (1995)[83] clarified the powers of the *Presidium of the RF SCC* (Article 391.12 of the RF Civil Procedure Code in regard to the RF SC). It stated that the Presidium of the RF SCC reviews in-force decisions of the commercial courts in the Russian Federation and examines individual issues arising in case law and informs commercial courts in the Russian Federation of the outcome of that process. While this provision has not been in force since 2014, Article 2 of Federal Constitutional Law of 5 February 2014 №3-FKZ «On the RF Supreme Court» provides similarly authority to the RF SC using the same language.

Accordingly, in terms of statutory law, the legally binding nature of decrees of the Presidium of the RF SCC / RF SC is predetermined by its capacity to review court decisions produced by the inferior courts where they do not reflect the legal positions formulated in decrees of the Presidium and/or resolutions of the Plenum of the RF SCC / RF SC.

Until August 2014, Chapter 36 of the RF Commercial Procedure Code (RF CPC) and, in particular, Article 292, envisaged that 'in-force judicial acts of the commercial courts in the Russian Federation may be judicially reviewed according to the rules of this chapter by the Supreme Commercial Court of the Russian Federation at the request of parties to the case, or other persons as specified in Article 42 of this Code and, in the cases specified in Article 52 of this Code, upon a representation from the prosecutor'. Since 2014 Chapter 36.1 and Article 308.1 have delegated the same authority to the RF Supreme Court.

Further, by virtue of Article 298 of the RF CPC (currently Article 308.4 of the RF CPC), the RF SCC / RF SC may even suspend execution of a judicial act rendered by an inferior court pending consideration of the matter of its revocation on the merits.

Article 304 of the RF CPC (currently Article 308.10 of the RF CPC) sets out in detail how the RF SCC/ RF SC is able to monitor the inferior courts' practice for compliance with the legal positions developed by it and expressed, *inter alia*, in decrees of the Presidium of the RF SCC / RF SC. The RF CPC establishes that '[i]n-force judicial acts of the commercial courts are subject to variance or revocation in the event

82. Federal Constitutional Law of 31 December 1996 №1-FKZ 'On the Judicial System in the Russian Federation'.
83. Federal Constitutional Law of 28 April 1995 №1-FKZ 'On Commercial Courts in the Russian Federation'.

that the Presidium of the Supreme Court of the Russian Federation establishes by judicial review that the contested judicial act ... breaches the uniformity of the commercial courts' interpretation and application of legal norms; ... [or] infringes the rights and lawful interests of an indefinite range of persons or other public interests'.

By virtue of this, both the RF SC itself and the lower courts often cite and apply both resolutions of the Plenum of the RF SCC/ RF SC and decrees of the Presidium of the RF SCC / RF SC. Recently, to support and encourage this practice, a specific direction was added to Article 170 of the RF CPC which states that the explanatory part of a judgment of commercial court may include references to resolutions of the Plenum of the Supreme Commercial Court / Supreme Court of the Russian Federation relating to questions of case law and decrees of the Presidium of the Supreme Commercial Court / Supreme Court of the Russian Federation[84]

Nearly the same approach to the judicial review and to the role of resolutions of the Plenum and decrees of the Presidium in Chapter 41.1 of the RF Civil Procedure Code can be seen in the area of the activity of the courts of general jurisdiction.

[3] Special Cases of Procedural Retroactivity in Judicial Interpretation

Decrees of the Presidium of the RF SCC/ RF SC acquired their additional governing weight and strong influence on case law when they began to be treated as grounds for a review of previously adopted, in-force judicial acts of the lower courts. The claimed judicial power to retrospectively examine previous lower decisions stands in contrast to tax legislation which, as a consequence of Article 5 of the Tax Code can only have a prospective application (the Article provides a general prohibition upon the retroactive application of tax legislation).

Many practitioners consider a 2007 Resolution of the Plenum of the RF SCC to be the most important step in the partial adoption in Russia of a common law precedent based system of law, particularly in the area of taxation, in which judicial doctrine already played an unusually large role in delimiting lawful and unlawful conduct. The Resolution indicated that appellate courts should take account of contrary subsequent appellate decrees of the RF SCC when asked to reviewing earlier lower court decisions.[85] This approach was upheld by the RF Constitutional Court.[86] The legal position of the RF SCC and the RF Constitutional Court concerning the governing role of decrees of the Presidium of the RF Supreme Commercial Court was subsequently incorporated

84. Article 170 of the RF CPC – 'Content of judgment' (version of 23 December 2010).
85. Resolution of the Plenum of the RF SCC of 12 March 2007 № 17 'On the Application of the RF Commercial Procedure Code in the Review of In-force Judicial Acts Based on Newly Discovered Facts' (version of 14 February 2008, Resolution of the Plenum of the RF SCC № 14). Now *see also*: Resolution of the Plenum of the RF SCC of 30 June 2011 № 52.
86. *See*, in particular, Decision of the RF Constitutional Court of 21 January 2010 № 1-P 'Verification of the Constitutionality of the Provisions of Part 4 of Article 170, Section 1 of Article 311 and Part 1 of Article 312 of the Commercial Procedure Code of the Russian Federation, Pursuant to Appeals from Closed Joint Stock Company Production Association Bereg, Open Joint Stock Company Karbolit, the Mikroprovod factory and Research and Production Enterprise Respirator.'

into statutory law.[87] A later decree of the Plenum of the RF SCC explicitly confirmed that previous inconsistent decisions can be reviewed retroactively directly by the courts which issued the respective decisions.[88]

[C] Judicial Interpretation and Anti-avoidance Doctrines in Russian Tax Law

[1] General Overview

A key concept in Russian tax law respected by courts but not actually mentioned in Russian tax legislation is that of a 'justified or unjustified tax benefit', a notion related to other unlegislated guiding concepts such as 'the good faith of the taxpayer'. An understanding of how the Russian tax authorities and courts currently interpret and apply the norms of the RF Tax Code concerning the procedure for calculating and paying corporate income and VAT requires an understanding of how the concept of 'justified or unjustified tax benefit' evolved and the particularities of how it is used.

Many countries, regardless whether they belong to the civil law or common law legal traditions, have incorporated a General anti-abuse rule (GAAR) directly into their legislation.[89] However, the Russian Federation uses general anti-abuse mechanisms based primarily on case law and legal interpretation. This point is clearly confirmed by various Decisions of the Plenum of the RF Supreme Commercial Court, Decrees of the Presidium of the RF Supreme Commercial Court / RF Supreme Court and Decisions and Rulings of the RF Constitutional Court.

[2] Fluctuations in Precedent

The origins of the modern general anti-avoidance principles are commonly traced to a 2001 Ruling of the RF Constitutional Court[90] considering an application from the RF Ministry of Taxes and Charges for clarification of how an earlier ruling on protection of private property would apply to a case in which the tax authority sought to recover unpaid taxes.[91]

87. Subsection 5 of s. 3 of Art. 311 of the Commercial Procedure Code – 'Grounds for review of judicial acts based on new or newly discovered facts' (version of 23 December 2010).
88. Resolution of the Plenum of the RF SCC of 30 June 2011 № 52 (version of 23 March 2012) 'On the Application of Provisions of the Commercial Procedure Code of the Russian Federation in the Reviewing of Judicial Acts on the basis of New or Newly Discovered Facts'.
89. *See*, for example, the provision of §42 (2) of Germany's Abgabenordnung (General Fiscal Law), Art. L. 64 of the French Livre de Procédures Fiscales (Tax Procedures Code) and Art. 25 of Spain's Ley General Tributaria (General Tax Law). As to common law jurisdictions, Australia, India, New Zealand, South Africa, the UK, and the US all have GAAPs as well.
90. Ruling of the RF Constitutional Court of 25 July 2001 № 138-O.
91. The earlier Decision of the RF Constitutional Court of 12 October 1998 № 24-P was based on the concept of 'the bona fide taxpayer'. The Decree states '(...) charging a bona fide taxpayer more than once for taxes that have not been paid to the budget infringes constitutional guarantees relating to private property. (...) The constitutional duty to pay taxes is deemed discharged at the

Other cases make it clear that the burden of proving bad faith on the part of the taxpayer lies with the competent state authorities. This is illustrated in a RF Supreme Court decision of 7 February 1997[92] that struck down as unreasonably onerous conditions imposed by the RF State Service on exporters seeking allowances available in respect of the taxation of exported goods. The court thought that the requirements that were intended to prevent the faking of exports, created an excessive burden for bona fide exporters, effectively and incorrectly shifting to legitimate exporters the duty to prove their good faith.

The issue of what actions by the taxpayer might constitute 'bad faith' has been the subject of many court disputes and for the most part case law is rather unfavourable to taxpayers as it does not clearly define the criteria for delimiting 'good faith' and 'bad faith' actions. Particular difficulties occurred in assessing good faith in the context of applying the provisions of a 1996 Order of the RF President aimed at increasing tax collections in the face of a budget crisis.[93] The concept of bad faith, when it is interpreted in conjunction with the provisions of the Order, has sometimes caused transactions, aimed at avoiding tax, to be declared invalid under Article 169 of the RF Civil Code and, consequently, assets of both parties to the transaction were confiscated and paid to the budget.[94] Later case law since 2006 proved considerably softer and more liberal towards taxpayers in the resolution of tax avoidance disputes.

The main document that currently defines judicial approaches to the interpretation of Russian anti-avoidance doctrines in tax law is the Resolution of the Plenum of the RF Supreme Commercial Court of 12 October 2006 №53, entitled 'Evaluation of Legitimacy of Tax Benefit Claimed by Taxpayer' (hereinafter 'Resolution №53'). The Resolution establishes a presumption of good faith on the part of taxpayers and thus a presumption that taxpayers are entitled to any tax benefits or concessions they seek, subject to a number of factors that could displace that presumption.

However, a tax benefit may be deemed unjustified, in particular, where operations have been taken into account for taxation purposes not in accordance with their true economic intent or operations have been taken into account which were not occasioned by reasonable economic or other grounds (business objectives). A tax benefit cannot be deemed justified if it was received by a taxpayer outside the context of genuine entrepreneurial or other economic activities (paragraphs 3 and 4 of Resolution №53).

time at which part of the bona fide taxpayer's property is actually expropriated within the framework of public-law relations.'

92. On application of paras 5, 6 and 7 of s. 22 of the Instruction of the RF State Tax Service of 11 October 1995 №39 (version of 22 August 1996).
93. Order of the RF President of 18 August 1996 №1212 entitled 'Measures to Increase the Collection of Taxes and Other Mandatory Payments to the Budget and to put in Order the Circulation of Cash and Non-Cash Money'.
94. The Resolution was subsequently supplemented by the Resolution of the Plenum of the RF SCC of 10 April 2008 №22, entitled 'Certain Issues of Practice in Consideration of Disputes Relating to the Application of Article 169 of the Civil Code of the Russian Federation', which restricted the application of Art. 169 of the RF Civil Code to tax relations. *See* now the Resolution of the Plenum of the RF SC of 23 June 2015 №25.

The factors that could be used to displace the presumption, focused on the economic substance of transactions, looking at whether they were part of genuine entrepreneurial activity, evidence of business purpose, and the impact of non-arm's length transactions on financing or timing decisions. Taxpayers have been able to use the enumerated list as a shield in debatable circumstances by arguing the tax authority had been able to show the taxpayer's claim was unambiguously an unjustified tax benefit in light of the specific factors. For example, in a 2007 case, № A40-11992/06-143-75, the RF SCC prevented the State Tax Service from denying a benefit available to exporters on the grounds of technical points related to the taxpayer's paperwork without evidence they impacted on the legitimacy of his transactions. By the following year, however, courts were moving to reduce the ability of taxpayers to use the 2006 Resolution № 53 as a shield when claiming deductions for corporate income tax and input-tax credits under VAT. Courts sometimes seized on section 1 of Resolution № 53, which provides that, under certain circumstances, the taxpayer can be stripped of tax advantages if the tax authority proves 'that information contained in (...) documents [that the taxpayer has submitted] is incomplete, inaccurate and (or) inconsistent' and section 4 of Resolution № 53, which says that a tax benefit cannot be received 'outside *the context of genuine entrepreneurial or other economic activities*', to deny taxpayers' claims. The new court decisions adopted strict views of the need for the accuracy of documents and the information they contain (understood in a formal sense) and the genuineness of business operations.

A turning point in the formulation of this approach was the Decree of the Presidium of the RF SCC of 11 November 2008 № 9299/08 (hereinafter 'Kestroi 1' or 'Decree № 9299/08'). The court dismissed the taxpayer's appeal against the tax inspectorate's assessment for additional profit tax, interest and fines for non-payment of the tax and a reduction of VAT rebates, in effect reversing the onus set out in 2006 Resolution № 53. The court decision noted that taxpayer's claims regarding the calculation of profits tax and entitlement to VAT rebates are recognized unless the tax authority proves that information contained in documents is incomplete, inaccurate or inconsistent but went on to say that the taxpayer's claims will be treated as legitimate only where there are accurate documents evidencing genuine economic operations, leaving the taxpayer with responsibility for proving entitlement to benefits rather than the tax authority accepting the taxpayer's report. Based on section 1 of Resolution № 53, the court was about to reject in whole the taxpayer's claims, pointing out that the tax invoices had been attributed to a natural person who did not sign them and who had nothing to do with that organization. In fact, the court pointed out there was no senior manager or chief accountant at the company able to sign the invoices, leaving the taxpayer with no primary accounting documents that would evidence the incurring of expenses. Strengthening the tax authority's case was evidence presented by the authority that the taxpayer lacked the management and technical staff, fixed assets, production assets, storage facilities and means of transport to carry on the economic activity claimed to be performed for taxation purposes.

The decision in *Kestroi 1* has become a powerful precedent. Since the decision, the taxpayer's intention to obtain an unjustified tax benefit ceased to be the determining factor (as required according to Resolution № 53) in resolving this category of disputes. The key question in determining the outcome of taxpayers' appeals has become whether the documents submitted by the taxpayer were accurate and whether they accurately demonstrated the genuineness of the commercial operations with named parties. If the documentation raises doubts as to the economic reality of the enterprises operations, it is not necessary for the tax authority to accept the taxpayer's claim and proceed with detailed calculations based on the claim. Decree № 9299/08 thus changed the distribution of the burden of proof between the tax authority and the taxpayer. From that point onwards it was the taxpayer who had to prove the reality of its business operations and the genuineness of documents if the representative of the taxpayer's counterparty in the business operation testified that she or he had not been involved in the operation.

The shifts in judicial approaches from 2006 following the release of 2006 Resolution № 53 and the swing of the pendulum in the other direction following the 2008 Decree № 9299/08 provides important insights into the dynamics of modern juridical interpretation in Russian Tax Law and the manner in which anti-avoidance judicial doctrine can evolve as the courts reconsider their role in the tax law system.

§12.05 INTERPRETATION OF TAX TREATIES IN THE RUSSIAN LEGAL SYSTEM

[A] General Overview

For the past 20 years the Russian Federation has pursued quite an active international tax policy; it has signed 86 conventions for the avoidance of double taxation with respect to taxes on income and on capital and at present, Russia has 80 double taxation conventions in force.[95] In addition, several double taxation conventions have been negotiated and signed but not yet ratified by the RF Parliament. Russian double taxation conventions generally follow the Organization for Economic Co-operation and Development (OECD) Model (or sometimes UN Model). However, articles derogating from these models can be found in certain treaties concluded by Russia. In principle, the Russian approach to double taxation conventions is reflected in the model treaty approved by the RF Government Regulation of 24 February 2010 № 84 (the previous model was approved by the RF Government Regulation of 28 May 1992 № 352). The differences between it and the OECD Model are not significant.

The tax treaties concluded by the RF as a rule do not contain any special procedural rules not found in the existing models (e.g., OECD Model). The exception is a tax treaty on indirect tax that the RF has concluded with its close trading partners. On 25 January 2008, a first treaty was signed between the Russian Federation, the Republic of Kazakhstan and the Republic of Belarus on procedures for collecting indirect taxes in the Customs Union; on 29 May 2014 it was replaced by the Treaty on Eurasian Economic Union / EEU (signed by the Russian Federation, the Republic of Kazakhstan,

95. Including two double taxation conventions (with Japan and Malaysia) concluded by the former USSR.

the Republic of Belarus, the Republic of Kyrgyzstan and the Republic of Armenia).[96] The Annexes to the Treaty on the EEU) contain a number of procedural rules in regard to filing a special tax return. Disputes have arisen concerning the question of whether it is possible to impose sanctions according to domestic legislation if a taxpayer did not file a tax return provided for only by the international treaty. The national courts of the signatory countries taking into account the purpose of the treaty, namely the harmonization of tax systems but as well as avoidance of double taxation usually allow the tax authorities of national states to apply sanctions set out in their domestic laws.

[B] Case Law on Thin Capitalization Rules and Non-discrimination Clause as Examples of Tax Treaty Interpretation

[1] General Overview

The methodology of tax treaty interpretation in the Russian legal system is still developing. One area that has given rise to litigation in recent years is the question of whether thin capitalization rules are compatible with the non-discrimination clause of the relevant tax treaty (Article 24 of the OECD MC).

Prior to 2001, taxpayers were nearly always successful in defeating the application of thin capitalization rules by arguing they were incompatible with the non-discrimination clause in Russia's double tax treaties. The decision of the RF CC in the *Severniy Kuzbass* case[97] of 15 November 2011 opened the door to an important shift in judicial approaches to this issue when the Court concluded that there are no direct contradictions between the non-discrimination clause of respective tax treaties and the Russian thin capitalization rules.[98] The subsequent adoption of the same conclusion by the RF SCC in a series of important cases[99] dealing with the application of the thin

96. The Protocol was signed on 23 March 2007 and ratified by the Federal Law of 1 April 2008 № 34-FZ.
97. RU: Supreme Commercial Court (SCC), 15 November 2011, *Severniy Kuzbass v. Russian Federation*, case 8654/11, Tax Treaty Case Law IBFD.
98. Danil V. Vinnitskiy, Russia: 'Thin Capitalization Rules and Non-Discrimination Clause' (Chapter 28), in Eric C.C.M., Kemmeren et al. (eds) *Tax Treaty Case Law around the Globe 2012* (Amsterdam: IBFD, 2013): 303–317.
99. *See*: the Ruling of the SCC of 15 May 2012 № VAS-6159/12 (Terminal Sibir case, the non-discrimination clauses of the Russian tax treaties with Finland and Cyprus were considered as non-applicable); the Ruling of the SCC of 5 April 2012 № VAS-3867/12 (Promlizing case, the non-discrimination clause of the tax treaty with Cyprus was considered as non-applicable); the Ruling of the SCC of 19 March 2012 № VAS-10350 (Dallesprom case, again the non-discrimination clause of the tax treaty with Cyprus was considered as non-applicable); the Ruling of the SCC of 13 January 2012 № VAS-17705 (Bryanskiy Mashinostroitelniy Zavod, the non-discrimination clause of the tax treaty with the Netherlands was considered as non-applicable).The only exception to this approach to interpretation is connected with the Ruling of the SCC of 2 March 2012 № VAS-13698/11 (Omskiy Zavod Polipropilena case, the non-discrimination clause of the tax treaty with Cyprus was applied) where the Court made reference to the principle of non-retroactivity and held that there were no grounds for the revision of the judgments previously held in favour of a taxpayer (the judgment of the respective court of cassation was held on 23 June 2011, i.e., before the SCC Ruling on 'Severniy Kuzbass' case of 15 November 2011).

capitalization rules had elevated the approach taken in *Severniy Kuzbass* to become a legal principle.

The Russian thin capitalization rules were introduced in 2001 but were mostly irrelevant until 2011, as taxpayers usually avoided them either through the sister-company loophole (a loan from an affiliated sister company is technically not subject to the thin capitalization rules) or on the basis that the rules were incompatible with the non-discrimination provisions in tax treaties. The sister-company loophole was eliminated by the RF SCC in the *NaryanmarNefteGaz* case,[100] where the court collapsed a loan arrangement made through a finance company related to the indirect owner of a Russian company (a US company had invested in the Russian company via a Dutch holding company). The tax authorities applied the domestic thin capitalization rules on the basis that the loan had been made through an affiliated finance company for no commercial reason other than to avoid the Russian thin capitalization rules. Relying on the consolidated financial statements and correspondence between the companies, authorities argued on the basis of substance over form that in its true economic and legal nature the loan was made in directly by the US shareholder of the Russian company.

On the key question of whether the non-discrimination Article of a tax treaty prevented the application of thin capitalization rules on the basis that the rule prohibits a signatory from denying deductions for payments to non-residents if similar payments to residents would be deductible,[101] the RF SCC in *NaryanmarNefteGaz* and a series of parallel cases[102] ruled that the non-discrimination article would not override the domestic thin capitalization rule.

[2] The Application of Domestic Anti-avoidance Measures to Deny Treaty Benefits

The argument presented by the taxpayer in NaryanmarNefteGaz rested on a number of limbs. One was the fact that Russian authorities had levied interest withholding tax on

100. №. VAS-7104/12 NaryanmarNefteGaz 21 June 2012.

101. '3. Except where the provisions of paragraph 1 of Article 7 (Adjustments to Income in Cases Where Persons Participate, Directly or Indirectly, in the Management, Control or Capital of Other Persons,) paragraph 4 of Article 11 (Interest), or paragraph 4 of Article 12 (Royalties) apply, interest, royalties, and other disbursements paid by a resident of a Contracting State to a resident of the other Contracting State shall, for the purposes of determining the taxable profits of the first-mentioned resident, be deductible under the same conditions as if they had been paid to a resident of the first-mentioned State. Similarly, any debts of a resident of a Contracting State to a resident of the other Contracting State shall, for the purposes of determining the taxable capital of the first-mentioned resident, be deductible under the same conditions as if they had been contracted to a resident of the first-mentioned State.4. A company which is a resident of a Contracting State, the capital of which is wholly or partly owned or controlled, directly or indirectly, by one or more residents of the other Contracting State, shall not be subjected in the first-mentioned State to any taxation or any requirement connected therewith which is more burdensome than the taxation and connected requirements to which other similar companies which are residents of the first-mentioned State (whether owned by residents of that State or of a third State) are or may be subjected.'

102. *See, supra* note 101.

payments to shareholders in treaty countries where the payments could have been treated as dividends had the thin capitalization rules applied. The application of interest withholding tax to the payments, the taxpayer claimed, was evidence of an implicit acceptance by Russian authorities that the thin capitalization rules were incompatible with the non-discrimination treaty article. The Court offered no support for this argument.

The primary argument put forward in the thin capitalization cases was that the application of thin capitalization rules treated foreign investors differently from domestic investors. The RF SCC's reasoning to support the conclusion that the non-discrimination article was compatible with domestic thin capitalization rules was based on the fact that the thin capitalization rules affected the taxable profits of resident companies, not foreign entities. The Court noted that it was only domestic firms owned by foreign shareholders that were affected by the thin capitalization rules but said the application of the rules did not increase the taxable profits of affected domestic enterprises to more than profit they would have realized if the loans were regarded as contributions to equity capital, which would have been the funding method used in arm's length arrangements.[103]

§12.06 CONCLUSION

The analysis above demonstrates the main directions in which two most principal types of legal interpretation in Russian tax law – administrative interpretation and judicial one – have developed.

The relevance of administrative interpretation is restricted by the fact that the expression of administration interpretation by way of rulings is not binding for the courts and taxpayers as it represents only the official position of the tax administration. However, it is binding for territorial subdivisions of the tax administration. Judicial interpretation, particularly in respect of the application of anti-avoidance measures, is emerging as an important factor in tax law in Russia.

The case law connected with international tax disputes in the Russian jurisdiction demonstrates the emergence of a relatively high degree of autonomy in the area of legal interpretation of tax treaties and domestic legislation as it related to cross-border transactions. The influence of international practice, in particular, OECD commentaries is becoming more significant. Recent decisions of the RF Supreme Court on international taxation issues demonstrate that it follows the main trends in the interpretation of tax treaties adopted by the former RF Supreme Commercial Court in the period of 2011–2014 (*see*, for instance, the decision on a new thin capitalization case – 'Novaya Tabacnaya Kompaniya'[104]).

---

103. In fact, the Courts cited clause 3 of the Commentary on Art. 9, para. 1 to the OECD Model convention (the version before 2010).
104. *See*: Ruling of the RF SC of 1 February 2016 № 305-KG15-14263.

CHAPTER 13

Legal Interpretation of Tax Law: Republic of South Africa

Robert C. (Bob) Williams

§13.01 INTRODUCTION

The Republic of South Africa, consisting of nine provinces, each with its own legislature, is a constitutional democracy. Legislative power in the national sphere of government is vested in a bicameral parliament, consisting of the National Assembly and the National Council of Provinces. Both of these chambers participate in the legislative process provided for in the Constitution.[1]

The Constitution empowers Parliament to pass legislation with regard to any matter,[2] implicitly including the imposition of tax.[3] The Constitution goes on to restrict the taxing powers of the provinces[4] and local authorities (called municipalities)[5] such

1. Constitution of the Republic of South Africa 108 of 1996, s. 42.
2. Section 43 of the Constitution provides as follows: '**Legislative authority of the Republic.** - In the Republic, the legislative authority - (a) of the national sphere of government is vested in Parliament, as set out in section 44; (b) of the provincial sphere of government is vested in the provincial legislatures, (c) of the local sphere of government is vested in the Municipal Councils, as set out as set out in section 104; and in section 156.'
3. Section 44 of the Constitution provides as follows: '**National legislative authority.** The national legislative authority as vested in, Parliament - (a) confers on the National Assembly the power - (i) to amend the Constitution; (ii) to pass legislation with regard to any matter ...'.
4. Section 228 of the Constitution provides as follows: '**Provincial taxes.** - (1) A provincial legislature may impose - (a) taxes, levies and duties other than income tax, value-added tax. general sales tax, rates on property or customs duties; and (b) flat-rate surcharges on any tax, levy or duty that is imposed by national legislation. Other than on corporate income tax, value-added tax, rates on property or customs duties.'
5. Section 229 of the Constitution provides as follows: '**Municipal fiscal powers and functions.** - ... [A] municipality may impose - (a) rates on property and surcharges on fees for services provided by or on behalf of the municipality; and (b) if authorised by national legislation, other taxes, levies and duties appropriate to local government or to the category of local government into

that they cannot impose income tax, value-added tax, general sales tax (since replaced by value-added tax), rates on property or customs duties. Consequently, the power to impose income tax (which includes capital gains tax), value-added tax, and customs duty is vested exclusively in Parliament.

In South Africa the apex court is the Constitutional Court. Originally, its jurisdiction was limited to constitutional issues, but in 2013 its jurisdiction was expanded to include any other case involving a matter of general public importance that it chooses to hear. Its decisions are binding on all other courts in South Africa.

The Supreme Court of Appeal (SCA) (previously called the Appellate Division) is the apex court in all except constitutional matters and other matters of general public importance that the Constitutional Court chooses to hear, and it exercises only an appellate jurisdiction.

Below the SCA is the High Court, previously called the Supreme Court, which has nine divisions, each with its seat in a specified geographical location in South Africa. The various divisions of the High Court exercise both an original and an appellate jurisdiction.

There are various specialist tribunals, of which the only ones relevant here are the Tax Court and the Tax Board, whose jurisdiction is limited to adjudicating disputed assessments to tax as between the South African Revenue Service (SARS) and taxpayers. Decisions of the Tax Board can be taken on appeal to the Tax Court. Decisions of the Tax Court can be taken on appeal to the High Court or, in certain circumstances,[6] directly to the SCA or (where the matter raises a constitutional issue, or in other cases in which the Constitutional Court agrees to hear the matter) to the Constitutional Court. As explained in more detail, below, the Tax Court and Tax Board are not courts in the strict sense, *inter alia*, because their decisions are binding only as between the SARS and the taxpayer in question and do not constitute judicial precedents.

The lower courts (previously called magistrates courts) have no jurisdiction in relation to the adjudication of disputed assessments to tax.

The Republic of South Africa currently imposes income tax on individuals, companies and other taxable entities (such as deceased and insolvent estates, trusts, associations and clubs), and also provides for donations tax, estate duty, customs and excise duties, plus a variety of other taxes. Capital gains tax is levied in terms of the Income Tax Act. In addition, transfer duty is payable on the transfer of immovable property, and property owners' pay rates and taxes. General sales tax has been replaced by value-added tax. A dividends tax came into effect on 1 April 2012.

The charging legislation of the South African tax system is laid down in the following statutes: the Transfer Duty Act,[7] the Estate Duty Act,[8] the Income Tax Act,[9]

which that municipality falls, but no municipality may impose income tax, value-added tax, general sales tax or customs duty.'

6. *See* the Tax Administration Act 28 of 2011 s. 133(2)(b).
7. Act 40 of 1949.
8. Act 45 of 1955.
9. Act 58 of 1962.

the Customs and Excise Act,[10] the Value-Added Tax Act,[11] the Tax on Retirement Funds Act,[12] the Securities Transfer Tax Act[13] (which repealed the Uncertificated Securities Tax Act)[14] and the Demutualisation Levy Act.[15]

The overarching administration of the charging legislation is provided for in the South African Revenue Service Act.[16] In terms of this Act, the SARS[17] is established as an organ of state within the public administration but outside the public service, and it functions within the general laws of the Republic.[18] In terms of section 3 of the SARS, the objective of SARS is 'the efficient and effective collection of revenue'.

Since it operates within the general laws of the Republic, the powers and the conduct of SARS are subject to the Constitution. In *First National Bank of SA Ltd t/a Wesbank v. Commissioner, South African Revenue Service And Another; First National Bank of SA Ltd t/a Wesbank v. Minister of Finance.*[19] Ackermann J, giving the judgment of the court, said that it is:

> necessary to emphasise that even fiscal statutory provisions, no matter how indispensable they may be for the economic well-being of the country – a legitimate governmental objective of undisputed high priority – are not immune to the discipline of the Constitution and must conform to its normative standards.

In the main, the administrative aspects of the tax system (as distinct from the charging provisions of fiscal legislation) are provided for in the Tax Administration Act 28 of 2011, as amended. Most aspects of tax administration have been deleted from the various tax Acts to coincide with the coming into force of that Act and have been relocated, sometimes in an amended form, in the Act. Many new provisions relating to tax administration have also been included in the Act.

The purpose of the Tax Administration Act is to ensure the effective and efficient collection of tax[20] *inter alia*, as follows: by aligning the administration of the various tax Acts as far as practically possible; by consolidating such provisions into a single piece of legislation; by determining the powers and duties of the SARS and its officials; by providing for the delegation of powers by the Commissioner; by prescribing the rights and obligations of taxpayers and other persons to whom the Act applies; by prescribing the powers and duties of persons engaged in the administration of a tax Act; and generally by giving effect to the objects and purposes of tax administration.[21]

For the purposes of the Tax Administration Act, 'tax' means not only a tax, but includes a duty, levy, royalty, fee, contribution, penalty, interest and 'any other

10. Act 91 of 1964.
11. Act 89 of 1991.
12. Act 38 of 1996.
13. Act 25 of 2007.
14. Act 31 of 1998.
15. Act 50 of 1998.
16. Act 34 of 1997, as amended.
17. As defined in s. 1 sv 'South African Revenue Service'.
18. Except for certain exemptions from transfer duty and stamp duty.
19. 2002 (4) SA 768 (CC) at 787B-D.
20. The Tax Administration Act 28 of 2011, referred to in what follows as 'the Tax Administration Act'.
21. Tax Administration Act, *supra* note 20, s. 2.

moneys imposed under a tax Act'.[22] It is implicit that the reference to a 'penalty' is to an administrative non-compliance penalty (such as is imposed under Chapter 15 of the Tax Administration Act) as distinct from a penalty imposed for the commission of a criminal offence, such as those provided for in Chapter 17 of that Act. Thus, administrative non-compliance penalties and interest may be collected in terms of the Tax Administration Act as though they were a 'tax'. In reality, however, an administrative penalty is not a tax and neither is interest on unpaid tax.

The SARS is responsible for the administration of the Tax Administration Act under the control or direction of the Commissioner for the SARS.[23]

The common law of the Republic of South Africa, Roman-Dutch law, does not impose any liability for tax, and the obligation to pay tax and the quantification of tax liability derive exclusively from statute. In the case of income tax, capital gains tax, the dividends tax and donations tax, the governing statute is the Income Tax Act 58 of 1962, as amended.

The provisions of fiscal legislation are central to the tax in question. However, this does not mean that the common law is irrelevant in matters of tax. Quite the contrary - South Africa's fiscal legislation is, in general, not a code, which is to say that (save where the legislation provides otherwise) it is not a comprehensive statement of the law and such legislation must be interpreted against the backdrop of the common law.

Thus, for example, in the context of income tax, although common law does not impose a charge to tax, many of key statutory concepts and terms of art (e.g., *income, capital, accrue, incur, repair*) are not defined in the Income Tax Act and their meaning must be sought in decisions of the courts. Moreover, common law principles of South Africa's law of contract are implicitly incorporated into the fiscal system in relation to issues such as whether a taxpayer, in given circumstances, had a *right* to a particular amount of income and whether the taxpayer had become subject to a legal *obligation* in relation to the incurring of a particular amount of expenditure.

Where judicial decisions are concerned, the authority of the judgment under scrutiny in relation, *inter alia*, to its interpretation of fiscal legislation - and whether the judgment is binding or merely persuasive in subsequent judicial proceedings on the same issue in that court or a different court - is determined by the principles of judicial precedent (*stare decisis*). Thus, the authority of a judicial decision depends on the status of the court in the judicial hierarchy.

As is discussed further, below, South Africa's Tax Courts and Tax Boards (the tribunals of first instance that adjudicate in a disputed assessment to tax) are not courts of law in the strict sense. Not only are they creatures of statute with no inherent jurisdiction such as is possessed by the superior courts, but their judgments do not constitute judicial precedents and do not bind even the Tax Court or the Tax Board itself in subsequent cases. Decisions of the Tax Court and the Tax Board are (subject to the right to appeal against the decision) binding only as between the SARS and the taxpayer in the particular matter.

22. Tax Administration Act, *supra* note 20, s. 1 sv 'tax'.
23. Tax Administration Act, *supra* note 20, s. 3(1).

§13.02 THE INTERPRETATION OF FISCAL LEGISLATION

In South Africa, the general principles of statutory interpretation[24] apply to fiscal legislation. Most of the administrative provisions of fiscal legislation have been withdrawn from the charging legislation and relocated to the Tax Administration Act.[25] Issues of interpretation can now arise in relation to the charging legislation and also in relation to aspects of tax administration contained in the latter Act.

Over the years, many *dicta* of the South African courts have addressed the interpretation of tax legislation, and some of these dicta give the impression that there are special rules for interpreting such legislation that are not applicable to other statutes. However, the Appellate Division (as it then was)[26] held that 'there seems little reason why the interpretation of fiscal legislation should be subjected to special treatment which is not applicable in the interpretation of ordinary legislation'.[27]

The following are the principles of interpretation of major importance in relation to the interpretation of legislation in South Africa, including fiscal legislation.

[A] The Intention of the Legislature

In interpreting a statute, the task of the court has traditionally been conceived as being to determine and give effect to 'the intention of the legislature'. Thus, in the Appellate Division decision in *S v. Toms; S v. Bruce*[28] Smalberger JA said:

> The primary rule in the construction of statutory provisions is to ascertain the intention of the Legislature. One does so by attributing to the words of a statute their ordinary, literal, grammatical meaning. Where the language of a statute, so viewed, is clear and unambiguous effect must be given thereto, unless to do so –
>
> 'would lead to absurdity so glaring that it could never have been contemplated by the Legisture, or where it would lead to a result contrary to the intention of the Legislature, as shown by the context or by such other considerations as the Court is justified in taking into account (...).[29]

It has subsequently been pointed out that there are three tacit premises in this proposition: first, that the legislature, as a body, does indeed have an 'intention'; second, that words invariably have an unambiguous 'ordinary meaning'; thirdly that the 'intention of Parliament' will necessarily coincide with the 'ordinary meaning' of

24. The standard works in South Africa are Lucas C. Steyn, *Die Uitleg van Wette* (Cape Town: Juta Legal and Academic Publishers, 5th edn, 1981) and George E. Devenish, *Interpretation of Statutes* (Cape Town: Juta Legal and Academic Publishers, 1992) *See also* Edwin A. Kellaway, *Principles of Legal Interpretation* (Durban: Butterworth 1995).
25. *Supra* note 20.
26. At the time of this decision, the Appellate Division was the apex court in South Africa. Currently, the apex court is the Constitutional Court.
27. *Glen Anil Development Corp Ltd v. SIR* 1975 (4) SA 715 (A), 37 SATC 319 at 333; Wallis M, *Is Tax Really Different*, 2016 (3) British Tax Review 299.
28. 1990 2 SA 802 (A) at 807H-808A.
29. Per Innes CJ in *R v. Venter* 1907 TS 910 at 915; *see also Shenker v. The Master* 1936 AD 136 at 142; *Summit Industrial Corporation v. Claimants against the Fund Comprising the Proceeds of the Sale of the MV Fade 15 Transporter* 1987 (2) SA 583 (A) at 596G-H.

words appearing in legislation. These points were made in the 2012 decision of South Africa's SCA in Natal Joint *Municipal Pension Fund v. Endumeni Municipality*[30] where Wallis JA, giving the judgment of the court, said:[31]

> Whilst this summary of the approach to interpretation [ie attempting to determine the 'ordinary meaning' of the words in question in order to arrive at the intention of the draftsperson] was buttressed by reference to authority it suffers from an internal tension because it does not indicate what is meant by the "ordinary meaning" of words, whether or not influenced by context, or why, once ascertained, this would coincide with the "true" intention of the draftsman.'

In addition to the tension between the three tacit premises, outlined above, each of the premises is flawed in its own right.

As to the first proposition, namely, that Parliament has an 'intention', Wallis JA pointed out[32] the implausibility of such a notion, for:

> legislation is drafted by legal advisers in a ministry, redrafted by the parliamentary draftsmen, subjected to public debate in committee, where it may be revised and amended, and then passed by a legislative body, many of whose members have little close acquaintance with its terms and are motivated only by their or their party's stance on the broad principles in the legislation. In those circumstances, to speak of an intention of parliament is entirely artificial.[33]

As to the second tacit proposition – that words, viewed in isolation, necessarily have an 'ordinary meaning' – Wallis JA said[34] that this assumption can lead to 'a studied literalism and denies resort to matters beyond the "ordinary grammatical meaning" of the words'.

To be fair, it has long been accepted that 'the intention of the legislature' must be derived from the words of the Act itself[35] and not by attempting to peer into the minds of the members of the assembly. But that qualification does not breathe life into the proposition that the interpretation of a statute involves a determination of 'the intention of the legislature', for if it is only the language of the Act that needs to be scrutinised, why is it necessary to seek or even mention 'the intention of the legislature' as an element of the inquiry? The artificiality of seeking and giving effect to 'the intention of the legislature' in any literal sense comes acutely to the fore in situations where legislation must be applied to circumstances that were non-existent at the time

30. 2012 (4) SA 593 (SCA) (for brevity, this judgment is referred to in the footnotes below, as *Natal Municipal Pension Fund)*; cited and applied by the Supreme Court of Appeal in *Bothma-Batho Transport (Edms) Bpk v. S Bothma & Seun Transport (Edms) Bpk*[2013] ZASCA 176; [2014] 1 All SA 517 (SCA) (28 November 2013).
31. *Natal Municipal Pension Fund, supra,* at para. 17.
32. *Natal Municipal Pension Fund, supra,* at 20.
33. *See* Lord Nicholls of Birkenhead in *My Kingdom for a Horse: The Meaning of Words* (2005) 121 LQR 577 at 589; *see also R v. Secretary of State for the Environment, Transport and the Regions, Ex parte Spath Holme Ltd* [2001] 2 AC 349 at 395 where he said that the intention of the legislature is 'a shorthand reference to the intention which the court reasonably imputes to Parliament in respect of the language used'.
34. *Natal Municipal Pension Fund, supra,* at para. [22].
35. *IRC v. Hinchy* [1960] AC 748 at 766; *Farrar's Estate v. CIR* 1926 TPD 501 at 507.

when Parliament enacted that legislation and therefore could not have had any 'intention' whatever in relation to those circumstances.[36]

In this same SCA judgment, Wallis JA went on to observe that:

> Over the last century there have been significant developments in the law relating to the interpretation of documents, both in this country and in others that follow similar rules to our own.[37]

Wallis JA then summarised[38] as follows what he called 'the emerging trend in statutory construction' (footnotes omitted):

> It clearly adopts as the proper approach to the interpretation of documents [that] from the outset one considers the context and the language together, with neither predominating over the other.

Nonetheless, the hallowed proposition that, for purposes of statutory interpretation, 'the intention of the legislature' needs to be determined and must be derived from the language of the legislation was reaffirmed by the SCA in *Natal Joint Municipal Pension Fund v. Endumeni Municipality*[39] and, four years after that judgment, some decisions of the South African courts continue to refer, in this context, to *the intention of the legislature.*[40] However, the important point is that such references must now be read as subject to the restrictive interpretation given to that proposition in the *Natal Joint Municipal Pension Fund* decision, namely,[41] that:

> The sole benefit of expressions such as 'the intention of the legislature' ... is to serve as a warning to courts that the task they are engaged upon is discerning the meaning of words used by others, not one of imposing their own views of what it would have been sensible for those others to say.

In other respects, also, this judgment of the SCA has taken the principles of statutory interpretation in a new direction and it will, henceforth, undoubtedly be regarded as the leading decision of the South African courts in matters of statutory interpretation.[42]

It was held in the *Natal Municipal Pension Fund* case that the process of interpretation involves attributing meaning to the words in a document, whether legislation or a contract, *having regard to the context.* Furthermore, that this process is objective, not subjective,[43] and is unrelated to whatever intention those responsible for the words may have had at the time they selected them.[44]

---

36. *See* for example *van Deventer v. Nedbank Ltd* 2016 (3) SA 633 (WCHC) at 35.
37. *Natal Municipal Pension Fund,* para. 18.
38. *Supra.*, para. 19.
39. 2012 (4) SA 593 (SCA); later cited and applied by the Supreme Court of Appeal in *Bothma-Batho Transport (Edms) Bpk v. S Bothma & Seun Transport (Edms) Bpk* [2013] ZASCA 176; [2014] 1 All SA 517 (SCA) (28 November 2013).
40. *See* for example *van Deventer v. Nedbank Ltd* 2016 (3) SA 622 (WCHC) at 35.
41. *Natal Municipal Pension Fund,* at para. 24.
42. *See Minister of Justice and Constitutional Development v. Southern Africa Litigation Centre* 2016 (3) SA 317 (CC) at footnote 75.
43. *Natal Municipal Pension Fund,* para.18.
44. *Supra.*, para. 23.

In short, the court held that the 'emerging trend in statutory construction',[45] is that from the outset it is necessary to consider the context and the language together, with neither predominating over the other. Wallis JA, speaking for the court, then made the portentous declaration that:

> This is the approach that courts in South Africa should now follow, without the need to cite authorities from an earlier era that are not necessarily consistent and frequently reflect an approach to interpretation that is no longer appropriate.

It is thus clear that the SCA intends that its decision in this case should now prevail over - and indeed should supplant - all previous decisions in regard to the principles by which statutory provisions should be interpreted.[46]

What, then, are the principles of statutory interpretation that should now be applied? Wallis JA, speaking for the court, said (footnotes omitted):

> The present state of the law can be expressed as follows: Interpretation is the process of attributing meaning to the words used in a document, be it legislation, some other statutory instrument, or contract, having regard to the context provided by reading the particular provision or provisions in the light of the document as a whole and the circumstances attendant upon its coming into existence. Whatever the nature of the document, consideration must be given to the language used in the light of the ordinary rules of grammar and syntax; the context in which the provision appears; the apparent purpose to which it is directed and the material known to those responsible for its production. Where more than one meaning is possible each possibility must be weighed in the light of all these factors. The process is objective, not subjective. A sensible meaning is to be preferred to one that leads to insensible or unbusinesslike results or undermines the apparent purpose of the document. Judges must be alert to, and guard against, the temptation to substitute what they regard as reasonable, sensible or businesslike for the words actually used. To do so in regard to a statute or statutory instrument is to cross the divide between interpretation and legislation; in a contractual context it is to make a contract for the parties other than the one they in fact made. The 'inevitable point of departure is the language of the provision itself', read in context and having regard to the purpose of the provision and the background to the preparation and production of the document.[47]

The court went on to quote with approval the words of Sir Anthony Mason CJ where he said:

> Problems of legal interpretation are not solved satisfactorily by ritual incantations which emphasise the clarity of meaning which words have when viewed in isolation, divorced from their context. The modern approach to interpretation insists that context be considered in the first instance, especially in the case of

45. *Bato Star Fishing (Pty) Ltd v. Minister of Environmental Affairs and Others* 2004 (4) SA 490 (CC) (2004 (7) BCLR 687; [2004] ZACC 15 para. 90.
46. The decision has since been referred to in many judgments, including a judgment involving, *inter alia*, the interpretation of a settlement agreement allegedly entered into between a taxpayer and the South African Revenue Service; *see Malema v. Commissioner for the South African Revenue Service* [2016] ZAGPPHC 263 at 72.
47. South Africa's Constitutional Court has described as 'settled' the principles of interpretation laid down by the Supreme Court of Appeal in this judgment; *see Minister of Justice and Constitutional Development v. Southern Africa Litigation Centre* 2016 (3) SA 317 (CC) at footnote 75.

> general words, and not merely at some later stage when ambiguity might be thought to arise.[48]

Such 'ritual incantations' are, it is submitted, exemplified in the decision in *CIR v. Delfos*[49] where Botha JA emphasised that 'in all cases of interpretation we must ... arrive at the true intention of the legislature'.

In *Natal Joint Municipal Pension Fund v. Endumeni Municipality* the SCA, as was noted above, emphatically rejected the notion that statutory interpretation entails a search for 'the intention of the legislature', in any literal sense, and said that:

> to characterise the task of interpretation as a search for such an ephemeral and possibly chimerical meaning is unrealistic and misleading.[50]

The court went on to warn that a search for 'the intention of the legislature' can lead to two extreme results:

> At one extreme, as has been the case historically, it leads to a studied literalism and denies resort to matters beyond the 'ordinary grammatical meaning' of the words. At the other judges use it to justify first seeking to divine the 'intention' of the legislature and then adapting the language of the provision to justify that conclusion.[51]

The court said that marginal notes to the Act, parliamentary debates,[52] ministers' statements as to the meaning of the Act and memoranda purporting to explain the Act cannot be used to ascertain the meaning of a statute. But that a court may properly have regard to the history of a provision of the Act and the form in which it appeared in earlier Acts.[53] And that it is also permissible to refer to a subsequent statute if it throws light on the meaning of a provision in an earlier statute.[54]

It remains accepted that, if legislation is expressed in clear, precise and unambiguous words, the court must interpret the words in their ordinary and natural sense[55] (except where those words are accorded a specific defined meaning in the Act) unless the plain meaning of the language leads to some absurdity, inconsistency, hardship or anomaly.[56]

---

48. *K & S Lake City Freighters Pty Ltd v. Gordon & Gotch Ltd* [1985] HCA 48 ((1985) 157 CLR 309) at 315.
49. 1933 AD 242.
50. *Natal Municipal Pension Fund,* at para. 22.
51. Wilson CJ identified the illegitimacy of this latter approach in *Richardson v. Austin* [1911] HCA 28 ((1911) 12 CLR 463 at 470) where he said – 'as to the argument from the assumed intention of the legislature, there is nothing more dangerous and fallacious in interpreting a Statute than first of all to assume that the legislature had a particular intention, and then, having made up one's mind what that intention was, to conclude that that intention must necessarily be expressed in the Statute, and then proceed to find it'.
52. Reference to what was said in Parliament is permissible to establish the particular mischief which the statute was intended to remedy; *see Federal Commissioner of Taxation v. Whitfords Beach Pty Ltd* (1982) 56 ALJR 240 at 242, 247.
53. *CIR v. Simpson* 1949 (4) SA 678 (A), 16 SATC 268; *New Union Goldfields Ltd v. CIR* 1950 (3) SA 392 (A), 17 SATC 1; *Buglers Post (Pty) Ltd v. SIR* 1974 (3) SA 28 (A), 36 SATC 71.
54. *National Health, Education and Allied Workers Union v. UCT* 2003 (3) SA 1 (CC) at 30H.
55. As in *Chilza v. Govender* 2016 (4) SA 397.
56. *R Koster & Son (Pty) Ltd v. CIR* 1985 (2) SA 831 (A), 47 SATC 24 at 32.

It is also still regarded as trite that a court must interpret fiscal legislation as it stands and cannot remedy a casus omissus[57] by supplying missing words.[58] To do so would be to usurp the function of Parliament.[59] But that if it is possible to reasonably construct the Act in a manner that does not lead to a casus omissus, then that interpretation is to be preferred to one which does.[60]

It has taken time for the sea-change in the fundamental approach to statutory interpretation, heralded by the decision in the Natal Municipal Pension Fund judgment to be fully understood and accepted by the South African courts, even though it has by since been affirmed numerous times by the SCA.[61] Even three years after the judgment Natal Municipal Pension Fund, there have been lower court decisions in which the judge seemed oblivious of that judgment and went on to articulate and apply the very approach that the SCA had so trenchantly disavowed.[62]

[B] There Is No Equity about a Tax

In *Partington v. The Attorney-General*[63] Lord Cairns said:

> If the person sought to be taxed comes within the letter of the law, he must be taxed, however great the hardship may appear to the judicial mind to be[64] (...) In other words, if there be an equitable construction, certainly such a construction is not admissible in a taxing statute (...).

This *dictum* was approved by South Africa's Appellate Division in *CIR v. George Forest Timber Co Ltd*[65] and in *CIR v. Delfos*.[66] In a decision of the English courts in *Cape Brandy Syndicate v. IRC*[67] Rowlatt J said that:

> in a taxing Act one has to look at what is clearly said. There is no room for any intendment. There is no equity about a tax. There is no presumption as to a tax. Nothing is to be read in, nothing is to be implied. One can only look fairly at the language used.

Unlike English law, South African law does not recognise 'equity' as a source of legal principles in its own right, distinct from the common law.[68] Consequently, the

57. A matter or contingency not catered for in the Act.
58. *Union Govt v. Thompson* 1919 AD 425.
59. *Hippo Holding Co Ltd v. CIR* 1949 (2) SA 503 (T), 16 SATC 112.
60. *CIR v. BP Southern Africa (Pty) Ltd* 1997 (1) SA 375 (C), 59 SATC 97 (Cape Provincial Division) at 104.
61. Most recently in *XO Africa Safaris v. CSARS* [2016] ZASCA 160.
62. *See* for example *Lifman v. C:SARS* (2015) 77 SATC 383.
63. 21 LT 370 at 375.
64. Of course the taxing legislation may contain provisions which are designed to alleviate hardship. *See*, for example, s. 89*quat*(3) and (3A), which give the Commissioner discretion to waive interest on underpaid amounts of tax where the taxpayer had reasonable grounds for contending that a particular amount was not taxable or that he was entitled to a particular allowance or deduction.
65. 1924 AD 516 at 531.
66. 1933 AD 242, 6 SATC 92 at 101.
67. [1921] 1 KB 64 at 71, 12 TC 358.
68. *Weinerlein v. Goch Buildings* 1925 AD 295.

exclusion of equitable principles in the interpretation of taxing statutes is significant in the United Kingdom but of little relevance in South Africa[69] except in so far as equitable principles are now expressly or impliedly enshrined in the Constitution.[70]

Thus, in South Africa, the proposition that 'there is no equity about a tax' must be qualified to the extent that the provisions of a taxing statute are unconstitutional and therefore invalid if they flout any of the rights contained in the constitutional Bill of Rights, for example, if the statute breaches the equality clause[71] or the right to lawful, reasonable and procedurally fair administrative action.[72]

The Constitution declares that it is 'the supreme law of the Republic' and that any law or conduct inconsistent with the Constitution is invalid.[73] Hence, provisions of fiscal legislation, such as the Income Tax Act, can (as with any other statute) be declared invalid on the grounds of inconsistency with the Constitution. Even where the taxing statute itself is not unconstitutional, 'conduct' by officials of the SARS may be in breach of the Constitution. For example, the manner in which such officials execute a search of the taxpayer's premises and effect a seizure of his property in terms of powers given under a fiscal statute could be challenged as infringing the Bill of Rights even if the statute itself is not unconstitutional.

In *Law Society of Zimbabwe v. Minister of Finance*[74] the Supreme Court of Zimbabwe expressed the view that the constitutionality of a tax cannot be questioned, 'however harsh and however ruinous to the economy'.[75] However, as was found to be so in that decision, a tax will be unconstitutional if the statutory criteria according to which it is collected are indiscriminate, arbitrary and irrational.

[C] *Contra Fiscum* Principle

The *contra fiscum* principle of interpretation[76] is merely 'a specific application of the rule that all legislation imposing a burden upon the subject should, in the case of an ambiguity, be construed in favour of the subject.'[77] Thus, where a provision of fiscal

69. The words *equity* and *equitable* are frequently found in judgments of the South African courts on income tax and other topics. For example, in *CIR v. Delfos* 1933 AD 242, 6 SATC 92 at 103 Wessels CJ said: 'It may well be that if it was sought to tax the taxpayer twice over in a particular case it may be possible to invoke equitable principles in order to avoid the double taxation'. It is submitted that this *dictum* means no more than that, on a proper interpretation of the Act, Parliament did not intend to impose double taxation; cf *Isaacs v. CIR* 1949 (4) SA 561 (A), 16 SATC 258. Even in English law the terms *equity* and *equitable* are sometimes used in different senses in different contexts; cf Peter St. J. Langan (ed), *Maxwell on the Interpretation of Statutes* (London: Sweet & Maxwell, 12th edn, 1969).
70. The Constitution of the Republic of South Africa 108 of 1996.
71. *Supra* note 52, s. 9.
72. *Supra* note 52, s. 33; *see also* the Promotion of Administrative Justice Act 3 of 2000.
73. *Supra* note 52, s. 2.
74. 61 SATC 458 (SCZ).
75. *Supra* at 468; *see also COT v. CW (Pvt) Ltd* 1989 (3) ZLR 361 (S).
76. *Estate Reynolds v. CIR* 1937 AD 57 at 70.
77. *Dibowitz v. CIR* 1952 (1) SA 55 (A) at 61.

legislation is reasonably capable of two constructions, the court will adopt the construction that imposes the smaller burden on the taxpayer.[78]

It seems, however, that this canon of construction applies only to the charging provisions of the Act; thus, it has been held[79] that, since section 103 of the Income Tax Act (the previous general anti-avoidance provision of that Act, now partially repealed and replaced by Part IIA of Chapter III of that Act) does not impose a tax, it should not be construed as a taxing measure, but in a way that will suppress the mischief against which it is aimed, and 'the discretionary powers conferred upon the [Commissioner] should therefore not be restricted unnecessarily by interpretation.'

It has also been held that, where there is ambiguity, that interpretation should be adopted which will best give effect to the intention of the legislature.[80] Where the Act is clear, precise and unambiguous, the court must give effect to the ordinary and natural meaning of the words[81] (unless the Act itself defines those words), even if the result is harsh or unfair to the taxpayer, inconvenient or unjust.[82]

There is an important distinction between an interpretation which is 'harsh' and one which is 'absurd'.[83] As Innes CJ said in *Venter v. R*:[84]

> [W]hen to give the plain words of the statute their ordinary meaning would lead to absurdity so glaring that it could never have been contemplated by the legislature or where it would lead to a result contrary to the intention of the legislature, as shown by the context or by such other considerations as the court is justified in taking into account, the court may depart from the ordinary effect of the words to the extent necessary to remove the absurdity and to give effect to the true intention of the legislature.

Where the language of the Act is clear, the fact that it permits avoidance of tax, if taken literally, does not justify a departure from the ordinary meaning of the language.[85]

In Australia, criticism that the courts were facilitating tax avoidance by adopting an excessively literalistic approach to the construction of tax legislation led to an amendment of that country's counterpart to South Africa's Interpretation Act to try to compel the courts to interpret such legislation more in accordance with its 'purpose'.[86] In South Africa, a leading authority on statutory interpretation stresses that deviation

78. *Estate Reynolds v. CIR* 1937 AD 57, 8 SATC 203 at 213.
79. *See Glen Anil Development Corp Ltd v. SIR* 1975 (4) SA 715 (A) at 727H–728A; quoted with approval in *Conshu (Pty) Ltd v. CIR* 1994 (4) SA 603 (A), 57 SATC 1 at 8.
80. *Astor v. Perry* [1935] AC 398 at 417.
81. *ITC 830* (1956) 21 SATC 305; *Loewenstein v. COT* 1956 (4) SA 766 (FC), 21 SATC 121.
82. *Cooper Brookes (Wollongong) Pty Ltd v. FCT* (1981) 55 ALJR 434 at 437.
83. Cf. *Cooper Brookes (Wollongong) Pty Ltd v. FCT* (1981) 55 ALJR 434 where a majority in the High Court of Australia sanctioned a departure from the literal interpretation of the Act on the grounds that this would lead to a result which was capricious and irrational. For an example of the departure from a literal interpretation to avoid absurdity, *see M v. COT* 1956 (4) SA 197 (SR), 21 SATC 16.
84. 1907 TS 910.
85. *P v. COT; LGM Ltd v. COT* 1966 (2) SA 208 (R), 28 SATC 55.
86. *See* s. 15A of the Acts Interpretation Act 1901.

from the literal interpretation of a statute is justified only where the intention of the legislature can be ascertained beyond doubt from other sources.[87]

If the objects and intention of the Act are clear but its language is not and, if taken literally, would render its provisions nugatory, then it may be permissible to supply omitted words or expressions in order to give effect to the clear intention of the legislature.[88]

Fiscal legislation is often clumsily expressed. It should be interpreted in such a way that - if possible - no clause, sentence or word is superfluous, void or tautologous.[89] A construction that avoids tautology is to be preferred to one that does not.[90]

[D] The *Natal Joint Municipal Pension Fund* Case

The recent decision of the SCA in *Natal Joint Municipal Pension Fund v. Endumeni Municipality*[91] is a watershed judgment in South Africa regarding the principles governing the interpretation of legislation and contracts, and it will henceforth be cited as the *locus classicus* in this regard.

The language of the judgment leaves no doubt that, in this decision, the SCA has deliberately drawn a line under earlier decisions on the interpretation of statutes and is trenchantly declaring that what it now lays down 'is the approach that courts in South Africa should now follow, without the need to cite authorities from an earlier era that are not necessarily consistent and frequently reflect an approach to interpretation that is no longer appropriate'.

The core of the modern approach, said the court, is that the process of interpretation is objective, not subjective. Giving the judgment of the court, Wallis JA said[92] that:

> Unlike the trial judge I have deliberately avoided using the conventional description of this process as one of ascertaining the intention of the legislature or the draftsman,[93] nor would I use its counterpart in a contractual setting, 'the intention of the contracting parties', because these expressions are misnomers, insofar as they convey or are understood to convey that interpretation involves an enquiry

87. Lucas C. Steyn, *Die Uitleg van Wette*, *supra* note 24, Ch 11; cf *Glen Anil Development Corp Ltd v. SIR* 1975 (4) SA 715 (A) at 727, 37 SATC 319 and *Loewenstein v. COT* 1956 (4) SA 766 (FC) at 772, 21 SATC 121.
88. *See* the judgment of Botha JA in *Glen Anil Development Corp v. SIR* 1975 (4) SA 715 (A), 37 SATC 319 at 336.
89. *Loewenstein v. COT* 1956 (4) SA 766 (FC), 21 SATC 121.
90. *CIR v. Louis Zinn Organisation (Pty) Ltd* 1958 (4) SA 477 (A), 22 SATC 85.
91. 2012 (4) SA 593 (SCA).
92. *Supra*, at para. 20.
93. 'A slippery phrase' according to Lord Watson in *Aron Salomon v. A Salomon & Co Ltd* [1897] AC 22 (HL) at 38. As to the usage of this expression, *see Ebrahim v. Minister of the Interior* 1977 (1) SA 665 (A) at 677-678 and the authorities there cited; *Protective Mining & Industrial Equipment Systems (Pty) Ltd (formerly Hampo Systems (Pty) Ltd) v. Audiolens (Cape) (Pty) Ltd* 1987 (2) SA 961 (A) at 991F-H; *Summit Industrial Corporation v. Claimants against the Fund Comprising the Proceeds of the Sale of the MV Jade Transporter* 1987 (2) SA 583 (A) at 596G-597B; *and Manyasha v. Minister of Law and Order* 1999 (2) SA 179 (SCA) at 185B-C.

> into the mind of the legislature or the contracting parties.[94] The reason is that the enquiry is restricted to ascertaining the meaning of the language of the provision itself.

In other words, expressions such as 'the intention of the legislature' are not to be construed as involving an enquiry into the mind of the legislature'.[95] The true inquiry, said the court, 'is restricted to ascertaining the meaning of the language of the provision itself'.

Modern statutory construction, said the court,[96] lays stress on identifying the mischief at which it is aimed. On the other hand, 'Courts do not set out to undermine legislative purpose but to give it effect within the constraints imposed by the language adopted by the legislature.'[97]

The sole purpose of expressions such as *the intention of the legislature*, said the court,[98] is 'to serve as a warning to courts that the task they are engaged upon is discerning the meaning of words used by others, not one of imposing their own views of what it would have been sensible for those others to say'[99] and that 'An interpretation will not be given that leads to impractical, unbusinesslike or oppressive consequences or that will stultify the broader operation of the legislation or contract under consideration'.[100]

The following dicta from the judgment are particularly noteworthy (footnotes omitted):

> [18] Over the last century there have been significant developments in the law relating to the interpretation of documents, both in this country and in others that follow similar rules to our own. The present state of the law can be expressed as follows: Interpretation is the process of attributing meaning to the words used in a document, be it legislation, some other statutory instrument, or contract, having regard to the context provided by reading the particular provision or provisions in the light of the document as a whole and the circumstances attendant upon its coming into existence. Whatever the nature of the document, consideration must be given to the language used in the light of the ordinary rules of grammar and syntax; the context in which the provision appears; the apparent purpose to which it is directed and the material known to those responsible for its production. Where more than one meaning is possible each possibility must be weighed in the light of all these factors. The process is objective, not subjective. A sensible meaning is to be preferred to one that leads to insensible or unbusinesslike results or undermines

94. In Kim Lewison, *The Interpretation of Contracts* (London: Sweet & Maxwell, 5th edn, 2011) para. 2.05, the heading reads: 'For the purpose of the interpretation of contracts, the intention of the parties is the meaning of the contract. There is no intention independent of that meaning.'

The discussion in this paragraph makes it clear that the international trend in countries with which we share some common heritage is to treat the 'intention of the parties' as a myth or abstraction remote from the reality of interpretation and unnecessary.

95. *Supra* note 73, para. 20.
96. *Supra* note 73, para. 21.
97. *Supra* note 73, para. 21.
98. *Supra* note 73, para. 24.
99. *Supra* note 73, para. 24.
100. *Supra* note 73, para. 26.

> the apparent purpose of the document. Judges must be alert to, and guard against, the temptation to substitute what they regard as reasonable, sensible or business-like for the words actually used. To do so in regard to a statute or statutory instrument is to cross the divide between interpretation and legislation; in a contractual context it is to make a contract for the parties other than the one they in fact made. The 'inevitable point of departure is the language of the provision itself', read in context and having regard to the purpose of the provision and the background to the preparation and production of the document.
>
> [19] All this is consistent with the 'emerging trend in statutory construction'. It clearly adopts as the proper approach to the interpretation of documents the second of the two possible approaches mentioned by Schreiner JA in Jaga v Dönges NO and Another; Bhana v Dönges NO, namely that from the outset one considers the context and the language together, with neither predominating over the other. This is the approach that courts in South Africa should now follow, without the need to cite authorities from an earlier era that are not necessarily consistent and frequently reflect an approach to interpretation that is no longer appropriate.

[E] Interpretation Notes and Advance Tax Rulings

The SARS has, over the years, released a considerable number of 'interpretation notes'. These do not have the force of law, nor do the courts generally pay any heed to them when interpreting the Act. Such interpretation notes merely reflect the view of the tax authorities on the interpretation of tax legislation on which there is no binding judicial precedent.

Thus, for example, in *Oceanic Trust Co Ltd NO v. CSARS*[101] the High Court was required to determine whether the 'effective management' of the company in question (and thus its tax residence) was located in Mauritius or in South Africa. The court simply ignored, and reached a decision inconsistent with, an Interpretation Note[102] previously issued by the SARS.

The Tax Administration Act 28 of 2011[103] provides that the SARS can issue advance tax rulings. These can take the form of a binding private ruling, a binding general ruling or a binding class ruling. The purpose of such rulings is to provide clarity, consistency and certainty as to the interpretation and application of a tax Act. Where an advance ruling applies to a person, SARS is statutorily obliged to interpret or apply the relevant tax Act to that person in accordance with that ruling.[104] A binding private ruling or binding class ruling may be cited only in proceedings involving the applicant for that ruling or a member of the relevant class.

The SARS is empowered to withdraw or modify an advance ruling at any time.[105]

101. [2012] JOL 28880 (WCC).
102. South African Revenue Service *Interpretation Note 6* issued in September 2011.
103. *See* Chapter 7 of the Tax Administration Act 28 of 2011.
104. Tax Administration Act, *supra* note 20, s. 82.
105. Tax Administration Act, *supra* note 20, s. 86(1).

§13.03 DISGUISED TRANSACTIONS

In interpreting a fiscal statute and applying it to a particular transaction, the courts have regard to the substance of that transaction and ignore any attempt by the parties to disguise its true nature or to attach false or misleading labels to the transaction.

As Viscount Simon said in *IRC v. Wesleyan and General Assurance Society:*[106]

> (...) the name given to a transaction by the parties concerned does not necessarily decide the nature of the transaction. To call a payment a loan if it is really an annuity does not assist the taxpayer any more than to call an item a capital payment would prevent it from being regarded as an income payment if that is its true nature. The question always is what is the real character of the payment, not what the parties call it.

In South Africa, the *locus classicus* on simulated transactions is Innes CJ's judgment in *Zandberg v. Van Zyl*[107] in which he said that:

> Not infrequently, however (either to secure some advantage which otherwise the law would not give, or to escape some disability which otherwise the law would impose) the parties to a transaction endeavour to conceal its true character. They call it by a name or give it a shape, intended not to express but to disguise its true nature. And when a court is asked to decide any rights under such an agreement, it can only do so by giving effect to what the transaction really is; not what in form it purports to be (...).

In a controversial decision, the SCA held in *CSARS v. NWK Ltd*[108] that, in order to determine whether a transaction is simulated, it is not sufficient merely to determine whether the parties intended to perform it according to its tenor; it is necessary to determine, in addition, whether the agreement made commercial sense. In that case, a convoluted borrowing arrangement, involving *inter alia* self-cancelling features and repayment of the loan *in specie*, that ostensibly gave rise to a large amount of tax-deductible interest, was held to be a simulated transaction on the grounds that aspects of the interlinked transactions lacked commercial sense and had been introduced only to generate such interest.

§13.04 DOUBLE TAXATION

It has been held that the same income is not subject to income tax twice in the hands of the same person unless the statute makes it clear that this was the intention of the legislature.[109] This, it has been held, is a 'necessary implication'.[110]

106. [1948] 1 All ER 555 (HL) at 557.
107. 1910 AD 302 at 309.
108. 2011 (2) SA 67 (SCA). The principles laid down in this judgment were reaffirmed by the Supreme Court of Appeal in *Roshcon (Pty) Ltd v. Anchor Auto Body Builders CC* [2014] ZASCA 40 (31 March 2014).
109. *Isaacs v. CIR* 1949 (4) SA 561 (A), 16 SATC 258; *ITC 554* (1944) 13 SATC 211; *Orkin Bros (Pretoria) Ltd v. CIR* 1935 AD 9, 7 SATC 179.
110. *CIR v. Delfos* 1933 AD 242, 6 SATC 92 at 112, *per* De Villiers JA; *see also* Curlewis JA at 108 and Wessels CJ at 103.

§13.05 NO DOCTRINE OF ECONOMIC EQUIVALENCE

It is trite that transactions that have similar economic effects (e.g., purchasing an item of equipment or leasing it) may have different tax consequences.[111] A doctrine of economic equivalence[112] – that transactions with the same economic result should be taxed equally – may be desirable in theory, but it is an unworkable basis for income tax liability, and it is not the law.

Innes CJ in *CIR v. George Forest Timber Co Ltd*[113] counselled that 'it is dangerous to depart from the actual facts; the true course is to take the facts as they stand (...)'. Viscount Simon observed in *IRC v. Wesleyan and General Assurance Society*[114] that:

> a transaction which on its true construction, is of a kind that would escape tax is not taxable on the ground that the same result could be brought about by a transaction in another form which would attract tax.

In *Badenhorst & Others v. CIR* it was said that:[115]

> if a person is liable to tax in a specified set of circumstances, he must not be held liable in different though analogous circumstances merely for the reason that because he is liable in the one case he should also be liable in the other.

§13.06 LATIN MAXIMS IN STATUTORY INTERPRETATION

The South African courts have accepted various Latin maxims as a shorthand way of expressing certain principles of statutory interpretation. These include the following.

[A] *Expressio Unius Est Exclusio Alterius*

This means that, where a statute expressly mentions one person or thing, it implies an intention to exclude other persons or things. The courts have warned that this maxim must be applied with great caution[116] – it is 'a valuable servant but a dangerous master'.[117] The implication expressed in the maxim is sometimes accepted by the courts as correctly reflecting the legislature's intention[118] and sometimes not.[119]

111. *See* the remarks of Centlivres CJ in *CIR v. Rand Selections Corp Ltd* 1956 (3) SA 124 (A) at 132 and of Lord Greene MR in *IRC v. Wesleyan & General Assurance Society* [1946] 2 All ER 749 at 751.
112. The phrase comes from *Europa Oil (NZ) Ltd v. IRC (NZ)* [1971] AC 760 at 772.
113. 1924 AD 516 at 523.
114. [1948] 1 All ER 555 (HL) at 557.
115. 20 SATC 39.
116. *COT v. Aktiebolaget Tetra Pak* 1966 (4) SA 198 (RA), 28 SATC 213 at 219.
117. *Colquhoun v. Brooks* [1888] 21 QBD 52, *per* Lopes LJ.
118. As in *SA Estates and Finance Corp Ltd v. CIR* 1927 AD 230, 2 SATC 193.
119. *See*, for example, *COT (SR) v. 'T' Company* 1957 (4) SA 90 (SR), 21 SATC 335.

[B] *Eiusdem Generis*

Where the statute uses particular words followed by general words (e.g., 'cattle and other animals') the *eiusdem generis* rule requires that the general words be interpreted as referring to things of the same nature as the particular (e.g., that 'other animals' be taken to mean other domesticated farm animals).

The exact nature of the genus to which the general words must be confined is often unclear and contentious.

[C] *Mutatis Mutandis*

This phrase means 'subject to the necessary alterations'[120] and is employed to avoid unnecessary repetition. It implies that appropriate changes must be read into the words of the statute where it applies to similar but not identical things. For example, 'the regulations applicable to the construction of houses shall apply *mutatis mutandis* to the construction of warehouses'.

§13.07 THE INTERPRETATION ACT

The Interpretation Act[121] applies in the interpretation of fiscal legislation, but in the case of conflict or inconsistency, the provisions of the latter override the former.

§13.08 STATUTORY DEFINITIONS

Fiscal legislation commonly embodies definitions of many (but not all) of its technical terms. In the context of income tax, many of the key definitions are set out in section 1 of the Income Tax Act 58 of 1962 – for example, the definitions of 'gross income', 'resident' and 'trade'.

Section 1 specifically provides that its definitions apply 'unless the context otherwise indicates'. In *CIR v. Simpson*[122] Watermeyer JA approved the principle that:

> A definition section does not necessarily apply in all the possible contexts in which a word may be found in the statute. If a defined expression is used in a context which the definition will not fit, it may be interpreted according to its ordinary meaning.

There is an important distinction between a statutory provision declaring that a particular word 'means' a certain thing, and one that says it 'includes' a certain thing. The former usually connotes an exhaustive (i.e., comprehensive) definition of the word. The latter is a 'term of extension'[123] – a non-exhaustive statement of some of the

120. *Touriel v. Minister of Internal Affairs, Southern Rhodesia* 1946 AD 535; *Big Ben Soap Industries Ltd v. CIR* 1949 (1) SA 740 (A), 16 SATC 22.
121. Act 33 of 1957.
122. 1949 (4) SA 678 (A) at 692, 16 SATC 268 at 282.
123. *Jones & Co Ltd v. CIR* 1926 CPD 1, 2 SATC 7 at 10.

things which the word comprehends. But the courts have observed that the word 'includes' can sometimes be equivalent to 'means', and is sometimes used to add unusual or less usual meanings to the one ordinarily borne by the defined word.[124]

§13.09 COMMENCEMENT OF STATUTES, RETROSPECTIVITY AND REPEAL

In terms of the Interpretation Act, a law (which includes a proclamation, an ordinance or an Act of Parliament) commences (i.e., comes into operation) on the day on which it is first promulgated (i.e., published) in the *Government Gazette*, unless the law in question fixes some other date for its commencement.[125]

Parliament has the power (subject to constitutional challenge) to change the law with retrospective effect, despite the unfairness that this may cause. A related phenomenon is that of what has been dubbed 'legislation by ministerial announcement'. This occurs where a cabinet minister announces in Parliament or in the press that a taxing Act is to be amended in a particular way and that the coming into force of the relevant amending legislation is to be made retrospective to the date of his announcement. In some instances, the ministerial announcement has been made in such general terms that the nature and scope of the proposed amendment was not clear, and in other instances the amending legislation has turned out to be different from that foreshadowed in the ministerial announcement.

§13.10 THE TAX COURT

The Tax Administration Act[126] provides[127] for the establishment of a specialised tribunal, called the Tax Court (previously called 'the Special Court for hearing income tax appeals') constituted in accordance with the provisions of the Act.[128] This is a relatively informal tribunal created for the purpose of adjudicating appeals against assessments,[129] including interlocutory applications in this regard and procedural matters.[130]

A taxpayer who is dissatisfied with an assessment[131] issued by the Commissioner has the right to lodge an objection against the assessment[132] and, if the objection is not resolved to the taxpayer's satisfaction, he is entitled to appeal against the disallowance

124. *Estate Brownstein v. CIR* 1957 (3) SA 512 (A), 21 SATC 262.
125. Interpretation Act 33 of 1957 s. 13(1)-(2).
126. *Supra* note 20.
127. Section 116 (1).
128. *See* John Newton, 'The Special Court – its Jurisdiction and Powers', (1987) 26 *Income Tax Reporter* 332.
129. Tax Administration Act, *supra* note 20, s. 117(1).
130. Tax Administration Act, *supra* note 20, s. 117(3).
131. The taxpayer's dissatisfaction may relate *inter alia* to the *quantum* of his taxable income or assessed loss as stated in the notice of assessment.
132. Tax Administration Act, *supra* note 20, s. 104(1).

of the objection. Such appeal is adjudicated in the first instance by the Tax Board[133] or the Tax Court,[134] which is empowered *inter alia* to amend, reduce or confirm the assessment.[135]

The Tax Court's jurisdiction and powers are laid down in the Tax Administration Act.[136] It is entirely a creature of statute, hence (unlike the High Court) it has no inherent jurisdiction and can decide only those matters specifically entrusted to it.[137] Indeed, it is not a court of law in the strict sense, being merely competent to decide issues between the parties and its decisions do not constitute precedents which bind the Commissioner in other cases.[138] Nor is it a Court of Appeal in the ordinary sense.[139] Thus, decisions of the Tax Court on the interpretation of tax legislation are binding only on the SARS and the taxpayer in question in the particular matter. Hearings in the Tax Court are not open to the public.[140]

Selected judgments and decisions of the Tax Court are published in the *South African Tax Cases* under a number and not under the taxpayer's name, in order to preserve confidentiality.

§13.11 THE TAX BOARD

The Tax Administration Act provides for the establishment of Tax Boards[141] as tribunals of first instance to hear appeals against assessments or certain stipulated decisions of the Commissioner[142] where the tax in dispute does not exceed an amount (which is relatively low) determined by the minister by public notice and where a senior official of the SARS and the taxpayer in question so agree.[143]

An appeal from a decision of the Board, at the instance of the taxpayer or the Commissioner, lies to the Tax Court, which then hears the matter *de novo*.[144]

§13.12 THE DOCTRINE OF JUDICIAL PRECEDENT

Although fiscal legislation, in common with all legislation, is (subject to a constitutional challenge) binding[145] on all courts in the Republic of South Africa, it is judges who interpret the often cryptic provisions of such legislation. Hence decisions of the

133. Tax Administration Act, *supra* note 20, s. 109(1).
134. Tax Administration Act, *supra* note 20, s. 117(2).
135. Tax Administration Act, *supra* note 20, s. 129(2).
136. Tax Administration Act, *supra* note 20, s. 117(1).
137. *CIR v. Taylor* 1936 AD 100, 7 SATC 1 at 8.
138. *CIR v. City Deep Ltd* 1924 AD 298, 7 SATC 1.
139. *Bailey v. CIR* 1933 AD 204, 6 SATC 69 at 76; *Rand Ropes (Pty) Ltd v. CIR* 1944 AD 142, 13 SATC 1 at 10.
140. Tax Administration Act, *supra* note 20, s. 124(1).
141. Tax Administration Act, *supra* note 20, s. 108(1).
142. Tax Administration Act, *supra* note 20, s. 108(2).
143. Tax Administration Act, *supra* note 20, s. 109(1)(a)-(b).
144. Tax Administration Act, *supra* note 20, s. 115(1)-(2).
145. There is no higher authority than an Act of Parliament – save for the Constitution – and no-one, not a judge, nor the Commissioner has any power to exempt a person from the operation of a statute.

superior[146] courts are in their own right a source of law. Indeed – in the context of income tax, as elsewhere – judges do not merely apply the law but also create it. Where the relevant statute is silent or ambivalent, the law on a particular issue may therefore be sought in judicial precedent.

In the interests of consistency and certainty, it is desirable that cases involving the same legal issue be decided in the same way. This common-sense principle has hardened into a set of legal rules – the doctrine of precedent,[147] also called *stare decisis*. This doctrine involves the recognition of a hierarchy of courts in which the *ratio decidendi*[148] of the decision of a higher court is absolutely binding on lower courts, but whose obiter dicta[149] have only persuasive authority.

A detailed treatment of the doctrine of precedent is not possible here.[150] It suffices to note that the *ratio decidendi* of a decision of the SCA is absolutely binding on all divisions of the High Court and on all inferior courts.

As was noted, above, the Tax Court and the Tax Board are not courts of law and their decisions are not binding on the inferior or superior courts of South Africa. Nor, indeed, is the Tax Court or the Tax Board bound by its own previous decisions, although, for obvious reasons, these tribunals try to be consistent. The Commissioner is not bound by a ruling given by the Tax Court except in that particular matter. Conversely, however, the Tax Court is bound by a decision of a superior court.

The decisions of the courts of the United Kingdom are, generally, of persuasive value in South Africa and decisions of the House of Lords and the Privy Council carry particular weight.[151] Such persuasive value attaches not only to the order of the court in question, but also to the force and validity of the reasoning on which that order is based.[152]

Decisions of the Australian courts are frequently cited by the South African courts in matters of income tax because of similarities between the two tax systems (South Africa's first income tax legislation was modelled on that of New South Wales), and decisions of the courts in the United States of America are occasionally cited.

146. The High Court, the Supreme Court of Appeal and the Constitutional Court. Magistrate's and regional magistrate's courts are termed *inferior courts*. The terms *superior* and *inferior* refer not to the quality of justice dispensed but to the status of the court in the hierarchy of South African courts.
147. The doctrine itself derives not from statute but from judicial decisions of the Appellate Division, now re-named the Supreme Court of Appeal, for example *Collett v. Priest* 1931 AD 290; *Harris v. Minister of the Interior* 1952 (2) SA 428 (A).
148. The legal principle on which the case was decided.
149. Literally a 'saying by the way'; in other words, a judge's pronouncement of a legal principle based on hypothetical facts, different from those of the matter before him.
150. For more detail, *see* W. J. Hosten, A. B. Edwards et al., *Introduction to South African Law and Legal Theory* (Durban: Butterworth, 1983), Ch. IV.
151. *See Reynolds Estate v. CIR* 1937 AD 70.
152. Per Rumpff JA in *Mooi v. SIR* 1972 (1) SA 675 (A), 34 SATC 1 at 13.

§13.13 INTERNAL PRACTICES OF THE SARS

There are many issues on which fiscal legislation is silent and which have not yet been resolved by the courts. To fill these gaps, and in the interests of the consistent treatment of like cases, the SARS has evolved a large number of departmental 'practices'.

Many of these practices are recorded in 'practice notes' published in the *Government Gazette* for the information of taxpayers and their advisers. These practices and practice notes do not have the force of law – indeed the Commissioner does not always assess taxpayers in accordance with such practice notes[153] – but the Act provides that the Commissioner cannot issue an additional assessment in respect of an amount which was assessed in accordance with 'the practice generally prevailing at the date of the assessment'.[154]

Many of the Commissioner's practices are recorded in what was previously a confidential in-house manual of practice, but which has now been published as the *South African Revenue Services Income Tax Practice Manual.*[155] When first published in 1997, it was sharply criticised as containing misleading and inaccurate material.[156] At that juncture, the Commissioner said:

> Although the manual is not an official publication of SARS, it is certainly the intention that the manual should reflect the official practice of the Commissioner. However, it is possible that outdated or revised practices contained in the manual may have slipped through in the editing process, in which case the Commissioner could well dispute the current applicability of a particular practice.[157]

Practices of SARS that have not been endorsed by the courts are open to challenge by taxpayers by way of an objection to an assessment that was issued in accordance with the contested practice.[158]

---

153. *See* for example *ITC 1675* (2000) 62 SATC 219 at 229.
154. Section 79(1) proviso (ii); as to the meaning of 'practice generally prevailing' *see CIR v. SA Mutual Unit Trust Management Co Ltd* 1990 (4) SA 529 (A).
155. Published by Lexis Nexis Butterworths.
156. (1997) 46 *The Taxpayer* 1 at 4.
157. *Supra* at 3.
158. But an amount paid by the taxpayer in terms of an assessment accepted by the taxpayer and made in accordance with the then generally prevailing practice is deemed to have been properly charged; *see* the proviso to s. 102(1). Conversely, the Commissioner is precluded from raising an additional assessment where his original assessment was made in accordance with a practice then generally prevailing; s. 79(1) proviso (iii) In *CSARS v. Executor Frith's Estate* 2001 (2) SA 261 at [46] the Supreme Court of Appeal said that, '*In Commissioners for Special Purposes of the Income Tax v. Pemsel* [1891] AC 531 (HL) at 591 it was recognised by the House of Lords – per Lord Macnaghten – that when tax legislation follows a continuous practice in the department responsible for its administration, repeating the very words on which the practice was founded, it is fair to infer that the Legislature in enacting the statute intended those words to be constructed in the manner understood by the department. This approach has been accepted as applicable in South Africa by Greenberg J in *Randfontein Estates Gold Mining Co, Witwatersrand, Ltd v. Minister of Finance* 1928 WLD 77 at 83 and 84. (*See also R v. Lloyd* 1920 AD 474 at 475 and "Practice as an Element in the Interpretation of Taxation Legislation" *Taxpayer* (1958) at 4–6.) I am in respectful agreement with this approach. Of course, the practice of the department cannot run counter to the language used by the Legislature and regard to continuous previous practice will only be permissible when the provisions to be interpreted are ambiguous. With these qualifications I find it a fair inference that the

§13.14 CONSTITUTIONAL ASPECTS OF TAX

The interim Constitution of the Republic of South Africa[159] came into effect on 27 April 1994 and the final Constitution[160] on 4 February 1997.[161]

The Constitution of the Republic of South Africa[162] declares that it is 'the supreme law of the Republic; law or conduct inconsistent with it is invalid, and the obligations imposed by it must be fulfilled'.[163]

As with all other statutes, any provision of fiscal legislation can now be challenged in the courts on the grounds that it is inconsistent with the Constitution and is therefore invalid. Of particular significance in this regard are the fundamental rights laid down in the Bill of Rights contained in Chapter 2 of the Constitution.

The following fundamental rights, enshrined in the Bill of Rights, are likely to be of particular significance in income tax disputes between taxpayers and the SARS:

- The right to equality before the law.[164]
- The right to privacy.[165]
- The right to property.[166]
- The right of access to information.[167]
- The right to lawful, reasonable and procedurally fair administrative action.[168]
- The right to have disputes resolved in a court hearing.[169]

The general limitation provision in the Constitution[170] states that the rights in the Bill of Rights may be limited only in terms of law of general application to the extent that the limitation is reasonable and justifiable in an open and democratic society based on human dignity, equality and freedom, taking into account all relevant factors, including the nature of the right, the importance of the purpose of the limitation, the nature and extent of the limitation, the relation between the limitation and its purpose and less restrictive means to achieve the purpose.

Of particular note in this regard was the decision in *Metcash Trading Ltd v. C: SARS*[171] where – in the context of value-added tax – the Constitutional Court held that the principle of 'pay now, argue later' (deriving from statutory provisions in terms of

Legislature intended the practice adopted by the department responsible for the administration of the legislative provisions over many years to be continued when the Legislature re-enacts the provision which forms the basis of the longstanding practice.'

159. The Constitution of the Republic of South Africa, Act 200 of 1993. Unless otherwise stated, all references to section numbers in this Chapter refer to sections of this Act.
160. The Constitution of the Republic of South Africa 108 of 1996.
161. Except for s. 160 (1) (*b*) which came into effect on 30 June 1997.
162. The Constitution of the Republic of South Africa 108 of 1996.
163. Section 2.
164. Section 9.
165. Section 14.
166. Section 25.
167. Section 32.
168. Section 33.
169. Section 34.
170. Section 36.
171. 2001 (1) SA 1109 (CC).

which the obligation to pay an assessed amount of tax is not suspended by an objection and appeal against the assessment) passes constitutional muster, *inter alia* because such provisions are accepted as reasonable in societies based on freedom, dignity and equality. Hence the limitation of fundamental rights that such provisions entailed was held to be constitutionally justifiable.

§13.15 DOUBLE TAX AGREEMENTS

South Africa currently has 22 international tax agreements (commonly called double tax agreements or DTAs) with other African countries and 62 with countries in the rest of the world.[172] The purpose of such agreements is the elimination of double taxation. There are also other categories of international agreements, such as air and sea agreements, estate duty agreements, exchange of information agreements, mutual administrative assistance agreements, trade agreements, one-stop border posts agreements.

There is close cooperation between the Australian Tax Office (ATO) and the SARS in harnessing to the full the provisions of the double tax agreement between the two countries. The latest evidence of such international cooperation appears from the decision of the Pretoria High Court in *Commissioner for the South African Revenue Service v. Krok*[173] where judgment was handed down on 31 January 2014.

The taxpayer who was the focus of this case was the South African billionaire, Mark Krok, and a British Virgin Islands company, Jucool Enterprises Inc whose sole shareholder was the Nova Trust which was also the trustee of the Jucool Trust, a discretionary trust governed by Jersey. The beneficiaries of the Jucool Trust were Krok and his children. In 2002, Krok had relocated from South Africa to Australia, at which juncture he gave up his South African tax residence status and became an Australian resident. In 2008, Krok relocated from Australia to the United Kingdom, by which time he had accrued a debt to the ATO of AUD 25.36 million plus interest for the period 2004–2009. His objection to these assessments had been disallowed.

The Australian Tax Office was naturally keen to collect this tax but Krok had managed his affairs in such a way that he had not accumulated assets in Australia that could be attached to secure payment of the tax. He did however still have assets in South Africa, and the ATO consequently had to look to these assets to try to collect the assessed Australian tax. Those South African assets had become 'blocked', that is to say frozen, in terms of South Africa's exchange control regulations when Krok emigrated from South Africa. He had applied repeatedly, but unsuccessfully, to the South African Reserve Bank for the release of some millions of rands from those funds.

The assessments issued to Krok by the ATO were based on the proposition that, contrary to his assertion that he had disposed of his interest in those blocked South

172. *See* the South African Revenue Service website in this regard at http://www.sars.gov.za/Legal/International-Treaties-Agreements/DTA-Protocols/Pages/default.aspx. Where income tax is concerned, such agreements are entered into in terms of s. 231 of the Income Tax 58 of 1962 read with s. 231(2) of the South Africa's Constitution.
173. [2014] ZAGPPHC 8.

African assets, he still retained a legal and beneficial interest in those assets and that he had omitted to declare to the ATO the income that he had derived from those assets whilst he was Australian resident.

The ATO made a formal request to SARS in terms of Article 25A of the double tax agreement between Australia and South Africa for assistance in the collection of Australian tax and the conservancy of Krok's assets in South Africa for this purpose.

At the time of the initial request, there was no specific provision in South Africa's tax legislation that entitled SARS to apply for orders to preserve assets and, at that juncture, SARS could only invoke the provisions of the common law in this regard.

In terms of South Africa's common law, an applicant for a preservation order (i.e., an injunction against the alienation of assets) had to prove on a balance of probabilities that the debtor's assets were about to be diminished with the specific intent of frustrating a claim.[174]

However, South Africa's Tax Administration Act[175] had came into force on 1 October 2012 and section 185 eased the way for SARS to apply for an order for the preservation of assets in terms of section 183 without having to discharge the heavy onus of proof imposed at common law.

Section 185 of that Act reads as follows:

> (1) If SARS has, in accordance with an international tax agreement received –
> (a) A request for conservancy of an amount alleged to be due by a person under the tax laws of the country where there is a risk of dissipation or concealment of assets by the person, a senior SARS Official may apply for a preservation order under section 163 as if the amount were a tax payable by the person under a Tax Act; or
> (b) a request for the collection from a person of an amount alleged to be due by the person under the tax laws of the other country, a senior SARS Official may, by notice, call upon the person to state, within the period specified in the notice, whether or not the person admits liability for the amount or for a lesser amount.
> (2) A request described in subsection (1) must be in the prescribed form and must include a formal certificate issued by the competent authority of the other country stating –
> (a) the amount of the tax due;
> (b) whether the liability for the amount is disputed in terms of the laws of the other country;
> (c) if a liability for the amount is so disputed, whether such dispute has been entered into solely to delay or frustrate collection of the amount alleged to be due; and
> (d) whether there is a risk of dissipation or concealment of assets by the person.
> (3) In any proceedings, a certificate referred to in subsection (2) is –
> (a) conclusive proof of the existence of the liability alleged; and
> (b) prima facie proof of the other statements contained therein.

174. *See Knox D'Arcy Ltd v. Jamieson* [1996] ZASCA 58; 1996 (4) SA 348 at 372 F-G and *Janse van Rensburg NO v. Minister of Trade and Industry* [2000] ZACC 18; 2001 (1) SA 29 CC at para. 33.
175. Act 28 of 2011.

The certificate referred to in subsection (3), above, is of critical importance, for the Act is explicit that such a certificate constitutes conclusive proof that the stated amount of tax is due and leaves the taxpayer free only to dispute other aspects of the request for assistance.

The main arguments put forward by Krok in contesting SARS' application to the High Court for the preservation order in relation to his South African assets to secure the tax due to Australia were twofold.

The first was that, properly interpreted, Article 25A of the double tax agreement with Australia could be invoked by the tax authorities only if the taxes due to the ATO had arisen in the tax years following the signing of the Protocol to the agreement. The court rejected this argument, holding that, in terms of the agreement, assistance could be granted even where the relevant tax debt had arisen prior to the entering into of the agreement.

The second argument was that Krok was no longer the beneficial owner of the assets that were the subject of the application for a preservation order and that no order could therefore be made in respect of those assets. The court rejected the argument that he was no longer the beneficial owner of those assets.

Significantly, the judgment noted that the purpose of the 1999 agreement between Australia and South Africa was the prevention of double taxation and fiscal evasion and that the agreement contained no provisions for mutual assistance in relation to fiscal evasion; however, with the coming into force of South Africa's Tax Administration Act on 1 October 2012, this *lacuna* had been filled, for section 185(1)(a) of the latter Act provides that SARS can apply for the preservation of assets in order to recover tax on behalf of a foreign government.

In the result, the court confirmed the provisional preservation order that it had made on 18 February 2013. The assets in question included a large portfolio of listed shares, certain fixed property, a ZAR 40 million property in the prestigious Cape Town coastal suburb of Clifton and a motor vehicle.

The effect of the court order was that no-one except the *curator bonis*, appointed by the court in terms of its earlier provisional order, was empowered to deal with those assets without SARS' permission. The *curator bonis* was to continue to function for as long as SARS was collecting tax from Krok for the Australian Tax Office or until SARS was satisfied that proper arrangements had been made to secure such assets for that purpose.

CHAPTER 14

Legal Interpretation of Tax Law: United Kingdom

John Snape[*]

§14.01 INTRODUCTION

This chapter offers a snapshot of approaches to the legal interpretation of tax law in the United Kingdom (UK) at a time of great political uncertainty, both as to the future size and shape of the British state, and as to the juristic effects of the UK's secession from the EU.

The chapter draws on, but does not reproduce, the approach taken in the author's earlier work. It starts from the data and is interpretative rather than idealistic. Whilst departing significantly from other approaches, the similarities and differences between it and them are easily discernible. The earlier work consists of a monograph[1] and subsequent writings developing various elements of the approach.[2]

The essential features of the chapter's viewpoint are these. Tax law is a practice of public law.[3] Tax law is therefore constitutive of the state (in this case, the UK of Great Britain and Northern Ireland).[4] Since it is so constitutive, tax law as public law is not confined to regulating the conduct of tax policy and administration. Instead, it shapes

* The author would like to thank: (a) the editors; (b) the anonymous reviewer; and (c) Dr Dominic de Cogan (Cambridge), each for their comments on the chapter. Any mistakes or omissions remain the author's responsibility.

1. John Snape, *The Political Economy of Corporation Tax: Theory, Values and Law Reform* (Hart: Oxford, 2011); [2012] BTR 672 (Dominic de Cogan), (2013) 72 CLJ 771 (John Tiley) and 23:1 LPBR 13 (George R. Crowley).
2. Referenced as relevant below.
3. Esp Martin Loughlin, *The Idea of Public Law* (Oxford: OUP, 2003); Martin Loughlin, *Foundations of Public Law* (Oxford: OUP, 2010).
4. For corporation tax, the UK comprises Great Britain (including the Isles of Scilly but excluding Guernsey, Jersey and the Isle of Man) plus Northern Ireland (IA 1978, sch 1; HMRC *Company*

the distribution of goods in society by allocating tax burdens and tax transfers in the furtherance of political decisions. The ability of tax law to do this is a matter of *capacity*, which is measured by the ongoing, relative, success of tax measures taken. Capacity, in turn, is promoted by political prudence, both in the formation of policy and legislation and in the interpretation of the latter. Responsibility for initiating and maintaining tax measures is a matter of *competence*, part of the set of specific duties and rights assigned to particular political institutions. This approach therefore reconciles pre-existing interpretations within a single framework, thereby highlighting differences between it and other viewpoints.

Within the theory just outlined, it is instructive to discuss, not only the role of HM judges, in understanding and applying tax legislation,[5] but also the role of the UK's principal tax authority, HM Revenue and Customs (HMRC),[6] in administering it. On Hamburger's definition, even *administration* involves the interpretation and application of rules purporting 'to bind not merely executive officers, but members of the public' also.[7] The chapter emphasises the political nature of tax law (tax law as 'political jurisprudence', embodying 'reason of state') and thus puts a high premium on the role of taxation relative to the 'administrative state'.[8] Essential to the administrative state is the administration's own burden of tax law interpretation.

The discussion consists of four sections: an analysis of the UK tax system; the deciphering of some general approaches to tax law interpretation; a focus on interpreting the law on corporate income tax ('corporation tax'); and, finally, a comparable focus on VAT.

§14.02 THE UK TAX SYSTEM

The UK tax system is complex, the legislation administered within it extensive and often unstable. The uncertainty thereby engendered is currently exacerbated by the prospect of working through the implications of the 'advisory referendum' of June 2016[9] as a result of which the UK will leave the EU. The system's complexity is often

---

Taxation Manual, at www.hmrc.gov.uk/manuals/ctmanual/CTM00505.htm (accessed 18 March 2017)). The Isle of Man is, however, part of the UK for VAT (Value Added Tax (Isle of Man) Order 1982, SI 1982/1067, reg 2).

5. Snape, *supra* n. 1 at 91–97.
6. A non-ministerial department and the single UK tax authority responsible for managing and collecting every tax not devolved to Scotland and Wales, except for duties of customs (Home Office, Border Force) and tax involved in financial crime (National Crime Agency, a non-ministerial government department). Wales and Scotland have national tax-management and tax-collection authorities (Revenue Scotland and Tax Powers Act 2014 and Tax Collection and Management (Wales) Act 2016).
7. Philip Hamburger, *Is Administrative Law Unlawful?* (Chicago: University of Chicago Press, 2014) 2.
8. John Snape, 'The "Sinews of the State": Historical Justifications for Taxes and Tax Law' in Monica Bhandari (ed.), *Philosophical Foundations of Tax Law* (Oxford: OUP, 2017) 9, 28–32.
9. European Union Referendum Act 2015; *R. (Miller and another) v. Secretary of State for Exiting the European Union (Birnie and others intervening)* [2017] UKSC 5.

bemoaned[10] and has prompted a number of simplification attempts.[11] Its instability, too, is concerning, expressing, as it does, both conflicts of ideologies of the state[12] and of the implications of the rule of law.[13]

Tax competences are spelt out in devolution and local government legislation, while the distribution of public revenue between the UK's constituent countries is governed, in part, by a 'block grant' under the non-statutory 'Barnett formula'[14] and, in part, by recent legislation permitting retention of specified tax proceeds.[15] Her Majesty's Government at Westminster is competent, subject to the devolution settlement, to legislate on matters involving direct and indirect taxation, in compliance hitherto with its EU competences.[16] Thus, personal income tax ('income tax'), national insurance contributions (NICs),[17] corporation tax, VAT, capital gains tax (CGT), inheritance tax, and various environmental levies are legislated for at Westminster. In none of the UK's countries is local government competent to legislate on taxation, except on business rates and council tax, which are each levied locally according to 'a rent-based valuation' for business rates (commercial premises) and council tax (residential premises).[18] Local government is competent to set the level of business rates and to retain 50% of the net proceeds.[19] December 2016 saw the first Scottish Government Budget. The Scottish Government's taxation competences comprise: local taxes; taxes on land and building transactions; (Scottish) landfill tax (LfT); (Scottish) aggregates levy; income tax rates and thresholds (but not for dividend income and savings income); and tax on air passenger transport. These competences are colloquially referred to as 'devolved functions'. The Welsh Government's taxation competences, again as contained in devolution legislation, comprise: local taxes; income tax rates within limits; tax on landfill disposals; and land transaction tax. The Northern Ireland

---

10. In *R v. Winstanley* (1833) 148 ER 1492, 1496 (quoted in David W. Williams, 'Taxing Statutes are Taxing Statutes: The Interpretation of Revenue Legislation' (1978) 41 MLR 404, 410), Lord Wynford opined that interpreting statutes literally would incentivise 'the legislature ... to speak plain and intelligible language'.
11. For example, Geoffrey Howe, 'Simplicity and Stability: the Politics of Tax Policy' [2001] BTR 113. Notably, there was the Tax Law Rewrite project (1996–2010), discussed in Daniel Greenberg (ed.), *Craies on Legislation: A Practitioners' Guide to the Nature, Process, Effect and Interpretation of Legislation*, 11th edn (London: Sweet and Maxwell, 2017) 89–94.
12. Snape, *supra* n. 1 at 173–174.
13. John Snape, 'Tax Law: Complexity, Politics and Policymaking' (2015) 24 SLS 155.
14. The basis for calculating portions of HMG's 'block grant' of public revenue to Wales, Scotland and Northern Ireland, '[t]he Barnett formula aims to give each country the same pounds-per-person change in funding', from year to year, as the change in funding for comparable government services in England (*see* House of Commons Library, *The Barnett Formula* (Briefing Paper No 7386, 13 April 2016), available at https//:researchbriefings.files.parliament.uk/documents/CBP-7386 (accessed 9 April 2017).
15. Scotland Act 2016 provides for the Scottish Government to retain a percentage of VAT revenues, revenues from business rates and council tax, and a percentage of income tax.
16. Glen Loutzenhiser, *Tiley's Revenue Law*, 8th edn (Oxford: Hart, 2016) Ch. 77.
17. In effect, a supplementary income tax charged on employees, employers and office-holders, as well as on the self-employed, payable voluntarily also by state benefit claimants (*see* David W. Williams, G. Morse & S. Eden, *Davies: Principles of Tax Law*, 8th edn (London: Sweet and Maxwell, 2016) 224–225).
18. *Supra* at 33. Domestic rates still apply in Northern Ireland.
19. *Supra* at 33.

Government is competent to alter the rate of corporation tax, as well as the rate of air passenger duty on long-haul flights starting in Northern Ireland.

There is a single system of tax tribunals for the whole of the UK.[20] The fact that appeals against HMRC go first to the UK First-tier Tribunal (UKFTT), and thence to the UK Upper Tribunal (UKUT), has considerably curtailed the tax jurisdictions of non-specialist courts.[21] This means, in turn, that the legal interpretation of tax law is effected almost exclusively in the administrative court system. Note that administration includes, but is not confined to, the executive. A tax tribunal 'is a non-executive tribunal that binds members of the public outside the regular courts and thus exercises administrative power'.[22] The UKUT's formidable expertise has made it extremely powerful. The UKFTT's judges hear both corporation tax and VAT appeals,[23] although, as tax law issues disgorge their constitutional implications, they are considered by less specialist judges further up the system. Hitherto, all of these institutions might, and sometimes, had to (under Article 267, TFEU) refer an EU law question to the Court of Justice of the European Union (CJEU).[24] It is not yet clear how, where there is any discretion, the likelihood of a reference has been affected by the activation of the Treaty on the Functioning of the European Union (TFEU), Article 50, on 29 March 2017.[25]

Critiquing these elements demonstrates the case for viewing tax law in the UK as a public law system. Dissentients might argue thus: there has, first, been no historical distinction between public law and private law in the UK; if there is such a distinction today, then, second, public law regulates only the conduct of institutions, it does not describe the nature of tax legislation itself; and, third, tax law uses private law concepts. The objections to such a standpoint are considerable, however: the first is an idealistic reason and denies a reality recognised by F.W. Maitland if not by A.V. Dicey;[26] the second ignores the administrative state's enhanced reliance on the executive; and the third understates the extent to which private law concepts are transformed and extended by legislation.

20. *Supra* at 26–28.
21. *Supra* at 447.
22. Hamburger, *supra* n. 7 at 4.
23. VATA 1994, s. 83.
24. Natalie Lee (ed.), *Revenue Law: Principles and Practice*, 34th edn (Haywards Heath: Bloomsbury, 2016) at 38.2.
25. Lee (ed.), *supra*. Department for Exiting the European Union, *Legislating for the United Kingdom's Withdrawal from the European Union* (Cm 9446, 2017).
26. Although A.V. Dicey (1835–1922) is often cited in support of the absence of a category of administrative law in the UK, the category was recognised by F.W. Maitland (1850–1906) (*see* Loughlin (2010), *supra* at 442–443).

§14.03 GENERAL PRINCIPLES OF TAX LAW INTERPRETATION IN THE UK

[A] Literal Versus Purposive

The gradual supplanting of the literal approach to tax law interpretation, by the purposive approach, tracks the decline in judicial loyalty to one ideal of the state and the recognition of another.

It is easy to argue for a literal approach if you believe in minimal government, abhor administrative discretion, and are zealously loyal to the foundational principle of representative consent to taxation. The purposive approach, however, demands a judicial viewpoint that accepts a need for large government, the inevitability of administrative discretion, and a pragmatic loyalty to representative consent.

The contrast between the two is well expressed in the distinction between the ideal of the state as a 'civil association', which is consistent with the literal approach, and that of the state as an 'enterprise association',[27] which conforms to the purposive approach. Judges do not refer explicitly to such ideologies but they do have their own views of the world. With the enterprise association (*universitas*), the state is seen as an enterprise,[28] its citizens having 'a common substantive purpose'. In such an enterprise association, 'land and natural resources ... are corporate property ... [with] property laws ... [being] understood as devices favourable to the prosecution of the joint enterprise'.[29] With the civil association (*societas*), however, there is no common purpose that links the state's citizens. Instead, the key unifying factors are values such as loyalty, legality (its 'kindred word'), and the rule of law.[30] This is the state as the focus of allegiance.[31] The tension between the two ideals has never been finally resolved.

The differences between the two views of law's function are apparent from the contrast between statutory interpretation as described by Sir Edward Coke, in his report of *Heydon*'s case,[32] and that stated by Lord Cairns LC, in *Partington v. Attorney-General*,[33] and in *Pryce v. Monmouthshire Canal and Railway*.[34] Each is the well-spring of a distinct interpretative tradition. In *Heydon's* case, the Exchequer barons had to consider whether a copyhold was an 'estate for life' within the wording of the 1539 act for the dissolution of the monasteries.[35] In deciding that it was, the judges allowed themselves to consider '[t]he true reason of the remedy',[36] and they did so after asking themselves '[w]hat remedy the Parliament hath resolved and appointed

27. Michael Oakeshott, *On Human Conduct* (Oxford: Clarendon, 1975) 199.
28. *Supra* at 187.
29. Loughlin 2003, *supra* n. 3 at 16–17; Oakeshott, *supra* n. 27 at 205.
30. Oakeshott, *supra* n. 27 at 201.
31. *Supra* at 187.
32. (1584) 76 ER 637.
33. (1869-70) LR 4 HL 100.
34. (1879) 4 App Cas 197.
35. 3 Stat Realm 733–739.
36. (1584) 76 ER 637, 638 (*see* Samuel E. Thorne, 'The Equity of a Statute and Heydon's Case' (1936) 31 Ill LR 202, 215).

to cure the disease of the commonwealth',[37] that is, the disorder of the state. This became known as 'the mischief rule'.[38] Though a case about property (taxation's antonym), *Heydon*'s case is nonetheless revealing.[39] In *Partington* and *Pryce*, by contrast, we encounter classical formulations of 'the literal rule'.[40] The issue in *Partington* was whether, on the true construction of stamp duty legislation, *ad valorem* stamp duty[41] was exigible on interest due on long-delayed transfers of estate property to next-of-kin. In holding that it was, Lord Cairns read the relevant provision literally, saying that:

> If the person sought to be taxed comes within the letter of the law he must be taxed, however great the hardship may appear to the judicial mind to be. On the other hand, if the Crown, seeking to recover the tax, cannot bring the subject within the letter of the law, the subject is free, however apparently within the spirit of the law the case might otherwise appear to be.[42]

Pryce involved an 1845 private Act of Parliament for a company to construct and operate a railway and a canal. One of the Act's clauses granted the company the right to levy tolls for 'a fraction of a mile beyond four miles', and the question was whether this allowed levies for lesser distances. In allowing it, a majority of the HL held that the wording of the Act covered the particular case. Earl Cairns LC explained the literal rule's rationale in terms that expressly disavowed the relevance of any 'common substantive purpose' to tax legislation. '[I]nasmuch [he said] as there was not any *à priori* liability in a subject to pay any particular tax, nor any antecedent relationship between the tax-payer and the taxing authority, no reasoning founded upon any supposed relationship of the tax-payer and the taxing authority could be brought to bear upon the construction of the Act, and therefore the tax-payer had a right to stand upon a literal construction of the words used, whatever might be the consequence'.[43]

That the purposive approach has thus far overtaken the literal one, in any case of disputed interpretation, is apparent from recent developments. In addition to the mischief rule, there had long been a much less contentious approach, known as 'the golden rule', less contentious because it is essentially a private law one.[44] This has allowed judges in tax cases to 'discard the ordinary meaning of any provision and adopt

37. (1584) 76 ER 637, 638.
38. Adrian Shipwright & Elizabeth Keeling, *Textbook on Revenue Law* (London: Blackstone, 1997) 55. The mischief rule is, indeed, difficult to reconcile with the idea of the state as *societas* (*see*, perhaps, Williams (*supra* n. 10 at 412–413), quoting *Hood Barrs (No 1) v. IRC* (1946) 27 TC 385, 400).
39. *Attorney-General v. Coote* (1817) 146 ER 433, 435 (Garrow B), cited in Williams (*supra*, n. 10 at 409).
40. Shipwright and Keeling, *supra* n. 38 at 55. *See* (even earlier) *R v. Winstanley* (1833) 148 ER 1492, 1496 (Lord Wynford, *supra* n. 10).
41. Early cases involving the interpretation of tax statutes tend to concern stamp duties (Williams, *supra* n. 10 at 408–409).
42. (1869-70) LR 4 HL 100, 122.
43. (1879) 4 App Cas 197, 203.
44. *Becke v. Smith* (1836) 150 ER 724, 726 (Parke B); *Grey v. Pearson* (1857) 10 ER 1216, 1234 (Lord Wensleydale). *See also Vestey v. IRC* (1979) 54 TC 503.

some other possible meaning' that would avoid 'an unreasonable result'.[45] Recent decades have however seen a much greater commitment to purposive construction.[46] The groundbreaking case was *McGuckian v. IRC*,[47] and the approach has been reaffirmed in *UBS AG v. CRC*.[48] Moreover, as will be seen presently, the purposive approach has become standard in corporation tax cases. In *McGuckian*, a bungled tax avoidance scheme attempted to prevent an income tax liability under the now ITA 2007, Part 13, Chapter 2 ('Transfer of Assets Abroad'). The scheme's essence was to re-characterise sums received by non-resident trustees from a company as capital rather than revenue. The HL cancelled the sought-for tax advantage and viewed the receipts as income. Lord Cooke said that 'in determining the natural meaning of particular expressions in their context, weight is given to the purpose and spirit of the legislation'.[49] This is a return to Coke by a judge closely associated with his thought. *UBS* concerned tax avoidance schemes implemented by two banks. The schemes sought to harness exemptions from income tax in ITEPA 2003, Part 7, Chapter 2, relating to 'restricted securities', namely, shares the award of which to employees might be forfeited on the occurrence of a contingency.[50] Discretionary bonuses under the schemes were utilised to pay for redeemable shares in specially formed non-UK-resident companies. The shares were then transferred to employees subject to contingencies that were commercially unlikely to be fulfilled. The UKSC accepted the crown's argument that the employees had received a benefit-in-kind of the cash equivalent of the bonuses awarded. First, although each case involved the application of different statutory provisions to specific facts, the court would follow a purposive construction, so as to ascertain the kind of transaction to which the legislation was designed to apply. Second, this particular legislation was not intended to cover shares subject to 'commercially irrelevant conditions whose only purpose is the obtaining of the exemption'.[51] Third, these shares were of this kind and therefore could not fall within the definition of restricted securities. Lord Reed stated the justices' unanimous conclusion:

> Approaching the matter initially at a general level, the fact that Chapter 2 was introduced partly for the purpose of forestalling tax avoidance schemes self-evidently makes it difficult to attribute to Parliament an intention that it should apply to schemes which were carefully crafted to fall within its scope, purely for the purpose of tax avoidance. Furthermore, it is difficult to accept that Parliament can have intended to encourage by exemption from taxation the award of shares to employees, where the award of the shares has no purpose whatsoever other than the obtaining of the exemption itself: a matter which is reflected in the fact that the shares are in a company which was brought into existence merely for the purposes of the tax avoidance scheme, undertakes no activity beyond its participation in the scheme, and is liquidated upon the termination of the scheme. The

45. *Luke v. IRC* [1963] AC 557, 579-580 (Lord Reid). *See* Hon Mr Justice Vinelott, 'Interpretation of Fiscal Statutes' (1982) 3 Stat LR 78, 82.
46. Loutzenhiser, *supra* n. 16 at 50–51.
47. (1997) 69 TC 1.
48. [2016] UKSC 13.
49. (1997) 69 TC 1, 84.
50. ITEPA 2003, ss 423, 425(2).
51. [2016] UKSC 13 [85].

> encouragement of such schemes, unlike the encouragement of employee share ownership generally, or share incentive schemes in particular, would have no rational purpose, and would indeed be positively contrary to rationality, bearing in mind the general aims of income tax statutes.[52]

The interpretative approach articulated in each of these cases illustrates the fact that the prompter to the new purposive approach is the perceived need to combat tax avoidance. Ours is not entirely an enterprise society but the judicial mind knows, when it sees it, a tax ploy designed to suborn the 'common substantive purpose' of our employment-tax legislation. 'Income tax is', after all, the engine room of the modern state'.[53] Though there are anomalous eighteenth- and nineteenth-century examples of purposive construction in tax cases,[54] it is obvious that judicial *dicta* in both *McGuckian* and *UBS* stand in stark contrast with statements of the literal rule. Purposive construction, as Williams writes, urges 'considerations of state'.[55] Indeed, the learned editors of *Bramwell* describe the approach in *UBS* as 'a fundamental shift ... in jurisprudential thinking', beyond even purposive construction, such that 'there is a stark affirmation that tax avoidance of ... [the kind in *UBS*] cannot have been intended by Parliament and on that basis alone a court can refuse to apply the legislative provisions'.[56]

Dead though the literal approach may appear, its pull might easily be underestimated. There are, of course, the overwhelming majority of uncontroversial cases in which it is easily applied, if not by judges, then by (other) administrators and by tax practitioners.[57] The literal approach owes much to the values of the 1688/1689 'Glorious Revolution', values with secure property rights at their centre, and ones that retain their appeal.[58] Such values have been of the greatest significance both in property law and in tax law[59] and are the foundation of 'the parliamentary state'.[60] The literal approach is entirely consistent, therefore, with liberal or conservative judicial outlooks in a confident, minimal state. When, in *Cape Brandy Syndicate v. IRC*,[61] Rowlatt J says 'there is no equity about a tax',[62] he is underlining this approach. This is a specific reference to the fact that the mischief rule was, in reality, a vestige of the

52. *Supra* [77].
53. John Prebble, 'Why Is Tax Law Incomprehensible?' [1994] BTR 380, 380 (but *see* Bret N. Bogenschneider, 'Wittgenstein on Why Tax Law Is Comprehensible' [2015] BTR 252).
54. Snape, *supra* n. 8 at 24; Williams, *supra* n. 10 at 409–410; Dominic de Cogan, 'Purposive Interpretation in the Age of Horse Trams' [2015] BTR 80.
55. Williams, *supra* n. 10 at 410.
56. Richard Bramwell, John Lindsay & Alun James et al., *Taxation of Companies and Company Reconstructions*, loose-leaf, release 22 (December 2016) (London: Sweet and Maxwell, 2009) [A13.1.5]. *See* also De Cogan [2016] CLJ 474.
57. Oliver Jones & Francis A.R. Bennion (eds), *Bennion on Statutory Interpretation: A Code*, 6th edn (London: LexisNexis, 2013) 914.
58. Loutzenhiser, *supra* n. 16 at 30, citing *Woolwich Equitable Building Society v. IRC* [1993] AC 70, 172E (Lord Goff).
59. Hubert Monroe, QC, *Intolerable Inquisition? Reflections on the Law of Tax* (London: Stevens, 1981) 49, quoted in Vinelott, *supra* n. 45 at 79; David W. Williams, 'Three Hundred Years On: Are Our Tax Bills Right Yet?' [1989] BTR 370.
60. Snape, *supra* n. 8 at 21–27.
61. (1921) 12 TC 358.
62. *Supra*, 366. *See Stewart and Another (trading as GT Shooting) v. CEC* [2001] EWCA Civ 1988 [42] (Laws LJ).

Aristotelian doctrine of the 'equity' of a statute.[63] The judicial attitude to the statute in *Heydon's* case was evinced in a period of near-absolutist rule, concerned a statute from such a period, and was reported in such a period. It is perhaps not surprising, therefore, that the purposive approach has resurfaced at a time of, in Lord Sumption JSC's vivid evocation, '[t]he complexity of the modern law and its progressive invasion of the interstices of daily life'.[64] Nowadays, the impetus for a return to something like the literal approach has come, not from the UK, but from America's intellectual descendants of the nineteenth-century strands of liberalism and conservatism mentioned above. Loutzenhiser cites Justice Scalia[65] in this connection and, whilst issuing the important *caveat* that American and UK legislative procedures are sufficiently different to awaken suspicion of easy transplants, nonetheless speculates that the combination of time, international legal education, and professional advancement may mean that the literal approach comes back.[66] Whether the literal approach is revived will depend, in part, on the evolving shape of the UK state after 'Brexit'. If, as seems possible, HM Government (HMG) does not conclude a deal with the EU within Article 50's two-year time period, and the UK becomes 'a low-tax, minimum-regulation country',[67] the literal approach may yet regain a wide importance.

What will now happen depends, too, in part on tax legislation retaining its current qualities and, in part, on the energy with which tax avoidance is pursued. Tax avoidance is less objectionable if you believe in a civil association rather than an enterprise association. More than that, to the 'literalist', successful tax avoidance is a vindication of the rights of the taxpayer in the face of government. This spirit runs through the majority speeches in *Duke of Westminster*, a personal income tax case that articulated the 'principle that if a transaction is genuine the courts cannot go behind it to some supposed underlying "substance"'.[68] It is no accident, to the author at least, that the case belongs to a period in which, for sure, the UK had developed an administrative state but that this was nothing compared with the administrative state after World War II. Each of the literal and purposive approaches is symptomatic of clashing ideologies, of the uneasiness our times: populism and neoliberalism; protectionism and free trade, etc. Either is a far cry from the 'consensus' approach, laid down by Lord Donovan in *Mangin v. CIR*,[69] and the mixing of elements of the mischief, literal and golden rules.

For completeness, it should be mentioned that, irrespective of literal or purposive approaches, there are certain presumptions of statutory construction, outside the scope

63. John H. Baker, *An Introduction to English Legal History*, 4th edn (London: Butterworths, 2002) 106, 209, 212.
64. *R (Prudential plc and another) v. Special Commissioner of Income Tax* [2013] UKSC 1.
65. Margaret Talbot, 'Supreme Confidence: The Jurisprudence of Justice Antonin Scalia' *New Yorker* (28 March 2005), available at http://www.newyorker.com/magazine/2005/03/28/supreme-confidence (accessed 25 January 2017).
66. Loutzenhiser, *supra* n. 16 at 51.
67. Martin Wolf, 'Brexiters must lose if Brexit is to succeed' *Financial Times* (London, 29 March 2017) 11.
68. Bennion, *supra* n. 57 at 914.
69. [1971] AC 739, 746C-F (*see also* Chapter 9 of this volume).

of this chapter.[70] Key here are the presumptions against taxation and the levying of charges and fees, which follow logically from the points made above.[71]

[B] International Tax Issues

It follows from the foregoing that the division of tax competences is crucial to understand judicial approaches to international tax texts. A common illustration is the absurdity of a UK 'tax on the Chinese income of a Chinaman resident in China'.[72] HM Government would be competent thus to legislate but its capacity in the matter would be non-existent. Treaty interpretation acknowledges this sensitivity.

Given this, judges have tended to take a more obviously purposive approach to the interpretation of Double Taxation Agreements (DTAs). Two examples are canonical. In *IRC v. Commerzbank AG,*[73] the issue was whether the receipt of US-source interest by the London branches of two non-UK nor US resident banks was exempted by the now-superseded 1966 UK/US DTA. In interpreting the DTA to exempt the receipt, Mummery J gave the relevant DTA article a 'purposive construction', on 'broad principles', in good faith, and without unnecessary reference to *travaux préparatoires.*[74] In *Indofood International Finance Ltd v. JP Morgan Chase Bank NA, London Branch,*[75] the issue was whether a subsidiary that had issued loan notes counted as 'beneficial owner' of interest paid to it by its parent under a loan intended to fund the subsidiary's payments to note-holders. Concluding that it did not, the CA rejected any 'technical and legal' interpretation of 'beneficial owner' and, instead, had regard 'to the substance of the matter'.[76]

Whilst Lisbon constituted the EU as a domestic legal order, it now seems appropriate to deal with EU tax law here. The interpretation of EU tax law has been exclusively concerned with competences.[77] The effect has probably been to enhance the UK's capacity to encourage inward investment. Two cases provide illustrations. In Case C-446/03, *Marks and Spencer plc v. Halsey,*[78] the issue was whether UK-residence restrictions on the group relief of trading losses were contrary to the fundamental freedoms of the European Treaties.[79] While recognising the need for public-revenue safeguards, the CJEU, in holding the UK provisions to breach the freedoms, offered inward investors to the UK from elsewhere in the EU an assurance of legality in a highly political area. In *Fleming (trading as Bodycraft) v. CRC; Condé Nast Publications Ltd v.*

70. But *see* Loutzenhiser, *supra* n. 16 at 48–49 and Shipwright and Keeling, *supra* n. 38 at 57–60.
71. Craies, *supra* n. 11 at 69–71.
72. Lee (ed.), *supra* n. 24 at [18.1].
73. [1990] STC 285.
74. *Supra* at 297h-298h, 303j-304g.
75. [2006] EWCA Civ 158.
76. *Supra* at [44].
77. HM Government, *Review of the Balance of Competences between the United Kingdom and the European Union: Taxation* (July 2013), available at https://www.gov.uk/government/uploads/system/uploads/attachment_data/file/224710/2901087_Taxation_acc.pdf (accessed 21 February 2017).
78. [2006] STC 237.
79. John Snape, 'Corporation Tax Reform: Politics and Public Law' [2007] BTR 374.

CRC,[80] the issue was whether or not a national three-year cut-off date for claiming an input VAT deduction was unlawful for infringing the EU-law effectiveness principle. The HL held the cut-off to be unlawful, holding that the cut-off period could not start until all affected taxpayers had been made aware of a transitional period for claiming historical input VAT deductions.[81] Again, this offered taxpayers an assurance of legality in the face of politics.

The decision in *Fleming*, some said, underlined 'the curbs' that EU VAT law imposed on Member States,[82] while *Marks and Spencer* illustrated a similar point for corporation tax. In fact, the opposite was the case: both cases enhanced the capacity of the UK to attract inward investors. Both, therefore, augmented the UK's political power. They did so even-handedly: Condé Nast, as publishers of *GQ* magazine, *Vogue*, etc., was a UK subsidiary of an American group; *Fleming* was a small-scale concern. The cases tend to support Milward's millennial observation that 'whenever the Community member-states had to implement their surrenders of sovereignty they produced an arrangement which left almost all political power with the nation-state'.[83]

[C] Domestic Tax Issues

Consistent with the transition referred to above, recent decades have seen a move away from the traditional blanket-ban on judges looking outside the wording of the legislative text when interpreting tax legislation. The milestone case, in relation to looking beyond the legislative wording, was *Pepper v. Hart*,[84] in which the question had arisen of whether the amount of a benefit-in-kind to a schoolmaster, for employment income purposes, was the 'marginal cost' of educating the schoolmaster's son at the school, rather than its 'average cost'. Prudence prevailed as the HL read the benefits-in-kind code as taxing the marginal cost, thereby averting swingeing (because of the time periods involved) and widespread (because of the likely commonplace nature of such arrangements) interest and penalties and, incidentally, opening up transcendent interpretative possibilities by allowing reference to the parliamentary record to establish parliamentary intention when interpreting 'legislation which is ambiguous or obscure'.[85]

The recognition of the need for greater flexibility may be rooted in the fact that, whilst it occasionally imports definitions from other areas of law, tax law often insists on idiosyncratic meanings, e.g., a 'company', as defined in CA 2006, is not coterminous with a 'company' in the CTAs;[86] a 'distribution', for CA 2006 purposes, is defined

80. [2008] UKHL 2.
81. Lee (ed.), *supra* n. 24 at [38.53].
82. Davies, *supra* n. 17 at 30.
83. Alan S. Milward, *The European Rescue of the Nation-State*, 2nd edn (London: Routledge, 2000) 435.
84. (1992) 65 TC 421; Jacqueline Dyson, 'Interpreting Tax Statutes', in M. Freeman (ed.), *Legislation and the Courts* (Dartmouth: Aldershot, 1997) 45, 53.
85. (1992) 65 TC 421, 483 (Lord Browne-Wilkinson).
86. John Snape, 'Corporate Income Tax Subjects in the United Kingdom' in D. Gutmann (ed.), *Corporate Income Tax Subjects* (Amsterdam: IBFD, 2015) 546.

differently from a CTA 'distribution';[87] 'beneficial ownership', for group relief, is a different concept from 'equitable ownership' for English private law.[88] This idiosyncrasy is behind the procedural rule applicable to the General Anti-Abuse Rule (the GAAR).[89] Section 211, FA 2013, allows reference, in interpreting the GAAR, to public 'guidance, statements or other material', as well as to 'evidence of' contemporary 'established practice'. There are also general rules of statutory interpretation, notably in the HRA 1998,[90] sections 2 and 3, although all of the provisions applicable to taxation are in some way qualified, either because of the way in which the Convention rights are framed, or because of the way in which the ECtHR has itself interpreted their scope.[91] The main constitutional restriction on creative interpretation is Article 4 of the Bill of Rights 1689,[92] which requires parliamentary consent for taxes and other financial levies. Article 4 was interpreted in *Bowles v. Bank of England*,[93] where Parker J held that, to comply, levies had to be imposed, not merely by House of Commons resolution, but by statute. The upshot is now PCTA 1968, which gives 'limited statutory force' to Budget resolutions from the start of the financial year until 5 August, by which time an FA will have been enacted.[94]

§14.04 INTERPRETING CORPORATION TAX LAW

[A] Literal Interpretation Generally Absent

In the wake of *Pepper v. Hart* and of *McGuckian v. IRC*, the HL, and the UKSC as its juridical successor, has embarked on the purposive interpretation of corporation tax legislation,[95] perhaps first and foremost, in *Barclays Mercantile Business Finance Ltd v. Mawson*.[96] There were three main issues. First, whether, for the purposes of capital allowances, Barclays Mercantile Business Finance (Barclays) had actually incurred GBP 91 million of expenditure. Second, if it had, whether that expenditure had been incurred in connection with providing the Irish Gas Board, *Bord Gáis Éireann*, with a pipeline. Third, if both these issues were resolved in the affirmative, whether Barclays had incurred the expenditure in the course of its trade. The pipeline in question was a major infrastructure project, the 200 + km First Interconnector, linking Ireland with Scotland, finished in 1993. In the circumstances, the HL held that Barclays was entitled

87. CA 2006, Pt 23; CTA 2009, Pt 9A; CTA 2010, Pt 23; TCGA 1992, s. 122.
88. *Bupa Insurance Ltd v. CRC* [2014] UKUT 262 (TCC).
89. FA 2013, Pt 5. *See*, esp, Bramwell, *supra* n. 56 at [A13]. Discussion in this chapter refers to the English GAAR, unless otherwise indicated. There are Scottish and Welsh GAARs (*see* Davies, *supra* n. 17 at 28–29).
90. Lady Justice Arden, 'The Interpretation of UK Domestic Legislation in the Light of European Convention on Human Rights Jurisprudence' (2004) 25 Stat LR 165.
91. Esp *Ferrazzini v. Italy* (Application No. 44759/98) [2001] STC 1314.
92. Also Claim of Right 1689, Art. 6 (Scotland).
93. [1913] 1 Ch 57.
94. Lee (ed.), *supra* n. 24 at [6.22]–[6.40].
95. *See*, e.g., Bill Dodwell & Kevin Prosser (eds), *The Red Book 2016-17*, 9 vols (Kingston-upon-Thames: Wolters Kluwer, 2016).
96. [2004] UKHL 51; also *CRC v. Tower MCashback LLP* (2011) 80 TC 641.

to the capital allowances, thereby resolving all three issues in the affirmative. The task of the court was, first, 'to give the statutory provision a purposive construction in order to determine the nature of the transaction to which it was intended to apply' and, second, 'to decide whether the actual transaction (which might involve considering the overall effect of a number of elements intended to operate together) answered to the statutory description ... The present case [said their Lordships] ... illustrates the need for a close analysis of what, on a purposive construction, the statute actually requires'.[97]

Whether this means that the literal approach has no place in the interpretation of corporation tax law remains to be seen, but there have been expressions of disquiet nonetheless, and a search for a third way. The purposive approach had earlier been criticised by Parker LJ and by Lord Oliver in *Craven v. White*,[98] while Lord Hoffmann sought a third way in *MacNiven v. Westmoreland Investments Ltd.*[99] In *Craven v. White*, a subsidiary question was whether CGT legislation could be read so as to re-characterise several transactions as just one chargeable disposal. The HL, by a majority of three to two, held not. Two judges, in the course of the litigation, were highly critical of the purposive approach. In the CA, Parker LJ had concluded that the judge was ultimately thrown back on the 'words of the section', given that 'the purpose was to tax some people and not others in respect of certain transactions and not others'.[100] In the HL, Lord Oliver stressed 'the continued validity'[101] of the approach taken in *Duke of Westminster v. IRC.*[102] In *MacNiven v. Westmoreland*, Lord Hoffmann's alternative approach had involved distinguishing 'between commercial concepts and juristic analysis'.[103] ' ... [I]t is first necessary [he said] to construe the statutory language and decide that it refers to a concept which Parliament intended to be given a commercial meaning capable of transcending the juristic individuality of its component parts. But there are many terms in tax legislation which cannot be construed in this way. They refer to purely legal concepts which have no broader commercial meaning.'[104]

It must be emphasised, however, that both of these alternatives have been superseded by *Barclays Mercantile Business Finance v. Mawson*, *McGuckian v. IRC* and *UBS*. Of *MacNiven v. Westmoreland*, Lord Nicholls said, in *Barclays Mercantile Business Finance v. Mawson*: 'we do not think that it was intended to provide a substitute for a close analysis of what the statute means. It certainly does not justify the assumption that an answer can be obtained by classifying all concepts a priori as either "commercial" or "legal". That would be the very negation of purposive construction'.[105] Of *Craven v. White*, Lord Cooke said, in *McGuckian v. IRC*: '*Craven v. White* ..., where the facts were distant from those of the present case, is a difficult case, partly

97. *Supra* at [32], [39].
98. (1988) 62 TC 1.
99. (2001) 73 TC 1.
100. (1988) 62 TC 1, 135.
101. *Supra* at 193.
102. (1935) 19 TC 490; *see* Bennion, *supra* n. 57 at 914.
103. Lee (ed.), *supra* n. 24 at [2.37].
104. (2001) 73 TC 1, 70.
105. 76 TC 446, 536. Lord Nicholls quoted *Collector of Stamp Revenue v. Arrowtown Assets Ltd* HKCFA (2003) 6 ITLR 454 [37] and [93] (Ribeiro PJ), and *Campbell v. IRC* [2004] STC (SCD)

because of the differences of opinion in your Lordships' House, but at least it can be said that one cardinal point of agreement was that essentially the question is one of construction'.[106]

[B] Legislative Amendment by Judges Occasionally Possible

As the growth of the purposive interpretation of tax legislation may well confirm, and as already strongly implied, traditionally, 'there are no special principles of construction applicable only to fiscal legislation'.[107] As Wills J stated, in *Styles v. Middle Temple Treasurer*,[108] '[t]hough I agree that every tax if it is to be supported, must be found within the clear language of an Act of Parliament, I am disposed to repudiate the notion of there being an artificial distinction between the rules to be applied to a taxing Act and the rules to be applied to any other Act'.[109] Nonetheless, just as judicial amendment of legislation is censored in other areas of law, it awakes acute sensitivities in relation to tax law. This is because, given the Bill of Rights, it sits at the outer limits of judicial competences. With taxes, perhaps more than any other area of law, 'a naked usurpation of the legislative function under the thin disguise of interpretation',[110] is undesirable. Nonetheless, there are various cases in which judicial amendment of non-corporation tax legislation has taken place and not raised serious objection.[111] Two corporation tax cases merit comment, *Mellham Ltd v. Burton*[112] and *Vodafone 2 v. CRC*.[113] In the former, the HL rejected a reading of ICTA 1988, section 14, which would have imposed a never-ending obligation to pay interest on an ACT liability, since it was 'so startling as to suggest that it would be a good reason for construing the statute more flexibly'.[114] That produced a decision in favour of the taxpayer. With the latter, discussed elsewhere in this volume,[115] the CA read legislative wording into the UK's former CFC code to ensure its conformity with CJEU case law and thus to prevent leakage of public revenue. That produced a decision against the taxpayer. *Vodafone 2* is, indeed, an example of reason of state at work in corporation tax law. It is unclear whether a general principle can be drawn out of such, admittedly rare, cases. The purposive approach would seem more tolerant of judicial amendment than would a literal approach.

---

396. The editors of Bennion, *supra*, n. 57 at 915n, *see MacNiven v. Westmoreland* as an application of *IRC v. Westminster*.
106. (1997) 69 TC 1, 85.
107. Vinelott, *supra* n. 45 at 78, quoted in Natalie Lee, 'A Purposive Approach to the Interpretation of Tax Statutes' (1999) 20 Stat LR 124, 127.
108. (1898) 4 TC 123, quoted in Shipwright and Keeling, *supra* n. 38 at 53.
109. *Supra*.
110. Lord Simonds' famous criticism of Denning LJ, in *Magor and St Mellons Rural District Council v. Newport Corporation* [1952] AC 189, 191.
111. *See* Lee, *supra* n. 107 at 127; Loutzenhiser, *supra* n. 16 at 47.
112. [2006] UKHL 6.
113. [2009] EWCA Civ 446.
114. *Supra* at [19].
115. *See* Chapter 6, this volume.

[C] Reception and Rejection of Transplanted Categories

Corporation tax legislation often seeks to transplant concepts from private law. One example of a transplanted concept is the test for corporate residence as it continues to apply to non-UK incorporated companies. Such companies are resident in the UK if they are centrally managed and controlled from the UK.[116] This common-law rule of tax law, writes Avery Jones, has its origins in the nineteenth-century law on the residence of railway companies for the purposes of county court jurisdiction.[117] A second example is the definition of a 'money debt' in the 'loan relationships' code,[118] part of the definition of which draws on contract law, being 'a debt which ... falls to be settled ... by the payment of money'.[119] A third example is the definition of 'plant', in relation to the availability of capital allowances, which has its origins in nineteenth-century tort law.[120]

The history of transplanting private law concepts to tax law has not however been a happy one, as such concepts tend to be easily manipulable. The common-law rule on non-UK incorporated companies is the residue of a rule curtailed when all UK-incorporated companies were made UK-resident, subject to DTA overrides, in 1988.[121] The loan relationships definition of a money debt was extended to include settlement by shares, as an anti-avoidance measure, in FA 2008.[122] Developments of the definition of plant considered to be against the public interest were curtailed by legislative intervention in FA 1994.[123] All this invites speculation as to the reasons for the unique pressure placed on definitions in tax law. An understandable judicial tendency to turn to equivalent concepts, in other areas of law, prompted perhaps by common-law judicial approaches and the doctrine of precedent, seems unequal to this pressure.[124]

[D] Statutory Interpretation and the GAAR

It is almost certainly true to say that the problems raised by the interpretation of tax legislation arise in their acutest form when judges are trying to analyse the taxation consequences of tax avoidance schemes. The countries of the UK now have, as already mentioned, GAARs, as one of a range of statutory counters to avoidance.[125] The GAAR

116. *Wood v. Holden* [2006] EWCA Civ 26.
117. John Avery Jones, 'Jurisdiction to Tax Companies: The Influences of the Jurisdiction of the Courts and of European Thinking' in John Tiley (ed.), *Studies in the History of Tax Law, Volume 4* (Oxford: Hart, 2010) 163, 165 (citing *Brown v. London and North Western Railway Co* [1861–1873] All ER Rep 487).
118. CTA 2009, Pts 5–7.
119. *Supra*, s. 303(1).
120. *Yarmouth v. France* (1887) 19 QBD 647.
121. CTA 2009, s. 14.
122. Loutzenhiser, *supra* n. 16 at 1185n.
123. *See* now CAA 2001, ss 21–23.
124. This observation was prompted by a comment of the anonymous reviewer, for which the author is grateful.
125. Davies, *supra* n. 17 at 61, 63; Loutzenhiser, *supra* n. 16 at 38.

covers 'arrangements' where 'it would be reasonable to conclude that the obtaining of a tax advantage was the main purpose, or one of the main purposes, of the arrangements'.[126] Arrangements 'are "abusive" if they are arrangements the entering into or carrying out of which cannot reasonably be regarded as a reasonable course of action in relation to the relevant tax provisions'.[127] In addition to the GAAR, there are piecemeal statutory anti-avoidance provisions, including TAARs, and disclosure schemes (DOTAS, POTAS, and VADR). Although there is no substantive judicial anti-avoidance doctrine of the type encountered in the United States, yet, in appropriate cases, the statutory-interpretation principles rehearsed above form part of the application of the principle of *WT Ramsay Ltd v. IRC*.[128] The effect of the cases discussed above is that the *Ramsay* principle has been re-characterised as a principle of statutory interpretation rather than a substantive constitutional law doctrine. Its application is far from straightforward, however, something that has induced Lewison J to formulate a 'Dworkinian' set of 14 propositions illustrating the process,[129] propositions subsequently adapted and applied.[130] In *Barclays Mercantile*, the HL's conclusions meant that the *Ramsay* principle did not come into play. In *IRC v. Scottish Provident Institution*,[131] however, it did. Extra-judicially, the South African judge, Malcolm Wallis, has argued that the 'statutory interpretation' view of the *Ramsay* principle shows that tax legislation is to be interpreted differently from other legislation,[132] despite the long-standing insistence of the UK's judges to the contrary.

The GAAR, which sits alongside *Ramsay*, is as yet relatively little-used, yet it is to be suspected that statutory interpretation approaches remain key. Indeed, the editors of *Bramwell* suggest, boldly, that the GAAR has been rendered otiose by *UBS*.[133]

126. FA 2013, s. 207(1). The editors of Bramwell, *supra* n. 56 at [A13.1.5], argue that *UBS* has made the GAAR redundant.
127. FA 2013, s. 207(2).
128. (1981) 54 TC 101. *See also Furniss v. Dawson* (1984) 55 TC 324, summed up at Davies, *supra* n. 17, 56–57. The *Ramsay* principle says that, even in the case of 'genuine' transactions, the absence of a commercial or business purpose and the presence of a tax avoidance purpose enables the court to ignore those transactions ('A subject is only to be taxed upon clear words, not upon "intendment" or upon the "equity" of an Act. Any taxing Act of Parliament is to be construed in accordance with this principle. What are "clear words" is to be ascertained upon normal principles: these do not confine the courts to literal interpretation. There may, indeed should, be considered the context and scheme of the relevant Act as a whole, and its purpose may, indeed should, be regarded' ((1981) 54 TC 101, 184 (Lord Wilberforce)). And *see* Judith Freedman, 'Interpreting Tax Statutes: Tax Avoidance and the Intention of Parliament' (2007) 123 LQR 53.
129. In *Berry v. CRC* [2011] UKUT 81 (TCC), [30], [31], quoted in Craies, *supra* n. 11, 981–984.
130. *See*, e.g., *Bupa Insurance Ltd v. CRC* [2014] UKUT 262 (TCC) [62]–[64].
131. [2004] UKHL 52.
132. Malcolm Wallis, 'Is Tax Really Different?' [2016] BTR 299, 308–309. Similar assumptions are shared, arguably, by parliamentary counsel (*see* Craies, *supra* n. 11 at 981).
133. Bramwell, *supra* n. 56 at [A13.1.5].

§14.05 INTERPRETING VALUE ADDED TAX LAW

[A] Distinctiveness of Administrative Approaches to Statutory Interpretation

Corporation tax and VAT have, for over a decade now, been administered by the merged HMRC, but this was not always so.[134] For over three decades from VAT's introduction in 1973, it had been administered by the now defunct HM Customs and Excise, a department with a strong maritime policing tradition dating back at least to Charles II's initial establishment, in 1671, of the Board of Customs Commissioners.[135] The distinctiveness of VAT administration still owes something to its origins in this tradition. Heavy use is made of delegated legislation as one of four sources of VAT regulation, the others being the VAT Recast Directive ('the Directive'),[136] VATA 1994 as amended by FAs, and VAT official Notices.[137] Delegated legislation may provide for a transaction to be regarded as a supply of goods, rather than a supply of services, and *vice versa*.[138] This can affect the rate of tax applied, along with other issues to do with the timing of the supply.[139] Certain sections of the Notices (notably, VAT Notice 700, *The VAT Guide*)[140] are given statutory effect.[141] In addition, there is a range of other material. Exceptionally, VAT is still replete with prerogatival extra-statutory concessions,[142] with agreements between HMRC and particular economic sectors, with parliamentary questions, information sheets and press releases.[143] This may be because, with VAT and other indirect taxes, the legislative niceties of the parliamentary state are even less honoured than with the direct taxes. It is important to recognise, therefore that despite – or perhaps because of – its EU origins, VAT is a classic manifestation of taxation in the administrative state.[144] Its system of penalties has long been so draconic that, exceptionally, the CA has mitigated its rigour by interpreting the relevant provision in VATA 1994, section 72, in the light of Article 6 of the ECHR.[145]

134. VATA 1994, sch 11, para. 1.
135. *See*, generally, Dorothy Johnstone, *A Tax Shall be Charged: Some Aspects of the Introduction of the British Value Added Tax* (London: HMSO, 1975) 7–8.
136. Directive 06/112/EU [2006] OJ L347/1, as amended, based on Art. 113, TFEU (*see* Davies, *supra* n. 17 at 434). *See* Lee (ed.), *supra* n. 24 at [37.5].
137. Davies, *supra* n. 17 at 447. FA 1972 brought VAT in; VATA 1983 was the first consolidation (Lee (ed.), *supra* n. 24 at [38.1]).
138. VATA 1994, s. 5 (*see* Davies, *supra* n. 17 at 454).
139. Davies, *supra* n. 17 at 455.
140. Available at https://www.gov.uk/government/publications/vat-notice-700-the-vat-guide/vat-notice-700-the-vat-guide (accessed 16 February 2017). (*See* Johnstone, *supra* n. 135 at 86).
141. VATA 1994, s. 97.
142. Lee (ed.), *supra* n. 24 at [38.2].
143. *See*, e.g., Bill Dodwell & Kevin Prosser (eds), *The Green Book 2016-17* (Kingston-upon-Thames: Wolters Kluwer, 2016).
144. Snape, *supra* n. 8 at 29. *See*, e.g., David Milne QC et al., *De Voil Indirect Tax Service*, 6 vols (London: LexisNexis, 2017) [V1.272]–[V1.273].
145. *Han (trading as Murdishaw Supper Bar) v. CEC* [2001] EWCA Civ 1040. Cultural memory may have had a part to play. VAT enforcement powers have always been considered draconic (Johnstone, *supra* n. 135 at 65–71).

[B] Irrelevance of Predecessor Taxes

The most tangible link between the structure of VAT and its predecessor taxes (selective employment tax and purchase tax)[146] is the range of so-called zero-rated supplies, yet the interpretation of VAT legislation owes little to those earlier taxes.[147] This range corresponds to the range of exemptions from the predecessor taxes.[148] Zero-rated supplies, *not quite* a uniquely British paradox,[149] are described in the Directive as 'exemptions with deductibility of the VAT paid at the preceding stage'[150] or as 'exemptions with credit'.[151] Though deplored by the EU Commission, on competition grounds, zero-rating is a permitted 'temporary measure' in the Directive.[152] It is, however, as Morse writes, intended to be confined to 'the essentials of life'.[153]

When the UK courts interpret VAT legislation,[154] they do so by reference to EU law, not UK law, and specifically to the CJEU's interpretations of the Directive.[155] The EU law is largely contained in the Directive, which has direct effect in Member States.[156] In addition, relevant principles of EU law apply, such as: fiscal neutrality[157] ('the reflection, in the context of VAT, of the principle of equal treatment');[158] legal certainty;[159] effectiveness;[160] legitimate expectation;[161] non-discrimination; equivalence[162] and proportionality.[163] In *Yoga for Health Foundation v. CEC*,[164] Nolan J emphasised this point, saying that he had to strive 'to adopt a European as distinct from a traditionally English approach to the question of construction', which approach required him to 'adopt what is often called a purposive or sometimes a teleological method of construction'.[165] The fiscal neutrality principle, as interpreted by the CJEU, has been applied by the HL, in ruling that HMRC breached the principle, by denying

146. Purchase tax related to specified goods, selective employment tax 'to distributive and other services' (*see* Johnstone, *supra* n. 135 at 6). Both 'were "single stage" taxes' (*ibid*).
147. VATA 1994, s. 30, sch 7A. But *see* references in De Voil, *supra* n. 144 at, e.g., [V1.241] and [V4.287].
148. Davies, *supra* n. 17 at 475.
149. *Marks and Spencer plc v. CRC: Note* [2009] UKHL 8 [13] (Auld LJ, quoted). As the anonymous reviewer of this chapter commented, 'both Canada and Australia also zero rate food', and also the Republic of Ireland.
150. Directive, Art. 110 (*see* Davies, *supra* n. 17 at 474).
151. *Marks and Spencer plc v. CRC: Note* [2009] UKHL 8 [6] (Lord Walker); Davies, *supra* n. 17 at 489.
152. Davies, *supra* n. 17 at 477.
153. Cited by Davies, *supra* n. 17 at 479.
154. *See*, generally, De Voil, *supra* n. 144 at [V1.241].
155. *Supra* 433. But *see* Department for Exiting the European Union, *supra* n. 25 generally.
156. *Fleming (trading as Bodycraft) v. CRC; Condé Nast Publications Ltd v. CRC* [2008] UKHL 2 [105] (Lord Neuberger).
157. *Rank Group plc v. CRC* (Cases C-259-260/10) [2012] STC 23, 34h-37g; Davies, *supra* n. 17 at 437.
158. *Marks and Spencer plc v. CRC: Note* [2009] UKHL 8 [20] (Lord Walker).
159. De Voil, *supra* n. 144 at [V1. 230G].
160. *Littlewoods Ltd and Others v. CRC* [2015] EWCA Civ 515. *See* Davies, *supra* n. 17 at 440–441.
161. De Voil, *supra* n. 144 at [V1. 230G].
162. *Supra* at [V1.230i].
163. *JP Commodities Ltd v. CRC* [2007] EWHC 2474 (Ch). *See* Davies, *supra* n. 17 at 436, 437, 441.
164. [1984] STC 630.
165. *Supra* at 634b-c.

repayment of overpaid output VAT to 'payment traders' but not to 'repayment traders'. The note of *Marks and Spencer plc v. CRC*[166] records Marks and Spencer's eventual success in arguing for an interpretation establishing that payment traders such as themselves were entitled to treatment equal to repayment traders in relation to unjust enrichment.

The EU reference-point affects statutory interpretation in cases involving VAT and abuse of rights.[167] The two-stage test laid down by the CJEU in Case C-255/02, *Halifax plc and Others v. CEC*[168] requires the court to consider: first, whether the application of VAT law provisions to the relevant transactions results 'in the accrual of a tax advantage the grant of which would be contrary to the purpose of those provisions'; and, second, whether it is 'apparent from a number of objective factors that the essential aim of the transactions concerned is to obtain a tax advantage'.[169] In *CRC v. Moorbury Ltd*,[170] the UKUT held that, if applicable, the test laid 'down a principle of construction', designed to re-characterise the transactions and 'secure that the correct tax ... [was] collected'.[171] A case in which there was found to be no abuse was *Newey (trading as Ocean Finance) v. CRC*.[172] There, the UKUT held that one Jersey-registered company's loan-broking activities constituted exempt supplies made in the UK, while another Jersey company's advertising services, supplied in Jersey, were outside the scope of VAT altogether. Therefore, Ocean Finance, which processed the loans in the UK, incurred no input VAT on its advertising costs, and made no exempt supplies in the UK. There was no abuse of rights, on the *Halifax* test, because Ocean Finance's tax advantage was not contrary to the purposes of the Directive. A contrasting case is *University of Huddersfield Higher Education Corporation v. CRC*,[173] where the CA held that the University's input VAT recovery scheme, involving the creation of a discretionary trust and various leasehold rights, was an abuse of rights.[174] Not only did it have 'no commercial effect other than to secure that [VAT] advantage',[175] but the whole purpose of the Directive was to prevent the obtaining of an input VAT deduction by someone, like the University, who made only exempt supplies.[176] The *Huddersfield* case casts an embarrassing light on the ethics of financing higher education in a significantly neoliberal state at a particular time.[177] Of course, the *Halifax* test might not be engaged in the first place. This happened in *WHA Ltd and*

166. [2009] UKHL 8.
167. Davies, *supra* n. 17 at 434.
168. [2006] STC 919.
169. *Supra* at 963c-d.
170. [2010] UKUT 360 (TCC).
171. *Supra* at [17] (Norris J).
172. [2015] UKUT 300 (TCC) (Warren J).
173. [2016] EWCA Civ 440.
174. *Supra* at [22] (Lewison LJ).
175. *Supra* n. 156 at [47].
176. *Supra* at [43]–[44].
177. 'Very regrettably, on the basis of the FTT's findings, when the University answered HMRC's questions about the rationale for the Trust it gave bogus answers' (*see* [2016] EWCA Civ 440 [5] (Lewison LJ)). *See also CRC v. Wakefield College* [2016] UKUT 19 (TCC) [56].

Another v. CRC,[178] where a scheme was found to be technically flawed to begin with. WHA, a UK motor insurance claims-handler, supplied services to Viscount Reinsurance, a Gibraltar-resident member of its group, in a scheme designed to reduce WHA's liability to input VAT on garage repairs. The UKSC held abuse of rights to be irrelevant because the scheme failed *a priori*: WHA suffered no input VAT burden: 'it pays the garage out of the float provided by Viscount, and its profit or loss is unaffected by the VAT';[179] moreover, 'WHA adds no value ... its inputs and its outputs in relation to that aspect of its business are identical'.[180] Lee points out that none of these cases discusses the initial relevance of abuse of rights to the interpretation of VAT directives, 'bearing in mind that a directive does not have direct effect against taxpayers'.[181]

Light was thrown upon this last issue, as well as on certain other aspects of abuse of rights, in *CRC v. Pendragon plc*.[182] The main issue in *Pendragon* was whether a technically flawless VAT-avoidance 'product', marketed by KPMG, the professional services firm, and designed to minimise Pendragon's output VAT by exploiting the secondhand cars 'margin scheme',[183] was nevertheless an abuse of rights. The UKSC held that it was. The margin scheme was designed to prevent a double VAT charge, whereas Pendragon had used the product to avoid any VAT at all, in a way flatly contrary to the scheme's purpose. That the essential aim of the product was VAT-avoidance was clear from the fact that it involved five distinct stages, the aim of which was to obtain input VAT deductions without a net output VAT liability. Abuse of rights (or 'abuse of law'),[184] according to Lord Sumption JSC (with whom the other justices agreed):

> is a concept derived from civil law jurisprudence, which is unknown to English common law but has been adopted by the law of the European Union. In its simplest form, it confines the exercise of legal rights to the purpose for which they exist, and precludes their use for a collateral purpose. For present purposes, the expression détournement de droit adopted by some French writers is probably a better description of its content. The application of the principle to tax avoidance schemes calls for a difficult balance to be drawn ... Like any other tax, VAT is due only in so far as its imposition is authorised by statute. It follows that although the courts may examine the commercial reality of transactions without being unduly hidebound by labels, they do not as a general rule enlarge the scope of a taxing provision by reference to considerations which affect neither the construction of its language nor the characterisation of transactions to which it is said to apply.[185]

It is noteworthy that abuse of rights principle places an arguably narrower competence in the hands of the judges than does the *Ramsay* principle. What its

178. [2013] UKSC 24; Lee (ed.), *supra* n. 24 at [2.44]; also *CRC v. Weald Leasing Ltd* [2008] EWHC 30 (Ch); [2008] STC 1601.
179. [2013] UKSC 24; [58] (Lord Reed).
180. *Supra*.
181. Lee (ed.), *supra* n. 24 at [2.44].
182. [2015] UKSC 37.
183. Lee (ed.), *supra* n. 24 at [40.108]–[40.109].
184. *See* Rita de la Feria, 'Prohibition of Abuse of (Community) Law: The Creation of a New General Principle of EC Law Through Tax' (2008) 45 CMLR 395.
185. [2015] UKSC 37 [5].

relationship with the *Ramsay* principle will be, once the UK has left the EU remains 'entirely uncertain'.

In addition to abuse of rights, the importance of EU principles in the interpretation process is highlighted by cases on the fraudulent evasion of VAT. The test now generally applied in 'missing-trader fraud' cases is that formulated by the CA in *Mobilx Ltd (in Administration) v. CRC.*[186] '[A] trader may be regarded as a participant where he should have known that the only reasonable explanation for the circumstances in which his purchase took place was that it was a transaction connected with such fraudulent evasion'.[187] '[I]t cannot matter a jot that that evasion precedes or follows that purchase'.[188] A trader will not, however, be regarded as a participant if he should have known that 'it was more likely than not that his transaction was connected with fraudulent evasion'.[189] This was based on the original test laid down by the CJEU in Joined Cases, C-439/04 and C-440/04, *Kittel v. Belgium* and *Belgium v. Recolta Recycling SPRL.*[190] Whilst at least one UKUT case has involved an argument that the *Mobilx* test was based on a mistranslation of the French text of *Kittel,*[191] the CA has confirmed *Mobilx* in *Fonecomp v. CRC.*[192]

[C] 'Economic Equivalence' Approaches

There are several comments to be made about UK acceptance, in relation to VAT concepts, of EU modes of interpretation. First, whilst a 'supply' in VATA 1994 'includes all forms of supply' except 'anything done otherwise than for a consideration',[193] consideration has a wider meaning under EU VAT law than in English contract law.[194] Contract law defines consideration as what an offeree gives in return for the offeror's promise,[195] while VAT law insists on 'payment' for a supply and a 'direct link' between the two.[196] Second, whilst supply generally denotes a bilateral commercial transaction, VATA 1994 law does not define it, and it has no non-English equivalent.[197] The CA, in *Stewart and Another (trading as GT Shooting) v. CEC,*[198] interpreted supply as including a gun retailer's surrender of handguns in return for compensation under a statutory scheme. 'It seems to me', said Laws LJ, ' ... inescapable that the surrender of the guns here pursuant to the scheme made under the ... [Firearms (Amendment) Act 1997] was a transfer of the whole property in goods within ... our municipal statute,

186. [2010] EWCA Civ 517.
187. *Supra* at [60] (Moses LJ).
188. *Supra* n. 168 at [62].
189. *Supra* at [60].
190. [2008] STC 1537.
191. *Powa (Jersey) Ltd v. CRC* [2012] UKUT 50 (TCC).
192. [2015] EWCA Civ 39; Davies, *supra* n. 17 at 443.
193. VATA 1994, s. 5(2)(a).
194. Davies, *supra* n. 17 at 450-451.
195. For example, *Currie v. Misa* (1874-1875) LR 10 Ex 153, 162 (Lush J).
196. *Apple and Pear Development Council v. CEC* (Case 102/86) [1988] STC 221.
197. Davies, *supra* n. 17 at 452.
198. [2001] EWCA Civ 1988.

and so constitutes a supply'.[199] Likewise, the CA declined to insist on a contractual nexus when interpreting the concept of 'supplier', and has instead interpreted the term in accordance with EU law. In *Telewest Communications plc and Another v. CEC*,[200] the court interpreted a supplier as including the person (A) who gets another (C) to transfer property in an asset to a third party (B) pursuant to A's contract with B. Generally, it is A, rather than C, who is the supplier. An exception, though, illustrated by *Telewest Communications* itself, is where A has transferred to C, by novation,[201] part of the burden of its contract with B, in which case the supplier is C. In that situation, legal certainty had to take precedence over the 'economic reality'.[202] Third, the foundational concept of a 'taxable person' has a different meaning under EU VAT law from that under VATA 1994.[203] Article 9 of the Directive provides that a taxable person is 'any person who, independently, carries out in any place any economic activity, whatever the purpose or results of that activity'. Section 3, VATA 1994, provides that a taxable person is a person that 'is, or is required to be, registered' for VAT.[204] Fourth, VATA 1994, section 80(7), denied a repayment of overpaid VAT that would otherwise have been permitted by restitution law, and the effectiveness principle might not apply so as to require restitution to be made.[205]

There are at least three reasons for the broader-brush approach of EU law. First, EU law has to take account of national legal variations, especially those of private law, across the Member States.[206] Second, while VAT is there to raise tax on value-added throughout the stages of manufacture, distribution and retail, contract law is there to ensure exact justice in private contractual relations.[207] Contract, along with property, is one of the two foundational concepts of private law. Tax is constitutive of the very fabric of the administrative state and therefore, as Morse writes, the collection of VAT must not be hampered by 'the legal niceties of a particular transaction'.[208] Third, which is a related point, fiscal neutrality denies the possibility of an all-purpose distinction between unlawful and lawful activity, at least where that activity can be performed lawfully.[209] Thus, dishonest activity with a credit card does not negate the making of a supply.[210]

199. VATA 1994, sch 4, para. 1(1). It might be queried whether this really is a matter of interpretation as such, since surrender to the government for compensation is included in the definition of a supply of goods (*see* Directive 06/112/EU [2006] OJ L347/1, Art. 14(2)(a)). The author is grateful to the editors for this observation.
200. [2005] EWCA Civ 102.
201. *Supra* at [19].
202. *Supra* n. 183 at [83].
203. Davies, *supra* n. 17 at 450.
204. '[T]hat a taxable person does not finally bear any tax but a non-taxable person does, is obvious joke-book material' (Johnstone, *supra* n. 135 at 76).
205. *CRC v. Investment Trust Companies* [2017] UKSC 29.
206. Davies, *supra* n. 17 at 451. *See also* Chapter 6, this volume.
207. *Supra* note 206.
208. *Supra* note 206.
209. *Supra*, citing *British American Tobacco International Ltd, Newman Shipping and Agency Company NV. v. Belgian State* (Case C-435/03) [2005] ECR I-7077.
210. *Dixon's Retail plc v. CRC* (Case C-494/12) [2014] STC 375 (*see* Davies (*supra* n. 17) 451).

Interpretative factors affecting zero-rating and exemption are different from each other. First, the categories of exempt supply are set out in Articles 131–166 of the Directive and transcribed into UK law in VATA 1994, section 31, and Schedule 9, with its 16 Groups.[211] Second, instead of appearing in the Directive, the categories of zero-rating appear in VATA 1994, Schedule 8, which consists of 18 Groups.[212] There are two interpretative themes to Schedule 8: first, the need to maintain the competitiveness of UK goods and services (zero-rated exports, transport, banknotes, etc);[213] second, the need to mitigate regressivity (food, domestic water and sewerage supplies, book, houseboats, etc.).[214] Three interpretative tropes have emerged from the case law on zero-rating. First, as held by the CA in *Sub One Ltd (trading as Subway) v. CRC*,[215] zero-rating categories have to be interpreted in accordance with the principle of fiscal neutrality,[216] notwithstanding that, as held by the CJEU in Case C-309/06, *Marks and Spencer plc v. CRC*,[217] 'a trader making ... [zero-rated] supplies does not have a directly enforceable Community-law right to have those supplies taxed at a zero rate of VAT'.[218] Second, as the court in *Sub One Ltd* also held, zero-rating categories should 'be "read down" in accordance with the *Marleasing* principle[219] to supply an objective test' of the meaning of the category.[220] Third, as illustrated by Case C-251/05, *Talacre Beach Caravan Sales Ltd v. CEC*:[221] the categories of zero-rating were frozen at 1 January 1991, zero-rating being a derogation from the standard rate, 'intended to prevent social hardship likely to follow from the abolition of exemptions provided for by the national legislature but not included in the Sixth Directive';[222] the categories of zero-rating, like exemption, must be 'strictly construed';[223] and the categories 'must be in accordance with Community law and ... only be established for clearly defined social reasons and for the benefit of the final consumer'.[224] The status of this third interpretative trope will have been affected by paragraph 15 of the European Council Conclusions of 17–18 March 2016.[225] The referendum has thrown it to the four winds.

211. Davies, *supra* n. 17 at 474, 484.
212. *Supra* at 476.
213. Davies, *supra* n. 17 at 476.
214. But *see* Robert F. van Brederode, 'VAT's Regressivity: Empirical Truth or Political Correctness' *International VAT Monitor* (March/April 2007) 86 (*see also* Davies, *supra* n. 17 at 477); Ian Crawford, Michael Keen, Stephen Smith, 'Value Added Tax and Excises' in S. Adam, T. Besley et al., (eds), *Dimensions of Tax Design: The Mirrlees Review* (Oxford: Oxford University Press, 2010) 275, 298–305.
215. [2014] EWCA Civ 773.
216. *Supra* at [64].
217. [2008] STC 1408.
218. *Supra* at 1433b.
219. *Marleasing SA v. La Comercial Internacional de Alimentacion SA* (Case C-106/89) [1990] ECR I-4135.
220. Davies, *supra* n. 17 at 478.
221. [2006] STC 1671.
222. *Supra*, 1683f-g, referring to the now recast Council Directive 77/388/EEC of 17 May 1977 [1977] OJ L145/1.
223. Davies, *supra* n. 17 at 477.
224. [2006] STC 1671, 1683b-c.
225. Available at http://www.consilium.europa.eu/en/press/press-releases/2016/03/18-european-council-conclusions/ (accessed 13 March 2017), discussed in Davies, *supra* n. 17 at 477.

[D] Mismatch Between Receipts and VAT Consideration

Examples of the differences between consideration for taxable supplies and receipts are as follows. There is a receipt (for corporation tax) but no such consideration (for VAT) where: a supply falls within one of the categories of exempt supply in VATA 1994, Schedule 9;[226] a supply is outside the scope of VAT as the transfer of a business as a going concern;[227] a supply is outside the scope of VAT as a change in the profit-sharing ratios of a partnership;[228] there is no supply for consideration but a receipt, as when a farmer receives a payment not to farm land.[229] Conversely, there is consideration (for VAT) but no receipt (for corporation tax) where, e.g., a charity carries on a trade.

The corporation tax and VAT definitions differ as follows. For corporation tax on income purposes, receipts can be trading or non-trading. Trading receipts, for corporation tax on income purposes, comprise only those that are revenue in nature and derived from a trade.[230] Non-trading receipts, for corporation tax on income purposes, are revenue receipts derived from a 'property business',[231] profits on non-trading or property business loan relationships,[232] but generally not dividends and other distributions.[233] Disposal proceeds, for chargeable gains purposes, generally consist of the sale proceeds, but can comprise, in whole or in part, the market value of the asset disposed of.[234] All three are exempted the recipient is a particular category of tax subject (e.g., a charity or local authority) or if the receipts or disposal proceeds are specifically exempt.[235] Receipts, for corporation tax purposes, do not necessarily correspond, therefore, to consideration for VAT, not least because bodies generally exempt from corporation tax (local authorities, other public bodies, charities) may nonetheless be liable to VAT.[236] When there is a disposal of a chargeable asset, output VAT on the supply forms no part of the chargeable gain[237] or allowable loss. Output VAT will not be due when a trader disposes of a non-business asset, though there may be liability for a chargeable gain.[238] Consideration, for VAT, is interpreted in accordance with the formula produced by the CJEU following the HL's reference in Case 102/86, *Apple and Pear Development Council v. CEC*.[239] 'The concept of the supply of services effected for consideration within the meaning of the Sixth Directive, Article

226. Davies, *supra* n. 17 at 486.
227. VATA 1994, s. 49; VAT (Special Provisions) Order 1995 (SI 1995 No 1268); Lee (ed.), *supra* n. 24 at [38.26].
228. Lee (ed.), *supra* n. 24, ch 44.
229. CTA 2009, s. 36; *Landboden-Agrardienste GmbH & Co KG v. Finanzamt Calau* (Case C-384/95) [1998] STC 171.
230. CTA 2009, ss 2, 35 and 49 (*see* Lee (ed.), *supra* n. 24 at ch 10).
231. CTA 2009, ss 2, 209.
232. Donald Drysdale, *Corporation Tax 2015/16* (Haywards Heath: Bloomsbury Professional, 2016) [15.21].
233. Lee (ed.), *supra* n. 24 at [41.46].
234. TCGA 1992, ss 17, 18, 19, 272, 273, 286 (*see* Lee (ed.), *supra* at [19.14]–[19.16]).
235. Snape, *supra* n. 86 at 549.
236. VATA 1994, s. 94 (Davies, *supra* n. 17 at 470); *ICAEW v. CEC* [1999] STC 398.
237. Lee (ed.), *supra* n. 24 at [38.10].
238. *Supra* at [38.21].
239. [1988] STC 221.

2(1), presupposes the existence of a direct link between the service provided and the consideration received'.[240] A direct link, in turn, means three things: first, the parties must be bound together by 'a legal relationship', as in *Stewart v. CEC*, above, where, 'once the [handgun surrender] scheme was promulgated and acted on, its beneficiaries could clearly insist on its fulfilment by the government, through the courts if necessary';[241] second, in pursuance of that relationship, there must be 'reciprocal performance';[242] and, third, 'the remuneration received by the service provider' must constitute 'the value actually given in return for the service supplied to the recipient'.[243] However, a direct link does *not* require that the payment must at least equal 'the cost of the supply'.[244] The interpretation of the need for a direct link is an example of a teleological approach at the level of the CJEU[245] that translates into a literal interpretation of the English-language text at national level.

The nature and purpose of VAT differs from corporation tax in the following respects. To the extent that corporation tax is borne by the tax subject, the company, it is a direct tax, while VAT is an indirect tax. Value added tax (VAT) is a tax on consumption, while corporation tax is a tax on income and applies to individual supplies, rather than to persons in respect of aggregated and adjusted transactions. Supplies, for VAT purposes, need have no commercial recipients (education, health, welfare, burials, etc.)[246] but trading must, by definition, be bilateral. Whilst, 'business includes any trade, profession or vocation', there is, with VAT, no need for a profit motive,[247] though there is for corporation tax purposes. Whilst an 'adventure in the nature of trade' can give rise to a trading receipt for corporation tax purposes, it is by itself not a business for VAT purposes.[248]

[E] Significance of Reduced-, Zero-rated and Exempt Supplies

Tax may be forgone, through tax expenditures, in various ways unique to VAT. First, zero-rating is much more favourable to the taxable person than is exemption as such.[249] Because it can allow a taxable person a full input VAT deduction on supplies received, while requiring that person not to charge VAT on its own supplies, zero-rating is a subsidy to those sectors making supplies in zero-rated categories.[250] Second, zero-rating is partly responsible for the repayment traders phenomenon referred to above. The cost to HM Treasury, in terms of public revenue foregone, was sufficiently great for HMG to mount an ill-fated attempt to challenge, almost, the very concept of

240. *Supra*, 237h-j.
241. [2001] EWCA Civ 1988 [44] (Laws LJ).
242. *Tolsma v. Inspecteur der Omzetbelasting Leeuwarden* (Case C-16/93) [1994] STC 509.
243. *Lebara Ltd v. CRC* (Case C-520/10) [2012] STC 1536.
244. *CRC v. Wakefield College* [2016] UKUT 19 (TCC) [52].
245. Dyson, *supra* n. 84 at 56.
246. Davies, *supra* n. 17 at 486.
247. *CEC v. Morrison's Academy Boarding Houses Association* [1978] STC 1; Lee (ed.), *supra* n. 24 at [38.28].
248. *Three H Aircraft Hire (A Firm) v. CEC* [1982] STC 653; Lee (ed.), *supra* n. 24 at [38.28].
249. Davies, *supra* n. 17 at 475.
250. *Supra*.

zero-rating, rejected by the CA, in *Marks and Spencer plc v. CEC*.[251] Third, zero-rating is damaging to the public revenue because it benefits the supplier rather than the Treasury.[252] For the latter to benefit, the zero-rated categories would instead have to be exempt *simpliciter*.[253]

Although much flexibility has been shown in interpreting categories of reduced rating[254] and zero-rating, there is no scope for altering categories of exemption, which means that zero-rating is intensely political,[255] in a way that exemption is not. In 2016, the UK Parliament refused to amend UK VAT law to reflect Case C-161/14, *Commission v. UK* and retained the VAT reduced rate on solar panels, while zero-rating women's sanitary products.[256] In each case, HMG was relying on the outcome of the March 2016 European Council meeting.[257] Solar panels were not within the reduced-rate categories in the Directive and the Directive required 'at least a reduced rate' to be applied to sanitary products.[258] It follows that there is no EU law right in relation to zero-rated supplies.[259] However, because of the interpretation principles mentioned above, equal treatment, and fiscal neutrality are nonetheless applicable.[260] *Sub One Ltd (trading as Subway) v. CRC* promulgated an objective test for the scope of zero-rating in relation to supplies of hot food.[261] Reading down the national legislation,[262] following *Marleasing*, McCombe LJ stipulated searching 'for the assumed common intention of the supplier and the consumer as to whether it is a term of the bargain that the product be supplied in order to be eaten hot'.[263] If so, as was the case here, the supply would be standard-rated. If not, it would be zero-rated. Supplies of food, in fact, have produced a whole range of baffling UKFTT interpretations: rabbit-food zero-rated, ferret-food not;[264] chocolate cakes zero-rated, chocolate biscuits not.[265] Hence the *Marks and Spencer* litigation on whether 'chocolate-covered teacakes' were 'chocolate-covered cakes' (zero-rated) or 'chocolate-covered biscuits' (standard-rated), an issue finally resolved in favour of the former.[266] In 2012, HMG provoked a backlash as elitist an

251. [2000] STC 16.
252. Davies, *supra* n. 17 at 488.
253. *Supra*.
254. VATA 1994, s. 29A, sch 7A.
255. This was always so (Johnstone, *supra* n. 135 at 2). On the historical reasons for zero-rating, see Office of Tax Simplification, *Review of Value Added Tax: Progress Report and Call for Evidence* (February 2017), available from https://www.gov.uk/government/uploads/system/uploads/attachment_data/file/564139/OTS_CT_Review_-_Progress_Report_.pdf (accessed 16 March 2017).
256. Davies, *supra* n. 17 at 436.
257. *Supra*.
258. *Supra*.
259. *Supra*.
260. *Supra* at 437, citing *Sub One Ltd (trading as Subway) v. CRC* [2014] EWCA Civ 773; and *JD Wetherspoon plc v. CRC* (Case C-302/07) [2009] STC 1022.
261. Davies, *supra* n. 17 at 438.
262. VATA 1994, sch 8, Pt II, Group 1, note 3(b).
263. [2014] EWCA Civ 773 [49].
264. *Supreme Petfoods Ltd v. CRC* [2011] UKFTT 19 (TC) (*see* Davies, *supra* n. 17 at 478).
265. Davies, *supra* n. 17 at 479.
266. *Marks and Spencer plc v. CEC* [2000] STC 16, 22j-23a (D Milne, QC, 'The Teacake Saga Nears Its End' *Tax Journal* (21 April 2008) 6). *See*, too, Davies, *supra* n. 17 at 479. Supplies of Jaffa Cakes, that most English of delicacies, are zero-rated as chocolate-covered cakes. The question

attempt to remove pasties and hot pies from 'the zero-rating umbrella', and subject them to a 'pasty tax', in the 'omnishambles' Budget of that year.[267] HMG wanted to include in the category of (standard-rated) supplies 'in the course of catering' food 'above the ambient air temperature at the time it is provided to the customer, other than freshly-baked bread'.[268] In the end, however, only food 'kept hot after being heated' was included in standard-rating, so zero-rating would continued to apply to food (including pasties) 'left to cool naturally'.[269] *Sub One Ltd (trading as Subway) v. CRC* stabilised the ensuing differences of interpretation.[270] Zero-rating provides a way of not imposing a tax on supplies falling outside the range of EU-mandatory exemptions.[271]

The only permissible exemption categories are delineated in the Directive.[272] Exemption has not therefore become political in the way of zero-rating. It should be, however. Financial services (Schedule 9, Group 5) and insurance (Schedule 9, Group 2) assume that it is difficult to isolate 'the value added in a financial supply such as a loan, or under insurance against a risk'.[273] Exemptions are therefore interpreted in accordance with CJEU decisions. The categories of exemption are obligatory,[274] and 'if the UK wording is narrower than the directive, the wider meaning of the latter will be applied'.[275] There is general agreement that the wording of VATA 1994, Schedule 9, has to be interpreted strictly but, as Chadwick LJ said, in *Expert Witness Institute v. CEC*,[276] '[a] strict construction is not to be equated, in this context, with a restricted construction'.[277] The issue was whether supplies by the institute to its members were exempt within Schedule 9, Group 9, on the basis that it had 'aims of a civic nature'. In holding that it did, Chadwick LJ said:

> I reject the premise that the proper approach to construction does require the court to confine the scope of an exemption if it can. The task of the court is to give the exempting words a meaning which they can fairly and properly bear in the context in which they are used.[278]

In this context, the purposive and literal interpretations are 'in tension'. In *CEC v. Electronic Data Systems Ltd*,[279] Jonathan Parker LJ said that, '[i]n my judgment, that

---

of cake/biscuit highlights the Humeian distinction between analytic and synthetic statements and its problematic nature (BBC Radio 4, 'Cake or Biscuit?' *The Philosopher's Arms* (22 February 2017), available at http://www.bbc.co.uk/programmes/b08ff180 (accessed 16 March 2017)).

267. Davies, *supra* n. 17 at 475.
268. Quoted by Davies, *supra* n. 17 at 480–481.
269. *Supra* at 481.
270. Davies, *supra* n. 17 at 481.
271. Davies, *supra* n. 17 at 488.
272. *Norbury Developments Ltd v. CEC* (Case C-136/97) [1999] STC 511. *See* Davies, *supra* n. 17 at 435.
273. Davies, *supra* n. 17 at 485.
274. *Commission v. UK* (Case 416/85) [1988] STC 456.
275. Davies, *supra* n. 17 at 484.
276. [2001] EWCA Civ 1882.
277. *Supra*.
278. *Supra* n. 259 at [19].
279. [2003] EWCA Civ 492.

tension falls to be resolved by interpreting the exemptions in a way which does not have the effect of extending their scope beyond their fair meaning, as ascertained by adopting a purposive approach to their interpretation'.[280] While, e.g., in relation to betting, Member States have a degree of discretion in framing an exemption, some differentiations thereby entailed are incompatible with fiscal neutrality.[281] For the final consumer, 'exempt supplies are in effect taxed supplies, while zero-rated taxable supplies are not'.[282]

§14.06 CONCLUSIONS

The UK tax system, as indeed the UK that it shapes and serves, is at a juncture unprecedented in the admittedly rather short history of the UK in its present form. Although the purposive approach to interpreting tax statutes has now prevailed for over two decades, it may – *just* may – not survive significant changes in the size and shape of the British state following the UK's secession from the EU. The purposive approach to the interpretation of corporation tax legislation has reduced the scope for avoidance, tacitly condoned judicial legislative amendment, accentuated the idiosyncratic and self-referential nature of corporation tax legislation, and raised the suspicion that there is a special judicial doctrine applicable to the interpretation of tax legislation, especially given the hitherto almost moribund nature of the GAAR. The strongly administrative quality of VAT, its historical interpretative reliance on the rulings of the CJEU, and its almost total uncoupling from concepts of private law, show similar interpretative features to those disclosed by corporation tax law. In the coming years, it will remain to be seen whether these characteristics evolve into assuming a national, rather than a European, significance, or whether – *just* possibly – they are gradually stripped away in a return to an interpretative literalism appropriate to a very different kind of British state.

280. *Supra*. (*see* Davies, *supra* n. 17 at 485).
281. Davies, *supra* n. 17 at 488.
282. *Supra* at 489.

CHAPTER 15

Legal Interpretation of Tax Law: United States of America

Steve R. Johnson

§15.01 GOVERNMENTAL, FISCAL, AND JUDICIAL STRUCTURES

[A] Governmental Structures

The United States (US) is a federal system consisting principally of the national government (hereafter the "federal government") and the 50 states.[1] The federal government and the state governments are independent sovereigns with separate revenue systems. Under the doctrine of intergovernmental fiscal immunity, the federal government cannot tax the state governments, and the state governments cannot tax the federal government.[2] The federal government makes substantial grants to the states, but the federal government and state governments do not otherwise share tax revenues they raise.[3]

The states have created numerous local governmental units, including counties, cities, towns, and various special use districts. Such units have only those regulatory and taxing powers conferred upon them by state law. A degree of revenue sharing sometimes occurs between states and their localities and instrumentalities. For example, states and their localities sometimes share real property tax revenues.

1. In addition, the United States has a number of territories, such as Puerto Rico, the American Virgin Islands, and Guam. Federal statutes provide the fundamental law in the territories, but such statutes authorize the territories to enact local laws as well.
2. For example, *Graves v. New York ex. rel. O'Keefe*, 306 U.S. 466, 477–478 (1939).
3. However, § 103 of the Internal Revenue Code (I.R.C.) exempts from the federal income tax interest received by investors who hold state and local bonds. This lowers the cost of state-local borrowing at the expense of the federal fisc, thus operating as a limited and indirect revenue transfer.

Through their ratification of the US Constitution, the states surrendered some of their sovereignty to the federal government. Under Article VI of the Constitution, federal law controls over state law when the two bodies of law conflict. However, federal statutes are protective of the states in a number of contexts. For instance, the Tax Injunction Act prohibits federal courts from interfering with the imposition or collection of state taxes as long as aggrieved taxpayers have a "plain, speedy and efficient remedy" in state court.[4] In addition, by a constructional preference known as federalism, the federal courts typically interpret ambiguous federal laws so as to minimize interference with state operations and areas of traditional state primacy.[5]

[B] Fiscal Structures

The federal government imposes personal and corporate income taxes, several types of wealth transfer taxes (the gift, estate, and generation-skipping transfer taxes), several types of payroll taxes (most prominently the Federal Insurance Contribution Act (FICA) tax to fund the Social Security System) and excise taxes on a wide variety of sales of goods and other transactions.[6] In fiscal year 2015, federal taxes brought in approximately USD 3.3 trillion. Of this, approximately 2.8 trillion (85% of the total) came from personal income and employment taxes, 390 billion (12% of the total) from business income taxes, 20 billion (0.6% of the total) from estate and gift taxes, and 77 billion (2.3% of the total) from excise taxes.[7] The federal government imposes no value added tax (VAT) or general sales tax.

Each state decides its own mix of taxes. Several major types of taxes are used in most states, including income taxes, real property taxes, and general and special sales taxes. In addition, a wide array of less common taxes are used in particular states, such as severance taxes on extraction of natural resources, taxes on gross receipts of businesses, death and gift taxes, documentary taxes, stock transfer taxes, and license taxes. State and local taxes totaled approximately USD 1,400,000,000 in 2012. Of this, approximately 22% came from the personal income tax, 4% from the corporate income tax, 23% from general and special sales taxes, and the remainder from other sources.[8]

[C] Judicial Structures

Federal tax law is set out in statutes, the most important of which are contained in the I.R.C. Gaps in the I.R.C. are filled mainly by regulations promulgated by the Department of the Treasury. "Only the legislature can legislate. Only Congress can enact tax

4. 20 U.S.C. § 1341. But *see Direct Marketing Ass'n v. Brohl*, 135 S. Ct. 1124 (2015)(reading the TIA narrowly).
5. For example, *Gregory v. Ashcroft*, 501 U.S. 452, 460–461 (1991).
6. These taxes are set out in subtitles A through E of Title 26 of the United States Code. Title 26 is the I.R.C.
7. *Internal Revenue Service Databook 2015*, tbl. 5.
8. United States Census Bureau, tbl. 1 www.census.gov/govs/gtax/index.html, May 9, 2013. But *see* National Ass'n of State Budget Officers, "Summary: Fall 2016 Fiscal Survey of States" (December 30, 2016) (noting a "softening" of state tax collections).

laws. However, since at least as early as 1828 ... the Treasury has been explicitly authorized by statute to promulgate 'regulations.' Such regulations acquire the force of law only derivatively, through statutes enacted by Congress."[9]

The I.R.C. and the regulations are applied by the Internal Revenue Service (IRS), a part of the Treasury Department. Taxpayers who believe the IRS has misapplied the I.R.C. and the regulations have both administrative and judicial remedies. The administrative remedy consists of appeal to the IRS Appeals Office, a part of the IRS structurally independent of the divisions that determine and collect tax liabilities. The Appeals Office settles most cases brought to it.[10]

Judicial remedies consist of the opportunity to bring suit in federal court. Depending on the type of tax at issue, suit may be brought either before or after payment of the additional tax determined by the IRS to be due and owing.

Trial of federal tax cases may occur in any of the four courts. The US Tax Court is a prepayment forum, most of whose cases involve income taxes. Federal district courts and the Court of Federal Claims are primarily refund fora.[11] Bankruptcy courts often decide tax issues involving insolvent taxpayers. In general, decisions of the tax trial fora may be appealed to the federal circuit courts of appeal. From there, cases may reach the US Supreme Court. Accepting such cases is discretionary with the Supreme Court, which typically hears four or fewer tax cases each year.

State practice is not uniform, but it broadly resembles federal practice. State legislatures enact tax statutes, which often are supplemented by regulations promulgated by state revenue agencies. In many states, disputes with taxpayers are heard first by hearing bureaus within the agency. Decisions by such bureaus may be appealed within the state court system. Federal courts typically review IRS determinations on a *de novo* basis. State courts also use *de novo* review or sometimes standards more deferential to the tax agency, such as "abuse of discretion." The decisions of state courts on state law matters may not be reviewed by the federal courts except with respect to possible conflicts between state law and federal law.

§15.02 INTERPRETATION OF INTERNATIONAL TAX AGREEMENTS

Under sections 8 and 10 of Article I of the US Constitution, only the federal government, not the states, may enter into treaties and agreements with foreign governments. The US has entered into tax treaties with over 100 other countries, territories, and dependencies. Most such treaties deal with income taxes. In some instances, they are supplemented by more limited vehicles, such as Mutual Legal Assistance Treaties and Tax Information Exchange Agreements. Unlike most US treaties, tax treaties are negotiated by the Treasury, not the Department of State.

9. *Feller v. Comm'r*, 135 T.C. 497 (2010) (Gustafson, J., dissenting).
10. *See* Steve Johnson, Jerome Borison & Samuel C. Ullman (3rd edn, Durham: Carolina Academic Press, 2016) *Civil Tax Procedure*, Chs 1, 4, 8 & 9, for more detailed discussion of the processes by which U.S. tax statutes and regulations are made and of the administrative and judicial remedies available to taxpayers.
11. For detailed description of prepayment and post-payment federal judicial remedies, *see* Steve R. Johnson, "Reforming Federal Tax Litigation - An Agenda" 41 *Fla. St. Univ. L. Rev.* 205 (2013).

The US has a Model Tax Treaty. This is the starting point for the US in negotiating new tax treaties, just as the OECD or United Nations models are starting points for many other countries. US courts often consider the Treasury commentary accompanying the US model and consider comparable provisions in the OECD and U.N. models in resolving disputes as to the meanings of tax treaties.[12] The treaties create Competent Authority procedures whereby administrators from the contracting countries attempt to resolve differences in interpretation between the countries. These procedures typically are quite slow and thus of limited utility.

"A tax convention or treaty is construed by the courts in the same manner as is a taxing statute."[13] What happens when tax treaties conflict with federal tax statutes? Most countries hold treaties superior to conflicting domestic law. The US has moved away from that approach although echoes of it still sometimes appear in the case law. Instead, the predominant position in the US is that the latter item controls. Thus, a subsequently ratified treaty controls over a previously enacted statute and a subsequently enacted statute controls over a previously ratified treaty.[14] The US' adherence to the "later in time" rule sometimes engenders diplomatic tensions, but these have proved manageable.

The US is not a party to the Vienna Convention on the Law of Treaties. Accordingly, US courts are free to develop their own rules for interpreting tax treaties. A fairly substantial body of scholarly literature has developed as to interpretation of treaties.[15]

Under Article VI of the Constitution, treaties are part of "the supreme Law of the Land." Thus, in the event of conflict, a tax treaty would control over state law under the Supremacy Clause of the Constitution. Such conflicts are not common, however. The states are not parties to the federal government's tax treaties, and those treaties typically address only national-level taxes. Accordingly, residents of the states, as well as nonresidents subject to state income taxes, cannot invoke the treaties to seek relief from state taxes.

§15.03 INTERPRETATION OF DOMESTIC LAW (VAT)

Probably no tax in the world is pure in a conceptual sense. All involve accommodations to economic exigencies, bureaucratic imperatives, and political realities.[16]

12. For example, *Taisei Fire & Marine Ins. Co., Ltd. v. Comm'r*, 104 T.C. 535, 549–550 (1995).
13. *Lewenhaupt v. Comm'r*, 20 T.C. 151, 160 (1953), aff'd, 221 F.2d 227 (9th Cir. 1955).
14. I.R.C. § 7852(d)(1). *See generally Xerox Corp. v. United States*, 41 F.3d 647 (Fed. Cir. 1994).
15. For example, William D. Popkin (5th edn, New York: Foundation Press, 2010) *Materials on Legislation: Political Language and the Political Process*, pp. 406–412; Edward K. Dennehy & Stephen E. Ehrlich, "Tax Treaty Interpretation and Conflicts with U.S. Federal Law" 122 *Tax Notes*, 1101 (2009); David Sachs, "Is the 19th Century Doctrine of Treaty Override Good Law for Modern Day Tax Treaties?" 47 *Tax Law*, 867 (1994); Robert T. Smith, "Tax Treaty Interpretation by the Judiciary" 49 *Tax Law*, 845 (1996).
16. For example, many significant features favoring savings – such as the realization requirement and tax advantages for pension plans and individual retirement accounts – have been engrafted onto the federal personal income tax. Thus, although it is still called an income tax, it now is

Broadly speaking, however, income taxes take as their base the economic inflows a taxpayer has during the taxable period, whether such inflows are consumed or saved. In contrast, VATs and retail sales taxes are consumption taxes. Retail sales taxes are imposed, typically at flat rates, on amounts spent to purchase consumption goods and sometimes services, regardless of whether the purchase is made with current income, borrowed funds, or funds previously saved. VATs are imposed at each stage as an article works its way through the phases of manufacture and distribution, rather than only at the time of retail sale to the ultimate consumer.

There are three different ways of computing VAT liability: the credit-invoice, subtraction, and addition methods. The first of these is applied on a transaction basis while the second and third are applied at the entity level. In the subtraction method, the tax base is calculated by finding the firm's gross receipts, then subtracting the value of the goods and services the firm purchased from others. In the addition method, the tax based is computed by adding the value of all the firm's untaxed inputs.[17]

[A] Absence of Federal VAT

Approximately 150 countries have some version of a VAT. The US is not among them. It is the only major country without a national-level VAT.

From time to time, proposals are made for adoption of a national VAT. For example, in the 1990s, Professors Robert Hall and Alvin Rabushka advanced a proposal to replace the federal corporate and income taxes.[18] The proposal was styled as a flat income tax. However, only wages were taxable under the wage tax component of the proposal. Returns on capitals (such as capital gains, interest, and dividends) would have been exempt under the wage tax component but would have been taxed under the VAT component if spent on consumption. These and other aspects made the proposal closer kin to an addition-method VAT than an income tax. The Hall-Rabushka plan was widely discussed but never came close to enactment.

The felt necessity to disguise the true nature of the Hall-Rabushka plan, the relative infrequency of VAT proposals and their failure to be enacted when proposed, all have a common explanation. A then-sitting chair of the House Ways and Means Committee, Al Ulmer, urged consideration of a value-added tax. He was then defeated when he stood for reelection. Rightly or wrongly, his defeat was attributed to his championing a VAT. Since then, this cause has been considered political poison in many circles in the US.[19]

---

more accurately characterized as a hybrid income tax/consumption tax. Edward J. McCaffery, "Tax Policy Under a Hybrid Income-Consumption Tax" 70 *Tex. L. Rev*, 1145 (1992).

17. *See* Sybren Cnossen, "A VAT Primer for Lawyers, Economists, and Accountants" 124 *Tax Notes*, 687 (2009); Harley Duncan & Jon Sedon, "How Different VATs Work" 125 *Tax Notes*, 1367 (2009).
18. Robert E. Hall & Alvin Rabushka (2nd edn, Stanford: Hoover Institution Press, 1995) *The Flat Tax*.
19. Reluctance to enact a value added tax has also reflected concerns about compliance, enforcement, and administrability. *See* generally Katherine O. Baer, "What International Experience Can Tell Us About the Potential Challenges of Administering a U.S. VAT" 66 *Nat'l Tax J.*, 447

[B] State VATs

Although sales taxes are standard features of state revenue structures, the states eschewed VATs for the great majority of the US' fiscal history. Cracks in this uniform façade started to emerge late in the twentieth century and in the first decades of the twenty-first century. Then, what were in substance, though not in name, state-level VATs were proposed with increasing frequency and, in some cases, were adopted.

In 1976, Michigan enacted the Single Business Tax (SBT).[20] It replaced the state's corporate income tax, franchise tax, intangibles tax, bank excise tax, personal property tax on inventory, and certain other taxes. The SBT had a variety of exotic features, especially after repeated amendments. At its core, the SBT was designed to be an addition-method VAT.[21] Effective in 2008, Michigan replaced the SBT with the modified gross receipts tax (MGRT), a tax on the gross receipts of a business minus purchases from other firms. "In some respects, the [MGRT] resembles a value-added tax [...,] although it has important features not found in a traditional VAT or in any known variation of that tax."[22]

In 1993, New Hampshire enacted a business enterprise tax (BET), imposed on "enterprise value," an amount equal to the value of the labor and capital resources of a business, measured by its payments of compensation, interest, and dividends. The BET replaced New Hampshire's principal general business tax, the business profits tax (BPT), an income tax.[23] The BET is best seen as an addition-method VAT.[24]

Since the nineteenth century, Texas has had a franchise tax.[25] Although its name has remained constant, its nature has changed over time. Throughout most of the twentieth century, the tax was computed on the corporation's net taxable capital, consisting of total assets minus debts. In the 1990s, the tax was revised so that its base became earned surplus, consisting of the corporation's profits plus compensation paid to directors and officers - essentially an income tax with an alternative minimum tax component.

Effective in 2007, Texas revamped the tax as a novel business entity tax typically called the margin tax. The prior version applied only to corporations and limited liability companies; the 2007 change extended the tax to most partnerships and professional associations. The tax base is total revenue minus the greatest of cost of

(2013); Robert F. van Brederode & Pierre-Pascal Gendron, "The Taxation of Cross-Border Interstate Sales in Federal or Common Markets" 2 *World J. VAT/GST L.*, 1 (2013).

20. Mich. Comp. Laws Ann. § 208.1 (repealed for tax years beginning after 2007).
21. Michael J. McIntyre & Richard D. Pomp, "A Policy Analysis of Michigan's Mislabeled Gross Receipts Tax" 53 *Wayne L. Rev.*, 1283 (2007).
22. *Supra*, p. 1284. *See* generally Steven M. Bieda, "Facing the Challenge of Replacing the Single Business Tax: The Development and Evolution of the Michigan Business Tax" 53 *Wayne L. Rev.*, 1149 (2007).
23. N.H. Rev. Stat. Ann. Ch. 77-E.
24. Alan Schenk & Oliver Oldman (Cambridge: Cambridge University Press (2007) *Value Added Tax: A Comparative Approach*, p. 395.
25. Tex. Tax Code Ch. 171.

goods sold, compensation, or 30% of total revenues. The result defies ready categorization. The margin tax is a hybrid of an income tax and gross receipts, with some attributes of a VAT.[26]

California's former governor Arnold Schwarzenegger charged the Commission on the twenty-first Century Economy with making recommendations to overhaul the state's tax structure. In 2009, the Commission proposed the business net receipts tax (BNRT) to replace revenues from the corporate income tax, much of the general sales tax, and part of the individual income tax. The BNRT would have been a subtraction-method VAT, but it was not enacted.[27]

Relatedly, to fill budgetary gaps, states from time to time consider and sometimes enact various forms of gross receipts taxes, which may have VAT-like aspects. Such proposals are often highly controversial, and the experiments have proved to be volatile.[28]

[C] Judicial Interpretation of State VATs

In countries with well-developed jurisprudence as to this type of tax, interpretational issues often arise as to VATs that are unique to them or at least receive different nuance from issues as to other types of taxes.[29] There is no such well-developed jurisprudence in the US.

Interesting questions have been raised as to treatment of state VATs under the federal Constitution. For example, the Supreme Court has held that, under the Commerce Clause of the Constitution, a business must have a physical presence in a state before that state can compel it to collect and remit the state's use tax.[30] A commentator has noted that, when the Court so held, almost no state had a VAT, and he questioned whether differences in compliance costs between the tax types might mean that the physical presence test could be applied differently to VATs than to traditional sales and use taxes.[31]

Questions also have been raised as to treatment of state VATs under state constitutions. New Hampshire's tax innovations have faced challenge under the state

26. *See* Texas Taxpayers & Research Ass'n, "Understanding the Texas Franchise – or 'Margin' – Tax" www.ttara.org/files/document/file-4ea5bda9239ed.pdf, October 2011.
27. For description and criticism of the proposed BNRT, *see* Charles E. McLure Jr., "The Business Net Receipts Tax: A Dog that Will Not Hunt" 37 *Hastings Con. L.Q.*, 745 (2010).
28. *See* Jamie Yesnowitz, Chuck Jones, Lori Stolly & Priya Nair, "United States: SALT Outlook, Trends and Predictions for 2017" (April 21, 2017), available at http://www.mondaq.com/article.asp?articleid=587614&email_access=on&chk=2076074&q=1488460 (noting gross receipts enactments in Ohio, Texas and Nevada).
29. *See* generally Alan Schenk, Victor Thuronyi & Wei Cui, (2nd edn, Cambridge University Press, 2015) *Value Added Tax: A Comparative Approach.*
30. *Quill Corp. v. North Dakota*, 504 U.S. 298, 314–318 (1992). Abrogation of this rule has often been urged, for example in *Direct Marketing Ass'n v. Brohl*, 135 S. Ct. 1124, 1134–1135 (2015)(Kennedy, J., concurring), but it remains in place.
31. William J. Kolarik II, "Untangling Substantial Nexus" 64 *Tax Law.*, 851, 885–886 (2011).

constitutional requirement that taxes be "proportional and reasonable."[32] The application of the Texas margin tax to partnerships was unsuccessfully challenged on the ground that it is inconsistent with the Texas constitutional provisions requiring equal and uniform taxation and approval by referendum of taxes on the net incomes of natural persons, including their shares of partnership incomes.[33]

However, most of the interesting questions have often gone without definitive judicial resolution. Certainly, no substantial body of jurisprudence has been produced. The causes of this include the small number of states with VATs, the hybrid nature of some of the taxes, the insularity of the issues and the thin volume of the cases. There is as yet no firm basis on which to conclude that American courts behave differently in interpreting VATs than they do in interpreting other types of taxes.

§15.04 INTERPRETATION OF DOMESTIC TAX LAW (NON-VAT)

Older commentary sometimes distinguished between the act of interpreting a statute and the act of construing it. That distinction has now been generally abandoned in the US. Construction and interpretation are used interchangeably.[34]

Below, we first explore the sources of American tax law. We then consider the elements to which the courts advert in the process of interpretation.

[A] Sources of Tax Law

Congress has authority to enact tax statutes under Article I, section 8 and, as to income tax, under the Sixteenth Amendment of the Constitution.[35] Federal tax statutes are invalid if inconsistent with the US Constitution. State tax statutes are invalid if inconsistent with either the US or the state constitutions. However, constitutional challenges fail far more often than they succeed.[36]

32. N.H. Const. pt II, Art. 5. *See* V. Hummel Berghaus & William F.J. Ardinger, "The Policy and Structure of the Business Enterprise Tax" 34 *N.H. Bar J.*, 5 (1993) (discussing this constitutional provision in the context of New Hampshire's value added tax).
33. *In re Allcat Claims Serv., L.P.*, 356 S.W.3d 455 (Tex. 2011).
34. Antonin Scalia & Bryan A. Garner (St. Paul: Thomson/West, 2012) *Reading Law: The Interpretation of Legal Texts*, pp. 13–15.
35. There also is authority that both the national and state governments' powers to tax do not depend wholly upon constitutions but exist as an inherent attribute of sovereignty. For example, *Society for Sav. v. Coite*, 73 U.S. (6 Wall.) 594, 606 (1867); *McCulloch v. Maryland*, 17 U.S. (4 Wheat.) 316, 431 (1819).
36. Among examples of successful constitutional challenges, *see United States v. United States Shoe Corp.*, 523 U.S. 360 (1998) (federal harbor maintenance tax held inconsistent with the Export Clause of the Constitution); *Allegheny Pittsburgh Coal Co. v. Commission of Webster Cty.*, 488 U.S. 336 (1989) (state property tax held inconsistent with the Equal Protection Clause of the Fourteenth Amendment of the Constitution).One common constitutional (and sometimes statutory) issue is whether a tax statute or regulation is excessively retroactive in effect. Retroactivity challenges sometimes succeed in state cases. They almost never succeed in federal cases when statutes are challenged but sometimes succeed when regulations are challenged. *See Markell Co., Inc. v. Comm'r*, T.C. Memo. 2014-86 (recognizing judicial disagreement as to retroactive application of a regulation targeting tax shelters); Steve R. Johnson, "Retroactive Tax Legislation," 81 *State & Local Tax Notes*, 529 (2016).

Federal and state tax classifications are presumed to be constitutional, and, in usual circumstances, the "burden is on the one attacking the legislative arrangement to negative every conceivable basis which might support it."[37] For example, equal protection concepts are strong in some non-US tax systems and can be strong in the US in some non-tax contexts.[38] But in normal US tax cases, equal protection arguments are exceedingly difficult for taxpayers to win.[39]

Subject only to such weak constitutional constraints, statutes are supreme in tax at both the federal and state levels. As one state Supreme Court observed:

> there is no natural law of ... tax liability. No brooding omnipresence nor invisible hand informs our consideration of such cases. The amount of ... tax a taxpayer owes to this state is determinable solely by reference to the positive provisions of the ... tax laws of this state and the regulations of the State Tax Commission promulgated within the scope of its authority.[40]

But supreme does not necessarily connote comprehensive. Tax legislation often has gaps. The legislature may constitutionally delegate its law-making power to an agency or to the courts. Such delegation may be either express (through direct delegation in a statute) or implied (by the existence of a statutory gap that must be filled in order to make the statute operative). Non-tax case law has developed an exception to this: the "too big" principle, under which some choices are of such importance that the legislature is presumed not to have delegated their decision to administrative agencies.[41] The principle has been applied in tax also but only rarely.[42]

Although tax is quintessentially statutory, there is in the US – consistent with the delegation notion – a considerable amount of judge-made tax law. In many instances, tax rules originating in case law later were codified in the I.R.C. or the regulations. For example, several requirements for eligibility for tax-free corporate reorganizations – such as business purpose, continuity of ownership, and continuity of enterprise – which first appeared in judicial decisions now are incorporated in the applicable regulations.[43]

Tax regulations come in several varieties. I.R.C. § 7805(a) delegates to the Treasury authority to "prescribe all needful rules and regulations for the enforcement of [the I.R.C.]" Regulations promulgated pursuant to this blanket authority are called "general authority regulations." In addition, hundreds of particular I.R.C. sections contain provisions allowing or directing Treasury to issue regulations to complement,

37. *Lehnhausen v. Lake Shore Auto Parts Co.*, 410 U.S. 356, 364 (1973).
38. *Smith*, a U.S. case, and *Symes*, a Canadian case, both involved disparate gender impact of facially neutral tax rules. Although the taxpayers ultimately lost in both cases, equal protection loomed much larger in *Symes*. Compare *Smith v. Comm'r*, 30 B.T.A. 1038 (1939), aff'd per curiam, 113 F.2d 114 (2d Cir. 1940); *Symes v. Canada*, [1993] 4 S.C.R. 695, [1994] 1 C.T.C. 40.
39. *See*, e.g., *Armour v. City of Indianapolis*, 566 U.S. 673 (2012); *Field v. Comm'r*, T.C. Memo. 2013-111.
40. *General Motors Corp. v. Mississippi State Tax Comm'n*, 520 So. 2d 498, 500 (Miss. 1987).
41. For example, *Industrial Union Dep't, AFL-CIO v. American Petroleum Inst.*, 448 U.S. 607, 687 (1980) (Rehnquist, J., concurring); *Arizona v. California*, 373 U.S. 546, 626 (1963) (Harlan, J., dissenting in part).
42. *See King v. Burwell*, 135 S. Ct. 2480, 2488–2489 (2015).
43. Treas. Reg. § 1.368-1(b) & (d).

extend, or even alter the thrust of the statute. Regulations promulgated pursuant to such provisions are called "specific authority regulations."[44] Prominent examples of specific authority delegations are I.R.C. §§ 385 (as to characterization of corporate instruments as debt or equity) and 1502 (as to filing of consolidated returns by affiliated corporations).

There were old cases suggesting that specific authority tax regulations are entitled to greater deference from the courts than general authority regulations. That view has now been rejected. The Supreme Court has instructed that, in general, both types of regulations have "force of law" effect as long as they have been promulgated under proper procedures and are compatible with the underlying statute.[45]

In addition to regulations, the IRS issues a variety of lower level guidance documents. The most prominent types are revenue rulings and revenue procedures. For the most part, these do not have "force of law" status, but courts may find them influential or persuasive in particular cases.[46]

State-level authorities go by various names. In substance, however, they typically resemble federal authorities, consisting of statutes, force-of-law regulations, and varieties of sub-regulation administrative guidance documents.

[B] Interpretational Elements

What are the sources to which American courts advert as they endeavor to construe tax statutes? The following are of principal significance: the text of the statute, its context, its purposes, canons of construction, administrative interpretations, and judicial precedents.

[1] Text and Context

The language used by the legislature obviously is of fundamental importance. A noted Supreme Court justice observed: "no one will gainsay that the function in construing a statute is to ascertain the meaning of the words used by the legislature."[47]

44. Treasury and the IRS persist in the habit of calling general authority regulations "interpretive regulations" and calling specific authority regulations "legislative regulations." This practice is wrong. "Interpretive" and "legislative" regulations are understood to have different meanings under American administrative law, denoting respectively nonbinding and binding interpretations. *See Altera Corp. v. Comm'r*, 145 T.C. 91, 115–117 (2015) (unanimously rejecting this position advanced by the IRS).
45. *Mayo Foundation for Med. Educ. & Research v. United States*, 562 U.S. 44, 56–58 (2011). For discussion of *Mayo* and of procedural and substantive challenges to the validity of tax regulations, *see* Steve R. Johnson, "Preserving Fairness in Tax Administration in the Mayo Era" 32 *Va. Tax Rev.*, 269 (2012).
46. For example, *Voss v. Comm'r*, 796 F.3d 1051 (9th Cir. 2015); *Validus Reins., Ltd. v. United States*, 786 F.3d 1039 (D.C. Cir. 2015)(both choosing not to defer to lower-level IRS guidance documents). *See* Johnson et al., *supra* n. 10, pp. 20–34 (identifying the varieties of IRS guidance documents and discussing deference issues).
47. Felix Frankfurter, "Some Reflections on the Reading of Statutes" 47 *Colum. L. Rev.*, 527, 528 (1947). Actually, some do gainsay that proposition, but it does represent the dominant view.

In general, however, the words are not taken in isolation. "The plainness or ambiguity of statutory language is determined by reference to the language itself, the specific context in which that language is used, and the broader context of the statute as a whole."[48] Language ambiguous in itself may take on a clear meaning when put in context.

Specific context includes how the language fits in the provision at issue and how the provision fits in the statute. Broader context includes statutes deemed to be *in pari materia* with the statute at issue and the historical pattern of enactments in the area. Typically, only other tax statutes are read as *in pari materia* with tax statutes. In rare situations, however, non-tax statutes may inform the interpretation of tax statutes.[49]

[2] Purpose

Virtually all American judges believe that legislative purpose is germane, but controversy has long existed as to the sources courts may consult in ascertaining that purpose. Some judges insist that purpose can legitimately be inferred only from the statute and its contexts.[50]

In contrast, other judges believe that they may legitimately hunt for purpose in sources extrinsic to the statute itself. Those sources can include reports produced by the tax-writing committees of Congress: the House Ways and Means Committee, the Senate Finance Committee, conference committees convened to reconcile differences between the House and Senate versions of the bill and the standing Joint Committee on Taxation.[51] Extrinsic indicators may also include occasional committee prints prepared for general informational purposes, pre-enactment versions of the bill, bills that failed to achieve enactment, testimony and statements made during committee hearings, floor debates included in the *Congressional Record*, Executive Branch documents and post-enactment events such as amendment of (or failure to amend) the statute.

Although numerous tax cases have delved into such extrinsic evidence, two caveats are appropriate. First, extrinsic sources should not be invoked when they are

48. *Robinson v. Shell Oil Co.*, 519 U.S. 337, 341 (1997); *see also United Sav. Ass'n v. Timbers of Inwood Forest Associates, Ltd.*, 484 U.S. 365, 371 (1988) (statutory construction "is a holistic endeavor"); *Loving v. IRS*, 742 F.3d 1013 (D.C. Cir. 2014); *Ridgely v. Lew*, 55 F. Supp. 3d 89 (D.D.C. 2014).
49. For example, *United States v. Cleveland Indians Baseball Co.*, 532 U.S. 200, 209–218 (2001) (reading the FICA tax in light of the Social Security Act).
50. For example, *Schindler Elevator Corp. v. United States*, 563 U.S. 401, 407 (2011); *Gross v. FBL Fin. Servs., Inc.*, 557 U.S. 167, 175–176 (2009) (both stating that, in construing statutes, courts "must begin with the language employed by Congress and the assumption that the ordinary meaning of that language accurately expresses the legislative purpose").
51. For major pieces of tax legislation, the Joint Committee typically produces a *General Explanation*, commonly called the "Blue Book." Because the Joint Committee is an adjunct, not itself the origin of tax proposals, and because Blue Books are prepared after enactment, some cases, including a unanimous Supreme Court tax decision, state that Blue Books are impermissible as guides to statutory interpretation. *United States v. Woods*, 134 S. Ct. 557, 568 (2013). However, litigants continue to cite them, and Treasury regulations list them as among the authorities that can be substantial in determining whether tax penalties may appropriately be imposed, Treas. Reg. § 1.6662-4(d)(3)(iii).

unreliable because, for example, they are ambiguous, are contradictory, reflect the views of only splinter legislators or represent attempts to strategically manipulate the outcomes of litigation.[52] American judges differ widely as to their degrees of suspicion of legislative history and similar indicia.[53]

Second, it is usually held that the proper role of extrinsic indicators of congressional purpose is to clarify ambiguous statues, not to "cloud a statutory text that is clear."[54] Thus, many decisions reject resort to legislative history when the statutory text has a plain meaning.[55] Other decisions, however, take a different tack, holding that "[i]t is a well-established canon of statutory construction that a court should go beyond the literal language of a statute if reliance on that language would defeat the plain purposes of the statute."[56]

[3] Canons of Construction

Canons are judicially developed principles, typically distilled from long experience, found useful in statutory explication. In some cases, they actually do produce or significantly influence the outcome of the case. In many instances, however, they serve as window-dressing: apparently objective bases on which to explain outcomes judges have determined to reach on grounds they prefer to leave behind the curtain.

No exhaustive enumeration of constructional canons exists; there are over a hundred canons. It is well established that canons are not rigid but instead are context-dependent rules of thumb to be modified or dispensed with if their application would interfere with more fundamental indicators of meaning.[57]

Canons are of two types: linguistic and substantive. Linguistic canons are based on how speakers of English communicate: how do speakers/writers express themselves and what do listeners/readers understand from various expressions? Common linguistic canons include *noscitur a sociis* (words are known by their neighbors), *eiusdem generis* (a general catch-all phrase following a specific, detailed list is limited to things of the same kind as the enumerated particulars), the presumption that words have consistent meaning throughout the text, the expectation that every word used is

52. For example, *State of Florida v. U.S. Dep't of Health & Human Servs.*, 648 F.3d 1235, 1318 (11th Cir. 2011), aff'd in part & rev'd on other grounds *sub nom. National Fed. of Independent Bus. v. Sebelius*, 567 U.S. 519 (2012).
53. For the dismissive view of one judge - himself a former legislator - of the reliability of floor speeches and committee reports, *see Oregon v. Ashcroft*, 192 F. Supp. 2d 1077, 1090–1091 (D. Or. 2002).
54. *Ratzlaf v. United States*, 510 U.S. 135, 147–148 (1994); *see also Milner v. Department of Navy*, 562 U.S. 562, 574 (2011).
55. For example, *Johnson v. United States*, 529 U.S. 694, 723 (2000); *Caminetti v. United States*, 242 U.S. 470 (1917).
56. *Bob Jones Univ. v. United States*, 461 U.S. 574, 586 (1983).
57. For example, *Connecticut Nat'l Bank v. Germain*, 503 U.S. 249, 253–254 (1992). For a list of canons used by the Supreme Court, *see* William N. Eskridge Jr. & Phillip P. Frickey, "The Supreme Court, 1993 Term - Forward: Law as Equilibrium" 108 *Harv. L. Rev.*, 26, 97–108 (1994).

intended to have significance, and *expressio unius est exclusio alterius* (express inclusion of some things implies exclusion of other things).[58]

Substantive canons, on the other hand, exist to advance important policies or to protect cherished values from accidental or ill-considered interference. These canons can be in tension, though. For example, while some canons - such as that I.R.C. § 61 (defining income) is to be interpreted broadly[59] and that exemptions and deductions are construed narrowly[60] - slant in favor of the tax collector, another canon holds that, when the case is closely balanced, it should be decided in favor of the taxpayer.[61] The strength of this canon at the federal level has risen and fallen on alternating ideological tides. The canon has always had force at the state level.[62] After being in eclipse for generations, it appears to be making a comeback at the federal level as well.[63]

[4] Administrative Interpretations

We have noted that, in the tax area, Treasury regulations typically have the force of law but lower-level IRS interpretations do not (although they may be influential). Under what standards have American courts decided which degree of weight to accord to which Treasury and IRS positions?

For most of the twentieth century, courts applied tax-specific lines of cases which generally evaluated Treasury regulations under a reasonableness standard and gave little shrift to lower-level IRS interpretations. Beginning in the last two decades of the twentieth century, however, tax-specific rules increasingly gave way to application in tax of general administrative law doctrines, of which three - *Chevron*, *Skidmore/Mead*, and *Auer/Seminole Rock* - are of principal significance.

In general, *Chevron* applies to agency positions which have gone through the notice-and-comment process prescribed by the Administrative Procedure Act.[64] When *Chevron* applies, the court will uphold the agency's position unless it is contrary to the

58. For examples of canons in federal and state tax cases, *see* Steve R. Johnson, "The 'Things of the Same Nature' Canon in State-Local Tax Construction" 67 *State Tax Notes*, 59 (2013); Steve R. Johnson, "The No Surplusage Canon in State and Local Tax Cases" 65 *State Tax Notes*, 793 (2012); Steve R. Johnson, "Supertext and Consistent Meaning" 52 *State Tax Notes*, 675 (2009).
59. For example, *Comm'r v. Glenshaw Glass Co.*, 348 U.S. 426 (1955).
60. For example, *INDOPCO, Inc. v. Comm'r*, 503 U.S. 79 (1992).
61. For example, *Int'l Harvester Cr. Corp. v. Goodrich*, 350 U.S. 537, 547 (1956).
62. *See* Steve R. Johnson, "Pro-Taxpayer Interpretation of State-Local Tax Laws" 51 *State Tax Notes*, 441 (2009); Steve R. Johnson, "Should Ambiguous Revenue Laws Be Interpreted in Favor of Taxpayers?" *Nev. Law.*, 15 (April 2002).
63. For example, *United Dominion Inds., Inc. v. United States*, 532 U.S. 822, 839 (2001)(Thomas, J., concurring); *id.* n.1 (Stevens, J., dissenting); *United States v. Marshall*, 798 F.3d 296, 318 (5th Cir. 2015); *Exxon Mobil Corp. v. Comm'r*, 689 F.3d 191, 199–200 (2d Cir. 2012).
64. 5 U.S.C. § 553. This consists of publication of the proposed agency position in the *Federal Register*, invitation of comments from the public, and agency consideration of those comments. Unless a statutory exception applies, a tax regulation not issued pursuant to these procedures is invalid. For example, *Cohen v. United States*, 853 F. Supp. 2d 138, 143 (D.D.C. 2012), aff'd, 751 F.3d 629 (D.C. Cir. 2014). It also is invalid if it is "arbitrary and capricious," i.e., does not appear to the courts to have been an exercise in reasoned decision making. For example, *Motor Vehicles Mfrs. Ass'n v. State Farm Mut. Auto. Ins. Co.*, 463 U.S. 29 (1983); *Dominion Resources, Inc. v. Unites States*, 681 F.3d 1313, 1318 (Fed. Cir. 2012).

statute or unreasonably interprets an ambiguous statute.[65] This standard typically applies to Treasury regulations but not to revenue rulings and other IRS positions.[66]

Courts usually evaluate such sub-regulation IRS positions under the 1940s *Skidmore* standard, revivified by the Supreme Court in 2001 in *Mead*. Courts applying this standard consider "the degree of the agency's care, its consistency, formality, and relative expertise, and ... the persuasiveness of the agency's position." This standard "has produced a spectrum of judicial responses, from great respect ... to near indifference."[67]

Auer and *Seminole Rock* apply when the issue turns on interpretation of a regulation, not a statute. They direct that the agency's interpretation of its own ambiguous regulation is "controlling" unless it is "plainly erroneous or inconsistent with the regulation."[68] The Supreme Court apples the doctrine strongly; most lower federal courts do so less enthusiastically; the Tax Court is hostile to the doctrine, avoiding it whenever possible.[69]

Deference doctrines at the state level fall into six patterns: (1) a high level of deference but without particularization of the standard; (2) state analogue of *Chevron*; (3) state analogue of *Skidmore/Mead*; (4) some deference, but without specification of degree; (5) little or no deference; and (6) deference on questions of fact but not on issues of law.[70]

Deference issues become even more intricate in states in which the initial adjudication occurs in, not a court, but a hearing function within the state revenue agency, with further administrative appeal before judicial review. For example, in a Nevada case, the state Department of Taxation determined that a large corporation owed additional sales taxes, and it made a deficiency assessment. The company filed a petition for redetermination of the deficiency. Pursuant to state law, the case was heard first by an Administrative Law Judge (ALJ), who held for the corporation. The Department appealed to the designated administrative body, the State Tax Commission, which reversed the ALJ's decision. The corporation appealed to state trial court, which reversed the Commission's decision and held for the corporation, a decision affirmed by the state Supreme Court.[71]

---

65. *Chevron U.S.A. Inc. v. Natural Resources Defense Council, Inc.*, 467 U.S. 837, 842–844 (1984). For an argument that *Chevron* has ceased to have outcome-determinative force, *see* Steve R. Johnson, "The Rise and Fall of *Chevron* in Tax: From the Early Days to *King* and Beyond," *Pepperdine L. Rev.*, 19 (2015).
66. For example, *Taproot Admin. Servs., Inc. v. Comm'r*, 133 T.C. 202, 208–209 (2009), aff'd, 679 F.3d 1109, 1115–1116 (9th Cir. 2012).
67. *United States v. Mead Corp.*, 533 U.S. 218, 228 (2001); *see Skidmore v. Swift & Co.*, 323 U.S. 134, 137 (1944).
68. *Auer v. Robbins*, 519 U.S. 482, 461 (1997); *see Bowles v. Seminole Rock & Sand Co.*, 325 U.S. 410, 413–414 (1945).
69. *See* Steve R. Johnson, "*Seminole Rock* in Tax Cases," *Yale J. on Regulation: Notice & Comment* (September 15, 2016); Steve R. Johnson, "*Auer/Seminole Rock* Deference in the Tax Court" 11 *Pitt. Tax Rev.*, 1 (2013).
70. *See* Steve R. Johnson, "Conditional Deference to Tax Authorities" 60 *State Tax Notes*, 269 (2011); Steve R. Johnson, "Deference – Questions of Fact versus Issues of Law" 59 *State Tax Notes*, 883 (2011); Steve R. Johnson, "Judicial Deference to State Tax Agencies – An Overview" 58 *State Tax Notes*, 633 (2010).
71. *State Dep't of Taxation v. Masco Builder Cabinet Group*, 265 P.3d 666 (Nev. 2011) (per curiam).

Under Nevada law, deference was owed to the opinion of the ALJ, not the opinion of the Commission. This is unusual. In most jurisdictions, deference is accorded to the agency's view, not that of its ALJ.[72] This type of deference issue does not arise at the federal level because the IRS does not adjudicate via ALJs or hearing boards.

[5] Judicial Precedents

Stare decisis is no less important in tax than in other areas of law. Indeed, the courts have recognized that the doctrine is even more important in heavily statutory areas (such as tax) - in which judicial decisions are always subject to possible reversal by Congress - than in constitutional law, in which the courts are effectively the last word.[73] The doctrine "represents an element of continuity in law, and is rooted in the psychological need to satisfy reasonable expectations."[74]

Tax decisions by the US Supreme Court (or the highest court in the state) are binding unless reversed by the legislature or the court itself.[75] Tax decisions by the federal circuit courts do not bind other circuits (but are influential to them) and bind only those trial courts within the circuit.

Under I.R.C. § 7482(b), Tax Court decisions are appealable to the circuit in which the individual taxpayer resides or the corporate taxpayer has its principal place of management. The Tax Court will adhere to clearly articulated law of the circuit to which the case is appealable - even if the Tax Court disagrees with the circuit's view.[76] This sometimes results in the Tax Court deciding essentially identical cases differently, simply because they are appealable to different circuits.

The Tax Court hears only tax cases, and - with rare exceptions - those nominated to be Tax Court judges had distinguished private sector and government careers in tax. Since the Tax Court is a specialized and expert tribunal, Tax Court decisions sometimes are accorded particular respect by generalist courts. Nonetheless, appellate courts are supposed to review Tax Court decisions "in the same manner and to the same extent as decisions of the" other tax trial tribunals.[77]

§15.05 INTERPRETATIONAL APPROACHES

This section describes and exemplifies the competing schools of statutory interpretation in the US. It then notes which approaches tend to prevail, taking into account

72. *See* Steve R. Johnson, "ALJs in State-Local Tax Cases: To Whom Is Deference Due?" 64 *State Tax Notes*, 785 (2012).
73. For example, *Payne v. Tennessee*, 501 U.S. 808, 827–828 (1991).
74. *Helvering v. Hallock*, 309 U.S. 106, 119 (1940).
75. The Supreme Court does sometimes reverse or modify its tax decisions. For example, *Arkansas Best v. Comm'r*, 485 U.S. 212 (1988) (limiting *Corn Prods. Refining Co. v. Comm'r*, 350 U.S. 46 (1955)).
76. *Golsen v. Comm'r*, 54 T.C. 742 (1970), aff'd, 445 F.2d 985 (10th Cir. 1971).
77. I.R.C. § 7482(a)(1); *see* Steve R. Johnson, "The Phoenix and the Perils of the Second Best: Why Heightened Appellate Deference to Tax Court Decisions Is Undesirable" 77 *Or. L. Rev.*, 235 (1998).

contextual differences. It concludes by noting that, despite arguments advanced by some commentators, American courts employ essentially the same approaches in tax and non-tax cases.

[A] Competing Approaches

The previous part of this chapter described the elements to which courts advert in construing tax statutes. Judges differ as to the weights to be attached to the elements and even as to the legitimacy of some of them. These differences have coalesced into different constructional schools, with which particular judges are more or less identified. Six such schools predominate: literalism, textualism, intentionalism, purposivism, dynamism, and pragmatism. These schools are described below and, by way of illustration, tax decisions reflecting each school are given.

[1] Literalism

This school of construction heavily emphasizes the particular statutory terms in controversy. The court must determine whether the legislature intended those words to be understood in an ordinary sense or a technical "term of art" sense.[78] In addition, words often have multiple recognized meanings. Thus, the court must choose from among them the meaning most apt to the occasion.[79]

In tax cases, as in other kinds of cases, courts often turn to dictionaries.[80] This is understandable, indeed often appropriate, but it can create a false impression of objectivity. One dictionary may offer multiple definitions of the key word(s); many dictionaries have gone through multiple editions; and there are numerous competing dictionaries. Which definition from which edition of which dictionary is best? Judges often have a wide range of choice and thus considerable opportunity to manipulate the outcome through "dictionary shopping."[81]

Even when it is performed carefully, however, literalism has been strongly criticized, as inappropriately truncating the judicial inquiry. A leading figure in mid-twentieth century American law remarked: "there is no surer way to misread any document than to read it literally."[82]

The *Gitlitz* case is a prominent example of literalism in American tax jurisprudence. The I.R.C. draws a distinction between C corporations and S corporations. C corporations are juridical entities separate from their owners. This has two effects. If

78. The presumption is in favor of an ordinary sense. For example, *FDIC v. Meyer*, 510 U.S. 471, 476 (1994).
79. "[W]ords are inexact tools at best, and hence it is essential that we place the words of a statute in their proper context." *Tidewater Oil Co. v. United States*, 409 U.S. 151, 157 (1972).
80. For example, *Comm'r v. Soliman*, 506 U.S. 168, 174 (1993).
81. *See*, e.g., Scalia & Garner, *supra* n. 34, Appendix; Ellen P. Aprill, "The Law of the Word: Dictionary Shopping in the Supreme Court" 30 *Ariz. St. L. J.*, 275 (1998); Note, "Looking It Up: Dictionaries and Statutory Interpretation" 107 *Harv. L. Rev.*, 1437 (1994).
82. Archibald Cox, "Judge Learned Hand and the Interpretation of Statutes" 60 *Harv. L. Rev.*, 370, 375–376 (1947).

the corporation is profitable, double taxation is possible: profits are taxed to the corporation and the amount left after taxes is taxed again when distributed to the shareholders as dividends. If, on the other hand, the corporation loses money, the losses are bottled up in the corporation: they can be used only to offset profits of the corporation in other years.

In contrast, some corporations (usually small and medium sized companies) are eligible to elect S status. If they do, they become pass-through entities in which both profits and losses immediately flow through to the shareholders. This obviates the possibility of double taxation and may result in faster utilization of the losses.

Basis is a crucial concept for S corporation shareholders, affecting the extent of losses they may deduct and the taxability of distributions and proceeds of stock sales. Basis was intended to measure the extent of the shareholder's investment in the corporation. However, the language Congress used in the basis statute at issue in *Gitlitz* was deficient. Under the language, if taken literally, shareholders could sometimes get more basis than Congress intended.

The issue eventually reached the Supreme Court. Reversing the Tax Court and the circuit court, the Supreme Court, by a vote of 8 to 1, held for the taxpayer. The Court applied the statutory language literally despite the bizarre policy result that ensued.[83]

[2] Textualism

Some commentators lump literalism and textualism together, but doing so is sloppy. Textualism shares with literalism attention to the statute language. However, textualism has a broader angle of vision. For the textualist, it is words in context, not words in isolation, that matter. To the textualist, statutory language "cannot be construed in a vacuum. It is a fundamental canon ... that the words of a statute must be read in their context and with a view to their place in the overall statutory scheme."[84]

An example of textualism in tax involves equitable tolling. Both corporate and individual taxpayers who overpay their liabilities may obtain refunds, but only if refund claims are filed within prescribed time periods. The doctrine of equitable tolling applies widely to non-tax statutes of limitations, allowing them to be suspended upon the occurrence of certain conditions when rigorous application of the statute would be fundamentally unfair.

The federal circuit courts were split as to whether equitable tolling was available as to the statute of limitations on federal tax refund claims. Based principally on the structure of the statute, the Supreme Court unanimously held against the taxpayers, emphasizing that the Code "set forth its time limitations in unusually emphatic form ...

83. *Gitlitz v. Comm'r*, 531 U.S. 206, 220 (2001). ("Because the Code's plain text permits the taxpayers here to receive these benefits, we need not address this policy concern [that the taxpayer would enjoy a double windfall].") The *Gitlitz* decision was widely criticized; it sometimes was read narrowly in later cases, for example, *Ball ex rel. Ball v. Comm'r*, 742 F.3d 552, 561–562 (3d Cir. 2014); and in short order Congress amended the statute to prospectively overturn the case, *see* IRC § 108(d)(7)(A).

84. *Roberts v. Sea-Land Servs.*, Inc., 566 U.S. 93, 103 (2012); *see also Brown v. Gardner*, 513 U.S. 115, 118 (1994). ("Ambiguity is a creature not of definitional possibilities but of statutory context.")

in a highly detailed technical manner [and] reiterates its limitation several times in several ways."[85] This highly articulated statutory structure left no room for supplementation or modification by a judicially crafted equitable doctrine.

Similarly, in a 2012 bankruptcy tax case, the Supreme Court rejected an interpretation of a statute that "strains the text beyond what it can bear." The Court acknowledged:

> certainly there may be compelling policy reasons for [the rejected approach]. But if Congress intended that result, it did not so provide in the statute. Given the statute's plain text, its context, and structure, it is not for us to rewrite that statute, particularly in this complex terrain of interconnected provisions and exceptions enacted over nearly three decades.[86]

[3] Intentionalism

A state tax case declared: "It is a fundamental rule ... to which all other rules are subordinate that the intent of the legislature governs when that intent can be ascertained."[87] Similar assertions are quite common in state tax cases, and they appear in some federal tax cases as well.

Unfortunately, courts using the same words often mean different things. Legislative intent can mean any of three things: actual subjective intent, imaginatively constructed subjective intent, or objective intent.

Actual intent exists when Congress or the state legislature had considered the issue at hand and formed a preference as to how it should be resolved. There are both theoretical and practical objections to basing statutory interpretation on such actual intent. Theoretically, if the legislature had formed such an intent, one would expect that it would have written it into the statute. In fact, in the great majority of cases in which the statute is silent on a matter, the reason is that the legislature never thought about the matter at all or that it did think about it but was unable to forge a consensus as to it.[88] Practically, if an unenacted actual intent existed, there can be formidable barriers to judges reliably ascertaining what it was. Legislative history will often be absent, opaque, contradictory, or reflective of the views of only some legislators. For such reasons, the notion that statutory interpretation can be routinely and reliably based on actual legislative intent is dubious.[89]

85. *United States v. Brockamp*, 519 U.S. 347, 349 (1997). Soon thereafter, Congress enacted a limited tolling rule. I.R.C. § 6511(h)(2)(A). Equitable tolling plays a larger role at the state level. *See* Steve R. Johnson, "Equitable Tolling in State and Local Tax Cases" 52 *State Tax Notes*, 917 (2009).
86. *Hall v. United States*, 566 U.S. 506 (2012).
87. *National Collegiate Athletic Ass'n v. Kansas Dep't of Revenue*, 781 P.2d 726, 729 (Kan. 1989).
88. "[W]ith respect to 99.99 percent of the issues of construction reaching the courts, there *is* no legislative intent." Antonin Scalia (1st edn, Princeton, Princeton University Press, 1997) *A Matter of Interpretation: Federal Courts and the Law*, p. 32 (emphasis in original). Some would quibble with the quantification, but the general thrust of the observation is surely correct.
89. *See*, e.g., William N. Eskridge Jr., Phillip P. Frickey & E. Garrett (2nd edn, New York: Foundation Press, 2006) *Legislation and Statutory Interpretation*, pp. 222–228.

The problems with actual intent cause some to turn instead towards imaginatively constructed intent. That is, the judge attempts to determine, from the evidence at hand, what position the legislature would have taken on the matter in controversy had it considered the particular point and had it reached agreement as to it.

Aristotle endorsed this method,[90] but it is dubious. Article I, § 7 of the Constitution, the Presentment Clause, provides that, in order to become law, a bill must pass both the House of Representatives and the Senate and be presented to the President for signing. Imaginative construction bypasses this required process by treating as law something that passed neither house and was never presented to the President. What judges think legislators would have done matters not; only what they actually did has constitutional significance.[91]

Courts and commentators sometimes refer to the text of a statute as "the best evidence of the legislative intent or will."[92] But unenacted intentions are not law. Only duly passed bills are.[93] Thus, imaginative construction is of doubtful constitutional legitimacy.

Moreover, reliability problems beset construction via imagination. When, in medieval England, judges often also sat in Parliament, they might have been able to intuit how the legislature would have dealt with a *casus omissus*. With contemporary separation-of-functions practice, however, any such advantage is gone. Can judges truly be confident that they can divine what the legislature would have done had it considered the particular matter and reached agreement as to it?

There was a time that British judges, when unsure about a statute's meaning, went to legislators directly and asked.[94] That certainly is not contemporary American practice.[95] Absent such direct evidence, the danger is great that the result the imaginative judge reaches will just happen to be the result that corresponds to the judge's personal view of wise policy.[96]

---

90. (New York: Macmillan, 1962, M. Ostwald transl.) *Nicomachean Ethics*, bk. V, § 10.
91. "[O]nly language that meets the constitutional requirements of bicameralism and presentment has true legal authority." *Weddel v. HHS*, 23 F.3d 388, 391 (Fed. Cir. 1994)(citing *INS v. Chadha*, 462 U.S. 919 (1983)).
92. For example, Norman J. Singer & J.D. Shambie Singer (7th edn, St. Paul: Thomson Reuters, 2007) *2A Statutes and Statutory Construction* § 46:3, p. 165.
93. "[I]t does not matter whether [the legislators] were fall-down drunk when they voted for it. So long as they voted for it, that text is the law." Antonin Scalia & John F. Manning, "A Dialogue on Statutory and Constitutional Interpretation" 80 *Geo. Wash. L. Rev.*, 1610, 1613 (2012) (remarks of Justice Scalia); *see also* Laurence H. Tribe, "Comment" in Scalia, *supra* n. 88, p. 65 ("it is the text's meaning, and not the content of anyone's expectations or intentions, that binds us as law").
94. Frederick J. de Sloovere, "Extrinsic Aids in the Interpretation of Statutes" 88 *U. Pa. L. Rev.*, 527, 537 (1940) n. 48.
95. In general, when American courts are trying cases in which construction of a statute is at issue, they do not admit as evidence proffered testimony by legislators as to what they intended in enacting the legislation. For example, *Bread Political Action Comm. v. FEC*, 455 U.S. 577, 582 n. 3 (1982).
96. This is one criticism that has been made of use of committee reports. For example, *Matter of Sinclair*, 870 F.2d 1340, 1343 (7th Cir. 1989). ("Often there is so much legislative history that a court can manipulate the meaning of a law by choosing which snippets to emphasize.") One judge described citing legislative history as akin to "looking over a crowd and picking out your

Judges concerned about the difficulties of subjective interpretation prefer to seek the objective intent in the statute, that is, "the intent that a reasonable person would gather from the text of the law, placed alongside the remainder of the *corpus juris*."[97] As on state court put it:

> The province of construction is to arrive at the true sense of the language of the act, not to supply language to help out a conjectured intent to be gathered from the words used. The question is not so much, What did the legislature intend to enact? as What did it mean by what it did enact?[98]

This approach is intentionalism in name only. It borrows the word "intent" only to keep peace in the judicial family by not expressly disagreeing with thousands of decisions saying that legislative intent is the touchstone of interpretation. In substance, though, "objective intent" is another name for textualism.

Subjective intentionalism in tax interpretation is exemplified by the Supreme Court's *Davis* decision. Ordinarily, a corporation's redemption of the stock of a shareholder qualifies for preferential income tax treatment as a sale. However, what is in form a redemption may in substance be a disguised dividend, which entails consequences less advantageous to the shareholder.

In *Davis*, the trial court and the circuit court held for the taxpayer. They concluded that there was a business purpose for the transaction, thus that it was not abusive and should not be recharacterized as a dividend. The Supreme Court reversed. Although conceding that the legislative history it cited "is certainly not free from doubt," the Court concluded that the committee reports disclosed Congress' intention to remove business purpose from the sale-versus-dividend test.[99]

[4] Purposivism

If it may be impossible to ascertain an actual specific intent and illegitimate to attempt to imagine one, the subjectively oriented judge may be driven to seek instead a general purpose. Even if the legislature had no particular intent as to the specific question at hand, at least there were general aims motivating enactment. Purposivism attempts to resolve statutory ambiguities by asking which of the candidate interpretations would better advance the general goals and objectives behind the statute.

Judge Learned Hand's statement remains a classic invocation of this interpretive approach. Although acknowledging that "the words used, even in their literal sense,

friends." Patricia M. Wald, "Some Observations on the Use of Legislative History in the 1981 Supreme Court Term" 68 *Iowa L. Rev.*, 195, 214 (1983) (citing remarks of Judge Harold Leventhal).

97. Scalia, *supra* n. 88, 16–17 ("despite frequent statements to the contrary, [judges] do not really look for subjective legislative intent. We look for a sort of 'objectified' intent").

98. *State ex rel. Seymour v. Gilfillan*, 1905 WL 824, at *7 (Ohio Com. Pl. 1905) (citations and internal punctuation omitted); *see* Steve R. Johnson, "The Two Kinds of Legislative Intent" 51 *State Tax Notes*, 1045 (2009).

99. *United States v. Davis*, 397 U.S. 301, 311–312 (1970).

are the primary, and ordinarily the most reliable, source of interpreting the meaning," Judge Hand added:

> it is one of the surest indexes of a mature and developed jurisprudence not to make a fortress out of the dictionary; but to remember that statutes always have some purpose or object to accomplish, whose sympathetic and imaginative discovery is the surest guide to their meaning.[100]

An aspect of this is the "legislative bargain" approach. This is most closely associated with the Public Choice model - which sees legislation as the result of bargaining between private economic interests - but is embraced by judges across a wide swathe of the ideological spectrum. The notion is that each piece of legislation represents compromise among groups represented by legislators. For example, a statute dealing with US taxation of transnational transactions may reflect the point of balance among groups interested in, respectively, facilitating international trade, reducing tax burdens on certain industries, simplifying the law, and enhancing federal revenues. The role of the courts is to discover the bargain struck by the parties and to enforce it in construing the statute.[101]

Purposivism drove *Lynch*, a 1986 circuit court tax opinion. The issue was what degree of involvement a former shareholder could have with the corporation that redeemed his stock in order for the redemption to qualify for favorable capital gains treatment. The Tax Court held for the taxpayer on the basis of a general facts-and-circumstances analysis. The Ninth Circuit appeals court reversed. It concluded that, in enacting the statute at issue, Congress sought to provide "definite standards in order to provide certainty in specific instances." The Tax Court's uncabined inquiry was the antithesis of definiteness and would undercut certainty and predictability. Inconsistent with the perceived general purpose, the Tax Court's approach could not stand.[102]

Albertson's, another case involving the Tax Court and the Ninth Circuit, is another striking example. The I.R.C. confers income tax advantages on compensation plans that meet certain qualification requirements. Subject to various limitations, it also allows taxpayers to take federal income tax deductions for interest expenses paid or accrued. The corporation had a nonqualified plan, and it accrued amounts, designated as interest, for deferred payments owed to the employees participating in the plan. The corporation deducted the amounts. The IRS disallowed the deductions.

The Tax Court held against the taxpayer, concluding that the nominal interest was actually additional compensation, deduction of which was limited by an I.R.C. provision. On appeal, the Ninth Circuit originally held for the taxpayer on the ground of plain statutory meaning. On the government's request for hearing, the Ninth Circuit withdrew its original opinion and issued a new opinion holding in favor of the IRS. It reasoned that upholding the taxpayer's arrangement would allow the taxpayer to reap the benefits of having a qualified plan without having to meet the burdensome qualification requirements. To protect the congressional purposes behind the qualified

100. *Cabell v. Markham*, 148 F.2d 737, 739 (2d Cir.), aff'd, 326 U.S. 404 (1945).
101. A classic exposition of this approach is F. Easterbrook, "Foreword: The Court and the Economic System" 98 *Harv. L. Rev.*, 4 (1984).
102. *Lynch v. Comm'r*, 801 F.2d 1176, 1179 (9th Cir. 1986).

plan regime, the court imposed a limitation not found in the I.R.C. itself. Contrary to the general movement of the courts towards textualism, the Ninth Circuit used purpose to trump clear text.[103]

In *Lynch* and *Albertson's*, application of purposivism led to decision for the IRS. This is by far the usual outcome. Purposive interpretation usually means defeat for the taxpayer.[104]

[5] Dynamism

Tax statutes may be on the books for generations. Is a statute to be interpreted the same way regardless of its vintage? May a court revise an old statute to better fit contemporary conditions, or is such updating a job exclusively for the legislature?

Dynamic interpretation theories would grant courts space to revise superannuated statutes. Leading American jurisprudence theorists have supported such theories,[105] but they remain more popular with scholars than with judges.

The most prominent dynamic American tax decision is *Bob Jones University.* Not-for-profit corporations are exempt from federal income tax if they meet certain conditions. Among these conditions, they must be organized and operated exclusively for one or more specified purposes, one of which is education. The university in question was organized as a not-for-profit corporation, and it exclusively pursued educational activities. Accordingly, the IRS originally recognized the university as tax exempt.

Subsequently, the IRS revoked such recognition because the university engaged in racially discriminatory practices. The statute made no reference to racial discrimination as a disqualifying condition. Indeed, comparable provisions had been in the law since the late nineteenth century, when school segregation was legal in the US.

Nonetheless, the Supreme Court upheld the revocation. The Court noted that the origins of the tax exemption were in "common law standards of charity – namely, that an institution ... serve a public purpose and not be contrary to established public policy." Such public policy can evolve. Racial discrimination was not against public policy when the statute was enacted, but it had become contrary to public policy by the 1970s, the tax years at issue.[106]

The Court reinforced this rationale by nothing that, in the dozen years since the IRS adopted its new policy, Congress did nothing to block it despite being "acutely

---

103. *Albertson's Inc. v. Comm'r*, 42 F.3d 537 (9th Cir. 1994), cert. denied, 516 U.S. 807 (1995). For discussion of *Albertson's*, *see* Jasper L. Cummings Jr., "Statutory Interpretation and *Albertson's*" 66 *Tax Notes*, 559 (1995).
104. *See* Steve R. Johnson, "Further Thoughts on Interpreting Tax Statutes" 17/4 *ABA Section of Tax'n Newsletter*, 11 (1998).
105. For example, Ronald Dworkin (1st edn, Cambridge: Belknap Press, 1986) *Law's Empire*, p. 348; Lon L. Fuller (1st edn, Chicago: Foundation Press, 1940) *The Law in Quest of Itself*, pp. 8–9 (describing a statute as "not something that is, but something that becomes; it is not a hard chunk of reality, but a fluid process").
106. *Bob Jones Univ. v. United States*, 461 U.S. 574, 588–592 (1983).

aware" of it. "Ordinarily, and quite appropriately, courts are slow to attribute significance to the failure of Congress to act," but the circumstances "[made] out an unusually strong case of legislative acquiescence in and ratification by implication of the revocation."[107]

Then Justice, later Chief Justice Rehnquist dissented. He argued that it was up to Congress to impose this limitation on tax exemption, that Congress had failed to do so and that "regardless of our view on the propriety of Congress' failure to legislate we are not constitutionally empowered to act for them."[108] The Supreme Court has stated: "There is a basic difference between filling a gap left by Congress' silence and rewriting rules that Congress has affirmatively and specifically enacted."[109] Whether the majority or then Justice Rehnquist was correct as to legitimacy may depend upon one's view as to on which side of this line *Bob Jones* falls.

[6] Pragmatism

Foundationalist theories - theories based on single foundations such as text, intent, or purpose - can be problematic because:

> our intellectual framework is not single-minded, but consists of a "web of beliefs," interconnected but reflecting different understandings and values. As a consequence, human decision making tends to be polycentric, spiral, and inductive, not unidimensional, linear, and deductive ... Thus, the goals of statutory interpretation may be multiple and the sources may be various.[110]

Pragmatic interpretation uses the best source thought to be available in the particular case or a combination of sources. It can be accused of being no method at all in that it is based as much or more on intuition as on defined principles. But theoretical purity often yields to necessity: the need to reach the perceived right result by whatever means are at hand. As Chief Justice John Marshall wrote for the Court: "where the mind labors to discover the design of the legislature, it seizes everything from which aid can be derived."[111]

The Supreme Court's *Engle* decision illustrates the pragmatic style. The I.R.C. allows holders of interests in mineral deposits (including oil and gas wells) to take depletion allowances as income tax deductions. *Engle* involved how to calculate the allowances. Reflecting the difficulty of the issue, the Tax Court and the circuit court had reached contrary conclusions.

The Supreme Court stated: "Our starting point, of course, is the language of the statute itself."[112] However, the Court found that each of several possible interpretations could be reconciled with the language of the statute. To resolve the conundrum, the

107. *Supra*; *see* Steve R. Johnson, "The Reenactment and Inaction Doctrines in State Tax Litigation" 50 *State Tax Notes*, 661 (2008).
108. 461 U.S. at 612.
109. *Mobil Oil Corp. v. Higginbotham*, 436 U.S. 618, 625 (1978).
110. Eskridge, Frickey & Garrett, *supra* n. 89, p. 249.
111. *United States v. Fisher*, 6 U.S. 358, 386 (1805).
112. *Comm'r v. Engle*, 464 U.S. 206, 214 (1984).

Court considered all of the following: remote history (going back to enactment of the country's early income tax laws), more recent history (committee reports from the Congress enacting the specific section and from a preceding Congress), the circumstances of enactment, the legislative process leading to enactment, related statutes, long-standing judicial and administrative constructions, Congress' general purpose, the "reenactment without change" canon, and the practical consequences of the competing positions.

[B] Prevalent Approaches

We have sketched the principal competing schools of statutory interpretation in the US. Which of them is dominant? In broad outline, American courts have:

> adopted a regular method for interpreting the meaning of a ... statute: first, find the ordinary meaning of the language in its textual context; and second, using established canons of construction, ask whether there is any clear indication that some permissible meaning other than the ordinary one applies.[113]

But considerable disagreement exists when one attempts to infuse this framework with greater specificity. One influential treatise stated: "The hard truth of the matter is that American courts have no intelligible, generally accepted, and consistently applied theory of statutory interpretation."[114] This could be read as meaning that pragmatism is the predominant constructional style. That might account for the fact that judges with different judicial philosophies nonetheless agree with each other to a high degree when it comes to resolving actual cases.[115]

However, it is more accurate to say that tax statutory interpretation in the US is highly contextualized than to say that it is random, unpredictable, or unprincipled. US tax statutory interpretation is contextual in that it varies according to the body doing the interpreting, the era in which the case is heard, and the reaction of the other actors in the tax law-making process.

[1] Interpretive Body

Courts are not the only or even first expositors of the meanings of statutes. A law suit is filed only if dispute has arisen between the taxpayer and the revenue agency. Moreover, taxpayers sometimes accede to the agency's interpretation, because they think the agency "got it right" or because the cost, time, and likelihood of success in

113. *Chisom v. Roemer*, 501 U.S. 380, 404 (1991) (Scalia, J., dissenting).
114. Henry M. Hart & Albert M. Sacks (New York: Foundation Press, William N. Eskridge, Jr. & Phillip P. Frickey eds., 1994, prepared from 1958 tentative edn) *The Legal Process*, p. 1169.
115. The Supreme Court resolves almost half its cases unanimously and many others by lopsided votes. *See* Paul H. Edelman, David E. Klein & Stefanie A. Lindquist, "Consensus, Disorder, and Ideology on the Supreme Court" 9 *J. Empirical Legal Stud.*, 129 (2012). Panels of lower courts resolve cases unanimously even more often. *See* Frank B. Cross (1st edn, Stanford: Stanford Univ. Press, 2007) *Decision Making in the U.S. Courts of Appeals*.

court make litigation unappetizing. Thus, revenue agencies, not courts, are always the first and sometimes the only governmental interpreters of tax statutes.

It is widely believed that the IRS and state tax agencies tend to be more intentionalist or purposivist than the courts. This is so for two reasons. First, the agencies often are involved in the process culminating in enactment of the legislation, giving them a privileged opportunity to know the aims. Second, legislators who perceive that an agency is insensitive to its purposes may make the administrators' lives uncomfortable in the next round of appropriations or oversight hearings. Legislators have less ability to punish courts for preferring text to imprecisely expressed intent.

When a tax case does reach court, interpretation can vary by the type of tribunal. The US Tax Court tends to be more purposive than the generalist courts. Presumably, this is because Tax Court judges - tax specialists for much or all of their careers - are more likely to perceive patterns in and pervading precepts underlying the tax laws. Courts in particular states tend to be textual or purposive in orientation, depending on whether that state's interpretive tradition emphasizes subjective or objective legislative intent.

[2] Era

The interpretational pendulum swings. Early in the life of the US, textual approaches predominated, in part because extra-textual legislative materials were sparse or nonexistent and because strict adherence to text could cabin statutes, minimizing their impact on the cherished common law.[116]

For much of the twentieth century, intentionalist and purposivist styles predominated in the US.[117] In part, this was attributable to the proliferation of extra-textual legislative materials (such as committee reports and floor debates) from which judges could glean perceived intent or purpose. In addition, early twentieth century tax statutes often were written in broad language, necessitating gap-filling by the courts, especially in the absence of on-point Treasury regulations.[118]

Beginning in the last several decades of the twentieth century, textualism - emphasizing context, not words in isolation - reclaimed much lost ground. In part this

116. The once powerful canon that statutes in derogation of the common law are narrowly construed has receded greatly in American law, particularly at the federal level. It is essentially extinct in federal tax jurisprudence. *See*, e.g., *United States v. Rodgers*, 461 U.S. 677, 716–717 (1983) (Blackmun, J., dissenting) (unsuccessfully asserting the canon in a case in which an I.R.C. provision as to foreclosure of tax liens contravened common law property rules).

117. So much so that it was sometimes said, only semi-jocularly, that the prevailing rule was "whenever the legislative history is ambiguous it is permissible to refer to the statute." Reed Dickerson (1st edn, Boston: Little, Brown & Co., 1975) *The Interpretation and Application of Statutes*, p. 164. *United States v. American Trucking Ass'ns, Inc.*, 310 U.S. 534 (1940), has been identified as "[t]he pivotal decision signaling the [Supreme] Court's acceptance of legislative history." Scalia & Manning, *supra* n. 93, at 617 n. 21.

118. As a result, during this period, judges felt free to gloss sparse statutes. For example, *United States v. Midland-Ross Corp.*, 381 U.S. 54, 57–58 (1965) (reading a purpose-based limitation into the capital gains/losses statutes).

was because of the intellectual power of new text-oriented judges, particularly US Supreme Court Justice Antonin Scalia and federal circuit court Judge Frank Easterbrook. In addition, purposivism was undermined by attacks from both the ideological left (represented by the Critical Legal Studies movement) and the ideological right (represented by the Law and Economics movement).[119] Finally, the increasing elaboration and specificity of tax statutes diminished the scope for judicial gloss.

Although exceptions exist, the contemporary dominant approach is that the text (in context) controls if it is clear. If the text is unclear, the courts will follow on-point Treasury regulations. Absent such regulations, the courts will consider legislative purpose, sub-regulation IRS guidance to the extent persuasive, and other extrinsic indicators. According to the Supreme Court:

> We must first determine whether the statutory text is plain and unambiguous and, if it is, we must apply the statute according to its terms. The plainness or ambiguity of statutory language is determined by reference to the language itself, the specific context in which that language is used, and the broader context of the statute as a whole.[120]

[3] Institutional Reactions

One who would understand American practice should avoid a sterile bipolar view. Tax law making and interpreting in the US is not just the legislature enacting statutes and the courts explicating them. The system is interactive as well as hierarchical. The participants in the system – legislatures, courts, revenue agencies, taxpayers, and their representatives – influence each other in ways sometimes obvious and sometimes subtle.[121]

Thus, some perceive a "collaborative model" of mutual feedback and influence, under which courts take an active role in molding statutes.[122] Congress can confirm or modify judicial constructions.[123] Under certain circumstances, regulations promulgated by tax agencies can trump judicial decisions.[124] And the regulations, to be politically viable over the long term, must be accepted by taxpayers and their

119. *See* Popkin, *supra* n. 15, §§ 4.03 & 4.04.
120. *Hardt v. Reliance Standard Life Ins. Co.*, 560 U.S. 242, 251 (2010); *see also Mass. Mut. Life Ins. Co. v. United States*, 103 Fed. Cl. 111, 146–152 (2012)(discussing these aspects plus canons of construction and agency deference doctrines); *The Limited, Inc. v. Comm'r*, 286 F.3d 324, 332 (6th Cir. 2002).
121. *See* Johnson, *supra* n. 11; *see* generally William S. Blatt, "Interpretive Communities: The Missing Element in Statutory Interpretation" 95 *Nw. U. L. Rev.*, 629 (2001).
122. For example, William D. Popkin, "The Collaborative Model of Statutory Interpretation" 61 *S. Cal. L. Rev.*, 541 (1988).
123. *See*, e.g., Nancy C. Staudt, René Lindstadt & Jason O'Connor, "Judicial Decisions as Legislation: Congressional Oversight of Supreme Court Tax Cases, 1954-2005" 82 *N.Y.U. L. Rev.*, 1340 (2007).
124. *National Cable & Telecommunications Ass'n v. Brand X Internet Servs.*, 545 U.S. 967 (2005) (holding that a regulation may trump a prior judicial construction of a statute as long as (1) the regulation qualifies for *Chevron* deference and (2) the prior judicial decision was not based on an unambiguous statute).

representatives.[125] Thus, whether a construction will endure may depend on reactions of other constituents of the interpretive process.

The Supreme Court's 2012 *Home Concrete* decision illustrates the potential for, and limits of, collaborative interpretation. The issue was whether the IRS had an extended statute of limitations within which to adjust tax shelter items claimed by a corporation. In a 1958 case, the Court had resolved a similar issue adversely to the IRS. But Congress had changed the statute in several ways after the years at issue in the 1958 case, and Treasury promulgated a new regulation purporting to clarify that the extended limitations period was available under the revised statute.

The lower courts divided as to the validity of the regulation, as did the Supreme Court. By a vote of five to four, the justices held against the IRS, on the ground that the 1958 decision remained controlling. The four dissenters invoked the collaborative model:

> Our legal system presumes there will be continuing dialogue among the three branches of Government on questions of statutory interpretation and application [....] These instructive exchanges [among Congress, the courts and agencies] would be foreclosed by an insistence on adhering to earlier interpretations of a statute even in light of new, relevant statutory amendments. Courts instead should be open to an agency's adoption of a different interpretation where, as here, Congress has given new instruction by an amended statute.[126]

Concurring in the judgment of the Court, Justice Scalia rejected the dissent's "continuing dialogue" contention, describing it as a "romantic, judge-empowering image [that had been] obliterated by this Court's [teaching]." Seeing "the dissent's vision of a troika partnership (legislative-executive-judicial) [as] a mirage," Justice Scalia maintained:

> What is needed for the system to work is that Congress, the Executive, and the private parties subject to their dispositions, be able to predict the meaning that the courts will give to their instructions. That goal would be obstructed if the judicially established meaning of a technical legal term ... could be overturned on the basis of [a new regulation supported by only "feeble" statutory indications].[127]

[4] Is Tax Different?

Should courts interpret tax statutes differently from the way they interpret other types of statutes? Scholars sometimes have argued that they should. They have suggested that tax legislation is more technocratic than ideological compared to some other areas of legislation, that tax law is a more coherent body of law (marked by a higher level of detail, frequent revision, and a largely self-contained nature) from which judges may

125. Monte A. Jackel, "Why the Tax Law Is So Dysfunctional" 138 *Tax Notes*, 891 (2013).
126. *United States v. Home Concrete & Supply, LLC*, 566 U.S. 478 (2012) (Kennedy, J., dissenting).
127. *Supra*. (Scalia, J., concurring in part & concurring in the judgment).

more easily derive general governing principles, and that the quality of committee reports in tax is unusually high.[128]

Such "tax is different" arguments have gained relatively little purchase in the courts. For the most part, courts (especially the generalist courts) treat tax statutes in much the same way as they treat other statutes. There are strong institutional reasons for this. The federal district and circuit courts have large and escalating caseloads. Docket management becomes a consuming drive, leaving little time, energy or inclination to develop and apply differing approaches to different types of cases.

Moreover, even differences in detail between treatment of tax and non-tax cases are diminishing. A 2009 study compared Supreme Court cases from 1969 to 2008 with respect to statutory interpretation in tax cases as opposed to workplace law cases. It found that, early in the period, the Court was more likely to rely on legislative history and structural canons (those involving the interrelationship of I.R.C. provisions) in tax cases. However, with changes in composition of the Court, there was movement later in the period towards more uniform, monolithic interpretation, suggesting that:

> [p]erhaps the philosophical arguments favoring one-size-fits-all statutory interpretation are [trumping] a pragmatic orientation that is more sensitive to differences among particular subject matter areas of federal law.[129]

§15.06 PARTICULAR INTERPRETATIONAL ISSUES

[A] Transplanted Character

For the most part, sales taxes and income taxes are self-contained and do not heavily advert to predecessor or parallel bodies of law. Exceptions, however, do exist.

[1] Accounting Principles

Occasional early decisions seemed willing to import accounting concepts into federal income tax law.[130] However, the Supreme Court later rejected that approach as a general matter. Stressing that financial accounting and tax accounting have "vastly different" objectives, the Court has held that the mere fact that a taxpayer's method satisfies generally accepted financial accounting principles creates no presumption that it meets the requirements of tax accounting.[131]

---

128. For example, Michael Livingston, "Practical Reason, 'Purposivism,' and the Interpretation of Tax Statutes" 51 *Tax L. Rev.*, 677 (1996); Michael Livingston, "Congress, the Courts, and the Code: Legislative History and the Interpretation of Tax Statutes" 69 *Tex. L. Rev.*, 819 (1991); Shannon W. McCormack, "Tax Shelters and Statutory Interpretation: A Much Needed Purposive Approach" *U. Ill. L. Rev.*, 697, 725–729 (2009).
129. James J. Brudney & Corey Ditslear, "The Warp and Woof of Statutory Interpretation: Comparing Supreme Court Approaches in Tax Law and Workplace Law" 58 *Duke L. J.*, 1231, 1311 (2009).
130. For example, *Dobson v. Comm'r*, 320 U.S. 489, 503–504 (1943).
131. *Thor Power Tool Co. v. Comm'r*, 439 U.S. 522, 543 (1979).

There are pockets of difference, however. For instance, subchapter J of Chapter 1 of the I.R.C. describes income taxation of estates, trusts, and their beneficiaries. This subchapter is heavily influenced by non-tax trusts and estates accounting concepts.

[2] Predecessor Regimes

The historical origins of a tax occasionally influence the interpretation of its current version. Above, we saw the *Bob Jones* case, in which the Supreme Court invoked the common law charitable public purposes doctrine in construing the modern tax-exempt organizations statute.[132] In addition, in the early years of the modern federal income tax, there was interplay between the income tax and the excess profits tax, especially as to consolidated returns.[133] And, of course, the patterns of amendment of a statute over time can show a court the direction charted by the legislature.

Occasional examples also exist at the state and local levels. For instance, a sale for sales tax purposes typically is understood as a transfer of property or services for consideration. Consideration in the sales tax context evolved from the concept of consideration in the law of contracts.[134] Thus, contract cases have sometimes been invoked to resolve sales tax consideration issues.[135]

Nonetheless, the above are not the norm. Predecessor regimes do not figure in most state or federal tax cases, and when they do appear they usually are compounding considerations, not outcome determinative factors.

[3] Law from Other Jurisdictions

Federal tax law sometimes incorporates state law for particular purposes. As examples, (1) the determination of whether individuals are married for federal tax purposes starts with state marriage rules (with a number of federal overlays); (2) state law creates property interests to which federal consequences then attach when the IRS seeks to effect collection via liens, levies, or foreclosure suits; and (3) state property law helps determine which assets are included in the decedent's gross estate for federal estate tax purposes.[136] Outside of such incorporation situations, however, state law definitions generally are not controlling in the federal tax context.[137]

132. *See* §15.05[A][5] *supra*.
133. *See* Harold Dubroff (Chicago, Commerce Clearing House, 1979) *The United States Tax Court: An Historical Analysis*, pp. 10–11.
134. *Monarch Beverage Co. v. Indiana Dep't of Revenue*, 589 N.E.2d 1209, 1212 (Ind. Tax Ct. 1992).
135. For example, *Sparks Nugget, Inc. v. State ex rel. Dep't of Taxation*, 179 P.3d 570, 575 n. 15 (Nev. 2008) (per curiam).
136. In ascertaining the meaning of state property laws, the federal courts consider themselves bound by decisions of the highest court of the state in question but do not consider themselves bound by decisions of lower state courts. *Comm'r v. Estate of Bosch*, 387 U.S. 456, 464–465 (1967); *see* Paul L. Caron, "The Role of State Court Decisions in Federal Tax Litigation: *Bosch, Erie*, and Beyond" 71 *Or. L. Rev.*, 781 (1992); William H. Scharf, "State Law in the Tax Court - Controlling Precedents" 26 *Tax Law*, 293 (1973).
137. For example, *Heiner v. Mellon*, 304 U.S. 271, 279 & n. 7 (1938).

American courts rarely advert to how the courts of other countries have decided similar issues. In one case, the Supreme Court found British decisions as to what constitutes income to be "quite without value" in defining income for federal tax purposes because of differences in context.[138] In a landmark case, the Court held that the availability of the foreign tax credit depends on federal standards not "foreign characterizations and classifications."[139]

States are far more likely to incorporate federal law. States income taxes, for example, often start with the federal income tax as their base, to which adjustments are then made. Similarly, state tax decisions quite often cite federal cases.[140]

[B] Legislative Direction of Interpretation

To what extent do American legislatures attempt to control the interpretive methods used by American courts? The most common and uncontroversial way is by defining the terms used in statutes. Such definitions are typical elements of particular sections. In addition, "dictionary acts" – that is, sections providing definitions to be applied widely across a body of statutes – are sometimes used. The US Code,[141] the I.R.C.,[142] and many state codes[143] have dictionary acts.

More assertively, legislatures could attempt to enact more or less specific, more or less comprehensive directions to courts as to interpretive methods to apply. Congress has not enacted such a general statute.[144] From time to time, some states have. Reflecting the ebb and flow of cherished values, the commands of such statutes have included: narrow construction of statutes in derogation of the common law, liberal construction to advance statutory purpose and promote justice and literal construction to prevent judges from substituting their notions of good policy for those of the legislature.[145]

The infrequency of American statutes prescribing or circumscribing interpretive methods reflects constitutional concerns. Statutes that go too far may violate the

---

138. For example, *Merchant's Loan & Trust Co. v. Smetanka*, 255 U.S. 509, 521–522 (1921).
139. *Biddle v. Comm'r*, 302 U.S. 573, 579 (1938). *Biddle* has been reaffirmed by later cases. For example, *PPL Corp. v. Comm'r*, 133 S. Ct. 1897, 1901 (2013) (holding that "the way a foreign government characterizes its tax is not dispositive with respect to the U.S. creditability analysis").
140. A striking example involves the *Chevron* doctrine. The Supreme Court announced it as a purely federal rule. States were in no respect bound by it. Nonetheless, many state courts follow *Chevron*, incorporating it into their own law. *See* Steve R. Johnson, "*Chevron* Deference to State Tax Agencies" 59 *State Tax Notes*, 285 (2011).
141. 1 U.S.C. §§ 1 et seq.
142. I.R.C. § 7701.
143. For example, Nev. Rev. Stat. tit. 0.
144. However, several bills have been introduced which, had they been enacted, would have prohibited the federal courts from deferring to agency interpretations in the manner of the previously discussed *Chevron*, *Auer*, and *Seminole Rock* cases. For example, "Separation of Powers Restoration Act," H.R. 5, §§ 201 & 202 (January 12, 2017).
145. *See* Popkin, *supra* n. 15, § 3.05(b)(iv); Steve R. Johnson, "Statutes Requiring Plain Meaning Interpretation" 53 *State Tax Notes*, 763 (2009).

separation of powers principle by infringing on core judicial functions.[146] Indeed, on rare occasion, such statutes have been declared unconstitutional by the courts.[147]

[C] Correcting Legislative Errors

American judges of all ideological stripe accept that it is a proper judicial function to correct evident errors of the legislature - not errors of policy or judgment but blatant errors of drafting execution.

The leading manifestations of this idea are the closely connected scrivener's error and absurdity doctrines. Examples would be: (1) when the court became convinced from all relevant sources that the legislature intended the statute to contain a "not," which happened to have been omitted from the enrolled bill that passed the legislature and was signed by the chief executive; and (2) when a criminal statute provided that the violator would be "fined ... or imprisoned ... and both." The disjunction and the conjunction contradicted each other, leading the court to construe the statute as meaning "fined ... or imprisoned ... or both."[148]

A Nebraska sales tax case is another example. A company brought suit challenging imposition of the tax on parts assembled into manufacturing machinery and equipment. That state Supreme Court held for the taxpayer:

> We must assume the Legislature intended a sensible rather than absurd result in enacting a statute. And it would make very little sense to exempt assembled machinery from sales and use taxes, and to exempt each and every part of that machinery from sales and use taxes if it is purchased to replace an original part, but to impose a tax on the purchase of the same parts when they are purchased to assemble the machinery in the first place.[149]

The scrivener's error and absurdity doctrines are accepted even by textualist judges.[150] Nonetheless, these are at least two serious objections to them. First, it is unclear why the textualist judge should feel free to rewrite the statute, as opposed to the alternative of holding the absurd law unconstitutional as lacking a rational basis.

Second, beyond obvious situations like incoherence, there is no easy place at which to draw the line separating the absurd (thus amenable to judicial rewriting) from the merely unwise (thus beyond judicial correction). This may tempt courts to overreach. For instance, some courts have applied the doctrine when the statute produced "unreasonable consequences" or mere inconvenience[151] - conditions which

146. Nicholas O. Rosenkranz, "Federal Rules of Statutory Interpretation" 115 *Harv. L. Rev.*, 2085 (2002).
147. For example, *Evans v. State*, 872 A.2d 539 (Del. 2005) (per curiam); *see* Thomas A. Bishop, "The Death and Reincarnation of Plain Meaning in Connecticut" 41 *Conn. L. Rev.*, 825 (2009).
148. *United States v. Pabon*, 391 F.3d 86 (2d Cir. 2004).
149. *Concrete Inds., Inc. v. Department of Revenue*, 766 N.W.2d 103, 107 (Neb. 2009). *See* generally Steve R. Johnson, "The 'Absurd Results' Doctrine in State and Local Tax Cases" 54 *State Tax Notes*, 195 (2009).
150. But *see* John F. Manning, "The Absurdity Doctrine" 116 *Harv. L. Rev.*, 2387 (2003) (criticizing the doctrine).
151. For example, *Haugen v. Henry Cty.*, 594 S.E.2d 324, 327 (Ga. 2004).

most would see as falling short of absurdity. Most American courts are not prepared to go that far.[152]

[D] Incidence of Tax

The legal and the economic incidences of a tax often diverge. Studies of economic incidence sometimes reach conflicting conclusions. For example, it once was the standard view that the economic burden of the American corporate income tax falls mainly on shareholders. Later scholarship, however, suggested that the corporations' workers bear the lion's share of the burden, in the form of reduced wages,[153] but this conclusion has been challenged by other studies.[154]

Ascertaining the economic incidence of taxes matters a great deal for tax legislation. It typically does not matter for tax statutory interpretation. Courts are not institutionally well equipped to make – and are not supposed to make – the essentially legislative judgments of economic incidence.

It is possible, of course, that judges' assumption about distribution of economic impact may influence their approach to particular cases. One scholar saw the movement of American tax decisions in the early and mid-twentieth century as going from formalism "to a purposive approach that has expanded the concept of income." He saw this movement "[t]hough unacknowledged by the Court" as being "in keeping with" the early purpose of the income tax as reduction of economic inequality.[155]

[E] Interpreting Concessions

Concessions can be deliberate, consciously written into the statute (or sometimes the regulation) in order to further some economic, social, or political value. Concessions also can arise inadvertently, as when the revenue authority misunderstands the statute and gives it a pro-taxpayer construction not intended by the legislature.

Numerous exemptions riddle most tax statutes. They exist to foster certain kinds of economic activities or to enhance the fairness of the distribution of tax burdens. The number and size of tax exemptions creates constitutional, policy, and interpretational issues.

---

152. For example, *Ball ex rel. Ball v. Comm'r*, 742 F.3d 552, 562 (3d Cir. 2014)("Although statutory text cannot be read in a way that creates an absurdity, the payment of some taxes and not others is not an absurdity, but rather a policy choice rightly left to Congress.").
153. *See* Daniel N. Shaviro (Washington, D.C., Urban Inst. Press, 2009) *Decoding the U.S. Corporate Tax*, pp. 57–71.
154. *See* generally Kimberly A. Clausing, "Who Pays the Corporate Tax in a Global Economy?" 66 *Nat'l Tax J.*, 151 (2013); Julie-Ann Cronin, Emily Y. Liu, Laura Power & Michael Cooper, "Distributing the Corporate Income Tax: Revised U.S. Treasury Methodology" 66 *Nat'l Tax J.*, 239 (2013); Jennifer C. Gravelle, "Corporate Tax Incidence: Review of General Equilibrium Estimates and Analysis" 66 *Nat'l Tax J.*, 185 (2013); Li Liu & Rosanne Altshuler, "Measuring the Burden of the Corporate Income Tax Under Imperfect Competition" 66 *Nat'l Tax J.*, 215 (2013).
155. William B. Barker, "Statutory Interpretation, Comparative Law, and Economic Theory: Discovering the Grund of Income Taxation" 40 *San Diego L. Rev.*, 821, 823 (2003).

First, exemption may be problematic at the constitutional level. Equal protection of the laws is enjoined upon the federal government by the Fifth Amendment and upon the states by the Fourteenth Amendment of the US Constitution. Typically, however, these are weak prohibitions.

For example, in one case, the taxpayer complained that it was similarly situated to another taxpayer. The other taxpayer received a favorable exemption in the federal statute, but the complaining taxpayer did not. A panel of the circuit court was sympathetic but ultimately held that the Fifth Amendment had not been violated. The full circuit court held that the panel should not even have reached the merits, that the complaining taxpayer lacked standing to challenge the disparate treatment.[156]

State constitutions usually have equal protection components as well. In addition, the great majority of state constitutions contain some type of uniformity provision. Some such provisions apply only to property taxes while others apply to all or nearly all types of taxes. Some require only that taxes be uniform while others demand they be uniform or proportional or fair and reasonable. For the most part, state uniformity provisions have not greatly limited sales tax and income tax exemptions.[157]

Second, at the level of tax policy, widespread concessions have given rise to tax expenditure budgets prepared by both the Treasury and Congress' Joint Committee on Taxation. These budgets identify and quantify the largest exceptions to "normal" income tax principles, both exemptions and deductions. The idea is that publicity helps constrain growth of the tax expenditures, but the concept has proved to be largely a failure.[158]

Third, at the level of tax interpretation, the standard canon in both state and federal courts is that the taxpayer has the burden of proving clearly that it comes within the statutory exemption. Such exemptions are to be strictly construed, and doubts concerning the applicability of the exemptions will be resolved in favor of taxation.[159]

Sometimes this is met with a counter canon. Each exemption was enacted by the legislature to remedy one or another perceived shortcoming in the law, and courts often hold that remedial measures are construed liberally to effectuate their purposes.[160]

This raises a larger interpretational issue. We have seen many canons - the pro-taxpayer canon, the narrow construction of exemptions, the liberal construction of remedial measures, the broad construction of income, and the like[161] - that slant

156. *Apache Bend Apartments, Ltd. v. United States*, 964 F.2d 1556 (5th Cir. 1992), rev'd en banc, 987 F.2d 1174 (5th Cir. 1993).

157. *See* Steve R. Johnson, "Uniformity Clause Limitations on State Taxes" 27/3 *ABA Section of Tax'n News Quarterly*, 16 (Spring 2008).

158. *See*, e.g., Douglas A. Kahn, "A Proposed Replacement of the Tax Expenditures Concept and a Different Perspective on Accelerated Depreciation" 41 *Fla. St. U. L. Rev.* 143 (2013); Daniel N. Shaviro, "Rethinking Tax Expenditures and Fiscal Language" 57 *Tax L. Rev.*, 187 (2004).

159. *Zebra Technologies Corp. v. Topinka*, 799 N.E.2d 725, 733 (Ill. App. 2003) (citations omitted); *see*, e.g., *Comm'r v. Schleier*, 515 U.S. 323, 328 (1995).

160. For example, *A.N.B. Corp. v. Comptroller*, 1990 WL 10957, at *7 (Md. Tax Ct. 1969); Steve R. Johnson, "Interpreting State Tax Exemptions, Deductions, and Credits" 51 *State Tax Notes*, 607 (2009).

161. For a more complete list of preferential canons in tax, *see* Steve R. Johnson, "The Canon that Tax Penalties Should Be Strictly Construed" 3 *Nev. L.J.*, 495-496 (2003).

interpretation in one direction or the other. Why should there be any thumb on the scale at all?

The alternative to tilted construction is construing the statute just as it is, with preference to neither taxpayers nor the IRS and to neither one type of statute nor another. Such constructional neutrality is not a new idea. Judge Cooley advocated it in his influential treatise,[162] and other judges and commentators have sought to keep the flame alive in ensuing generations.[163] Despite official endorsement of neutral interpretation in some decisions,[164] the courts have yet to rid themselves of the various preferential canons.

Concessions also may arise as a result of mistakes in enforcement. The IRS states that its revenue rulings and procedures may generally be relied upon as precedents,[165] and the IRS usually does adhere to the positions it takes in such guidance documents. Sometimes, however, the IRS takes audit or litigation positions contrary to such guidance - without having formally revoked that guidance.

What if, as a matter of substantive tax law, the guidance document was wrong and the subsequent, inconsistent IRS audit or litigation position is right? Can taxpayers ask the courts to hold the IRS to the earlier, incorrect position? Doing so would promote administrative consistency but at the cost of enshrining substantive error.

The issue has been litigated sporadically for generations. Yet, unfortunately, the matter remains unsettled. The majority view, and the better view, is that there is no judicially enforceable duty of consistency on the IRS in such situations.[166] However, some cases - especially Tax Court cases - are to the contrary.[167]

[F] Abuse of Law

American courts have been schizophrenic in their reactions to tax minimization schemes that adhere to the letter of the law but produce results which seem "too good to be true." For instance, in one case, a corporation engaged in a convoluted multi-party transaction admittedly for no purpose other than to achieve an income tax result better than would have obtained under a straight-forward deal structure. The Tax Court held against the corporation, but the circuit court reversed.[168] In another case, a corporation reorganized its operations to move income out of the US in order to defer imposition of US tax. The Tax Court upheld both the deficiency and the penalties

162. Thomas M. Cooley (2nd edn, Chicago, Callaghan, 1886) *A Treatise on the Law of Taxation*, p. 272.
163. For example, Scalia & Garner, *supra* n. 34, § 62; Steve R. Johnson, "Tilted versus Reasonable Interpretation of Tax Laws" 58 *State Tax Notes*, 277 (2010).
164. For example, *White v. United States*, 305 U.S. 281, 292 (1938).
165. For example, IRS Proc. Reg. § 601.601(d)(2)(v)(e).
166. *See* Steve R. Johnson, "An IRS Duty of Consistency: The Failure of Common Law Making and a Proposed Statutory Solution" 77 *Tenn. L. Rev.*, 563 (2010) (discussing the cases and their rationales).
167. For example, *Dixon v. Comm'r*, 141 T.C. 173, 185–188 (2013).
168. *Chamberlin v. Comm'r*, 207 F.2d 462, 471–472 (6th Cir. 1953).

determined by the IRS, but the circuit court reversed, holding the transaction valid for tax purposes.[169]

The confusion is attributable primarily to three causes. First, American courts (and the IRS) have been exceedingly sloppy in defining and applying anti-abuse doctrines. These doctrines include sham, substance-over-form, lack of business purpose, step transaction doctrine, and economic substance doctrine.[170] They have been applied in thousands of cases, but courts have disagreed as to: (1) whether they are separate tests or the same tests bearing names; (2) if they are separate, which tests should be applied when; (3) what the elements of each test are; and even (4) whether particular tests are legitimate at all.

A high-water mark of such disagreement occurred in the *Coltec* case. The trial court, the Court of Federal Claims, upheld benefits claimed via a corporate tax shelter. In so doing, the court saw one of the key anti-abuse rules, the economic substance doctrine, as unconstitutional, as a judge-made rule adding substantive requirements Congress omitted from the statute. The court said:

> where a taxpayer has satisfied all statutory requirements established by Congress ... use of the economic substance doctrine to trump mere compliance with the [I.R.C.] would violate the separation of powers.[171]

The appellate court reversed and held for the government. It held that the separation of powers is not traduced "when the judiciary goes beyond the literal language of a statute in order to give effect to its purpose."[172]

The second root of the confusion is the failure of the Supreme Court to lay down clear principles for lower courts to follow. *Gregory v. Helvering* was a pivotal early case. The taxpayer wanted to receive a dividend from her corporation but did not want to pay the high tax attaching to a dividend. Accordingly, she structured the transactions to come within the corporate reorganization provisions, yielding lower tax if the scheme succeeded. The trial court (the ancestor of the current Tax Court) held for the taxpayer. The circuit court reversed, and the Supreme Court agreed with the circuit court. The Court conceded:

> The legal right of a taxpayer to decrease the amount of what otherwise would be his taxes, or altogether avoid them, by means which the law permits, cannot be doubted.[173]

169. *United Parcel Serv. of Am., Inc. v. Comm'r*, 254 F.3d 1014 (11th Cir. 2001).
170. "[T]ax law deals in economic realities, not legal abstractions." *Comm'r v. Southwest Exploration Co.*, 350 U.S. 308, 315 (1956). For description of some of the anti-abuse rules, *see* Joseph Bankman, "The Economic Substance Doctrine" 74 *S. Cal. L. Rev.*, 5 (2000). Boris I. Bittker, "Pervasive Judicial Doctrines in the Construction of the Internal Revenue Code" 21 *How. L. J.*, 693 (1978).
171. *Coltec Inds., Inc. v. United States*, 62 Fed. Cl. 716, 755–756 (2004).
172. 454 F.3d 1340, 1354 (Fed. Cir. 2006).
173. *Gregory v. Helvering*, 293 U.S. 465, 469 (1935). There is an extensive literature on *Gregory* and its aftermath. For example, Assaf Likhovski, "The Duke and the Lady: Helvering v. Gregory and the History of Tax Avoidance Adjudication" 25 *Cardozo L. Rev.*, 953 (2004).

Nonetheless, the Court held against the taxpayer. It concluded, without textual support, that when Congress used the term "reorganization," it intended to embrace only transactions motivated by business purposes, not by tax reduction motives.

In ensuing decades, opinions differed as to whether this approach was limited to the corporate reorganization provisions or was a tool of statutory interpretation applicable to the entire I.R.C. Compounding the difficulty, ensuing Supreme Court tax decisions sometimes took a strict "letter of the I.R.C." tack but other times leavened text with anti-abuse rationales.[174]

The third root of the problem is Congress. Despite the evident confusion of the courts, Congress was slow to intervene. Numerous specific anti-avoidance statutes existed, as did the judicial anti-abuse doctrines noted above. Finally, in 2010, Congress enacted the country's first general anti-abuse rule: I.R.C. § 7701(o). It provides in key part:

> In the case of any transaction to which the economic substance doctrine is relevant, such transaction shall be treated as having economic substance only if—
> (A) the transaction changes in a meaningful way (apart from Federal income tax effects) the taxpayer's economic position, and
> (B) the taxpayer has a substantial purpose (apart from Federal income tax effects) for entering into such transaction.[175]

This is an improvement over the pre-codification version of the economic substance doctrine. Courts had disagreed whether, in order for the claimed tax benefits of a transaction to be upheld, there had to be both economic effect and non-tax business purpose. They also had disagreed as to the quanta of economic effect and business purpose required. The statute clarifies that the requirement is conjunctive and that the required quanta are "meaningful" and "substantial."

Yet "meaningful" and "substantial" are hardly terms of crystal clarity. Moreover, the introductory phrase clouds the matter considerably. By its terms, the codified economic substance doctrine does not apply to all transactions. The statute itself does not define when the doctrine is "relevant" and when it is not. Non-authoritative legislative history suggests that history, not logic, is the touchstone of relevance.[176] It is plain that § 7701(o) will be controversial for decades.

---

174. *Compare Gitlitz*, § VA1 above (literal interpretation) *to Frank Lyon Co. v. United States*, 435 U.S. 561, 583–584 (1978) (offering a multi-factoral test without clarifying whether it applies only to sale-leaseback transactions or more generally) *to Knetsch v. United States*, 364 U.S. 361, 366 (1960) (using a broad, common law anti-abuse approach). The majority view is that *Gregory* applies broadly rather than being limited to corporate reorganizations. *See Higgins v. Smith*, 308 U.S. 473, 476 (1940).

175. I.R.C. § 7701(o)(1). To put further teeth in the requirement, a penalty of as much as 40% of the understatement can be imposed as to tax benefits claimed in violation of the economic substance requirement. I.R.C. §§ 6662(b)(6) & (i).

176. Staff of Jt. Comm. on Tax'n (March 21, 2010) *Technical Explanation of the Revenue Provisions of the "Reconciliation Act of 2010," as Amended, in Combination with the "Patient Protection and Affordable Care Act,"* p. 152 (referring to transactions respected under "longstanding judicial and administrative practice" and listing examples); *see also* IRS Notice 2010-62, 2010-2 C.B. 411.

Later case law continues the muddle. On the one hand, many courts continue to say that literal compliance with the requirements set out in an I.R.C. section is not enough if the underlying transaction does not comport with a perceived or imagined congressional purpose behind the section.[177] But other cases have reined in what they saw as abuse by the IRS, not the taxpayer, i.e., the IRS inappropriately using generalized anti-abuse doctrines to deny taxpayers benefits to which they were entitled under the I.R.C. sections at issue.[178] The trial court/circuit court disagreements described above are mirrored in subsequent federal cases.[179]

For the most part, the states do not have well-developed general anti-abuse tax rules. They fall into three patterns. Some take a generally pro-taxpayer view. Others rely on specific anti-abuse rules supplemented by the substance-over-form doctrine.[180] Only a few states have well-developed economic substance or comparable rules.[181]

177. For example, *Countryside Ltd. P'ship v. Comm'r*, T.C. Memo. 2008-3.
178. For example, *Summa Holdings, Inc. v. Comm'r*, 848 F.3d 779, 781 (6th Cir. 2017)(comparing the position of the IRS to Caligula's tax practices and rejecting the IRS's denial of "relief to a set of taxpayers who complied in full with the printed and accessible words of the tax laws"); *Wright v. Comm'r*, 809 F.3d 877, 884-85 (6th Cir. 2016)(finding no sensible tax policy that is advanced by the statute at issue but holding for the taxpayers because they complied with the statute as written).
179. In both *Summa* and *Wright, supra*, the circuit court reversed Tax Court decisions in favor of the IRS. A different case was reminiscent of the *Coltec* controversy described above. The trial court held for the taxpayer and sharply criticized the IRS' overreaching in applying the anti-abuse doctrines. The circuit court found no overreaching and held for the IRS. *Santander Holdings USA, Inc. v. United States*, 844 F.3d 115 (1st Cir. 2016), rev'g, 977 F. Supp. 2d 46 (D. Mass. 2013) & 144 F. Supp. 3d 239 (D. Mass. 2015).
180. *See* Steve R. Johnson, "Substance and Form in State Taxation" 50 *State Tax Notes*, 239 (2008).
181. *See*, e.g., Peter L. Faber, "Business Purpose and Economic Substance in State Taxation" 55 *State Tax Notes*, 331 (2010); Jeffrey C. Glickman & Clark R. Calhoun, "The 'States' of the Federal Common Law Tax Doctrines" 61 *Tax Law.*, 1181 (2008).

Bibliography

CHAPTER 1: A REFLECTION ON METHODS AND ISSUES

Alexy, Robert. *A Theory of Legal Argumentation*. Translated by Ruth Adler & Neil MacCormick (Oxford: Clarendon Press, 1989).

Augustine, Saint. *The Work of Saint Augustine: A Translation for the 21st Century*, Part II/2, Letters (Epistulae) 100-155. Translated by Ronald Teske (Hyde Park, NY: New City Press, 2003).

Benson, Robert. *The Interpretation Game: How Judges and Lawyers Make the Law* (Durham, NC: Carolina Academic Press, 2008).

Brożek, Bartosz. *Defeasibility of Legal Reasoning* (Kraków: Zakamycze, 2004).

Dworkin, Ronald. *Taking Rights Seriously* (Cambridge: Harvard University Press, 1978).

Dworkin, Ronald. 'Law as Interpretation'. 60 *Texas Law Review* 527 (1982).

Dworkin, Ronald. *Law's Empire* (Cambridge: Harvard University Press, 1986).

Epstein, Lee and Jack Knight. 'The New Institutionalism, Part II'. 7(2) *Law & Cts.*: 4 (1997).

Fish, Stanley E. *Is There a Text in This Class?: The Authority of Interpretive Communities* (Cambridge: Harvard University Press, 1980).

Fish, Stanley E. *Doing What Comes Naturally: Change, Rhetoric, and the Practice of Theory in Literature and Legal Studies* (Durham, NC: Duke University Press, 1989).

Galilei, Galileo. *Edizione nazionale delle Opere di Galileo Galilei*, A. Favaro (ed.), edition of 1968, vol. V.

Gilman, Howard. 'The New Institutionalism, Part I: More and Less Than Strategy: Some Advantages to Interpretative Institutionalism in the Analysis of Judicial Politics'. 7(1) *Law & Cts.*: 6 (1997).

Hacking, Ian. *Why Does Language Matter to Philosophy?* (Cambridge: Cambridge University Press, 1975).

Hart, Herbert L.A. *The Concept of Law* (Oxford: Oxford University Press, 1961).

Heise, Michael. 'The Past, Present, and Future of Empirical Legal Scholarship: Judicial Decision Making and the New Empiricism'. 4 *University of Illinois Law Review* 819-850 (2002).

Kalinowski, Jerzy. *La Logique des normes* (Paris: Presses Universitaires de France, 1972).

Moore, George E. *Principia Ethica* (Cambridge: Cambridge University Press, 1903).

Moore, Michael S. 'The Interpretive Turn in Modern Theory: A Turn for The Worse?' 41(4) *Stanford Law Review* 871-957 (1989).

Perelman, Chaim and Lucie Olbrechts-Tyteca. *Traité de l'argumentation: La nouvelle rhétorique* (Paris: Presses Universitaires de France, 1958).

Perelman, Chaim and Lucie Olbrechts-Tyteca. *The New Rhetoric: A Treatise on Argumentation*. Translated by John Wilkinson and Purcell Weaver (Notre Dame: University of Notre Dame Press, 1969).

Posner, Richard A. 'What Do Judges Maximize? (The Same Thing Everybody Else Does)'. 3(1) *Supreme Court Economic Review* 1-42 (1993).

Rowland, C.K. and Robert A. Carp. *Politics and Judgment in Federal District Courts* (Lawrence: University Press of Kansas, 1996).

Russell, Bertrand. *Principles of Mathematics* (Cambridge: Cambridge University Press, 1903).

Viehweg, Theodor. *Topik und Jurisprudenz*. 5th edn (München: C.H. Beck, 1974).

Wittgenstein, Ludwig. *Philosophical Investigations*. Translated by G.E.M. Anscombe. 3rd edn (New York: MacMillan Publishing Co., 1958).

CHAPTER 2: AUSTRALIA

Avery Jones, John, Luc De Broe, Maarten Ellis, Kees van Raad, Jean-Pierre Le Gall, Henri Torrione, Toshio Miyatake, Sidney Roberts, Sanford Goldberg, Jürgen Killius, Guglielmo Maisto, Federico Giuliani, Richard Vann, David Ward and Bertil Wiman. 'Treaty Conflicts in Categorizing Income as Business Profits Caused by Differences in Approach between Common Law and Civil Law'. 57(6) *Bulletin for International Taxation* 237-248 (2003).

Bailey, Kenneth H. 'The Uniform Income Tax Plan (1942)'. In W. Prest and R.L. Mathews (eds), *The Development of Australian Fiscal Federalism: Selected Readings* (Canberra: Australian National University Press, 1980), 309-327.

Bain, Kathrin, Richard Krever and Anthony van der Westhuysen. 'The Influence of Alternative Model Tax Treaties on Australian Treaties'. 26(1) *Australian Tax Forum* 31-49 (2011).

Bevan, Chris. 'GST on Long-Term Non-reviewable Contracts: Unresolved Transitional Problems'. 9(1) *The Tax Specialist* 28-38 (2005).

Blackstone, William. *Commentaries on the Laws of England* (Oxford: Clarendon Press, 1765).

Boucher, Trevor. *Blatant, Artificial and Contrived: Tax Schemes of the 70s and 80s* (Canberra: Australian Taxation Office, 2010). Available at: http://www.ato.gov.au/super/content.aspx?menuid = 39504&doc = /content/00244226.htm&page = 3#P63_15145 (accessed on 8 March 2013).

Brooks, Neil. 'The Responsibility of Judges in Interpreting Tax Legislation'. In Graeme Cooper (ed.), *Tax Avoidance and the Rule of Law* (Amsterdam: IBFD, 1997), 93-129.

Butlin, Sydney J. and Carl B. Schedvin. *War Economy, 1942-1945* (Canberra: Australian War Memorial, 1977).

Cassidy, Julie. *Concise Income Tax*. 5th edn (Sydney: Federation Press, 2010).

Committee on Uniform Taxation (Professor R.C. Mills, chair), *Report* (Canberra: Commonwealth Government Printer, 28 March 1942).

De Jonge, Alice. 'Australia'. In Dinah Shelton (ed.), *International Law and Domestic Legal Systems: Incorporation, Transformation, and Persuasion* (Oxford: Oxford University Press, 2011), 23-54.

Dick, Robert A. 'A Loss of State Autonomy: Implications of the *Ha* and *Hammond* Decisions'. 27(1) *Australian Tax Review* 30-40 (1998).

Ebrill, Liam, Michael Keen, Jean-Paul Bodin and Victoria Summers. *The Modern VAT* (Washington, DC: International Monetary Fund, 2001).

Edmonds, Justice Richard. 'Interpretation of s 11-15: Significance of the Text, Context and History'. 12(3) *Australian GST Journal* 79-89 (2012).

Edmundson, Peter. 'GST and Involuntary Supplies'. 6(2) *Journal of Australian Taxation* 224-244 (2006).

Evans, Michael. 'Commentary: Taxation of Goods and Services in Australia'. In Chris Evans and Richard Krever (eds), *Australian Business Tax Reform in Retrospect and Prospect* (Sydney: Thomson, 2009), 563-571.

de la Feria, Rita and Richard Krever. 'Ending VAT Exemptions: Towards a *Post*-Modern VAT'. In Rita de la Feria (ed.), *VAT Exemptions: Consequences and Design Alternatives* (Alphen aan den Rijn: Kluwer Law International, 2013), 3-36.

Freiberg, Arie. 'Enforcement Discretion and Taxation Offences'. 3(1) *Australian Tax Forum* 55-92 (1986).

French, Chief Justice Robert. 'If they could see us now – what would the founders say?.' John Curtin Prime Ministerial Library Anniversary Lecture, 18 July 2013. Available at: http://www.hcourt.gov.au/publications/speeches/current/speeches-by-chief-justice-french-ac (accessed on 6 September 2013).

Gerangelos, Peter. 'Tax Coordination between Regions in Australia – Role of the Courts'. In Michael Lang, Pasquale Pistone, Josef Schuch and Claus Staringer (eds), *Horizontal Tax Coordination* (Amsterdam: IBFD, 2012), 53-80.

Gordon, Justice Michelle. 'The Commonwealth's Taxing Power and Its Limits – Are We There Yet?'. 36(3) *Melbourne University Law Review* 1037-1063 (2013).

Hanks, Peter. 'Constitutional Issues of Australian Taxation'. In Richard Krever (ed.), *Australian Taxation: Principles and Practice* (Melbourne: Longman Professional, 1987), 37-61.

Harris, Peter. *Metamorphosis of the Australasian Income Tax, 1866-1922* (Sydney: Australian Tax Research Foundation, 2002).

Hill, Hon. Justice Graham. 'Some Thoughts on the Principles Applicable to the Interpretation of the GST'. 6(1) *Journal of Australian Taxation* 1-31 (2003).

Hill, Justice Graham. 'The Interpretation of Double Taxation Agreements – The Australian Experience'. 57(8) *Bulletin for International Taxation* 320-327 (2003).

Hill, Peter. 'Taxation of Goods and Services in Australia: Past, Present, and Future'. In Chris Evans and Richard Krever (eds), *Australian Business Tax Reform in Retrospect and Prospect* (Sydney: Thomson, 2009), 547-561.

James, Kathryn. *The Rise of the Value-Added Tax* (New York: Cambridge University Press, 2015).

Kobetsky, Michael. *International Taxation of Permanent Establishments: Principles and Policy* (Cambridge: Cambridge University Press, 2011).

Krever, Richard. 'Tax Reform in Australia: Base-Broadening Down Under'. 34(2) *Canadian Tax Journal*: 346-394 (1986).

Krever, Richard. 'Involuntary and Statutory Supplies – The Australian GST Base Narrows'. 16(1) *International VAT Monitor*: 19-22 (2005).

Krever, Richard. 'Interpreting Income Tax Laws in the Common Law World'. In Markus Achatz, Tina Ehrke-Rabel, Johannes Heinrich, Roman Leitner and Otto Taucher (eds), *Steuerrecht Verfassungsrecht Europarecht: Festschrift für Hans Georg Ruppe* (Vienna: Facultas Verlags- und Buchhandels AG, 2007), 354-378.

Krever, Richard. Book Review: *The Future of Indirect Taxation: Recent Trends in VAT and GST Systems Around the World* (T. Ecker, M. Lang and I. Lejeune, eds, Wolters Kluwer, 2012). 12(4) *Australian GST Journal* 186-188 (2012).

Krever, Richard and Peter Mellor, 'The Development of Centralised Income Taxation in Australia, 1901-1942'. In Peter Harris and Dominic de Cogan (eds), *Studies in the History of Tax Law, Vol. 7* (Oxford: Hart Publishing, 2015), 363.

Krever, Richard and Peter Mellor, 'Australia'. In Michael Lang, Jeffrey Owens, Pasquale Pistone, Alexander Rust, Josef Schuch and Claus Staringer (eds), *GAARs: A Key Element of Tax Systems in the Post-BEPS World* (Amsterdam: IBFD Publications, 2016), 45.

Krever, Richard and Jonathan Teoh, *Justice Edmonds and Interpretation of Australia's GST Legislation*, 45(2) Australia Tax Review 121 (2016).

Lang, Michael and Florian Brugger. 'The Role of the OECD Commentary in Tax Treaty Interpretation'. 23(2) *Australian Tax Forum* 95-108 (2008).

Law Reform Commission of Victoria. *Redraft of Division 16E of Part III of the Income Tax Assessment Act 1936*. Melbourne: Law Reform Commission of Victoria, 1992.

Lehmann, Geoffrey. 'The Income Tax Judgments of Sir Garfield Barwick: A Study in the Failure of the New Legalism'. 9(3) *Monash University Law Review* 115-156 (1983).

Lehmann, Geoffrey and Cynthia Coleman. *Taxation Law in Australia*. 5th edn (Sydney: Butterworth, 1998).

Maddock, Rodney. 'Unification of Income Taxes in Australia'. 28(3) *Australian Journal of Politics and History* 354-366 (1982).

Mellor, Peter. 'Origins of the Judicial Concept of Income in Australia'. 25(3) *Australian Tax Forum* 339-360 (2010).

Millar, Rebecca. 'What's VAT Got to Do with It?' 12(3) *Australian GST Journal* 99-124 (2012).

Morabito, Vince. 'The Constitutional Restriction on Taxes Imposed on Crown Property'. 1(1) *Journal of Australian Taxation* 41-56 (1998).

New South Wales Treasury. *Budget Paper No. 2, Budget Statement 2012-13*. Sydney: New South Wales Treasury, 12 June 2012.

OECD. *Transfer Pricing Guidelines for Multinational Enterprises and Tax Administrations* (Paris: OECD, 2010).

OECD. *Aligning Transfer Pricing Outcomes with Value Creation, Actions 8-10: Final Reports*, OECD/G20 Base Erosion and Profit Shifting Project (Paris: OECD Publishing, October 2015).

Olding, Robert. 'Interpretation of the GST Act – Towards a Principled Basis?'. In Christine Peacock (ed.), *GST in Australia: Looking Forward from the First Decade* (Sydney: Thomson, 2011), 77-96.

Parsons, Ross. 'Income Taxation: An Institution in Decay'. 13(3) *Sydney Law Review* 435-474 (1991).

Pinder, Greg. 'The Coherent Principles Approach to Tax Law Design'. (Autumn, 2005) *Economic Roundup*: 75-90.

Prebble, John. 'Income Taxation: A Structure Built on Sand'. 24(3) *Sydney Law Review*: 301-318 (2002).

Saunders, Cheryl. 'Vertical Fiscal Imbalance: Constitutional Origins'. In David Collins (ed.), *Vertical Fiscal Imbalance and the Allocation of Taxing Powers* (Sydney: Australian Tax Research Foundation, 1993, 55-64).

Saunders, Cheryl. 'The High Court, Section 90 and the Australian Federation'. In Neil Warren (ed.). *Reshaping Fiscal Federalism in Australia* (Sydney: Australian Tax Research Foundation, 1997), 21-39.

Saunders, Cheryl. 'The Uniform Income Tax Cases'. In H.P. Lee and George Winterton (eds), *Australian Constitutional Landmarks* (Cambridge: Cambridge University Press, 2003), 62-84.

Sievers, Christopher. 'GST and Compulsory Acquisitions of Land: Can You Have an "Involuntary Supply"?'. 12(4) *Australian GST Journal* 165-173 (2012).

Slater, A.H. 'Part IVA: An International Perspective'. 42(3) *Australian Tax Review* 149-159 (2013).

Smith, Julie. *Taxing Popularity*. Rev. ed. (Sydney: Australian Tax Research Foundation, 2004).

Story, Joseph. *Commentaries on the Constitution of the United States* (Boston: Hilliard, Gray, 1833).

Turnbull, I.M.L., QC. 'Clear Legislative Drafting: New Approaches in Australia'. 11(3) *Statute Law Review* 161-183 (1990).

Vann, Richard. 'Income as a Tax Base'. In Richard Krever (ed.), *Australian Taxation: Principles and Practice* (Melbourne: Longman Professional, 1987), 62-79.

Walpole, Michael. 'Sharing the "Magic Pudding" – An Australian Approach to Allocation of Taxing Rights'. In Michael Lang and Peter Melz (eds), *Value Added Tax and Direct Taxation: Similarities and Differences* (Amsterdam: IBFD, 2009), 1171-1196.

Wigney, Michael, SC. 'Text, Context and the Interpretation of a "Practical Business Tax"'. 40(2) *Australian Tax Review* 94-107 (2011).

Wattel, Peter and Otto Marres. 'The Legal Status of the OECD Commentary and Static or Ambulatory Interpretation of Tax Treaties'. 43(7/8) *European Taxation* 222-235 (2003).

CHAPTER 3: BRAZIL

Amaro, Luciano. *Direito Tributário Brasileiro.* 17th edn (São Paulo: Saraiva, 2011).

Becker, Alfredo Augusto. *Teoria Geral do Direito Tributário.* 2nd edn (São Paulo: Saraiva, 1972).

Bellan, Daniel V. 'Algumas considerações sobre a tributação dos royalties pagos a beneficiários residentes ou domiciliados no exterior'. In Heleno Tôrres (ed.), *Direito tributário internacional aplicado* (São Paulo: Quartier Latin, 2003).

Blank, Joshua and Nancy Staudt, 'Corporate Shams'. 87 (6) *New York University Law Review* (December 2012).

Cais, Cleide Previtalli. *O processo tributário* (São Paulo: Revista dos Tribunais, 2004).

Canto, Gilberto de Ulhôa. 'Elisão e Evasão'. In Ives Gandra da Silva Martins (ed.), *Elisão e Evasão Fiscal* (São Paulo: Resenha Tributária, 1988).

Carrazza, Roque Antonio. *ICMS* (São Paulo: Malheiros, 2004).

Cavalcante, Miquerlam Chaves. '"O propósito negocial e o planejamento tributário no ordenamento jurídico brasileiro'" ('"Business Purpose and the Tax Planning in the Brazilian Law'"). *Revista da PGFN* (Brasília, n. 1, 2011): 139-162.

Carvalho, Paulo de Barros. 'O absurdo da interpretação econômica do "fato gerador" - direito e sua autonomia - o paradoxo da interdisciplinariedade'. *Revista de Direito Tributário*, No. 97, 2007.

Costa, Alcides Jorge. *ICM na Constituição e na Lei Complementar* (São Paulo: Resenha Tributária, 1978).

Dória, Antonio Roberto Sampaio. *Discriminação de Rendas Tributárias* (São Paulo: José Bushatsky, 1972).

Dória, Antonio Roberto Sampaio. *Elisão e Evasão Fiscal.* 2nd edn (São Paulo: José Bushatsky, 1977).

Falcão, Amílcar de Araújo. *Introdução ao Direito Tributário* (Rio de Janeiro: Forense, 1959).

Greco, Marco Aurélio. 'Constitucionalidade do parágrafo único do artigo 116 do CTN' ('Constitutionality of the Sole Paragraph of Article 116 of the National Tax Code'). In Valdir Rocha Oliveira (ed.), *O planejamento tributário e a Lei Complementar 104* (São Paulo: Dialética, 2001).

Greco, Marco Aurélio. *Planejamento Tributário* ("*Tax Planning*") (São Paulo: Dialética, 2004).

Gutierrez, Miguel Delgado. '"O Planejamento Tributário e o Business Purpose'" ('"Tax Planning and Business Purpose'"). *Revista Dialética de Direito Tributário* (São Paulo, 2014), n. 231

Huck, Hermes Marcelo., *Evasão e Elisão: rotas internacionais ("Tax Evasion and Tax Avoidance: International Routes)"* (São Paulo: Saraiva, 1997).

Jardim Neto, José Gomes. 'Os produtos digitais vendidos na Internet e o ICMS'. In Luís Eduardo Schoueri (ed.), *Internet: o direito na era virtual* (Rio de Janeiro: Forense, 2001).

Leonardos, Gabriel Francisco. 'O imposto de renda de fonte sobre os pagamentos ao exterior por serviços técnicos - análise de um caso de renúncia fiscal do Brasil.' In *Revista dialética de direito tributário*, no. 40 (São Paulo: Dialética, 1999).

Machado, Hugo de Brito. 'ISS e o arrendamento mercantile' (in *Revista Dialética de Direito Tributário*, No. 185, 2011).

Machado, Hugo de Brito. *Mandado de segurança em matéria tributária* (*Writ of Mandamus in Tax Matters*) S(ão Paulo: Revista dos Tribunais, 2006).

Machado, Hugo de Brito. *Curso de Direito Tributário*. 5th edn (Rio de Janeiro: Forense, 1992).

Martins, Ives Gandra da Silva (ed.). *Elisão e Evasão Fiscal* (São Paulo: Resenha Tributária, 1988).

Martins, Ives Gandra da Silva. 'Norma Antielisão é incompatível com o sistema constitucional brasileiro'. In Valdir Rocha Oliveira (ed.), *O planejamento tributário e a Lei Complementar 104* (São Paulo: Dialética, 2001).

Mello, José Eduardo Soares de. *ICMS: teoria e prática* (São Paulo: Dialética, 2008).

Nogueira, Johnson Barbosa. *A Interpretação Econômica no Direito Tributário* (São Paulo: Resenha Tributária, 1982).

OECD. *Model Tax Convention on Income and on Capital - Condensed Version* (OECD: Paris, 2010).

Pereira, Caio Mário da Silva. *Instituições de Direito Civil*. Vol. I, 23rd edn (Rio de Janeiro: Forense, 2009).

Pereira, Caio Mário da Silva. *Instituições de Direito Civil*. Vol. II, 19th edn (Rio de Janeiro: Forense, 2000).

Pietruszkiewicz, Christopher M. 'Economic Substance and the Standard of Review'. 60 *Alabama Law Review* 346-347 (2009).

Ribeiro, Ricardo Lodi. O dever de comunicar à Fazenda Pública o planejamento fiscal no Brasil ('"The obligation to disclose tax planning to Tax Authorities in Brazil'"), in (242) *Revista Dialética de Direito Tributário*: 101 (São Paulo, 2015).

Rocha, Sérgio A. 'O Ato Declaratório n. 1/2000 e a ilegalidade da obrigação de retenção do imposto de renda na fonte'. In *Revista dialética de direito tributário*, no. 58 (São Paulo: Dialética, 2000).

Rodrigues, Silvio. *Direito Civil*. Vol. II (São Paulo: Saraiva, 2002).

Rolim, João Dácio. *Normas antielisivas tributárias* ("*Anti-avoidance Tax Rules*). São Paulo: Dialética, 2001.

Rothmann, Gerd W. 'Problemas de qualificação na aplicação das convenções contra a bitributação internacional'. In *Revista dialética de direito tributário*, no. 76 (São Paulo: Dialética, 2002).

Schoueri, Luís Eduardo. 'O desafio do planejamento tributário'. In Luís Eduardo Schoueri (ed.), *Planejamento tributário e o 'propósito negocial'* (São Paulo: Quartier Latin, 2010).

Schoueri, Luís Eduardo and Ricardo André Galendi Jr. Transparência Fiscal e Reciprocidade nas Perspectivas Interna e Internacional. In Valdir de Oliveira Rocha (ed.),

Grandes Questões Atuais do Direito Tributário, vol. 19 (São Paulo: Dialética, 2015), 252-254.

Schwarz, Jonathan. *Schwarz on Tax Treaties* (Surrey: Wolters Kluwer, 2009).

Souza, Rubens Gomes de. *Interpretação no Direito tributário* (São Paulo: Saraiva, 1975).

Takata, Marcos Shigueo. '"Empresa-veículo e a amortização fiscal do ágio: há um problema real?'" ('"Conduit Company and goodwill amortization: is there a real problem?')". In Roberto Quiroga Mosquera and Alexsandro Broedel Lopes (eds), *Controvérsias jurídico-contábeis (aproximações e distanciamentos)*. Vol. 5 (São Paulo: Dialética, 2014).

Venosa, Silvio de Salvo. *Direito Civil*. Vol II (São Paulo: Atlas, 2001).

Vogel, Klaus. *Double Taxation Conventions* (London: Kluwer Law, 1996).

Xavier, Alberto. *Direito tributário internacional do Brasil* (Rio de Janeiro: Forense, 2004).

CHAPTER 4: CANADA

Arnold, Brian, et al. *Timing and Income Taxation: The Principles of Income Measurement for Tax Purposes*. 2nd edn (Canadian Tax Foundation, 2015).

Brooks, Neil. 'The Appropriate Role of Courts in Interpreting GST Legislation: Reflections on the Canadian Experience'. 6 *Australian GST Journal* 1 (2006).

Brooks, Neil. 'The Responsibility of Judges in Interpreting Tax Legislation'. In Graeme S. Cooper, *Tax Avoidance and the Rule of Law* (International Bureau of Fiscal Documentation, 1997), 93.

Brooks, Neil and Kim Brooks. 'The Supreme Court's 2012 Tax Cases: Formalism Trumps Pragmatism and Good Sense'. 64 *Supreme Court Law Review* 267 (2014).

Brooks, Neil and Kim Brooks. 'The Supreme Court's 2013 Tax Cases: Side-Stepping the Interesting, Important and Difficult Issues'. 68 *Supreme Court Law Review* 335 (2015).

Christians, Allison. 'While Parliament Sleeps: Tax Treaty Practice in Canada'. 10 *Journal of Parliamentary & Political Law* 15 (2016).

Constitution Act, 1867 (UK), 30 & 31 Vict, c 3, ss 91(3), 92(2), 92(9), reprinted in RSC 1985, Appendix II, No 5.

Convention on Mutual Administrative Assistance on Tax Matters (4 April 1995), ETS No 127.

Department of Finance Canada. *Tax Treaties: In Force*. https://www.fin.gc.ca/treaties-conventions/in_force--eng.asp.

Department of Finance Canada. *Tax Information Exchange Agreements*, http://www.fin.gc.ca/treaties-conventions/tieaaerf-eng.asp.

Department of Justice. *Harmonization Acts and Related Information*, http://www.justice.gc.ca/eng/csj-sjc/harmonization/bijurilex/harmonization-loisdharmonisation.html.

Department of Justice. *Policies and Directives*, http://www.justice.gc.ca/eng/csj-sjc/harmonization/bijurilex/policies-politiques.html.

Duff, David G. 'Interpreting the Income Tax Act – Part I: Interpretative Doctrines'. 47 *Canadian Tax Journal* 464 (1999).

Duff, David G. 'Interpreting the Income Tax Act – Part II: Toward a Pragmatic Approach'. 47 *Canadian Tax Journal* 741 (1999).

Duff, David G. 'Justice Iacobucci and the 'Golden and Straight Metwand' of Canadian Tax Law'. 57 University of Toronto Law Journal 525 at 567 (2007).

Excise Tax Act. RSC 1985, c E-15.

Graham, Randal N. *Statutory Interpretation: Theory and Practice*. 1st edn (Toronto: Emond Montgomery Publications, 2001).

Income Tax Act, RSC 1985, c 1 (5th Supp).

Income Tax Conventions Interpretation Act, RSC 1985, c I-4.

Income Tax Regulations, CRC, c. 945.

Larre, Tamara. 'Supreme Court of Canada Tax Judgements of Justice LeBel'. 70 *Supreme Court Law Review* (2015).

Li, Jinyan and David Piccolo. 'Reviving the Modern Rule in the Interpretation of Tax Statutes: Baby Steps Taken in Canada Trustco, Mathew, Placer Dome and Imperial Oil'. 38 Supreme Court Law Review 519 (2007).

MacGregor, Ian, et al. 'The Development of the Tax Court of Canada'. 58 (Supp) Canadian Tax Journal 87(2010).

Magyar, John James. *The Evolution of Hansard Use at the Supreme Court of Canada: A Comparative Study in Statutory Interpretation*. 33 *Statute Law Review* 363 (2012).

Official Languages Act, RSC 1970, c O-2, repealed in 1988 SC 1988, c 38, s 110.

Sullivan, Ruth. 'Statutory Interpretation in the Supreme Court of Canada'. 30 *Ottawa Law Review* 175 (1999).

Sullivan, Ruth. 'Sullivan and Driedger on the Construction of Statutes'. 4th edn (Markham: Butterworths, 2002), 3.

CHAPTER 5: CHINA

Cai, Qiaoping. 'Issues of Reduction in Effectiveness of China's Tax Law' (in Chinese). 2 *Finance and Tax Law Review* (2002).

Chen, Yanzhong. *Interpretation Issues of International Tax Treaties: A Preliminary Study* IScience Press, 2010).

Cui, Wei. 'What is the "Law" in Chinese Tax Administration?'. 19(1) *Asia Pacific Law Review* 75-94. (2011).

Cui, Wei. 'Fiscal Federalism in Chinese Taxation'. 3(3) *World Tax Journal* 455-480 (2011).

Cui, Wei. 'Foreign Administrative Law and International Taxation: A Case Study of Treaty Implementation in China'. 64(1) *Administrative Law Review* 191-233 (2012).

Cui, Wei. 'Does Judicial Independence Matter? A Study of the Determinants of Administrative Litigation in an Authoritarian Regime', https://papers.ssrn.com/sol3/papers.cfm?abstract_id=2707436, August 2015.

Duan, Alex. 'Income from Sale of Carbon Credits Is Taxable Dividend, Chinese Tax Authority Says'. Tax Analysts: *Worldwide Tax Daily*, 16 November 2011.

Gao, Yang. 'Review of the Recent Development on Hong Kong Tax Regime' (in Chinese). 11 *International Taxation* 57-60 (2012).

Gu, Guoxian. 'Reflection and Perfection of the Existing Tax Litigation Mechanism' (in Chinese). 11(2) *Journal of Taxation College of Yangzhou University* 37-41 (2006).

Hu, Yuhong. *Principles and Techniques of Law* (in Chinese) (China University of Political Science and Law Press, 2002).

Ji, Weidong. 'Truth in the Law Interpretation (Part II)' (in Chinese). 1 *Peking University Law Journal* 1-12 (1999).

Jones, William C. 'Trying to Understand the Current Chinese Legal System'. In C. Stephen Hsu (ed.). *Understanding China's Legal System: Essays in Honor of Jerome A. Cohen* (New York: New York University Press, 2003).

Kong, Xiaohong. 'Legal Interpretation in China'. 6 *Connecticut Journal of International Law* 491-506 (1990).

Li, Jin. 'Teaching Taxation Law in China'. 62(5) *Bulletin for International Taxation* 183-190 (2008).

Li, Jinyan. 'The Great Fiscal Wall of China: Tax Treaties and Their Role in Defining and Defending China's Tax Base'. 66(9) *Bulletin for International Taxation* 452-479 (2012).

Liu, Jianwen. 'How the Tax Legislative Powers may be Returned to the NPC' (in Chinese). *Economic Information Daily*, 27 March 2013.

Liu, Xin and Wang Lingguang. 'Statutory Taxation and Legislation Reservation' (in Chinese). 3 *Administrative Law Review* 81-91 (2008).

Mo, Zhang. 'The Socialist Legal System with Chinese Characteristics: China's Discourse for the Rule of Law and a Bitter Experience'. 24 *Temple International & Comparative Law Journal* 1-64 (2010).

Qiu, Dongmei. 'The Concept of Beneficial Ownership in Chinas Tax Treaties – The Current State of Play'. 67(2) *Bulletin for International Taxation* 593-621 (2013).

Shen, Fujun. 'Relationship Between the Courts and Administrative Organs from the Perspective of Administrative Litigation' (in Chinese). 4 *Legal Science* 34-38 (2010).

Shen, Kui. 'Administrative Self-regulation and Rule of Administrative Law: A Preliminary Investigation' (in Chinese). 3 *Administrative Law Research* 12-17 (2011).

Sun, Jianbo. *Research on Tax Law Interpretation* (in Chinese) (Law Press, 2006).

Wang, Hongmao. 'An Analysis on the Defect in China's Tax Administrative Procedural System' (in Chinese). 290 *Taxation Research* 63-67 (2009).

Wei, Shengqiang. 'Some Thoughts on How to Improve China's Court Decisions' (in Chinese). 5 *Science of Law* 72-77 (2012).

Wei, Shengqiang. 'We Need a Uniform Legal Interpretation Law' (in Chinese). 1 *Legal Science* 32-41 (2007).

Wu, Jingsong. 'Reflection on Tax Administrative Interpretation in China' (in Chinese). 3 *Taxation Research* 69-72 (2010).

Xiong, Wei, et al. 'Discussion Forum on "The Meaning and Inspiration of the Questioning Raised by Taxpayers on the Legality of the Tax Normative Rules"' (in Chinese). 1(1) *Tax Law and Case Review*, Law Press, 1-22 (2010).

Yang, Haikun and Zhu Zhongyi. 'Investigation into the Stagnancy of the Administrative Litigation' (in Chinese). 4 *Administrative Law Review* 70-76 (1999).

Ye, Jinyu. 'Justification and Operation Guarantee of Interpretation Power of SAT' (in Chinese), 6 *The Jurist* 112-125 (2016).

Yuan, Mingsheng. 'The Legality Crisis of the Tax Administrative Crisis and the Solution' (in Chinese). 1 *Studies in Law and Business* 52-57 (2010).

Zhang, Xuebo. 'Research on Legitimacy of Tax Administrative Document' (in Chinese). 10 *Journal of South East University of Political Science and Law* 3-7 (2008).

Zhou, Yongkun. 'The Conflict Between Legal Interpretation and Government in Accordance with a System of Law' (in Chinese). 27 *Modern Law Science* 3-9 (2006).

CHAPTER 6: EUROPEAN UNION

Amand, Christian. 'VAT for Public Entities and Charities – Should the Sixth Directive Be Renegotiated?'. 6 *International VAT Monitor* 433-443 (2006).

Beaumont, P.R. 'Indirect Effect of Directives and Stare Decisis'. 55(3) *Scottish Law Gazette* 77-78 (1987).

Bengoetxea, Joxerramon. *The Legal Reasoning of the European Court of Justice* (Oxford: Oxford University Press, 1993).

Bijl, Jeroen. 'The European Union's New VAT Rules for Vouchers: The Emperor's New Clothes?'. (27) 6 *International VAT Monitor* 407-410 (2016).

Boyle, David P. 'Circumstances in Which Stare Decisis Applies'. 31(5) *Irish Law Times* 68-69 (2013).

van Brederode, Robert F. 'The Re-emergence of Gross Receipt Taxes in the US'. 19(3) *International VAT Monitor* 182-191 (2008).

van Brederode, Robert F. 'Third Party Risks and Liabilities in Case of VAT Fraud in the EU'. (34)1 *International Tax Journal* 31-39 (2008).

van Brederode, Robert F. *Systems of General Sales Taxation: Theory, Policy and Practice* (Alphen aan den Rijn: Wolters Kluwer, 2009).

Brokelind, Cecile (ed.). *Towards a Homogeneous EC Direct Tax Law: an Assessment of the Member States* (Amsterdam: IBFD, 2007).

Cappelletti, Mauro. 'The Law-Making Power of the Judges and Its Limits: A Comparative Analysis'. 8 *Monash University Law Review* 15-67 (1981-1982).

Cappelletti, Mauro. 'Is the European Court of Justice Running Wild?'. 12 *European Law Review*: 3-17 (1987).

Craig, Paul P. and Gráinne De Búrca. *EU Law: Text, Cases, and Materials* (Oxford: Oxford University Press, 2007).

Davis, Roy W. 'Liability in Damages for a Breach of Community Law: Some Reflection on the Question of Who to Sue and the Concept of "the State"'. 31(1) *European Law* Review 69-80 (2006).

Derlén, Mattias. *Multilingual Interpretation of European Union Law* (Alphen aan den Rijn: Kluwer Law International, 2009).

Ecker, Thomas. *A VAT/GST Model Convention*. Doctoral Series 25 (Amsterdam: IBFD, 2013).

Edge, Peter W. 'Decisions of the Judicial Committee of the Privy Council in other Jurisdictions: Limits of Stare Decisis in Commonwealth Jurisdictions'. 20(2) *Commonwealth Law Bulletin*: 720-727 (1994).

Edward, David. 'Judicial Activism – Myth or Reality?'. In David Campbell and Meropi Voyatzi (eds), *Legal Reasoning and Judicial Interpretation of European Law* (Essays in honour of Lord Mackenzie-Stuart) (Gosport: Trenton Publishing, 1996), 29-67.

Emmert, Frank. 'Stare Decisis: A Universally Misunderstood Idea'. 6(2) *Legisprudence*: 207-227 (2012).

Englisch, Joachim. 'Tax Coordination between member States in the EU – Role of the ECJ'. In Michael Lang et al. (eds), *Horizontal Tax Coordination* (Amsterdam: IBFD, 2012).

Fennelly, Nial. 'Legal Interpretation at the European Court of Justice'. 20(3) *Fordham International Law Journal* 656-879 (1996).

Graetz, Michael J. and Alvin C. Warren Jr. 'Dividend Taxation in Europe: When the ECJ Makes Tax Policy'. 44 *Common Market Law Review* 1577-1623 (2007).

Hahn, Walter. *Steuerpolitische Willensbildungsprozeße in der Europäischen Gemeinschaft: das Beispiel der Umsatzsteuer-Harmonisierung* (Frankfurt am Main, 1988).

Hartley, Trevor C. *The Foundations of European Community Law: An Introduction to the Constitutional and Administrative Law of the European Community*, 6th edn (Oxford: Oxford University Press, 2007).

Horspool, Margot and Matthew Humphreys. *European Union Law*, 4th edn (Oxford: Oxford University Press, 2006).

Kapteyn Paul J.G., Alison M. McDonnell, Kamiel J.M. Mortelmans and Christiaan W.A. Timmermans (eds). *The Law of the European Union and the European Communities*. 4th rev. edn (The Netherlands: Wolters-Kluwer, 2008).

Keeleng, D. 'In Praise of Judicial Activism, but What Does It Mean? And Has the European Court of Justice Ever Practiced It?'. In Curti Gialdino (ed.), *Scritti in Onore di G.F. Mancini* (Milano: Giuffré, 1998).

Kemmeren, Eric C.C.M. 'Double Tax Conventions on Income and Capital and the EU: Past, Present and Future'. 21(3) *EC Tax Review* 157-177 (2012).

Lasser, Mitchel. *Judicial Deliberations. A Comparative Analysis of Judicial Transparency and Legitimacy* (Oxford: Oxford University Press, 2004).

Littlewood, Michael. 'The Privy Council, the Source of Income and Stare Decisis'. 2 *British Tax Review* 121-145 (2004).

Maduro, Miguel P. 'Interpreting European Law: Judicial Adjudication in a Context of Constitutional Pluralism'. 1(2) *European Journal of Legal Studies* 1-21 (2007).

Manin, Philippe. 'The Nicolo case of the Conseil d'Etat: French Constitutional Law and the Supreme Administrative Court's Acceptance of the Primacy of Community Law over Subsequent National Statute Law'. *Common Market Law Review* 499 (1991).

Mikesell, John L. *Gross Receipt Taxes in State Government Finances: A Review of Their History and Performance*. Background Paper, no. 53 (Washington, DC: Tax Foundation, January 2007).

Morse, Geoffrey and Rita de la Feria. 'HMRC v Aimia Coalition Loyalty UK Ltd (UKSC): A Question Too Far?'. 3 *BTR* 287-298 (2013).

Neill, Patrick. *The European Court of Justice: A Case Study in Judicial Activism*. Evidence submitted to the House of Lords Select Committee on the European Communities, Sub-committee on the 1996 Intergovernmental Conference, Minutes of Evidence, House of Lords Session 1994-95, 18th report, p. 218.

Neville Brown, Lionel, John Bell and Jean-Michel Galabert. *French Administrative Law*, 5th edn (Oxford: Oxford University Press, 1998).

Oppenheimer, Andrew (ed.). *The Relationship between European Community Law and National Law: The Cases*. Vol. 2 (Cambridge: Cambridge University Press, 2003).

O'Shea, Tom. 'Marks and Spencer v Halsey (HM Inspector of Taxes): Restriction, Justification and Proportionality'. 15(2) *EC Tax Review* 66-82 (2006).

O'Shea, Tom. 'From Avoir Fiscal to Marks & Spencer'. 41 *Tax Notes International* 587-612 (2006).

O'Shea, Tom. 'Dividend Taxation Post-Manninen: Shifting Sands or Solid Foundations?'. 45 *Tax Notes International* 887-918 (2007).

O'Shea, Tom. *EU Tax Law and Double Tax Conventions* (London: Avoir Fiscal Limited, 2008).

O'Shea, Tom. 'EU Tax Regulatory Framework'. 955 *The Tax Journal* 21-24 (2008).

O'Shea, Tom. 'Cartesio: Moving a Company's Seat Now Easier in the EU'. 47 *Tax Notes International* 394-397 (2009).

O'Shea, Tom. 'European Tax Controversies: Quis Custodies Ipsos Custodes?'. 1 *EC Tax Journal* 39-98 (2011/12).

O'Shea, Tom. 'CFC Reforms in the UK - Some EU Law Comments'. 13(1) *EC Tax Journal*: 65-89 (2012/13).

O'Shea, Tom. 'European Tax Controversies: A British-Dutch Debate: Back to Basics and Is the ECJ Consistent?'. 1 *World Tax Journal* 100-127 (2013).

Pollicino, Oreste. 'Legal Reasoning of the Court of Justice in the Context of the Principle of Equality Between Judicial Activism and Self Restraint'. 5(3) *German Law Journal* 283-317 (2014).

Prime, T. and G. Scanlan. 'Stare Decisis and the Court of Appeal; Judicial Confusion and Judicial Reform?'. 23 *Civil Justice Quarterly* 212-227 (2004).

Rasmussen, Hjalte. 'Between Self-restraint and Activism: A Judicial Policy for the European Court'. 13 *European Law Review* 28-38 (1988).

Schermers Henry, G. and Denis F. Waelbroeck. *Judicial Protection in the European Communities*. 6th edn (Deventer: Kluwer Law International, 2001).

Schockweiler, Fernand. 'La Cour de justice des Communautés européennes dépasse-t-elle les limites de ses attributions?' ['Does the European Court of Justice Exceed Its Competences?']. 18 *Journal des Tribunaux, Droit Européen* 73-80 (1995).

Scully-Hill, Anne and Hans Mahncke. 'The Emergence of the Doctrine of Stare Decisis in the World Trade Organization Dispute Settlement System'. 36(2) *Legal Issues of Economic Integration* 133-156 (2009).

Slynn, Gordon. 'The Court of Justice of the European Communities'. 33 *International and Comparative Law Quarterly* 409-429 (1984).

Solan, Lawrence M. 'The Interpretation of Multilingual Statutes by the European Court of Justice'. 34(2) *Brooklyn Journal of International Law* 277-301 (2009).

Stein, Eric. 'Lawyers, Judges and the Making of a Transnational Constitution'. 75(1) *American Journal of International Law* 1-27 (1981).

Terra, Ben J.M. and Peter J. Wattel. *European Tax Law*. 6th edn (Deventer: Wolters Kluwer, 2012).

Toscani, Gerd. 'Translation and Law – The Multilingual Context of the European Union Institutions'. 30 *International Journal of Legal Information* 288-307 (2002).

Tridimas Takis. *The General Principles of EU Law*. 2nd edn. Oxford EC Law Library (Oxford: Oxford University Press, 2006).

Tridimas, Takis. 'The European Court of Justice and Judicial Activism'. 21 *European Law Review* 199-210 (1996).

de Waele, Henri. 'The Role of the European Court of Justice in the Integration Process: Contemporary and Normative Assessment'. 6(1) *Hanse Law Review* 3-26 (2010).

Wattel, Peter J. 'Exit Taxation in the EU/EEA before and after National Grid Indus'. *Tax Notes International* 371 (2012).

CHAPTER 7: FRANCE

Austry, Stéphane. '"QPC fiscale et effets de la décision dans le temps'." 33 *Nouveaux Cahiers du Conseil constitutionnel* (October 2011).

Sophie Boyron, Sophie. *The Constitution of France: A Contextual Analysis* (Oxford: Hart Publishing, 2012).

Brunet, Pierre. '"Le style déductif du Conseil d'État et la ligne de partage des mots'." 3 (91) *Droit et Société*: 545-561 (2015).

Collet, Martin. '"Le juge fiscal français et le contentieux TVA'". 128 *Revue française de finances publiques*: 125 et seq. (2014).

Collet, Martin. *Droit Fiscal*, 6th edn (Paris: PUF, 2017).

Combacau, Jean and Serge Sur. *Droit International Public*. 12th edn (Paris: LGDJ, 2016).

Conseil d'Etat. *Rapport Public 2016* (Paris: La documentation française, 2016).

Cour des Comptes. *Les relations de l'administration fiscale avec les particuliers et les entreprises*. Rapport public thématique, February 2012.

Cozian, Maurice and Louis Trotabas. '"Propos désobligeants sur une "'tarte à la crème"': l'autonomie et le réalisme du droit fiscal'". 13 *Droit fiscal* 100–125 (31 March 1999).

David, René. *French Law – Its Structure, Sources, and Methodology* (Baton Rouge: Louisiana State University Press, 1972).

Deboissy, Florence. '"Retour sur un principe controversé: l'indépendance des procédures pénale et fiscale'", 51-52 *Droit fiscal*: Etude no 692 (2014).

De La Mardière, Christophe. '"Le pouvoir créateur du juge de l'impôt'". in *Archives de philosophie du droit - La création du droit par le juge*, t. 50: 229 et seq. (2007).

Dubut, Thomas. '"Modélisation des normes et normativité des modèles. Le caractère normatif ambivalent du Modèle de Convention fiscale concernant le revenu et la fortune de l'OCDE en droit international public'." 1 *Revue belge de droit international* 212-239 (2009).

Dubut, Thomas. '"Les Commentaires du Modèle de Convention fiscale de l'OCDE et l'interprétation des conventions bilatérales contre la double imposition. Contribution à l'étude de la normativité sans efficacité en droit international public'." 34 (3) *Revue de la recherche juridique – Droit prospectif* 1449-1472 (2009).

Dubut, Thomas, '"Chapter 13: France'." In M. Lang, P. Pistone, J. Schuch, C. Staringer and A. Storck (eds), *General Anti-Avoidance Rules (GAARs) – A Key Element of Tax Systems in the Post-BEPS Tax World?* (Amsterdam: IBFD, 2016).

Dussart, Vincent. '"Les avis contentieux du Conseil d'Etat en matière fiscal'." 210 *Les Petites affiches* 3-12 (20 October 2004).

Fouquet, Olivier, *Améliorer la sécurité juridique des relations entre l'administration fiscale et les contribuables: une nouvelle approche*. Rapport au ministre du Budget, Paris: La Documentation Française, June 2008.

Gest, Guy, '"L'affaire des crédits d'impôt brésiliens, ou les limites de l'interprétation littérale des Conventions fiscales'." 50 (69) *Droit fiscal* (14 December 2006).

Guez, Julien. '"L'interprétation jurisprudentielle en droit fiscal doit-elle être spécifique? Retour sur le principe d'interprétation stricte en droit fiscal'." in *L'année fiscale* (Paris: PUF, 2004).

Guillaume, Marc. '"La question prioritaire de constitutionnalité et le droit fiscal'." 14 *Revue de droit fiscal* (7 April 2011).

Gutmann, Daniel. '"Tax Treaty Interpretation in France, the Relevance of EC Law'." 10 (4) *EC Tax Review* 204 (2001).

Gutmann, Daniel. '"Tax Treaty Interpretation in France'." In Lang et al. (eds), *Tax Treaty Interpretation* (The Netherlands: Kluwer Law International, 2001).

Gutmann, Daniel. '"Sanctions fiscales et Constitution'". 33 *Nouveaux Cahiers du Conseil constitutionnel*: 41 et seq. (October 2011).

Gutmann, Daniel. *Droit fiscal des affaires*, 7th edn (Paris: Montchrétien, 2016).

Jestaz, Philippe. *Les sources du droit*, 2nd edn (Paris: Dalloz, 2015).

Marchessou, Philippe. '"Réflexions contemporaines sur l'interprétation des textes fiscaux'". In *Mélanges Paul Amselek* (Bruxelles: Bruylant, 2005).

Martin, Philippe. '"L'interprétation des conventions fiscales internationales'". 24 *Droit fiscal* (13 June 2013).

Neville Brown, Lionel, John Bell and Jean-Michel Galabert. *French Administrative Law*, 5th edn (Oxford-New York: Clarendon Press-Oxford University Press, 1998).

OECD. *Model Tax Convention on Income and on Capital* (Paris: OECD, 2015).

Pfersmann, Otto. '"Contre le néo-réalisme juridique. Pour un débat sur l'interprétation'". *Revue française de droit constitutionnel* 279-334 (2002).

Pfersmann, Otto. '"Concrete Review as Indirect Constitutional Complaint in French Constitutional Law: A Comparative Perspective'." 6(2) *European Constitutional Law Review* 223-248 (2010).

Philip, Loic. *Droit fiscal constitutionnel: Evolution d'une jurisprudence* (Paris: Economica, 2014).

Picard, Etienne. '"Contre la Théorie réaliste de l'interprétation juridique'". In Gilles Darcy, Véronique Labrot and Mathieu Doat (eds), *L'office du juge* (Paris: Les colloques du Sénat, 2006).

Picard, Etienne and Georges A. Bermann. '"Administrative Law'". In E. Picard and G.A. Bermann (eds), *Introduction to French Law* (The Netherlands: Kluwer Law International, 2008).

Pierre, Jocelyn. '"Mettre en ligne du droit: l'expérience BOFIP-Impôts, des réponses informatiques à des questions juridiques'." *Revue générale du droit on line* (2013), no10887 (www.revuegeneraledudroit.eu/?p = 10887).

Plagnet, Bernard. '"Le raisonnement économique dans la jurisprudence fiscale'." In *Études en l'honneur de Loïc Philip* (Paris: Economica, 2005).

Stirn, Bernard. '"La place de la coutume internationale en droit public français'." 12 *The Law and Practice of International Courts and Tribunals* 267-271 (2013).

Taly, Michel. "'Le code général des impôts, Elephant Man juridique'". 4(151) *Pouvoirs* 87-97 (2014).

Taly, Michel. *Les coulisses de la politique fiscale* (Paris: PUF, 2016).

Troper, Michel. *La théorie du droit, le droit, l'Etat* (Paris: PUF, 2001).

Troper, Michel, Véronique Champeil-Desplats and Christophe Grzegorczyk (eds). *Théorie des contraintes juridiques* (Bruxelles-Paris: Bruylant-LGDJ, 2005).

Troper, Michel. '"Constitutional Law'." In E. Picard and G.A. Bermann (eds), *Introduction to French Law* (The Netherlands: Kluwer Law International, 2008).

Vapaille, Laurence. *La doctrine administrative fiscale* (Paris: L'Harmattan, 2000).

Viala, Alexandre. *Les réserves d'interprétation dans la jurisprudence du Conseil constitutionnel* (Paris: LGDJ, 1999).

CHAPTER 8: GERMANY

Ball-Kaduri, Kurt Jacob. *Steuerrecht und Privatrecht* (Mannheim: Bensheimer, 1924).

Barth, Rainer. *Richterliche Rechtsfortbildung im Steuerrecht* (Berlin: Duncker und Humblot Verlag, 1996).

Bydlinski, Franz. *Juristische Methodenlehre und Rechtsbegriff*. 2nd edn (Vienna: Springer-Verlag, 1991).

Bydlinski, Franz. *Grundzüge der juristischen Methodenlehre*. 2nd edn (Vienna: Facultas-Verlag, Vienna, 2012).

Canaris, Claus-Wilhelm. *Die Feststellung von Lücken im Gesetz*. 2nd edn (Berlin: Duncker und Humblot Verlag, 1983).

Debatin, Helmut. 'Doppelbesteuerungsabkommen und innerstaatliches Recht'. 23 *DStR*, Beihefter, 1 (1992).

Drüen, Klaus-Dieter. '§ 4 AO'. In Klaus Tipke and Heinrich Wilhelm Kruse (eds), *AO/FGO* (Cologne: Dr. Otto Schmidt Verlag, loose-leaf, 2014).

Drüen, Klaus-Dieter. '§ 42 AO'. In Klaus Tipke and Heinrich Wilhelm Kruse (eds), *AO/FGO* (Cologne: Dr. Otto Schmidt Verlag, loose-leaf, 2016).

Englisch, Joachim. 'Rechtsanwendung im Steuerrecht'. In Klaus Tipke et al. (eds), *Steuerrecht*, 22nd edn (Cologne: Dr. Otto Schmidt Verlag, 2015).

di Fabio, Udo. *Das Recht offener Staaten* (Tübingen: Mohr Siebeck, 1998).

Frenz, Walter. *Europarecht* (Berlin: Springer-Verlag, 2011).

Förster, Guido. 'Die Gesamtplanrechtsprechung im Steuerrecht'. In Dieter Carlé et al. (eds), *Festschrift for Klaus Korn* (Bonn-Berlin: Stollfuß Verlag, 2005).

Grosche, Nils. *Rechtsfortbildung und Unionsrecht* (Tübingen: Mohr Siebeck, 2011).

Grzesdzick, Bernt. 'Art. 20 GG'. In Theodor Maunz and Günter Dürig (eds), *Grundgesetz Kommentar* (*Commentary on the German Constitutional Law*) (Munich: Beck-Verlag, loose-leaf, 2016).

Hahn, Hartmut. 'Treaty Overriding sine ira et studio'. *Internationales Steuerrecht* 863 (2011).

Heck, Philipp. 'Begriffsjurisprudenz und Interessenjurisprudenz'. In Günter Ellscheid and Winfried Hassemer (eds), *Interessenjurisprudenz* (Darmstadt: Wissenschaftliche Buchgesellschaft, 1974).

Herzog, Roman and Bernd Grzesdzick. 'Art. 20 GG'. In Theodor Maunz and Günter Dürig (eds), *Grundgesetz Kommentar* (Munich: Beck-Verlag, loose-leaf, 2013).

Hey, Johanna, 'Einführung zum EStG' ('Introduction to the Individual Income Tax Code'). In Carl Herrmann et al. (eds), *Einkommensteuer- und Körperschaftsteuergesetz* (*Individual and Corporate Income Tax Code*) (Cologne: Dr. Otto Schmidt Verlag, loose-leaf, 2016).

Hirsch, Günter. 'Auf dem Weg zum Richterstaat?'. *Juristen Zeitung* 853 (2008).

Höpfner, Clemens and Bernd Rüthers. 'Grundlagen einer Europäischen Methodenlehre'. *Achiv für die civilistische Praxis* 1 (2009).

Knobbe-Keuk, Brigitte. 'Die Betriebsaufspaltung – ein "Rechtsinstitut"?'. In Franz Hörstmann et al. (eds), *Steuerberater-Jahrbuch 1980/81* ICologne: Verlag Dr. Otto Schmidt, 1981).

Kroll-Ludwigs, Kathrin and Markus Ludwigs. 'Die richtlinienkonforme Rechtsfortbildung im Gesamtsystem der Richtlinienwirkung'. *Zeitschrift für das juristische Studium* 7 (2009).

Lang, Joachim. 'General Rules of Statute Interpretation in Germany'. In Klaus Vogel (ed.). *Interpretation of Tax Law and Treaties and Transfer Pricing in Japan and Germany* (The Hague: Kluwer Law International, 1998).

Lang, Michael et al. *Die Auslegung von Doppelbesteuerungsabkommen in der Rechtsprechung des Bundesfinanzhofs* (Vienna: Linde Verlag, 1998).

Larenz, Karl. *Methodenlehre der Rechtswissenschaft*, 6th edn (Berlin: Springer-Verlag, 1991).

Lehner, Moris. 'Interpretation of Tax Treaties according to German Theory and Practice'. In Klaus Vogel (ed.), *Interpretation of Tax Law and Treaties and Transfer Pricing in Japan and Germany* (The Hague: Kluwer Law International, 1998).

Lutter, Markus. 'Die Auslegung angeglichenen Rechts'. *Juristen Zeitung* 593 (1992).

Neuner, Jörg. *Die Rechtsfindung contra legem*, 2nd edn (Munich: C.H. Beck Verlag, 2005).

Neuner, Jörg. 'Die Rechtsfortbildung'. In Karl Riesenhuber (ed.), *Europäische Methodenlehre*, 3rd edn (Berlin: De Gruyter Verlag, 2015).

Osterloh-Konrad, Christine. '"Quelle" und die Folgen: kein Nutzungsersatz bei Ersatzlieferung'. *Computer und Recht* 545 (2008).

Reimer, Ekkehart. 'Tax Treaty Interpretation in Germany'. In Michael Lang (ed.), *Tax Treaty Interpretation* (Vienna: Linde Verlag, 2001).

Roth, Wulf-Henning and Christian Jopen. 'Die richtlinienkonforme Auslegung'. In Karl Riesenhuber (ed.), *Europäische Methodenlehre*, 3rd edn (Berlin: De Gruyter Verlag, 2015).

Ruppe, Hans G. 'Einführung zum EStG'. In Carl Herrmann et al. (eds), *Einkommensteuer-und Körperschaftsteuergesetz* (Cologne: Dr. Otto Schmidt Verlag, loose-leaf, 2014).

Rust, Alexander and Ekkehart Reimer. 'Treaty Override im deutschen Internationalen Steuerrecht'. *Internationales Steuerrecht* 843 (2005).

Schaumburg, Harald. *Internationales Steuerrecht*, 3rd edn (Cologne: Dr. Otto Schmidt Verlag, 2011).

Schnitger, Arne. 'Die Einbeziehung des OECD-Kommentars in die Rechtsprechung des BFH'. *Internationales Steuerrecht* 402 (2002).

Schön, Wolfgang. *Die Auslegung europäischen Steuerrechts* (Cologne: Otto Schmidt Verlag, 1993).

Schön, Wolfgang. 'Interpretation of Tax Statutes'. In Klaus Vogel (ed.), *Interpretation of Tax Law and Treaties and Transfer Pricing in Japan and Germany* (The Hague: Kluwer Law International, 1998).

Schön, Wolfgang. 'Gestaltungsfreiheit und Belastungsgleichheit als Grundlagen des Steuerrechts'. In Rainer Hüttemann (ed.), *Gestaltungsfreiheit und Gestaltungsmissbrauch im Steuerrecht*, DStJG. Vol. 33 (Cologne: Dr. Otto Schmidt Verlag, 2010).

Schön, Wolfgang. 'Legalität, Gestaltungsfreiheit und Belastungsgleichheit als Grundlage des Steuerrechts'. In Rainer Hüttemann (ed.), *Gestaltungsfreiheit und Gestaltungsmissbrauch im Steuerrecht*, DStJG, Vol. 33 (Cologne: Dr. Otto Schmidt Verlag, 2010).

Sparrer, Claudia. *Sonderbetriebsvermögen* (Berlin: LIT Verlag, 2007).

Spindler, Wolfgang. 'Der "Gesamtplan" in der Rechtsprechung des BFH'. *DeutschesSteuerrecht* 1 (2005).

Spindler, Wolfgang. 'Richterliche Rechtsfortbildung und Rechtssicherheit'. In Hanno Kube et al. (eds), *Leitgedanken des Rechts II* (Heidelberg: C. F. Müller, 2013).

Tanzer, Michael. 'Der Gesamtplan im Rahmen steuerlicher Tatbestände'. In Rainer Hüttemann (ed.), *Gestaltungsfreiheit und Gestaltungsmissbrauch im*, DStJG. Vol. 33 (Cologne: Dr. Otto Schmidt Verlag, 2010).

Tappe, Henning. *Die Begründung von Steuergesetzen: Normatives Ermessen im Steuerrecht zwischen Gesetzmäßigkeit und Gestaltungsfreiheit* (Habilitations thesis. Münster, 2012).

Tipke, Klaus. *Die Steuerrechtsordnung*. Vol. I, 2nd edn (Cologne: Dr. Otto Schmidt Verlag, 2000).

Tipke, Klaus. *Die Steuerrechtsordnung*. Vol. III, 2nd edn (Cologne: Dr. Otto Schmidt Verlag, 2012).

Vogel, Klaus and Alexander Rust. 'Introduction'. In Ekkehart Reimer and Alexander Rust (eds), *Klaus Vogel on Double Taxation Conventions*, 4th edn (Alphen aan den Rijn: Kluwer Law International, 2015).

Vogel, Klaus. 'Grundzüge des Finanzrechts des Grundgesetzes'. In Josef Isensee and Paul Kirchhof (eds), *Handbuch des Staatsrechts*. Vol. IV, 2nd edn (Heidelberg: C.F. Müller, 1999).

Vogenauer, Stefan. 'Eine gemeineuropäische Methodenlehre des Rechts – Plädoyer und Programm'. *Zeitschrift für Europäisches Privatrecht* 234 (2005).

Weber-Grellet, Heinrich. *Steuern im modernen Verfassungsstaat* (Cologne: Dr. Otto Schmidt Verlag, 2001).

Wendt, Michael. '§ 42 AO vor dem Hintergrund der Rechtsprechung'. In Rainer Hüttemann (ed.), *Gestaltungsfreiheit und Gestaltungsmissbrauch im Steuerrecht*. DStJG, Vol. 33 (Cologne: Dr. Otto Schmidt Verlag, 2010).

CHAPTER 9: HONG KONG

Evans, Chris, Judith Freedman and Richard Krever (eds). *The Delicate Balance: Tax, Discretion and the Rule of Law* (Amsterdam: IBFD, 2011).

Freedman, Judith. 'Interpreting Tax Statutes: Tax Avoidance and the Intention of Parliament'. 123 *The Law Quarterly Review* 53 (2007).

Ghai, Yash. *Hong Kong's New Constitutional Order: the Resumption of Chinese Sovereignty and the Basic Law*. 2nd edn (Hong Kong: Hong Kong University Press, 1999).

Halkyard, Andrew. 'Common Law and Tax Avoidance: Back to the Future?'. 14 *Revenue Law Journal*: 19 (2004).

Halkyard, Andrew and Stephen Phua. 'Taxation of Income in Singapore and Hong Kong'. *Singapore Journal of Legal Studies* 1 (2007).

Law Commission Report. *The Interpretation of Statutes*. HC 256 at p. 14 (1969).

Littlewood, Michael. 'Taxation Without Representation: The History of Hong Kong's Troublingly Successful Tax System'. *British Tax Review* 212 (2002).

Littlewood, Michael. 'How Simple Can Tax Law Be? The Instructive Case of Hong Kong'. 38 *Tax Notes International* 689 (2005).

Littlewood, Michael. *Taxation Without Representation: The History of Hong Kong's Troublingly Successful Tax System* (Hong Kong: Hong Kong University Press, 2010).

Millett, Lord. 'Ramsay Comes to Hong Kong'. 31 *Hong Kong Law Journal* 20 (2001).

Smith, Adam. *The Wealth of Nations* (London: W. Strahan and T. Cadell, 1776).

Wesley-Smith, Peter. 'Literal or Liberal: The Notorious Section 19'. 12 *Hong Kong Law Journal* 203 (1982).

Yun, Davy and Finsen Chan. 'Hong Kong: No Deduction for Manufacturing Assets Used in China, Court Says'. 69(2) *Tax Notes International* 148 (14 January 2013).

CHAPTER 10: ITALY

Antonini, Enrico. 'Norma di legge, standard giuridico ed interpretazione ministeriale'. (1979) 1 *Riv. Dir. Fin.* 425.

Beghin, Mauro. *Diritto Tributario* (Torino: Giappicchelli, 2011).

Benatti, Francesco. 'Principio di buona fede ed obbligazione tributaria'. 12 *Boll. trib.* 94 (1986).

Berliri, Antonio. *Principi di diritto tributario*. Vol. I (Milano: Giuffrè, 1967).

Bizioli, Gianluigi. 'Tax Treaty Interpretation in Italy'. In Michael Lang (ed.), *Tax Treaty Interpretation* (London: Kluwer Law International, 2001).

Bobbio, Norberto. 'Lacune del diritto'. In *Nov. mo dig. it.* Vol. IX (Torino: UTET, 1963), 423.

Bobbio, Norberto. *Giusnaturalismo e positivismo giuridico* (Milano: Edizioni di Comunità, 1965).

Bobbio, Norberto. *Positivismo giuridico* (Torino: Giappichelli, 1979).

Boria, Pietro. *L'interesse fiscale* (Torino: Giuppichelli, 2002).

Braccini, Raffaello. 'Mutamenti nelle basi del diritto tributario: la crisi dell'idea di "sistema"'. IV *Giurisprudenza Italiana* 313 (1997).

Braithwaite, John. 'Large Businesses and the Compliance Model'. In Valerie Braithwaite (ed.), *Taxing Democracy: Understanding Tax Avoidance and Evasion* (Burlington, VT: Ashgate,2003).

Braithwaite, Valerie. *Responsive Regulation and Taxation*, 29 Law and Policy 3 (2007).

Conte, Amedeo G. 'Completezza'. In *Digesto IV* (Discipline civilistiche) (Torino: UTET, 1988).

Crisafulli, Vezio. 'Disposizione (e norma)'. In *Enciclopedia del Diritto*. Vol. XIII (Milano: Giuffrè, 1964).

Della Valle, Eugenio. 'Revirement ministeriale e buona fede nell'esercizio della funzione impositiva'. 1 *Rivista Diritto Tributarii* 587 (1995).

Dworkin, Ronald. *Law's Empire* (Cambridge: Harvard University Press, 1986).

Falsitta, Gaspare. 'L'interpretazione antielusiva della norma tributaria come clausola generale immanente al sistema e direttamente ricavabile dai principi costituzionali'. *Corriere Giuridico* 296 (2009).

Falsitta, Gaspare. *Manuale di diritto tributario* (Padova: CEDAM, 2015).

Garbarino, Carlo. 'Alcune considerazioni sulle Convenzioni per evitare le doppie imposizioni'. *Diritto del commercio internazionale* 51 (1989).

Garbarino, Carlo. *Manuale di tassazione internazionale* (Deventer: Kluwer, 2008).

Garbarino, Carlo. 'An Evolutionary Approach to Comparative Taxation: Methods and Agenda for Research'. *American Journal of Comparative Law* 677 (2009).

Garbarino, Carlo. 'Comparative Taxation and Legal Theory: The Tax Design Case of the Transplant of General Anti-Avoidance Rules'. 11(2) *Theoretical Inquiries in the Law* 764-790 (2010).

Giannini, Massimo S. 'L'interpretazione e l'integrazione delle leggi tributarie'. 1 *Rivista Diritto Finanziario* 123 (1941).

Gianoncelli, Stefania. 'Contrasto all'elusione fiscale in materia di imposte sui redditi e divieto comunitario di abuso del diritt'o'. *Giurisprudenza Italiana* 129 (2008).

Guastini, Riccardo. *Dalle fonti alle norme* (Torino: Giappichelli, 1992).

Guglielmi, Stefano. 'Il caso Philip Morris nelle recenti modifiche al Commentario OCSE'. *Fiscalità Internazionale* 148-157 (2006).

Hart, Herbert L.A. *The Concept of Law*, 2nd edn (Oxford: Clarendon Press, 1961).

Ingrosso, Manlio. 'Diritto, sistema e giustizia tributaria'. *Rassegna tributaria* 183 (1990).

Innamorato, Caterina. 'An Unwritten Anti-abuse Principle in the Italian Tax System'. 8 *European Taxation'* 449 (2008).

Jarach, Dino. 'La considerazione del contenuto economico nella interpretazione delle leggi d'imposta'. *Rivista Diritto Finanziario* 56 (1937).

Jori, Mario (ed.). *Legal Positivism* (Aldershot: Dartmouth: The International Library of Jurisprudence, 1992).

Kelsen, Hans. *General Theory of Law and State.* Translated by Anders Wedberg (New York: Russell & Russell, 1961).

Kelsen, Hans. *Dottrina pura del diritto.* Translated by M. G. Losano (Torino: Einaudi, 1966).

La Rosa, Salvatore. 'Esenzioni ed agevolazioni tributarie'. In *Enc. Giur. Treccani*. Vol. XIII (Roma: 1989).

Logozzo, Maurizio. 'Capacità contributiva ed interpretazione della legge tributaria'. *Bollettino Tributario* 1653 (1990).

Logozzo, Maurizio. *L'ignoranza della legge tributaria* (Milano: Giuffrè, 2002).

Lovisolo, Antonio. 'Abuso del diritto e clausola generale antielusiva alla ricerca di un principio'. I *Rivista Diritto Tributarii* 89 (2009).

Lupi, Raffaello and Dario Stevanato. 'Tecniche interpretative e pretesa immanenza di una norma generale antielusiva'. 6 *Corriere Tributario* 403 (2009).

Marello, Enrico. 'Il divieto di doppia imposizione come principio generale del sistema tributario'. 6 *Giurisprudenza costituzionale* 4127 (1997).

Marongiu, Gianni. 'Abuso del diritto o abuso del potere?'. 13 *Corriere Tributario* 1077 (2009).

Melis, Giuseppe. 'L'interpretazione delle convenzioni internazionali in materia di imposte sul reddito e sul patrimonio'. *Rassegna tributaria* 1966 (1995).

Melis, Giuseppe. *L'Interpretazione nel Diritto Tributario* (Padova: Cedam, 2003).

Murphy, Kristina. 'Moving towards a more effective model of regulatory enforcement in the Australian Tax Office'. *British Tax Review* 603 (2004).

Owens, Jeffrey. 'The "'Enhanced Relationship"': A Challenge for Revenue Bodies and Taxpayers'. *European Taxation* 351 (July 2008).

Paparella, Franco. 'Riflessioni in margine all'art. 10 della Legge 1990, No. 408, relativo alla ristrutturazione delle imprese'. 6 *Diritto e pratica tributaria* 1835 (1995).

Pedrotti, Francesco. 'Il principio giurisprudenziale comunitario di abuso del diritto come strumento di contrasto alle operazioni elusive domestiche: il caso del cd. Dividend stripping (o usufrutto azionario)', 2 *Diritto e Pratica Tributaria Internazionale* 1010 (2008).

Potito, Enrico. 'Le "valide ragioni economiche" di cui all'art. 37 - bis del D.p.r. n. 600/1973: considerazioni di un economista d'azienda'. 1 *Rassegna tributaria* 63 (1999).

Prebble, John and Zoë Prebble. 'Comparing the General Anti-Avoidance Rule of Income Tax Law with the Civil Law Doctrine of Abuse of Law'. 4 *Bulletin for International Taxation* 151 (2008).

Raz, Joseph. *The Concept of a Legal System: An Introduction to the Theory of Legal System* (Oxford: Clarendon Press, 2003).

Ross, Alf. *On Law and Justice*. Translated by Margaret Dutton (London: Stevens & Sons, 1958).

Sacco, Rodolfo and Pier G. Monateri. 'Legal Formants'. In Peter Newman (ed.), *The New Palgrave Dictionary of Economics and the Law* (London: MacMillan, 1998).

Scarpelli, Uberto. *Cos'è il positivismo giuridico* (Milano: Edizioni di Comunità, 1965).

Tarello, Giovanni. *Studi sulla teoria generale dei precetti, I. Introduzione al linguaggio precettivi* (Milano: 1968 (estratto da *Annali Giurisprudenza Genova, I,* 1968)).

Tarello, Giovanni. *Diritto, enunciati, usi* (Bologna: Il Mulino, 1974).

Tarello, Giovanni. 'L'interpretazione della legge'. In Antonio Cicu, Francesco Messineo and Luigi Mengoni (eds), *Trattato di diritto civile* (Milano: Giuffrè, 1980).

Twining, William and David Miers. *Come fare cose con regole*. Translated by Carlo Garbarino (Milano: Giuffrè, 1990).

Vanoni, Ezio (1932). 'Natura ed interpretazione delle leggi tributarie'. Reprinted in F. Forte and C. Longobardi (eds). Ezio Vanoni, *Opere Giuridiche*. Vol. I (Milano: Giuffrè, 1961), 2002.

Zizzo, Giuseppe. 'Ragioni economiche e scopi fiscali nella clausola antielusione'. 1 *Rassegna tributaria*: 170 (2008).

Zoppina, Giancarlo. 'Prospettiva critica della giurisprudenza "antielusiva" della Corte di Cassazione (1969 - 1999)'. 1 *Rivista Diritto Tributarii* 919 (1999).

CHAPTER 11: JAPAN

Ault, Hugh J. and Brian Arnold. *Comparative Income Taxation: A Structural Analysis*, 3rd edn (Alphen aan den Rijn: Kluwer, 2010).

Cooper, Graeme S. (ed.). *Tax Avoidance and the Rule of Law* (Amsterdam: IBFD, 1997).

Dibout, Patrick. 'L'inapplicabilité de l'article 209 B du CGI face à la convention fiscale franco-suisse du 9 septembre 1966'. 36 *Revue de Droit Fiscal* 1133-1141 (2002).

Ecker, Thomas. *A VAT/GST Model Convention: Tax Treaties as Solution for Value Added Tax and Goods and Services Tax Double Taxation* (Amsterdam: IBFD, 2013).

Evans, Chris, Judith Freedman and Richard Krever (eds). *The Delicate Balance: Tax Discretion and the Rule of Law* (Amsterdam: IBFD, 2011).

de la Feria, Rita (ed.). *VAT Exemptions: Consequences and Design Alternatives* (Alphen aan den Rijn: Kluwer, 2013).

Ishi, Hiromitsu. *The Japanese Tax System*, 3rd edn (Oxford: Oxford University Press, 2001).

Kaneko, Hiroshi. 'The Principle of Statute-based Taxation in Japan'. In Paul Kirchhof et al. (eds), *Staaten und Steuern, Festschrift für Klaus Vogel zum 70. Geburtstag* (Heidelberg: C.F. Müller, 2000).

Kaneko, Hiroshi, Hideaki Sato, Yoshihiro Masui and Masahiro Shibuya. *Casebook Sozeiho [Casebook Tax Law]*, 4th edn (Kobundo, 2013).

Masui, Yoshihiro. 'Statutory Interpretation as a Process of Tax Law Making: The Case of Japan'. In Klaus Vogel (ed.), *Interpretation of Tax Law and Treaties and Transfer Pricing in Japan and Germany* (Alphen aan den Rijn: Kluwer, 1998).

Masui, Yoshihiro. 'The Responsibility of Judges in Interpreting Tax Legislation: Japan's Experience'. 52(2) *Osgood Hall Law Journal* 491-512 (2015).

Milhaupt, Curtis J., J. Mark Ramseyer and Mark D. West. *The Japanese Legal System*, 2nd edn (New York: Foundation Press, 2012).

Murai, Tadashi. 'Japan'. In 'IFA, Form and Substance in Tax Law', 87a *Cahier de droit fiscal international* 379 (2002).

Nakazato, Minoru and Yoshihiro Masui (eds). *Sozeiho Hanrei Roppo* [*Tax Law: Principal Statutes, Regulations, and Cases*], 2nd edn (Yuhikaku, 2015).

Nakazato, Minoru et al. (eds). *Sozei Hanrei Hyakusen* [*100 Cases in Tax Law*], 6th edn (Yuhikaku, 2016).

Nishiyama, Yumi. 'Case Note: Tokyo District Court of 8 August 1997'. In Tadatsune Mizuno et al. (eds) *Sozei Hanrei Hyakusen* [*100 Cases in Tax Law*], 5th edn (Yuhikaku, 2011).

Okada, Yukihito. 'Case Commentary'. 63(7) *Hoso Jiho* [*Lawyers Association Journal*] 1731 (2011).

Yoon, Ji-Hyun. 'An End of a Journey or a New Beginning? - The 2012 Trilogy of Supreme Court Decisions on International Tax'. 19(3) *Asia-Pacific Tax Bulletin* 190 (2013).

CHAPTER 12: RUSSIAN FEDERATION

Aleskeyev, Sergey S. *General Theory of Law*. Vol. 1 (Moscow: Yuridicheskaya literatura, 1981).

Kopina, Anna A. 'The Place of Judicial Practice within the System of Sources of Tax Law'. *Finansovoye pravo* № 12 (2008).

Miroshnik, Svetlana V. and Valeriy V. Raygorodskiy. 'Decisions of the RF Constitutional Court as a Source of Tax Law', *Nalogi (newspaper)* № 21 (2008).

Mkrtumyan, Arman Yu. 'Judicial Practice as a Source of Russian Law: Historical and Legal Aspects'. *Istoriya gosudarstva and prava* № 9 (2008).

Mozolin, Viktor P. 'Future Paths for Development of Civil Law', *Zhurnal rossiyskogo prava* № 3 (2007).

Notin, Sergey A. *Judicial Practice within the System of Sources of Tax Law: The EU and the RF as Examples*: Dissertation for Ph.D. in Law, 2003.

Perevalov, Viktor D. *Theory of State and Law*, 2nd edn (Moscow: Urait, 2012).

Sorokin, Vitaliy V. 'Judicial Practice as a Source of Law: For and Against'. *Sibirskiy yuridicheskiy vestnik* № 3 (2003).

Sviridenko, Oleg. M. 'Judicial Practice - A Source of Russian Law?'. *Sovremennoye pravo* № 10 (2010).

Tille, Anatoliy A. *Socialist Comparative Jurisprudence* (Moscow, 1975).

Tonenkova, Olga A. 'Judicial Practice as a Source of Administrative Law'. *Administrativnoye pravo and protsess* № 2 (2010).

Tsyganova, Elena M. 'Judicial Practice as a Source of Law'. *Yuridicheskiy mir* №2 (2006).

Vinnitskiy, Danil V. 'Russia: Thin Capitalization Rules and Non-discrimination Clause'. In Eric C.C.M., Kemmeren et al. (eds), *Tax Treaty Case Law around the Globe 2012* (Amsterdam: IBFD, 2013).

CHAPTER 13: SOUTH AFRICA

Devenish, George E. *Interpretation of Statutes* (Cape Town: Juta Legal and Academic Publishers, 1992).

Lord Grabiner QC. 'The Iterative Process of Contractual Interpretation'. 128 *The Law Quarterly Review* 41 (2012).

Lord Nicholls of Birkenhead. 'My Kingdom for a Horse: The Meaning of Words'. 121 *The Law Quarterly Review* 577 (2005).

Hosten W.J., et al. *Introduction to South African Law and Legal Theory* (Durban: Butterworth, 1983).

Kellaway, Edwin A. *Principles of Legal Interpretation* (Durban: Butterworth, 1995).

Langan, Peter St.J. (ed.). *Maxwell on the Interpretation of Statutes*, 12 edn (London: Sweet & Maxwell, 1969).

Lewison, Kim. *The Interpretation of Contracts*, 5th edn (London: Sweet & Maxwell, 2011).

Newton, John. 'The Special Court – Its Jurisdiction and Powers'. 26 *Income Tax Reporter* 332 (1987).

Spigelman, James J. 'From Text to Context: Contemporary Contractual Interpretation', an address to the Risky Business Conference in Sydney, 21 March 2007. Published in Castle, Timothy D. (ed.), *Speeches of a Chief Justice: James Spigelman 1998–2008* (Neutral Bay, NSW: CS2N Publishing, 2008).

Steyn, Lucas C. *Die Uitleg van Wette*, 5th edn (Cape Town: Juta Legal and Academic Publishers, 1981).

Wallis, M. 'Is Tax Really Different'. 3 *British Tax Review* 299 (2016).

CHAPTER 14: UNITED KINGDOM

Arden, Lady Justice. 'The Interpretation of UK Domestic Legislation in the Light of European Convention on Human Rights Jurisprudence'. *Statute Law Review* 165 (2004).

Avery Jones, John. 'Jurisdiction to Tax Companies: The Influences of the Jurisdiction of the Courts and of European Thinking'. In John Tiley (ed.), *Studies in the History of Tax Law, Volume 4* (Oxford: Hart, 2010).

Baker, John H. *An Introduction to English Legal History*, 4th edn (London: Butterworths, 2002).

Bogenschneider, Bret N. 'Wittgenstein on Why Tax Law is Comprehensible'. *British Tax Review* 252 (2015).

Bramwell, Richard, John Lindsay, Alun James, et al. *Taxation of Companies and Company Reconstructions*, loose-leaf, release 22 (December 2016).

van Brederode, Robert F., 'VAT's Regressivity: Empirical Truth or Political Correctness'. *International VAT Monitor* 86 (March/April 2007).

Crawford, Ian, Michael Keen, Stephen Smith. 'Value Added Tax and Excises'. In S. Adam, T. Besley et al., (eds), *Dimensions of Tax Design: The Mirrlees Review* (Oxford: Oxford University Press, 2010).

de Cogan, Dominic, 'Purposive Interpretation in the Age of Horse Trams'. *British Tax Review* 80 (2015).

de Cogan, Dominic, '"Case Comment: Defining Tax Avoidance: Flirting With Chaos, Again'". *Cambridge Law Journal* 474 (2016).

de la Feria, Rita. 'Prohibition of Abuse of (Community) Law: The Creation of a New General Principle of EC Law Through Tax'. 45 *Common Market Law Review* 395 (2008).

Department for Exiting the European Union. *Legislating for the United Kingdom's Withdrawal From The European Union* (Cm 9446, 2017).

Dodwell, Bill and Kevin Prosser (eds). *The Green Book 2016-17* (Kingston-upon-Thames: Wolters Kluwer, 2016).

Dyson, Jacqueline. 'Interpreting Tax Statutes'. In M. Freeman (ed.), *Legislation and the Courts* (Dartmouth: Aldershot, 1997), 45.

Freedman, Judith. 'Interpreting Tax Statutes: Tax Avoidance and the Intention of Parliament'. 123 *The Law Quarterly Review* 53 (2007).

Greenberg, Daniel (ed.). *Craies on Legislation: A Practitioners' Guide to the Nature, Process, Effect and Interpretation of Legislation*, 11th edn (London: Sweet and Maxwell, 2017).

Hamburger, Philip. *Is Administrative Law Unlawful?* (Chicago: University of Chicago Press, 2014).

HM Government, *Review of the Balance of Competences Between the United Kingdom and the European Union: Taxation* (July 2013).

House of Commons Library. *The Barnett Formula* (Briefing Paper No 7386, 13 April 2016).

Howe, Geoffrey. 'Simplicity and Stability: the Politics of Tax Policy'. *British Tax Review* 113 (2001).

Johnstone, Dorothy. *A Tax Shall be Charged; Some Aspects of the Introduction of the British Value Added Tax* (London: HMSO, 1975).

Jones, Oliver and Francis A.R. Bennion (eds). *Bennion on Statutory Interpretation: A Code*, 6th edn (London: LexisNexis, 2013).

Lee, Natalie. 'A Purposive Approach to the Interpretation of Tax Statutes'. 20 *Statute Law Review* 124 (1999).

Lee, Natalie (ed.). *Revenue Law: Principles and Practice*, 34th edn (Haywards Heath: Bloomsbury, 2016).

Loughlin, Martin. *The Idea of Public Law* (Oxford: OUP, 2003).

Loughlin, Martin. *Foundations of Public Law* (Oxford: OUP, 2010).

Loutzenhiser, Glen. *Tiley's Revenue Law*, 8th edn (Oxford: Hart, 2016).

Milward, Alan S. *The European Rescue of the Nation-State*, 2nd edn (London: Routledge, 2000), 435.

Monroe QC, Hubert. *Intolerable Inquisition? Reflections on the Law of Tax* (London: Stevens, 1981).

Oakeshott, Michael. *On Human Conduct* (Oxford: Clarendon, 1975).

Prebble, John. 'Why Is Tax Law Incomprehensible?'. *British Tax Review* 380 (1994).

Shipwright, Adrian and Elizabeth Keeling. *Textbook on Revenue Law* (London: Blackstone, 1997).

Snape, John. 'Corporation Tax Reform: Politics and Public Law'. *British Tax Review* 374 (2007).

Snape, John. *The Political Economy of Corporation Tax: Theory, Values and Law Reform* (Hart: Oxford, 2011).

Snape, John. 'Tax Law: Complexity, Politics and Policymaking'. 24 Social and Legal Studies 155 (2015).

Snape, John. 'Corporate Income Tax Subjects in the United Kingdom'. In D. Gutmann (ed.), *Corporate Income Tax Subjects* (Amsterdam: IBFD, 2015), 546.

Snape, John. 'The "Sinews of the State": Historical Justifications for Taxes and Tax Law'. In Monica Bhandari (ed.), *Philosophical Foundations of Tax Law* (Oxford: OUP, 2017), 9.

Talbot, Margaret. 'Supreme Confidence: The Jurisprudence of Justice Antonin Scalia'. *New Yorker* (28 March 2005).

Thorne, Samuel E. 'The Equity of a Statute and Heydon's Case'. 31 *Illinois Law Review* 202 (1936).

Vinelott, Hon Mr Justice. 'Interpretation of Fiscal Statutes'. *Statute Law Review* 78 (1982).

Wallis, Malcolm. 'Is Tax Really Different?'. *British Tax Review* 299, 308-309 (2016).

Williams, David W. 'Taxing Statutes Are Taxing Statutes: The Interpretation of Revenue Legislation'. 41 *Modern Law Review* 404 (1978).

Williams, David W. 'Three Hundred Years On: Are Our Tax Bills Right Yet?'. *British Taw Review* 370 (1989).

Williams, David W., Geoffrey Morse and Sandra Eden. *Davies: Principles of Tax Law*, 8th edn (London: Sweet and Maxwell, 2016).

Wolf, Martin. 'Brexiters Must Lose If Brexit Is to 'Succeed'. *Financial Times* (London, 29 March 2017), 11.

CHAPTER 15: UNITED STATES OF AMERICA

Aprill, Ellen P. 'The Law of the Word: Dictionary Shopping in the Supreme Court'. 30 *Arizona State Law Journal* 275 (1998).

Aristotle. *Nicomachean Ethics.* Translated by M. Ostwald (New York: Macmillan, 1962).

Baer, Katherine O. 'What International Experience Can Tell Us about Administering a U.S. VAT'. 66 *'National Tax Journal* 447 (2013).

Bankman, Joseph. 'The Economic Substance Doctrine'. 74 *South California Law Review* 5 (2000).

Barker, William B. 'Statutory Interpretation, Comparative Law, and Economic Theory: Discovering the Grund of Income Taxation'. 40 *San Diego Law Review* 821 (2003).

Berghaus, V. Hummel and William F.J. Ardinger. 'The Policy and Structure of the Business Enterprise Tax'. 34 *New Hampshire Bar Journal* 5 (1993).

Bieda, Steven M. 'Facing the Challenge of Replacing the Single Business Tax: The Development and Evolution of the Michigan Business Tax'. 53 *Wayne Law Review* 1149 (2007).

Bishop, Thomas A. 'The Death and Reincarnation of Plain Meaning in Connecticut'. 41 *Connecticut Law Review* 825 (2009).

Bittker, Boris I. 'Pervasive Judicial Doctrines in the Construction of the Internal Revenue Code'. 21 *Howard Law Journal* 693 (1978).

Blatt, William S. 'Interpretative Communities: The Missing Element in Statutory Interpretation'. 95 *Northwestern University Law Review* 629 (2001).

van Brederode, Robert F. and Pierre-Pascal Gendrón. 'The Taxation of Cross-Border Interstate Sales in Federal or Common Markets'. 2 *World Journal of VAT/GST Law* 1 (2013).

Brudney, James J. and Corey Ditslear. 'The Warp and Woof of Statutory Interpretation: Comparing Supreme Court Approaches in Tax Law and Workplace Law'. 58 *Duke Law Journal* 1231 (2009).

Caron, Paul L. 'The Role of State Court Decisions in Federal Tax Litigation: *Bosch, Erie*, and Beyond'. 71 *Oregon Law Review* 781 (1992).

Clausing, Kimberly A. 'Who Pays the Corporate Tax in a Global Economy?'. 66 *'National Tax Journal* 151 (2013).

Cnossen, Sybren. 'A VAT Primer for Lawyers, Economists, and Accountants'. 124 *Tax Notes* 687 (2009).

Cooley, Thomas M. *A Treatise on the Law of Taxation*, 2nd edn (Chicago: Callaghan, 1886).

Cox, Archibald. 'Judge Learned Hand and the Interpretation of Statutes'. 60 *Harvard Law Review* 370 (1947).

Cronin, Julie-Ann, Emily Y. Lin, Laura Power and Michael Cooper. 'Distributing the Corporate Income Tax: Revised U.S. Treasury Methodology'. 66 *'National Tax Journal* 239 (2013).

Cross, Frank B. *Decision Making in the U.S. Courts of Appeals* (Stanford: Stanford University Press, 2007).

Cummings Jr, Jasper L. 'Statutory Interpretation and *Albertson's*'. 66 *Tax Notes* 559 (1995).

Dennehy, Edward K. and Stephen E. Ehrlich. 'Tax Treaty Interpretation and Conflicts with U.S. Federal Law'. 122 *Tax Notes* 1101 (2009).

Dickerson, Reed. *The Interpretation and Application of Statutes* (Boston: Little, Brown & Co., 1975).

Dubroff, Harold. *The United States Tax Court: An Historical Analysis* (Chicago: Commerce Clearing House, 1979).

Duncan, Harley and Jon Sedon. 'How Different VATs Work'. 125 *Tax Notes* 1367 (2009).

Dworkin, Ronald. *Law's Empire* (Cambridge: Belknap Press, 1986).

Easterbrook, Frank H. 'Foreword: The Court and the Economic System'. 98 *Harvard Law Review* 4 (1984).

Edelman, Paul H., David E. Klein and Stefanie A. Lindquist. 'Consensus, Disorder, and Ideology on the Supreme Court'. 9 *Journal of Empirical Legal Studies* 129 (2012).

Eskridge Jr, William N. and Phillip P. Frickey. 'The Supreme Court 1993 Term – Forward: Law as Equilibrium'. 108 *Harvard Law Review* 26. (1994)

Eskridge Jr, William N., Phillip P. Frickey and Elizabeth Garrett. *Legislation and Statutory Interpretation*, 2nd edn (New York: Foundation Press, 2006).

Faber, Peter L. 'Business Purpose and Economic Substance in State Taxation'. 55 *State Tax Notes* 331 (2010).

Frankfurter, Felix. 'Some Reflections on the Reading of Statutes'. 47 *Columbia Law Review* 527 (1947).

Fuller, Lon L. *The Law in Quest of Itself* (Chicago: Foundation Press, 1940).

Glickman, Jeffrey C. and Clark R. Calhoun. 'The "States" of the Federal Common Law Tax Doctrines'. 61 *Tax Law* 1181 (2008).

Gravelle, Jennifer C. 'Corporate Tax Incidence: Review of General Equilibrium Estimates and Analysis'. 66 *'National Tax Journal* 185 (2013).

Hall, Robert E. and Alvin Rabuska. *The Flat Tax*, 2nd edn (Stanford: Hoover Institution Press, 1995).

Hart Jr, Henry M. and Albert M. Sacks. *The Legal Process: Basic Problems in the Making and Application of Law* (New York: Foundation Press, William N. Eskridge Jr and Phillip P. Frickey (eds), 1994, from 1958 tentative edn).

Internal Revenue Service. *Internal Revenue Service Databook* (Washington, DC: IRS, 2012).

Jackel, Monte A. 'Why the Tax Law Is So Dysfunctional'. 138 *Tax Notes* 891 (2013).

Johnson, Steve, Jerome Borison and Samuel C. Ullman. *Civil Tax Procedure*, 3rd edn. Durham: Carolina Academic Press, 2016.

Johnson, Steve R. '"*Seminole Rock* in Tax Cases'." *Yale Journal on Regulation: Notice & Comment* (September 15, 2016).

Johnson, Steve R. 'Retroactive Tax Legislation'. 81 *State & Local Tax Notes* 529 (2016).

Johnson, Steve R. 'The Rise and Fall of *Chevron* in Tax: From the Early Days to *King* and Beyond'. *Pepperdine Law Review* 19 (2015).

Johnson, Steve R. '*Auer/Seminole Rock* Deference in the Tax Court'. 11 *Pittsburgh Tax Review* 1 (2013).

Johnson, Steve R. 'Reforming Federal Tax Litigation – An Agenda'. 41 *Florida State University Law Review* 205 (2013).

Johnson, Steve R. 'The "Things of the Same Nature" Canon in State-Local Tax Construction'. 67 *State Tax Notes* 59 (2013).

Johnson, Steve R. '"Preserving Fairness in Tax Administration in the Mayo Era'". 32 *Virginia Tax Review* 269 (2012).

Johnson, Steve R. 'The No Surplusage Canon in and Local Tax Cases'. 65 *State Tax Notes* 675 (2012).

Johnson, Steve R. 'ALJs in State-Local Tax Cases: To Whom Is Deference Due?'. 64 *State Tax Notes* 785 (2012).

Johnson, Steve R. 'Conditional Deference to Tax Authorities'. 60 *State Tax Notes* 269 (2011).

Johnson, Steve R. 'Deference – Questions of Fact Versus Issues of Law'. 59 *State Tax Notes* 883 (2011).

Johnson, Steve R. '*Chevron* Deference to State Tax Agencies'. 59 *State Tax Notes* 285 (2011).

Johnson, Steve R. '"An IRS Duty of Consistency: The Failure of Common Law Making and a Proposed Statutory Solution'." 77 *Tennessee Law Review* 563 (2010).

Johnson, Steve R. 'Judicial Deference to State Tax Agencies – An Overview'. 58 *State Tax Notes* 633 (2010).

Johnson, Steve R. 'Tilted versus Reasonable Interpretation of Tax Laws'. 58 *State Tax Notes* 277 (2010).

Johnson, Steve R. 'The "Absurd Results" Doctrine in State and Local Tax Cases'. 54 *State Tax Notes* 195 (2009).

Johnson, Steve R. '"Pro-Taxpayer Interpretation of State-Local Tax Laws'." 51 *State Tax Notes* 441 (2009).

Johnson, Steve R. 'Statutes Requiring Plain Meaning Interpretation'. 53 *State Tax Notes* 763 (2009).

Johnson, Steve R. 'Equitable Tolling in State and Local Tax Cases'. 52 *State Tax Notes* 917 (2009).

Johnson, Steve R. 'Supertext and Consistent Meaning'. 52 *State Tax Notes* 675 (2009).

Johnson, Steve R. 'The Two Kinds of Legislative Intent'. 51 *State Tax Notes* 1045 (2009).

Johnson, Steve R. 'Interpreting State Tax Exemptions, Deductions, and Credits'. 51 *State Tax Notes* 607 (2009).

Johnson, Steve R. 'The Reenactment and Inaction Doctrines in State Tax Litigation'. 50 *State Tax Notes* 661 (2008).

Johnson, Steve R. '"Uniformity Clause Limitations on State Taxes'." 27/3 *ABA Section of Tax'n News Quarterly* 16 (Spring 2008).

Johnson, Steve R. 'Substance and Form in State Taxation'. 50 *State Tax Notes* 239 (2008).

Johnson, Steve R. 'The Canon That Tax Penalties Should Be Strictly Construed'. 3 *Nevada Law Journal* 495 (2003).

Johnson, Steve R. 'Should Ambiguous Revenue Laws Be Interpreted in Favor of Taxpayers?'. *Nevada Law Journal* 15 (April 2002).

Johnson, Steve R. 'The Phoenix and the Perils of the Second Best: Why Heightened Appellate Deference to Tax Court Decisions Is Undesirable'. 77 *Oregon L. Review* 235 (1998).

Johnson, Steve R. 'Further Thoughts on Interpreting Tax Statutes'. 17(4) *ABA Section of 'Taxation Newsletter* 11 (1998).

Kahn, Douglas A. 'A Proposed Replacement of the Tax Expenditures Concept and a Different Perspective on Accelerated Depreciation'. 41 *Florida State University Law Review* 143 (2013).

Kolarik II, William J. 'Untangling Substantial Nexus'. 64 *Tax Law* 851 (2011).

Likhovski, Assaf. 'The Duke and the Lady: Helvering v. Gregory and the History of Tax Avoidance Adjudication'. 25 *Cardozo Law Review* 953 (2004).

Liu, Li and Rosanne Altschuler. 'Measuring the Burden of the Corporate Income Tax under Imperfect Competition'. 66 *'National Tax Journal* 215 (2013).

Livingston, Michael. 'Practical Reason, "Purposivism," and the Interpretation of Tax Statutes'. 51 *Tax Law Review* 677 (1996).

Livingston, Michael. 'Congress, the Courts, and the Code: Legislative History and the Interpretation of Tax Statutes'.) 69 *Texas Law Review*: 819 (1991).

Manning, John F. 'The Absurdity Doctrine'. 116 *Harvard Law Review* 2387 (2003).

McCaffery, Edward J. 'Tax Policy under a Hybrid Income-Consumption Tax'. 70 *Texas. Law Review* 1145 (1992).

McCormack, Shannon W. 'Tax Shelters and Statutory Interpretation: A Much Needed Purposive Approach'. *University of Illinois Law Review* 697 (2009).

McIntyre, Michael J. and Richard D. Pomp. 'A Policy Analysis of Michigan's Mislabeled Gross Receipts Tax'. 53 *Wayne Law Review* 1283 (2007).

McLure Jr, Charles E. 'The Business Net Receipts Tax: A Dog that Will Not Hunt'. 37 *Hastings Constitutional Law Quarterly* 745 (2010).

National Ass'n of State Budget Officers. '"Summary: Fall 2016 Fiscal Survey of States'" (December 30, 2016).

Note. 'Looking It Up: Dictionaries and Statutory Interpretation'. 107 *Harvard Law Review* 1437 (1994).

Popkin, William D. 'The Collaborative Model of Statutory Interpretation'. 61 *Southern California Law Review* 541 (1988).

Popkin, William D. *Materials on Legislation: Political Language and the Political Process*, 5th edn (New York: Foundation Press, 2010).

Rosenkranz, Nicholas O. 'Federal Rules of Statutory Interpretation'. 115 *Harvard Law Review* 2085 (2002).

Sachs, David. 'Is the 19th Century Doctrine of Treaty Override Good Law for Modern Day Tax Treaties?'. 47 *Tax Law* 867 (1994).

Scalia, Antonin. *A Matter of Interpretation* (Princeton: Princeton University Press, 1997).

Scalia, Antonin and Bryan A. Garner. *Reading Law: The Interpretation of Legal Texts* (St. Paul: Thomson/West, 2012).

Scalia, Antonin and John F. Manning. 'A Dialogue on Statutory and Constitutional Interpretation'. 80 *The George Washington Law Review* 1610 (2012).

Scharf, William H. 'State Law in the Tax Court – Controlling Precedents'. 26 *Tax Law* 293 (1973).

Schenk, Alan and Oliver Oldman. *Value Added Tax: A Comparative Approach* (Cambridge: Cambridge University Press, 2007).

Schenk, Alan, Victor Thuronyi and Wei Cui. *Value Added Tax: A Comparative Approach*, 2nd edn (Cambridge: Cambridge University Press, 2015).

Shaviro, Daniel N. 'Rethinking Tax Expenditures and Fiscal Language'. 57 *Tax Law Review* 187 (2004).

Shaviro, Daniel N. *Decoding the U.S. Corporate Tax* (Washington, D.C.: Urban Institute Press, 2009).

Singer, Norman J. and J.D. Shambie Singer. *Statutes and Statutory Construction*, 7th edn (St. Paul: Thomson Reuters, 2007).

Sloovere, Frederick J. de. 'Extrinsic Aids in the Interpretation of Statutes'. 88 *University of Pennsylvania Law Review* 527 (1940).

Smith, Robert T. 'Tax Treaty Interpretation by the Judiciary'. 49 *Tax Law* 845 (1996).

Staudt, Nancy C., René Lindstädt and Jason O'Connor. 'Judicial Decisions as Legislation: Congressional Oversight of Supreme Court Tax Cases, 1954-2005'. 82 *New York University Law Review* 1340 (2007).

Texas Taxpayers & Research Ass'n. 'Understanding the Texas Franchise - Or "Margin" - Tax'. www.ttara.org/files/document/file-4ea5bda9239ef.pdf, October 2011.

Tribe, Lawrence T. 'Comment'. In Antonin Scalia (ed.), *A Matter of Interpretation* (Princeton: Princeton University Press, 1997).

United States Census Bureau. www.census.gov/govs/gtax/index.html.

Wald, Patricia M. 'Some Observations on the Use of Legislative History in the 1981 Supreme Court Term'. 68 *Iowa Law Review* 195 (1983).

Yesnowitz, Jamie, Chuck Jones, Lori Stolly and Priya Nair. '"United States: SALT Outlook, Trends and Predictions for 2017'." (April 21, 2017), available at http://www.mondaq.com/article.asp?articleid = 587614&email_access = on& chk = 2076074&q = 1488460.

Table of Cases

Chapter 1: A Reflection on Methods and Issues

United States

Name	*Reported*	*Page*
Riggs v. Palmer	115 N.Y. 506; 22 N.E. 188 (1889)	4

Chapter 2: Australia

Australia and United Kingdom

Name	*Reported*	*Page*
Bouch v. Sproule	(1887) 12 App. Cas. 385 (H.L.)	25
In re the Income Tax Acts (No. 2)	(1901) 27 VLR 39	25
Commissioner of Income Tax (Queensland) v. The Brisbane Gas Company	(1907) 5 CLR 96	25
Harding v. Federal Commissioner of Taxation	(1917) 23 CLR 119	23
Cornell v. Deputy Federal Commissioner of Taxation (South Australia)	(1920) 29 CLR 39	23
Scott v. Commissioner of Taxation	(1935) 35 SR (NSW) 215	25
Matthews v. Chicory Marketing Board (Vic.)	(1938) 60 CLR 263	17, 20
Sun Newspapers Ltd. and Associated Newspapers Ltd. v. Federal Commissioner of Taxation	(1938) 61 CLR 337	27
Inland Revenue Commissioners v. British Salmson Aero Engines, Ltd.	[1938] 3 All ER 283	27

Name	*Reported*	*Page*
South Australia v. Commonwealth (First Uniform Tax Case)	(1942) 65 CLR 373	19
Resch v. Federal Commissioner of Taxation	(1942) 66 CLR 198	23, 25, 45
Parton v. Milk Board (Vic.)	(1949) 80 CLR 229	17
Moore v. Commonwealth	[1951] HCA 10; 82 CLR 547	21
Broken Hill Theatres Pty. Ltd. v. Federal Commissioner of Taxation	(1952) 85 CLR 423	27
Victoria v. Commonwealth (Second Uniform Tax Case)	(1957) 99 CLR 575	19
BP Australia Ltd. v. Federal Commissioner of Taxation	(1965) 112 CLR 386	28
Fairfax v. Federal Commissioner of Taxation	(1965) 114 CLR 1	20
Federal Commissioner of Taxation v. Westraders Pty. Ltd.	(1980) 144 CLR 55; 11 ATR 24	29, 30
Cooper Brookes (Wollongong) Pty. Ltd. v. Federal Commissioner of Taxation	(1981) 147 CLR 297	29, 31
Hematite Petroleum Pty. Ltd. v. Victoria	(1983) 151 CLR 599	18
MacCormick v. Federal Commissioner of Taxation	(1984) 158 CLR 622	21
Queensland v. Commonwealth	[1987] HCA 2; 162 CLR 74; 18 ATR 158	22
Air Caledonie International v. Commonwealth	(1988) 165 CLR 462	21
Harper v. Minister for Sea Fisheries	[1989] HCA 47; 168 CLR 314	21
Thiel v. Federal Commissioner of Taxation	[1990] HCA 37; 171 CLR 338	43
Federal Commissioner of Taxation v. Consolidated Fertilizers Ltd.	(1991) 22 ATR 281	28
Mutual Pools & Staff Pty. Ltd. v. Federal Commissioner of Taxation	[1992] HCA 4; 173 CLR 450; 22 ATR 856	23
Deputy Commissioner of Taxation v. State Bank of New South Wales	[1992] HCA 6; 174 CLR 219; 23 ATR 1	22
South Australia v. Commonwealth	[1992] HCA 7; 174 CLR 235; 23 ATR 10	22
ANZ Savings Bank Ltd. v. Federal Commissioner of Taxation	(1993) 25 ATR 369	32
Mutual Pools & Staff Pty. Ltd. v. Commonwealth	[1994] HCA 9; 179 CLR 155; 27 ATR 357	22
Ha v. New South Wales	[1997] HCA 34; 189 CLR 465; 36 ATR 319	17

Name	*Reported*	*Page*
Applicant A v. Minister for Immigration & Ethnic Affairs	[1997] HCA 4; 90 CLR 225	43
Federal Commissioner of Taxation v. Lamesa Holdings B.V.	[1997] FCA 785; 36 ATR 589	43, 44
Airservices Australia v. Canadian Airlines International Ltd.	[1999] HCA 62; 202 CLR 133; 43 ATR 246	21
Commissioner for Australian Capital Territory Revenue v. Kithock Pty. Ltd.	(2000) FCA 1098	18
Interchase Corporation Limited v. ACN 010 087 573 Pty. Ltd. & Ors.	[2000] QSC 13; 45 ATR 445	37
Shaw v. Director of Housing and State of Tasmania (No. 2)	[2001] TASSC 2; 46 ATR 242	37
Walter Construction Group Ltd. v. Walker Corporation Ltd. & Ors.	[2001] NSWSC 283; 47 ATR 48	37
Unisys Corporation Inc. v. Federal Commissioner of Taxation	[2002] NSWSC 1115; 51 ATR 386	44
CSR Ltd. v. Hornsby Shire Council	[2004] NSWSC 946; 57 ATR 201	36
Orr v. Wendt	[2005] WASCA 199	25
ACP Publishing Ltd. v. Federal Commissioner of Taxation	[2005] FCAFC 57; 59 ATR 98	40
HP Mercantile Pty. Ltd. v. Federal Commissioner of Taxation	[2005] FCAFC 126; 60 ATR 106	36, 37, 38
Sterling Guardian Pty. Ltd. v. Federal Commissioner of Taxation	[2005] FCA 1166; 60 ATR 502	37
McDermott Industries (Aust.) Pty. Ltd. v. Federal Commissioner of Taxation	[2005] FCAFC 67; 59 ATR 358	43, 44
Toyama Pty. Ltd. v. Landmark Building Developments Pty. Ltd.	(2006) 62 ATR 73	42
Sterling Guardian Pty. Ltd. v. Federal Commissioner of Taxation	[2006] FCAFC 12; 62 ATR 119	38
Westley Nominees Pty. Ltd. v. Coles Supermarkets Australia Pty. Ltd.	[2006] FCAFC 115; 62 ATR 682	40
Federal Commissioner of Taxation v. DB Rreef Funds Management Ltd.	[2006] FCAFC 89; 62 ATR 699	40
Cascade Brewery Company Pty. Ltd. v. Federal Commissioner of Taxation	[2006] FCA 821; 64 ATR 28	41
Saga Holidays Ltd. v. Federal Commissioner of Taxation	[2006] FCAFC 191; 64 ATR 602	38
P. & N. Beverages Australia Pty. Ltd. V. Federal Commissioner of Taxation	[2007] NSWSC 338; 65 ATR 391	41

Name	*Reported*	*Page*
Reliance Carpet Co. Pty. Ltd. v. Federal Commissioner of Taxation	[2007] FCAFC 99; 66 ATR 117	38
Reliance Carpet Co. Pty. Ltd. v. Commissioner of Taxation	[2008] HCA 22; 68 ATR 158	39
KAP Motors Pty. Ltd. v. Federal Commissioner of Taxation	[2008] FCA 159; 68 ATR 927	38
Virgin Holdings S.A. v. Federal Commissioner of Taxation	[2008] FCA 1503; 70 ATR 478	45
JMB Beverages Pty. Ltd. v. Federal Commissioner of Taxation	[2009] FCA 668; 73 ATR 191	41
Travelex Ltd. v. Federal Commissioner of Taxation	[2009] FCAFC 133; 73 ATR 463	38
Procter & Gamble U.K. v. Revenue and Customs Commissioners	[2009] STC 1990	42
JMB Beverages Pty. Ltd. v. Federal Commissioner of Taxation	[2010] FCAFC 68; 76 ATR 76	41
Federal Commissioner of Taxation v. Secretary to the Department of Transport (Victoria)	[2010] FCAFC 84; 76 ATR 306	38
Travelex Ltd. v. Commissioner of Taxation	[2010] HCA 33; 76 ATR 329	39
Sunchen Pty. Ltd. v. Federal Commissioner of Taxation	[2010] FCAFC 138; 78 ATR 197	42
Lansell House Pty. Ltd. v. Federal Commissioner of Taxation	[2011] FCAFC 6; 79 ATR 22	41, 42
Russell v. Federal Commissioner of Taxation	[2011] FCAFC 10; 79 ATR 31	44
Roy Morgan Research Pty. Ltd. v. Federal Commissioner of Taxation	[2011] HCA 35; 244 CLR 97; 80 ATR 1	21
Qantas Airways Limited v. Federal Commissioner of Taxation	[2011] FCAFC 113; 81 ATR 816	38
Federal Commissioner of Taxation v. Multiflex Pty. Ltd.	[2011] FCAFC 142; 82 ATR 153	38
Federal Commissioner of Taxation v. SNF (Australia) Pty. Ltd.	[2011] FCAFC 74; 82 ATR 680	45
Commissioner of Taxation v. Qantas Airways Ltd.	[2012] HCA 41; 247 CLR 286; 83 ATR 1	39
Mills v. Federal Commissioner of Taxation	[2012] HCA 51; 250 CLR 171; 83 ATR 514	32
MTAA Superannuation Fund (R. G. Casey Building) Property Pty. Ltd. v. Federal Commissioner of Taxation	[2012] FCAFC 89; 84 ATR 349	40

Name	*Reported*	*Page*
Fortescue Metals Group Ltd. v. Commonwealth	[2013] HCA 34; 250 CLR 548; 89 ATR 1	22
Commissioner of Taxation v. MBI Properties Pty. Ltd	[2014] HCA 49, 254 CLR 376	39
Queensland Nickel Pty. Ltd. v. Commonwealth	[2015] HCA 12; 255 CLR 252	22
Eclipse Resources Pty. Ltd. v. WA (No. 4)	[2016] WASC 62	17
Eclipse Resources Pty. Ltd. v. Minister for Environment (No. 2)	[2017] WASCA 90	17
Federal Commissioner of Taxation v. Seven Network Ltd.	[2016] FCAFC 70; 103 ATR 253	45
Tech Mahindra Ltd. v. Federal Commissioner of Taxation	[2016] FCAFC 130; 103 ATR 813	43
Chevron Australia Holdings Pty. Ltd. v. Federal Commissioner of Taxation	[2017] FCAFC 62	21

European Union

C-408/98 Abbey National	*[2001] ECR I-1361*	*36*

United States

Patton v. Brady, Executrix	*[1902] 184 US 608*	*17*

Chapter 3: Brazil

Brazil

Supreme Court

Case	*Name*	*Date of Decision*	*Reported*	*Page*
EA, No. 103.778	*Federal Union v. Cobesca Manchester*	09.18.1985	OG, 12.13.1985	56
EA, No. 150.755	*Federal Union v. Nordeste*	11.18.1992	OG, 10.22.1993	56
EA, No. 148.754-2/RJ	*Itaparica v. Federal Union*	06.24.1993	OG, 03.04.1994	56
DAU, No. 1	*Arguition of the Constitutionality of COFINS*	12.01.1993	OG, 06.16.1995	56

Administrative Council of Administrative Appeals (CARF)

Superior Court of Justice

Chapter 4: Canada

Canada and United Kingdom

Name	*Reported*	*Page*
Inco Ltd v. Canada	2004 TCC 373	84
Inco Ltd v. Canada	2005 FCA 44, [2005] 1 CTC 367	84
Canada Trustco Mortgage Co. v. Canada	2005 SCC 54, [2005] 2 SCR 601	81, 95
Mathew v. Canada	2005 SCC 55, [2005] 2 SCR 643	95
Imperial Oil Ltd. v. Canada; Inco Ltd. v. Canada	2006 SCC 46, [2006] 2 SCR 447	89
Placer Dome Canada Ltd. v. Ontario (Minister of Finance)	2006 SCC 20, [2006] 1 SCR 715	81, 83, 86
A.Y.S.A. Amateur Youth Soccer Association v. CRA	2007 SCC 42	81
Lipson v. Canada	2009 SCC 1, [2009] 1 SCR 3	95
Prévost Car Inc. v. Canada	[2009] FCJ No 241, 176 ACWS (3d) 278	97
United Parcel Service Canada Ltd. v. Canada	2009 SCC 20, [2009] 1 SCR 657	96
Husky Oil Ltd v. Canada	2010 FCA 125	94
Copthorne Holdings Ltd. v. Canada	2011 SCC 63, [2011] 3 SCR 721	95
Canada v. Craig	2012 SCC 43, [2012] 2 SCR 489	82
Calgary (City) v. Canada	2012 SCC 20, [2012] 1 SCR 689	96
Fundy Settlement v. Canada	2012 SCC 14, [2012] 1 SCR 520	82
Agence du Revenu du Quebec v. Service Environmentaux AES Inc.	2013 SCC 65	85
Envision Credit Union v. Canada	2013 SCC 48, [2013] 3 SCR 191	82
High-Crest Enterprises Ltd. v. Canada	2015 TCC 230	96
Canada (National Revenue) v. Thompson	2016 SCC 21	88, 93
French v. Canada	2016 FCA 64	91
Jean Coutu Group (PJC) Inc v, Canada (AG)	2016 SCC 55	91
Canada (AG) v, Fairmont Hotels Inc.	2016 SCC 56	91

Chapter 5: China

Higher People's Court of Beijing

20 December 2002	*PanAmSat*	*Gaoxingzhongzi*	*(2002) 248*	*117*

People's Court of Huancui District, Weihai City

November 2010	*Weihai Donghe Shiye Inc.*	*Guoshuibanfa*	*[2011] No. 34*	*123*

Chapter 6: European Union

Court of Justice of the European Union (ECJ)

Case	*Name*	*Reported*	*Page*
26/62	*Van Gend & Loos*	[1963] ECR 3	134
28/62 and 30/62	*Da Costa en Schaake*	[1963] ECR 11	139
90/63 and 91/63	*Commission v. Luxembourg and Belgium*	[1964] ECR 121	134
6/64	*Costa v. E.N.E.L*	[1964] ECR 119	134
29//68	*Milch- Fett und Eierkontor GmbH*	[1969] ECR 165	139
6/72	*Europemballage Corp. & Continental Can Co.*	[1973] ECR 215	145
166/73	*Rheinmühlen* (II)	[1974] ECR 33	139
8/74	*Dassonville*	[1974] ECR 837	169
45/75	*Rewe-Zentrale*	[1976] ECR 181	167
48/75	*Jean Noël Royer*	[1976] ECR 497	135
33/76	*Rewe*	[1976] ECR 198	135, 146
45/76	*Comet*	[1976] ECR 2043	146
51/76	*VNO*	[1977] ECR 113	134
38/77	*Enka*	[1977] ECR 2203	135
70/77	*Simmenthal*	[1978] ECR 1453	146
93/78	*Mattheus*	[1978] ECR 2203	142
120/78	*Cassis de Dijon*	[1979] ECR 649	170
168/78	*Commission v. France*	[1980] ECR 347	167
265/78	*Ferwerda*	[1980] ECR 617	146
244/80	*Foglia*	[1981] ECR 3045	142
64/81	*Nicolaus Corman*	[1982] ECR 13	134

Case	*Name*	*Reported*	*Page*
89/81	*Hong Kong*	[1982] ECR 1277	158
283/81	*CILFIT*	[1982] ECR 3415	141–143
292/82	*Merck*	[1983] ECR 1-3781	145
14/83	*Von Colson & Kamann*	[1984] ECR 1891	151
268/83	*Rompelman*	[1985] ECR 655	158, 159
270/83	*Commission v. France (Avoir Fiscal)*	[1986] ECR 273	171–174, 180
106/84	*Cie v. Denmark*	[1986] ECR 833	167
152/84	*Marshall*	[1986] ECR 723	152
81/87	*Daily Mail*	[1988] ECR 05483	174, 175
122/87	*Commission v. Italy*	[1988] ECR 2685	156
230/87	*Naturally Yours*	[1988] ECR 6365	161
348/87	*SUFA*	[1989] ECR 1737	156
51/88	*Knut Hamann*	[1989] ECR 767	145
C-126/88	*Boots*	[1990] ECR I-1235	161
C-175/88	*Biehl*	[1990] ECR I-01779	170
C-372/88	*Milk Marketing Board*	[1990] ECR I-1345	157
C-106/89	*Marleasing*	[1990] ECR I-4135	151
C-213/89	*Factortame I*	[1990] ECR I-2433	146
C-230/89	*Commission v. Greece*	[1991] ECR I-1909	167
C-6/90 and C-9/90	*Francovich*	[1991] ECR I-5357	134, 135, 147, 148
C-204/90	*Bachmann*	[1990] ECR I-00249	171
C-267/91 & C-268/91	*Keck*	[1993] ECR I-06097	189
C-46/93 & C-48/93	*Brasserie du Pêcheur & Factortame III)*	[1996] ECR I-1029	147
C-279/93	*Schumacker*	[1995] ECR I-225	168, 173, 178, 189
C-367/93 to 377/93	*Roders et al*	[1995] ECR I-2229	167
C-453/93	*Bulthuis-Griffioen*	[1995] ECR I-2341	156
C-468/93	*Gemeente Emmen*	[1996] ECR 1-1756	145
C-55/94	*Gebhard*	[1995] ECR I-4165	170
C-110/94	*INZO*	[1996] ECR I-857	159
C-178/94, C-179/94, C-188/94, C-189/94 C-190/94	*Dillenkofer*	[1996] ECR I-4845	147

Case	*Name*	*Reported*	*Page*
C-237/94	*O'Flynn*	[1996] ECR I-02617	170
C-317/94	*Elida Gibbs*	[1996] ECR I-5339	162, 163
C-25/95	*Otte v. Germany*	[1996] ECR 1-3745	145
C-250/95	*Futura*	[1997] ECR I-02471	171
C-261/95	*Palmisani v. INPS*	[1997] ECR I-4025	146
C-283/95	*Karlheinz Fischer*	[1998] ECR I-3369	166
C-124/96	*Commission v. Spain*	[1998] ECR I-2501	165
C-264/96	*ICI*	[1998] ECR I-04695	171
C-336/96	*Gilly*	[1998] ECR I-2793	178
C-349/96	*Card Protection Plan*	[1999] ECR I-973	151
C-149/97	*Institute of the Motor Industry*	[1998] ECR I-7053	157
C-216/97	*Gregg*	[1999] ECR I-4947	164, 165
C-307/97	*Saint Gobain*	[1999] ECR I-6161	180, 181
C-384/98	*D. v. W.*	[2000] ECR I-6795	156
C-397/98 & C-410/98	*Metallgesellschaft*	[2001] ECR I-1727	148
C-481/98	*Commission v. France*	[2001] ECR I-3369)	164
C-76/99	*Commission v. France*	[2001] ECR I-249	158
C-55/00	*Gottardo v. INPS*	[2002] ECR I-0413	179
C-112/00	*Schmidberger*	[2003] ECR I-5659	142
C-144/00	*Matthias Hoffmann*	[2003] ECR I-2921	165
C-212/01	*Unterpertinger*	[2003] ERC I-13859	156
C-224/01	*Gerhard Köbler*	[2003] ECR I-10239	147
C-307/01	*d'Ambrumenil*	[2003] ECR I-13989	158
C-397-403/01	*Pfeiffer*	[2004] ECR I-8835	152
C-255/02	*Halifax et al*	[2006] ECR I- 01609	183
C-319/02	*Petri Manninen*	[2004] ECR I-7477	142, 169, 176, 177
C-365/02	*Lindfors*	ECLI:EU:C:2004:449	168
C-453/02 & C-462/02	*Linneweber*	[2005] ECR I-1131	166
C-105/03	*Maria Pupino*	[2005] ECR I-5285	152
C-152/03	*Ritter-Coulais*	[2006] ECR I-01711	170
C-173/03	*Traghetti*	[2006] ECR I-5177	147
C-403/03	*Schempp*	[2005] ECR I-06421	168
C-411/03	*SEVIC*	[2005] ECR I-10805	175
C-446/03	*Marks & Spencer*	[2005] ECR I-10837	170, 171, 178, 183

Case	*Name*	*Reported*	*Page*
C-513/03	*van Hilten-van der Heijden*	[2006] ECR I-1957	169, 173, 178, 181, 182
C-94/04 and	*Cipola v. Fazari*	[2006] ECR I-11421	141
C-202/04	*Macrino v. Meloni*	[2006] ECR I-11421	141
C-196/04	*Cadbury Schweppes*	[2006] ECR I-7995	178, 184–186
C-212/04	*ELOG*	[2006] ECR I-6057	152
C-265/04	*Bouanich*	[2006] ECR I-923	181
C-290/04	*Scorpio*	[2006] ECR I-09461	171
C-292/04	*Meilicke*	[2007] ECR I-01835	142
C-347/04	*Rewe Zentralfinanz*	[2007] ECR I-2647	178
C-374/04	*Act IV GLO*	[2006] ECR I-11673	182
C-446/04	*Test Claimants in the FII Group Litigation*	[2006] ECR I-11753	139
C-470/04	*'N'*	[2006] ECR I-7409	178
C-513/04	*Kerckhaert-Morres*	[2006] ECR I-10967	169
C-524/04	*Thin Cap GLO*	[2007] ECR I-2107	178, 186
C-106/05	*L.u.P.*	[2006] ECR I-5123	165
C-170/05	*Denkavit France*	[2006] ECR I-11949	183
C-201/05	*CFC and Divided GLO*	[2008] ECR I-2875	178
C-231/05	*Oy AA*	[2007] ECR I-6373	178
C-277/05	*Société thermale d'Eugénie-les-Bains*	[2007] ECR I-6415	163
C-379/05	*Amurta*	[2007] ECR I-9569	178, 183
C-432/05	*Unibet*	[2007] ECR I-2271	146
C-205/06	*Commission v. Austria*	[2009] ECR I-01301	179
C-210/06	*Cartesio*	[2008] ECR I-9641	175
C-249/06	*Commission v. Sweden*	[2009] ECR I-01301	179
C-414/06	*Lidl Belgium*	[2008] ECR I-3601	169, 178
C-437/06	*Securenta*	[2008] ECR I-1597	160
C-43/07	*Arens-Sikkens*	[2008] ECR I-6887	183
C-105/07	*Lammers & Van Cleeff*	[2008] ECR I-173	178
C-118/07	*Commission v. Finland*	[2009] ECR I-10889	179
C-157/07	*Krankenheim*	[2008] ECR I-08061	171
C-303/07	*Aberdeen Property Fininvest Alpha*	[2009] ECR I-5145	178
C-572/07	*Tellmer*	[2009] ECR I-4983	140, 142
C-67/08	*Block*	[2009] ECR I-883	169
C-96/08	*CIBA*	[2010} ECR I-2911	169
C-127/08	*Metock*	[2008] ECR I-06241	189

Case	*Name*	*Reported*	*Page*
C-128/08	*Damseaux*	[2009] ECR I-6823	169
C-153/08	*Commission v. Spain ("Lotteries")*	[2009] ECR I-9735	170, 174
C-311/08	*SGI*	[2010] ECR I-487	169, 178, 183, 186
C-582/08	*Cie v. United Kingdom*	[2010] ECR I-7195	154
C-86/09	*Future Health Technologies*	[2010] ERC I-5215	157
C-269/09	*Commission v. Spain*	ECLI:EU:C:2012:439	178
C-277/09	*RBS Deutschland*	[2010] ECR I-13805	184
C-259/10 & C-260/10	*The Rank Group*	[2011] ECR I-10947	166
C-371/10	*National Grid Indus*	[2011] ECT I-12273	178
C-591/10	*Littlewoods*	ECLI:EU:C:2012:478	149
C-35/11	*Test Claimants in the FII Group Litigation 2*	ECLI:EU:C:2012:707	139
C-44/11	*Deutsche Bank*	ECLI:EU:C:2012:484	168
C-85/11	*Cie v. Ireland*	ECLI:EU:C:2013:217	154
C-123/11	*A Oy*	ECLI:EU:C:2013:84	169
C-174/11	*Ines Zimmermann*	ECLI:EU:C:2012:716	165, 167, 168
C-322/11	*K*	ECLI:EU:C:2013:716	178
C-371/11	*Punch Graphix*	ECLI:EU:C:2012:647	151
C-362/12	*Test Claimants in the FII Group Litigation 3*	ECLI:EU:C:2013:834	139
C-282/12	*Itelcar*	ECLI:EU:C:2013:629	186
C-10/14, C-14/14 & C-17/14	*Joined case Miljoen & Société Générale*	ECLI:EU:C:2015:608	183
C-112/14	*Commission v. United Kingdom of Great Britain and Northern Ireland*	ECLI:EU:C:2014:2369	186

France

Conseil d'Etat

22 December 1978	*Cohn-Bendit*	*[1978] Recueil Lebon* 524	*143*
3 February 1989	*Compagnie Alitalia*	[1989] *Recueil Lebon* 44	143
20 October 1989	*Nicolo*	[1989] *Recueil Lebon* 190	143

Germany

Bundesverfaßungsgericht

8 April 1987	*Case 2 BvR 687/85*	*[1988] 3 CMLR 1*	*143*

United Kingdom

London, Chatham and Dover Railway Co v. South Eastern Railway Co.	*[1893] AC 429*	*148*
Machado v. Fontes	(1897) 2 QB 231	189
Young v. Bristol Aeroplane Co. Ltd.	(1944) 1 KB 718	189
Trans Trust SPRL v. Danubian Trading Co Ltd.	[1952] 2 QB 297	148
Boys v. Chaplin	[1968] 2 WLR 328	189
Jones v. Wrotham Park Settled Estates	[1980] AC 74	154
Garland v. British Railways Engineering Limited	[1983] 2AC 751, 771	151
Westdeutsche Landesbank Girozentrale v. Islington London Borough Council	[1996] AC 669	148
Sempra Metals Limited v. Commissioners of Inland Revenue	[2007] UKHL 34	148
Vodafone 2 v. HMRC	[2009] EWCA Civ 446	153
Test Claimants in the FII Group Litigation v. HMRC	[2012] UKSC 19	150
HMRC v. Aimia Coalition Loyalty UK Limited	[2013] UKSC 15	140

The Netherlands

Hoge Raad

6 October 1982	*Case 20260*	*Hong Kong*	*[1982] BNB 312*	*152*

Chapter 7: France

Court of Justice of the European Union (ECJ)

Case	*Name*	*Reported*	*Page*
C-409/04	*Teleos*	[2007] ECR I-7797	210

Conseil Constitutionnel

Case	*Name*	*Date of Decision*	*Reported*	*Page*
80-119 DC	Loi portant Validation d'actes administratifs	22 July 1980	www.conseil-constitutionnel.fr/decision/1980/80119dc.htm	192
89-256 DC	Loi portant dispositions diverses en matière d'urbanisme et d'agglomérations nouvelles	25 July 1989	www.conseil-constitutionnel.fr/decision/1989/89256dc.htm	195
2010-28, QPC	*Association Sportive Football Club de Metz [Taxe sur les salaires]*	17 September 2010	www.conseil-constitutionnel.fr/decision/2010/49362dc.html	199
2012-298 QPC	*SARL Majestic Champagne [Taxe additionnelle à la contribution sur la valeur ajoutée des entreprises - Modalités de recouvrement]*	28 March 2013	www.conseil-constitutionnel.fr/decision/2013/136568dc.html	199
2013-351 QPC	*Société Boulanger [Taxe locale sur la publicité extérieure II]*	25 October 2013	www.conseil-constitutionnel.fr/decision/2013/138461dc.html	199
2013-679 DC	Loi relative à la lutte contre la fraude fiscale et la grande délinquance économique et financière	4 December 2013	www.conseil-constitutionnel.fr/decision/2013/2013679dc.htm	202
2014-435 QPC	*M. Jean-François V.* [Contribution exceptionnelle sur les hauts revenus]	5 December 2014	www.conseil-constitutionnel.fr/decision/2014/2014435qpc.htm	206

Case	*Name*	*Date of Decision*	*Reported*	*Page*
2016-545 QPC	*M. Alec W. et autre* [Pénalités fiscales pour insuffisance de déclaration et sanctions pénales pour fraude fiscale]	24 June 2016	www.conseil-constitutionnel.fr/decision/2016/2016545qpc.htm	206
2016-546 QPC	*M. Jérôme C.* [Pénalités fiscales pour insuffisance de déclaration et sanctions pénales pour fraude fiscale]	24 June 2016	www.conseil-constitutionnel.fr/decision/2016/2016546qpc.htm	206

Court de Cassation

Case	*Name*	*Date of Decision*	*Reported*	*Page*
N/A	*Société française des câbles télégraphiques*	5 February 1943	Sirey 1944, I53	203
94-50.002	*Préfet de la région Midi-Pyrénées c/ Bechta*	28 June 1995	Bulletin 1995 II N° 221, 127	206

Conseil d'Etat

Case	*Name*	*Date of Decision*	*Reported*	*Page*
97.719	*Mlle X*	5 May 1976	RJF 7-8/76, 326	202
01.683	*Richard*	31 March 1978	Rec. Lebon,168	202
11.798	*Comité de propagande de la banane*	14 December 1979	RJF 1/80, 99	202
34.588	*SA Renfort Service*	27 July 1984	RJF 10/84, 564	204

40.686	*M. X*	12 January 1987	RJF 3/87, 292	201
38.607	*Le Prestre*	13 December 1989	RJF 2/90, 199	201
86.113	*Min. du Budget c/ Cercle militaire mixte de la caserne Mortier*	22 December 1989	Rec. Lebon, 260	209
78.519	*Gisti*	29 June 1990	RJF 9/90, 1096	207
63.266	*SPA Raffaella*	22 May 1992	RJF 7/92, 960	208
115.052	*SA 'La Cinq'*	11 March 1994	Rec. Lebon, 118	206
154.217	*SA Quartz d'Alsace*	6 May 1996	RJF 6/98, 731	204
169.219	*Koné*	3 July 1996	Rec. Lebon, 255	209
148683	*Aquarone*	6 June 1997	Rec. Lebon, 206	192
190.083	*SA Banque française de l'Orient*	13 October 1999	RJF 12/99, 1587	208
172.003	*SA Fabricauto-Essarauto*	19 April 2000	RJF 5/00, 631	205
189.572	*Boniface*	14 February 2001	RJF 5/01, 614	204
215.124	*SA Golay Buchel France*	27 July 2001	RJF 11/01, 1428	208
219.840	*Simoens*	5 June 2002	RJF 8-9/02, 934	206
233618	*Mme Duvignères*	18 December 2002	Rec. Lebon, 463	200
233.944	*Guth*	2 July 2003	RJF 10/03, 1110	205
239.677	*Heskes*	17 December 2003	RJF 3/03, 249	207
233.894	*Andritz*	30 December 2003	RJF 2/04, 238	208
266.997	*Sté Lever Faberger*	2 June 2006	RJF 8-9/2006, 995	202
284.930	*Sté Natexis Banques Populaires*	26 July 2006	RJF 11/06, 1421	209

285.201	*Sté Kaufman & Broad Participations*	4 August 2006	RJF 11/06, 1330	203
295.689	*SARL Alain Palanchon*	1 July 2009	RJF 10/09, 822	210
312-165	*Mme Dubosque*	27 July 2009	RJF 12/09, 1102	204
337.656	*M. Regazzacci*	27 July 2012	RJF 11/12, 1012	207

Chapter 8: Germany

Bundesverfassungsgericht (Federal Constitutional Court)

Date	*Number*	*Reported*	*Page*
21 May 1952	2 BvG 2/52	1 BVerfGE 299	215
18 December 1953	1 BvL 106/53	3 BVerfGE 225	223
17 January 1957	1 BvL 4/54	6 BVerfGE 55	215
12 November 1958	2 BvL 4/56 et al.	8 BVerfGE 274	215
15 December 1959	1 BvL 10/55	10 BVerfGE 234	215
17 May 1960	2 BvL 11/59, and 2 BvL 11/60	11 BVerfGE 126	215
24 January 1962	1 BvR 232/60	13 BVerfGE 318	219
24 January 1962	1 BvR 845/58	13 BVerfGE 331	220
15 July 1969	1 BvR 457/66	26 BVerfGE 327	221, 223
14 February 1973	1 BvR 112/65	34 BVerfGE 269	223, 224, 226
10 February 1976	2 BvG 1/74	41 BVerfGE 291	215
17 January 1978	1 BvL 13/76	47 BVerfGE 109	215
11 October 1978	1 BvR 84/74	1979 NJW 305	224
25 January 1983	2 BvE 1-4/83	62 BVerfGE 1	215
18 December 1984	2 BvL 22/82	68 BVerfGE 337	230
12 March 1985	1 BvR 571/81, 1 BvR 494/82, 1 BvR 47/83	69 BVerfGE 188	224
14 May 1985	1 BvR 233/81, 1 BvR 341/81	69 BVerfGE 315	224
14 May 1985	2 BvL 19/84	72 BVerfGE 278	230

Date	*Number*	*Reported*	*Page*
14 January 1986	1 BvR 209/79, 1 BvR 221/79	71 BVerfGE 354	226
8 April 1987	2 BvR 687/85	1988 NJW 1459	231
27 December 1991	2 BvR 72/90	1992 BStBl II 212	221
22 December 1992	1 BvR 1333/89	1993 NJW 2734	224
30 March 1993	1 BvR 1045/89, 1 BvR 1381/90, 1 BvL 11/90	88 BVerfGE 145	225
28 May 1993	2 BvF 2/90, 2 BvF 4/90, 2 BvF 5/92	88 BVerfGE 203	230
20 March 2002	2 BvG 1/01, 2 BvG 2/02	105 BVerfGE 135	215
14 October 2004	2 BvR 1481/04	111 BVerfGE 307	234
11 January 2005	2 BvR 167/02	112 BVerfGE 164	230
15 January 2009	2 BvR 2044/07	122 BVerfGE 248	226
26 September 2011	2 BvR 2216/06, 2 BvR 469/07	19 BverfGK 89	233
15 December 2015	2 BvL 1/12	2016 HFR 405	237

Bundesfinanzhof (Federal Fiscal Court)

21 February 1964	*IV 26/62 S*	*1964 BStBl III 188*	*216*
14 October 1964	II 175/61 U	1964 BStBl III 667	227, 228
5 February 1965	VI 338/63 U	1965 BStBl III 258	235
10 December 1969	I R 43/67	1970 BStBl II 310	219
28 April 1970	II 56/65	1970 BStBl II 597	220
17 September 1970	IV R 178/67	1971 BStBl II 87	221
19 August 1971	V R 18/71	1972 BStBl II 75	220
14 November 1972	VIII R 22/68	1973 BStBl II 182	220
14 May 1974	VIII R 95/72	1974 BStBl II 572	215–218
1 August 1974	IV R 120/70	1975 BStBl II 12	216
7 October 1976	IV R 50/72	1977 BStBl II 201	221
7 March 1979	I R 145/76	1979 BStBl II 527	235
11 November 1982	IV R 117/80	1983 BStBl II 299	221
29 November 1982	GrS 1/81	1983 BStBl II 272	227, 228
20 October 1983	IV R 175/79	1984 BStBl II 221	224
21 November 1983	GrS 2/82	1984 BStBl II 160	219
11 January 1984	II R 187/81	1984 BStBl II 327	218, 219
25 June 1984	GrS 4/82	1984 BStBl II 751	219, 221

3 August 1984	VI R 129/79	1984 BStBl II 809	222
5 October 1984	III R 192/83	1985 BStBl II 151	216
23 January 1985	II R 36/83	1985 BStBl II 339	221
25 January 1985	III R 130/80	1985 BStBl II 309	221
21 August 1985	I R 63/80	1986 BStBl II 4	235
5 June 1986	IV R 268/82	1986 BStBl II 659	235
22 October 1986	I R 261/82	1987 BStBl II 171	236
7 May 1987	IV R 150/84	1987 BStBl II 670	215
23 November 1987	GrS 1/86	1988 BStBl II 180	222
21 January 1988	I R 241/83	1988 BStBl II 574	235
10 June 1988	III R 118/85	1988 BStBl II 782	222
12 July 1988	IX R 149/83	1988 BStBl II 942	227, 228
30 November 1989	IV R 97/86	1991 BFH/NV 432	228
22 August 1990	I R 27/86	1991 BStBl II 413	222
28 November 1990	X R 109/89	1991 BStBl II 327	227
27 February 1991	I R 15/89	1991 BStBl II 444	235
23 May 1991	IV R 94/90	1991 BStBl II 800	224
19 June 1991	IX R 134/86	1991 BStBl II 904	229
31 October 1991	X R 9/91	1992 BStBl II 241	219, 220
10 January 1992	VI R 117/90	1992 BStBl II 720	219
26 February 1992	V R 118/87	1992 BStBl II 937	236
10 November 1993	I R 53/91	1994 BStBl II 218	236
7 April 1994	VIII R 79/88	1992 BStBl II 786	225
16 March 1994	I R 140/93	1994 BStBl II 508	236
25 January 1995	X R 191/93	1995 BStBl II 586	219, 220
31 May 1995	I R 74/93	1995 BStBl II 683	235
19 July 1995	I R 56/94	1996 BStBl II 28	222
12 September 1995	IX R 54/93	1996 BStBl II 158	227, 228
19 October 1995	IV R 11/95	1996 BFH/NV 464	222
13 December 1995	XI R 43-45/89, XI R 43/89, XI R 44/89, XI R 45/89	1996 BStBl II 232	221
26 March 1996	IX R 51/92	1996 BStBl. II 443	227
12 August 1997	VII R 107/96	1998 BStBl II 131	225
13 August 1997	I R 65/95	1998 BStBl II 21	236
21 November 1997	VI R 93/95	1998 BStBl II 208	216
17 June 1998	X R 68/95	1998 BStBl II 667	227
19 October 1998	I R 67/09	2011 BStBl II 367	221
15 December 1998	VIII R 77/93	1999 BStBl II 168	221
16 December 1998	I R 40/97	1999 BStBl II 207	236

3 February 2000	III R 30/98	2000 BStBl II 438	216
9 November 2000	IV R 60/99	2001 BStBl II 101	227
25 April 2001	II R 14/98	2001 BFH/NV 1457	221
18 July 2001	I R 48/97	196 BFHE 128	227, 228
25 July 2001	VI R 77/00	2002 BGBl II 12	236
17 October 2001	III R 3/01	2002 BStBl II 793	225
19 June 2002	III R 28/99	2002 BStBl II 753	225
16 October 2002	I R 17/01	2003 BStBl II 631	235
5 November 2002	IX R 48/01	2003 BStBl II 646	222
20 March 2003	IV R 42/00	2003 BStBl II 798	225
17 September 2003	I R 91 et al.	2004 BFH/NV 182	222
12 May 2004	X R 59/00	2004 BStBl II 607	221
2 June 2005	III R 86/03	2005 BStBl II 756	216
27 October 2005	IX R 76/03	2006 BStBl II 359	227–229
29 March 2006	X R 59/00	2006 BStBl II 661	221
18 May 2006	III R 21/03	2006 BStBl II 776	225
28 June 2006	III R 13/06	2007 BStBl II 714	219
10 August 2006	II R 59/05	2009 BStBl II 758	235
21 September 2006	VI R 47/05	2007 BStBl II 47	219
14 February 2007	II R 66/05	2007 BStBl II 621	224
17 April 2007	IX R 40/06	2007 BStBl II 608	221
26 June 2007	IV R 9/05	2007 BStBl II 893	221, 225
17 October 2007	I R 5/06	2009 BStBl II 356	235
25 February 2009	IX R 24/08	2009 BStBl II 587	224
11 February 2010	V R 38/08	2010 BStBl II 873	225
15 April 2010	IV B 105/09	2010 BStBl II 971	225
19 May 2010	I B 191/09	2011 BStBl II 156	236
22 September 2010	VI R 54/09	2010 BFHE 231	230
21 October 2010	IV R 23/08	2011 BStBl II 277	215
15 December 2010	VIII R 50/09	2011 BStBl II 506	222
9 February 2011	I R 54/10, 55/10	2012 BStBl II 106	236
3 March 2011	V R 23/10	2012 BStBl II 74	224
24 May 2011	VIII R 3/09	2012 BStBl II 254	222
25 May 2011	I R 95/10	234 BFHE 63	236
31 August 2011	X R 11/10	2012 BStBl II 312	225
9 November 2011	X R 60/09	2012 BStBl II 638	228
10 January 2012	I R 66/09	236 BFHE 304	237
18 April 2012	X R 5/10	237 BFHE 106	225
18 April 2012	X R 5/10	2013 BStBl II 785	215
12 July 2012	I R 23/11	238 BFHE 344, 177	227, 228

30 August 2012	III R 40/10	2013 BFH/NV 193	222
26 September 2012	IX R 50/09	2013 BStBl II 231	221
22 January 2013	IX R 18/12	2013 BFH/NV 1094	227, 228
30 January 2013	I R 54/11	2013 BStBl II 1048	222
21 February 2013	V R 27/11	2013 DB 1155	225
10 April 2013	I R 80/12	2013 BStBl II 1004	226
11 April 2013	III R 11/12	2013 BStBl II 665	225
26 June 2013	I R 48/12	2013 DB 2657	235
18 July 2013	II R 37/11	2013 BStBl II 934	227
24 July 2013	I R 40/12	2014 BStBl II 272	223
20 August 2013	IX R 38/11	2013 BStBl II 1021	227
22 August 2013	V R 19/09	243 BFHE 8	233
28 August 2013	XI R 5/11	243 BFHE 51	222
11 September 2013	II R 60/11	2014 BFH/NV 297	228
11 September 2013	II R 61/11	243 BFHE 376	227
25 September 2013	XI R 41/12	2014 BStBl II 135	215
23 October 2013	X R 3/12	2014 BStBl II 58	215
12 November 2013	VIII R 36/10	2014 BStBl II 168	222
11 December 2013	I R 4/13	2014 BStBl II 791	236
16 January 2014	I R 30/12	2014 BStBl II 721	236
2 April 2014	I R 68/12	2014 BStBl II 875	235
4 December 2014	IV R 53/11	2015 BStBl II 483	221
29 January 2015	V R 5/14	2015 BStBl II 567	221
11 February 2015	X R 36/11	2015 BStBl II 545	221
15 July 2015	II R 11/14	2015 HFR 1062	221
23 July 2015	III R 26/12	2016 BFH/NV 65	221
17 September 2015	III R 49/13	252 BFHE 17	221
25 November 2015	I R 50/14	253 BFHE 52	236
14 April 2016	III R 10/15	2016 HFR 924	221
1 June 2016	XI R 17/11	254 BFHE 164	221
14 June 2016	IX R 15/15	254 BFHE 246	221
6 July 2016	XI R 1/15	254 BFHE 283	221
20 July 2016	I R 50/15	254 BFHE 365	235
21 July 2016	IV R 26/14	254 BFHE 371	221
22 September 2016	IV R 35/13	2016 HFR 405	221

Bundesgerichtshof (Federal Court of Justice)

26 November 2008	*VIII ZR 200/05*	*179 BGHZ 27*	*233*
28 November 2013	5 StR 576/13	2014 NJW 576	230

Court of Justice of the European Union (ECJ)

Case	*Name*	*Reported*	*Page*
11/70	*Internationale Handelsgesellschaft*	[1970] ECR 1125	230
14/83	*von Colson and Kamann*	[1984] ECR 1891	151, 231
79/83	*Dorit Harz*	[1984] ECR 1921	231
80/86	*Kolpinghuis*	[1987] ECR 3969	232
C-397-403/01	*Pfeiffer*	[2004] ECR I-8835	152, 232
C-105/03	*Pupino*	[2005] ECR I-5285	152, 232
C-212/04	*Konstantinos Adeneler*	[2006] ECR I-6057	152, 232
C-268/06	*Impact*	[2008] ECR I-2483	232
C-404/06	*Quelle*	[2008] ECR I-2685	233

Chapter 9: Hong Kong

Australia

FCT v. Spotless Services Ltd	*(1996) 186 CLR 404*	*246*
IRC v. McGuckian	[1997] 1 WLR 991	244, 247, 260
MacNiven v. Westmoreland Investments Ltd	[2001] STC 237	247

Hong Kong

CIR v. Chan Tin-chu	*(1966) 1 HKTC 284*	*243, 250*
Elson-Vernon Knitters Ltd v. Sino-Indo-American Spinners Ltd	[1972] HKLR 468	249
CIR v. Howe	(1977) 1 HKTC 936	245
Asia Television Ltd v. CIR	(1987) 2 HKTC 198	243
Leung Shee-wing v. CIR	(1989) 3 HKTC 209	250

Foo Ying v. CED	[1989] 2 HKLR 376 (CFI); (1990) 3 HKTC 372 (CA)	244
Glynn v. CIR	[1990] 2 WLR 633	253
Pepper v. Hart	[1992] 3 WLR 1032	248, 383, 384
CIR v. Lee Lai-ping	[1993] HKPLR 141	251
Harvest Sheen Ltd v. Collector of Stamp Revenue	[1997] 4 HKTC 750	251
CIR v. Emerson Radio Corp	(1999) 2 HKCFAR 501	252, 258, 259
Hong Kong Clays & Kaolin Co Ltd v. Director of Lands	[1999] 1 HKLRD 527	248
CIR v. Loganathan	[2000] 1 HKLRD 914	244
Shiu Wing Ltd v. Commissioner of Estate Duty	[2000] 3 HKLRD 76	244, 246, 247, 255
Medical Council of Hong Kong v. Chow Siu Shek	(2000) 3 HKCFAR 144	245
CIR v. Secan Ltd	(2000) 3 HKCFAR 411	249
Commissioner of Rating & Valuation v. Agrila Ltd	[2001] 2 HKLRD 36	248
Director of Immigration v. Chong Fung Yuen	(2001) 4 HKCFAR 211	245
Ng Siu Tung v. Director of Immigration	(2002) 5 HKCFAR 1	253
Director of Lands v. Yin Shuen Enterprises Ltd	(2003) 6 HKCFAR 1	248, 249
CSR v. Arrowtown Assets Ltd	[2004] 1 HKLRD 77	242, 244, 246, 254
Town Planning Board v. Society for the Protection of the Harbour	(2004) 7 HKCFAR 1	245
PCCW-HK Telephone Ltd v. Telecommunications Authority	[2005] 3 HKLRD 235	248, 249
Ho Choi Wan v. Hong Kong Housing Authority	[2005] 4 HKLRD 706	245
Lam Soon Trademark Ltd v. CIR	(2006) 9 HKCFAR 391	244
HKSAR v. Lam Kwong Wai	(2006) 9 HKCFAR 574	245
CIR v. HIT Finance Ltd	HCIA 15/2005 (CA); (2007) 10 HKCFAR 717 (CFA)	247
Weson Investment Ltd v. CIR	[2007] 2 HKLRD 567	251
Poon Chau Nam v. Yim Siu Cheng	[2007] 1 HKLRD 951	251
A Solicitor v. Law Society of Hong Kong	[2008] 2 HKLRD 576	253
Ngai Lik Electronics Co Ltd v. CIR	(2009) 12 HKCFAR 296	246
China Field Ltd v. Appeal Tribunal (Buildings) (No.2)	(2009) 12 HKCFAR 342	245

HKSAR v. Cheung Kwun Yin	(2009) 12 HKCFAR 568	245, 249
CIR v. Nam Tai Trading Co. Ltd	(2009) 4 HKLRD 675	251
CIR v. Datatronic Ltd	(2009) 4 HKLRD 675	252
CIR v. Shelcore Hong Kong Limited	(2011) DCTC 5209/2009	251
Lee Yee Shing v. Board of Review and CIR	(2012) 2 HKLRD 981	251
Braitrim (Far East) Ltd v. CIR	(2012) CACV 45/2012	255
Turner Entertainment Networks Asia, Inc v. CIR	(2012) HCIA 4/2010 and (2015) 3 HKLRD 295	257, 258
Moulin Global Eyecare Trading Ltd (in liquidation)	[2012] 2 HKLRD 911	249
CIR v. Nice Cheer Investment Ltd	(2013) 16 HKCFAR 813	250
HKSAR v. Fugro Geotechnical Services Ltd	(2014) 17 HKCFAR 755	245
Good Mark Industrial Limited v. CIR	[2015] 2 HKLRD 16	249
Wong Chak Sin v. CSD	(2016) DCSA 19/2014	251
Ho Kwok Tai v. CSD	(2016) CACV 52/2016	248, 249, 257

United Kingdom and Privy Council

Partington v. Attorney General	*(1869) LR 4 HL 100*	*242, 377*
Yarmouth v. France	(1887) 19 QBD 647	240, 387
Cape Brandy Syndicate v. IRC	(1921) 12 TC 358	242, 243, 356, 380
IRC v. Duke of Westminster	[1936] AC 1	245
D'Avigdor-Goldsmid v. IRC	[953] AC 347	243
Mangin v. IRC	[1971] AC 739	243
IRC v. WT Ramsay Ltd	[1982] AC 300	244
Furniss v. Dawson	[1984] AC 474	244
Grays Timber Products Ltd v. HMRC	[2010] UKSC 4	260

USA

Gilbert v. Commissioner of Inland Revenue	*248 F.2d 399 (1957)*	*255*

Chapter 10: Italy

Italy

Corte di Cassazione

Date	*Number*	*Recorded*	*Page*
1 February 1985	not appl.	(1985) I *Rass. Avv. Stato,* 346	300
3 April 1990	No. 2702	See below at 1	276
19 January 1994	not appl.	(1994) II *Foro. It.*, 408	301
28 October 1995	No. 11313	(1996) I *Giur. It.* 449	302
25 September 1996	No. 8456	(1997) I(1) *Giur. it.*, 1055	277
2 February 2000	No. 1122	See below at 2	299
13 March 2000	No. 2868	(2000) I *Foro. It.*, 1465	302
1 August 2000	No. 10062	(2002) II *Diritto e Pratica Tributaria*, 483	299
10 November 2000	No. 14619	See below at 3	294
21 April 2001	No. 5927	See below at 4	298
7 March 2002	No. 3368	See below at 5	299
25 May 2002	No. 7682	See below at 6	299
10 December 2002	No. 5768	(2000) II *Riv. dir.trib.*, 312	280, 293
10 December 2002	No 17576	(2003) I(1) *Giur. It.*, 2194	282
14 July 2004	No. 13056	See below at 7	301
5 May 2006	No. 10353	See below at 8	301
24 May 2006	No. 12301 and 12302	See below at 9	287
29 September 2006	No. 21220	See below at 10	295
4 October 2006	No. 21371	See below at 11	287
13 October 2006	No. 22023	See below at 12	288
12 February 2007	No. 3022	See below at 13	301
17 April 2007	No. 13579	(2007) 29 *Corriere tributario*, 2353	297
4 May 2007	No. 10273	See below at 14	288
2 November 2007	No. 23031	See below at 15	294
21 December 2007	No. 26996	See below at 16	287
4 April 2008	No. 8772	See below at 17	286–288

Date	*Number*	*Recorded*	*Page*
21 April 2008	No. 10257	See below at 18	287
6 August 2008	No. 21154	See below at 19	294
17 October 2008	No. 25374	See below at 20	287, 288
23 December 2008	No. 30055, 30056, 30057	See below at 21	286–288
21 January 2009	No. 1465	See below at 22	285, 286
6 February 2009	No. 2931	See below at 23	286
25 February 2009	No. 4501	See below at 24	270
1 October 2010	No. 20527	See below at 25	301
31 January 2011	No. 2221	See below at 26	282
22 March 2011	No. 6583	See below at 27	296
27 June 2011	No. 14071	See below at 28	282
6 October 2011	No. 20450	See below at 29	282
18 January 2012	No. 634	See below at 30	282
3 February 2012	No. 1550/2012	See below at 31	296
23 February 2012	No. 7080	See below at 32	278
11 May 2012	No. 7355/2012	See below at 33	296
30 November 2012	No. 21390	See below at 34	288
7 February 2013	No. 2869	See below at 35	278
27 February 2013	No. 4901	See below at 36	289
19 July 2013	No. 17673	See below at 37	282
26 February 2014	No. 4604	See below at 38	289
30 October 2015	No. 43809	See below at 39	278
25 November 2015	No. 24024	See below at 40	289
17 June 2016	No. 12548	Not yet on the website	289

1. http://0-bd46.leggiditalia.it.lib.unibocconi.it/cgi-bin/FulShow?NAVIPOS = 1&DS_POS = 0&KEY = 46SE1000187216&FT_CID = 751832&OPERA = 46

2. http://0-bd46.leggiditalia.it.lib.unibocconi.it/cgi-bin/FulShow?NAVIPOS = 1&DS_POS = 1&KEY = 46SE1000419285&FT_CID = 635326&OPERA = 46

3. http://0-bd46.leggiditalia.it.lib.unibocconi.it/cgi-bin/FulShow?NAVIPOS = 1&DS_POS = 0&KEY = 46SE1000419673&FT_CID = 624147&OPERA = 46

4. http://0-bd46.leggiditalia.it.lib.unibocconi.it/cgi-bin/FulShow?NAVIPOS = 1&DS_POS = 0&KEY = 46SE1000423232&FT_CID = 617704&OPERA = 46

5. http://0-bd46.leggiditalia.it.lib.unibocconi.it/cgi-bin/FulShow?NAVIPOS = 1&DS_POS = 0&KEY = 46SE1000446431&FT_CID = 608153&OPERA = 46

6. http://0-bd46.leggiditalia.it.lib.unibocconi.it/cgi-bin/FulShow?NAVIPOS = 1&DS_POS = 0&KEY = 46SE1000449034&FT_CID = 605404&OPERA = 46

7. http://0-bd46.leggiditalia.it.lib.unibocconi.it/cgi-bin/FulShow?NAVIPOS = 1&DS_POS = 0&KEY = 46SE0000126143&FT_CID = 552155&OPERA = 46

8. http://0-studiolegale.leggiditalia.it.lib.unibocconi.it/#id = 10SE0000332634,_m = document

9. http://0-bd46.leggiditalia.it.lib.unibocconi.it/cgi-bin/FulShow?NAVIPOS = 1&DS_POS = 0&KEY = 46SE0000361786&FT_CID = 441146&OPERA = 46 and http://0-bd46.leggiditalia.it.lib.unibocconi.it/cgi-bin/FulShow?NAVIPOS = 1&DS_POS = 0&KEY = 46SE0000361820&FT_CID = 441144&OPERA = 46

10. http://0-bd46.leggiditalia.it.lib.unibocconi.it/cgi-bin/FulShow?NAVIPOS = 1&DS_POS = 0&KEY = 46SE0000448527&FT_CID = 423688&OPERA = 46

11. http://0-bd46.leggiditalia.it.lib.unibocconi.it/cgi-bin/FulShow?NAVIPOS = 1&DS_POS = 0&KEY = 46SE0000366566&FT_CID = 423361&OPERA = 46

12. http://0-studiolegale.leggiditalia.it.lib.unibocconi.it/#id = 10SE0000367807,_m = document

13. http://0-bd46.leggiditalia.it.lib.unibocconi.it/cgi-bin/FulShow?NAVIPOS = 1&DS_POS = 0&KEY = 46SE0000410319&FT_CID = 405755&OPERA = 46

14. http://0-studiolegale.leggiditalia.it.lib.unibocconi.it/#id = 10SE0000429456,__m = document

15. http://0-bd46.leggiditalia.it.lib.unibocconi.it/cgi-bin/FulShow?NAVIPOS = 1&DS_POS = 0&KEY = 46SE0000504642&FT_CID = 368105&OPERA = 46

16. http://0-bd46.leggiditalia.it.lib.unibocconi.it/cgi-bin/FulShow?NAVIPOS = 1&DS_POS = 0&KEY = 46SE0000522829&FT_CID = 361344&OPERA = 46

17. http://0-bd46.leggiditalia.it.lib.unibocconi.it/cgi-bin/FulShow?NAVIPOS = 1&DS_POS = 0&KEY = 46SE0000564768&FT_CID = 343498&OPERA = 46

18. http://0-bd46.leggiditalia.it.lib.unibocconi.it/cgi-bin/FulShow?NAVIPOS = 1&DS_POS = 0&KEY = 46SE0000572164&FT_CID = 340511&OPERA = 46

19. http://0-bd46.leggiditalia.it.lib.unibocconi.it/cgi-bin/FulShow?NAVIPOS = 1&DS_POS = 0&KEY = 46SE0000614384&FT_CID = 319451&OPERA = 46

20. http://0-bd46.leggiditalia.it.lib.unibocconi.it/cgi-bin/FulShow?NAVIPOS = 1&DS_POS = 0&KEY = 46SE0000633128&FT_CID = 310548&OPERA = 46

21. http://0-bd46.leggiditalia.it.lib.unibocconi.it/cgi-bin/FulShow?NAVIPOS = 1&DS_POS = 0&KEY = 46SE0000658869&FT_CID = 300955&OPERA = 46 and http://0-bd46.leggiditalia.it.lib.unibocconi.it/cgi-bin/FulShow?NAVIPOS = 1&DS_POS = 0&KEY = 46SE0000658610&FT_CID = 300952&OPERA = 46 and http://0-bd46.leggiditalia.it.lib.unibocconi.it/cgi-bin/FulShow?NAVIPOS = 1&DS_POS = 0 &KEY = 46SE0000658845&FT_CID = 300949&OPERA = 46

22. http://0-bd46.leggiditalia.it.lib.unibocconi.it/cgi-bin/FulShow?NAVIPOS = 1&DS_POS = 0&KEY = 46SE0000661277&FT_CID = 296705&OPERA = 46

23. http://0-bd46.leggiditalia.it.lib.unibocconi.it/cgi-bin/FulShow?NAVIPOS = 1&DS_POS = 0&KEY = 46SE0000672843&FT_CID = 293744&OPERA = 46

24. http://0-bd46.leggiditalia.it.lib.unibocconi.it/cgi-bin/FulShow?NAVIPOS = 1&DS_POS = 0&KEY = 46SE0000678307&FT_CID = 290400&OPERA = 46

25. http://0-bd46.leggiditalia.it.lib.unibocconi.it/cgi-bin/FulShow?NAVIPOS = 1&DS_POS = 0&KEY = 46SE0000930018&FT_CID = 199278&OPERA = 46

26. http://0-bd46.leggiditalia.it.lib.unibocconi.it/cgi-bin/FulShow?NAVIPOS = 1&DS_POS = 0&KEY = 46SE0000961798&FT_CID = 182226&OPERA = 46

27. http://0-studiolegale.leggiditalia.it.lib.unibocconi.it/#id = 10SE0000986107,_m = document

28. http://0-studiolegale.leggiditalia.it.lib.unibocconi.it/#id = 10SE0001028269,_m = document

29. http://0-studiolegale.leggiditalia.it.lib.unibocconi.it/#id = 10SE0001065803, m = document

30. http://0-studiolegale.leggiditalia.it.lib.unibocconi.it/#id = 10SE0001103696, m = document

31. http://0-studiolegale.leggiditalia.it.lib.unibocconi.it/#id = 10SE0001111524, m = document

32. http://0-studiolegale.leggiditalia.it.lib.unibocconi.it/#id = 10SE0001118017, m = document

33. http://0-studiolegale.leggiditalia.it.lib.unibocconi.it/#id = 10SE0001160517, m = document

34. http://0-studiolegale.leggiditalia.it.lib.unibocconi.it/#id = 10SE0001229832, m = document

35. http://0-studiolegale.leggiditalia.it.lib.unibocconi.it/#id = 10SE0001255627,_m = document

36. http://0-studiolegale.leggiditalia.it.lib.unibocconi.it/#id = 10SE0001262032,_m = document

37. http://0-studiolegale.leggiditalia.it.lib.unibocconi.it/#id = 10SE0001320039,_m = document

38. http://0-studiolegale.leggiditalia.it.lib.unibocconi.it/#id = 10SE0001391500,_m = document

39. http://0-studiolegale.leggiditalia.it.lib.unibocconi.it/#id = 10SE0001619132,_m = document

40. http://0-studiolegale.leggiditalia.it.lib.unibocconi.it/#id = 10SE0001626917,_m = document

Corte Cost

10 December 1981	*No. 18*	*Giur. it.*, 1982, I, 1, 800	*293*
3 March 1989	No. 84	*Giur. It.*, 1990, I, 1, 1379	269
4 April 1990	No. 155	*Giur. cost.*, 1990, 952	291
28 December 1990	No. 244	*Giur. cost.*, 1990, 3284	292
25 July 1995	No. 376	*Foro. it.*, 1997, I, 346	291, 293
3 September 1995	No. 430	*Giur. It.*, 1990, I, 1, 1379	269
23 December 1997	No. 432	*Giur. cost.*, 1997, 3858	293
12 March 1999	No. 84	*Giur. It.*, 1999, I, 1, 1565	280
27 July 2000	No. 374	*Giur. cost.*, 2000, 2656	293
23 July 2002	No. 375	*Giur. It.*, 1990, I, 1, 1379	269

10 March 2006	No. 244	*Boll. trib.*, 2006, 637	280
24 July 2009	No. 244	*Rass. trib.*, 2009, 1783	280
17 June 2010	No. 217	*Giur. Cost.*, 2010, 2495	280

Regional Commercial Court of Florence

18 January 2008	*No. 61*	*See below at 1*	*278*

1.http://0studiolegale.leggiditalia.it.lib.unibocconi.it/#id=10SE0000733572,__m=document.

Court of Justice of the European Union (ECJ)

Case C-330/91	*Commerzbank*	*[1993] ECR I-4017*	*302*
Case C-279/93	*Schumacker*	[1995] ECR I-0225	302
Case C-250/95	*Futura*	[1997] ECR I-2471	302
Case C-255/02	*Halifax et al*	[2006] ECR I-1609	302
Case C-223/03	*University of Huddersfield*	[2006] ECR I-1751	302
Case C-425-06	*Part Service*	[2008] ECR I-0897	287, 302

Chapter 11: Japan

Japan

Supreme Court

Date	**Name**	**Reported**	**Page**
7 October 1960	*Suzuya Finance*	Minshu Vol. 14, No. 12, 2420	311
27 October 1961	*Kangyo Keizai*	Minshu Vol. 15, No. 9, 2357	301
14 December 1973	*Tsukamoto Shoji*	Shomu Geppo Vol. 20, No. 6, 146	313
21 April 1978	*Korakuen Hotel*	Shomu Geppo Vol. 24, No. 8, 1694	313
27 March 1985	*Ohshima*	Minshu Vol. 39, No. 2, 247	304

Fukuoka High Court

18 July 1990	*Mice scheme*	*Hanrei Jiho No. 1395, 34*	*312*

Tokyo High Court

28 March 1996	*Corresponding adjustment*	*Hanrei Jiho No. 1574, 57*	*310*
31 May 1999	*Pachinko Heiwa*	Shomu Geppo Vol. 51, No. 8, 2135	313
28 June 2007	*Guidant*	Hanrei Jiho No. 1985, 23	310

Tokyo District Court

8 August 1997	*Lease termination*	*Gyoshu Vol. 48, No. 7=8, 539*	*308*

France

Conseil d'Etat

28 June 2002	*Case No. 232276*	*Schneider Electric*	*RJF 10/02, no. 1080*	*310*

Chapter 12: Russian Federation

RF Constitutional Court

Date	*Case No*	*Name*	*Reported*	*Page*
25 April 1995	3-P	*L.N. Sitalova*	VCC, 1995, No. 2-3	327
17 December 1996	20-P	*MKM Ltd, 5M Ltd*	VCC, 1996, No. 5	320
21 March 1997	5-P	*Constitutional Court of the Republic of Komi, etc.*	VCC, 1997, No. 4	326
1 December 1997	18-P	*RF President*	VCC, 1997, No. 6	327
12 October 1998	24-P	*AO Kondopozhskiy kombinat khleboproduktov, NITSIAMT*	VCC, 1999, No. 1	340

Date	*Case No*	*Name*	*Reported*	*Page*
15 July 1999	11-P	*AO Bolshevik, AO Svet, etc*	VCC, 1999, No. 5	327
25 July 2001	138-O	*RF MTC*	VCC, 2002, No. 2	328, 340
16 July 2004	14-P	*A.D. Egorov, N.V. Chuev*	VCC, 2004, No. 6	326, 328
5 July 2005	246-O	*I.V. Kuznetsov*	VCC, 2005, No. 6	334
21 January 2010	1-P	*ZAO PO Bereg, OAO Karbolit, Zavod Mikroprovod, and NPP Respirator*	VCC, 2010, No. 2	339

RF Supreme Court

Date	*Case No*	*Name*	*Reported*	*Page*
7 February 1997	N/A	*OAO Novolipetskiy metallurgicheskiy kombinat*	EDP "KP"	341
20 January 2003	2	*Plenum of the Court*	Rossiyskaya Gazeta No. 15, 25/01/2003	330
27 December 2005	GKPI05-1625	*F.*	EDP "KP"	331
29 November 2007	48	*Plenum of the Court*	Rossiyskaya Gazeta No. 276, 08/12/2007	331
1 February 2016	305-KG15-14263	Novaya Tabacnaya Kompaniya	EDP "KP"	346

RF Supreme Commercial Court

Date	*Case No*	*Name*	*Reported*	*Page*
26 January 2005	16141/04	*OAO*	VSCC, 2005, No. 4	331
12 October 2006	53	*Plenum of the Court*	VSCC, 2006, No. 12	341
10 July 2007	A40-11992/06-143-75	*PricewaterhouseCoopers*	VSCC, 2007, No. 10	342

Date	*Case No*	*Name*	*Reported*	*Page*
12 March 2007	17	*Plenum of the Court*	VSCC, 2007, No. 4	339
10 April 2008	22	*Plenum of the Court*	VSCC, 2008, No. 5	341
30 June 2011	52	*Plenum of the Court*	VSCC, 2011, No. 9	340
11 November 2011	9299/08	*Kestroi 1*	VSCC, 2009, No. 3	342
15 November 2011	8654/11	*Severniy Kuzbass*	VSCC, 2012, No. 3	344
13 January 2012	VAS-17705	*Bryanskiy Mashinostroitelniy Zavod*	EDB "KP"	344
2 March 2012	VAS-13698/11	*Omskiy Zavod Polipropilena*	EDB "KP"	344
19 March 2012	VAS-10350	*Dallesprom*	EDB "KP	344
5 April 2012	VAS-3867/12	*Promlizing*	EDB "KP	344
15 May 2012	VAS-6159/12	*Terminal Sibir*	EDB "KP	344
21 June 2012	VAS-7104/12	*NaryanmarNefteGaz*	EDB "KP	345

Commercial Court of the East Siberian federal district

Date	*Case No*	*Name*	*Reported*	*Page*
1 July 2004	A78-552/04-C2-28/74-Ф02-2381/04-C1	*OOO KET-tovary Zabaykalya*	EDB "KP"	331

Commercial Court of the Moscow federal district

13 January 2005	*KA-A41/12802-04*	*Tax Inspectorate*	*EDB "KP"*	*335*

Commercial Court of the North-Western federal district

Date	*Case No*	*Name*	*Reported*	*Page*
22 March 2004	A05-9051/03-20	*FGUP SPO Arktica*	EDB "KP"	335
4 March 2005	A56-26746/04	*OOO PO Kirish NefteOrgSintez*	EDB "KP"	335

Commercial Court of the Volgo-Vyatskiy federal district

Date	*Case No*	*Name*	*Reported*	*Page*
23 December 2004	A79-5685/2004-CK1-5372	*Tax Inspectorate*	EDB "KP"	335
10 November 2004	A43-14279/2003-31-632	*Tax Inspectorate*	EDB "KP"	335

Commercial Court of the West Siberian federal district

Date	*Case No*	*Name*	*Reported*	*Page*
22 December 2004	A56-276/04	*ZAO Nevskaya Kosmetika*	EDB "KP"	335

Chapter 13: South Africa

South Africa and United Kingdom

Name	*Reported*	*Page*
Partington v. The Attorney-General	(1869) LR 4 HL 100 (21 LT 370)	356
Colquhoun v. Brooks	[1888] 21 QBD 52	363
Commissioners for Special Purposes of the Income Tax v. Pemsel	[1891] AC 531 (HL)	368
Aron Salomon v. A Salomon & Co Ltd	[1897] AC 22 (HL)	359
R v. Venter	1907 TS 910	358, 361
Zandberg v. Van Zyl	1910 AD 302	362
Richardson v. Austin	[1911] HCA 28 ((1911) 12 CLR 463	355
Union Govt v. Thompson	1919 AD 425	356
R v. Lloyd	1920 AD 474	368
Cape Brandy Syndicate v. IRC	[1921] 1 KB 64, 12 TC 358	356
CIR v. City Deep Ltd	1924 AD 298, 7 SATC 1	366
CIR v. George Forest Timber Co Ltd	1924 AD 516	356, 363
Weinerlein v. Goch Buildings	1925 AD 295	356
Farrar's Estate v. CIR	1926 TPD 501	352
Jones & Co Ltd v. CIR	1926 CPD 1, 2 SATC 7	364
SA Estates and Finance Corp Ltd v. CIR	1927 AD 230, 2 SATC 193	363

Name	*Reported*	*Page*
Loewenstein v. COT	1956 (4) SA 766 (FC), 21 SATC 121	358, 359
CIR v. Rand Selections Corp Ltd	1956 (3) SA 124 (A)	363
Estate Brownstein v. CIR	1957 (3) SA 512 (A), 21 SATC 262	365
COT (SR) v. 'T' Company	1957 (4) SA 90 (SR), 21 SATC 335	363
M v. COT	1956 (4) SA 197 (SR), 21 SATC 16	358
CIR v. Louis Zinn Organisation (Pty) Ltd	1958 (4) SA 477 (A), 22 SATC 85	359
IRC v. Hinchy	[1960] AC 748	352
P v. COT; LGM Ltd v. COT	1966 (2) SA 208 (R), 28 SATC 55	358
COT v. Aktiebolaget Tetra Pak	1966 (4) SA 198 (RA), 28 SATC 213	363
Europa Oil (NZ) Ltd v. IRC	*(NZ)* [1971] AC 760	363
Mooi v. SIR	1972 (1) SA 675 (A), 34 SATC 1	367
Buglers Post (Pty) Ltd v. SIR	1974 (3) SA 28 (A), 36 SATC 71	355
Glen Anil Development Corp Ltd v. SIR	1975 (4) SA 715 (A), 37 SATC 319	351, 358, 359
Ebrahim v. Minister of the Interior	1977 (1) SA 665 (A)	359
Cooper Brookes (Wollongong) Pty Ltd v. FCT	(1981) 55 ALJR 434	358
Federal Commissioner of Taxation v. Whitfords Beach Pty Ltd	(1982) 56 ALJR 240	355
K & S Lake City Freighters Pty Ltd v. Gordon & Gotch Ltd	[1985] HLA 48; (1985) 157 CLR 309	355
R Koster & Son (Pty) Ltd v. CIR	1985 (2) SA 831 (A), 47 SATC 24	355
Summit Industrial Corporation v. Claimants against the Fund Comprising the Proceeds of the Sale of the MV Fade 15 Transporter	1987 (2) SA 583 (A)	351, 359
Protective Mining & Industrial Equipment Systems (Pty) Ltd (formerly Hampo Systems (Pty) Ltd) v. Audiolens (Cape) (Pty)Ltd	1987 (2) SA 961 (A)	359
S v. Toms; S v. Bruce	1990 (2) SA 802 (A)	351
CIR v. SA Mutual Unit Trust Management Co Ltd	1990 (4) SA 529 (A)	368
Conshu (Pty) Ltd v. CIR	1994 (4) SA 603 (A), 57 SATC 1	358

Name	*Reported*	*Page*
Knox D'Arcy Ltd v. Jamieson	[1996] ZASCA 58; 1996 (4) SA 348	371
CIR v. BP Southern Africa (Pty) Ltd	1997 (1) SA 375 (C), 59 SATC 97	356
Manyasha v. Minister of Law and Order	1999 (2) SA 179 (SCA)	359
ITC 1675	(2000) 62 SATC 219	368
Metcash Trading Ltd v. C: SARS	2001 (1) SA 1109 (CC)	369
Janse van Rensburg NO v. Minister of Trade and Industry	2001 (1) SA 29 (CC)	371
CSARS v. Executor Frith's Estate	2001 (2) SA 261	368
Natal Joint Municipal Pension Fund v. Endumeni Municipality	[2001] 2 AC 349	352, 353
First National Bank of SA Ltd t/a Wesbank v. Commissioner, South African Revenue Service and Another; First National Bank of SA Ltd t/a Wesbank v. Minister of Finance	2002 (4) SA 768 (CC)	349
National Health, Education and Allied Workers Union v. UCT	2003 (3) SA 1 (CC)	355
Bato Star Fishing (Pty) Ltd v. Minister of Environmental Affairs and Others	2004(4) SA 490 (CC); (2004) (7) BCLR 687; [2004] ZACC 15	354
CSARS v. NWK Ltd	2011 (2) SA 67 (SCA)	362
Natal Joint Municipal Pension Fund v. Endumeni Municipality	2012 (4) SA 593 (SCA)	355, 359
Oceanic Trust Co Ltd NO v. CSARS88	[2012] JOL 28880 (WCC)	361
Bothma-Batho Transport (Edms) Bpk v. S. Bothma & Seun Transport (Edms) Bpk	[2013] ZASCA 176; [2014] 1 All SA 517 (SCA)	352
Roshcon (Pty) Ltd v. Anchor Auto Body Builders CC	[2014] ZASCA 40 (31 March 2014)	362
Commissioner for the South African Revenue Service v. Krok	[2014] ZAGPPHC 8	370
Lifman v. C:SARS	(2015) 77 SATC 383	356
van Deventer v. Nedbank Ltd	2016 (3) SA 633 (WCHC) 35	353
Malema v. Commissioner for the South African Revenue Service	[2016] ZAGPPHC 263	354
Minister of Justice and Constitutional Development v. Southern Africa Litigation Centre	2016 (3) SA 317 (CC)	353, 354

Name	*Reported*	*Page*
Chilza v. Govender	2016 (4) SA 397	355
XO Africa Safaris v. CSARS	[2016] ZASCA 160	356

Zimbabwe

COT v. CW (Pvt) Ltd	*1989 (3) ZLR 361 (S)*	*357*
Law Society of Zimbabwe v. Minister of Finance	(1999)61 SATC 458 (SCZ)	357

Chapter 14: United Kingdom

Court of Justice of the European Union (ECJ)

Case	*Name*	*Reported*	*Page*
102/86	*Apple and Pear Development Council v. CEC*	[1988] STC 221	393, 396
C-106/89	*Marleasing SA v. La Comercial Internacional de Alimentacion SA*	[1990] ECR I-4135	395
C-16/93	*Tolsma v. Inspecteur der Omzetbelasting Leeuwarden*	[1994] STC 509	397
C-384/95	*Landboden-Agrardienste GmbH & Co KG v. Finanzamt Calau*	[1998] STC 171	396
C-136/97	*Norbury Developments Ltd v. CEC*	[1999] STC 511	399
C-255/02	*Halifax plc and Others v. CEC*	[2006] STC 919	391
C-435/03	*British American Tobacco International Ltd, Newman Shipping and Agency Company NV. v. Belgian State*	[2005] ECR I-7077	394
C-446/03	*Marks and Spencer plc v. Halsey*	[2006] STC 237	382
C-439/04 and C-440/04	*Kittel v. Belgium* and *Belgium v. Recolta Recycling SPRL*	[2008] STC 1537	393
C-251/05	*Talacre Beach Caravan Sales Ltd v. CEC*	[2006] STC 1671	395
C-309/06	*Marks and Spencer plc v. CRC*	[2008] STC 1408	395

Case	*Name*	*Reported*	*Page*
C-302/07	*JD Wetherspoon plc v. CRC*	[2009] STC 1022	398
C-259-260/10	*Rank Group plc v. CRC*	[2012] STC 23	390
C-520/10	*Lebara Ltd v. CRC*	[2012] STC 1536	397
C-494/12	*Dixon's Retail plc v. CRC*	[2014] STC 375	394
C-161/14	*Commission v. UK*	[2015] STC 1767	398

United Kingdom and Hong Kong

Attorney-General v. Coote	*(1817) 146 ER 433*	*378*
Barclays Mercantile Business Finance Ltd v. Mawson	[2004] UKHL 51; (2004) 76 TC 446	384
Becke v. Smith	(1836) 150 ER 724	378
Berry v. CRC	[2011] UKUT 81 (TCC)	388
Bowles v. Bank of England	[1913] 1 Ch 57	384
Brown v. London and North Western Railway Co	[1861-1873] All ER Rep 487	387
Bupa Insurance Ltd v. CRC	[2014] UKUT 262 (TCC)	384, 388
Campbell v. IRC	[2004] STC (SCD) 396	385
Cape Brandy Syndicate v. IRC	(1921) 12 TC 358	356, 380
CEC v. Electronic Data Systems Ltd	[2003] EWCA Civ. 492; [2003] STC 688	399
CEC v. Morrison's Academy Boarding Houses Association	[1978] STC 1	397
Collector of Stamp Revenue v. Arrowtown Assets Ltd	HKCFA (2003) 6 ITLR 454	385
Craven v. White	(1988) 62 TC 1	385
CRC v. Investment Trust Companies	[2017] UKSC 29	394
CRC v. Moorbury Ltd	[2010] UKUT 360 (TCC); [2010] STC 2715	391
CRC v. Pendragon plc	[2015] UKSC 37; [2015] 1 WLR 2838	392
CRC v. Tower MCashback LLP	(2011) 80 TC 641	384

Chapter 15: United States

Supreme Court

Comm'r v. Schleier	515 U.S. 323 (1995)	433
Skidmore v. Swift & Co.	323 U.S. 134 (1944)	414
Society for Sav. v. Coite	73 U.S. 594 (1867)	408
Comm'r v. Soliman	506 U.S. 168 (1993)	416
Comm'r v. Southwest Exploration Co.	350 U.S. 308 (1956)	435
Thor Power Tool Co. v. Comm'r	439 U.S. 522 (1979)	428
Tidewater Oil Co. v. United States	409 U.S. 151, 157 (1972)	416
United Dominion Inds., Inc. v. United States	532 U.S. 822, 839 (2001)	413
United Sav. Ass'n v. Timbers of Inwood Forest Associates, Ltd.	484 U.S. 365 (1988)	411
United States v. United States Shoe Corp.	523 U.S. 360 (1998)	408
White v. United States	305 U.S. 281 (1938)	434
United States v. Woods	134 S. Ct. 557, 568 (2013)	411

Other Federal Courts

Albertson's Inc. v. Comm'r	*42 F.3d 537 (9th Cir. 1994), cert. denied 516 U.S. 807 (1995)*	*422*
Altera Corp. v. Comm'r	145 T.C. 91, 115-17 (2015)	410
Apache Bend Apartments, Ltd. v. United States	964 F.2d 1556 (5th Cir. 1992), rev'd en banc, 987 F.2d 1174 (5th Cir. 1993)	433
Ball ex rel. Ball v. Comm'r	742 F.3d 552, 561-62 (3d Cir. 2014)	417, 432
Cabell v. Markham	148 F.2d 737 (2d Cir.), aff'd, 326 U.S. 404 (1945)	421
Chamberlin v. Comm'r	207 F.2d 462 (6th Cir. 1953)	434
Cohen v. United States	853 F. Supp. 2d 138, 143 (D.D.C. 2012), aff'd, 751 F.3d 629 (D.C. Cir. 2014)	413
Coltec Inds., Inc. v. United States	62 Fed. Cl. 716 (2004), *vacated*	435
Countryside Ltd. P'ship v. Comm'r	T.C. Memo. 2008-3	437

Dominion Resources, Inc. v. Unites States	681 F.3d 1313, 1318 (Fed. Cir. 2012)	413
Exxon Mobil Corp. v. Comm'r	689 F.3d 191, 199-200 (2d Cir. 2012)	413
Feller v. Comm'r	135 T.C. 497 (2010)	403
Field v. Comm'r	T.C. Memo. 2013-111.	409
Golsen v. Comm'r	54 T.C. 742 (1970), aff'd, 445 F.2d 985 (10th Cir. 1971)	415
Lewenhaupt v. Comm'r	20 T.C. 151 (1953), aff'd, 221 F.2d 227 (9th Cir. 1955)	404
Loving v. IRS	F.3d 1013 (D.C. Cir. 2014)	411
Lynch v. Comm'r	801 F.2d 1176 (9th Cir. 1986)	421
Markell Co., Inc. v. Comm'r	T.C. Memo. 2014-86	408
United States v. Marshall	798 F.3d 296, 318 (5th Cir. 2015)	413
Mass. Mut. Life Ins. Co. v. United States	103 Fed. Cl. 111, 146-52 (2012)	426
Oregon v. Ashcroft	192 F. Supp. 2d 1077, 1090-1091 (D. Or. 2002)	412
United States v. Pabon	391 F.3d 86 (2d Cir. 2004)	431
Ridgely v. Lew	55 F. Supp. 3d 89 (D.D.C. 2014)	411
Santander Holdings USA, Inc. v. United States	844 F.3d 115 (1st Cir. 2016)	437
Sinclair, Matter of	870 F.2d 1340 (7th Cir. 1989)	419
Smith v. Comm'r	30 B.T.A. 1038 (1939) aff'd per curiam, 113 F.2d 114 (2d Cir. 1940)	409
State of Florida v. U.S. Dep't of Health & Human Servs.	648 F.3d 1235 1318(11th Cir. 2011), aff'd in part & rev'd on other grounds *sub nom. National Fed. of Independent Bus. v. Sebelius,* 132 S. Ct. 2566 (2012)	412

State Courts

Sparks Nugget, Inc. v.	*State ex rel. Dep't of Taxation* 179 P.3d 570 (Nev. 2008) (per curiam)	429
State Dep't of Taxation v. Masco Builder Cabinet Group	265 P.3d 666 (Nev. 2011) (per curiam)	414
State ex rel. Seymour v. Gilfillan	1905 WL 824 (Ohio Com. Pl. 1905)	420
Zebra Technologies Corp. v. Topinka	799 N.E.2d 725 (Ill. App. 2003)	433

Canada

Symes v. Canada	*[1993] 4 S.C.R. 695, [1994] 1 C.T.C. 40*	*409*

SERIES ON INTERNATIONAL TAXATION

1. Alberto Xavier, *The Taxation of Foreign Investment in Brazil,* 1980 (ISBN 90-200-0582-0).
2. Hugh J. Ault & Albert J. Rädler, *The German Corporation Tax Law with 1980 Amendments,* 1981 (ISBN 90-200-0642-8).
3. Paul R. McDaniel & Hugh J. Ault, *Introduction to United States International Taxation,* 1981 (ISBN 90-6544-004-6).
4. Albert J. Rädler, *German Transfer Pricing/Prix de Transfer en Allemagne,* 1984 (ISBN 90-6544-143-3).
5. Paul R. McDaniel & Stanley S. Surrey, *International Aspects of Tax Expenditures: A Comparative Study,* 1985 (ISBN 90-654-4163-8).
6. Kees van Raad, *Nondiscrimination in International Tax Law,* 1986 (ISBN 90-6544-266-9).
7. Sijbren Cnossen (ed.), *Tax Coordination in the European Community,* 1987 (ISBN 90-6544-272-3).
8. Ben Terra, *Sales Taxation. The Case of Value Added Tax in the European Community,* 1989 (ISBN 90-6544-381-9).
9. Rutsel S.J. Martha, *The Jurisdiction to Tax in International Law: Theory and Practice of Legislative Fiscal Jurisdiction,* 1989 (ISBN 90-654-4416-5).
10. Paul R. McDaniel & Hugh J. Ault, *Introduction to United States International Taxation* (3rd revised edition), 1989 (ISBN 90-6544-423-8).
11. Manuel Pires, *International Juridicial Double Taxation of Income,* 1989 (ISBN 90-6544-426-2).
12. A.H.M. Daniels, *Issues in International Partnership Taxation,* 1991 (ISBN 90-654-4577-3).
13. Arvid A. Skaar, *Permanent Establishment: Erosion of a Tax Treaty Principle,* 1992 (ISBN 90-6544-594-3).
14. Cyrille David & Geerten M.M. Michielse (eds), *Tax Treatment of Financial Instruments,* 1996 (ISBN 90-654-4666-4).
15. Herbert H. Alpert & Kees van Raad (eds), *Essays on International Taxation,* 1993 (ISBN 90-654-4781-4).
16. Wolfgang Gassner, Michael Lang & Eduard Lechner (eds), *Tax Treaties and EC Law,* 1997 (ISBN 90-411-0680-4).
17. Glória Teixeira, *Taxing Corporate Profits in the EU,* 1997 (ISBN 90-411-0703-7).
18. Michael Lang et al. (eds), *Multilateral Tax Treaties,* 1998 (ISBN 90-411-0704-5).
19. Stef van Weeghel, *The Improper Use of Tax Treaties,* 1998 (ISBN 90-411-0737-1).
20. Klaus Vogel (ed.), *Interpretation of Tax Law and Treaties and Transfer Pricing in Japan and Germany,* 1998 (ISBN 90-411-9655-2).
21. Bertil Wiman (ed.), *International Studies in Taxation: Law and Economics; Liber Amicorum Leif Mutén,* 1999 (ISBN 90-411-9692-7).
22. Alfonso J. Martín Jiménez, *Towards Corporate Tax Harmonization in the European Community,* 1999 (ISBN 90-411-9690-0).

23. Ramon J. Jeffery, *The Impact of State Sovereignty on Global Trade and International Taxation,* 1999 (ISBN 90-411-9703-6).
24. A.J. Easson, *Taxation of Foreign Direct Investment,* 1999 (ISBN 90-411-9741-9).
25. Marjaana Helminen, *The Dividend Concept in International Tax Law: Dividend Payments Between Corporate Entities,* 1999 (ISBN 90-411-9765-6).
26. Paul Kirchhof, Moris Lehner, Kees van Raad, Arndt Raupach & Michael-Rodi (eds), *International and Comparative Taxation: Essays in Honour of Klaus Vogel,* 2002 (ISBN 90-411-9841-5).
27. Krister Andersson, Peter Melz & Christer Silfverberg (eds), *Liber Amicorum Sven-Olof Lodin,* 2001 (ISBN 90-411-9850-4).
28. Juan Martín Jovanovich, *Customs Valuation and Transfer Pricing: Is It Possible to Harmonize Customs and Tax Rules?,* 2002 (ISBN 90-411-9888-1).
29. Stefano Simontacchi, *Taxation of Capital Gains under the OECD Model Convention: With Special Regard to Immovable Property,* 2007 (ISBN 978-90-411-2549-1).
30. Michael Lang, Josef Schuch, & Claus Staringer (eds), *Tax Treaty Law and EC Law,* 2007 (ISBN 978-90-411-2629-0).
31. Duncan Bentley, *Taxpayers' Rights: Theory Origin and Implementation,* 2007 (ISBN 978-90-411-2650-4).
32. Sergio André Rocha, *Interpretation of Double Taxation Conventions: General Theory and Brazilian Perspective,* 2008 (ISBN 978-90-411-2822-5).
33. Robert F. van Brederode, *Systems of General Sales Taxation: Theory, Policy and Practice,* 2009 (ISBN 978-90-411-2832-4).
34. John G. Head & Richard Krever (eds), *Tax Reform in the 21st Century: A Volume in Memory of Richard Musgrave,* 2009 (ISBN 978-90-411-2829-4).
35. Jens Wittendorff, *Transfer Pricing and the Arm's Length Principle in International Tax Law,* 2010 (ISBN 978-90-411-3270-3).
36. Marjaana Helminen, *The International Tax Law Concept of Dividend,* Second Edition, 2017 (ISBN 978-90-411-8394-1).
37. Robert F. van Brederode (ed.), *Immovable Property under VAT: A Comparative Global Analysis,* 2011 (ISBN 978-90-411-3126-3).
38. Dennis Weber & Stef van Weeghel, *The 2010 OECD Updates: Model Tax Convention & Transfer Pricing Guidelines - A Critical Review,* 2011 (ISBN 978-90-411-3812-5).
39. Yariv Brauner & Martin James McMahon, Jr. (eds), *The Proper Tax Base: Structural Fairness from an International and Comparative Perspective—Essays in Honour of Paul McDaniel,* 2012 (ISBN 978-90-411-3286-4).
40. Robert F. van Brederode (ed.), *Science, Technology and Taxation,* 2012 (ISBN 978-90-411-3125-6).
41. Oskar Henkow, *The VAT/GST Treatment of Public Bodies*, 2013 (ISBN 978-90-411-4663-2).
42. Jean Schaffner, *How Fixed Is a Permanent Establishment?*, 2013 (ISBN 978-90-411-4662-5).

43. Miguel Correia, *Taxation of Corporate Groups*, 2013 (ISBN 978-90-411-4841-4).
44. Veronika Daurer, *Tax Treaties and Developing Countries*, 2014 (ISBN 978-90-411-4982-4).
45. Claire Micheau, *State Aid, Subsidy and Tax Incentives under EU and WTO Law*, 2014 (ISBN 978-90-411-4555-0).
46. Robert F. van Brederode & Richard Krever (eds), *Legal Interpretation of Tax Law*, Second Edition, 2017 (ISBN 978-90-411-8473-3).
47. Radhakishan Rawal, *Taxation of Cross-border Services*, 2014 (ISBN 978-90-411-4947-3).
48. João Dácio Rolim, *Proportionality and Fair Taxation*, 2014 (ISBN 978-90-411-5838-3).
49. Paulo Rosenblatt, *General Anti-avoidance Rules for Major Developing Countries*, 2015 (ISBN 978-90-411-5839-0).
50. Gaspar Lopes Dias V.S., *Tax Arbitrage through Cross-Border Financial Engineering*, 2015 (ISBN 978-90-411-5875-8).
51. Geerten M.M. Michielse & Victor Thuronyi (eds), *Tax Design Issues Worldwide*, 2015 (ISBN 978-90-411-5610-5).
52. Oktavia Weidmann, *Taxation of Derivatives*, 2015 (ISBN 978-90-411-5977-9).
53. Chris Evans, Richard Krever & Peter Mellor (eds), *Tax Simplification*, 2015 (ISBN 978-90-411-5976-2).
54. Reuven Avi-Yonah & Joel Slemrod (eds), *Taxation and Migration*, 2015 (ISBN 978-90-411-6136-9).
55. Alexander Bosman, *Other Income under Tax Treaties: An Analysis of Article 21 of the OECD Model Convention*, 2015 (ISBN 978-90-411-6610-4).
56. John Abrahamson, *International Taxation of Manufacturing and Distribution*, 2016 (ISBN 978-90-411-6664-7).
57. Frederik Boulogne, *Shortcomings in the EU Merger Directive*, 2016 (ISBN 978-90-411-6713-2).
58. Angelika Meindl-Ringler, *Beneficial Ownership in International Tax Law*, 2016 (ISBN 978-90-411-6833-7).
59. Andreas Waltrich, *Cross-Border Taxation of Permanent Establishments: An International Comparison*, 2016 (ISBN 978-90-411-6832-0).
60. Sergio André Rocha & Allison Christians (eds), *Tax Sovereignty in the BEPS Era*, 2017 (ISBN 978-90-411-6707-1).

www.ingramcontent.com/pod-product-compliance
Lightning Source LLC
Chambersburg PA
CBHW071235230926
51849CB00001B/109
* 9 7 8 9 0 4 1 1 8 4 7 3 3 *